NORTHERN CALIFORNIA DISCOVERY GUIDE

A remarkably useful travel companion
for motorists, RVers and other explorers

By Don W. Martin & Betty Woo Martin

Pine Cone Press • Columbia, California

BOOKS BY DON AND BETTY MARTIN

NORTHERN CALIFORNIA DISCOVERY GUIDE • 1993
OREGON DISCOVERY GUIDE • 1993
THE ULTIMATE WINE BOOK • 1993
THE BEST OF NEVADA • 1992
THE BEST OF THE WINE COUNTRY • 1991
INSIDE SAN FRANCISCO • 1991
COMING TO ARIZONA • 1991
THE BEST OF ARIZONA • 1990; revised 1993
THE BEST OF THE GOLD COUNTRY • First printing, 1987; second printing, 1990; revised 1992
SAN FRANCISCO'S ULTIMATE DINING GUIDE • 1988
THE BEST OF SAN FRANCISCO • 1986; revised 1990, 1994

Library of Congress Cataloging-in-Publication Data
Martin, Don and Betty—
Northern California Discovery Guide
Includes index.
1. California—description and travel
2. California—history

ISBN: 0-942053-12-5
Library of Congress catalog card number 92-91153

Illustrations • **Bob Shockley,** Mariposa, Calif.
Cartography • **Dianne Shannon & Dave Bonnott**, Columbine Type and Design, Sonora, Calif.

THE COVER • Guests of Lake Tahoe Balloons take flight for a sky-high view of the rugged eastern face of the Sierra Nevada, one of Northern California's most beautiful regions.
—**Don W. Martin**

*San Francisco, Northern California's most popular tourist destination, glitters
in this nighttime view from Treasure Island.* — **Don W. Martin**

*I shall be telling this with a sigh
Somewhere ages and ages hence:
Two roads diverged in a wood, and I—
I took the one less traveled by,
And that made all the difference.*
— **Robert Frost, *Road Not Taken* (1916)**

**This book is dedicated to the next generation, daughter Kimberly
Martin Schultz and son Daniel C. Martin, who—unlike their father—are
native to this place.**

CONTENTS

MAPS

INTRODUCTION

THIS BOOK WAS WRITTEN FOR YOU, whether you're among the nearly 30 million Californians looking for backyard discoveries, or the 25 million annual visitors from elsewhere.

If you're a resident, you've probably compiled a long list of places you intend to visit in the state's scenic northern half "when you get around to it." This book is designed to get you going.

If you're a visitor—or if you're contemplating a visit—the book will help you make sense of this large and complex region.

Further, this is a Discovery Guide, which separates the fun and the fascinating from the ordinary and the obvious. It was written for travelers with a sense of adventure, not for tourists who merely collect locations.

California is the most populated and one of the largest and most complex states in the Union. We would hardly expect you to do as we did, and cover the entire northern half in one monumental exploration. As a visitor from the outside, you can use our guide as a sampler to select a specific region, since we've picked the best that Northern California has to offer. Each chapter will fit comfortably into a one or two week vacation. As a resident, you can keep the book handy for future reference, pulling it from shelf or glove compartment whenever you want to spend a long weekend or a vacation in your state.

Like many Californians, I came from elsewhere. My first view of the state was through a chain link fence at Marine Corps Recruit Depot in San Diego. I was too intimidated by my glowering drill sergeant to be impressed by the December sunshine and palm trees. After being shuttled about the globe by the Corps, I was returned to California and turned loose.

I've never left—except to travel—and the view of my adopted state has improved considerably. During the past 40 years, I've worked here as a newspaperman and as a travel writer and photographer. With my wife Betty—who *is* a native, I've explored nearly every square mile of the Golden State.

After writing regional guidebooks on San Francisco, the Gold Country and the Wine Country, we decided to place all of Northern California under one handy wrapper. This was no small task, given the area's complexity. We didn't want to create an encyclopedic tome that wouldn't fit into your glove compartment. And we certainly didn't want to flog you with facts about every obscure hamlet.

We elected to research a book that is both comprehensive and selective, covering all of Northern California's more interesting regions. We ignore communities with limited appeal (sorry about that, Madera), while focusing on areas that visitors want to visit. After spending many months in a detailed review of our back yard, we've uncovered the delightfully obscure and we've updated the obvious, to create a book that is indeed a Discovery Guide.

We've sorted through the wonders of this amazing state's northern half, and saved the very best just for you.

Don W. Martin
Columbia, Tuolumne County, California

THE WAY THINGS WORK

When most folks go on vacation, they either drive their family sedan or RV, or they fly to a city and rent a car. We have thus written this book for the way you travel, steering you along major highway and minor byway to the state's most appealing places.

The **Northern California Discovery Guide** takes you mile by mile, with attendant maps, from one corner of this region to the other. Along the way, we suggest interesting stops, and detours to little discoveries that other guidebooks may have missed. In towns with visitor appeal, we review its lures, activities and places to sleep or camp, and we recommend some good restaurants. We guide you carefully through larger cities, suggesting a driving route that will take you to its most interesting areas.

ATTRACTIONS

As the book follows Northern California's highways and scenic byways, it takes attractions as they come, describing them briefly and listing hours and prices (if any). In communities that offer several lures, we suggest driving routes and list points of interest along the way.

Don't rely too much on times in this book because many places seem to change their hours more often than a deadbeat changes his address. Also, summer and winter hours may vary. If you're going out of your way to visit an attraction, call to ensure that it's open. Prices change, too, inevitably upward, so use those shown only as guidelines.

SPECIAL PLACES

☺ Our little smiling faces mark Northern California's special places—the best visitor lures in each area. These range from major attractions and excellent museums to undiscovered jewels. Several restaurants and lodgings earn grins in addition to their regular ratings because of their particular charm, exceptional facilities or food, great views or other distinctive features.

DINING

Our intent is to provide a selective dining sampler. We focus on restaurants in or near visitor attractions, so we won't send you to a neighborhood shopping center in search of smashed beans and rice. We *do* recommend tucked away diners that have become legend for their food and atmosphere. Restaurants suffer a high attrition rate, so don't be crushed if one that we recommend has become a laundromat by the time you get there.

Choices are based more on overviews of food, service and dècor, not on the proper doneness of a specific pork chop. Further, we try to offer the typical regional dining experience, from California *nouveau* to fresh-from-the-surf seafood to country fried chicken.

Of course, one has to be careful when recommending restaurants. People's tastes differ. Also, the chef might have a bad night, or your waitress might be recovering from one. Thus, your dining experience may be quite different from ours. Restaurants are graded with one to four wedges, for food quality, service and ambiance.

Δ **Adequate**—A clean cafè with basic but edible grub.

ΔΔ **Good**—A well run establishment that offers fine food and service.

ΔΔΔ **Very good**—Substantially above average; excellent fare, served with a smile in a fine dining atmosphere.

△△△△ **Excellent**—We've found culinary heaven, and it has great *polenta* and a good wine list!

Price ranges are based on the tab for an average dinner, including soup or salad (but not wine or dessert). Obviously, cafés serving only breakfast and/or lunch are priced accordingly.

$—Average dinner for one is $9 or less

$$—$10 to $14

$$$—$15 to $24

$$$$—$25 and beyond

Ø—Smoke free dining. Most Northern California restaurants have non-smoking sections; they're required in San Francisco and many other cities. Our symbol indicates a place that's entirely non-smoking or one that has a completely separate smoke free dining room.

LODGING

Our sleeping selections are somewhat arbitrary, since the book can't list them all. Nor does it attempt to; the idea is to recommend facilities near points of interest as you drive through Northern California. The guidebook suggests clean, well run accommodations in all price ranges. In choosing pillow places, we often rely on the judgment of the American Automobile Association because we respect its high standards. We also include some budget lodgings that may fall short of Triple A ideals, but still offer a clean room for a fair price. Of course, one can't anticipate changes in management or the maid's day off, but hopefully your surprises will be good ones.

Bed & breakfast inns and historic hotels are part of the Northern California vacation experience, and we've made a point of seeking these out. We use little Monopoly © style symbols to rate the selected lodgings:

⌂ **Adequate**—Clean and basic; don't expect anything fancy.

⌂⌂ **Good**—A well run place with comfortable beds and most essentials.

⌂⌂⌂ **Very good**—Substantially above average, often with facilities such as a pool, spa or restaurant.

⌂⌂⌂⌂ **Excellent**—An exceptional lodging with beautifully appointed rooms and extensive amenities.

Ø—Non-Smoking rooms are available, or the entire facility is smoke free (common with bed & breakfast inns). Incidentally, most B&Bs do not allow pets. Inquire when you make reservations so your poor pooch doesn't have to spend the night sulking in the back seat of your car.

Our price ranges are based on figures provided by the establishments. They are, of course, subject to change. Price codes below reflect the range for a standard room during high season. Call ahead to confirm current price and availability. It has been our experience that the lower end rooms are the first to go.

$—a double room for $35 or less

$$—$36 to $49

$$$—$50 to $74

$$$$—$75 to $99

$$$$$—$100 and beyond

It's always wise to make advance reservations, particularly during weekends and local celebrations (listed at the end of each community write-up). If you don't like the place and you're staying more than a day, you can always shop around after the first night and—hopefully—change lodgings.

CAMPING

California offers a variety of camping facilities, especially in the state's northern end, making it a *nirvana* for RVers and happy tenters. Many of its state parks offer campsites, and national forests abound with campgrounds as well, primarily in mountainous regions such as the Sierra Nevada. In the Gold Country along the foothills of the Sierra, most county fairgrounds offer RV parking, often with hookups and showers. Most communities, of course, have a goodly number of RV parks. Even metropolitan areas such as San Francisco offer full hookup asphalt camping. Listed prices indicate a camp-site for two people per night. Some outfits charge more for extra bodies; others do not.

As the most populous state in the Union, California generates its own camping crowds, so make reservations as early as possible, particularly on summer weekends. For details, see **Getting camped** in Chapter one.

A BIT ABOUT THE AUTHORS

This is the tenth guidebook by husband and wife Don and Betty Martin, who make their home in California's Gold Country. Don, who provides most of the adjectives, has been a journalist since he was 17. He was a Marine correspondent in the Orient, then he worked on the editorial side of several California newspapers. Later, he served as associate editor of the California State Automobile Association's travel magazine. A member of the Society of American Travel Writers, he now devotes his time to writing, photography, travel and—for some curious reason—collecting squirrel and chipmunk artifacts.

Betty, who does much of the research, photography and editing, offers the curious credentials of a doctorate in pharmacy and a California real estate broker's license. A California native, she's also a freelance travel writer and photographer who has sold material to assorted newspapers and magazines.

A third and most essential member of the team is *Ickybod*, a green 1979 Volkswagen camper, the Martins' home on the road. Without *Ick*, they might have been tempted to solicit free lodging and meals, and this guidebook wouldn't be quite so honest.

A FEW WORDS OF THANKS

In a sense, guidebooks are written by committee. The authors only provide the research, the adjectives and the editing, while hundreds of other sources furnish facts and background information. Among our primary helpers were director **John Poimiroo,** media relations manager **Fred Sater** and associate tourism specialist **Sharon Smith-Hangsen** of the California Office of Tourism; **John A. Dell'Osso,** chief of interpretation for Point Reyes National Seashore; **Elizabeth Knight,** chief naturalist for Lassen Volcanic National Park; **John W. Wise,** chief interpreter for Redwood National Park; **Larry Waldron,** chief naturalist for Sequoia/Kings Canyon National Parks; the **interpretive staff** of Yosemite National Park; **Michele Moore,** interpretive ranger for Lava Beds National Monument; **Esther Goodhue** of Monterey State Historic Park; **Sharon J. Rooney** and **Nenita Ramos** of the San Francisco Convention & Visitors Bureau; **Lucy Steffens,** assistant tourism director for the Sacramento Convention & Visitors Bureau; **Maryjane Cavioli,** public information officer for Inyo National Forest.

Also, dozens of folks at city and county chambers of commerce and visitors bureaus, and offices of the U.S. Forest Service, National Park Service and Bureau of Land Management contributed to this work as well.

CLOSING INTRODUCTORY THOUGHTS:
Keeping up with the changes

Nobody's perfect, but we try. This guidebook contains thousands of facts and a few are probably wrong. If you catch an error, let us know.

Information contained herein was current at the time of publication, but of course things change. Drop us a note if you discover that an historic museum has become an auto repair shop or the other way around; or if a restaurant, motel or attraction has opened or closed. Further, we'd like to know if you discover a great undiscovered attraction, restaurant or hideaway resort. And we certainly want to learn if you have a bad experience at one of the places we've recommended.

All who provide useful information will earn a free copy of a Pine Cone Press publication. (See listing in the back of this book.) Address your comments to:

Pine Cone Press
P.O. Box 1494
Columbia, CA 95310

TRAVEL TIPS

Whether you travel by car, RV or commercial transit, these tips will help make any trip more enjoyable and economical.

Reservations ● Whenever possible, make advance room reservations. Otherwise, you'll pay the "rack rate," the highest rate that a hotel or motel charges. Also, with a reservation, you won't be shut out if there's a convention or major local celebration.

Car rentals ● The same is true of rental cars; you'll often get a better rate by reserving your wheels ahead. **Important note:** Car rental firms may try to sell you "insurance" (actually collision damage waiver) to cover the vehicle. However, you may already have this protection through your own auto insurance company. Check before you go and take your policy or insurance card as proof of coverage.

Trip insurance ● If you're flying, trip insurance may be a good investment, covering lost luggage, accidents and missed flights (essential if you have a no-refund super saver). Most travel agencies can arrange this coverage.

Medical needs ● Always take spare prescription glasses and contacts. Take the prescriptions for your lenses and any drugs you may be taking. Don't forget sun protection, such as a wide brimmed hat and sun block, since you may be spending more time outdoors.

Cameras and film ● If you haven't used your camera recently, test it by shooting a roll of film before you go. Test and replace weak camera and flash batteries. If you're flying, hand carry your camera and film through the security check.

Final checklist

There's more to trip departure than putting out the cat. Check off these essentials before you go:

___ Stop newspaper and other deliveries; put a hold on your mail.

___ Lock off or unplug your automatic garage door opener.

___ Arrange for indoor plant watering, landscaping and pet care.

___ Make sure your phone answering machine is turned on; most of these devices allow you to pick up messages remotely.

___ Don't invite burglars by telling the world via answering machine or voice mail that you're gone. Put several lights on timers and make sure newspapers and mail don't accumulate outside.

___ If you're going on a long trip, arrange for future mortgage and other payments to avoid late charges.

___ Take perishable food from the refrigerator and lower the fridge and water heater temperatures to save energy.

___ Double check the clothes you've packed (extra shoes, matching belts); make sure your shaving and cosmetic kits are complete.

___ Take more than one type of credit card, so you won't be caught short if one is lost or stolen.

___ Get travelers checks and/or take your bank debit card.

___ Have your car serviced, including a check of all belts, tires and fluid levels. For long desert stretches, take extra water and oil.

___ Turn out the lights, turn off the heat and put out the cat.

Northern California

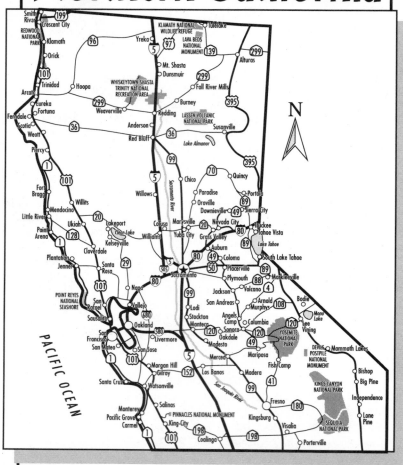

Chapter one

CALIFORNIA

Getting to know you

CALIFORNIA! Say the word and a kaleidoscopic vision leafs through your mind, like flickering images on a Hollywood moviola. This is the state of the Golden Gate, redwoods, well-aged Zinfandel, the Fortyniners, loggers and joggers, weathered missions and Silicon Valley.

According to the state's office of tourism, California is a plural. The state's brochures separate it into different tourist regions, which it originally referred to as "the Californias." This is helpful, since the state as a whole is a mind boggling mass of varied terrain, mega-sprawl cities, and scores of places to amuse and amaze.

Reaching about 800 miles north to south, California is whatever the visitor wants it to be: thick forests, rocky or sandy seacoasts, snowcapped peaks, rolling farmlands, high prairies and deserts both high and low. Placed over the Atlantic Seaboard, it would stretch from Massachusetts through South Carolina. Its communities range from skyrise cities to scattered suburbs, historic gold rush towns, tiny farm hamlets and glossy resort villages. Although it's America's most populous state, it contains vast expanses of lonesome landscape. It has some of the most enormous and least populated counties in the country.

It's difficult to cover such an enticing demographic octopus in a single publication, so we've verbally sawed our home state in half. We had to draw a line somewhere, so we decided that "Northern California" starts at the Oregon border and ends below Big Sur in Monterey County. Our line extends eastward between Monterey and San Luis Obispo counties and continues across the San Joaquin Valley between King and Kern Counties. It then swings northward, following Highway 395 through the Owens Valley to take in the Sierra Nevada range, while leaving Death Valley where it belongs, in the Southern California desert.

In escorting you through the upper end of the state, we've taken a cue from the California Office of Tourism and sliced it into manageable portions. On the pages that follow, we will lead you by the hand through the Golden State's northern "Californias," advising you what to see and what you might choose to ignore.

We begin where the modern day state began—in our favorite city of San Francisco. Technically, the state traces its roots to a 1769 Spanish mission near present day San Diego. However, today's California blossomed with the discovery of gold in the northern Sierra Nevada foothills in 1848. San Francisco, port of entry for the flood of argonauts who came by sea, was its first substantial city. It remained its largest until well into this century. (For more detail on everybody's favorite city, see our *Best of San Francisco* (Chronicle Books, © 1986, 1990, 1994) and *Inside San Francisco* (Pine Cone Press, © 1991).

Starting from that city, we'll take you north to the wine country of Sonoma and Napa. We'll venture into the beautiful North Coast and its redwoods, and then south through Monterey to Big Sur. Returning to the Bay Area, we'll head east through the Delta to Sacramento and the Gold Country. We'll continue to Lake Tahoe and the High Sierra. Finally, we'll travel across the mountainous top of the state, and then south through its "Big Valley"—the San Joaquin.

When we finish, we will have taken you several thousand miles through the best of Northern California. Of course, we don't expect you to tackle the enormity of this area in a single extended outing. Each chapter is designed to fit comfortably into a one or two week vacation.

Is it still golden?

California bashing has become rather fashionable during the Decade of the Nineties, even in other travel guides. They talk of the California dream becoming a nightmare.They talk of high unemployment, of street people, of AIDS, of Rodney King and race riots, of high taxes, of the exodus of industry. Indeed, this once booming state—the leading socio-technological edge of America—struggled during the early nineties as the blunted edge of the recession.

Has the Golden State lost its golden touch? Has the fun gone out of Fantasyland?

Not hardly. It's still the most appealing, the most versatile and intriguing state in America. More than 25 million visitors are drawn here each year and the vast majority of them go away happy. It is true that some residents have abandoned ship—even though it isn't sinking. Many are moving next door to Oregon, Nevada and Arizona. Despite this exodus, California had a larger total population gain than any other state during the 1980s. Alaska, Nevada and Arizona were higher in percentage gain, but the Golden State led the nation in numbers.

In fact, it is America's leading state by most economic and population measures. (This isn't necessarily good news to those caught in a San Francisco-Oakland Bay Bridge traffic jam.) It leads the country in total agricultural and industrial production. It is number one in aerospace and computers, medical equipment, food processing, film and television production. It produces much of the nation's cotton, more than half of its fruit and 75 percent of its wine. If it were an independent nation, it would be the seventh wealthiest in the world!

California also is the Nation's greatest trend setter. The state gave birth to Levi's, the freeway, the motel, drive-in movies and restaurants, the John Birch Society, Carol Doda, tofu sushi, designer pizza, frozen yogurt, the microchip and personal computer, property tax limitation, farm labor organizations and the ecology movement. The first environmental legislation in the United States—perhaps in the world—was enacted here in 1884 to stop gold dredging runoff from fouling farmers' fields. California is home to the Sierra Club and Greenpeace, and it certainly has its share of spotted owls.

Among its inventions are Hollywood, student anti-Vietnam protests, *nouveau* cuisine, fast food parlors, flower children, Richard Nixon, Ronald Reagan (born elsewhere but invented in Hollywood), the Beach Boys, hippies and yuppies. Thousands of World War II veterans remained here after returning from the Pacific Theatre to form the fertile nucleus of America's Baby Boom.

Today's Californians certainly know how to enjoy life. Perhaps it stems from a mentality born of earthquake fear. "Live today, for tomorrow ye may fall into the San Andreas Fault." Whatever the reason, its citizens lead the nation in most areas of leisure, from travel and physical fitness to that curious local pastime called the backyard barbecue. Surfing, invented in Hawaii, came here early in this century to create a suntanned, idyllic leisure class of blonde beach bums and bunnies, enjoying endless summers.

According to surveys from the American Automobile Association, Californians travel more, hold more passports and eat out more than any one else in America. They drive more miles, take more mini-vacation trips, buy more ski and backpacking equipment and probably hit the beach more. They like to live on the naughty side, too. This was America's first state to legalize bottomless dancing and topless beaches.

The true melting pot

California—not New York—is America's melting pot. It has the country's largest Latino and Asian population, and nearly 100 different languages are spoken in the public school systems. One in ten residents is Asian, and this is the fastest growing racial group in the state—mostly by immigration. By the end of this decade, the state's white majority will be outnumbered by collective minorities. Other ethnic groups already outnumber honkeys in the public school system.

For the visitor, this melting pot provides a hearty stew of experiences, from colorful ethnic neighborhoods to a tremendous mix of restaurants. Where but in San Francisco, for instance, would you find Yellow Page listings for 47 different ethnic cafès?

Northern California's melting pot began boiling early. On January 24, 1848, an itinerant carpenter named James Wilson Marshall discovered a few gold flakes in the tailrace of a lumber mill. He'd been employed by Swiss entrepreneur John Sutter to build the water powered mill on the banks of the American River, about 35 miles east of present day Sacramento.

Months passed before the rest of the world learned of the discovery, but when word got out, it spurred an international stampede. Argonauts came from Europe, China, Australia and South America, inciting history's first gold rush. Between the dash for California's gold and free land in Oregon, more than half a million people moved across the continent, around Cape Horn or across the Isthmus of Panama. At no time before or since have so many people moved so quickly from one place to another.

Although California traces its roots to the discovery of gold, its human history goes back much further. The first residents, of course, were Native Americans who met the boats of Spanish explorers. New findings by archaeologists keep pushing back the date of North America's first human occupation. It's currently established at about 14,000 years ago.

Natives here enjoyed the good life, blessed with the same benign climate that still draws hoards to the state. They were semi-nomadic for the most part—hunter-gatherers who drifted with the seasons from the foothills to the valleys in search of game and acorns. Although their basketry was quite advanced, their weapons and dwellings were more primitive than those who had to combat harsher climates in other areas. They rarely formed into tribal groups. Instead, they clustered into extended families sharing common territories and dialects. As many as 500 different tongues have been identified. With little concern for tribal identity, most groups merely referred to themselves as "the people." Nor was territorial imperative important. Wars never extended much beyond family feuds.

Scholars suggest that native population density here was eight times greater than in the rest of the United States. Estimates range between 250,000 and 400,000. When Spanish missionaries and later American settlers came to this land, they found a Stone Age culture that was easily subjugated. The padres literally enslaved them, separated the men from the women into crowded compounds, punished them like errant children when they tried to flee, and systematically destroyed their culture. It was the Indians, not the missionaries, who built the chain of California missions.

Proud but unable to resist high tech swords and muskets, they fell by the hundreds of thousands to disease, mistreatment and persecution. As unspeakable as it seems today, some authorities even posted bounties on these "pesky natives," who offered little organized resistance but had a penchant for petty thievery. Although strong native tribal groups still exist in other parts of the nation—particularly in Arizona—many California bands were literally obliterated.

Perhaps the last truly free man in America was a Northern California native called Ishi. The sole survivor of the Yahi band, he was found cowering in a meat shed near Oroville in 1911. He was taken to the University of California's Museum of Anthropology in San Francisco, where he became a friend and object of study for Professor Alfred Kroeber. Like legions before him, Ishi died of a white man's disease, succumbing to tuberculosis in 1916.

A myth becomes reality

California existed in a Spanish myth before it became a real place. In 1510, Garci Ordonez de Montalvo penned *Las Sergas de Esplanadian,* a fanciful story about an island "at the right hand of the Indies" ruled by a black Amazonian named Califia.

Spanish mariners touched Cape San Lucas at the tip of Baja California around 1533. They named their discovery "Califia's Land," or California, since they thought it was an island. This misconception persisted for decades as sailors cruised along the coast but failed to probe inland. The first coastal voyager probably was Portuguese navigator Juan Rodriguez Cabrillo, sailing under the flag of Spain. Departing Mexico in 1542, he cruised as far north as the Big Sur coast before dying of injuries sustained in a shipboard accident. His pilot Bartolomè Ferrelo carried on, sailing up the California coast and probably reaching Oregon the following year. As more of the coast was explored, the name "California" was extended farther northward.

In 1579, England's gentleman pirate Sir Francis Drake sought refuge for ship repairs on California's north coast. He landed in northern San Francisco Bay, Drake's Bay on the Point Reyes Peninsula or Bodega Bay, depending on your historian. He called the region *Nova Albion,* claimed it for his queen and sailed away, apparently not giving the area much more thought. Sebastian Viscaino made a more careful exploration in 1602 and 1603, discovering Monterey Bay and sailing well up the Oregon Coast. Naturally, he claimed all of this for *his* queen.

More than a century passed before anyone bothered to settle this much-claimed land. In the mid-1700s, Czarist Russia began scouting Alaska and working south down the coast. Spanish officials, by this time well settled in Mexico, saw the need to establish a foothold in present day California. They dispatched a diminutive, gimpy-legged friar named Junìpero Serra to install the first of a string of missions on San Diego Bay. The chain eventually stretched more than 500 miles to Sonoma, north of San Francisco Bay.

Bibles and muskets

These were not cities, but church-run agricultural outposts whose only government was the word of the friars, enforced by swords and muskets of accompanying soldiers. The docile natives were rounded up, herded into the missions and made to do most of the work, under the guise of being Christianized. *Presidios* or military posts were established at San Diego, Santa Barbara, Monterey and San Francisco to quell any uprisings.

Although the first mission was established at San Diego, it was not California's first city. That honor goes to the Northern California *pueblo* of San Josè. It was founded in 1777 by an entourage of men, women, children and livestock that had marched overland from Mexico.

With an abundance of free labor, the missions became successful businesses for the Catholic Church and funded much of the government of New Spain. Tens of thousands of cattle roamed the great grasslands, providing meat, hides and tallow for trade. Settlers began drifting into the area, forming more communities. Many of the residents were former soldiers from the presidios, who sent for their families from Mexico.

Revolts against Spanish rule in Mexico City in the early 1800s caused little stir among the *Californios* to the north. In 1822, however, the territory learned that Mexico had gained its independence, so it proclaimed allegiance to the new government. In fact, the northernmost mission in Sonoma was established under Mexican rule.

Shortly thereafter, however, Mexico decided to dismantle the mission complexes. The new government converted them into secular churches and granted their extensive landholdings to *Californios* who had supported the independence movement. These became huge *rancherias,* fostering the first of California's golden eras. Proud *dons* rode about their endless acres, supervising the work of their *vaqueros.* The Mexican ranchers built great adobe and tile roofed homes and regally entertained travelers along *El Camino Real,* the "Royal Road" linking the former missions and the settlements.

California's first golden age lasted only couple of decades. By the 1840s, pioneers were following a rutted wagon trail to Oregon, lured by offers of

Reversal of fortunes? This cartoon from a museum wall in Murphys, in California's Gold Country, ponders the wisdom of the thousands who came seeking golden wealth in California

free land. A few began filtering into California. The cross-country immigrant route split off in present day Idaho to form separate Oregon and California trails. The tragedy of the Donner party, caught on the wrong side of the Sierra Nevada by an early snow in 1846, did little to stem the growing westward tide.

Back east, a writer coined the phrase "manifest destiny," suggesting that it was both logical and inevitable that America extend its borders to the Pacific. Captain John C. Frèmont was dispatched by the government to survey the West and size it up for an American takeover.

James Knox Polk, perhaps the most underrated leader in American history, was the man primarily responsible for pushing the borders to the Pacific. President from 1845 until 1849, this stern, no nonsense Tennessean ignited the U.S. war with Mexico, resulting in the ceding of Texas, Arizona, New Mexico and California to the United States. He also pressured England into a boundary settlement that brought the future Oregon, Washington and Idaho into the fold.

During his four-year term, he encouraged Westward migration and signed the Organic Land Act. This was the forerunner of the Homestead Act, giving pioneers free land just for the working of it. When gold was discovered in California, he waved a nugget under the collective noses of Congress, driving home the importance of making the new territory our 31st state. We find it ironic, as we travel about our home state, that there is no major monument to this hard working Tennessee lawyer who was to become California's champion.

In football, politics and history, timing is everything. Had gold been discovered a few years earlier, had James K. Polk not been President, Mexico would not have surrendered this land so easily. By the time Polk started his westward push, Americans already had their feet in California's door. Gringo settlers had married into prominent Mexican families, started ranches around *El Pueblo de Los Angeles* and established businesses in *Yerba Buena* on San Francisco Bay.

The declaration of war with Mexico in 1846 started a ripple of unrest in this area. Frèmont gathered several area settlers, bivouacked them near Marysville and told them to stay on the alert. On June 14, the anxious gringos jumped the gun. Led by William B. Ide, this rag tag band took over the pueblo of Sonoma. The raiders declared the land to be a republic and locked Northern California's governor-general Mariano Guadalupe Vallejo in his own barracks.

The California Republic, bannered by the famous bear flag, lasted only a few days, saving Frèmont and historians considerable embarrassment. On July 7, Commodore John Drake Sloat landed at Monterey, Mexico's California capital, and claimed the territory for the United States. As in Sonora, not a shot was fired and the Mexicans quickly acceded to their new rulers. In fact, Vallejo became one of the new state's most prominent citizens.

The war with Mexico dragged on for more than a year after the American occupation. Then California was formally ceded to the United States by the Treaty of Guadalupe Hidalgo on February 2, 1848. Talk about timing. Gold had been discovered at Sutter's Mill just 15 days before!

The Sutter factor

Swiss-born John Sutter arrived in Monterey via Hawaii in 1839 and charmed Mexican officials out of 47,827 acres of land. He began creating a vast agricultural empire called New Helvetia, headquartered at his civilian fort on the banks of the American River. The first non-Latin settlement in California, Sutter's Fort became an important commercial and social center for both the Mexicans and the few Americans that had begun filtering into the area.

Sutter established the state's first factories and was its first major employer. He had as many as 450 on his payroll—a mix of sailors, Kanakas (Hawaiians), Mexican *vaqueros* and Indians. The fort, with its tannery, carpentry shops, bakery, distillery and kitchens, became the future state's first shopping and industrial center.

Gregarious and generous (particularly with other people's money), Sutter hosted the likes of John C. Frèmont and Kit Carson. He sent a rescue squad to aid the Donner party and nurtured its survivors at the fort. When those gringos raised the bear flag in Sonora, he placed Vallejo under loose house arrest at his fort. During his genial confinement, the pair sipped wine and discussed California's future.

That future took an unexpected twist that led to Sutter's bankruptcy. In 1847, he contracted with James Marshall to build a sawmill on the American river, since his growing empire was in urgent need of lumber.

What happened next, as they say, is history.

Checking the millrace after a rain in early 1848, Marshall found two tiny pieces of gold worth maybe 50 cents. He and his boss agreed to keep the discovery a secret until the mill was completed. However capitalistic Mormon Sam Brannan, a guest of Sutter's, got wind of it and headed for San

Francisco to spread the word.

Despite Brannan's announcement, more than a year passed before the first wave of "Fortyniners" reached the foothills of the Sierra Nevada. The wave soon turned into a flood, changing the face and the fortunes of California forever. Within months, eager argonauts were scrabbling for gold along a 200-mile front. The state's population leaped from about 15,000 in 1848—not counting Native Americans—to 225,000 in four years. Until Marshall's moment, America essentially ended at the Missouri frontier. In the mad dash for gold, argonauts ignored and overshot mid-America, leaving the Great Plains, the Rockies and the Great Basin for later settlers.

When word of the discovery reached Washington, California was rushed into statehood, joining the Union in 1850 without ever having been a territory. It came so quickly that the fledgling state had no government and no place to put it. The capital bounced from San José to Vallejo to Benicia before finally settling near Sutter's Fort in Sacramento.

Once thought to be an island, California was in fact a socio-political isle, tied to the rest of the nation by thin, dusty wagon tracks. Communication with eastern America required months, via the uncertainties of ocean travel around Cape Horn, across the malaria ridden isthmus of Panama or by Butterfield stage south through the New Mexico Territory. Although settlers poured westward along the California Trail, there was no scheduled mail or supply traffic in the other direction. Early miners sent their laundry to China by clipper ship, for that was quicker than getting it back to Mom in Boston.

Officials in San Francisco and in Washington saw the need to tie the fragile young nation—about to engage in a great civil war—together. The Gold Rush, then, became the reason for the Pony Express, the transcontinental telegraph and railroad. When the war came, the South sought to lure California into the Confederacy. Skirmishes were fought between Union and Rebel sympathizers as far west as Arizona. It was gold from California and silver from Nevada that helped the Union win the war.

The Gold Rush peaked by the mid-1850s, leaving behind an interesting scatter of old towns and landmarks along present-day Highway 49. However, adventurers, dreamers and opportunists found new wealth in vast farmlands, ranches, thick forests and fertile offshore waters. The state continued to grow. It suffered the usual lags during the Depression and assorted recessions, but generally fared better than the rest of the country.

Spain's gentle legacy is still evident here, in musical place names and a large Mexican-American population that adds much of the flavor to the California of today. However, the *real* California—America's most populous, wealthiest, most racially mixed and sometimes wackiest state—is a bastard child of the Gold Rush. It attracted a mixed bag of people to create a rich sociological stew: adventurers, opportunists, plutocrats, free thinkers, snake oil peddlers, preachers, whores, noble men and women, highwaymen and thieves.

Welcome to the Golden State, the Union's most fascinating province!

GETTING THERE & ABOUT

It's no exaggeration that nearly all roads lead to California, since it occupies such a large chunk of the West Coast. Of the five major cross-country interstate highways, three terminate here. Northern California's major corridor is Interstate 80, which enters the state over that fateful Donner Pass just west of Reno and terminates in San Francisco.

Interstate 5 is the primary north-south artery, heading south from Oregon. It climbs the Siskiyou Summit north of Yreka, then slices down the middle of the state through Sacramento, continuing to Los Angeles and San Diego. It was completed in the 1970s to relieve congestion on old U.S. 99. The original highway still runs through the heart of the San Joaquin Valley agricultural belt, linking together its cities and farm towns.

State Highway 1, among the most scenic routes in America, crawls patiently along the coast. Its companion, U.S. 101, shares the same route in some areas, then swings inland through coastal mountains in others. Above San Francisco, Route 1 stays with the coast while 101 travels through the Sonoma wine country to the redwoods.

California has more miles of freeway than any other state, and the northern end certainly has its share. However, this book is not designed to take you over all of them. More often than not, we'll steer you along those thinner red lines—the roads less traveled.

Flying

To list the airlines serving this end of the state would be to name virtually every major carrier in the world. Obviously, many leading airlines serve busy San Francisco International Airport (SFO). If you're doing a fly-drive, you might ask your travel agent to route you into the less crowded fields of Oakland, San José or Sacramento. Oakland is one of our favorite airports—uncrowded, clean and easily accessible. And it isn't much farther from downtown San Francisco than SFO. It's served by frequent shuttles to the Bay Area Rapid Transit System that will whisk you into the city in minutes.

Training

Amtrak has daily service to Oakland (with bus links to San Francisco), offering an extensive rail network along the coast and through the San Joaquin Valley. The San Joaquin Route is becoming increasingly popular with San Francisco-Stockton-Fresno-Bakersfield-Los Angeles travelers. They find the coaches to be more comfortable than buses. A new Capitol Route serves Sacramento from San Francisco-Oakland, with bus connections on to Reno. For complete details on Amtrak schedules, call **(800) USA-RAIL**.

Some of the state's larger cities are getting into commuter training. The Key System that linked San Francisco to East Bay cities was dismantled decades ago. Then planners realized the foolishness of their ways and began bringing rail transit back. First was BART—Bay Area Rapid Transit. Now over 25 years old, it's still one of the most advanced rail systems in the country. BART brings tens of thousands of commuters and visitors to San Francisco each day from the East Bay counties of Alameda (Oakland) and Contra Costa. It's augmented by CalTrain, offering service south from San Francisco to San José, with a bus link to the beach resort of Santa Cruz.

In recent years, San José and Sacramento have established light rail systems to help cope with their growing commuter traffic.

Busing

Greyhound offers frequent service up and down the state on highways 101 and 99. It also runs buses east and west to tie the state to Reno, Las Vegas, Phoenix and beyond. Service thins out considerably in the "cow counties" of the Gold Country and northern mountains. However, most counties have a local transit service funded by a special state gasoline tax. If you're among the backpacking set, call county offices in rural areas for schedule information.

Greyhound's Ameripass provides unlimited travel during specified times and an international version is available for foreign travelers. For information on Greyhound routing and special passes, call **(214) 744-6500** or the Greyhound office in the nearest community.

The **Green Tortoise,** started years ago as a counter-culture bus service for the free wheeling set, still thrives. It's based in San Francisco, offering service to several California cities, with regular runs along Interstate 5 north to Portland and Seattle. It also features Yosemite excursions and scenic tours of California. Call **(800) 227-4766** outside the state or **(415) 821-0803** within. The address is P.O. Box 24459, San Francisco, CA 94124.

Touring

Several firms offer guided bus and train tours of California. Check with your travel agent for specifics. Among firms with tour packages in the state are **California Parlor Car Tours,** 1101 Van Ness Ave., San Francisco, CA 94109; (800) 227-4250 or (415) 474-7500; **Tauk Tours,** 11 Wilton Rd., Westport, CT 06880, (203) 226-6911; and **Maupintour,** 1515 Saint Andrews Dr., Lawrence, KS 66046; (800) 255-6162.

Elderhostel specializes in inexpensive learning vacations for seniors, using college dorms and classrooms in several communities. Outings range from cultural studies to bird watching. If you're 60-plus, contact the folks at 75 Federal St., Boston, MA 02110-1941; (617) 426-8056. They'll send you a thick tabloid brochure listing outings here and throughout the Northern Hemisphere.

With its proclivity for fitness and outdoor living, California is a major center for adventure travel. This is particularly true in the northern half. You can take rock climbing classes in Yosemite National Park, run whitewater rivers or take conducted hikes with packs on your backs. Two of the world's leading adventure travel firms are based here. For specifics on trekking in this state and throughout the world, contact **Mountain Travel** in El Cerrito, (800) 227-2384, and **Oars-Sobek** in Angels Camp at (209) 736-4677. Local chambers of commerce can put you in touch with other outdoor adventure outfits.

Getting camped

With its huge population, California generates its own crowds. They inevitably fill up every available campsite at the beach and in most mountain areas on summer weekends. Only in the most distant reaches can you escape this self-bred congestion.

If possible, plan your camping outings away from the weekends, or at least during the off-season. Otherwise, make reservations as far in advance as possible, for both public and commercial camping areas. Realistically, it's difficult to make spontaneous travel plans during peak season in such a populated state.

California has one of the nation's most extensive state park systems, preserving everything from redwood groves and ocean beaches to historic missions and mining towns. Many of these parks offer campsites. Facilities range from hot showers and flush potties to primitive sites with little more than a place to pitch a tent. Overnight prices range from $14 down. Day use fees are $3 to $5 per vehicle, although many parks are free. State parks have some of the state's most attractive campsites, often in wooded, scenic areas. Sites are usually better spaced than those in commercial campgrounds.

Many of these campsites are on an advance reservation system, operated under contract with Mistix, a commercial ticket agency. You can make phone reservations with a major credit card in hand, or you can reserve by phone and follow up with a check if you call far enough in advance. Mail reservations may be made by sending a completed form with payment. Contact **Mistix,** P.O. Box 85705, San Diego, CA 92138-5705. Within California, call (800) 444-PARK (7275) or (800) 274-PARK for the hearing impaired. From out of state, call (619) 452-1950.

Campsite applications are available from Mistix or the **California Department of Parks and Recreation,** P.O. Box 942896, Sacramento, CA 94296; (916) 653-6995. The department will send you *California Escapes,* a complete guide to state parks. Mistix also handles Yosemite, Sequoia/Kings Canyon and most other national park camping reservations, with a different number: (800) 365-CAMP.

Several **U.S. Forest Service** campgrounds in the state also are on the Mistix advance reservation system, accepting requests up to 120 days ahead. For information, call (800) 283-CAMP. As in most other states, California's forest service campgrounds generally do not have hookups or showers, and many have chemical toilets. However, the price is right—from $9 down to nothing. Many rival state park campgrounds in the beauty of their settings and isolation of individual campsites.

U.S. Forest Service "Camp Stamps" save about 15 percent of campsite costs. They're also convenient, since most campgrounds are self-service. With Camp Stamps, you won't have to worry about having the right amount of money to poke into those little slots. You can purchase any amount in denominations of $1, $2, $3, $5 and $10 by sending a check or money order to: Camp Stamps, U.S. Forest Service, P.O. Box 96090, Washington, DC 20090-6090.

Persons who qualify can get a 50 percent discount at Forest Service campgrounds by obtaining **Golden Age** (for those 62 and over) and **Golden Access** (for the disabled) passes. They're available at any Forest Service office and at national parks and monuments.

Finding a place to camp in the state's two popular national parks, **Yosemite** and **Sequoia,** is particularly tough in summer. Make reservations as early as possible by contacting Mistix at (800) 365-CAMP. Sites generally are available without reservation during the off-season, particularly on weekdays. During the summer, a good time to catch a vacancy is Sunday afternoon as the weekend crowds are checking out.

The **Bureau of Land Management** administers much of the state's deserts and other remote regions, maintaining several campgrounds and permitting informal camping in designated areas. For a map of federal campgrounds in the state, send a dollar to: California State Office, BLM, 2800 Cottage Way, Sacramento, CA 95825; (916) 978-4754.

Pacific Gas & Electric, which provides power to much of northern and central California, maintains campgrounds and other recreational facilities at many of its reservoirs. For a free guide to these sites, write: Land Department, Pacific Gas & Electric Company, 77 Beale St., San Francisco, CA 94106; (415) 972-5552.

Getting auto clubbed

Although the American Automobile Association is active throughout the country, nowhere is AAA service more saturated than in California. Two clubs serve the state, dividing it roughly through the middle. The **California State Automobile Association** provides service for Northern California and all of Nevada, with headquarters at 150 Van Ness Ave. (P.O. Box 1860), San Francisco, CA 94101; (415) 565-2012. California's lower half is handled by the **Automobile Club of Southern California,** 2601 S. Figueroa St., Los Angeles, CA 90007; (213) 741-3111.

Both maintain dozens of district offices and their emergency road service program blankets the state. Of course, your AAA card from other states is accepted here. You'll find more attractions and lodgings listed the AAA California-Nevada TourBook than in this guide—although it isn't nearly as much fun to read. The auto clubs also publish other area guides and maps.

HANDICAPPED TRAVELERS

People with mobility problems can get a special permit to use handicapped parking spaces by applying at any California **Department of Motor Vehicles** office. Proof of impairment must be provided. These permits aren't limited to the driver; they can be used if any occupant of the car is physically impaired. Incidentally, there is a stiff fine if able bodied persons park in handicapped spaces.

Golden Access Passes, available free to handicapped persons at national park and U.S. Forest service offices, provide half price camping at national forest campgrounds and free admission to all national parks and monuments. **Golden Bear Passes** for handicapped persons and folks aged 62 and older, provide free access to day use facilities at most state parks. They're available at parks, or contact: Department of Parks and Recreation, P.O. Box 942896, Sacramento, CA 94296; (916) 653-4000.

Among agencies that handicapped travelers will find useful are: **Travel Information Center,** 12th Street and Tabor Rd., Philadelphia, PA 19141, (215) 329-5715; **Society for the Advancement of Travel for the Handicapped,** 26 Court St., Brooklyn, NY 11242; (718) 858-5483; **American Foundation for the Blind,** 15 W. 16th St., New York, NY 10011; (800) 323-5463; and **Mobility International USA,** P.O. Box 3551, Eugene, OR 97403. Two federal government pamphlets, *Access Travel* and *Access to the National Parks,* are available by writing: **U.S. Government Printing Office,** Washington, DC 20402.

An extremely helpful publication is *Access to the World—A Travel Guide for the Handicapped* by Louise Weiss. Available at many bookstores, it's published by Holt, Rinehart & Winston of New York.

SENIOR TRAVELERS

Anyone 62 or older can obtain a free **Golden Age Pass** that provides the same advantages as the Golden Access Pass for the handicapped. This also is true of **Golden Bear Passes** for state parks (see above). Nearly every attraction and museum in the country now offers senior discounts. They're also available on most public transit systems, and many restaurants, motels and hotels offer reduced rates as well.

A fine organization serving the interests of seniors is the **American Association of Retired Persons,** 1919 K Street Northwest, Washington,

DC 22049; (202) 872-4700. For a nominal annual fee, AARP members receive information on travel and tour discounts and other stuff of interest to retired folk.

Elderhostel is a useful travel oriented organization for 60-plus seniors; contact the organization at 75 Federal St., Boston, MA 02110-1941; (617) 426-8056. (See "Touring" above.)

THE LAY OF THE LAND

Basically, Northern California is comprised of two major north-south mountain ranges separated by broad valleys, occasionally crossed by smaller east-west mountains.

One of its distinctive topographic-climatic features is the Coast Range. This buffer zone, separating much of the north coast from inland areas, creates curious weather patterns found in few other parts of the world. On any given July day, for instance, it may be 55 degrees, cold, damp and drizzling in San Francisco while it's 100 degrees, dry and sunny less than ten miles inland. Mark Twain once said: "The coldest winter I ever spent was a summer in San Francisco."

Working north to south, the state is laid out in this fashion:

A jumble of mountains fill its most northern reaches—a confusing tangle of the Cascades, Siskiyous, Coast Range and Sierra Nevada. Northeastern California is a remote area of high prairies and wooded tablelands, giving way to the Great Basin of southeastern Oregon and northwestern Nevada. The Coast Range continues south along the shorefront for several hundred miles, extending deeply into Southern California. These are relatively gentle mountains, covered mostly with oaks and madrones, although the northern reaches shelter California's magnificent redwood forests.

The coast itself stretches 840 miles from the Oregon border to Mexico. When you count all the kinks, bays and tidal estuaries, it measures a remarkable 3,427 miles, more than any other state except Alaska.

The great Sierra Nevada marches in a south by southeast curve along the California-Nevada border. Among the most rugged mountain ranges in America, it created a formidable barrier to westward migration. Ironically, these granite peaks also cultivated the gold that lured the migrants. Through the millennia, the coveted metal was leached downward into foothill streams and gravel bars. Spanish miners called the main gold vein *La Vetra Madre,* the Mother Lode. Today, these mountains and foothills harbor most of the state's ski resorts, rivers, lakes, alpine recreation areas and its two most popular national parks. The Pacific Crest Scenic Trail winds along the Sierra heights on its long trek from Canada to Mexico.

The Coast·Range and Sierra Nevada merge just above Los Angeles to form the transverse Tehachapi, San Bernardino and San Gabriel mountains. To the east, much of southern California is wrapped into the Mojave, California's largest desert, which extends into Nevada and Arizona. Although much of it is relatively high desert, some areas sink well below sea level, including Death Valley east of the lower Sierra Nevada and the Salton Sink northeast of San Diego.

California's great middle, forming America's largest agricultural basin, is simply called the Central Valley. From 40 to 50 miles wide, it extends 400 miles from Red Bluff to the Tehachapi foothills. Although topographically a single unit, it's called the Sacramento Valley north of the state capital and the San Joaquin Valley to the south.

Because of its great topographic diversity, California is *the* state for all seasons. Covering more degrees of longitude than any states except Alaska and Texas, it offers nearly every kind of climate and terrain imaginable, from rain forests to sand dunes to alpine tundra.

It has the highest and lowest spots in the Lower 48—Mount Whitney at 14,496 feet and Death Valley at 282 feet below sea level. Curiously, they're only 85 miles apart. Annual rainfall varies from 90 inches north of Crescent City to a couple of inches in Death Valley. Temperatures on a given day can dance above 120 in the desert and plummet below zero on a Sierra peak.

For the most part, however, the state has a relatively benign climate. Although gold drew the first immigrant masses to the land, California's moderate weather motivate much of the later migration. Most of the 20th century growth has occurred in the sunnier reaches of Southern California, which now claims two-thirds of the state's population. This comes as a relief to many northlanders.

Folks in the two halves of the state often are at odds with one another. This rivalry, extending back to the earliest days of the Gold Rush, ranges from friendly joshing to downright animosity. Northerners kid Southlanders about their crowds and smog, while contributing to those elements by hurrying to Disneyland and other attractions. Southern Californians boast of their climate and sunny beaches, while migrating north to escape the heat and beach crowds. Things get downright nasty when dry, thirsty Southern California keeps demanding more of Northern California's water.

WHERE TO DO WHAT WHEN

There is no main tourist season for this end of the state, although summer draws the largest crowds simply because that's when school is out. Most residents will suggest that summer is the *worst* time to visit here.

Unlike many other regions, this area does not suffer a serious shutdown of museums and tourist attractions during the off-season. With many locals to draw from, most establishments can afford to stay open the year around.

Weather rarely inhibits travel, although mountain passes can be shut temporarily by snow. Interstate 80, I-5 and U.S. 50 are plowed after each storm; less traveled Sierra passes are closed in winter. Snowfall is rare below 2,000 feet except in the most northern reaches, so you can move freely about throughout the winter.

If we lived elsewhere and were planning a trip to here, we'd target the seasons this way:

Spring ● This is the season for the coast, with its uncrowded beaches and blooming wildflowers, the Redwood Country and the Monterey Peninsula. The weather offers a mix of sunshine and light, infrequent rains.

Summer ● Head for the mountains above Redding and the lakes areas of the Whiskeytown-Shasta-Trinity National Recreation Area. Northern California's hometown crowds tend to focus on the Sierra Nevada and the coast during the summer; you won't trip over as many people in these northern reaches. The often overlooked northeast, with beautiful Mount Lassen National Park and Lava Beds National Monument, also is a good summer destination.

Fall ● Hit the heights of the Sierra Nevada, including Yosemite and Sequoia national parks, before the snow flies. You've got two good months—

September and October—to enjoy the Sierra without the crowds. While you're there, follow Highway 49 through the Gold Country, which combines fall color with its history. And don't overlook the Wine Country (countries, actually), where you can watch the crush while sampling good Zinfandel. The long California coastline also is in fine form during the fall, when it's relatively free of summer fogs and winter rains.

Winter ● Naturally, it's ski season for the many Sierra Nevada resorts. Also, head coastward for spectacular vistas of wave-tossed beaches—*if* you don't mind wind-driven rains.

For all seasons ● There is no bad time to visit San Francisco and the Bay Area. Indifferent to the seasons, it draws visitors throughout the year. The museums and great restaurants don't go by the calendar, and attraction hours change little from summer to winter. Although visitor facilities are crowded in summer, commuter traffic drops slightly as local folks vacation elsewhere. And never mind what Mark Twain said. San Francisco has as many sunny days as foggy ones in summer. Just bear in mind that this isn't a beach resort, so leave the halter tops and shorts packed.

JUST THE FACTS

Size ● 158,693 square miles; third largest state. About 840 miles long at the coastline and 770 miles in a straight line inland; width varies from 150 to 300 miles.

Population ● About 32 million; ranks first. Los Angeles is the largest city with 3,458,000; followed by San Diego with 1,110,000; San Josè with 782,200 and San Francisco with 724,000.

Elevations ● Highest point is Mount Whitney at 14,496 feet; lowest point is Badwater in Death Valley at 282 feet below sea level.

Admitted to the Union ● September 9, 1850, as the 31st state. Ceded to the United States by the Treaty of Guadalupe Hidalgo on February 2, 1848; was never designated as a territory.

Time zone ● Pacific

Area codes ● Thirteen, the most of any state. They are: Sacramento and California's inland rural north (916), north coastal California (707), San Francisco and Marin counties (415), East Bay (510), San Joaquin Valley and the Gold Country (209), San Josè to Monterey (408), central coast and inland to Bakersfield (805), northern Los Angeles County (818), metropolitan Los Angeles (213), western and southeastern Los Angeles County (310), Orange County (714), western and central San Bernardino and Riverside counties (909), San Diego County, Palm Springs area and north to the eastern Sierra (619).

Traffic laws ● Same speed limit as most other states—55 on highways unless otherwise posted and 65 on rural freeways. Some but not all units of the California Highway Patrol use radar, but they aren't fanatics. Law requires RVs and other slow moving vehicles to seek turnouts and let faster traffic pass. Safety belts must be used by all occupants of private vehicles.

Taxes ● Current sales tax is 7.25 percent and many counties and cities have tacked on extra amounts, to go as high as 8.25 percent. Supermarket food items but not restaurant foods are exempt from sales tax. Per gallon gasoline tax is 17 cents state, 14.1 cents federal plus state sales tax. With this tax load, it's hard to find gasoline bargains, although average prices are about the same as the rest of the nation. They can vary considerably from area to area—usually with no logical reason.

Border inspections ● Stations at points of entry check to see if you're carrying any fresh fruits or vegetables that might be harboring unsuitable bugs. Pets brought into the state must have proof of a rabies vaccination within the last year if they're over four months old.

Alcoholic beverages ● Bottled goods are freely available in liquor stores, supermarkets and drug stores. There is no state price support, so shop for bargains. A tip: wine often is less expensive at discount liquor stores and supermarkets than at the wineries, although tasting rooms often have sales. One liter of booze may be brought in from other states or countries. Agricultural inspection stations do not check for bottles. Legal drinking age is 21 and bar hours are 6 a.m. to 2 a.m., with no Sunday blue laws.

DWI ● California, the home of Mothers Against Drunk Driving (MADD) is tough on drinking and driving, so don't *even* think about it. A night in the slammer is mandatory, along with a stiff fine. If you're suspected of being drunk behind the wheel, you must submit to a blood, breath or urine test. Blood alcohol level for presumption of intoxication was dropped recently from .10 to .08. The California Highway Patrol and other law enforcement agencies routinely set up check points, particularly during holidays.

Fishing and hunting ● Fishing licenses are required for anyone over 14 years of age, and they may be obtained from most sporting goods stores, and tackle and bait shops. A license isn't required for ocean fishing off a pier, but it is for clamming. Because of California's warm coastal waters, mussel and clam gathering is quarantined during most of the summer months. For specifics on clamming and fishing, request a booklet from the Department of Fish and Game, 3211 S St., Sacramento, CA 95816; (916) 227-2244. A Hunting license is required for most anything you kill and there are strict bag limits. You can get details at the same office.

Official things ● **State motto**—"Eureka!" which means "I have found it," referring to the gold discovery, not to a hidden loophole in the state tax code. **State Song**—"California, Here I Come"; **nickname**—the Golden State; **state flower**—golden poppy; **state bird**—California valley quail; **state tree**—California redwood; **state animal**—grizzly bear which, ironically, is now extinct in California.

To learn more

California Office of Tourism, P.O. Box 9278, Department 1003, Van Nuys, CA 91409; (800) 862-2543 or (800) TO-CALIF.

California Department of Parks and Recreation, P.O. Box 942896, Sacramento, CA 94296; (916) 653-6995. For campground reservations, contact **Mistix,** P.O. Box 85705, San Diego, CA 92138-5705; call (800) 444-PARK within California or (619) 452-1950 from out of state. (See **Getting camped** above for more details.)

U.S. Forest Service, Office of Information, 630 Sansome St., San Francisco, CA 94111; (415) 556-0122. For **National Forest campground reservations** call (800) 283-CAMP.

Bureau of Land Management, California State Office, BLM, 2800 Cottage Way, Sacramento, CA 95825; (916) 978-4754.

California Department of Fish and Game, 3211 S St., Sacramento, CA 95816; (916) 227-2244.

PHOTO TIPS: PRETTY AS A PICTURE?

As we travel, we've watched scores of people take hundreds of photos and shoot thousands of feet of videotape. We can tell by their set-ups that most of the shots will be poor and they'll be disappointed when they get back home. By following a few simple steps, you can greatly improve your images. These pointers won't make you a pro, but they'll bring better results the next time you point and shoot.

Still cameras

Most of these suggestions work with the simplest fixed focus cameras, even the disposables, in addition to more complex ones.

1. Get the light right. In photography, light is everything. Avoid shooting objects that are hit by direct sunlight; it washes them out. Try to catch light coming from an angle to accentuate shadows, giving depth and detail to your subject. Photo light is best from sunup to mid-morning and from mid-afternoon to sunset.

2. Frame your photos. Before you shoot, compose the image in the viewfinder. Eliminate distracting objects such as signs or utility poles by changing your position. Or, line up your shot so the offending sign is behind a bush. When shooting people, make sure a utility pole or tree isn't sprouting from a subject's head.

3. Create depth, not clutter. If you're shooting scenery, give dimension to the photo with something in the background (craggy mountains), the middleground (someone in the meadow) and the foreground (a tree limb to frame the photo). On the other hand, if you're focusing on a specific object such as wildlife or an intriguing rock formation, keep the photo simple; don't clutter it.

3. Take pictures, not portraits. Endless shots of Auntie Maude standing in front of the scenery and squinting into your lens are pretty boring. Everyone already knows what she looks like, so let professionals at home shoot the family portraits.

4. Put life in your lens. On the other hand, people *do* add life to scenic photos. Instead of posing them in front of the scenery, let them interact with it. The kids can scramble over the redwood log to show how big that monster really is. Ask your mate to stroll from the historic building or perch carefully on the canyon rim. Maybe Aunt Maude can extend a tentative finger toward the prickly cactus. Also, have people wear bright clothes to add splashes of color to the photo.

Video cameras

1. Follow the above principles for lighting, framing and posing. You may want to create your own titles by shooting identifying signs.

2. Plan ahead. Think of what you're going to shoot before you pull the trigger. Be a good director and plot each sequence.

3. Hold her steady. You're shooting *moving* pictures, which means that the subjects should be moving, not the video camera. Keep it steady and let people walk in and out of the picture. Limit your panning; give viewers a chance to focus on the scenery.

4. Don't doom your zoom. A zoom lens is a tool, not a toy. Keep your zooming to a minimum, or you'll make your audience seasick.

TRIP PLANNER

WHEN TO GO ● The Bay Area has no "tourist seasons," although you may have preferences. The best weather is in the fall and cultural activities peak in winter. With its popularity as a tourist and convention destination, San Francisco keeps virtually all of its attractions going the year around. It's obviously most crowded in summer, when you'll have to struggle to get onto a cable car. This also is the chilly season, so bring a sweater and leave your shorts and halter tops packed.

WHAT TO SEE ● In San Francisco: Golden Gate Park with its many attractions, Fort Point, the National Maritime Museum, Hyde Street pier's historic ships and Alcatraz. Elsewhere in the Bay Area: Oakland Museum, University of California campus; Point Bonita Light, Muir Woods National Monument, Mount Tamalpais and China Camp State Park in Marin; Rosicrucian Museum and Tech Museum in San José and Great America in Santa Clara.

WHAT TO DO ● Hike to the top of one of the Twin Peaks, take an elevator up Coit Tower in San Francisco and Sather Tower on the campus of UC Berkeley, climb from Fort Point to the Golden Gate Bridge then walk across that grand span, stroll San Francisco's oceanfront at Baker Beach and its bayfront on the Golden Gate Promenade, hike the landscaped rim of Lake Merritt in Oakland, catch ferries from San Francisco to Sausalito and Tiburon, and take the ferry from Tiburon to Angel Island. And good grief, ride a cable car!

Useful contacts

San Francisco Visitors Bureau, P.O. Box 429097, San Francisco, CA 94142-9097; (415) 391-2000. Events hotline, (415) 391-2001. The **San Francisco Visitor Information Center** is in Hallidie Plaza at the Powell BART station at Powell and Market, open weekdays 9 to 5:30, Saturday 9 to 3 and Sunday 10 to 2. Essential numbers: **Municipal railway** (cable cars and city buses), (415) 673-MUNI; **Golden Gate Ferries,** (415) 332-6600; **Red & White Fleet,** (800) 445-8880; **San Francisco International Airport,** (415) 761-0800.

Berkeley Chamber of Commerce, 1834 University Ave., Berkeley, CA 94703; (415) 549-7000.

Golden Gate National Recreation Area, Building 201, Fort Mason, San Francisco, CA 94123; (415) 556-0560.

Oakland Convention & Visitors Bureau, Trans Pacific Centre, 1000 Broadway, Suite 200, Oakland, CA 94607-4020; (415) 839-9000.

Redwood Empire Association, 785 Market St., San Francisco, CA 94103; (415) 543-8334.

San José Convention & Visitors Bureau, 333 W. San Carlos St., Suite 1000, San José, CA 95110-2720; (408) 283-8833.

Bay Area radio stations

KSAN-FM, 94.9—country
KQED-FM, 88.5—NPR
KIOI-FM, 101—rock
KOIT-FM, 95.6—light rock
KJAZ-FM, 92.7—jazz
KYA-FM, 93—rock
KFOG-FM, 104.5—new wave

KBAY-FM, 100.3—easy listening
KABL-FM, 98.1—60s to 90s pop
KSFO-AM, 560—light rock, news
KGO-AM, 810—news and talk
KCBS-AM, 740—news
KFRC-AM, 610—easy listening

Chapter two

SAN FRANCISCO & SURROUNDS
Ambling around the Bay Area

THE ENTIRE San Francisco Bay Area in a single chapter? No way, San José. One could do books on this immensely popular area. We offer instead an exploration of San Francisco, by every measure the region's premiere attraction, and then highlight tours to other areas. These are drive-park-and-stroll trips designed to reveal the best of everybody's favorite city and its Bay Area neighbors.

A fine way to introduce yourself to this region is to climb to the top of one of the city's Twin Peaks. They're treeless mounds rising from San Francisco's hilly backbone. Native Americans, more romantically inclined than cartographers, called them the "Maidens' Breasts." Nearly a thousand feet above sea level, they provide a clear topographical introduction to the Bay Area, particularly on a clear day.

Hilly San Francisco lies at your feet, spilling toward the Pacific to the west and the bay to the east. Mount Diablo, the highest point in the Bay Area, dominates the eastern horizon, beyond the Oakland and Berkeley hills. Immediately north of your perch is the Golden Gate Bridge, with the headlands of Marin County yonder. To the south, the knobby peninsula widens into the wooded hills of San Mateo County, with the broad basin of San José's Silicon Valley beyond.

All rivers flow into the sea, yet the sea is not full, says the Bible. In Northern California, most of them flow into San Francisco Bay, after merging in the San Joaquin Delta behind Mount Diablo. This gathering of the waters then pours through the mile-wide Golden Gate to reach the Pacific and fulfill the biblical proclamation.

Water provides not only life, but transit. Thus, it was here that modern

California began. San Josè is its oldest city, founded on the shores of the south bay by a handful of Spanish colonists in 1777. San Francisco was its first great metropolis, since the huge harbor was a natural gathering place for gold seekers. The rivers—particularly the Sacramento and San Joaquin—provided passage toward the gold fields. During the last half of the last century, Mississippi style riverboats plied these waters, hauling passengers and cargo to Sacramento and Stockton. Not surprisingly, these were California's second and third largest cities during much of that era, after San Francisco. Late in the 19th century, Los Angeles ranked a mere 18th.

Like a great open hand, San Francisco Bay reaches 50 miles east and south; its San Pablo arm stretches 30 miles northeast. One of the largest natural inlets in America, it covers more than 900 square miles. In that coverage, it touches most of the areas we'll explore in this chapter.

What forces created this huge inland waterway? Rivers flowing westward from the Sierra Nevada and southwest from the Siskiyous and Cascades merged in the San Joaquin Valley and puddled up behind the Coast Range. Eventually, they found a weak link in the low mountains, breaking through to carve out the headlands of the Golden Gate. When glaciers of the last ice age began melting 10,000 years ago, the ocean level rose, spilling into the river-carved valleys to form a huge tidal estuary.

Early offshore explorers missed the often fog-shrouded entrance to the bay. The Spanish began settling California without realizing that the natural harbor existed. It was discovered by an overland expedition led by Josè Francisco de Ortega in the fall of 1769. Six years later, a ship piloted by Juan Manuel de Alaya became the first non-Indian craft to sail into the bay. Now realizing the immensity of this natural waterway, the Spanish hurried to colonize it before Russians from the north took a foothold. A party led by Lieutenant Josè Moraga and Father Francisco Palòu established a presidio and mission on the tip of the southern peninsula in 1776. The mission and bay were named for St. Francis of Assisi. The following year, Captain Juan Bautista de Anza arrived overland to start the *pueblo* of San Josè and settlement began in earnest.

Lots of folks

Today, the Bay Area is California's second largest population center, after the Los Angeles Basin. Although San Francisco itself ranks only fourth among California's cities, with 724,000 residents, the huge megaloptic sprawl surrounding it shelters nearly four million.

This teeming center of humanity can intimidate the visitor. However, we'll sort it all out with a series of driving trips to its highlight attractions. Although the Bay Area is congested, its traffic jams aren't nearly as monumental as those in the Los Angeles Basin. Nor is its suburban sprawl so extensive. An hour's drive from San Francisco in any direction delivers you to farm country, vinelands or reasonably uncrowded seacoasts. To the surprise of visitors and the delight of residents, the greater Bay Area contains extensive woodlands, forest-clad peaks, miles of hiking and biking trails and quiet groves of redwoods.

On the pages that follow, we'll take you by the hand to explore counties touched by San Francisco Bay. Directly across the pond is Alameda County with its principal communities of Oakland and Berkeley, home to the University of California. This area, plus a string of nondescript communities to the south, is known generically as the East Bay. Just above, Contra Costa

San Francisco Bay Area

County—Spanish for "opposite coast"—is bounded by northern San Francisco Bay and San Pablo Bay to the northeast. Its heartland is the Diablo Valley at the foot of Mount Diablo. This contains a merged-together sprawl of bedroom communities that range from upscale to blue collar. The Diablo Valley is a nice place to live, but it doesn't offer much to intrigue the visitor.

Immediately south of San Francisco is San Mateo County, named for St. Matthews. Locals call it "the Peninsula," even though it's only a piece of one. Like the Diablo Valley, it consists mostly of commuter communities. With the wooded backbone of the San Bruno Mountains, it shelters some very appealing forest enclaves. At the bottom of it all is Santa Clara County, where vineyards and fruit orchards have in recent decades surrendered to the cultivation of computer chips. Principal city San José passed San Francisco in recent years to become California's third largest city, after San Diego.

"Marvelous Marin"

Marin County, playing out its own parody of upscale hot tub self indulgence, occupies the thickly wooded peninsula across the Golden Gate from San Francisco. Beyond are Napa and Sonoma counties, California's finest premium wine producing areas, which we shall visit in the next chapter.

All of this sprawl is roped together by a series of freeways that can become protracted parking lots during commute hours. Five bridges and the submerged BART tube reach across the bay to bring Oakland and other neighbors into the fold. Curiously, there are no railroad bridges, so cross-country train travel begins in Oakland.

The Bay Area's major north-south artery is Highway 101, called The Bayshore south of San Francisco. It loses freeway status in the city, sending unsuspecting travelers into a tangle of surface streets. Highway 101 eventually finds the Golden Gate Bridge and continues northward. Interstate 280, the Junipero Serra Freeway, parallels U.S. 101, following the higher ridges through San Mateo County. Generally less congested and definitely more attractive than the Bayshore, it's our preferred route south.

The San Francisco-Oakland Bay Bridge, one of the world's busiest water crossings, is the main link to the East Bay. Having survived this passage, you can head north on Interstate 80 through Berkeley and eventually east across the country, or south on I-880 through Oakland. Also known as the Nimitz, I-880 is a tough, homely and crowded freeway knifing through the East Bay's industrialized heart. Interstate 580 parallels 880, traveling inland through a more attractive area at the foot of the Oakland Hills.

If you continue eastward from the Bay Bridge on Highway 24, you'll tunnel through those hills and emerge into the Diablo Valley. The route merges with I-680, which was designed to accomplish a wide, sweeping bypass of the Bay Area. With recent growth surging eastward from the city, the "bypass" has been buried by suburbia. During non-commute hours, however, it still offers a fairly rapid route north to south.

DISCOVERING THE BAY AREA

Thus armed with this rough sketch of the Bay Area, we begin our exploration. Before setting forth, equip yourself with detailed maps to augment our simple locator maps. If you're an AAA member, pick up area maps at the main office at 150 Van Ness Avenue in San Francisco; (415-565-2012).

If you're planning a fly-drive, you might consider the alternates of **Oakland International Airport** (510-444-4444) or **San José Airport** (408-

277-4759) to the busier **San Francisco International** (415-761-0800). Further, lodgings generally are cheaper in the outlying areas than in San Francisco itself.

For a much more detailed look at the city by the Golden Gate, pick up a copy of our *Inside San Francisco*; details are in the back of this book.

San Francisco

Population: 724,000   **Elevation: 63 feet**

No longer the Bay Area's largest city, San Francisco is still its urban focal point, the hub of the wheel, the center of the action. This is where local political power is brokered, where headlines are written, where people come to wine, dine and play. In Bay Area jargon, it's simply "the city." Indeed, one local newspaper has the presumption to capitalize it.

San Francisco also is a difficult city to navigate. A glimpse at a map will reveal that it sits at a 45-degree angle to itself. Downtown grids are diagonal to those south of Market, and streets become hopelessly entangled with one another as they climb into the city's hills. We'll endeavor to keep you on the right track as we explore.

RV Advisory: Before you begin motoring through the city, bear in mind that driving is only difficult. Downtown parking is close to impossible if you have a high-rise RV and totally impossible with a trailer. It's best to explore the heart of the city by public transit, foot or cab. Our driving trips (except the Mount Tam climb in Marin) can be navigated by RVs; it's parking that's the problem.

A **49-mile Scenic Drive** offers a good motoring view of the city and its ramparts, but it can be tricky to follow. Unknown persons have a penchant for tearing down the directional signs. Also, it takes you through some heavily congested areas and some rather tricky turns. Our route, we modestly insist, is easier to follow. Like any driving tour of the city, it involves a bit of hill climbing. You *will* encounter traffic, so avoid it during the rush hour.

It was suggested at the top of this chapter that you begin your Bay Area exploration atop one of the Twin Peaks. Getting there is relatively easy. From the downtown area, find Market Street and start driving away from the bay. Never mind the swirl of traffic; you won't get lost if you keep the Ferry Building in your rearview mirror.

As Market passes Castro Street in the **Castro District** of gay liberation fame, it swerves to the right and climbs toward your destination. Use that ungainly red and white **Sutro Tower,** the city's major radio and TV antenna, as a beacon. At the top of the climb (with a dazzling city view behind), you'll pass through a stoplight at Clipper Street, where Market becomes Portola Drive.

A few blocks beyond, take a hard turn to your right up Twin Peaks Boulevard. The road twists around to **Twin Peaks Vista Point.** Park, walk the short distance back to the north peak and begin your climb. It's not difficult, since railroad tie steps have been set into its slopes.

Having absorbed the view, loop around the peaks and retrace your route to Portola Drive. Turn right and follow its winding course past the mix of tidily small and elaborately elegant homes of the **Twin Peaks District.** To see the most opulent of these, turn left onto Santa Rosa Avenue for a brief drive through **St. Francis Wood.** Back on Portola, take a half right onto Sloat at a five-point intersection and follow it west toward the ocean. You're

San Francisco

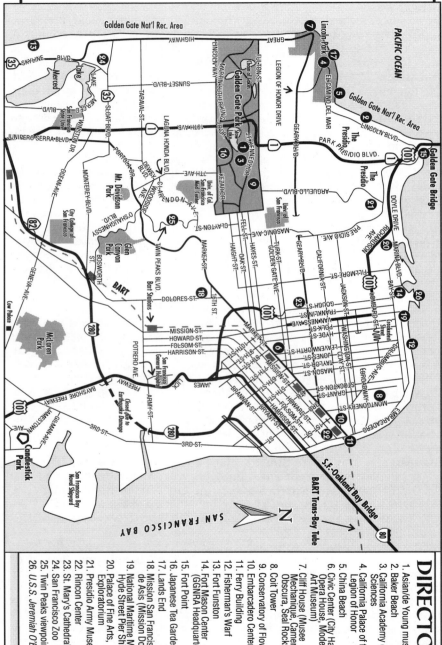

now in the **Sunset District,** an area of reclaimed sand dunes anchored down with endless rows of little mix-and-match stucco houses.

Cross the landscaped expressway of Sunset Boulevard, then take a quick half left onto Skyline Boulevard at the edge of the **San Francisco Zoo.** Follow Skyline (Highway 35) south; you'll skim the edge of **Lake Merced** and shortly encounter **Fort Funston.** It's a former coastal battery perched atop bluffs 200 feet above the Pacific, offering impressive coastal views. The area is a favorite hangout of hang gliders. After you've finished watching them dance with the wind, you can follow a short path to concrete bunkers left over from the fort's earlier days.

Fort Funston is part of the **Golden Gate National Recreation Area,** a glorious gathering of historic and natural sites established in 1972. Covering a scattered patchwork of 144 square miles, it's the world's largest urban park and the most visited element of America's national park system. It encompasses nearly all of San Francisco's ocean front, several bayside beaches and the Marin Headlands across the Golden Gate. We'll encounter its diverse elements frequently during our spin around San Francisco. From Fort Funston, retrace your route up Skyline Boulevard, perhaps pausing to take a drive around Lake Merced and its kelly green golf courses.

Departing Fort Funston, make the right-turn-only onto Skyline, drive up a few blocks and make a U-turn in front of the entrance to the Olympic Club Country Club. This points you back toward the city. Opposite Lake Merced, get into the left lane and blend onto the Great Highway, which fronts the city's long and sandy beachfront.

Follow the highway north about three miles, turn right onto Lincoln Avenue at a traffic signal and follow signs into the city's premiere showplace, **Golden Gate Park.** One of the largest and most attractive manmade parks in the world, this 1,017-acre facility was shaped from drifting sand more than a century ago. We won't suggest a specific course through the park since you'll probably get lost anyway. Just keep your eye to the west and return to the Great Highway when you've finished. While you're in there, stop by some of the city's leading attractions, such as the **Academy of Sciences, Conservatory of Flowers, DeYoung** and **Asian** art museums, and **Japanese Tea Garden.**

Continue northward on the Great Highway, swerving uphill to the **Cliff House,** one of the city's most enduring landmarks. Communicate with the seals on the offshore **Seal Rocks,** study historic exhibits and pick up information at the **GGNRA Visitor Center.** Step into the **Camera Obscura,** and look at the amusing gadgetry of **Musee Mechanique.** Consider an oceanview lunch or a sunset dinner or cocktails and the Cliff House restaurant and cocktail lounge. Arrive early if you want a sunset view from the Cliff House's nautically old fashioned **Phineas T. Barnacle** pub.

Your route becomes Point Lobos Avenue as it curves past the Cliff House. Follow it inland briefly, then turn left onto El Camino Del Mar opposite Seal Rock Inn for pleasing ocean views from **Point Lobos Overlook.** From here, you'll enjoy the first of many postcard glimpses of the **Golden Gate Bridge.** If you like to hike, you can pick up GGNRA's **Coastal Trail,** which winds along the headlands, through groves of cypress and eucalyptus, with frequent Golden Gate vistas. Just beyond Point Lobos is the superstructure of the *U.S.S. San Francisco,* a battle scarred World War II battleship. Return to Point Lobos Avenue and follow it inland, where it soon blends into Geary Boulevard. Start counting down the numbered avenues and turn left onto 34th.

This takes you through the lush links of **Lincoln Park Golf Course** and to one of the city's finest art museums, the **Palace of the Legion of Honor** (closed for renovation until 1995). Featuring an outstanding collection of European art, it's a marble columned twin to the Legion of Honor in Paris. Nearby is the **Holocaust,** a stark monument that recalls the horrors of Jewish death camps in World War II.

Turn right onto El Camino del Mar and follow it into **Seacliff,** the gloriously landscaped grotto of San Francisco's super rich. Before you lose yourself in a fit of envy, watch carefully for Seacliff Drive, take a sharp left and follow it to **China Beach**. One of the city's authentic hidden jewels, this is a thumbnail of strand at the base of Seacliff's mansions. The water level view of the Golden Gate Bridge and the rugged coastal bluffs is awe-inspiring, yet this tiny enclave is rarely visited.

As El Camino del Mar weaves through Seacliff, it becomes Lincoln Boulevard and takes you through the eucalyptus, redwood and pine forests of the **Presidio.** Headquarters for the U.S. Sixth Army, this thickly wooded coastal bluff becomes part of the GGNRA in 1995. As you enter the Presidio, fork to the left and follow signs down to **Baker Beach.** On warm days, it's a popular spot for the bronzed bikini set. If you hike a few hundred yards up the beach, you'll see all bronze; no bikini. While not prohibiting beach nudity, GGNRA park rangers ask skinny dippers remain in the rocky coves, out of sight of mom, pop and wide-eyed kids.

Battery Lowell A. Chamberlain, a gun emplacement turned mini-museum, is a short hike up the beach. You'll see exhibits on coastal fortifications and unusual disappearing rifles—artillery pieces that recoiled out of sight after firing a round.

To experience one of the Bay Area's most striking hikes, keep walking past the Chamberlain battery, past the nudies and rock ribbed coves all the way to the Golden Gate Bridge. It can be accomplished safely *only* during low tide. You still may have to do a bit of scrambling to get up and over some of the rocky outcroppings.

Caution: Do not climb the seacliffs above Baker Beach. The rocks are loose and the sand is slippery. Every year, foolhardy hikers are injured when they try to play mountain goat on this fragile terrain.

The drive through the Presidio offers frequent glimpses of the Golden Gate, framed in coastal cypress, and several turnouts invite you to pause. As you approach the bridge, watch on your left for Merchant Drive, which takes you to **Battery Godfrey** and **Battery Marcus Miller,** two elaborate gun emplacements that are often missed by visitors.

Continuing on Lincoln Boulevard, you'll pass under elevated Doyle Drive and arrive at the popular **Golden Gate Bridge viewpoint**. You'll be hard pressed to find a parking place on a busy day. Even if you do, you'll have to interrupt your explorations to feed hungry parking meters. We have a better idea. Continue past the viewpoint for about half a mile and take a sharp left, following signs down to **Fort Point National Historic Site**.

Our favorite place in the city, Fort Point is an imposing brick citadel tucked under the south anchorage of the Golden Gate Bridge. Officially called Fort Winfield Scott, it was completed in 1861 to head off a Confederate naval attack that never came. After exploring the fort and absorbing

Towers of the Golden Gate Bridge reach toward a canopy of fog; the great brick citadel of Fort Point sits under its massive arch.
—Don W. Martin

awesome city, bay and bridge views, you can take a set of stairs back up to the bridge viewpoint. They're steep but vistas are great, so take your time and enjoy.

Who will argue that this is the most beautiful bridge in the most striking setting in the world? To appreciate it fully, leave the crowds and diesel bus fumes and hike across this span. The sidewalk is open daily from 5 a.m. to 9 p.m. The round trip is three miles; if time is short, at least go to mid-span. Feel its strength shudder beneath your feet. Admire the distant cityscape, looking now like a model in a blue diorama of sky and bay. Stare dizzily down to the Pacific, 200 feet below, and watch toy ships pass.

No, the bridge isn't golden. The official color is International Orange. Actually, the name precedes the bridge. This narrow strait was first called the Golden Gate by explorer John C. Frèmont when he saw it in 1846. Presumably, he was moved by the magic of sunset on the water. And why is this bridge orange while most others are painted silver? Because it's more visible in the frequent fogs that cloak the bay's entrance.

Return to your Fort Point parking place and continue driving along Lincoln Boulevard. As your route twists and turns past the parade ground and administrative area, pause at the **Presidio Army Museum** on your right at Lincoln and Mesa Street, offering a mix of military lore in several rooms of the former station hospital. Just beyond, as you pass **Letterman Army Medical Center,** turn left onto Lombard Street. Pass through the Presidio Gate and do an immediate left onto Lyon. Follow it down to Richardson Avenue (Highway 101) and do a right-left zig-zag across it, with the help of a traffic light.

Lyon takes you to the **Palace of Fine Arts,** a splendid Beaux Arts structure mirrored in a reflection pool. Neither a palace nor an art museum, it's a reconstructed survivor of the 1915 Panama-Pacific International Exposition. Tucked in behind this domed structure is the **Exploratorium,** a hands-on science museum that's a required stop for the curious child that lurks in all of us.

From the Exploratorium, follow Baker Street toward the bayfront to Marina Boulevard and the **Marina Green,** an emerald rectangle along the bayfront. Take a break to watch frisbees, footballs and Technicolor kites fly about, and stroll past the pleasure boats at rest in three adjacent small craft harbors. The **Golden Gate Promenade,** the city's most popular walking/biking trail, extends three and a half miles west along the bayfront from the Marina Green to Fort Point.

Anchoring the east side of the Green is **Fort Mason,** a former Army supply depot, now turned into a simmering sociological center. It also houses the GGNRA headquarters. Once colorless cargo sheds are now alive with cultural-political-educational activity, ranging from Greenpeace headquarters to performing arts groups to ethnic awareness centers. Among its visitor attractions are the **Mexican Museum, San Francisco Craft and Folk Art Museum, Museo Italo Americano** and the **African-American Cultural Society Museum.** The outstanding **Greens Restaurant** offers tasty vegetarian dishes and splendid bay views. Its **Tassajara Bakery** sells whole earth breads and pastries that will make you renounce junk food. Two historic vessels are parked next to Fort Mason—**U.S.S. Jeremiah O'Brien,** America's only fully operational World War II liberty ship, and the steam tug *Hercules*.

Beyond the fort, follow signs toward Fisherman's Wharf, which will put you onto Bay Street. Cross the wide Van Ness Avenue, then turn left down Polk Street, headed directly toward the **National Maritime Museum.** Fashioned like the superstructure of an Art Deco ship, it offers a delightful cargo of nautical lore. Take a right onto Beach Street in front of the museum and start looking for a parking place. (Good luck on a summer weekend!) Near the museum is **Hyde Street Pier,** one of the more appealing attractions of the GGNRA, with a wonderful collection of old ships.

That pleasant rattling chime reaching your ear is the siren call of the San Francisco cable car, the city's most endearing and enduring landmark. Dropping off Hyde Street Hill, the little wooden cars clatter onto a turntable at the edge of Aquatic Park. Tourists stand in long queues, eager for a ride on one of America's only mobile landmarks. Street musicians, willing to perform for a smile and an occasional tip, soothe the long wait for the riders.

The smell of crab pots signals your arrival at **Fisherman's Wharf,** the most heavily impacted tourist area in the city. A few decades ago, Fisherman's Wharf was one of the city's most appealing areas—a John Steinbeck vision of weathered fish processing sheds, seafood cafés and brightly painted fishing boats. It is today a gaudy parody of itself, a garish potpourri of wax museums, novelty rides, tacky souvenir shops and sidewalk T-shirt vendors.

All is not lost to the sultans of schlock, however. Bright-hulled fishing boats still bob in their slips at Jefferson Street Lagoon, glittering catches of fish are still hauled into the processing plants of Pier 45, and steaming crab pots permeate the salty air. The wharf also offers the city's greatest concentration of seafood restaurants (although not the best), plus its largest gathering of boutiques and curio shops.

Of the shopping complexes, **Ghirardelli Square** at North Point and Polk offers the most upscale galleries and boutiques, followed closely by the **Cannery** at Beach Street and the foot of Columbus Avenue. The **Anchorage** at Jefferson and Jones offers a mix of souvenir and specialty shops. **Cost Plus,** just up from the wharf at Taylor and North Point, is Northern California's largest import shop complex.

Just east of the wharf, along the Embarcadero, is ticky-tacky **Pier 39.** This blend of boutiques, restaurants and carnival midway is the area's busiest tourist shopping facility. It boasts some of the most tightly focused shops in the tourist trade. Where else can you find a store specializing in refrigerator magnets? About the only natural attraction at Pier 39 is a troupe of sea lions that annexed part of the pier's boat basin a few years ago.

You'll pass the **U.S.S. Pampanito** as you approach Pier 39. It's a battle-scarred World War II submarine permanently berthed here as a visitor attraction. Nearby, at Pier 41, is the ticket office for the **Red and White Fleet,** offering bay cruises and trips to **Alcatraz.** The famed prison is now part of the GGNRA. Once you're delivered ashore by the Red and White Fleet, you can follow a self-guiding tour to points of interest in this notorious lock-up that hosted Al Capone and Machine Gun Kelly.

The **Embarcadero,** Spanish for "place of embarkation," is a wide thoroughfare leading east from the wharf, following the gentle curve of the city's waterfront. If several years have passed since you last visited, you'll note a pleasant absence. The Embarcadero Freeway, the concrete eyesore that ran along the waterfront, was demolished after suffering damage in the 1989 Loma Prieta earthquake.

Once the leading seaport on the West Coast, San Francisco's waterfront has lost most of its shipping business to the more aggressive Port of Oakland. Many of the cavernous cargo piers, reaching into the bay like giant, chubby fingers, stand empty. Others, like Pier 39, have been given over to tourism. In the years ahead, we will witness a transition to promenades, bay view restaurants, townhouses and office space. This is not an unpleasant alternative to cargo ships sitting in oily waters.

As you travel follow the Embarcadero along the waterfront, note the contoured brick **Levi's Plaza,** a stylish office and shopping complex on your right, across the Embarcadero from Pier 33. Telegraph Hill rises behind and above, topped by Coit Tower; we'll get you to this noted landmark later.

Approaching the Ferry Building, you'll see the slender highrises of **Embarcadero Center,** the city's most extensive and attractive urban renewal project. Covering several city blocks, the complex consists of four office towers with tiered shopping galleries at their bases. With its landscaped patios, elevated shops, monumental artwork and slender highrises, Embarcadero Center has the feel of an Orwellian city of the future. Adjacent is the **Golden Gateway,** an upscale residential complex linked to the center by crosswalks. Conceivably, a resident could spend years here without ever touching feet to the ground.

After prowling about the Embarcadero shops, step into the great indoors of the **Hyatt Regency** hotel. Admire the Buck Rogers style elevators scurrying up inner walls and a giant steel orb suspended above a spill-over reflection fountain. Retire for drinks at **The Other Trellis** lobby bar, or take one of those passenger rockets up to the **Equinox,** a revolving restaurant offering overpriced food, cocktails and interesting low-level views of the city's waterfront.

At the base of Embarcadero Center is **Justin Herman Plaza,** a wonderful urban open space busy with skateboarders, bench sitters, sun worshipers and brown-baggers. The ground floor of Embarcadero Four is lined with take-out restaurants, so this is a nice spot for an urban picnic. Street artists set up their stalls on the south side of the plaza; they're particularly numerous on weekends.

A focal point here is the squarish and garish **Vaillancourt Fountain,** which appears to have been assembled from concrete packing crates. With the Embarcadero Freeway gone, it's now unchallenged as the ugliest thing on the waterfront. However, it's fun to crawl among its innards and tip-toe across square stepping stones of the dirty reflection pool.

Across the way is the durable **San Francisco Ferry Building** at the foot of Market Street, with a 230-foot clock tower modeled after the campaniles of Seville's cathedral. Once host to 100,000 daily ferry passengers, the 1896 facility has come full circle. Swift passenger boats of the **Red and White Fleet** (415-546-BOAT) and **Golden Gate Ferries** (415-332-6600) operate from slips on either side of the structure, carrying commuters about the bay. They can carry you, the visitor, as well. Particularly popular are the Golden Gate Ferry run to Sausalito, the Red and White ferry trip to Tiburon and Red and White's long haul across the bay and up Carquinez Strait to Vallejo.

Step inside the Ferry Building's **World Trade Center** to admire simplified Pacific Rim picture maps painted for the 1939 Golden Gate International Exposition. A bit of irony here: That exposition celebrated the completion of the Golden Gate and San Francisco-Oakland Bay Bridges, which spelled the death knell for the auto ferries. Just beyond the Ferry Building is the **Embarcadero Promenade** at the foot of Mission Street, a series of concrete risers and walkways. It's a fine spot for viewing the **Bay Bridge,** which leapfrogs from pier to pier en route to Yerba Buena Island and Oakland beyond.

For an outstanding example of renewal and preservation, walk two blocks up to **Rincon Center** at Mission and Spear. Once the Art Deco Rincon Annex post office, it was converted recently into an atrium shopping center, with office and apartment towers rising behind. Step into the old post office lobby, where the Depression era **California history murals** by Anton Refregier have been preserved. The adjacent atrium features a distinctive "rain column" fountain. Chairs, tables and assorted snack and beverage shops make this is an easy place to linger. Incidentally, as you walk up to Rincon Center, notice the handsome Mansard roofed **Audiffred Building** at 100 Mission. It's a survivor of the 1906 earthquake and a fine example of 19th century commercial architecture.

We presume that you've parked your vehicle and haven't been trying to absorb all this through your windshield. If so, leave it parked. This is a good area to begin a public transit exploration of the city, since the foot of Market serves as a transportation hub. **Bay Area Rapid Transit** and the San Francisco Municipal Railway's **Metro Muni** run beneath your feet, reached from Embarcadero Station, just up Market. Many of the city's bus lines branch from Market or cross over it. Maps in the BART station and on a kiosk outside offer details of the transit system.

The **California Street cable car** terminates here as well. This stop is never as crowded as those at Fisherman's Wharf or Powell and Market. Hop a car here for a short ride to the heart of **Chinatown** at Grant and California. Or continue to the top of the hill at Powell Street, and transfer to a car headed for the wharf. (However, wedging yourself onto a wharf-bound cable car is no easy task on a summer weekend.)

If you're in a walking mood, you can reach the heart of downtown from here, with its mix of restaurants, shops, sunny plazas and other lures. Meanwhile, since this is a driving guide, we'll try to steer you to a few more highlights and get you out of town before the traffic hits. Get a good downtown map and stay alert, because it gets a little complicated from this point.

Head up Market Street into the heart of the city. Market doesn't reach the Embarcadero, so take a right up Mission, an immediate right on Steuart, and then a left up Market. Your progress up Market will be slow, although it's manageable most of the time. *Don't* try this during rush hour. Incidentally, this is the area where the city sits at a 45-degree angle to itself, so it's easy to become confused.

About a mile and a half from the waterfront, take a half right onto Hayes Street, in front of a tall office, shopping and residential complex called **Fox Plaza.** There's parking underneath, reached via Hayes.

You're in the **Civic Center,** with its splendid collection of French renaissance architecture. You'll likely want to wander through San Franciso's **City Hall** with its sweeping grand staircase. It's modeled after the nation's capital, with a copper dome that's 16 feet higher. Nearby, side-by-side on Van Ness Avenue, are the look-alike **Veterans' Memorial** and **San Francisco Opera House,** and the splendid **Davies Symphony Hall.** Headquarters for the **California State Automobile Association** is close by, at Hayes and Van Ness Avenue.

The Civic Center also is the city's cultural core. The **San Francisco Museum of Modern Art** is housed in the Veterans' Memorial (although a new home is under construction elsewhere). The Opera House is home to the San Francisco Ballet and San Francisco Opera, while the San Francisco Symphony performs at Davies Hall. Several art galleries stand along Hayes Street, just beyond Van Ness Avenue, and you'll find a fine art and book store on the ground floor of the Veterans' Memorial.

If you prefer cabbage to culture, you can shop the **Heart of the City Farmers Market,** which happens on United Nations Plaza every Sunday and Wednesday. **Civic Center Plaza**, opposite City Hall between Polk and Larkin streets, is a popular venue for anti-government protests—city, state and federal. When it isn't filled with placard-waving protesters poking holes in the air with their fingers, it's busy with pigeons and slumbering street people. **Brooks Hall** exhibit center is cleverly tucked beneath the sod of Civic Center Plaza.

The Civic Center was designed by noted architect Daniel Burnham, and built in stages early in this century. Burnham chose the French renaissance style because of its timeless look. However, latter-day additions with their puffy rounded corners, such as **Davies Hall,** and the **Edmund G. Brown California Office Building** at Van Ness and McAllister, appear to have been inspired by the Michelin tire man.

You have undoubtedly seen that photo of the "Painted Ladies," a matched set of six Victorian row houses, with the city skyline rising behind them. They're in the Alamo Square Historic District, not far from the Civic Center. We'll wander through there, hop across Market Street to visit the mission where San Francisco began, then return to the Civic Center to complete our drive.

To reach the "Ladies," cross Van Ness Avenue on Hayes Street and follow it eight blocks to **Alamo Square**. This sloping park is bounded by Hayes, Scott, Fulton and Steiner. The Victorian row houses are on Steiner, and are best viewed from the park's tilted greens. Other fine examples of Victorian architecture surround Alamo Square. Note particularly the **Archbishop's Mansion** and **Russian Consulate,** both on Fulton. To see more, drive a block north on Scott (beside the Consulate), then go right onto McAllister past a row of elaborate Italianate Victorians. Hang a left onto Steiner and watch for an imposing fairy castle conglomeration at Steiner and Golden Gate. It's **Chateau Tivoli,** an 1892 gingerbread confection now housing a bed and breakfast (listed below).

Reverse directions on Steiner and head back to Alamo Square. You will have effectively looped the historic district. To reach the mission from here, continue south on Steiner for about seven blocks to small **Duboce Park.** Jog left on Duboce Avenue, take an immediate right onto Sanchez Street and cross upper Market after a few blocks.

Travel one block, turn left onto 16th street, drive about three blocks to Dolores Street and you're beside **Mission San Francisco de Asis.** That grand edifice with ornate baroque towers isn't the mission. That's the **Basilica of San Francisco,** completed in 1926. The humble whitewashed mission kneels in the basilica's shadow. The city's most venerated building and one of its oldest, it was completed in 1791. The original chapel, founded a short distance away in 1776, no longer exists.

From the mission, cross Dolores on 16th Street, follow it two blocks east and turn left onto Valencia. After two blocks, watch on your left for an old-style yellow building. This structure houses history of another sort. It's the oldest surviving factory of the apparel giant, **Levi Strauss & Co**, built in 1906 after the earthquake destroyed company headquarters near the waterfront. Plant tours are conducted on Wednesdays (see "Activities" below).

Just beyond the Strauss structure, you'll hit Market Street again. Turn right, then immediately get into a double left turn lane that will swing you north onto Gough Street. Drive about eight blocks, turn right onto one-way Golden Gate Avenue, drive two blocks and turn left up the broad boulevard of Van Ness Avenue.

After a couple of roller-coaster miles, turn right onto California Street at a cable car terminus, drive four blocks to Hyde Street and turn left. This puts you on another cable car line. We're setting you up for the proper approach to **"the crookedest street in the world."** For the uninitiated, this is a one block section of Lombard that spirals down through terraced hillside homes and gardens. Climb to the top of Hyde Street Hill, turn right onto Lombard and there it is!

RV advisory: The street is too crooked for all but the smallest RVs, so don't attempt it. You'll get hung up and cause a traffic mess. To stay with our driving tour, continue a block to Chestnut, go downhill to the right, then go right again to pick up Lombard at the base of the squiggle. Follow it several blocks as it cuts across diagonal Columbus Avenue, climbs uphill and ends at a scenic overlook to the bay. Curling around to your right is Telegraph Hill Boulevard, which winds to the top of **Telegraph Hill,** crowned by **Coit Tower.**

If it's a summer day, don't *even* try to fight the bumper-to-bumper traffic to the top. The reason it's stalled is because people up there are waiting for a place to park. City-savvy visitors find a parking spot down below—difficult but not impossible—and stroll a tree-shaded path to Coit Tower. It's a better approach both esthetically and temperamentally. Having achieved this height, you can pay a modest fee to ride an elevator to the top of Coit Tower for stellar city views.

Some of the city's most pleasurable walks descend from here, following steep wooden stairways past thick foliage and homes cantilevered into the slopes of Telegraph Hill. To begin your descent, look for a set of stairs leading bay-ward, near the entrance to the parking area; a "Greenwich" sign marks the spot. As you wind downward, enjoying the views and the closeness of lush gardens, remember that it's 494 steps back to the top. If you've conned a travel companion into meeting you at the bottom with the car, mention that you'll emerge on Sansome Street, opposite Levi's Plaza.

From Telegraph Hill, backtrack four blocks down Lombard. Go left onto Mason, then take an immediate half left onto Columbus Avenue. It cuts a diagonal swath into the Italian heart of **North Beach.** This is one of the city's oldest neighborhoods, with a satisfying mix of 18th century Victorians and bay-windowed post-earthquake structures. At Union and Columbus, you'll nip the edge of **Washington Square,** a grassy *piazza* in this urban enclave. Here, old men of Italy doze in the sun while their grandchildren toss frisbees instead of rolling boccè balls. Watching over them are the twin spires of **Saints Peter and Paul Church,** a 1924 edifice done up in classic European filigree.

The city's finest Italian restaurants are focused in this area and many offer sidewalk tables. Parking is a chore here, but if you can find a spot, take an outdoor lunch break or sip cappuccino at one of the *al fresco* cafès and watch people and traffic pass. Or step into a deli, build a sandwich and join those old men in the sun on Washington Square. Don't forget the frisbee.

At the busy intersection of Columbus, Grant and Broadway, you'll nip the edge of **Chinatown** and pass what's left of the city's **topless bars.** More interesting are three remnants of the area's artist colony and Beat Generation. Clustered together for reassurance, half a block below on Broadway, are **Vesuvio's Bar,** where Jack Kerouac, William Saroyan and Allen Ginsberg once warmed the bar stools, and poet Lawrence Ferlinghetti's very literate and liberal **City Lights Bookstore.** Across the way is a pub with the odd name of **Spec's 12 Adler Museum Cafè,** another wonderful relic of those liberated Sixties.

As you approach the lower end of Columbus, you'll note that the pointed **Transamerica Pyramid** seems to be blocking your path. Swing to the right to avoid colliding with its leggy concrete buttresses. This puts you on Montgomery Street, in the heart of the **Financial District.** And this returns you to Market Street and the end of our drive.

You probably noticed, as you drove through North Beach, that there was no beach. The area's name survives from gold rush days when the bay intruded much farther inland. The water reached into Yerba Buena Cove, a block up from the Pyramid on Washington Street. This is now the site of **Portsmouth Square,** the town's original plaza. Had the bay not been filled, the Pyramid would be up to its buttresses in water.

SAN FRANCISCO ATTRACTIONS
(In order of appearance)

☺ *San Francisco Zoological Gardens* ● *One Zoo Road (at Sloat); (415) 753-7172. Daily 10 to 5. Adults $6, kids 12 to 15 and seniors, $3. Zebra Train ride $2 for adults and $1 for kids and seniors; Children's Zoo $1; carousel rides 75 cents.* Stare quizzically at your ancestral cousins, then learn about them with hands-on exhibits at the Primate Discovery Center, the zoo's best feature. Other major attractions are Gorilla World, housing America's only zoo gorilla family, and the old fashioned lion house, where the big cats are fed from 2 to 3 daily.

☺ *California Academy of Sciences* ● *Off the Music Concourse, Golden Gate Park; (415) 750-7145 or 750-7111; 750-7141 for planetarium/Lasarium. Daily 10 to 5 (to 7 from July 4 to Labor Day). Adults $4, kids 12-17 and seniors $2, kids 6-11, $1. Planetarium: adults $2.50, seniors and kids $1.25; Lasarium shows: adults $6, kids 6 to 12 and seniors $4.* One of America's premiere science centers, the academy includes Steinhart Aquarium and Laserium, Morrison Planetarium and outstanding science, wildlife and anthropology exhibits. Graphics, lasers, videos and computers help this lively place come to life.

Conservatory of Flowers ● *John F. Kennedy Drive (just beyond McLaren Lodge), Golden Gate Park; (415) 666-7017. Daily 9 to 5 (until 6 from March through September). Adults $1.50, kids and seniors free.* Fashioned after London's Kew Garden Conservatory, this grand Victorian greenhouse contains a lush jungle of orchids and other tropical plants. Pictorial flower beds out front are changed periodically to reflect seasonal themes.

☺ *M.H. de Young Memorial Museum and Asian Art Museum* ● *Tea Garden Drive, near the Music Concourse, Golden Gate Park; (415) 750-3600 and 668-8921. Wednesday-Sunday 11 to 5. Adults $4, kids 12 to 17 and seniors $2.* Although they're separate entities, the de Young and Asian Art museums share the same building and the same admission ticket. De Young features American art—primarily paintings, sculpture and furnishings, as well as exhibits from England and from Pacific cultures. The Asian Museum has an outstanding collection of artifacts, statuary and scrolls from China, Japan, India and Tibet.

Japanese Tea Garden ● *Tea Garden Drive (just beyond de Young), Golden Gate Park; (415) 666-7024. Daily 8:30 to 5:30. Adults $2, kids and seniors $1.* Walk the cobbled paths of this lushly landscaped formal garden, then pause for a spot of green tea and cookies in the teahouse. A gift shop sells things Japanese.

Camera Obscura ● *1096 Point Lobos Ave. (behind the Cliff House); (415) 750-0415. Daily 10 to sunset; Adults $1, kids 50 cents.* Images of the area are reflected onto a parabolic screen; several holographs are on exhibit.

Musee Mechanique ● *1090 Point Lobos Ave. (behind the Cliff House); (415) 386-1170. Weekdays 11 to 6, weekends 10 to 7; free.* It brims with dozens of early day music boxes, Nickelodeons and Rube Goldberg devices.

☺ *California Palace of the Legion of Honor* • *Legion of Honor Drive (Lincoln Park); currently undergoing a major renovation; scheduled for re-opening in 1995. For an update, call the de Young at (415) 750-3600.* When reopened, this colonnaded palace will exhibit eight centuries of European art. Its collections include an exceptional Rodin sculpture retrospective, elegant porcelains and paintings by Van Gough, Renoir, Monet and other past masters.

☺ *Fort Point National Historic Site* • *Off Lincoln Boulevard; (415) 556-1693. Wednesday-Sunday 10 to 5; free.* This grand brick edifice offers impressive views of the city and the Golden Gate Bridge that arches directly over it. Massive corridors and rooftop ramparts invite exploration. Features include historic exhibits in several of the rooms, cannon drills, guided tours, videos and a bookstore.

Presidio Army Museum • *Lincoln Boulevard (Funston); (415) 561-3319. Tuesday-Sunday 10 to 4; free.* Two hundred years of Bay Area military and civilian history are on display. Exhibits include military uniforms and weapons and an outstanding collection of 1906 San Francisco earthquake photos.

☺ *Palace of Fine Arts & Exploratorium* • *3601 Lyon St. (Baker); (415) 563-7337 or 561-0360 for recorded information. Wednesday 10 to 9:30, Thursday-Sunday 10 to 5. Adults $6, seniors $3, kids 6 to 17, $2 (all tickets good for six months).* Occupying a wing of the palace, the Exploratorium invites you to make lightning, create color spectrums, fiddle with magnetism, check the latest weather satellite photo and such. The palace is a leftover from the 1915 Pan-Pacific Exposition, worth a look for its classic Beaux Arts rotunda and colonnade. Stop by at night, when it's bathed in floodlights and mirrored in a reflection pool.

Mexican Museum • *Fort Mason Center Building D; (415) 441-0404. Wednesday-Sunday noon to 5. Adults $3, seniors and kids $2.* The Mexican-American experience is reflected in folk art and fine art in this well organized museum. A gift shop with ethnic art and handicrafts is adjacent.

San Francisco Craft and Folk Art Museum • *Fort Mason Center Building A; (415) 775-0990. Tuesday-Sunday 11 to 5; adults $1.* It's one of the city's better small museums. Changing shows range from American and foreign folk art to costume jewelry, furnishings and crafts. Special theme exhibits sometimes occupy the entire museum.

Museo Italo Americano • *Fort Mason Center Building C; (415) 673-2200. Wednesday-unday noon to 5; free.* This small museum features changing and permanent exhibits of Italian-American art and artists.

African-American Cultural Society Museum • *Fort Mason Center Building C; (415) 441-0640. Wednesday-Sunday noon to 5. Adults $1, kids 50 cents.* A combined museum and handicrafts shop, it features Black American arts and crafts as well as artifacts from Africa.

☺ *U.S.S. Jeremiah O'Brien Liberty Ship* • *Pier 3, Fort Mason; (415) 441-3101. Weekdays 9 to 3, weekends 11 to 4. Adults $3, seniors and kids $1, families $6.* Prowl the welded steel decks and engine room of America's only fully operational Liberty Ship. Three thousand were built to carry troops and supplies overseas during World War II.

☺ *National Maritime Museum of San Francisco* • *Beach and Polk streets; (415) 556-3002. Free. Daily 10 to 5.* This excellent museum pre-

The 1886 Balclutha is one of several historic ships at Hyde Street Pier near Fisherman's Wharf. The city skyline rises beyond. — **Don W. Martin**

serves a century of Bay Area maritime history. Exhibits are thematic, covering river boats, ferryboats, fishing and sailors' arts such as scrimshaw, knot-tying and—surprisingly—macrame. On display are fine examples of model ships, figureheads, old photos and pieces of historic ships.

☺ **Hyde Street Pier Historic Ships** ● *Foot of Hyde Street; (415) 556-6435. Daily 10 to 6 May-October and 10 to 5 November-April; ranger-led tours hourly 11 to 4. Adults $3; seniors and kids under 16 free.* Walk about the decks and crawl through the holds of ships that made maritime history. The collection includes the square-rigged 1886 *Balclutha*, the 1895 *C.A. Thayer* sailing cargo ship, the 1890 sidewheel ferry *Eureka*, the 1904 paddle-wheel steam tug *Eppleton Hall*, the 1891 scow schooner *Alma*, and the *Wapama*, a steam schooner built in 1915.

☺ **U.S.S. Pampanito submarine** ● *Pier 45; (415) 929-0202. Adults $4, kids 12 to 18, $2; kids 6 to 11 and seniors, $1. Daily 9 to 9 (shorter hours in the off-season).* A self-guiding taped tour takes you through the cozy confines of this sub that sank six enemy ships during World War II. Kids will be fascinated by the myriad of knobs, dials and levers and the gleaming torpedoes—disarmed, of course—still sitting in their cradles.

☺ **Alcatraz** • *Reached via Red and White Fleet shuttle boat from Pier 41; (415) 546-2800. Adult roundtrip $5.50, seniors $4.60, kids 5 to 11, $3. Cell house tour audio tapes $3. MC/VISA.* Self-guiding tours take you past the home of Al Capone, Robert "Birdman of Alcatraz" Stroud and other notorious jailbirds. Special ranger programs are conducted periodically. Originally built as a military post, it served as a federal maximum security prison from 1934 until the 1960s.

☺ **Embarcadero Center** • *Just off the waterfront, between Sacramento, Sansome and Clay streets; (415) 772-0500. Most shops open weekdays 10 a.m. to 6 p.m., 10 to 5 Saturday and noon to 5 Sunday; restaurant hours vary. Validated parking; free parking on weekends.* Shops and restaurants line lower terraces of the four Embarcadero Center complexes. Elevated walkways, basins of flowering plants, artwork, fountains and patios make this the city's most attractive shopping area.

Ferry Building • *Foot of Market Street on the Embarcadero; open to the public weekdays 7 a.m. to 6 p.m.* The Ferry Building's 230-foot clock tower was modeled after the campaniles of Seville's cathedral. Youngsters will enjoy the oversized wall maps depicting the people, animals and native shelters of the nations of the Pacific Rim.

☺ **Rincon Center** • *Mission Street between Spear and Steuart. Daily 7 a.m. to 11 p.m.* The old Rincon Annex post office, a national architectural landmark, is the handsome façade of this new center. Several California history murals line the historic lobby, and museum cases contain artifacts found in local excavations. New murals depicting contemporary city life rim the walls of an adjacent atrium lobby.

☺ **City Hall** • *Polk between Grove and McAllister.* San Francisco's City Hall is one of America's most opulent public buildings, a showplace worthy of the grand city it represents. The interior is resplendent in marble columns, statuary in ornate niches and a sweeping marble stairway.

Heart of the City Farmers' Market • *United Nations Plaza between Market and Larkin; (415) 647-9423. Sunday 8 to 5, Wednesday 8 to 5:30.* Dozens of turnip farmers, peach pickers and even fishmongers set up stalls under bright blue awnings two days a week.

San Francisco Museum of Modern Art • *Veteran's Memorial Building, Van Ness at McAllister; (415) 863-8800. Adults $4, seniors and kids under 16, $1.50; Tuesday is free day. Open Tuesday, Wednesday, Friday 10 to 5, Thursday 10 to 9, weekends 11 to 5, closed Monday.* Some exhibits here stretch your definition of art, and well they should. SFMMA is one of America's leading museums on the leading edge of the art world.

☺ **Mission San Francisco de Asis** • *Dolores at 16th Street; (415) 621-8203. Daily 9 to 4; $1 donation.* Self-guiding tours take you into this historic mission's sanctuary, through a small museum and into cemetery-garden. The basilica next door also is open to visitors, except during services.

☺ **Coit Tower** • *Atop Telegraph Hill (via Lombard Street); (415) 362-8037. Adults $3, seniors $2, kids (6 to 12) $1. Daily 10 to 4:30.* When Lillie Hitchcock Coit bequeathed $125,000 "for the purpose of adding to the beauty of San Francisco," designers came up with this fluted Art Deco column, completed in 1933. Study interesting WPA murals on the inner walls, depicting Californians at work. Then take the clunking old elevator to the top for impressive city views.

ACTIVITIES AND TOURS

Blue and Gold Fleet sails from the west marina of Pier 39, offering scenic bay cruises and weekend dinner cruises; (415) 781-7877.

Golden Gate Ferries make frequent runs between the San Francisco Ferry Building and the Marin communities of Sausalito and Larkspur; (415) 332-6600.

Golden Gate Tours conducts city outings that cross the Golden Gate Bridge to Sausalito; (415) 788-5775.

Gray Line has its usual assortment of tours within the city and throughout Northern California; (415) 558-9400.

Great Pacific Tours offers city trips, plus jaunts to Muir Woods, Monterey and the vinelands; (415) 626-4499.

Hornblower Dining Yachts feature dinner-dances nightly and lunch cruises on Fridays, departing Pier 33; (415) 394-8900. (See "Where to dine" below.)

Near Escapes has a variety of theme tours and activities in the Greater Bay Area, plus self-guiding auto tape tours; (415) 921-1392.

Pier 39 Cable Car Company runs city tours in motorized cable cars; (415) 39-CABLE.

Red and White Fleet offers scenic bay cruises, shuttle trips to Angel Island, Tiburon and Vallejo's Marine World, and weekend dinner cruises; (800) 445-8880 outside California or (415) 546-BOAT.

Walking tours

Chinatown tours are conducted by the Chinese Culture Center; some include a dim sum lunch; (415) 986-1822. **Chinatown Discovery Tours** include walks through Chinatown, dim sum lunches and Chinese dinner tours; (415) 982-8839. The **"Wok Wiz,"** Shirley Fong-Torres conducts behind-the-scenes Chinatown tours; (415) 355-9657.

Civic Center, City Hall, Japantown and city tours are conducted free by Friends of the Library's City Guides; (415) 557-4266.

Golden Gate Park strolls are sponsored by Friends of Recreation and Parks, May through October; (415) 221-1311.

Levi's factory tours are conducted at the plant at 250 Valencia on Wednesdays at 10:30 and 2; free; reservations required. (415) 565-9153.

Mural tours past the Mission District's many Mexican murals are sponsored by Precita Eyes Mural Center; (415) 285-2287.

ANNUAL EVENTS

International Boat Show in Moscone Center, first week of January; (415) 521-2558.

Chinese New Year's Celebration, determined by a complex lunar calendar formula, usually in February (sometimes in early March); (415) 974-6900.

Great Outdoors Adventure Fair, Concourse Exhibition Center, Eighth and Brannan, late February; (415) 771-1111.

San Francisco International Film Festival at Kabuki 8 Cinemas, Post and Fillmore, early March; (415) 931-3456.

St. Patrick's Day Parade, downtown, the Sunday before March 17; (415) 467-8218.

Opening Day of the yachting season, first Sunday of Daylight Savings

Time; hundreds of sails on the bay; (415) 974-6900.

Cherry Blossom Festival in Japantown (*Nihonmachi*), middle weekends of April; (415) 563-2313.

Cinco de Mayo, celebrated in the Mission District, closest weekend to May 5; (415) 826-1401.

Historic Trolley Festival, May through October; vintage trolleys operate on Muni's Market Street route; (415) 673-MUNI.

Bay to Breakers race from downtown to Ocean Beach, third Sunday in May; (415) 777-7770.

Stern Grove Midsummer Music Festival in Sigmund Stern Grove, Sundays from mid-June through August; (415) 398-6551.

Lesbian-Gay Freedom Gay Parade, Market Street to Civic Center, date varies; (415) 864-3733.

Fourth of July Celebration with fireworks off Crissy Field and other events; (415) 556-0560.

San Francisco Marathon through the city's streets, a mid-July Sunday; (415) 681-2322.

Nihonmachi **Street Fair** in Japantown, weekend in early August; (415) 922-8700.

San Francisco Hill Stride, scenic walking race over the city's hills, late summer; (415) 626-1600.

San Francisco County Fair, at Fort Mason Center and Civic Center, urban version of a county fair, late August; (415) 558-3623.

San Francisco Blues Festival at Fort Mason's Great Meadow, mid-September; (415) 826-6837.

Festa Italiana, Italian festival at Fisherman's Wharf and North Beach, late September-early October; (415) 673-3782.

Festival 2000, city-wide ethnic cultural festival, through October; (415) 864-4237.

Fleet Week, celebration of the U.S. Navy, early October; (415) 765-6056.

Columbus Day festivities at North Beach and Fisherman's Wharf, nearest weekend to Oct. 12; (415) 434-1492.

Harvest Festival every weekend from late October to mid-November; (707) 778-6300.

International Auto Show at Moscone Center, late November; (415) 673-2016.

Christmas festivities include poinsettia decorations at **Embarcadero Center** with 17,000 white lights framing the high-rises; window decorations at **Macy's** at Stockton and Geary; large lighted yule trees at **Union Square**, the entrance to **Golden Gate Park** and **Ghirardelli Square**; holiday floral theme at **Conservatory of Flowers; The Nutcracker** performed by the San Francisco Ballet; **Handel's Messiah** by the San Francisco Symphony; and Dickens' **A Christmas Carol** by American Conservatory Theater.

WHERE TO DINE

Where, indeed! It is said that San Francisco has more restaurants per capita than any other city in the world, although Hong Kong challenges that claim. With about 4,000 restaurants and cafés, the city could accommodate its entire population in less than two sittings! We've focused on places in the downtown area and along our driving route. Since *several hundred* restaurants open and close each year, don't be startled if one of our selections has disappeared by the time you arrive. Incidentally, all San Francisco restaurants are required to have non-smoking sections.

Downtown/Nob Hill

Bardelli's Restaurant ● ∆∆ $$

243 O'Farrell St. (Powell); (415) 982-0243. Italian-continental; full bar service. Weekdays 11:30 to 10, Saturday 5 to 10. Major credit cards. Warm woods, stained glass and tuxedo-clad waiters mark this as classic San Francisco. In business since 1909, Bardelli's serves good, honest fare, ranging from fresh fish to Italian veal and pasta.

☺ The Big Four ● ∆∆∆∆ $$$$ Ø

1075 California St. (in the Huntington Hotel at Taylor); (415) 771-1140. Continental; full bar service. Daily 7 to 10 a.m., lunch weekdays 11:30 to 3 and dinner nightly 5:30 to 10 p.m. Jackets required at dinner. Major credit cards. It's one of the city's pre-eminent restaurants, offering attentive service and creative cuisine in an atmosphere of quiet elegance. The stylish dècor celebrates the city's glory days, from the Gold Rush to the railroad barons— for whom it is named.

☺ Carnelian Room ● ∆∆∆ $$$

Atop Bank of America building at 555 California St. (Montgomery); (415) 443-7500. American-continental; full bar service. Dinners nightly 6 to 10:30. Jackets required. Major credit cards. At 52 stories, the city's loftiest skyroom predictably offers the finest views. Perhaps surprisingly, the food is generally excellent, emerging from a creative *nouveau* kitchen. Rich wood paneling and old world tapestries add to the allure of this dining aerie.

☺ Garden Court at the Sheraton Palace ● ∆∆∆∆ $$$

Two New Montgomery (Market); (415) 392-8600. California nouveau; *full bar service. Daily 7 a.m. to 11 p.m.; Sunday brunch. Jackets recommended. Major credit cards.* A sparkling jewel from yesterday, the Garden Court sparkles after a recent renovation. With a leaded-glass domed ceiling and gilded chandeliers, it's the most eye-appealing restaurant space in the city. We particularly recommend it for Sunday brunch.

☺ John's Grill ● ∆∆∆ $$$

63 Ellis (Powell); (415) 986-0069. American-continental; full bar service. Monday-Saturday 11 to 10, Sunday 5 to 10. MC/VISA, AMEX. Dashiell Hammett's mention of the Grill in *The Maltese Falcon* has turned this longtime establishment into a mecca for Sam Spade fans. It's a virtual museum of Hammett lore, with photos, clippings and other regalia; the dècor is stylish early San Franciscan.

Kuleto's ● ∆∆∆ $$$$

221 Powell St. (Geary); (415) 397-7720. Northern Italian with California nouveau *accent; full bar service. Daily 7 a.m. to 11 p.m. Major credit cards.* One of the city's trendy power luncheon spots, Kuleto's gets serious about things garnished with air-dried tomatoes and sun-dried cherries. Or is it the other way around? The innovative fare is consistently good, although it comes close to being over-priced. The look is a decorator's dream in upscale Italian deli.

Masa's ● △△△△ $$$$$ Ø

648 Bush St. (Powell); (415) 989-7154. French; prix fixe dinners; full bar service. Tuesday-Saturday 6 to 9:30. Reservations essential and jackets requested. Major credit cards. The best French restaurant west of New York and possibly west of the Seine, Masa's issues impeccably prepared fare in an atmosphere of understated opulence. Service is attentive and never hovering. The dining room is smoke free. Excellence has its price; expect to part with $150 to $200 per couple, including a proper wine and dessert.

Ristorante Donatello ● △△△△ $$$$$ Ø

501 Post St. (Donatello Hotel, at Mason); (415) 441-7182. Regional Italian; full bar service. Daily 7 to 10:30 a.m. and 5:30 to 11 p.m. Coat and tie for dinner. Major credit cards. One of the city's premiere restaurants, award-winning Donatello offers intimate dining in small, luxuriant rooms.

Rotunda Restaurant ● △△△ $$$

150 Stockton St. (in Neiman-Marcus at Geary); (415) 362-4777. Light continental; full bar service. Lunch daily 11 to 3, tea time 5 to 5. AMEX only. This beaux arts restaurant is tucked under the Neiman-Marcus stained glass dome, offering a welcome retreat for tired shoppers' feet. It's all a bit pretentious, but the setting and view of Union Square are nice.

☺ Silks ● △△△△ $$$$ Ø

222 Sansome St. (California, in the Mandarin Oriental); (415) 986-2020. California-Asian; full bar service. Breakfast Monday-Saturday 7 to 10:30, Sunday brunch 8 to 2, lunch weekdays 11:30 to 2, dinner nightly 6 to 10. Coats and ties advised. Major credit cards. The menu at Silks changes frequently; you may happen across lobster yakitori or grilled ginger chicken with buckwheat noodles. The setting is elegantly subdued: an inviting space in peach, beige and teal.

Victor's ● △△△△ $$$$ Ø

335 Powell St. (atop Westin St. Francis at Geary); (415) 956-7777. California and contemporary French cuisine; full bar service. Daily 6 p.m. to 10:30 p.m., Sunday brunch 10 to 2:30. Dressy; jackets for dinner. Major credit cards. Nestled on the 32nd floor of the Westin St. Francis, Victors is at the same time intimate and grandiose. It's a special occasion restaurant with a constantly changing menu, lush dècor and sweeping city views.

Chinatown

Brandy Ho's ● △△ $$

217 Columbus Avenue (Pacific); (415) 788-7527. Mandarin (Hunan); wine and beer. Daily 11:30 to midnight. MC/VISA, AMEX. Lively Brando Ho's is a good place to sample Hunan-Szechuan food. The helpful waitstaff will explain the menu—and the kitchen will go easy on the peppers if you ask.

Hang Ah Tea Room ● △△ $ Ø

One Hang Ah St. (off Sacramento); (415) 982-5686. Cantonese, dim sum; wine and beer. Daily 10 a.m. to 9 p.m., dim sum 10 to 3. No credit cards. Dating from the turn of the century, Hang Ah claims to be Chinatown's oldest dim sum parlor. It serves these tasty little morsels until 3 p.m., then switches to Cantonese entrèes.

Sam Wo ● △ $

813 Washington St. (Grant); (415) 982-0596. Cantonese; no alcohol.

Daily 11 a.m. to 3 a.m. No credit cards. Slumming yuppies, starving students and lovers of a rice gruel called *jook* have made this shabby, skinny, three-story place legendary. The food varies, from excellent *jook* and noodle dishes to rather greasy stir-fried veggies. So tramp through the noisy ground floor kitchen, climb the stairs, find a seat and hope the cook's in a good mood.

North Beach

☺ *Basta Pasta* ● △△△ $$ ∅

1268 Grant Ave. (Vallejo); (415) 434-2248. Italian; full bar service. Daily 11:30 a.m. to 2 a.m. Major credit cards. Sporting a handsome new tiled interior, this longtime North Beach place is one of our favorite Italian cafés. Try tasty veal dishes, fine fresh fish or pizza and calzone done to a proper turn in an imposing wood burning oven.

Caffè Trieste ● △△ $

601 Vallejo (Grant); (415) 392-6739. Coffee house with light meals; wine and beer. Weekdays 7 a.m. to 11:30 p.m. and weekends 7 a.m. to 12:30 a.m. No credit cards. Inhale the aroma of fresh coffee and nibble a piroshki, pizza or deli style salad in this seedy survivor of the Beat Generation.

☺ *The Gold Spike* ● △△△ $$

527 Columbus Ave. (Green); (415) 421-4591. Italian; full bar service. Monday-Tuesday-Thursday 5 to 10, Friday-Saturday 5 to 10:30, Sunday 4:30 to 9:45, closed Wednesday. MC/VISA, DISC. A wonderful scatter of eclectic clutter adorns the walls of this hangout, dating back to Prohibition. Tummy-topping six-course dinners include everything from antipasto to dessert.

Il Pollaio ● △ $

555 Columbus Ave. (Union); (415) 362-7727. Italian-Argentinean; wine and beer. Daily except Sunday 11:30 to 9. Major credit cards. This tiny Italian *rosticceria* (roasted meats) offers the best meal prices in North Beach. Four dollars gets you half a chicken; with salad and fries it's only $6.25.

San Francisco Brewing Company ● △△ $

155 Columbus Ave. (Pacific); (415) 434-3344. American; light fare; beer and wine. Weekdays 11:30 to 10 p.m., weekends noon to 10 (bar open until 2 a.m.). AMEX only. Hearty beers and ales are brewed in a big copper kettle right before patrons' eyes. Pub grub such as fish and chips and assorted sandwiches accompany your pint of Albatross or Emperor Norton lager.

☺ *Washington Square Bar and Grill* ● △△△ $$$

1707 Powell St. (Union); (415) 982-8123. American with an Italian tilt; full bar service. Lunch Monday-Saturday from 11:30; dinner Sunday 4 to 10, Monday-Thursday 5:30 to 10:30, Friday-Saturday 5:30 to 11:30. Major credit cards. It's the classic San Francisco restaurant, with honest food served by knowledgeable waiters, a great bar, live music and a good crowd of regulars. In this city, the "Square" is very in.

Fisherman's Wharf & the waterfront

☺ *Buena Vista* ● △△△ $$

2675 Hyde St. (Beach); (415) 474-5044. American; full bar service. Weekends 8 a.m. to 2 a.m., weekdays 9 to 2. No credit cards. It's the landmark tourist bar that introduced Irish coffee to America. This Victorian pub also serves tasty breakfasts and light entrées. Pull up a chair (tables are expected to be shared) and enjoy a light bite, an "Irish" and a view of the waterfront.

Gaylord ● △△△△ $$$

Ghirardelli Square (North Point); (415) 771-8822. Indian; full bar service. Daily noon to 2 and 5 to 11. Major credit cards. The East Indian dècor is exquisite and so are the bay views from Gaylord's high perch. It features lightly seasoned northern India dishes cooked in the round clay *tandoor*, accompanied by *kulcha* bread, steaming hot from the oven. Voted by locals as the city's best Indian restaurant.

☺ Greens ● △△△ $$$ Ø

Fort Mason Center (Building A); (415) 771-6222. Vegetarian; wine and beer. Lunch Tuesday-Saturday 11:30 to 2:15, dinner Tuesday-Saturday 6 to 9:30, Sunday brunch 10 to 2, bakery counter Tuesday-Saturday 10 to 4:30 and Sunday 10 to 3. MC/VISA. Using mushroom magic, cheeses, polenta, creative pasta and clever seasonings, Greens assembles entrèes so hearty that you'll never ask: "Where's the beef?"

☺ Harbor Village ● △△△△ $$$ Ø

Four Embarcadero Center (Drumm and Clay); (415) 781-8833. Chinese; full bar service. Lunch weekdays 11 to 2:30, weekends 10:30, dinner nightly 5:30 to 9:30. Major credit cards. This handsome restaurant is both resplendent and understated, with touches of rosewood, teak and crystal in small, canopied dining areas; many tables with bay views. The fare is upscale Hong Kong style, consistently well-prepared; innovative *dim sum* is a specialty.

Hornblower Dining Cruises ● △△△ $$$$

Pier 33, off the Embarcadero; (415) 394-8900, ext. 7. Continental; prix fixe dinners $52 to $65, including bay cruise, live entertainment and band for dinner-dancing; lunch cruises $26; full bar service. Dinner voyages depart 7:30 daily, lunch cruises at noon Fridays only. MC/VISA, AMEX. Hornblower's dining yachts are nicely done in turn-of-the-century brass and glass, with stylish table service. Cruise itineraries vary with the weather and the whims of the captain.

Neptune's Palace ● △△△ $$$ Ø

Far end of Pier 39; (415) 434-2260. Seafood; full bar service. Sunday-Thursday 11:30 to 9:30, Friday-Saturday 11:30 to 10. Major credit cards. Early San Francisco dècor provides an opulent setting, and the end-of-pier position provides nice bay views. Although large, Neptune's is divided into intimate dining rooms; some are smoke free.

Pizzeria Uno ● △△△ $

2323 Powell St. (Bay), (415) 788-4055; and Two Embarcadero Center, (415) 397-8667. Pizza; full bar service. Monday-Thursday 11 to 11, Friday-Saturday 11 to midnight, Sunday 11:30 to 11. MC/VISA, AMEX, DISC. Uno serves the city's best pizza—a deep-dish Chicago style that arrives piping hot in its own personal skillet. Salads, sandwiches and soups are peddled as well.

Scott's Seafood Grill & Bar ● △△△ $$$

Three Embarcadero Center; (415) 981-0622. Seafood; full bar service. Monday-Thursday 10 to 11, Friday-Saturday 11 to 11, Sunday 4:30 to 9:30. Major credit cards. Spacious, attractive restaurant with a versatile, daily-changing menu, based on what's just been caught. The locally popular restaurant has kept pace with culinary trends, with an emphasis on lighter sauces, fresh herbs and vegetables.

Tarantino's ● △△△ $$

206 Jefferson St. (Taylor); (415) 775-5600. Seafood-Italian; full bar service. Daily 11 to 11. Major credit cards. Founded by Irishmen, not Italians, this venerable place is popular with visitors, yet it doesn't display a tourist mentality. Fish is properly cooked and it brews up a fine cioppino. Views over the boat basin and across the bay are nice.

Civic Center and ocean beach

The Cliff House ● △△△ $$$

1090 Point Lobos Ave.; (415) 386-3330 or 387-5847. American, seafood, pasta; full bar service. Sunday-Thursday 9 a.m. to 10:30 p.m., Friday-Saturday 9 to 11. Major credit cards. It's actually three restaurants: the early San Francisco style **Upstairs at the Cliff House** and **Seafood and Beverage Company** and the **Phineas T. Barnacle**, an oldstyle pub with libations and light fare.

Enoteca Lanzone ● △△△△ $$$$ Ø

601 Van Ness Ave. (in Opera Plaza at Golden Gate); (415) 928-0400. Upscale Italian; full bar service. Lunch weekdays 11:30 to 2:30, dinner Monday-Saturday from 5. Major credit cards. This stylish restaurant serves creative northern Italian fare in a setting of quiet opulence. The cozy dining rooms are virtual galleries, decorated with the modern art collection of founder Modesto Lanzone.

Hayes Street Grill ● △△△ $$$ Ø

320 Hayes St. (Franklin); (415) 863-5545. Seafood; full bar service. Lunch weekdays 11:30 to 2, dinners Monday-Thursday 5 to 10, Friday 5 to 11, Saturday 6 to 11. MC/VISA, DISC. This busy bistro is the city's best seafood restaurant. Fish is properly cooked and offered with a variety of sauces, such as herb shallot butter, Szechuan peanut sauce and *beurre blanc.* This is a popular if somewhat noisy business lunch spot.

☺ Stars ● △△△△ $$$$

150 Redwood Alley (between McAllister and Golden Gate); (415) 861-7827. Contemporary American; full bar service. Weekdays from 11:30 a.m., weekends from 12:30 p.m., oyster bar service to midnight. Major credit cards. One of the Bay Area's early California *nouveau* restaurants, this noisy, barnlike bistro is decorated with awards immodestly posted by its founder, Jeremiah Tower. It's the city's yuppie social center and power lunch haven.

Straits Cafe ● △△△ $$

3300 Geary Blvd. (Parker Street), (415) 668-1783. Singaporean; full bar service. Daily 11:30 to 10. Major credit cards. The city's only Singapore restaurant features tasty and spicy Southeast Asian fare, served in a light and cheery space beneath a clever street scene facade. The name comes from the Strait of Malacca and the cuisine is a crossroads blend Thai, Malaysian, Indonesian, Indian and Chinese cuisine.

Polk Gulch

Harris' ● △△△△ $$$$ Ø

2100 Van Ness Ave. (Pacific); (415) 673-1888. American; full bar service. Lunch Wednesday 11:30 to 2, dinner 5 to 10 week nights and 5 to 10:30 weekends. Major credit cards. Harris serves the city's best steaks and prime rib in a luxuriant setting. High ceilings, deep booths and paneled walls give it a genteel men's club ambiance.

Hard Rock Café ● △△ $

1699 Van Ness Ave. (Sacramento); (415) 885-1699. American; full bar service. Daily 11:30 to 11:30. MC/VISA, AMEX. As with other cafès Hard Rock, this one is more interesting for the dècor than the food: football helmets, guitars, a candy apple red Cadillac emerging from one wall. We've said it before: they should charge admission and give away the food.

☺ Tommy's Joynt ● △△ $

1101 Geary Blvd. (Van Ness); (415) 775-4216. Hofbrau; full bar service. Daily 10 a.m. to 2 a.m. Major credit cards. Decorated with a maniacal jungle of bric-a-brac, Tommy's is the penultimate San Francisco hofbrau. Corned beef and pastrami sandwiches are fine, the buffalo stew is more curious than tasty and 90 beers are available for washing it all down. Splendidly garish early San Francisco murals cover the outer walls of this landmark.

WHERE TO SLEEP

Lodgings are not inexpensive in San Francisco. An ordinary hotel room with a view of a brick wall across the alley can go for $100 and beyond. However, it's possible to get a suitable room for less than $50. We offer here a sampler of hotels, motels and inns listed by price range.

Although motels and hotels are scattered throughout the city, most are grouped in four areas: downtown/Financial District, Fisherman's Wharf, on Van Ness Avenue north of the Civic Center and along Lombard Street—the city's motel row. Price ranges shown are for a double room during the summer tourist season.

Rooms for $100 and up

The Donatello ● ⌂⌂⌂ $$$$$ (downtown)

501 Post St. (Mason), San Francisco, CA 94102; (800) 792-9837 in California, (800) 227-3184 outside, (415) 441-7100. Couples $155 to $165, singles $140 to $160, suites $200 to $375. Major credit cards. The dècor might be described as elegantly modern Italian. TV movies, room phones, morning newspaper, other amenities; some refrigerators. Locally acclaimed **Ristorante Donatello** listed above.

Cartwright Hotel ● ⌂⌂ $$$$$ Ø (downtown)

524 Sutter St. (Powell); San Francisco, CA 94102; (800) 227-3844 or (415) 421-2865. Couples $99, singles $90, suites $140 to $160. Major credit cards. This refurbished 114-room hotel features TV movies and room phones; refrigerators and hair dryers available. **Teddy's Restaurant** serves breakfast daily, 7 to 11:30.

☺ The Fairmont ● ⌂⌂⌂⌂ $$$$$ Ø (Nob Hill)

950 Mason St. (California); (800) 527-4727 or (415) 772-5000. Couples $175 to $265, singles $145 to $235, suites $450 to $2,000. Major credit cards. Built at the turn of the century by silver magnate William Fair, the Fairmont is rich in history and opulence. Its 595 rooms and suites have TV movies, room phones and all other amenities; shopping arcade, several bars including a sky room lounge. Five restaurants, including locally popular **Squire** and **Mason's**; dinners $15 to $40.

☺ Four Seasons Clift ● △△△ $$$$$ Ø (downtown)

495 Geary St. (Taylor), San Francisco, CA 94102; (800) 332-3442 or (415) 775-4700. Couples and singles $170 to $335, suites $350 to $810. Major credit cards. The city's only Mobil five-star and AAA five-diamond hotel. A hundred eight rooms with TV movies, room phones, bathrobes, other amenities; limo service to the Financial District. **The French Room** serves 6:30 a.m. to 10:30 p.m., California cuisine; prix fixe dinners from $28 or entrées from $25; historic

Holiday Inn ● △△△ $$$$$ Ø (Financial District/Chinatown)

750 Kearny St. (Washington), San Francisco, CA 94108; (800) HOLIDAY or (415) 433-6600. Couples $114 to $150, singles $99 to $139, suites $350 to $450. Major credit cards. A 566-room hotel with panoramic city views. TV movies, room phones, outdoor pool. **Lotus Blossom Restaurant** serves 6:30 a.m. to 2 p.m. and 5:30 to 10; California and Oriental fare; dinners $9 to $16; luncheon buffet.

☺ The Huntington ● △△△ $$$$$ (Nob Hill)

1075 California St. (Taylor), San Francisco, CA 94108; (800) 652-1539 in California, (800) 227-4683 outside, (415) 474-5400. Couples $185 to $235, singles $165 to $215, suites $250 to $645. Major credit cards. An outstanding small hotel with 140 rooms and suites, individually decorated with antiques and artwork. Its quiet refinement is often sought by visiting celebrities. TV movies, room phones, luxury amenities; complimentary tea, sherry and limo service. **Big Four** restaurant listed above.

☺ Hyatt Regency ● △△△ $$$$$ Ø (waterfront)

Five Embarcadero Center (Market), San Francisco, CA 94111; (800) 233-1234 or (415) 788-1234. Couples from $238, singles from $218, suites from $315. Curiously typewriter-shaped from the outside, it has the city's most striking lobby—a 17-story atrium with a spill-over fountain; 803 rooms. TV movies, room phones, self service bar, other amenities. **Mrs. Candy's, The Market Place** and rotating rooftop **Equinox** restaurants serve from 6 a.m. to 1 a.m.; American and California cuisine; dinners $12 to $25.

Hyde Park Suites ● △△△ $$$$$ Ø (Fisherman's Wharf)

2655 Hyde St. (North Point), San Francisco, CA 94109; (800) 227-3608 or (415) 771-0200. All suites with full kitchens, $165 to $220. Major credit cards. Small suite hotel with 24 kitchen units. TV, room phones, free newspaper; continental breakfast, nightly wine; weekday morning limo drop-off.

King George Hotel ● △△△ $$$$$ (downtown)

334 Mason St. (Geary), San Francisco, CA 94102; (800) 288-6005 or (415) 781-5050. Couples $102, singles $92, suites $194. Major credit cards. Charming English style hotel, with a tinkling lobby piano, marble staircase and cage elevator. TV movies and phones in rooms. **Bread and Honey Tearoom** serves buffet breakfast from 7 to 10 and English High Tea, Monday-Saturday afternoon 3 to 6:30.

☺ Mandarin Oriental ● △△△ $$$$$ Ø (Financial District)

222 Sansome St. (California), San Francisco, CA 94104; (800) 622-0404 or (415) 885-0999. Couples and singles $255 to $390, suites $540 to $1,200. Major credit cards. The Mandarin is one of the city's premier mid-sized hotels, with 160 exquisitely furnished rooms; all have city views. Amenities include remote TV with movies, room phones, mini-bar refrigerators and—oh, my—bathtubs with a city view. The hotel was completely refurbished in 1992. Locally popular **Silks** restaurant listed above.

Parc Fifty Five ● △△△△ $$$$$ Ø (downtown)

55 Cyril Magnin St. (Eddy), San Francisco, CA 94102; (800) 338-1338 or (415) 392-8000. Couples and singles $155 to $195. Major credit cards. This luxury hotel has San Francisco style bay windows on its 1,003 rooms and 23 suites; downtown near Macy's and Nordstrom's. TV movies, room phones; health club and business service center. **Rikyu** serves *nouveau* Japanese cuisine; the more casual **Veranda Restaurant** is open from 6:30 a.m. to 10:30 p.m.

☺ Sheraton Palace ● △△△△ $$$$$ Ø (Financial District)

Two Montgomery St. (Market), San Francisco, CA 94103; (800) 325-3535 or (415) 392-8600. Couples $200 to $260, singles $180 to $240, suites $350 to $1,500. Major credit cards. Sparkling new after a complete renovation, the legendary Sheraton has 550 stylishly furnished rooms. TV movies, room phones, refrigerators, free newspapers; health club, spa and business center. The **Garden Court** with its splendid 1800s atrium skylight is a focal point, listed above.

☺ Stouffer Stanford Court ● △△△△ $$$$$ Ø (Nob Hill)

905 California St. (Powell), San Francisco, CA 94108; (800) 622-0957 in California and (800) 227-4736 elsewhere, or (415) 989-3500. Couples $225 to $280, singles $195 to $250. Major credit cards. Upscale 392-room hotel with carriage entry; European dècor. TV movies, room phones, complimentary coffee and newspapers, all amenities. **Fournou's Ovens** serves from 6:30 a.m. to 2:30 p.m. and 5:30 to 11 p.m.; contemporary American cuisine; dinners $30 to $50.

Travelodge ● △△△ $$$$$ Ø (Fisherman's Wharf)

250 Beach St. (Powell), San Francisco, CA 94133; (800) 255-3050 or (415) 392-6700. Couples $107 to $175, singles $95 to $175, suites $225 to $300. Major credit cards. Most of its 250 rooms have bay or city views. TV with pay-per-view movies, room phones, morning coffee and newspaper; free parking. Adjacent to Pier 39. **Johnny's Rockets** is a Fifties style cafè with a singing waitstaff; American fare.

☺ Westin St. Francis ● △△△△ $$$$$ Ø (downtown)

335 Powell St. (Geary), San Francisco, CA 94102; (800) 228-3000 or (415) 397-7000. Couples $180 to $225, singles $150 to $225, suites $300 to $1,575. Major credit cards. One of San Francisco's world class hotels; 1,200 rooms; stylish lobby; shopping arcade. TV movies, room phones, refreshment centers, all luxury amenities. **Five restaurants** serve seafood, California, continental and American cuisine, various hours, dinners $7 to $30.

Rooms from $50 to $99

Amsterdam Hotel ● △△ $$$ (downtown/Nob Hill)

749 Taylor St. (Sutter), San Francisco, CA 94108; (800) 637-3444 or (415) 673-3277. Couples $50 to $70, singles $45 to $69. MC/VISA, AMEX. Pension style hotel with 34 rooms; TV, room phones, free breakfast.

Commodore Hotel ● △△ $$$ (downtown)

825 Sutter St. (Jones), San Francisco, CA 94109; (800) 338-6848 or (415)

923-6800. *Couples $70 to $100, singles $60 to $90. Major credit cards.* Older, refurbished 113-unit hotel with TV and phones in rooms. **Coffee shop** serves breakfast and lunch from 7 to 2; American, meals from $6; full bar.

Day's Inn San Francisco ● △△△ $$$ Ø (near park and zoo)

2600 Sloat Blvd. (Great Highway), San Francisco, CA 94116; (800) 325-2525 or (415) 665-9000. Couples and singles $60 to $80, suites $105 to $130. Major credit cards. New 33-room motel across from San Francisco Zoo. TV, room phones, microwaves, refrigerators; free continental breakfast.

Essex Hotel ● △△ $$$ (downtown/Civic Center)

684 Ellis St. (Larkin), San Francisco, CA 94109; (800) 44-ESSEX in California, (800) 45-ESSEX elsewhere; (415) 474-4664. Couples and triples $59 to $69, singles $49, suites $79. MC/VISA, AMEX. Refurbished 100-room hotel; TV, room phones; free coffee in lobby.

Great Highway Motor Inn ● △△ $$$ (near Golden Gate Park)

1234 Great Highway (Lincoln), San Francisco, CA 94122; (415) 731-6644. Couples $60 to $78, singles $54 to $72. Major credit cards. Located near ocean beach and Cliff House; 54 rooms with TV and room phones.

Pacific Bay Inn ● △△ $$$ (downtown)

520 Jones St. (Geary), San Francisco, CA 94102; (415) 673-0234. Couples $65 to $75, singles $55, lower weekly rates. Major credit cards. Attractive small hotel with 84 rooms; TV, room phones. **Dottie's True Blue Café** serves breakfast and lunch weekdays 7 to 2 and weekends 7 to 1 (closed Wednesdays); American menu; Fifties décor; meals from $7; wine and beer.

Royal Pacific Motor Inn ● △△ $$$$ Ø (Chinatown)

661 Broadway (Grant), San Francisco, CA 94133; (800) 545-5574 or (415) 781-6661. Couples $76. Major credit cards. Located on the outer edge of Chinatown; TV, room phones, in-room coffee; sauna, coin laundry; restaurant next door.

San Remo Hotel ● △ $$$ (Fisherman's Wharf)

2237 Mason St. (Chestnut), San Francisco, CA 94133; (800) 352-REMO or (415) 776-8688. Couples $55 to $75, singles $35 to $45, weekly rates from $100; rates include continental breakfast. Major credit cards. European style hotel with 62 rooms, shared baths. **San Remo Restaurant** serves Wednesday-Sunday 5 to 10; Italian-continental; dinners $7 to $16; Victorian décor; full bar service.

Seal Rock Inn ● △△△ $$$ (Ocean beach)

545 Point Lobos Ave. (48th Avenue), San Francisco, CA 94121; (415) 752-8000. Couples $70 to $92, singles $66 to $88, kitchenettes $4 more (two day minimum). Major credit cards. Attractive inn near the Cliff House with 27 ocean view rooms. TV, room phones, refrigerators, some fireplaces; pool, free parking. **Seal Rock Inn Restaurant** serves weekdays 7 a.m. to 4 p.m. and weekends 7 to 6; breakfast and lunch.

Rooms under $50

Grant Plaza Hotel ● △△ $$ (downtown/Chinatown)

465 Grant Ave. (Pine), San Francisco, CA 94108; (800) 472-6805 in California and (800) 472-6899 elsewhere, locally (415) 434-3883. Couples $42 to $65, singles $37 to $55, suites $82. Major credit cards. Budget priced, newly renovated hotel; 72 rooms with TV movies and room phones.

Lombard Plaza Motel ● △ $$ (Marina)
2026 Lombard St. (Fillmore), San Francisco, CA 94123; (415) 921-2444. Couples and singles $39 to $69. Major credit cards. Thirty-two rooms; TV movies, room phones; guest parking.

Temple Hotel ● △ $$ (Financial District/Chinatown)
469 Pine St. (Kearny), San Francisco, CA 94109; (415) 781-2565. Couples $35 to $45, singles $30 to $40, weekly rates. No credit cards. Clean, older hotel with 88 rooms, 19 with private baths.

Bed & breakfast inns

Alamo Square Inn ● △△△ $$$ Ø (Alamo Square)
719 Scott St. (Fulton), San Francisco, CA 94117; (415) 922-2055. Couples $70 to $150. Some private, some shared baths; full breakfast. MC/VISA, AMEX. Restored Victorian mansion; 15 rooms furnished in Victorian and early American antiques. Attractive parlor and dining room with wood burning fireplaces; landscaped gardens; patios; decks.

☺ Chateau Tivoli ● △△△△ $$$$ Ø (near Alamo Square)
1057 Steiner St. (Golden Gate), San Francisco, CA 94115; (800) 228-1647 or (415) 776-5462. Couples and singles $80 to $125, suites $160 to $200. Some private, some shared baths; expanded continental breakfast. MC/VISA, AMEX. Striking 1892 French Renaissance chateau style structure with five rooms and two suites. Furnished with Victorian and French antiques and rare artwork, it's one of the city's most attractive and elaborate 19th century mansions.

☺ Mansions Hotel ● △△△△ $$$$$ (Pacific Heights)
2220 Sacramento St. (Laguna), San Francisco, CA 95115; (415) 929-9444. Couples $129 to $350. Private baths; full breakfast. Side-by-side Victorian mansions with 21 guest rooms. Fully restored and delightfully overdone with antiques, a stuffed monkey, live macaw and Lawrence Welk bubble machine. **Mansions Restaurant** features continental fare with pre-dinner concerts or comedy entertainment.

Obrero Hotel ● △ $$ Ø (Chinatown-North Beach)
1208 Stockton St. (Pacific), San Francisco, CA 94133; (415) 989-3960. Couples from $45. Share baths; full breakfast. No credit cards. Small European style pension with homey décor. **Obrero Basque Restaurant** serves family style dinners; nightly seating at 6:30.

Washington Square Inn ● △△△ $$$$ (North Beach)
1660 Stockton St. (Filbert), San Francisco, CA 94133; (800) 388-0220 or (415) 981-4220. Couples and singles $85 to 180. Some private, some shared baths; continental breakfast. MC/VISA, AMEX. Fifteen rooms; contemporary décor with French and English country antiques; afternoon tea and evening wine service.

White Swan Inn & Petite Auberge ● △△△△ $$$$$ Ø (downtown)
845 and 863 Bush St. (Mason), San Francisco, CA 94108; (415) 775-1755. Couples $145 to $160. Private baths; full buffet breakfast. MC/VISA, AMEX. Twin inns, each with 26 nicely appointed rooms. Library, afternoon tea, morning newspaper. The White Swan features a 19th century English look; the Petite Auberge is decorated in a French country motif.

WHERE TO CAMP

Candlestick RV Park ● *650 Gilman St. (Candlestick park exit from U.S. 101), San Francisco, CA 94124; (800) 888-CAMP or (415) 822-2299. RV sites only, $28 to $32. Reservations accepted; MC/VISA.* Adjacent to ballpark; full hookups, showers, coin laundry, mini-mart, game room with big screen TV; fee shuttle to downtown San Francisco.

San Francisco RV Park ● *250 King St. (Fourth Street, south of Market), San Francisco 94107; (800) 548-2425 or (415) 986-8730. RV sites only, $28 to $32. Reservations accepted; MC/VISA.* The only rec vehicle park near downtown San Francisco. Full hookups, showers, coin laundry and a convenience store. Near several bus lines.

EAST BAY LOOP

We won't pretend that the eastern reach of San Francisco Bay is a tourist mecca. Its largest city **Oakland** is a blue collar extension of San Francisco, with a population pushing 400,000. Next door **Berkeley,** home to the outstanding University of California, is noted more for liberal politics than for visitor attractions. Extending north and south from the Oakland-Berkeley metro-glop are several nondescript residential towns nudging up to the bayfront.

Taken as a whole, the area offers several interesting lures, and we shall guide you to them with a loop drive from San Francisco.

Find your way onto the **San Francisco-Oakland Bay Bridge** and head east. For an outstanding view back to the city skyline, get into the left lane as you approach Yerba Buena Island tunnel at mid-bay, and take the **Treasure Island** exit. Built over a series of shoals to form a base for the 1939-40 Golden Gate International Exposition, "TI" has been a naval station since the start of World War II. Mere civilians can't enter the base without a permit—which is a pity, since some of the buildings and landmarks of the world's fair survive. However, if de-commissioning plans go through, it may be opened to the public.

You can enjoy the view back to the city from a parking area outside the main gate. And you're certainly welcomed at the **Treasure Island Museum,** just inside the gate. To get there, ask the sentry for a walk-on pass. Exhibits cover the Pacific history of the Navy, Marine Corps and Coast Guard, and the world's fair. Hours are 10 to 3:30 daily and it's free; (415) 395-5067.

Retrace your route, heading back to the wooded nub of **Yerba Buena Island,** which adjoins Treasure Island. It's a U.S. Coast Guard facility and is open to through traffic. Fork to the left, following signs to Oakland. This takes you over the Yerba Buena Island tunnel, offering an imposing view of the San Francisco skyline, filtered through the cables of the bay bridge. The road wraps around the far side of the island and blends back onto the bridge.

As you leave the bridge and draw near the giant cranes of the busy Oakland waterfront, take the Oakland Army Base exit to the right, then veer left after about half a mile onto West Grand Avenue. It takes you through several blocks of traffic lights and finally to Broadway, where you turn right to drive through the heart of downtown Oakland. A faster freeway approach is no longer possible, since this is the area where the infamous Cypress section collapsed during the 1989 earthquake.

Follow Broadway toward the waterfront to **Jack London Square.** Built on the site of the famous author's former waterfront hangout, is Oakland's most serious tourist trap, with several seafood restaurants and curio shops. Pause at the deliberately scruffy **Heinhold's First and Last Chance Saloon,** where a barkeep sometimes regales visitors with tales of the adventuring author. Nearby is half of **Jack London's cabin,** in which he wintered during the Yukon Gold Rush. Half? The crumbling shanty was discovered in the Yukon wilds several years ago by some folks from Dawson City. Dawson and Oakland agreed to share the logs, so that each could display an "authentic" cabin. Just north of the square is the **Bret Harte Boardwalk,** named for another scribe who spent his youth here. Along Fifth Street between Jefferson and Clay, it's comprised of shops and restaurants housed in attractively restored Victorians.

The next stop is one of California's outstanding museums. To find it, follow Embarcadero south from Jack London Square about five blocks to a stop sign and turn right onto Oak Street. This takes you under the freeway and to the museum at Tenth and Oak.

☺ *Oakland Museum* ● *1000 Oak St.; (510) 273-3401 or 834-2413 for a recording about exhibits. Wednesday-Saturday 10 to 5 and Sunday noon to 5; free.* Built into a three-level landscaped bunker, this excellent archive devoted to the ecology, art, natural and human history of California. Your visit begins with "A walk through California" as you view ecology exhibits concerning the state's primary life zones. After studying the rocks, critters and climates that comprise the Golden State, adjourn to the second level history hall filled with artifacts of California's yesterdays. The state's arts and artists are honored on the third level. Permanent and changing exhibits focus on the amazing spectrum of California creativity.

☺ If you continue northeast on one-way Oak, it becomes Lakeside, which takes you to **Lake Merritt,** Oakland's fine aquatic jewel. The largest saltwater lagoon within a city, it's rimmed by parks, walking paths and a glittering **Necklace of Lights,** which is illuminated after dusk. A series of right turns on surrounding streets will wrap you around the lake. To stay close, turn right into **Lakeside Park** (requires a $2 parking fee). As you near the completion of your circuit, swerve to the right onto 14th Street, pass the Greek-Modern **Alameda County Courthouse,** cross over Lakeside, continue a block to Madison and turn left. Follow it southwest to Seventh Street and turn right.

This takes you into **Oakland Chinatown.** It lacks the color and tourist gimmickry of the much larger San Francisco version, although it offers some fine and inexpensive restaurants.

Follow Seventh back to Broadway, turn right, and then left onto 12th. Just before it crosses the sunken I-990, turn right onto Castro and then fork left to drop down onto this freeway. Follow San Francisco I-580 signs, and then signs to I-80 and Berkeley. After about three miles, turn right onto University Avenue and follow it through downtown **Berkeley,** toward that lofty fraternity of higher learning.

☺ Red tile rooftops of the **University of California's** home campus create a handsome picture, tucked randomly into the wooded slopes of the Berkeley Hills. University Avenue curls into the campus, although parking is virtually impossible there on class days. It's best to park outside and explore the campus on foot. With luck, you'll find a two-hour meter along Oxford, which fronts the campus.

☺ Pick up a map at a kiosk near the entrance and use it to guide your feet to the great school's attractions. Head for the 307-foot **Campanile** (Sather Tower) and invest 50 cents in an elevator ride to the top for a glorious Bay Area view. It operates Monday-Saturday 10 to 3:30 and Sunday 10 to 1:45. Other worthy lures are **Sproul Plaza,** site of student unrest in the 1960s; **Bancroft Library,** with its outstanding collection of Western Americana and the an excellent museum of anthropology:

☺ *Phoebe Apperson Hearst Museum of Anthropology* ● *Kroeber Hall on Bancroft Way; (510) 643-7648. Tuesday-Friday 10 to 4:30 and weekends noon to 4:30. Adults $1.50, less for kids and seniors; free on Thursdays.* This fine facility is abrim with exhibits on anthropology and ethnology, including displays concerning Ishi, California's last "free" Native American.

Near the Hearst and worth a visit are the **University Art Museum** and adjacent **Pacific Film Archive**; (510) 642-1207; Wednesday-Sunday 11 to 5; adults $5, seniors and kids $4; free on Thursday; (510) 642-1207.

The anthropology and art museums border Bancroft Way, which you can follow back to your vehicle. En route to your ticking parking meter, take a stroll up America's quintessential campus commercial fringe, **Telegraph Avenue.** Predictably, it's lined with small cafés, coffee houses, bookstores, record shops and street vendors selling tie-dyed shirts. Hungry? Try **La Bodega** at 2311 Telegraph for sandwiches and quiche, or **Musical Offering,** near the art museum at 2430 Bancroft, offering classic music with your veggie sandwich or Greek salad.

Back in your driver's seat, follow Oxford north, curve to the right around the edge of the campus and turn left onto Spruce. This street winds past terraced hillside homes into the heights of the Oakland/Berkeley Hills. At a stop sign at the top, turn right onto Grizzly Peak Boulevard and follow it southward along the ridge line through **Tilden Regional Park**. It's the first of a string of hilltop parklands providing a fine woodland retreat amidst all this suburbia. The parks offer miles of hiking trails, a golf course, picnic areas, riding stables and other outdoor lures. For specifics, including hiking trail maps, contact the **East Bay Regional Parks District,** 11500 Skyline Blvd., Oakland, CA 94619; (415) 531-9300.

After driving 1.5 miles on Grizzly Peak Boulevard, turn right onto Centennial Drive and follow it down a fine science center on the upper fringe of the UC campus:

☺ *Lawrence Hall of Science* ● *Centennial Drive; (510) 642-5132. Weekdays 10 to 4:30 and weekend 10 to 5. Adults $5, students and seniors $4. Holt Planetarium shows daily in summer, weekends and holidays the rest of the year, at 1, 2:15 and 3:30; admission $1.50.* The Hall of Science is impressive both for its Bay Area views and its leading edge scientific exhibits. They're designed to intrigue all ages. Since kids love the science hall, avoid it on school days when great, shouting busloads swarm through the place.

Return to Grizzly Peak and continue your eucalyptus-lined parade route across the top of the Bay Area. Views improve as you continue south, and occasional turnouts invite you to pull over to absorb them. You'll pass through the area devastated by the Oakland Hills Fire of 1990. The scars remain and the rebuilding continues, several years later.

At some point—it's not important where—Grizzly Peak becomes Skyline Boulevard, which carries you through the redwood and eucalyptus fringes of **Redwood** and **Chabot** regional parks. Meandering Skyline takes a hard swing to the right and hits a stop sign at an intersection with Joaquin Miller Road. Go left to stay on Skyline. By this time, your views are across the broad southern arm of San Francisco Bay, over San Francisco International Airport to the peninsula cities of San Mateo County.

Finally, Skyline tucks around to the right, changes its name to Grass Valley Road and drops quickly out of the hills. Curl around to the right again at a Y-intersection and you're on Golf Links Road. It takes you to **Knowland Park** and down to a merger with I-580 freeway. Park entry is $3 per vehicle. Inside, you'll find the once shabby but rapidly improving **Oakland Zoo,** open daily 10 to 4. Admission is $3.50 for adults and $1.50 for seniors and kids; (415) 632-9523.

From I-580, it's a quick run to wherever you need to go next. Head north to complete your loop back to Oakland, and then follow Bay Bridge signs into San Francisco.

MARIN COUNTY LOOP

The county to the north of San Francisco is much more than a Yuppie joke revolving around BMWs, hot tubs and ostrich feathers. Nature has made it the prettiest of the seven counties rimming San Francisco Bay. It has one of the area's mildest and wettest climates, accounting for a particularly thick thatch of pines, madrones, redwoods and green pasturelands.

Marin County has some of the most attractive sections of the Golden Gate National Recreation Area. We shall touch most of them in our loop trip. One of "Marvelous Marin's" nicest lures is its portal, that noble Golden Gate Bridge. However, to reach it, you must deal with surface traffic, since no freeway links San Francisco to Marin. Avoid starting out during morning or late afternoon commute hours. Our preferred approach is to drive west about 3.5 miles on one of three major streets from downtown—Turk, Geary or California—then turn right onto Park Presidio Boulevard. (Geary, which becomes an expressway for a pair of miles, is the fastest.) Landscaped Park Presidio cuts through the ancient eucalyptus and pines of the **Presidio,** then merges onto Highway 101 just short of the bridge toll plaza.

Once across the Golden Gate, take the right lane exit for the **Vista Point,** which offers a rewarding view of the city's skyline. However, it pales when compared with our next lookout. Continuing north from the vista point, stay on the freeway's shoulder lane and exit onto Alexander Avenue. Soon, a brown sign advises you to fork left and head toward Marin Headlands of the GGNRA. You cross under the freeway, head briefly back toward the bridge, then veer off to the right and start climbing.

Before the national recreation area was established, this headlands drive was rarely explored by visitors. Today, it's a chore to find a parking place up there on a sunny weekend. Schedule your visit on a weekday if possible.

☺ Of all the places where man and nature have joined to create eye appeal, few rival the **Marin Headlands** with its stellar views of San Francisco and the Golden Gate. It's right up there with the Rio de Janeiro vista from Sugarloaf. The first turnout offers perhaps the finest of the headland views. The ramparts of the old **Battery Russell** gun emplacement stand in the foreground, with the dazzling white city skyline beyond, filtered through the harp string cables of the bridge's north tower.

For a vantage point rarely seen by visitors, take the half mile hike from Battery Russell down to **Kirby Cove.** Here, the skyline is tucked under the bridge, and the Pacific shore laps at your feet.

As you continue driving the winding headlands road, each curve and swerve reveals a new angle to the awesome vista. Turnouts and picnic areas encourage lingering. At road's end near a radar installation, turn north onto McCulloch Road, following Point Bonita signs. Cross over the headlands rim and down into **Rodeo Valley,** cradled by grassy hills that were shorn of trees during past San Francisco building sprees.

Staying with those Point Bonita signs, you'll encounter the **Marin Headlands Visitor Center,** in the former Fort Barry Chapel. It's open daily 8:30 to 4:30; (415) 331-1540. Exhibits here feature the flora, fauna and history of the region. Pick up a copy of the Golden Gate NRA map/brochure, if you don't already have one.

☺ Pressing onward, you pass several abandoned artillery bunkers and reach the parking area for **Point Bonita Lighthouse.** The San Francisco Peninsula, hidden since you came over the rise, is now back in glorious view. Point Bonita Light, occupying a razorback ridge extending into the Pacific, is open only on weekends, from 12:30 to 3:30. Even when it's closed, you can walk out toward the light for nice views back to the city. A guided sunset walk—a glorious experience—is scheduled every first and third Wednesday.

The winding road ends at **Rodeo Lagoon,** with a sandy beach across its mouth, popular with summer sun lovers. Picnic areas and walk-in campgrounds are plentiful in this area. Hiking paths gallop off in all directions, including the **Coastal Trail** that links the Marin Headlands with Point Reyes National Seashore.

As an alternate approach to Rodeo Valley, you can stay on the coastal route, continuing past the radar station. It clings to the headlands and spirals steeply down to the valley. However, this route isn't always open to the public, and it's *not* recommended for trailers and large RVs.

After you've done the valley, retrace your route over the headlands, enjoying reverse angle views of the Golden Gate and San Francisco as you drive, then follow Alexander Avenue into **Sausalito.** This saucy little village seems transplanted from some Mediterranean shore, with its red tile roofs and white stucco, terraced into steep slopes. Bridgeway, the main street, is a bayfront promenade lined with smart boutiques and galleries. Pricey restaurants stand on pilings, offering views of **Angel Island State Park,** and the thickly wooded **Belvedere Peninsula,** where some of the Bay Area's most expensive homes are hidden.

You don't need to dine to enjoy those views, since most of Bridgeway is open to the bay. You *will* have trouble finding a parking place if you venture into Sausalito on a summer weekend. A preferred weekend approach is to bring a **Golden Gate Ferry** from San Francisco.

If you do decide to dine, try one of these:

The Chart House ● △△△ $$$

201 Bridgeway; (415) 332-0804. American; full bar service. Dinner nightly from 6. Major credit cards. Seascape Victorian décor with picture window views of the bay from its pier perch. The fare—generally well prepared—

ranges from grilled seafood, steaks and chops to an occasional chicken.

Casa Madrona ● △△△△ $$$$ Ø

801 Bridgeway; (415) 332-0502. American nouvelle; full bar service. Breakfast, lunch and dinner daily. Major credit cards. One of the Bay Area's most romantic dining spots, housed in a splendidly refurbished 1885 Victorian tucked into a brushy hillside. The views are excellent, as is the fare, ranging from well prepared fresh seafood to roast quail with *pancetta*.

Continuing down Bridgeway past yacht harbors and warehouses, you'll see a sign directing you to the Army Corps of Engineer's **Bay Model**. Sheltered under two acres of warehouse, this miniaturization of the great Bay Area drainage is used to study the action of tides, silting and saltwater intrusion. Although it's activated infrequently, you can take a self-guiding tour and—with a "magic wand" clapped to your ear—learn about tide and time. It's free, open Tuesday-Saturday 9 to 4; (415) 332-3870.

Your route out Bridgeway brushes the edge of 101 north of Sausalito, then you soon peel off to the right, following a Muir Woods-Mount Tamalpais sign. You're on Highway 1, which skirts the edge of **Mill Valley** and takes you back toward the coast. Before reaching the beach, we'll explore the cool depths of Muir Woods National Monument and the heights of Tamalpais State Park.

RV advisory: Signs advise that vehicles over 35 feet are not recommended on the route we're about to follow. The same goes for trailers.

This drive takes you past the tree-shrouded homes of **Tamalpais Valley**, then winds steeply upward through a pine and eucalyptus forest. Turn right onto the aptly named Panoramic Highway at the Muir Woods-Mount Tamalpais sign. After an uptilted mile, you can go downhill to Muir Woods or continue upward to Mount Tamalpais State Park. We'd recommend that you take time for both.

☺ **Muir Woods National Monument** ● *c/o Site Manager, Mill Valley, CA 94941; (415) 388-2595. Daily 8 to sunset; free.* This is a walk-in national monument, with a thick grove of Coast redwoods in a narrow creek valley. Its popularity spoils the solitude, although a stroll through the eternal twilight beneath these giant trees is still a moving experience. A short walk takes you along Redwood Creek to a grand cluster of giants at Cathedral Grove. Serious hikers can follow the Panoramic Trail from here up to Mount Tam, or the Dipsea Trail down to the coast. Park facilities include a snack bar and gift shop and a visitor center where you can learn about these primeval trees.

☺ **Tamalpais State Park** ● *801 Panoramic Highway, Mill Valley, CA 94941; (415) 388-2070. Daily 7 a.m. to sunset. Day use parking fee $5 per car at the summit. Primitive camping $12 near Pan Toll park headquarters. Mountain Theater presents outdoor plays in summer; call (415) 383-0155 for details.* Mount Tam State Park is reached by returning to Panoramic Highway from Muir Woods and continuing your twisting ascent. After passing the Pan Toll headquarters and continuing your drive toward Mount Tam, you begin catching previews of the panoramic view that awaits. About the time you pass a radar facility, the vista unfolds—a living topo map of the entire bay and sections of nine counties.

From a parking area at the end of the road, a rocky and steep but mercifully short trail leads to the very top, at 2,571 feet. It's occupied by Gardiner

Lookout, which no longer is open. A longer and less strenuous trail loops for 1.1 miles around the shoulders of the peak. Back at the parking lot, you can find picnic tables, a small concession stand and visitor center.

Return to Pan Toll Station and turn right, following signs down to **Stinson Beach,** back on Highway 1. This small coastal town, which we explore in greater depth in Chapter four, offers yet another state preserve. **Stinson Beach State Park** has a sandy strand beyond seagrass dunes, picnic areas and a small ranger station. Expect it to be absolutely mobbed on summer weekends. To complete your Marin County loop, press north on Highway 1 for about 14 miles to **Olema.** You're on Point Reyes Peninsula, birthplace of the infamous (for nervous residents) San Andreas Fault. Most of this promontory is contained within Point Reyes National Seashore, also covered in Chapter four.

From Olema, head inland on Sir Francis Drake Boulevard, which takes you over **Bolinas Ridge,** through dairy lands and oak-thatched glens to **Samuel P. Taylor State Park.** This 2,700-acre park contains several stands of Coast redwoods and offers developed campsites at $12 per night, picnic areas and hiking trails; (415) 488-9897.

Continue driving over hill and pretty dale and you soon enter the back door of two very Marin communities, **San Anselmo** and **Fairfax.** Separated by name only, they're near identical twins, containing stylish business areas and homes sheltered by thick woods. Just beyond, even more upscale, is **Ross,** comprised mostly of grand old redwood shaded estates.

Although this wooded maze of homes and businesses can confuse, you'll keep on course if you stay with Sir Francis Drake Boulevard. When it seems that the Yuppie suburban sprawl will never end, you suddenly encounter U.S. 101 freeway. Head back toward San Francisco, then—after three miles—take the Tiburon Boulevard-East Blithedale exit and go left over the freeway.

Your destination is **Tiburon,** an aquatic version of the tree trimmed communities you just left. It offers more for the visitor, such as splendid views across the bay to San Francisco, a disarmingly cute business district along the bayfront and several tempting restaurants. Parking is scarce on weekends, although you can arrive on a **Red and White Fleet** ferry from San Francisco. Call (415) 546-2628 for schedule information.

With the convenient ferry service, Tiburon is a great lunch stop. Among your restaurant choices:

Sam's Anchor Café ● ▵▵ $$

27 Main St.; (415) 435-4527. American, mostly seafood; full bar service. Monday-Thursday 11 to 10, Friday 11 to 10:30, Saturday 10 to 10:30, Sunday 9:30 to 10. MC/VISA, AMEX. Something of a local legend, Sam's has been dishing up ample portions of seafood since 1920. Walk through the funky up-front bar to the simple dining room in the rear. On nice days, continue to the outside deck, offering great bay views.

Guaymas ● ▵▵▵ $$$ ∅

5 Main St.; (415) 435-6300. Contemporary Mexican; full bar service. Daily from 11 a.m. Major credit cards. Handsome upscale Mexican place with exposed beams and ceramic tile accents; patio dining at bayside. Mexican *nouveau* menu features several mesquite grilled seafoods and Southwest savories such as veal with peanut-chili sauce. All non-smoking.

Main Street Grill ● ΔΔΔ $$

15 Main St.; (415) 435-3440. Eclectic menu; wine and beer. Sunday and Tuesday-Thursday 11:30 to 9, Friday-Saturday 11:30 to 10, closed Monday. Major credit cards. Innovative menu bounces from egg plant garlic and red onion pizzas to pot stickers, grilled salmon and stuffed chicken breast. Pleasing contemporary dècor, with salmon-turquoise trim and white enameled bentwood chairs. Outdoor dining with a bay view.

Sweden House ● ΔΔ $

35 Main St.; (415) 435-9767. Bakery-conditori. Monday-Friday 8 to 5, Saturday-Sunday 8:30 to 6. MC/VISA. This cheerful cafe with Scandinavian trim and a small outdoor deck is a great spot for a creative breakfast, quick snack or light lunch. Try Swedish pancakes with lingonberries, open-faced sandwiches or tasty pastries such as Florentine rolls and Lindsor shortbread.

☺ **Angel Island State Park** is just offshore, reached by a funky old passenger ferry; (415) 435-2131. Runs are hourly and daily in summer, weekends and holidays only the rest of the year. Fare is $5 for adults, $3 for kids and $1 for bikes. Do take a bike if you have one, since the thickly wooded, traffic free island is laced with trails offering ever changing panoramas of the surrounding Bay Area. In addition to woods and bay vistas, the island has a large collection of structures dating back to the Civil War, when it was fortified for a Rebel invasion that never came. It later was used as an Asian immigration station, earning it the title of "Ellis Island of the West," and as a Japanese detention center during World War II.

If you'd like to drive past the pricey homes of **Belvedere** adjacent to Tiburon, continue on Main Street to a stop sign and turn left. Once you've completed your envy-riddled Belvedere loop, return to U.S. 101 on Tiburon Boulevard, or follow Paradise Drive in the opposite direction. It takes you around the northern edge of the peninsula, through the **Tiburon Uplands Nature Preserve** and finally back to the freeway in **Corte Madera.**

☺ En route, pause at **China Camp State Park,** a partial reconstruction of a turn-of-the-century Chinese fishing village. In the small museum, open 9 to 5 daily in summer and weekends the rest of the year, you'll learn that Chinese dominated shrimp fishing on the bay until discriminatory laws banned them in 1900. Although most of the buildings here are reconstructions, one going business remains: Frank Quan sells bait, serves sandwiches and offers fresh shrimp. In addition to the fishing camp, the state park covers about 1,600 acres of adjacent woodlands and marshes, with hiking and picnicking. Walk-in primitive camping is $8 a night.

KNOWING YOUR WAY THROUGH SAN JOSE

If you're a Bay Area community bent on attracting an occasional tourist, it's no fun being San Francisco's neighbor. The Golden Gate city gets most of the action, and the favorable publicity that goes with it. However, its neighbor to the south—even larger than San Francisco—should not be ignored, for it offers a few interesting lures.

Your first impression of San Josè is that it has a very Los Angeles look. The third largest city in California with a population of 782,000, it strikes the eye as an endless sprawl of concrete and asphalt. These fused-together neighborhoods stretch west to the Santa Cruz Mountains and east to the Mount Hamilton Range.

In recent decades, the broad Santa Clara Valley between them has earned the title of Silicon Valley. Here, William Hewlett and David Packard of Hewlett-Packard, and Steve Jobs and Steve Wozniak of Apple revolutionized the computer industry. Working in their garages, they created small, user friendly machines that even hack writers such as myself could manipulate. Other firms were drawn here to form the microchip center of the world. Here's a bit of irony: Although silicon is the world's second most abundant element after oxygen, none exists in Silicon Valley. It must be brought in from elsewhere.

Most San José-bound visitors head south on U.S. 101, the Bayshore freeway. However, we have a more scenic alternate. Begin your trip on the Bayshore, then west on Interstate 280 just south of the city. You'll shortly enter San Mateo County and pass through **Daly City,** a nondescript town whose low hills are covered with unending strings of row houses. They inspired that 1950s song about *Little houses made of ticky-tack.* Just to the south is **Colma,** with the unfortunate distinction of serving as the Bay Area's burial ground.

Below Colma's cemeteries, your route becomes more appealing. Now called the Junípero Serra Freeway, it climbs the knobby spine of the **San Bruno Mountains,** offering woodsy views west and east. As you pass high above **San Bruno,** San Francisco International Airport spreads out below you, looking like an elaborate toy model.

This peninsular thighbone of San Mateo County is thickly populated. It houses some of the Bay Area's more upscale communities, such as **Burlingame, Belmont, San Carlos, Atherton, Menlo Park** and the county seat of **San Mateo.** However, you're riding high above this congestion on I-280. It's just as well. Although these tree-shrouded communities are nice places to live, they offer little reason to visit.

After skimming several hilly open space preserves, you'll drop down into Santa Clara County and its attendant sprawl. As you pass through **Cupertino** and enter the western edge of San José, watch for a cluster of highrises marking the downtown area. Take the Almaden Boulevard exit and head north into that cluster. When you see the **San José Convention Center** at Almaden and Santa Clara Street, start looking for a parking place.

Within the complex, which looks like an oversized quonset hut, you'll find the **visitor center** of the San José Convention and Visitors Bureau. Enter the convention center foyer from Santa Clara Street and walk to the left. The visitor facility is open weekdays 8 to 5:30 and weekends 11 to 5. Here, you can pick up a walking map of what's left of historic downtown San José, plus abundant other material.

In recent years, as San José multiplied manifold, it has attempted to upgrade its old downtown area, focused around the elliptical 1797 Plaza Park. This former site of bull and bear fights, public hangings and other amusements is a pleasant green retreat from the encircling buildings. What surrounds you is a mix of geometric modern, yesterday brick and some architectural afterthoughts.

Among things to see in this random yet spacious downtown area are the **Tech Museum of Innovation** at 145 W. San Carlos Street, across from the convention center, and the Frank Lloyd Wright style **Center for the Performing Arts** just beyond at San Carlos and Almaden. Now stroll northeast to **Plaza Park** at Market and San Carlos. Turn left and walk a couple of blocks to the **San José Museum of Art** at 110 S. Market, and the intriguing multi-domed **St. Joseph's Cathedral,** just beyond at 90 S. Market.

Continue your hike to the only survivor of San José's founding. Follow Market to St. John Street, turn left and walk a pair of blocks to the **Peralta Adobe.** Built before 1800, it now crouches timidly in the shadow of downtown commercialism.

Return to wherever you parked your vehicle and we'll guide you on a short driving tour of San José's other lures. Although the city rivals Los Angeles in its sprawl, most of its attractions are conveniently bunched. Several are gathered in **Kelley Park,** a bit over a mile from downtown. To get there, head southeast on Market (which becomes Monterey), cross under I-280 and turn left onto Keyes Street. After about ten blocks, turn right onto Senter Road and you're at the corner of the park. Its **Happy Hollow Zoo, Japanese Friendship Garden** and **Historic San José** outdoor museum are lined up along Senter.

Now, retrace your route to Market and follow it through downtown to Santa Clara Avenue. Turn left, cross under Highway 87 freeway and the route becomes The Alameda. If you'd like to visit an urban wine tasting room, turn right onto Lenzen Avenue for a pause at **J. Lohr Winery.** Then continue on The Alameda four blocks, turn left onto Naglee Avenue and you'll shortly arrive at the **Rosicrucian Museum** at Park and Naglee. (The entrance is on Park.)

Continue southwest on Naglee (which changes its name to Forest), cross under I-880, go about five blocks to Winchester Boulevard and hang a left. The **Winchester Mystery House** comes up shortly, on your right, within view of I-280. Cross under that freeway, take an immediate left onto Moorpark, follow it less than two miles and it will blend onto the freeway. You might want to continue on over to U.S. 101 and head north for a visit to **Great America,** the large thrill ride park in neighboring Santa Clara.

ATTRACTIONS
(In order of appearance)

☺ *Tech Museum of Innovation* • *145 W. San Carlos St.; (408) 279-7150. Tuesday-Sunday 10 to 5. Adults $6, youths $4; MC/VISA.* Where else but in Silicon Valley would you find a fine little museum with hands-on exhibits concerning the leading edge of technology? Eventually, it will become a fine *big* museum, since plans are afoot to relocate it in a 170,000-square-foot facility on the nearby Guadalupe River. Displays range from bicycle aerodynamics and DNA to robotics and space age plastics. An excellent exhibit focuses on computer chips, taking you through the production and use of these incredibly complex silicon wafers. In another intriguing display, you can sit before a video camera while a multi-task robot sketches your picture.

San José Museum of Art • *110 S. Market St.; (408) 294-2787. Wednesday-Sunday 10 to 5 (until 8 Thursday), closed Monday-Tuesday. Adults $4, seniors and kids $2; Thursday is free day.* The curiosity value of this museum depends on what's showing, since most exhibits are changed periodically. They're generally contemporary, ranging from a Martin Luther King photo essay to Plexiglas art. There *is* a curiosity value to the structure, consisting of a modern building fused into an old Gothic brownstone. The latter houses a fine art book and gift shop.

St. Joseph's Cathedral • *80 S. Market St.; (408) 283-8100.* Step into this architectural beauty and admire the elaborate coffered domed ceilings and beautiful stained glass windows. Complimenting the circular ceiling, the navè forms a rounded cross—very unusual for a Catholic church.

Peralta Adobe • *St. John and Terrine streets; (408) 287-2990. Park open daily; adobe tours by appointment.* Sergeant Louis Maria Peralta served as San Josè's *comisionado* of civil affairs from 1807 until 1822. He lived in this simple mud house until his death in 1851 at the age of 91. His whitewashed, shingle-roofed shed is all that survives of that era. Standing in the shadow of highrises, the place could use a little TLC and patching. Display cases in the adjacent park contain maps and other graphics concerning the town's Spanish and Mexican period.

☺ **San José Historical Museum** • *1600 Senter Road in Kelley Park; (408) 287-2290. Weekdays 10 to 4:30, weekends noon to 4:30. Adults $2, seniors $1.50, kids $1, parking fee $3.* This outdoor museum is appealing if you're interested in 19th century architecture. Several buildings, mostly Victorian, have been moved here from other areas or replicated to form an early San Josè village. Many are furnished to the period. Of particular interest are A.P. Giannini's Bank of Italy which became the Bank of America, and a 327-foot electric light tower, one of four erected in 1881 and said to be the inspiration for Alexander Eiffel's tower in Paris. Adjacent are the peaceful **Japanese Friendship Garden,** open daily 10 to dusk. Next to that is **Happy Hollow,** a family oriented playground and kiddie zoo. It's open Monday-Saturday 10 to 5 and Sunday 11 to 6; adults $2.50, seniors and kids $2.

J. Lohr Winery • *1000 Lenzen Ave.; (408) 288-5057. Daily 10 to 5; MC/VISA.* Although it's located in an industrial area, this urban winery is quite inviting, with a redwood paneled tasting room.

☺ **Rosicrucian Museums** • *1342 Naglee Ave.; (408) 287-9171. Daily 9 to 5. Adults $6, students and seniors $4, kids $3.50.* Doubters are usually surprised to learn that this privately run museum contains the finest collection of Egyptian artifacts in western America. Mummies, elaborately decorated coffins, funeral urns and such paint a vivid picture of the land of pharaohs. Other exhibits concern ancient Mesopotania, Assyria and Babylonia, featuring jewelry, papyrus fragments, pottery and such. Adjacent is a second facility housing a planetarium and science center. Should you wonder, the Rosicrucians are a nonsectarian group preoccupied with natural and cosmic laws.

Winchester Mystery House • *525 S. Winchester Ave.; (408) 247-2000. Daily 9 to 5. Adults $12.50, seniors $9.50, kids $6.50. MC/VISA.* If you're a Californian, you've heard the story before. Sarah Winchester, widow of the rifle maker, came to town in 1884 with $20 million in the bank and royalties rolling in at the rate of a thousand dollars a day. A mystic convinced her that she was haunted by the ghosts of those killed by her husband's rifles, and she could fend them off with a non-stop building project. Keeping a crew of carpenters busy 24 hours a day until she died in 1922, she turned her seven-room farmhouse into a bizarre 750-room crazy-quilt mega-mansion. Only 160 rooms survive, and a tour guide takes you through 120 of them, pointing out blind stairways, trapdoors to nowhere and such. It's not our favorite place and the admission price is a bit steep for a tour of an empty building—albeit a rather amazing one. If you're moved by statistical excess—2,000 doors, 47 fireplaces, 40 staircases and 10,000 windows—you might want to stop by.

☺ **Great America** • *Great America Parkway, Santa Clara; (408) 988-1800. Daily 10 to 9 in summer, weekends only the rest of the year. Adults and students $23.95, seniors $16.95, kids 3 to 6, $11.95; price includes all rides and attractions.* Test your equilibrium and your lunch on some of America's wildest rides, from upside-down roller coasters to a free fall that'll roll your eyeballs. This fine, well run park also offers a bevy of restaurants, an IMAX wide-screen 3-D movie and live entertainment. It sounds pricey, but the ticket gets you into everything; a better and livelier deal than the mystery house. And never mind that they call the Yukon Territory part of "great America." You go there for fun, not for history lessons.

WHERE TO DINE

Should you want to pause for lunch or linger for dinner, one of these downtown San José restaurants may tempt you. Three are side-by-side, on a Market Street mini-restaurant row.

Bellino Restaurant & Bar • ΔΔΔ $$
95 S. Market St. (second floor); (408) 277-0690. Italian; full bar service. Lunch weekdays from 11:30, dinner Monday-Saturday from 5:30. MC/VISA, AMEX. Stylishly modern *trattoria* with a wide range of pasta dishes, creative wood-fired pizzas and a few steak, seafood and poultry entrèes. Highly regarded by area critics.

China Wok • ΔΔ $
Nine N. Market St.; (408) 280-6688. Chinese; wine and beer. Lunch and dinner daily. MC/VISA, DISC. A cut above your typical mom and pop vinyl and chrome place, it's an appealing cafè done in modern green and beige. The menu covers the full Chinese spectrum, including clay pot specials and many seafood dishes.

☺ Rue de Paris • ΔΔΔ $$$
19 Market N. St.; (408) 298-0704. French; wine and beer. Lunch weekdays 11 to 2, dinner Monday-Thursday 5:30 to 10 and Friday-Saturday 5:30 to 11. Major credit cards. Exceptionally cute French cafè right off a Paris side street, with dark woods, wainscotting, print wallpaper and lace curtains. Local critics praise the menu with all those classic, hard-to-pronounce French entrèes.

Thepthai Restaurant • ΔΔ $$
23 N. Market St.; (408) 292-7515. Southeast Asian; wine and beer. Lunch weekdays 11 to 3 and weekends noon to 3, dinner nightly 5 to 10. MC/VISA. Bright, cheerful Thailand restaurant with terrace seating beneath white beams and pillars. The 100-dish menu ranges from satay and sautèed scallops to ground chicken salad with scallions, mint leaf, cilantro and chilies.

TRIP PLANNER

WHEN TO GO ● There is no closed season on winery touring. Fall is great when the grapes are being harvested and the leaves put on their own special autumn display. However, weekends are very crowded then. Springtime can be striking, when many vineyards are carpeted with yellow mustard blooms.

WHAT TO SEE ● Our favorite wineries are Ferrari-Carano, Hop Kiln, Chateau DeBaun in northern Sonoma County; Sebastiani, Viansa, Gloria Ferrer, Buena Vista and Gundlach-Bundschu in the Sonoma Valley; and Domaine Carneros, the Hess Collection, Rutherford Hill Winery, Clos du Val, Chateau Montelena, Clos Pegase, Sterling Vineyards and Cuvaison in the Napa Valley. Among other attractions, visit Sonoma State Historic Park, the Sonoma Mission, Jack London State Park, Bale Grist Mill State Historic Park, and the Silverado Museum in St. Helena. Vintage 1870 is the best of the shopping complexes.

WHAT TO DO ● Other than winery touring, go canoeing down the Russian River in northern Sonoma County; take a glider ride from Calistoga or a hot air balloon ride above the vines; hike to the Silverado Mine and the valley lookout at Robert Louis Stevenson State Park; do lunch on the Napa Valley Wine Train.

Useful contacts

Calistoga Chamber of Commerce, 1458 Lincoln Ave. (in the Calistoga Depot), Calistoga, CA 94515; (707) 942-6333.

Calistoga Resort Owners' Association, P.O. Box 3, Calistoga, CA 94515.

St. Helena Chamber of Commerce, P.O. Box 124 (Main and Pope streets), St. Helena, CA 94574; (707) 963-4456.

Sonoma State Historic Park, P.O. Box 176, Sonoma, CA 95476; (707) 547-1414.

Sonoma Valley Visitors Bureau, 453 E. First St. (east side of the plaza), Sonoma, CA 95476; (707) 966-1090 or 966-1033.

Yountville Chamber of Commerce, 6795 Washington St., Yountville, CA 94599; (707) 0904.

Napa-Sonoma area radio stations

San Francisco and Sacramento stations reach California's wine country, in addition to these locals:

KVYN-FM, 99.3, Napa—top 40 & news
KMGG-FM, 97.7, Santa Rosa—top 40 oldies
KZST-FM, 100.1, Santa Rosa—adult contemporary
KHTT-FM, 92.9, Santa Rosa—adult contemporary
KXFX-FM, 101.7, Santa Rosa—rock
KRPQ-FM, 105, Rohnert Park—country
KVON-AM, 1440, Napa—news and talk
KSRO-AM, 1350, Santa Rosa—popular music and talk

Chapter three

THE WINE COUNTRY

Tripping and sipping through the vineyards

WE BEGIN THIS CHAPTER with a misleading title. There is no single "wine country" in California. In fact, wine is produced in 45 of the state's 48 counties. California has nearly 800 wineries scattered about, producing 90 percent of the nation's supply.

However, in only a few areas are climate and soil conditions ideal for the creation of the finest premium wines. For decades, these regions were limited to Sonoma and Napa counties north of San Francisco and the Livermore and Santa Clara valleys south of the city. Today, fine wine grapes are grown from Mendocino county north of Sonoma to the Temecula Valley of San Diego County. And these represent only 15 percent of the state's total output. About 85 percent of its wines—those notorious generic burgundies, chablis and rosès—are produced in the hot San Joaquin Valley.

Still, when someone mentions California winery touring, Sonoma and Napa quickly come to mind. And for this book's purposes, they shall be The Wine Country.

In recent years, winery touring and tasting has become one of the state's most popular pastimes. Many wineries offer delis and picnic areas—perfect partners for an idyllic luncheon *al fresco*. Adding to this recipe for rhapsody is the proliferation of cozy bed and breakfast inns and fine restaurants in the Wine Country.

Predictably, such a popular pastime generates congestion. A day in the vineyards loses its luster when you have to shoulder through crowds—plastic glass clutched in hand—to summon a sip of Semillon. Your wine knowledge suffers little gain when you're hurried through a quickie tour, with programmed tastes of three wines—red, white and pink—at the end. It's enough to make you blue.

To curtail the crowds, some wineries now charge for tasting, or sell you a souvenir glass. Others accommodate the crowds by turning their tasting rooms into wine country supermarkets. A few vintners even require reservations for their picnic tables.

The visitor comes away with claustrophobia, little wine tasting knowledge and a set of mismatched glasses. There must be a better way.

There is and that's why we call this a Discovery Guide. Our tours will take you off the heavily trod paths to a kinder, gentler wine country. Here, tasting rooms are rarely crowded and the winemakers themselves may be pouring your samples. We also will mention other attractions along the way, to give this tour a bit more depth.

A few thoughts before we sally forth:

● If possible, avoid the Wine Country on summer and fall weekends. Crowds are thinner on off-season weekends and the same wines are available, being poured by people in better moods.

● The best time to tour is on an autumn weekday, during the "crush" when the grapes are being harvested and brought to the winery. During your tour, you may be able to stare into frothy vats where tomorrow's Zinfandel is beginning its metamorphosis. Some wineries may even pour you a little "must," the freshly-crushed juice.

● Limit your stops to four or five wineries a day, and limit your samples as well. If you taste too many wines, their differences will begin to blur. So will your vision.

● Be sensible if you're the designated driver. Save the urge to party until you're back to your lodgings or RV park, off the road and close to the floor. Only about two percent of people arrested for driving while intoxicated where drinking wine. We'd like to keep it that way.

We won't list all the wineries we pass on our tours. Instead, we'll select the more interesting ones. For a more detailed guide that covers all of the state's premium wine producing areas, pick up a copy of our **Best of the Wine Country.** (See the back of this book.)

NORTHERN SONOMA COUNTY WINERY TOUR

We're going to run in reverse of the typical Sonoma tour. We'll first visit less crowded wineries of north county, then enter through the popular Sonoma Valley's back door.

Head north on U.S. 101, going to and through Santa Rosa, then turn west onto River Road about five miles above the town. Within a few hundred feet, you'll encounter two wineries—the castle-like **Chateau DeBaun** on your right and the pleasantly funky **Z Moore Winery,** housed in an old hop-drying kiln on your left. Continuing west, you're headed into the **Russian River Valley,** an appealing mix of vineyards, forest-clad hills, redwood groves and—of course—the Russian River.

After about ten miles, you'll cross the Russian River and soon see the imposing stone **Korbel Champagne Cellars** upslope on your right. It will *not* be uncrowded on summer weekends. Reverse your route from Korbel, then after about a mile, fork to the left onto Westside Road. If you re-cross the river, you've missed it.

You'll find no prettier vineland than this rolling hill country thatched with oaks, madronas, pines and ancient vines. The wineries begin cropping up after a few miles: **Davis Bynum** on the left, the attractive **Hop Kiln** on

Sonoma & Napa Valley Wineries

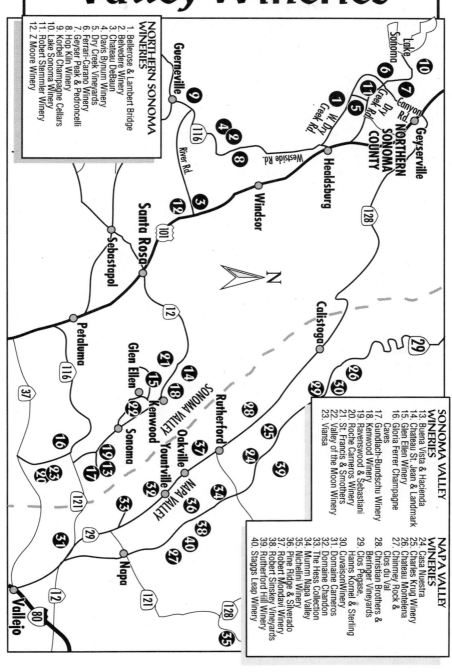

NORTHERN SONOMA WINERIES

1. Bellerose & Lambert Bridge
2. Belvedere Winery
3. Chateau DeBaun
4. Davis Bynum Winery
5. Dry Creek Vineyards
6. Ferrari-Carano Winery
7. Geyser Peak & Pedroncelli
8. Hop Kiln Winery
9. Korbel Champagne Cellars
10. Lake Sonoma Winery
11. Robert Stemmler Winery
12. Z Moore Winery

SONOMA VALLEY WINERIES

13. Buena Vista & Hacienda
14. Chateau St. Jean & Landmark
15. Glen Ellen Winery
16. Gloria Ferrer Champagne Caves
17. Gundlach-Bundschu Winery
18. Kenwood Winery
19. Ravenswood & Sebastiani
20. Roche Carneros Winery
21. St. Francis & Smothers
22. Valley of the Moon Winery
23. Viansa

NAPA VALLEY WINERIES

24. Casa Nuestra
25. Charles Krug Winery
26. Chateau Montelena
27. Chimney Rock & Clos du Val
28. Christian Brothers & Beringer Vineyards
29. Clos Pegase, Hanns Kornel & Sterling
30. Cuvaison Winery
31. Domaine Carneros
32. Domaine Chandon
33. The Hess Collection
34. Mumm Napa Valley
35. Nichelini Winery
36. Pine Ridge & Silverado
37. Robert Mondavi Winery
38. Robert Sinskey Vineyards
39. Rutherford Hill Winery
40. Staggs Leap Winery

the right and **Belvedere** on the left.

Westside turns into Mill Street as it ducks under U.S. 101 freeway and takes you into **Healdsburg.** It's a handsome old town built around a landscaped plaza. You'll find a bevy of boutiques, antique shops and a good restaurant or two. Several winery tasting rooms are near the plaza. In our opinion, tasting parlors divorced from their wineries aren't that interesting. If you disagree, get a locator map from the chamber of commerce (see "Trip planner").

Retrace your route on Mill Street and, after about a mile, turn right onto West Dry Creek Road and drive north. Two small wineries, **Bellerose** and **Lambert Bridge,** soon appear on your left. A short distance above Lambert Bridge, turn right onto Lambert Bridge Road. You'll see **Robert Stemmler Winery** on the left and **Dry Creek Vineyard** on the right.

Dead ahead, you'll run into **Dry Creek General Store,** sitting at the intersection of Lambert Bridge and Dry Creek Road. It's an inviting old mercantile offering a deli, groceries and local wine selections, with a couple of picnic tables out front. Head north on Dry Creek Road, watching for a country lane leading up to **Timber Crest Farms.** The small retail room sells pricey but tasty specialty foods such as dried fruits and vegetables, pasta sauces and preserves. About four miles beyond, you'll encounter the strikingly modern **Ferrari-Carano Winery** on the left.

Follow Dry Creek Road toward **Warm Springs Dam** and **Lake Sonoma,** offering boating access, a campground and typical reservoir recreation. Before you reach the dam, watch for **Lake Sonoma Winery,** uphill on your right. Now, reverse yourself on Dry Creek Road. About a mile and a half beyond Ferrari-Carano, turn left up Canyon Road. Two wineries appear on your left: **J. Pedroncelli,** and—just short of the freeway—**Geyser Peak.**

A quick sprint south on the freeway will return you to Santa Rosa and the beginning of our next vineland tour.

The wineries

☺ *Chateau DeBaun* ● *5007 Fulton Rd., Fulton, CA 95439; (707) 571-7500. Daily 10 to 5; major credit cards. Most varieties tasted; landscaped picnic area; vineyard tours by appointment.* Chateau indeed. This opulent wine estate begs to be nestled on a high slope above the Rhine or alongside a meandering stream in Burgundy. Inside, it's a study in old world opulence, with brass chandeliers, etched glass and carefully selected artworks.

Z Moore Winery ● *3364 River Road, Windsor, CA 95492; (707) 544-3555. Daily 10 to 5. Most varieties tasted; picnic area under a huge, gnarled oak.* Housed in a triple-towered hop kiln, Z Moore offers sanctuary from busy River Road traffic hurrying toward Freeway 101. The distinctive tasting room occupies one of the drying towers of the hop kilns, affording views of vineyards, ancient apple orchards and distant peaks.

☺ *Korbel Champagne Cellars* ● *13250 River Rd., Guerneville, CA 95446; (707) 887-2294. Daily 9 to 5; MC/VISA, AMEX. All varieties except brandy tasted; landscaped picnic areas. Winery tours daily every 45 minutes in summer, and hourly from 10 to 3 the rest of the year; garden tours daily at 11 and 2.* Started in 1882, Korbel has evolved into a baronial estate with vine covered stone buildings, a tower right out of medieval Germany and oldstyle European gardens. The setting is equally impressive, in a narrowing of the

Russian River Valley, rimmed by wooded hills on one side and a vineyard tilting toward the river on the other.

Davis Bynum Winery • *8075 Westside Rd., Healdsburg, CA 95448; (707) 433-5852. Daily 10 to 5; MC/VISA. Most varieties tasted free; small fee for some limited release wines. Picnic patio beside winery; guided tours by reservation.* Straightforward masonry block structures cluttered with equipment are trademarks of the Davis Bynum Winery, sitting just above a farmyard off Westside Road.

☺ **Hop Kiln Winery** • *6050 Westside Rd., Healdsburg, CA 95448; (707) 433-6491. Daily 10 to 5; MC/VISA, AMEX. Most varieties tasted; picnic tables under sheltering fig tree, others near a pond.* This intriguing winery is housed in an old hop kiln, with of the original equipment still in place. The tasting room occupies a mezzanine above the winery. A tour thus consists of walking to a railing and peering down at stainless steel vats and wooden barrels.

Belvedere Winery • *4035 Westside Rd., Healdsburg, CA 95448; (707) 433-8236. Daily 10 to 4:30; MC/VISA. All varieties available for tasting (limit of four samples). Nice selection of wine-related gift items and works by local artists; picnic area.* Belvedere is a comely winery in a nice locale, set amongst hillside vineyards. Lawns and blooming flowers give it a park-like quality. Honeysuckle droops from a porch overhanging the tasting room.

Bellerose Vineyard • *435 W. Dry Creek Rd., Healdsburg, CA 95448; (707) 433-1637. Tuesday-Thursday 1 to 4:30, Friday-Sunday 11 to 4:30, closed Monday; MC/VISA, DISC. Most varieties tasted. Picnic area. Group tours only, by appointment.* Earthy, organic Bellerose more resembles an old farmyard than a modern winery. Two draft horses, Rowdy and Curly, who contribute generously to the organic concept, are honored with their portraits on Bellerose' Workhorse Red Cabernet Sauvignon. The tasting room consists of a plank counter, not far from a cluttered office desk.

Lambert Bridge Vineyards • *4085 W. Dry Creek Rd., Healdsburg, CA 95448; (707) 433-5855 or (800) 634-2680. Daily 10 to 4:30; MC/VISA. Select varieties tasted. Gazebo and picnic area overlooking Dry Creek Valley; tours by appointment.* Perched in a wooden glen above the road, Lambert Bridge is one of the area's more attractive small wineries. The tasting room is in a shingle-sided redwood structure resembling a national park chalet.

Robert Stemmler Winery • *3805 Lambert Bridge Rd., Healdsburg, CA 95448; (707) 433-6334. Daily 10:30 to 4:30; MC/VISA. Most varieties tasted; picnic tables near tasting room.* Wine harvest prints from ancient Flemish tapestries decorate Stemmler's wine labels and tasting room, which might be described as an elegant lean-to. The small winery sits on a wooded knoll above the vineyards.

Dry Creek Vineyard • *3770 Lambert Bridge Rd. (P.O. Box T), Healdsburg, CA 95448; (707) 433-1000. Daily 10:30 to 4:30; MC/VISA. Most varieties tasted; picnic area on a lawn.* The tasting room of this mid-sized winery occupies a sturdy structure suggestive of a manor house, covered with climbing ivy and rimmed by old trees and new lawns.

☺ **Ferrari-Carano Vineyards and Winery** • *8761 Dry Creek Rd., Healdsburg, CA 95448; (707) 433-6700. Daily 10 to 5; MC/VISA, AMEX. Selected wines tasted; tours by appointment Tuesday-Saturday at 10 and 2.* This large facility is a striking blend of castle and leading-edge winery. Fronted by a formal entryway and billiard-green lawns, it's the most palatial of the Dry Creek area wineries.

Ancient vines and an old farm house create a bucolic scene in northern Sonoma County's Russian River Valley
— Betty Woo Martin

Lake Sonoma Winery ● *9990 Dry Creek Rd., Geyserville, CA 95441; (707) 431-1550. Daily 10 to 5. Most varieties tasted; deli with picnic fare and specialty foods. Shaded picnic areas; informal winery tours.* A gravel road pitches steeply upward through hillside vineyards to this small new winery. The view of nearby Warm Springs dam and the valley from the cheerful, airy tasting room and its wrap-around balcony is impressive.

J. Pedroncelli Winery ● *1220 Canyon Road, Geyserville, CA 95441; (707) 857-3531. Daily 10 to 5; MC/VISA, AMEX. Most varieties tasted. Small deck with picnic tables. Guided tours by reservation.* The tasting room of this long-established winery is an attractive, airy space with high ceilings and a curving bar. Picnic tables near the vineyards encourage visitors to linger in this bucolic setting. It's all part of a pleasant ranch style complex of redwood buildings among vines and oak-thatched hills.

Geyser Peak Winery ● *22281 Chianti Rd., Geyserville, CA 95441; (707) 857-9463. Daily 10 to 5; MC/VISA. Most varieties tasted; covered patio picnic area.* This large operation features terraced patios and a stone faced ivy covered winery built against a wooded hillside. Hiking trails wander about the grounds; one leads to a picnic area near the Russian River. It's difficult to believe that freeway traffic is but an exhaust belch away.

ACTIVITIES & ATTRACTIONS

Bicycle rentals ● Spoke Folk Cyclery, 249 Center St., Healdsburg; (707) 433-7171.

Canoeing ● Bob Trowbridge Canoe trips, Healdsburg, one to four days with return shuttle; (707) 433-7247.

Farm products ● For a map and guide to direct outlet farms selling fresh and prepared fruits, vegetables, meats, dairy products and wines, contact *Sonoma County Farm Trails*, P.O. Box 6674, Santa Rosa, CA 95406; (707) 544-4728 or pick up free map at most member outlets.

Guided winery tours ● "Surrey & Sip" horse-drawn or antique car wine tours with picnic lunch; (707) 894-5956. Five Oaks Farm Horse-Drawn Vineyard Tours with lunch or early dinner; (707) 433-2422.

Hot air ballooning ● Air Flamboyant, (707) 575-1989; Airborn of Sonoma County, (707) 433-3210; Once in a Lifetime, (707) 578-0580.

Winery tour maps ● Free *Russian River Wine Road* map of wineries, restaurants and lodgings, available throughout the area, or contact Russian River Wine Road, P.O. Box 46, Healdsburg, CA 95448; (707) 433-6782 or (800) 648-9922 (California only). Mattioli's *In Your Pocket Guide* to wineries and other attractions, in many tasting rooms, or call (707) 965-2006.

Museums

Edwin Langhart Historical Museum ● *221 Matheson Street, Healdsburg; (707) 431-3325. Tuesday-Sunday noon to 5.* Local history exhibits in a classic Carnegie library building.

Sonoma County Wine Library Collection ● *City Library, 139 Piper St., Healdsburg; (707) 433-3772. Free; hours vary.* A few early winery artifacts and extensive collection of wine-oriented books and documents.

ANNUAL EVENTS

Russian River Barrel Tasting, early March; (707) 433-6782.

Russian River Wine Festival, mid-May, $10; (800) 648-9922.

Polo, Wine and All That Jazz, early June, Sonoma County Wine Library Association, P.O. Box 15225, Santa Rosa, CA 95402; (707) 571-1926.

Sonoma County Harvest Fair, early October; (707) 545-4203. Individual wineries also sponsor various events throughout the year.

WHERE TO DINE

Catelli's The Rex ● ΔΔ $$

21047 Geyserville Ave., Geyserville; (707) 857-9904. Italian-American; dinner $9 to $17; full bar service. Lunch Monday-Friday 11:30 to 2, dinner nightly 5 to 9. MC/VISA. Geyserville's local hangout; expect to see an occasional cluster of vintners seriously discussing the Zinfandel crop. A plain front shields an ordinary interior with ceiling fans, tables and a few booths.

☺ *Chateau Souverain Restaurant* ● ΔΔΔ $$$$ Ø

400 Souverain Rd., Geyserville; (707) 433-8281. American-continental; dinner $25 to $35; full bar service. Lunch in the café Wednesday-Sunday noon to 10; lunch in the restaurant Wednesday-Saturday 11:30 to 3 and dinner Wednesday-Sunday 5:30 to 9, Sunday brunch 10:30 to 2:30; restaurant and café closed Monday and Tuesday. MC/VISA, AMEX. Elegant restaurant at Chateau Souverain Winery. Changing eclectic menu, offering such fare as roast salmon with celery root crust, and macadamia nut Hawaiian sea bass. Smaller **Souverain Café** leans toward *hors d'oeuvres* and light fare.

Healdsburg Coffee Company ● Δ $ Ø

312 Center St., Healdsburg; (707) 431-7941. American; light fare; wine and beer. Monday-Friday 7:30 to 6, Saturday-Sunday 8 to 6. MC/VISA, AMEX. A cheerful place offering soup, salad, sandwiches, quiche, espresso and local wine. On Healdsburg Plaza, with homey oak-antique décor.

Jacob Horner ● ΔΔΔ $$$ Ø

106 Matheson St. (on the Plaza), Healdsburg; (707) 433-3939. California nouveau; full bar service. Lunch Monday-Saturday 11:30 to 2, dinner Tuesday-Saturday 5:30 to 9 (to 9:30 Friday-Saturday). MC/VISA, AMEX. Locally popular place with stylish Victorian décor; changing menu with items such as Sonoma *cassoulet*, Petaluma duck and Sonoma County chicken *paillard*, along with some vegetarian dishes.

☺ *Madrona Manor Restaurant* ● ΔΔΔΔ $$$$ Ø

1001 Westside Rd., Healdsburg; (800) 258-4003. California nouveau; wine and beer. Dinner nightly 6 to 9, Sunday brunch 11 to 2. Reservations advised; required on Saturdays. Major credit cards. Northern Sonoma County's most opulent restaurant, housed in a Victorian mansion. Menu features entrées such as Peking duck with almond coconut rice, stuffed mild chilies, and salmon with mixed herbs. Multi-course prix fixe dinners.

WHERE TO SLEEP

The list below represents lodgings near northern county vinelands. Nearby Santa Rosa offers a considerably larger selection.

Best Western Dry Creek Inn ● ΔΔ $$$ Ø

198 Dry Creek Rd. (at U.S. 101), Healdsburg, CA 95448; (800) 222-5784 or (707) 433-0300. Couples and singles $55 to $79. Major credit cards. A 104-room motel with TV movies, room phones and in-room coffee service. Pool, spa; gift bottle of wine and free continental breakfast.

Fairview Motel ● Δ $$ Ø

74 Healdsburg Ave. (at U.S. 101), Healdsburg, CA 95448; (707) 433-5548. Couples $44 to $46, singles $38. Major credit cards. Eighteen rooms with TV movies and phones; pool, spa and playground.

Huckleberry Springs ● ⌂⌂⌂ $$$$$

8105 Old Beedle Rd. (end of Tyrone Road; P.O. Box 400), Monte Rio, CA 95462; (707) 865-2683. Cottages $175 including dinner and breakfast. Five units with private baths. MC/VISA, AMEX. Rustic, luxurious country lodge on 56 acres. Contemporary furnishings in cottages; oldstyle lodge with antiques, folk art and graphics collection.

☺ **Madrona Manor** ● ⌒⌒⌒ $$$$$ Ø
1001 Westside Rd. (P.O. Box 818), Healdsburg, CA 95448; (707) 433-4231. Rooms $110 to $200. Major credit cards. Beautifully restored 1881 Victorian mansion. Twenty-one rooms with antique and modern furnishings, fireplaces in many. Music room lounge with fireplace, books, piano and light food service. Located on eight wooded, landscaped acres. **Madrona Manor Restaurant** listed above.

Bed & breakfast inns

☺ **Belle de Jour Inn** ● ⌒⌒⌒ $$$$$ Ø
16276 Healdsburg Ave. (opposite Simi Winery), Healdsburg, CA 95448; (707) 431-9777. Couples $115 to $185, singles $110 to $180. Four cottages with private baths; full breakfast. MC/VISA. Posh accommodations in ranch style complex near downtown Healdsburg. Antique and modern furnishings; fireplaces, spas, refrigerators in rooms. Vintage car winery tours available.

Campbell Ranch Inn ● ⌒⌒⌒ $$$$$ Ø
1475 Canyon Rd. (1.6 miles west of 101), Geyserville, CA 95441; (707) 857-3476. Couples $100 to $145, singles $90 to $135. Five rooms with private baths; full breakfast selected from menu. MC/VISA, DISC. Modern ranch style B&B on a wooded knoll with vineyard views. Spa, tennis courts, pool and gardens. Four rooms in main house, one cottage.

Grape Leaf Inn ● ⌒⌒⌒ $$$$ Ø
539 Johnson St. (Grant Street), Healdsburg, CA 95448; (707) 433-8140. Couples $85 to $130, singles $55 to $100. Seven rooms with private baths; full breakfast. MC/VISA. Refurbished 1900 Queen Anne Victorian. Nicely appointed rooms with whirlpool tubs, skylight roofs, air conditioning.

Healdsburg Inn on the Plaza ● ⌒⌒⌒ $$$$ Ø
110 Matheson St. (Healdsburg Avenue), Healdsburg, CA 95448; (707) 433-6991. Couples and singles $75 to $160. Nine rooms, all with TV, phones and private baths; full breakfast, including champagne on weekends and holidays. MC/VISA. Oldstyle inn with Victorian furnishings and original artworks. Bright, cheerful rooms; some overlooking Healdsburg Plaza.

☺ **Hope-Bosworth & Hope-Merrill houses** ● ⌒⌒⌒ $$$$ Ø
21238 and 21253 Geyserville Ave. (P.O. Box 42), Geyserville, CA 95441; (707) 857-3356. Bosworth—$65 to $90, four rooms with private baths; Merrill—$95 to $125, seven rooms with private baths; full breakfast. MC/VISA. Two turn of the century Victorians across the street from one another in downtown Geyserville, furnished with antiques. The 1904 Hope-Bosworth is American country style; 1870s Hope-Merrill is Victorian.

WHERE TO CAMP

Cloverdale KOA ● *26460 River Rd. (P.O. Box 600), Cloverdale, CA 95425; (707) 894-3337. RV and tent sites, $14.50 to $16.50. Reservations accepted; MC/VISA.* Just off U.S. 101, eight miles north of Healdsburg. Full hookups; some shaded sites; showers, coin laundry, mini-mart, swimming pool, playground, rec room, miniature golf.

Lake Sonoma ● *3333 Skaggs Springs Rd., Geyserville, CA 95441; (707) 433-9483. Liberty Glen campground with RV and tent sites; $10. No credit cards.* Above Warm Springs Dam; water and electric, barbecues, nature trails, amphitheater; hiking, biking and equestrian trails.

SONOMA VALLEY WINERY TOUR

As you pass through Santa Rosa on U.S. 101 freeway, watch for a turnoff for eastbound Highway 12. It leads through this city of 100,000 and into the attractive **Valley of the Moon,** praised in prose by Jack London, who spent his final days here.

You'll traverse several miles of country homes, curvaceous green farmlands and hills blanketed by oak before you encounter your first vines. The tasting begins with the new **Landmark Vineyards** on your left, at Highway 12 and Adobe Canyon Road. A steep drive up Adobe Canyon will take you to **Sugarloaf Ridge State Park,** offering camping, hiking trails and some stellar views of the countryside.

Back on Highway 12, as you approach the prim hamlet of **Kenwood, Chateau St. Jean** and **St. Francis** wineries stand opposite one another. Just beyond, look on your right for the **Smothers Brothers Wine Store** (yes, Tom and Dickey). **Kenwood Winery** is uphill, on your left.

A three-mile drive takes you to Arnold Drive and the picturesque town of **Glen Ellen.** Author London used to come down from his ranch to hang out at the false front bars and stores here. His spread is now enshrined in **Jack London State Park,** up a steep road from the town. En route, pause at **Glen Ellen Winery** on your right. Return to town and turn right onto Arnold Drive. On your left is **Jack London Village,** a themed shopping center built into an old winery and brandy distillery. This collection of boutiques and restaurants was rather scruffy the last time we looked.

Just beyond, you pass through the lushly landscaped grounds of **Sonoma State Hospital,** an stately institution for the troubled of mind. A mile or so beyond the hospital, turn left onto Madrone Road; the old **Valley of the Moon Winery** soon appears on your left.

You hit Highway 12 again after less than a mile; go right and head for the town of Sonoma. En route, you'll pass through the scruffy scatters of **Agua Caliente, Fetters Hot Springs** and **Boyes Hot Springs.** These tattered towns, once boasting stylish health spas, do no justice to the pretty valley that surrounds them. One elegant resort remains—the completely renovated **Sonoma Mission Inn.**

Remember that Bear Flag business? When a ragtag band of Americans took over Sonoma in 1846 and locked Mexican governor Mariano Vallejo in his own barracks? You're about to enter the town where it all happened—one of the most historic and appealing communities in California.

☺ Carefully restored and basking in wealth wrought by tourism, Spanish style **Sonoma** is built around the largest plaza in California. The *piazza* itself could occupy a good piece of the day, with a kids' playground, duck-feeding ponds, picnic and barbecue areas, rose garden and a monument heralding the Bear Flag Revolt. Old **Sonoma City Hall** sits in the middle, with four identical sides, so all the merchants on the quadrangle get a front view. Today's merchants, basking in the sunlight of tourism, operate boutiques, restaurants and specialty shops.

Elements of **Sonoma State Historic Park** stand opposite the plaza to the north, including **Sonoma Barracks, La Casa Grande** (an adobe fragment that was once part of Vallejo's home) and the restored **Toscano Hotel.** At the northeast corner stands the humble adobe chapel of **Mission San Francisco Solano.** Informally called the Sonoma Mission, it's the only one founded after Mexico took California from Spain. About half a mile west of the plaza, off West Spain Street, is **Lachryma Montis** (*"Tears of the Mountain"*), Vallejo's ornate 1854 Victorian style home.

If you have kids in tow, Sonoma offers respite from the monotony of winery touring. Turn them loose at the plaza playground or take them to **Train Town,** less than a mile south of the plaza on Broadway. Here, scale model ride-upon trains chug through a mini-western town.

Should all this activity work up an appetite, you've come to the right place. Sonoma is noted for its culinary culture, both from restaurants that surround the plaza and from specialty food shops. Most of the shops offer samples.

Start with **Sonoma Cheese Factory** (707-996-1931) on the north side of the plaza on Spain Street. Monterey jack is a special cheese produced hereabouts and you can watch it being made through viewing windows in this large deli. Then load up on goodies, have a sandwich tailored from the large selection of meats and cheeses, pick up a bottle of wine and adjourn to the plaza or to a nearby winery for a picnic. The cheese factory offers indoor tables and a latticework patio.

The **Sonoma Sausage Company** on the west side of the plaza at 453 First Street (707-938-8200) offers a tasty selection of locally made patès, salads and every kind of sausage from British bangers to bratwurst.

On the opposite side of the square, **Sonoma French Bakery** (707-996-2691) makes some of the best sourdough bread in Northern California, along with sundry other savories. Get there early, since the bread supply often runs out.

A block east of the mission on Spain Street, then a block north at 315 Second is **Vella Cheese Company,** a smaller but equally appealing cheese factory. Housed in a 1905 rough-cut stone brewery building, it offers assorted cheeses and other specialty foods.

Should you wish something other than wine to rinse all this down, try the rich fruit juices of the **Cherry Tree.** It has two outlets—about five miles south on Highway 121, and at 1901 Fremont Drive (Highways 12/121 headed for Napa).

The Sonoma Chamber of Commerce **Sonoma Valley Visitors Bureau** occupies an old Carnegie library building on the plaza's east side. You can purchase a *Sonoma Walking Tour* map and pick up assorted free brochures.

Since you're about to ask, there *are* wineries around here. Lots of them, and the community has posted signs to help you seek them out. Head east from the Plaza on East Napa Street, turn left onto Fourth Street and you'll shortly encounter **Sebastiani Vineyards.** By this time, you've likely noticed the Sebastiani name on an old theater off the plaza. Immigrant Samuele Sebastiani came to this valley in 1904, and the family is still a major presence in the town. The winery tasting room, incidentally, will not be uncrowded on summer weekends, although it's large enough to accommodate quite a herd.

From here, head east into the vineyards on Spain Street, then go uphill on Gehricke Road to **Ravenswood,** tucked among the trees. Continue east on Spain (it becomes Lovell Valley Road), then head northeast on Castle Road to **Hacienda Wine Cellars.** Retreat to Lovell Valley, continue east briefly, then turn left onto Old Winery Road, lined with huge eucalyptus trees. At the end is one America's oldest wineries, dug into limestone caverns, **Buena Vista.** Backtrack on Old Winery Road, jog to the right onto Napa Street then left onto Denmark Street. With luck, you'll wind up at pleasantly rustic **Gundlach-Bundschu Winery,** tucked into a hollow.

Return to the Sonoma Plaza, turn left onto Broadway, go south about 3.5 miles to **Schellville** and blend to the right onto Highway 121. This takes you into the **Carneros region,** an old flood plain between the Sonoma and Napa valleys. New vines and new wineries are sprouting in this area. Watch for **Gloria Ferrer Champagne Caves** uphill on your right, Sam Sebastiani's stylish **Viansa** and then **Roche Carneros,** both on the left.

The wineries

Landmark Vineyards ● *101 Adobe Canyon Rd., Kenwood, CA 95452; (707) 833-0053. Daily 10 to 4:30; MC/VISA. Selected wines tasted; picnic tables near the tasting room. Guided tours by appointment.* This enticing new facility of beige stucco with shake roofs is built around a large Spanish style courtyard. A tile floor, vaulted ceiling tasting room and a stylish gift and gourmet food shop occupy one wing.

☺ **Chateau St. Jean** ● *8555 Sonoma Hwy., Kenwood, CA 95452; (707) 833-4134. Daily 10 to 4:30; MC/VISA, AMEX. Selected wines tasted; shaded picnic areas. Self-guided tours daily from 10:30 to 4.* St. Jean ("jean" as in denims) is a chateau in every sense of the word. Tasting room and offices are in the Spanish style manor house of a former country estate. The winery occupies a beige stucco creation with a distinctive witch's hat tower.

St. Francis Winery ● *8450 Sonoma Hwy., Kenwood, CA 95452; (707) 833-4666. Daily 10 to 4:30. Most varieties tasted; choice of four from the list. Shaded picnic garden; tours by appointment.* Smaller than St. Jean and also well groomed, neighbor St. Francis has an affluent rural European look. The matched winery buildings have shingled roofs and cupolas, with burgundy awnings accenting the handsome oak tasting room.

Smothers Brothers Wine Store ● *9575 Sonoma Hwy. (P.O. Box 789), Kenwood, CA 95452; (707) 833-1010. Daily 10 to 4:30; MC/VISA, AMEX. All wines tasted for a fee.* This facility is a blend of tasting room, wine store and curio shop. The musical-comedy brothers' winery is elsewhere. However, their presence is evident here, with the Tom Smothers yo-yo collection and assorted other SmoBro souvenirs. Some of their gold records adorn a wall.

Kenwood Vineyards ● *9592 Sonoma Hwy., Kenwood, CA 95452; (707) 833-5891. Daily 10 to 4; MC/VISA. Most varieties tasted.* Kenwood is located in a wood-sided ranch structure amidst the vineyards. The grounds are carefully tended and the spacious tasting room suggests an oversized chalet, with wood paneled walls and open beams.

Glen Ellen Winery ● *1883 London Ranch Rd., Glen Ellen, CA 95442; (707) 935-3047. Daily 10 to 4:30; MC/VISA, DISC. Most varieties tasted; informal tours; picnic area in a redwood grove.* Started just a few years ago, this facility now ships 3.7 million cases of wine worldwide. The operation is housed in a random scatter of neat white clapboard buildings, shaded by mature oaks. The tasting room is in a cheery knotty pine cottage.

Valley of the Moon Winery ● *777 Madrone Rd., Glen Ellen, CA 95442; (707) 996-6941. Daily 10 to 5; all major credit cards. Selected wines tasted; tree-shaded picnic area.* Crouched behind an ancient bay laurel, this century-old winery's tasting room is housed in a weathered stone building. The winery was established in the 1800s and was operated at one time by Senator

George Hearst. Closed by Prohibition, it was brought back to life by the Parducci family in 1942.

☺ **Sebastiani Vineyards** • *389 E. Fourth St., Sonoma, CA 95476; (707) 938-5532. Daily 10 to 5. Most varieties tasted; picnic areas near the winery and along the vineyards on Spain Street. Tours every half hour from 10:30 to 4.* The ancient cut-stone winery is on the edge of a tidy old residential area, while vineyards stretch toward low hills. Heavy beams hold up the tasting room ceiling and a stained glass window glitters with the family logo. Note the remarkable collection of wood carvings on barrel ends and just about every other exposed wood surface. They were done by employee Earle Brown, who took up the craft as a retirement project and continued carving for more than a decade.

Ravenswood • *18701 Gehricke Rd., Sonoma, CA 95476; (707) 938-1960. Daily 10 to 4:30; MC/VISA. Selected wines tasted. Picnic area with hillside and vineyard views; guided tours by appointment.* This is where you go for a little Zin. The stone winery, tucked into a wooded slope and besieged by vineyards, specializes in Zinfandel. A picnic terrace offers fine views of vines, pines, giant eucalyptus trees and the edges of Sonoma below.

Hacienda Wine Cellars • *1000 Vineyard Lane (P.O. Box 416), Sonoma, CA 95476; (707) 938-3220. Daily 10 to 5; MC/VISA. Most varieties tasted. Oak-shaded picnic area overlooking the vineyards; guided tours by appointment.* The "villa" catches your eye before you see the winery. Crowning a hill to your left, it's a reconstruction of the Pompeiian villa erected in 1857 by Count Agoston Haraszthy, one of California's early wine pioneers. It isn't open to the public, but the winery tasting room just up the road is. It's housed in a century-old, oak-shaded Spanish-California structure that once served as a community hospital.

☺ **Buena Vista Winery** • *18000 Old Winery Rd. (P.O. Box 1842), Sonoma, CA 95476; (707) 938-1266. Daily 10 to 5; major credit cards. Most varieties tasted; some free, others for a fee. Historical presentations at 11:30 and 2 in summer, 2 p.m. only the rest of the year. Picnic areas in the winery courtyard, and terraced on a steep slope.* Founded in 1857 by Count Haraszthy, the winery is shaped from rough blocks quarried from its own tunnels, bunkered into a steep slope. It exudes the mystique of a viticultural Mayan ruin. Prowling the tunnels of the ancient winery or its next-door Press House, you can see the pick marks where Chinese laborers dug the tunnels.

Gundlach-Bundschu Winery • *2000 Denmark St., Sonoma, CA 95476; (707) 938-5277. Daily 11 to 4:30; MC/VISA. Selected wines tasted; picnic area up a slope with a valley view.* Gundlach-Bundschu combines antiquity, a modern wine facility and humor. The weather-worn stone winery was built in the 1860s. Inside, a contemporary winery functions. The funky tasting room is decorated with off-beat Gundlach-Bundschu advertising posters. One shows a highway patrolman telling a motorist in an old Kaiser: *If you can't say "Gundlach-Bundschu Gewürztraminer," you shouldn't be driving!*

☺ **Gloria Ferrer Champagne Caves** • *23555 Highway 121, Sonoma, CA 95476; (707) 996-7256. Daily 10:30 to 5:30; MC/VISA. Sparkling wines by the glass from $3.50 to $7.50. Guided tours hourly from 11 to 4.* The tile-roofed winery with its graceful Spanish arches shields an underground *cava*, where sparkling wines are coaxed into graceful maturity. Tours take you past fermenting tanks and a bottling line, then descend into gunnited caves under 20 feet of earth.

☺ **Viansa Winery** • *25200 Arnold Dr. (Highway 121), Sonoma, CA 95476; (707) 935-4700. Daily 10 to 5; MC/VISA. Most varieties tasted. Deli, picnic and gourmet food items. Valley view picnic area; informal peek into the winery, or guided tours by appointment.* Fashioned as a Tuscan villa, Sam and Vickie Sebastiani's stylish winery is tucked into the brow of a hill high above the Carneros. The tasting room is aptly described as an "Italian marketplace." Murals embellish the walls, and a century old Italian wine cart is the focal point of an extensive giftware and specialty food shop.

Roche Carneros Estate Winery • *28700 Arnold Dr. (Hwy. 121), Sonoma, CA 95476; (707) 935-7115. Daily 10 to 5 (to 6 in summer); MC/VISA, AMEX. Most wines tasted free, fee for some reserves. Picnic area; tours by appointment.* Housed in a double-pitched roof structure suggestive of an urban barn, Roche offers a pleasurable view of the Carneros region, San Pablo Bay, and Sonoma Valley. The tasting room is spacious and inviting, like an oversized living room.

ACTIVITIES & ATTRACTIONS

Auto racing • Sears Point International Raceway, auto and cycle races most weekends, Highway 37 at 121; (707) 938-8448.

Farm products • For a map and guide to direct outlet farms selling fresh and prepared fruits, vegetables, meats, dairy products and wines, contact *Sonoma County Farm Trails,* P.O. Box 6674, Santa Rosa, CA 95406; (707) 544-4728 or pick up free map at most member outlets.

Horseback riding • Guided trail rides through Jack London and Sugarloaf Ridge state parks by Sonoma Cattle Company, (707) 996-8566.

Hot air ballooning • Air Flamboyant, (707) 456-4711; Sonoma Thunder, (707) 538-7359.

Scenic flights • Aero-Schellville (open cockpit biplane), (707) 938-2444; Helicopter Network, 252-7874; Sonoma Sky Park, 935-9745.

Train rides • Train Town, 20264 Broadway, Sonoma; (707) 938-3912.

Wine country tours • Sonoma Charter & Tours, (707) 938-4248; Linda Viviandi Touring Company, 938-2100; Wine Country Wagons, 833-2724.

Winery maps • Free *Sonoma Valley Viticultural Area* map, at area wineries and Sonoma Valley Visitors Bureau, or write Sonoma Valley Vintner's Association, P.O. Box 238, Sonoma, CA 95476. *Official Sonoma Valley Visitors Guide* available at visitors bureau and local wineries and shops.

Museums & historical exhibits

Sonoma State Historic Park • *P.O. Box 167, Sonoma; (707) 938-1578. Daily 10 to 5; modest admission charge (one ticket good for all units of the park).* The park includes Mission San Francisco Solano, Sonoma Barracks, La Casa Grande and Toscano Hotel, all on Sonoma Plaza; and General Vallejo's Home, south of the plaza off Spain Street.

Jack London State Historic Park • *London Ranch Road, Glen Ellen; (707) 938-5216. Daily 10 to 5; modest admission charge.* Author's ranch, Wolf House ruins and wife Charmian's elaborate stone home, filled with London memorabilia.

ANNUAL EVENTS

Heart of the Valley barrel tasting at eight Kenwood area wineries, mid-March; 833-4666.

Sonoma Valley Wine Festival, mid-July; (707) 938-6791.

Sonoma Vintage Festival, oldest in California with parade, grape stomps, wine tasting, late September; (707) 996-2109.

WHERE TO DINE

Depot 1870 Restaurant • ∆∆∆ $$
241 First St. West (Spain Street), Sonoma; (707) 938-2980. Northern Italian; wine and beer. Lunch Wednesday-Friday 11:30 to 2, dinner Wednesday-Sunday from 5. Major credit cards. Chef owned restaurant with dining at poolside in a landscaped garden, or in a historic Sonoma setting indoors.

Kenwood Restaurant • ∆∆∆ $$$ Ø
9900 Sonoma Highway, Kenwood; (707) 833-6326. French country cuisine; full bar service. Daily except Monday 11:30 to 9. MC/VISA. An open, cheerful place among the vineyards, with an outdoor dining patio. Changing menu with a strong *nouveau* tilt, featuring local fare meats and produce.

Magliulo's Restaurant • ∆∆∆ $$
691 Broadway, Sonoma; (707) 996-1031. Italian-American; full bar service. Open daily, lunch 11 to 2:30 and dinner 5 to 9. MC/VISA, DISC. Attractive restaurant in an early American home with warm woods, ironwork, cut glass and potted plants. Menu focuses on Italian fare, topped off by homemade desserts. Lantern-lit dining garden.

Oreste's Golden Bear • ∆∆ $$$
1717 Adobe Canyon Rd., Kenwood; (707) 833-2327. Northern Italian; wine and beer. Monday-Saturday 11:30 to 9:30, Sunday 11 to 2 and 4:30 to 9:30. MC/VISA, AMEX. Rustically casual restaurant built across a small creek, in an inviting wooded setting; a popular local hangout for decades. Menu is essentially Italian, some a few American chicken, chops and seafood entrèes.

Ristorante Piatti • ∆∆∆ $$$ Ø
405 First St. West (in the El Dorado Hotel), Sonoma; (707) 996-2351. Regional Italian; full bar service. Daily from 11:30, various closing hours. MC/VISA. Lively *trattoria*, popular as a business lunch hangout. Open kitchen with wood-burning rotisserie. Tree-shaded dining patio.

WHERE TO SLEEP

Best Western Sonoma Valley Inn • ⌂⌂⌂ $$$$$ Ø
550 Second St. West (a block west of plaza), Sonoma, CA 95476; (800) 334-5784 or (707) 938-9200. Couples and singles $90 to $132; rates include continental breakfast. Major credit cards. Nicely appointed 72-unit motel with pool, spa, coin laundry. Rooms have TV movies, phones, refrigerators; some with fireplaces or spa tubs.

El Dorado Hotel • ⌂⌂⌂ $$$$ Ø
405 First St. West (west side of plaza), Sonoma, CA 95476; (800) 289-3031 or (707) 996-3030. Couples $85 weekdays, $120 to $130 weekends (with continental breakfast). MC/VISA. Refurbished 27-room mission style hotel. Attractive rooms with terraces overlooking courtyard or plaza; continental furnishings with Spanish accents; swimming pool. **Ristorante Piatti** listed above.

Sonoma Hotel • ∆∆ $$$
110 W. Spain St. (northwest corner of plaza), Sonoma, CA 95476; (707) 996-2996. Couples $62 to $105 (includes continental breakfast and nightly

bottle of wine). MC/VISA, AMEX. Restored 1874 hotel; 17 rooms furnished with Victorian and early California antiques. Five rooms with private baths; others share. **Sonoma Hotel Bar & Grill** serves daily 11:30 to 8; American, mostly light fare and sandwiches; dinners $10 to $15; full bar service.

☺ **Sonoma Mission Inn & Spa** ● ⌂⌂⌂⌂ $$$$$ Ø
18140 Sonoma Highway, Boyes Hot Springs; mailing address P.O. Box 1447, Sonoma, CA 95476; (800) 862-4945 in California or (800) 358-9022 elsewhere, locally (707) 938-9000. Couples and singles $99 to $325. Major credit cards. Elegantly restored Mediterranean style resort on seven acres with a complete health spa, tennis courts and two pools. Stylish rooms have TV with VCRs, room phones and typical resort amenities. **The Grille** serves daily 11:30 to 2:30 and 6 to 9; California *nouveau*; dinners $25 to $40; overlooking pool and gardens; full bar service.

Bed & breakfast inns

Gaige House ● ⌂⌂⌂ $$$$ Ø
13540 Arnold Dr. (north of Warm Springs Road), Glen Ellen, CA 95442; (707) 935-0237. Couples $90 to $160, singles $80 to $145. Eight rooms, all with private baths; full breakfast. MC/VISA, DISC. An Italianate Victorian dating from 1890, furnished with English and American antiques. Spacious yard, pool; some rooms with fireplaces; one with tub spa.

Sonoma Chalet ● ⌂⌂⌂ $$$$ Ø
18935 Fifth St. West (Verano Avenue), Sonoma, CA 95476; (707) 938-3129. Couples $75 to $135. Three rooms and three cottages, some private and some share baths; continental breakfast. MC/VISA, AMEX. Country style farm house; rooms furnished with country antiques; fireplaces, wood-burning stoves. Spa, bicycles, complimentary sherry.

Thistle Dew Inn ● ⌂⌂⌂ $$$$ Ø
171 W. Spain St. (a block west of plaza), Sonoma, CA 95476; (707) 938-2909. Couples and singles $80 to $135. Six rooms, all with private baths; full breakfast. MC/VISA, AMEX. Lodgings in an 1869 Victorian and a 1905 early American home; modern furnishings, decorated with antique furnishings, arts and crafts. Spa, bicycles, afternoon *hors d'oeuvres.*

Victorian Garden Inn ● ⌂⌂⌂ $$$$ Ø
316 E. Napa St. (block and a half east of plaza), Sonoma, CA 95476; (707) 996-5339. Couples $79 to $139. Four rooms, all with private baths, one cottage with fireplace; full breakfast. MC/VISA, AMEX. An 1880 Greek Revival style home furnished with country antiques. Pool, landscaped grounds and patio; complimentary evening wine.

Trojan Horse Inn ● ⌂⌂⌂ $$$$$ Ø
19455 Sonoma Hwy. (between West Napa and Spain), Sonoma, CA 95476; (707) 996-2430. Couples $110 to $130. Six rooms, all with private baths; full breakfast. MC/VISA, AMEX. Victorian style farmhouse with landscaped grounds on banks of Sonoma Creek. Rooms furnished with English and American antiques; armoires, brass beds. Complimentary bicycles.

WHERE TO CAMP

Sugarloaf Ridge State Park ● *2605 Adobe Canyon Rd., Kenwood, CA 95452; (707) 833-5712. RV and tent sites, $10. Reservations via Mistix, (800) 444-PARK, or write: P.O. Box 85705, San Diego, CA 92138-5705.* Attractive mountainside campsites; flush potties, no hookups or showers. Hiking and equestrian trails.

NAPA VALLEY WINERY TOUR

Sugarloaf Ridge and the Mayacamas Mountains separate America's two most famous vineyard valleys. For an easy transition from the Sonoma to the Napa Valley, head east from **Schellville** on Highway 121/12, across the Carneros flood plain. The more adventurous may want to go back toward Glen Ellen and take **Trinity Grade.** After topping the Mayacamas, the winding but all-paved route spills down **Oakville Grade,** offering a stunning view of vineyards and mountains.

If you take the 121/12 route, your first winery vision will be an impressive one—chateau like **Domaine Carneros** on your right. You then swing north onto Highway 29, skirting the edge of **Napa.** Initially, you catch no clue to the fabled wineland. The town itself has all the charm of Boise, Idaho. However, as you approach a traffic light where Trancas and Redwood roads meet at Highway 29, a *Falcon Crest* vision of the Napa Valley spreads before you. Sun dappled vines dance off in all directions, filling the valley floor and climbing to the wooded foothills of the cradling mountains. Far up the valley, **Mount St. Helena** stands silent watch.

If you stay on Highway 29, you'll run a vinicultural gauntlet through the greatest concentration of wineries in the world. The valley's total is nearly 250. They crowd along Highway 29 and crawl into foothills of the Mayacamas Mountains to the west and the Vaca Range to the east. They're all here—classic chateaux, stylish new cellars built by the spoiled rich, gimmick places that sell more souvenirs and sourdough bread than wine, and little family owned wineries untouched by all this.

You can catch glider flights and hot air balloon flights and take a ride on the Wine Train. You can shop 'til you flop and dine 'til your tummy whines. You can even taste some wine, but you'll have to pay a fee at many of these places. And you'll need patience; some of the more popular wineries draw 300,000 sippers a year!

There is, as we said in the beginning, a better way. Instead of plunging undaunted down Highway 29, turn left onto Redwood Road and start climbing into the Mayacamas. You're seeking a single winery and it's a stunner—the **Hess Collection,** several miles up this pretty, winding mountain road. From Hess, retrace your tire tracks and cross over Highway 29 onto Trancas Street. After two miles, go left onto a less traveled route with an attractive name, the Silverado Trail. It prowls along the wooded foothills of the Vaca Range, taking you to tasting rooms untrammeled by the tour bus set.

The wineries begin arriving after a couple of miles—**Clos du Val, Chimney Rock** and **Stag's Leap** on your right, then **Pine Ridge** and **Silverado** on your left. Just beyond Yountville Cross Road, **Robert Sinskey Vineyards** occupies a ridge on your right. Another pair of miles takes you to the **Mumm Napa Valley** sparkling wine cellars on the left. For a nice diversion, follow Highway 128 east into the mountains past **Lake Hennessey Recreation Area.** After several miles, you'll find rustic **Nichelini Winery** straddling a pine tree ridge.

Back in the valley, your northern march takes you to the very attractive **Rutherford Hill Winery,** up a tree-canopied slope to your right. You have a mile or so to catch your breath, then you see charmingly funky **Casa**

Nuestra, sitting down to the left off Silverado, just past Glass Mountain Road. A mile beyond, turn left onto Larkmead Lane for **Hans Kornell Winery.** Return to Silverado for a stop at **Cuvaison** on the right, then dip into Dunaweal Lane for impressive **Clos Pegase** on the right and **Sterling Vineyards** with its gimmicky sky bucket over the vines, down a shady lane to the left.

Returning to the Silverado Trail, you intersect Highway 29 as you reach charming old **Calistoga.** A 1930s spa undergoing a yuppie/tourism renaissance, it's noted for boutiques and restaurants, a glider port, mineral spas and mud baths. Pause for a peak at **Old Faithful Geyser** off Tubbs Lane. It spews a thin streak of steamy water fitfully every 40 minutes or so. Nearby is a particularly attractive tree-shrouded winery, **Chateau Montelena.**

If you remain on Highway 29, you'll climb the steep flanks of Mount St. Helena with its dramatic ramparts called the Palisades. Expect to see gliders flitting through the thermals up there, as free and easy as J. Edgar Swoop. You soon reach a turnout to **Robert Louis Stevenson State Park.** It's undeveloped but never mind that. Follow a trail from the parking area to the old **Silverado Mine,** and hike higher for simply awesome valley views.

Stevenson spent his honeymoon here in the summer of 1880, with his new wife, her son and their dog. Some honeymoon.

When you return from the mountain, plan a glider ride for the ultimate trip over the valley. The **Calistoga Glider Port** is at the northern edge of town. If you like trees turned to stone, take Petrified Forest Road southeast out of Calistoga to **Petrified Forest.** Stevenson visited there and found "Petrified Charlie," the gruff but affable owner, to be more interesting than the stiff trees.

We've deprived you of some of the sights and attractions along Highway 29, so you may want to go back that way. **Bothe-Napa Valley State Park** encompasses a nice slice of Mayacamas foothills, with camping and hiking trails. One of those trails leads to **Bale Grist Mill State Historic Park.** Or you can motor a bit farther south on Highway 29 and drive up to the mill.

If you just want to sample assorted wines, **Vintners Village** shopping center offers several tasting rooms divorced from their wineries. It's on your right, just south of Bale Mill. A bit beyond, you pass under an impressive canopy of Dutch elms as you enter the town of **St. Helena.** It isn't quite as charming as Calistoga, but—spurred by tourists and their money—it's getting there.

Assuming you like imposing old winery architecture, you might brave the crowds at three venerable institutions clustered at the town's north edge—**Christian Brothers Greystone Cellars, Charles Krug Winery** and **Beringer Vineyards** with its elegant Rhine House. And if you'd like to see where Angela sat at poolside to hatch plots against her *Falcon Crest* family, take Madrona Avenue west to Spring Mountain Road and follow it to **Spring Mountain Vineyards.** You can join a tour through the grounds of Angela's Victorian style lair, which in real life is the home of Spring Mountain winery owner Michael Robbins.

A pair of museums in St. Helena offer diversion from winery tripping and sipping. To reach the **Silverado Museum,** rich with Stevenson lore, turn left from Highway 29 (Main Street) onto Adams, driving two blocks to Library Lane and go left again. The museum is in the library complex. Continuing through town, you'll see the **Napa Valley Museum** on your right. Just short of it is the **St. Helena Chamber of Commerce,** on the left at Main and Pope.

As you clear the northern edge of town, swing left onto Charter Oak (at the vine-covered Tra Vigna restaurant) and follow it to **Napa Valley Olive Oil Manufacturing Company.** It's a wonderful Italian family deli cluttered with cheeses, spiced meats, fresh pasta and great jugs of olive oil. Walls are papered with thousands of calling cards and the "cash register" is a rolltop desk.

After ten miles of Highway 29 vines and wineries, follow signs to your right into **Yountville,** another old town all dressed up with tourist money. The visitor center of the **Yountville Chamber of Commerce** is in a shopping center called **Washington Square,** at the north edge of town. You'll find still more shops in the long established **Vintage 1870,** a nice gathering of brick and ivy that once housed a winery. One of the valley's better restaurants is at **Domaine Chandon,** a winery reached by crossing under the Highway 29 overpass from downtown Yountville.

The wineries

☺ *Domaine Carneros* ● *1240 Duhig Rd. (at Highway 121; P.O. Box 5420), Napa, CA 94558; (707) 257-0101. Daily 10:30 to 5:30 May through October, Friday-Tuesday 10:30 to 4:30 the rest of the year; MC/VISA. Sparkling wines sold by the glass for $3.50. Guided tours at 11, 1 and 3; self-guiding tours at other times.* Styled after an 18th century French chateau, this is an imposing presence, crowning a low hill in the heart of the Carneros. After admiring the portrait of Madame Pompadour, the beaded glass chandeliers, high coffered ceilings and the view, you can seat yourself in a cane-backed chair at a brass and glass table for a bit of the bubbly. On warm days, you can adjourn to an outdoor deck.

☺ *The Hess Collection* ● *4411 Redwood Rd. (P.O. Box 4140), Napa, CA 94558; (707) 255-1144. Daily 10 to 4; MC/VISA. Cabernet Sauvignon and Chardonnay tasted for a $2.50 fee. Self-guiding tour of the art museum, with views into the winery.* A new winery housed in an ancient cut stone building, Hess is one of the most impressive inner spaces in the wine country. Pause for a sip at an island counter tasting salon, peek into the winery and visit the art gallery with dazzling white walls set against old stone.

☺ *Clos du Val* ● *5330 Silverado Trail (P.O. Box 4350), Napa, CA 94558; (707) 252-6711. Daily 10 to 4; MC/VISA. Three wines tasted from the list; no fee. Oak-shaded picnic tables; tours by appointment.* Sitting upslope in a wooded grove, cathedral-like Clos du Val is one of the first of the valley's grand "new generation" wineries. The tasting room is an imposing space—a stunning abbey-like affair with 50-foot ceilings, accented by ornate woods, conglomerate walls and tile floors. Windows offer views into the winery.

Chimney Rock Winery ● *5350 Silverado Trail, Napa, CA 94558; (707) 257-2461. Daily 10 to 4; MC/VISA, DISC. Current releases tasted for $2.50 fee (includes glass, or can be applied to wine purchase). Guided tours by appointment.* With its ornate Dutch Colonial architecture, Chimney Rock is one of the valley's most striking small wineries. The two-building complex was fashioned after a winery in the Cape Colony of South Africa. Note the elaborate frieze on the main building, portraying Ganymede, cup bearer to Zeus and other Mount Olympus celestials.

Stag's Leap Wine Cellars • *5766 Silverado Trail, Napa, CA 94558; (707) 944-2020. Daily 10 to 4; MC/VISA. Most varieties tasted for $2 fee (includes glass). Oak-shaded picnic area; guided tours by appointment.* Stag's Leap is tucked into a pleasantly wooded niche on the mountain side of Silverado. Gnarled oaks glamorize the modest looking Spanish style complex. The tasting room is a simple counter at one end of the main winery building. From here, one can watch the business of winemaking.

Pine Ridge Winery • *5901 Silverado Trail, Napa, CA 94558; (707) 253-7500. Daily 11 to 4; MC/VISA. Most varieties tasted; no fee. Small picnic area with a swing set; tours of winery and caves 10:15 daily, by appointment.* Tucked into the pine shaded hollow of a hill, Pine Ridge is folksy and casual. You can peek into the winery and into several cooling caves, or arrange for a more formal tour.

Robert Sinskey Vineyards • *6320 Silverado Trail, Napa, CA 94558; 944-9090. Daily 10 to 4:30; MC/VISA. Most varieties tasted for a $3 fee (includes glass or credit toward purchase). Guided tours at 11, 1 and 3.* The Sinskey facility is architecturally intriguing, with a high, ridge-like wooden center flanked by low stone-trimmed wings. The interior is a nice mix of wood and stone.

☺ **Mumm Napa Valley** • *1111 Dunaweal Lane (P.O. Drawer 500), Rutherford, CA 94573; (707) 942-4219. Daily 10:30 to 4:30; MC/VISA, AMEX. Sparkling wine by the glass, $3.50 to $4.50. Tours hourly on the half hour from 10:30 to 4:30.* France's legendary Mumm set up shop in the Napa Valley in the mid-1980s. The structure is architecturally curious—a wood-sided creation suggestive of a king-sized California barn. It hovers low to the ground; the tour reveals that much of it is underground, in true French champagnery fashion.

Nichelini Winery • *2950 Sage Canyon Rd., St. Helena, CA 94574; (707) 963-0717. Weekends only, 9 to 6 April-October and 9 to 5 November-March. MC/VISA. Most varieties tasted; wooded picnic areas.* This delightfully rustic winery seems to cling to the edge of the highway, threatening to topple into a canyon. On nice days, tasting is conducted outdoors. You can settle onto a nearby bench to sip your wine and listen to the soft sounds of the forest.

☺ **Rutherford Hill Winery** • *200 Rutherford Hill Rd., Rutherford, CA 94573; (707) 963-7194. Weekdays 10 to 4:30, weekends 10 to 5; MC/VISA, AMEX. Most varieties tasted for a $3 fee (includes the glass). Wooded picnic area with a valley view. Tours of caves and winery.* Rutherford Hill occupies a monumental weathered wooden structure with flying buttresses, set in a wooded notch high above the valley. Tours take visitors through aging caves tunneled into the hillside, then into the state-of-the-art winery.

Casa Nuestra • *3473 Silverado Trail, St. Helena, CA 94574; (707) 963-5783. Friday-Sunday 11 to 5; MC/VISA. Most varieties tasted; shaded picnic area.* As rural and simple as Rutherford Hill is grand, this winery's tasting room is tucked into a little yellow farmhouse. It even has a fireplace and easy chairs for sitting and sipping. A tree-shaded picnic area with a hammock reinforces the laid-back, down-home impression.

Hanns Kornell Champagne Cellars • *1091 Larkmead Lane (P.O. Box 249), St. Helena, CA 95474; (707) 963-1237. Daily 10 to 4:30; most major credit cards. Selected sparkling wines tasted after tour, no fee. Guided tours* *about every 20 minutes, from 10 to 3:45.* Hanns Kornell fled Nazi Germany in 1939. He arrived in New York flat broke, scraped and saved and eventually opened a winery in 1952. Now eighty or so, he still keeps his hand in things but leaves most of the work to other family members. After a very informative tour, tastings are held in a simple, cottage style hospitality center.

☺ **Cuvaison Winery** ● *4550 Silverado Trail (P.O. Box 384), Calistoga, CA 94515; (707) 942-6266. Daily 10 to 5; MC/VISA, AMEX. Most varieties tasted for $2.50 fee (includes glass). Shaded picnic area near tasting room; guided tours by appointment.* This is a genuine jewel—a comely Spanish mission style winery with an architecturally matching tasting room shaded by ancient oaks. A woodsy picnic area on a downslope offers views of vineyards and the distant Mayacamas Mountains.

☺ **Clos Pegase** ● *1060 Dunaweal Lane, Calistoga, CA 94515; (707) 942-4901. Daily 10:30 to 5. Selected wines tasted for $3 fee (includes glass). Guided tours by appointment; wine and art lectures the third Saturday of each month, by appointment.* This opulent new winery is at once imposing and stark—a towering, columned presence enclosing a simple courtyard. A giant mural of Bacchus rises behind the counter in the large tasting room, taunting you to another sip.

☺ **Sterling Vineyards** ● *1111 Dunaweal Lane (P.O. Box 365), Calistoga, CA 94515; (707) 942-4219. Daily 10:30 to 4:30; MC/VISA, AMEX. Tram ride $5 (includes tasting of three wines; $2 credited toward wine purchase); self-guiding tours.* Reached by an aerial tram, Sterling gleams from a hillock among the vines like a misplaced Moorish monastery. The walk-through tour is among the best of the wine country, adorned with explanatory graphics, historic wine art reproductions and quotes about the grape.

☺ **Chateau Montelena Winery** ● *1429 Tubbs Lane, Calistoga, CA 94515; (707) 942-5105. Daily 10 to 4; MC/VISA. Selected wines tasted for $5 (credited toward wine purchase). Guided tours by appointment at 11 and 2.* A mini-medieval castle beneath sheltering trees and an Oriental lake comprise one of the valley's most serene winery retreats. Visitors can stroll the perimeter of Jade Lake, cross bright red arched bridges to tiny islands, converse with ducks and pause under the quietude of Japanese maples.

ACTIVITIES & ATTRACTIONS

Bicycling ● Bryan's Napa Valley Cyclery (bike tours), 4080 Byway East, Napa, CA 94558; Napa Valley Bike Tours, (707) 255-3377.

Bike rentals ● Jules Culver Bicycles, 1227 Lincoln Ave., Calistoga, CA 94515, (707) 942-0421; and St. Helena Cyclery, 1156 Main St., St. Helena, CA 94574; (707) 963-7736.

☺ **Glider rides** ● Calistoga Gliders, 1546 Lincoln Ave., Calistoga, CA 94515; (707) 942-5000.

"Falcon Crest" tours ● Tour of the grounds of Victorian estate used in TV's *Falcon Crest*, at Spring Mountain Winery, 2805 Spring Mountain Rd., St. Helena; (707) 963-5233; hourly from 11 to 4; $4.

Helicopter tours ● Helicopter Network International, (800) 662-6886 or (707) 255-5135; Napa Valley Helicopter Tours, (800) 876-5559 or (707) 252-7874.

Hiking, swimming ● Bothe-Napa Valley State Park, 3801 North St. Helena Hwy., Calistoga, CA 94515; (707) 942-4575.

Dr. Edward Bale's grist mill ground flour for Napa Valley's earliest settlers. The 1846 mill is now a state park.
—Betty Woo Martin

Hot air ballooning ● The Napa Valley has the greatest concentration of hot air balloon companies in California, and possibly in the entire country. Among the operators are: Above the West, (800) 627-2759; Adventures Aloft, (707) 255-8688; American Balloon Adventures, (800) 333-4359 or (707) 944-8117; Balloon About the Napa Valley, (707) 257-1001; Balloon Aviation of Napa Valley, (800) 367-6272; Balloons Above the Valley, (800) 233-7681; Bonaventura Balloon Co., (707) 944-2822; Napa Valley Balloons, (800) 253-2224; Napa's Great Balloon Escape, (707) 253-0860; Once In a Lifetime Balloon Co., (707) 942-6541; and Napa Valley Balloon Safaris, (800) 255-0125.

Napa Valley Wine Train ● 1275 McKinstry St., Napa, CA 94559; (800) 522-4142 or (707) 253-2111. A lunch and dinner train that makes a slow-motion cruise through the valley between Napa and Calistoga.

Wine country tours ● Napa Valley Tourist Bureau, (707) 258-1957; Napa Valley Bike Tours, (707) 255-3377; Antique Auto Adventures, (707) 226-3988.

Wine country maps ● *Napa Valley Tour Map*, available at many wineries and gift shops for $2.50 or contact Napa Valley Art Studio, 1028 Summit Ave., Napa, CA 94559; (707) 253-0204. Mattioli's *In Your Pocket Guide* to Yountville, Oakville and Rutherford is one dollar; available in many gift shops and tasting rooms, or call (707) 965-2006.

Museums and historic exhibits

☺ **Bale Grist Mill State Historic Park** • *Highway 29, three miles north of St. Helena; (707) 963-2236. Daily 9 to 5; admission fee.* Restored grist mill built by Dr. Edward T. Bale in 1846; it's furnished with old milling and farm equipment.

Napa Valley Museum • *473 Main St., St. Helena, CA 94574; (707) 963-7411. Monday-Friday 9 to 12 and 1 to 4.* Changing exhibits of the valley's history, art and sociology.

Old Faithful Geyser • *1299 Tubbs Lane, Calistoga, CA 94515; (707) 942-6463. Daily 9 to 6 in summer, 9 to 5 the rest of the year; admission fee.* Smaller than Yellowstone's but reasonably faithful, erupting about every 40 minutes; picnic area, gift and snack shop.

Petrified Forest • *Petrified Forest Rd. (five miles west), Calistoga, CA 94515; (707) 942-6667. Daily 9 to 6 in summer, 9 to 5 off-season; admission fee.* A scattering of petrified trees, museum, gift shop and picnic area.

☺ **Robert Louis Stevenson State Historic Park** • *Seven miles above Calistoga on Highway 29.* Site of the author's 1880 honeymoon. Although undeveloped, the park has several hiking trails and a monument at the cabin site where Stevenson and his bride stayed.

Sharpsteen Museum and Sam Brannan Cottage • *1311 Washington St., Calistoga, CA 94515; (707) 942-5911. Daily 10 to 4 from April to October, noon to 4 the rest of the year.* Historic museum with a scale model of Sam Brannan's resort and a restoration of one of his cottages. Brannan was a founder of Calistoga.

☺ **Silverado Museum** • *1490 Library Lane (P.O. Box 409), St. Helena, CA 94574; (707) 963-3757 or 963-3002. Noon to 4 daily except Mondays and holidays.* Excellent collection of objects concerning Robert Louis Stevenson and his 1880 visit to the Napa Valley.

ANNUAL EVENTS

Wine appreciation courses sponsored by the Napa Valley Wine Library Association; (707) 963-3535.

Mondavi Pops Festival and Summer Music Festival, June-August; (707) 963-9611.

Napa County Fair in Calistoga, featuring local winery exhibits, early July; (707) 942-5111.

Napa Town & Country Fair in Napa, featuring local winery exhibits, early August; (707) 253-4900.

Napa Valley Wine Festival, early November; (707) 253-3563. Individual wineries also sponsor various events throughout the year.

WHERE TO DINE

Since it draws hundreds of thousands of visitors including many San Francisco Bay Area regulars, the Napa Valley supports some of Northern California's better restaurants.

Brava Terrace • △△ $$
3010 St. Helena Hwy., St. Helena; (707) 963-9300. French-American; wine and beer. Daily noon to 9. Major credit cards. Charming bistro with *nouveau* accents, featuring local meats and produce and fresh pasta. Eclectic menu varies from roast chicken thighs with pistachio nuts to pork tender-

loin with bell peppers and cilantro. Outdoor dining terrace.

California Café • ΔΔ $$$

6795 Washington St. (Washington Square), Yountville; 944-2330. California nouveau; full bar service. Monday-Thursday 11:30 to 9, Friday-Saturday 11:30 to 10, Sunday 10 to 9:30. Major credit cards. Contemporary café with an Art Deco look; eclectic menu touches on grilled fresh fish, chicken and chops and pastas, enlivened with Mediterranean touches.

Compadres Mexican Bar & Grill • ΔΔ $$

6539 Washington St. (in Vintage Estate), Yountville; (707) 944-2406. Mexican; full bar service. Weekdays from 10 a.m., weekends from 9 a.m., various closing times. Major credit cards. The usual smashed beans and rice dishes, plus specialties such as Huajolote (charbroiled turkey breast marinaded in chilies, spices and tequila). The look is bright, cheery upscale California-Mexican; patio dining.

Depot Restaurant • ΔΔ $$

1458 Lincoln Ave. (in the Calistoga Depot), Calistoga; (707) 942-6411. American; wine and beer. Monday-Thursday 7 a.m. to 9 p.m., Friday-Sunday 7 to 10. MC/VISA, DISC. Dining inside the historic Calistoga depot or in a wine garden. Family style atmosphere, basic American menu featuring steaks, prime rib, chops and seafood; salad bar.

☺ Domaine Chandon Restaurant • ΔΔΔΔ $$$$ Ø

California Drive, Yountville; (707) 944-2892. California-French; wine. Open Wednesday-Sunday; lunch 11:30 to 2:30, dinner 6 to 9:30. Reservations essential (two weeks in advance for weekends). Major credit cards. One the valley's more striking restaurants, with glass walls offering vineyard views. Nouveau menu ranges from tuna pepper steak with potato puree and leek coulis to venison tournedos with sweet potato Napoleon, crepes and huckleberry sauce. Extensive California wine list.

☺ The French Laundry • ΔΔΔΔ $$$$$ Ø

Washington and Creek Streets (P.O. Box 3450), Yountville; (707) 944-2380. California-French country; prix fixe dinners about $46; wine and beer. Wednesday-Sunday, dinners only. Reservations essential (well in advance). No credit cards. Fashionable French Country café in a century-old brick laundry building, with fireplace, European antiques, artworks and gardens. One seating nightly for five-course dinners.

☺ Mustards • ΔΔΔ $$$Ø

7399 St. Helena Hwy. (just north of Yountville), Napa; (707) 944-2424. California-American upscale grill; full bar service. Daily 11:30 to 10. Reservations advised. MC/VISA, DISC. California nouveau café with a Yuppie American grill look. Changing menu offers smoked and grilled fish, fowl and beef served with fresh vegetables and innovative seasonings; good wine list.

Ristorante Piatti • ΔΔΔ $$$ Ø

6480 Washington St. (downtown), Yountville; (707) 944-2070. Regional Italian; full bar service. Monday-Thursday 11:30 a.m. to 10 p.m. (closed 2:30 to 5), Friday 11:30 to 11 (closed 2:30 to 5), Saturday 11:30 to 11, Sunday 11:30 to 10. MC/VISA. Cozy trattoria with bright, airy California décor and a versatile Italian menu. Specialties include angel hair pasta, spinach ravioli in lemon cream sauce, black and white fettuccine with fresh mussels, and grilled seafoods; also a wood burning pizza oven. Outdoor tables.

Trilogy ● △△△ $$$ Ø
1234 Main St. (Hunt Street), St. Helena; (707) 963-5507. California and French; wine and beer. Lunch Tuesday-Friday noon to 2, dinner Tuesday-Sunday from 6 p.m. MC/VISA. Cozy little place offering interesting fare from an often-changing menu. Outdoor dining; large wine list featuring valley labels.

WHERE TO SLEEP

☺ Auberge du Soleil ● △△△△ $$$$$ Ø
180 Rutherford Hill Rd, Rutherford, CA 94573; (800) 348-5406 or (707) 963-1211). Couples and singles $295 to $380, suites $465 to $840. MC/VISA, AMEX, DISC. Opulent 48-unit French country inn terraced up a hillside with panoramic valley views. Rooms feature fireplaces, terraces, TV movies, phones and mini-bars. Pool, health spa with masseuse and steam rooms; tennis courts. **Auberge du Soleil Restaurant** serves "wine country cuisine"; breakfast 7 to 10:30, lunch 11:30 to 2:30, dinner 5:30 to 10:30.

Best Western Inn ● △△△ $$$$ Ø
100 Soscal Ave. (Imola Street), Napa, CA 94558; (800) 528-1234 or (707) 257-1930. Couples $69 to $89, singles $65 to $79, suites $119 to $149. Major credit cards. Attractive 68-unit motel with TV movies, phones, in-room coffee; some room refrigerators. Pool, spa. **Denny's Restaurant** serves 24 hours; dinners $8 to $15; wine and beer.

Calistoga Inn ● △ $$$
1250 Lincoln Ave. (Cedar), Calistoga, CA 94515; (707) 942-4101. Rooms $45 to $55, including continental breakfast. MC/VISA. Oldstyle 17-room inn with shared baths and no-frills furnishings; it dates from the turn of the century. **Napa Valley Brewing Company** microbrewery and restaurant serves American fare from 8 a.m. (various closing times); dinners $8 to $19; wine and beer.

Calistoga Village Inn & Spa ● △△ $$$ Ø
1880 Lincoln Ave. (Silverado Trail), Calistoga, CA 94515; (707) 942-0991. Couples $65 to $175, singles $55 to $150. Major credit cards. A 42-room inn with spa, featuring mud baths, mineral baths, massages and facials; swimming pool. Room have TV movies and phones. **Lincoln Avenue Grill** serves dinners only, Tuesday-Sunday 5:30 to 9; intimate candlelight décor; wine and beer; all non-smoking.

Comfort Inn ● △△△ $$$$ Ø
1865 Lincoln Ave. (near downtown, off Silverado Trail), Calistoga, CA 94515; (800) 228-5150 or (707) 942-9400. Doubles $90 to $120, singles $80 to $110. Major credit cards. A 54-unit motel with landscaped grounds, mineral water pool, hot tub, sauna and steam room. TV movies and phones in rooms.

Dr. Wilkinson's Hot Springs ● △△ $$$ Ø
1507 Lincoln Ave. (Fairway), Calistoga, CA 94515; (707) 942-4102. Couples $49 to $94, singles $44 to $84, kitchenettes $56 to $84. MC/VISA, AMEX. A 42-room motel and spa; TV and room phones. Full spa facilities with three warm water mineral pools, plus mud baths, massages and facial salon.

El Bonita Motel ● △△△ $$$ Ø
195 Main St., St. Helena, CA 94574; (707) 963-3216. Couples $53 to $95, singles $48 to $91, kitchenettes and suites $71 to $98. Major credit cards. A 41-room art deco motel, recently remodeled, with landscaped grounds. TV,

room phones and some room refrigerators. Pool, spa, volleyball court.

☺ Meadowood Napa Valley ● ◠◠◠◠ $$$$$
900 Meadowood Lane, St. Helena; (800) 458-8080 or (707) 963-3646. Rooms and suites $200 to $525; major credit cards. Luxurious, secluded French country style resort with opulently furnished rooms. Extensive landscaped grounds; golf, tennis, pool, spa and hiking trails. **The Restaurant** features California cuisine; **Fairway Grill** is a bistro style café; meal service from 11:30 to 10; dinners $23.50 to $35.50; full bar service; reservations essential.

☺ Silverado Country Club ● ◠◠◠◠ $$$$$ Ø
1600 Atlas Peak Rd. (at Monticello), Napa, CA 94558; (800) 532-0500 or (707) 257-0200. Suites $175 to $465. Major credit cards. Long established luxury resort with two 18-hole PGA golf courses, tennis courts, swimming pool and spa; and cycling, jogging paths. Suites and cottages have kitchens, fireplaces, TV movies, phones and other amenities. Three restaurants— **Vintners Court, Royal Oak** and **Bar and Grill**, serve continental and American regional cuisine; dinners $20 to $30; full bar service.

Vintage Inn ● ◠◠◠ $$$$$ Ø
6541 Washington St. (downtown), Yountville, CA 94599; (800) 351-1133 in California, (800) 982-5539 elsewhere, or (707) 944-1112. Doubles $134 to $184, singles $124 to $184, suites $174 to $194; rates include breakfast buffet. Major credit cards. American country style resort with 80 rooms; TV movies, phones, wine and spa tubs. Two restaurants, **Café Kinyon** (California) and **Compadres** (Mexican); breakfast, lunch and dinner; $12 to $18 for dinner; full bar service.

Wine Country Inn ● ◠◠◠ $$$$
1152 Lodi Lane (Highway 29), St. Helena, CA 94574; (707) 963-7077. Couples $97 to $211, singles $77 to $191, including continental breakfast. MC/VISA. New 25-room inn fashioned like an early American country home. Stylish rooms and common areas with wood paneling and print wallpaper; antique furnishings.

Bed & breakfast inns

☺ Burgundy House ● ◠◠◠ $$$$$ Ø
6711 Washington St. (P.O. Box 3156), Yountville, CA 94599; (707) 944-0889. Couples $110 to $120, singles $100 to $110. Five rooms with private baths; full buffet breakfast. MC/VISA. Intriguing 1870 stone building fashioned into an elegant French country style inn; originally built as a brandy distillery and listed on the National Register of Historic Places. Furnished with American and French antiques.

☺ Cinnamon Bear Bed & Breakfast ● ◠◠ $$$$ Ø
1407 Kearney St. (Adams), St. Helena, CA 94574; (707) 963-4653. Couples $65 to $145, singles $55 to $145. Four rooms with private baths; full breakfast. MC/VISA. Early 20th century redwood home with shady front porch. Furnished with antiques and early American arts and crafts; teddy bear theme.

☺ Forest Manor ● ◠◠◠◠ $$$$$ Ø
415 Cold Springs Rd. (Deer Park Road), Angwin, CA 94508; (707) 965-3538. Couples and singles $99 to $199. Three rooms with private baths; conti-

nental breakfast. MC/VISA. Striking English Tudor home on 20-acre estate, in the mountains above the Napa Valley. English antiques, Oriental art and Persian rugs; pool and spa. Some rooms with fireplaces, one with spa.

The Ink House ● ⌂⌂⌂ $$$$$ Ø
1575 St. Helena Hwy. (Whitehall Lane), St. Helena, CA 94574; (707) 963-3890. Couples and singles $125 to $165. Four rooms with private baths, TV and phones; continental breakfast. MC/VISA. Elegant 1884 Italianate mansion. American and English antiques; 12-foot ceilings; large stylishly furnished guest rooms. Complimentary bicycles and pool table.

Larkmead Country Inn ● ⌂⌂⌂ $$$$$ Ø
1103 Larkmead Lane (between Highway 29 and Silverado), Calistoga, CA 94515; (707) 942-5360. Couples $100 to $115, singles $75. Four rooms with private baths; continental breakfast. No credit cards. Imposing 1918 California winery estate furnished with English antiques, Persian carpets and artworks. Extensive landscaped grounds with mature hardwoods.

☺ Magnolia Hotel ● ⌂⌂⌂ $$$$ Ø
6529 Yount St., Yountville, CA 94599; (800) 788-0369 or (707) 944-2056. Couples $89 to $169. Twelve rooms, all with private baths; full breakfast. No credit cards. Restored 1873 stone and brick hotel with Victorian antiques; five rooms with fireplaces. Gardens and decks, pool and spa.

☺ Silver Rose Inn ● ⌂⌂⌂ $$$$$ Ø
351 Rosedale Rd. (Silverado Trail), Calistoga, CA 94515; (707) 942-9581. Couples $115 to $200. Nine rooms with private baths and TV; full breakfast. MC/VISA, DISC. Stylish modern/rustic country home on oak knoll; guest rooms with valley views. Early American, Oriental and modern dècor. Landscaped grounds with pool, flagstone paths and rock garden.

WHERE TO CAMP

Bothe-Napa Valley State Park ● *3801 N. St. Helena Highway, Calistoga, CA 94515; (707) 942-4575. RV and tent sites; $10. Reservations through Mistix, (800) 444-PARK, or write: P.O. Box 85705, San Diego, CA 92138-5705.* Fairly well-spaced units, many shaded; flush potties, no showers or hookups; nature trails, visitor center and museum, fishing.

Napa County Fairgrounds ● *1435 Oak St., Calistoga, CA 94515; (707) 942-5111. RV and tent sites; water and electric $14. No credit cards.* Some pull-throughs, showers and flush potties, rec field.

Outdoor Resorts of Napa Valley ● *500 Lincoln Ave., Napa, CA 94558; (707) 252-7777. RV sites only; $23 to $30. Reservations accepted; MC/VISA.* Attractive RV resort with some pull-throughs; coin laundry, mini-mart, pool, sauna, rec room, playground.

TRIP PLANNER

WHEN TO GO ● Fall is the finest time on the North Coast, when the rainfall lets up a bit and the wind calms down. Spring also is appealing, when flowers decorate the moors. Expect crowds in summer and expect to get wet in winter—but those coastal storms present awesome sights!

WHAT TO SEE ● The Marin Headlands portion of Golden Gate National Recreation Area, Point Reyes National Seashore, Fort Ross State Historic Park, Stillwater Cove Regional Park, Richardson's Grove and Humboldt Redwoods state parks, Benbow Inn, Scotia Inn, Carson Mansion in Eureka, the coastal town of Trinidad, Redwood National Park, Jedediah Smith Redwoods State Park, Patrick's Point State Park.

WHAT TO DO ● Watch for whales at coastal promontories from December through March, hike the Earthquake Trail at Point Reyes, explore tidepools and ecological terraces at Salt Point State Park, catch the spring booms at Kruse Rhododendron Preserve, prowl the shops and galleries of Victorian Mendocino and Ferndale, hike the wooded ravines of Van Damme and Russian Gulch state parks, ride the Skunk Train from Fort Bragg, pig out at the Samoa Cookhouse in Eureka, drive the Avenue of the Giants.

Useful contacts

Crescent City-Del Norte County Chamber of Commerce, 1001 Front St., Crescent City, CA 95531; (800) 343-8300 or (707) 464-3714.

Eureka/Humboldt County Convention & Visitors Bureau, 1034 Second St., Eureka, CA 95501; in California (800) 338-7352, elsewhere (800) 346-3482, or (707) 4432-5097.

Ferndale Chamber of Commerce, P.O. Box 325, Ferndale, CA 95536; (707) 786-4477.

Fort Bragg-Mendocino Chamber of Commerce, P.O. Box 1141 (332 N. Main St.), Fort Bragg, CA 95437; (800) 726-2780 or (707) 961-8300.

Garberville-Redway Chamber of Commerce, P.O. Box 445 (773 Redwood Dr.), Garberville, CA 95440; (707) 923-2613.

Golden Gate National Recreation Area, Fort Mason, San Francisco, CA 94123; (415) 331-1540.

Point Reyes National Seashore, Point Reyes Station, CA 94956; (415) 663-1092.

Redwood Empire Association, 785 Market St., 15th floor, San Francisco, CA 94103; (415) 543-8334.

Redwood National Park, 1111 Second St., Crescent City, CA 95531; (707) 464-6101.

Trinidad Chamber of Commerce, P.O. Box 356, Trinidad, CA 95770; (707) 677-0591.

North coast radio stations

KMGG-FM, 97.7, Santa Rosa—top 40 oldies
KZYX-FM, 90.7, Philo—National Public Radio
KSOY-FM, 98.5, Fort Bragg—light rock
KEKA-FM, 101.5, Eureka—country
KREV-FM, 95.3, Mendocino—classic rock
KMUD-FM, 91.1, Garberville—National Public Radio
KRED-FM, 92.3, Eureka—rock and classic oldies.
KPOD-FM, 97.9, Crescent City—country
KATA-AM, 1340, Eureka—top 40, easy listening
KFLI-AM, 790, Eureka—country
KFBR-AM, 1310, Crescent City—easy listening

Chapter four
THE COAST NORTH
Finding foggy moors and redwood forests

CALIFORNIA SHEDS ITS STEREOTYPES when you follow the coast north of San Francisco. Here, it is not the land of orange groves, Sierra peaks, dusty deserts, sunny strands or suburban megasprawls. It reveals instead a American Northwest personality, with touches of Cape Cod.

North Coast California is wilderness beaches, rain-drenched forests, windy moors and weather-worn fishing villages. Shores are mostly rocky, often wind-whipped and frequently foggy—suitable more for strolling and bundling than for swimming. Unlike much of America's most populous state, this region is uncrowded and usually unplowed. The only town of any size between San Francisco and the Oregon border is Eureka, with 27,000 residents. In fact the Oregon coast, with easy access from the Willamette Valley, is more settled.

This is not to say that California's North Coast is a tourist backwater. With three federal preserves, scores of parks and the famous redwoods, it's one of the state's most visited regions. Legions of travelers are drawn to the Marin Headlands section of the Golden Gate National Recreation Area, Point Reyes National Seashore and Redwood National Park. In summer, you'll be pressed to find a parking place in the New England style art colony of Mendocino. Campsites in the state's many beach and redwood parks go quickly in summer; most are booked up weeks in advance.

Our preferred period for north coastal exploration is fall through winter. Autumn gets more sunshine than summer, and winter is a fine time for coastal storm watching. Snow is virtually nonexistent and your only serious climatic risk is an occasional soaking from wind-driven rainstorms. Fog is more often poetic than obscuring, changing headlands and seastacks into

103

surrealistic art forms. Notorious San Joaquin Valley style zero/zero fogs are not frequent, although they can occur, so one must drive with caution.

During fall and winter, there are vacancies aplenty in most coastal resorts, ocean-view motels and campgrounds. However, fall salmon runs bring crowds to towns on river estuaries. Some museums and other attractions close or shorten their hours in the off season, but you'll miss little of cultural consequence. Discovering that Confusion Hill has shut early or that the Trees of Mystery walk was closed by darkness probably won't ruin your day.

This damp, thinly populated land presents a splendid visual spectacle. The colliding plates that generate California's frightening earthquakes have rumpled the coast into near vertical bluffs, wave-lashed seastacks and wooded mountains. Rain-fed streams have carved hidden coves and inlets, and fog-shrouded inland valleys shelter silent stands of old growth redwoods.

RV advisory: Highway 1 north of San Francisco is often steep, narrow and winding, although RVs and trailers can negotiate it. However, this means that RVs must take it slowly, causing frustrating delays for more nimble cars behind. **Please** use turnouts and let the faster folks pass.

Fishing, clamming and diving

Coastal towns such as Fort Bragg, Eureka, Trinidad and Crescent City offer party boat fishing offshore. The catch can include king and silver salmon, rockfish, halibut, ling cod, sole and cabezon. Harbor and jetty fishing or surf casting can yield similar dinner candidates. Many rivers invite you to wet a line to seek salmon and trout in the estuaries or upstream. The fall steelhead run up the Klamath River lures hundreds of fisherpersons, who stand shoulder-to-shoulder on opening day.

Several bays offer clamming opportunities, including Tomales and Drakes at Point Reyes, Bodega Harbor and the vast tidal flats of Eureka's Humboldt Bay. The latter is by far the best place to catch your shellfish supper. Pick up a copy of state fish and game regulations and a tide table; both are available at tackle shops and coastal bait shops.

Clamming is not permitted during summer months because of a noxious plankton that shellfish may consume in the coast's relatively warm waters. Regional quarantines can extend beyond the warm months, so check before you start digging.

A California fishing license is required for fishing and clamming, but not for pier fishing. There are catch limits, of course, so be informed before you go. For specifics, contact: Department of Fish and Game, 3211 S St., Sacramento, CA 95816; (916) 227-2244.

The coast's rocky subterranean formations, which contain abundant sea life, are popular with scuba enthusiasts. Several state preserves are considered diving parks—particularly Salt Point, Van Damme and Russian Gulch. Diving for abalone is permitted at most areas along the coast, although size and catch limits are regulated and a fishing license is required. For those preferring to stay above the surface, the coast has exceptional tidepool areas for studying sea life.

Whale watching

The annual 6,000-mile migration of the magnificent gray whale is well chronicled. These noble sea beasts feed off the coast of Alaska during summer months, consuming vast quantities of krill and other small, shrimp-like critters. Then, well stocked with a foot-thick layer of blubber, they head south in winter, not stopping or eating until they reach warm lagoons off Mexico. There, females give birth, are impregnated, and head back to Alaska. A handy 12-month gestation period fits well into this cycle of being perpetually pregnant (but not barefoot and starry eyed).

Since they skim close to the coast, they can be spotted from promontories such as Bodega Head, Salt Point State Park, Manchester State Beach at Point Arena, Mendocino's seacliffs, Shelter Cove, Trinidad and Patrick's Point north of Eureka and Point St. George near Crescent City. Best whale spotting periods are mid-December to early February (southbound) and March to early April (northbound).

You can book offshore whale watching trips from Bodega Bay, Fort Bragg, Eureka, Trinidad and Crescent City.

Coming to the coast

Much of this land remained unknown for eons, beyond the reach of early explorers. The first outsider to see this untamed shore probably was Bartolomè Ferrelo. He sailed as far north as Crescent City and possibly beyond in 1543. Bart was chief pilot for the Juan Rodrìguez Cabrillo; he took over after the great navigator died following a shipboard mishap off the Santa Barbara coast.

England's Sir Francis Drake put his *Golden Hind* ashore for repairs in Drake's Bay in 1579. He decided that the nearby beige cliffs resembled those at Sussex and named the place Nova Albion (New Britain). Two centuries rolled by before anyone else paid much attention to the North Coast. The Russians came in 1812 to build Fort Ross, slaughter sea otters and plant crops to support their Alaska colonies. They ventured as far south as Sebastopol in Sonoma County. The Mexicans, who until this time had ignored the area, hurried to establish a mission in the town of Sonoma.

The Russians withdrew after virtually exterminating the otters, the Mexicans lost California to the United States, and gringo occupation of the coast began. The first settlement was Trinidad north of Eureka, established in 1850 as a supply and fishing port for inland gold seekers. Eureka followed within a year. However, it was redwood, not gold, that brought most settlers to the North Coast. Within five years, 140 lumber schooners were hauling the "harvested" trees from dozens of sawmills.

Sturdy, long lasting redwood was the material of choice for the construction boom spurred by the California Gold Rush. Thousands of board feet were sent south to San Francisco Bay. Virtually all of that city's Victorians were built of redwood and many survive to this day. The Russians also had used it in the construction of Fort Ross. Tree cutting continued at such a furious pace that vast tracts of the North Coast's redwood forests were gone before organizations such as the Save-the-Redwoods League began campaigning for their preservation early in this century.

Contrary to what some may assume, redwood is not a rare tree. It once was a relatively common conifer, ranging from Monterey north to the southern Oregon coast. Today, only a few virgin stands survive, mostly in state parks and in Redwood National Park. Outside the preserves, the noble trees are still being harvested to provide decks and patios for suburbia. Most cutting is in second growth stands, since redwood is a relatively fast-growing tree. However, as you explore the North Coast, you may see fallen giants trundle past, so massive that only one chunk of trunk will fit on a logging truck.

Still, logging has been reduced, which has cast much of the North Coast into a chronic economic slump. Many of the huge mills have closed. Tourism and fishing are gaining on lumbering as leading industries. Curiously, marijuana cultivation may be the area's major cash crop (see box).

SAN FRANCISCO TO MENDOCINO/FORT BRAGG

If you're in San Francisco, begin your North Coast drive by finding and crossing the Golden Gate Bridge, which should be no great chore for the visitor. However, you'll have to contend with surface street traffic, since no freeway reaches that grand span from downtown.

As mentioned in Chapter two, our favorite approach works this way: Drive west for 3.5 miles on one of three major streets from downtown—Turk, Geary or California—then turn right onto Park Presidio Boulevard. This landscaped expressway cuts through the ancient eucalyptus and pine groves of the **Presidio,** then merges onto Highway 101 just short of the bridge toll plaza.

☺ As you clear the bridge, you might want to get into the right lane and stop at the **Vista Point** for a final glimpse back at the city. From here, you can explore the **Marin Headlands** section of the Golden Gate National Recreation Area (covered in detail in Chapter two). Another option as you start north from the Vista Point is to take the Alexander Avenue exit into Mediterranean-like **Sausalito,** also described in Chapter two. Traffic is very congested in this idyllic town on weekends, however.

Bridgeway, Sausalito's main street, delivers you back U.S. 101. Exit immediately onto State Highway 1, following Stinson Beach-Mount Tamalpais signs. After a couple of miles, fork to the left at **Tam Junction,** staying on Route 1. This will be your asphalt carpet through the North Coast for about 200 miles, until it rejoins U.S. 101 at Leggett.

Although Marin County is thickly populated, virtually all of this density is inland. Despite its beauty, the Marin coast is sparsely settled, since there is no industry here except recreation and little flat land for farming. Twisting Highway 1 discourages commuting back to the Bay Area. Once you've cleared Tam Junction, you'll see scores of wood-shrouded homes and beach havens, but no towns of significant size. For the visitor, this is a blessing, since much of this appealing coastline is still being shaped by nature, not by developers.

Highway 1 squiggles up to a cleft in the Coast Range, thick with eucalyptus and conifers. At the ridgeline, you can turn right onto the Panoramic Highway for an exploration of **Muir Woods** and **Mount Tamalpais,** also covered in Chapter two. If you remain on Highway 1, you'll spiral downward and touch the Pacific at **Muir Beach,** where a shallow valley reaches the ocean to form a sandy cove. Facilities include a picnic area and potties. Should you choose to spend the night, nearby **Pelican Inn** (listed below) offers stylish Old English ambiance.

RV advisory: This coiling section of Highway 1 is negotiable by carefully driven RVs and trailers. However, the Panoramic Highway is not recommended for anything over 35 feet.

A few miles beyond Muir Beach, you'll encounter tiny **Stinson Beach,** boasting a population of 486. It's strung along Highway 1 for a few blocks,

CANNABIS: THE COAST'S CASH CROP

The Indian hemp plant is relatively useful in the Near East, since its strong fibers are suitable for rope-making. However, to toy with words, it's the kind of rope that often trips some entrepreneurs of California's North Coast.

The region's moist, warm climate is ideal for the cultivation of *Cannabis sativa*, and this area is said to be America's largest supplier of the illicit weed. Marijuana cultivation began with Flower Children who filtered into the area during the 1960s, feeling the need to return to the soil. They planted subsistence crops and, to keep themselves mellow, began experimenting with high-potency strains of *cannabis.* "Mary Jane" went commercial in the following two decades when some economically-depressed residents sought ways to augment their income.

Thick coastal forests provide suitable camouflage for these "plantations." Pot cultivation has become so prevalent that it's reportedly the North Coast's major cash crop. Unfortunately, the potential for big money has attracted a mean criminal element. Violence, even murder, has become a byproduct of this illegal industry.

California has created a special task force to combat the spread of marijuana and its related violence in the North Coast. Using everything from helicopters to sniffer-dogs, the Campaign Against Marijuana Planting (CAMP) has discovered, uprooted and destroyed hundreds of thousands of hemp plants. Under the Comprehensive Crime Control Act, officials can confiscate the growers' implements, vehicles used for pot transport, bank accounts and even the land where the stuff grows. Are they winning the war? It depends on whether you talk with CAMP officials or folks from NORML, the National Organization for the Reform of Marijuana Laws. The latter group feels that it's unfair to include pot with such nasty drugs as cocaine and heroine.

Earlier in this century, marijuana was regarded as a medical tool, listed on the U.S. pharmacopoeia as an analgesic and sedative. It later was dropped when researchers decided that its value was limited. The Merck Pharmaceutical Index advises that a dose of 120 milligrams or more will induce "euphoria, delirium, hallucinations, weakness, hyporeflexia and drowsiness." Its use was prohibited by the Marihuana Tax Act of 1937. Latter-day experiments have found the weed useful in the treatment of glaucoma and as a pain reliever for cancer patients. Debate continues to rage over its use.

Several years ago, in an attempt to head off the weed's growing international use, the World Health Organization began research to develop a hemp plant that didn't contain the intoxicating resins.

We offer no moral or medical judgment concerning its use or usefulness. (Like President Clinton, we tried it once; didn't care for it.) However, if you're hiking in the backwoods of the North Coast and come across a thatch of plants with multiple-spiked leaves, we'd suggest that you quickly change direction. You wouldn't a lawman hiding in the bushes to mistake you for a grower.

Or visa versa.

---

with a modest collection of galleries and curio shops. People come mostly to play in the sand of adjacent **Stinson Beach State Park;** (415) 556-0734. It's tucked behind low dunes shaded by a cypress grove. Facilities include a snack bar, restrooms and picnic areas. Protected by Bolinas Lagoon, this is the closest thing to a swimming beach you'll find on the North Coast. You'll also find it swamped with visitors on summer weekends. The beach is nearly three miles long, so you can shake some of the crowd by walking north toward the lagoon entrance.

North of Stinson, your route borders the broad, calm lagoon. **Audubon Canyon Ranch,** in a vale on your right, shelters a nesting site for great blue herons, egrets and dozens of other shorebirds. A small visitor center and bookstore occupies a 19th century farmhouse. Trails from here lead to the nesting areas in a pretty canyon. The facility is free (donations appreciated) although hours are limited. It's generally open on weekends and holidays 10 to 4 during the nesting season, March through July; (415) 383-1644. Adjacent Bolinas Lagoon also is a sanctuary, luring a variety of sea and shore birds.

Across the lagoon, tucked among eucalyptus trees where residents hope no one will notice them, is the village of **Bolinas.** The occupants of this old coastal charmer are so bent on privacy that a group routinely removes signs directing visitors there from Highway 1. At the risk of angering this "Bolinas border patrol," we'll tell you how to get there. Simply take the next left turn, a mile or so past Audubon Canyon Ranch, and follow it to the end. The route, canopied with eucalyptus, is called Bolinas-Olema Road, although that sign also was missing when we last visited.

This town of a few hundred citizens perches pleasantly on a low headland. It's a charming and quiet little place, with a few weathered houses—Victorian and otherwise—and a small business district offering the requisite whole earth bakery and a couple of tie-dyed galleries. The **Bolinas General Store** sells what few essentials residents require, and the **Bolinas Bay Bakery and Café** (listed below) offers an organic menu.

Since the sign swipers are thorough in their work, the sandy beach is rarely crowded. From this vantage point, you can enjoy visual irony—a view from sleepy Bolinas to distant San Francisco, one of the most congested cities on the West Coast.

Continuing north from Bolinas, you soon encounter one of the most fascinating land forms of the California coast. Here, intrigue begins, both geologically and historically.

☺ *Point Reyes National Seashore* ● *Point Reyes Station, CA 94956; (415) 663-1092. Bear Valley Visitor Center open daily 9 to 5; Ken Patrick Visitor Center at Drake's Beach open weekends and holidays 10 to 5; and Point Reyes Lighthouse Visitor Center open Thursday-Monday 10 to 5; all facilities free. Various ranger programs and hikes. Camping at hike-in sites only, which can be reserved by calling the main park number between 9 and noon.*

Named for the Feast of the Three Kings, *La Punta de los Reyes* is a wedge-shaped peninsula with a hook forming Drake's Bay. Skewered by slender Tomales Bay to the north, it seems ready to break away from the mainland.

Break away, indeed. Tomales Bay is a trench formed by the notorious San Andreas Fault, father of California earthquakes. From here, the fracture extends hundreds of miles, ending in the Southern California desert. The San Francisco earthquake of '06 was born here, as was the Loma Prieta shaker, witnessed on TV by millions of World Series fans on October 17, 1989. At this precise point, the North American and Pacific plates are in slow motion collision, grinding together and suddenly releasing, sending shock waves through the state.

The peninsula is a fascinating island in time. Although the national seashore is but a few decades old, the area has suffered little development.

San Francisco To Fort Bragg

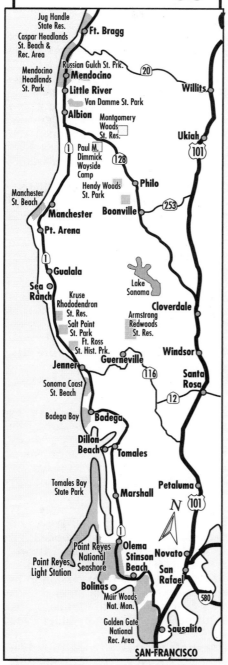

Once a Spanish land grant, it later fell into the hands of San Francisco bankers, who leased it out to dairy farmers. Those bucolic pasturelands remain, operating under special arrangement with the National Park Service. Surrounding them are rocky headlands with wilderness beaches, thickly forested ridges and hidden vales where sunny skies hide from coastal fogs. Life at Point Reyes National Seashore moves to the beat of the surf, the bleat of an elk at the Tule Elk Reserve, the glide of a hawk, the surrealistic ballet of morning fog.

The first intruder probably was gentleman pirate Sir Francis Drake, who lurched his *Golden Hind* into Drake's Estuary in the summer of 1579 and stayed five weeks. Some question whether this was Drake's landing site. In 1936, a so-called "plate of brass" that Drake supposedly nailed to a post was found far to the south, at Point San Quentin in San Francisco Bay. It has since been proven to be a forgery. However, the "San Quentin school" still has its protagonists, insisting that Drake sailed through the Golden Gate, not into Drake's Bay.

Spanish explorer Sebastian Rodriguez Cermeno may have been the next outsider to land here. And he landed the hard way; his ship was driven aground by a storm in 1595. Survivors built a launch from the pieces and miraculously made it back to Mexico. Don Sebastian Viscaino passed by on January 6, 1603, and named the peninsula.

Begin your Point Reyes visit with a stop at the **Bear Valley Visitor Center** near the hamlet of Olema. You can pick up a park brochure, hiking maps, lists of area lodgings and restaurants and check out exhibits on the flora, fauna and certainly the geology of the area. A seismograph will tell you whether unsaintly San Andreas has begun twitching again. From the attractive heavy beamed visitor center, the **Earthquake Trail** takes you to ground zero of the 1906 quake. Here, the peninsula suddenly shifted 16 feet northward. An old fence, its sunbleached posts still offset, stands in silent testimony to the big one. Nearby is a reconstruction of a Coast Miwok settlement.

Point Reyes is a hikers' and backpackers' paradise. Dozens of miles of trails fan out from Bear Valley, traveling along the wooded Inverness Ridge and reaching over it to wilderness beaches.

To continue your vehicular exploration of the park, drive north from the visitor center on Bear Valley Road, along the shore of Tomales Bay, past the settlements of **Inverness Park** and **Inverness.** They offer dining and lodging, listed below. From Inverness, roads cross Inverness Ridge and branch into the park. The beaches, though beautiful, are surf-pounded and unsafe for swimming. If you wish to dip a toe, head for **Tomales Bay State Park,** an inholding surrounded by the national seashore. Bay waters are calmer and considerably warmer.

The main park roadway, an undulating strip of narrow asphalt called Sir Francis Drake Highway, leads past moors and "historic dairies" to the 1870 **Point Reyes Lighthouse** at the peninsula's tip. A visitor center here is open Thursday-Monday 10 to 5 and a steeply inclined path to the light is open until 4:30. Although the light itself is closed to the public, this is a great spot for whale watching during the migration season. Take time to enjoy the view and catch your breath, since the hike back is equivalent to climbing a 30-story building.

From the main park road, a spur leads to **Drake's Beach,** and the **Ken Patrick Visitor Center,** open weekends and holidays from 10 to 5, with a small cafeteria. Exhibits focus on Drake's visit, and a short trail takes strollers to the mouth of Drake's Estuary, his alleged landing site. Other branch roads lead to **Point Reyes Beach, McClures Beach** and the **Tule Elk Reserve.** A trail takes you into the preserve itself. As you leave Point Reyes, you may want to pause at **Johnson's Oyster Farm,** open Tuesday-Sunday 8 to 4:30; (415) 669-1149.

After you've done the peninsula, return to Highway 1 at **Point Reyes Station** to continue your journey north. Quite small and quite rustic, the town offers a few shops and an ornate red brick building that was empty when we last passed. **Toby's Feed Barn,** on the right as you enter town, is an interesting combination specialty food, curio and country crafts shop. Just north of town, **Tomales Bay Oyster Company** offers another chance to get 'em in the raw.

The drive north from here is pleasant if not awesome, with the slate gray Tomales Bay on your left and English style moors and hardwood groves on the passenger side. **Marconi Conference Center,** cresting a wooded hill on the right, is a recent addition to the state historic park system. It preserves the site of one of Guglielmo Marconi's wireless stations, opened in 1914. You probably know that Marconi invented wireless transmission in Italy at the age of 21 and eventually established a worldwide communications company. A museum to chronicle Marconi's genius is planned for the future. For the moment, there isn't much here to intrigue the visitor, unless you need a nice conference site; (415) 663-9020.

Just beyond Marconi, the town of **Marshall** perches on a narrow shelf between the highway and the bay. Many of the structures are built on stilts

Visitors to Point Reyes Light get a good workout on their return trip; it's equivalent to climbing a 30-story building. — **Betty Woo Martin**

over the water. When I was managing editor of the Petaluma *Argus-Courier* over the hill a few decades ago, Marshall was a popular escape, offering funky restaurants and pubs. When we last passed, however, many of its shabby buildings were boarded up. **Pony's** is a rustic seafood place that may or may not be open. Hours were noon to 8:30 weekends only when we stopped by.

The gentle hills between here and **Petaluma** offer appealing side trips. Pick your route—from Point Reyes Station, Marshall or Tomales. You'll be rewarded with a pleasant meander through pasturelands marked with rocky outcroppings and past small canyons thatched with oak groves. We'd recommend taking the Petaluma-Point Reyes Road, then returning via the Petaluma-Marshall route.

☺ Driving inland, you'll pass the **Marin French Cheese Company,** producers of *Rouge et Noir* brand camembert, brie and other French style cheeses. You can sample the pungent stuff in a sales room, take a tour of the facility and buy wine and cheese for a picnic beside a duck pond. Sales room hours are daily 9 to 5; tours are 10 to 4.

Petaluma has a splendid selection of Victorian and early American homes and an old fashioned business district lined with rare iron front stores. Built on bedrock, it survived the 1906 earthquake relatively intact, accounting for this fine collection of old buildings. The town wears its funny name with good humor, sponsoring such events as the annual Ugly Dog Contest and the World's Wristwrestling Championships.

Back on Highway 1, you soon encounter **Tomales,** another Marin coast hamlet. Looking considerably more stable than Marshall, it has a fine assortment of 19th century brick and false front buildings. Check out the 1875 **Diekmann's General Store,** a neat old place with wooden floors and an awesome assortment of goods that nearly reach its high ceilings.

Turn left in downtown Tomales and follow a narrow road to reclusive **Dillon Beach,** one of the least visited seaside towns on the California coast. There's not much to the place, although its setting in a rock-ribbed canyon is imposing. So is the sandy beach accented with seastacks, at the base of near vertical cliffs. **Lawson's Resort Store** is the sole business here, offering basic essentials and collecting a $5 beach parking fee. It's open daily 9 to 5, a bit later on weekends. Mudflats beyond contain a primitive campground and a good clam digging area—for which Lawson's also collects a fee.

Just north of Tomales, Highway 1 departs Marin and enters Sonoma County near the tiny town of **Valley Ford.** Ahead lies a place made famous by a great movie teaser: "The Birds is coming."

WHERE TO DINE ON THE MARIN COAST

Towns en route to Point Reyes offer a restaurant or two, and you'll find several grouped around the park, in Olema and Inverness. We list our selections as they appear, traveling south to north:

Stinson Beach Grill ● ΔΔ $$
3465 Shoreline Highway, Stinson Beach; (415) 868-2002. American; wine and beer. Daily 9 to 9 (to 9:30 Friday-Saturday). MC/VISA. Cozy board and batten place a block from the beach, with knotty pine interior and a crackling stove. A mixed menu ranges from fresh seafood to Southwest *nouveau* to Italian fare. An outdoor deck is open when the weather cooperates.

Bolinas Bay Bakery and Café ● Δ $$ Ø
Bolinas; (415) 868-0211. American; wine and beer. Monday-Tuesday and Friday 7 to 9, Wednesday-Thursday 7 to 8, weekends 8 to 9. MC/VISA, DISC. The place is properly funky for Bolinas, set back off the main street in an old clapboard house, with oilcloth tables and local art on the walls. Fare is mostly light—chicken potstickers, lasagna and whole-grain baked goods.

Olema Farm House Restaurant ● ΔΔ $$
10005 Highway 1, Olema; (415) 663-1264. Contemporary American; full bar service. Weekdays 11 to 9, weekends 8 to 10. MC/VISA, AMEX. American *nouveau* fare, plus a few continental creations are served in an 1873 shingle-sided former stage stop. It's primly cozy with early American décor, including the West Coast's largest collection of decanters. An outdoor dining patio is open in summer. Among menu features are oysters Waldorf and chicken Parmesan.

Olema Inn Restaurant ● ΔΔΔ $$$
10000 Sir Francis Drake Blvd. (at Highway 1), Olema; (415) 663-9559. American; wine and beer. Lunch and dinner daily. MC/VISA. Early American style B&B and restaurant, with California *nouveau* touches to the menu. It's housed in a white clapboard 1876 Victorian, with an attractive garden patio. Try stuffed pork tenderloin, veal medallions or grilled fresh swordfish.

Vladimir's ● ΔΔ $$$
Inverness; (415) 669-1021. European; wine and beer. Tuesday 4 to 9, Wednesday-Sunday noon to 9. MC/VISA. Cozy European dining room featuring Czech and other eastern European fare such as chicken *paprikash* with sour cream and mushrooms, Moravian cabbage roll and of course *wiener schnitzel*. Full Czechoslovakian dinners $16.50, served from 5.

☺ Manka's Inverness Lodge & Restaurant • ΔΔΔΔ $$$

Inverness; (415) 669-1034. European and American nouveau; full bar service. Thursday-Monday 6 p.m. to 9 p.m., closed Tuesday-Wednesday. MC/VISA. This tree-cloaked old world style cafè with a crackling fireplace and warm, dark woods is tucked into a 1917 hunting lodge. The daily-changing menu is mostly modern, with fare such as venison with pecan wild rice, and crispy duckling with sweet potato puree and roasted fennel. It's not inexpensive, but worth the trip; our favorite Marin coast hideaway.

Station House Café • ΔΔΔ $$ ∅

Point Reyes Station; (415) 663-1515. American; full bar service. Sunday-Thursday 8 a.m. to 9 p.m., Friday-Saturday 8 to 10. MC/VISA. One of the best dining deals on the coast; relatively inexpensive and well prepared food has won raves from critics. Weekly-changing menu offer full course dinners for under $15 and light suppers for $7; several health conscious entrées are featured. It's served in a railroad station atmosphere (in homage to the town's name), with bentwood chairs, wainscotting and beamed ceilings.

William Tell House • ΔΔ $$

26955 Highway 1, Tomales; (707) 878-2403. Italian-American; full bar service. Tuesday-Thursday 5 to 9. Friday-Saturday 5 to 10, Sunday 3 to 9. MC/VISA. The look is early American, although there's a strong Italian accent in the kitchen. Meals are hearty and well prepared, ranging from assorted pastas and fresh fish to London broil and prime rib.

WHERE TO SLEEP

Most Marin coast lodgings are clustered around Inverness, ranging from medium-sized resorts to bed & breakfast inns. For a list of area rooms, contact: Inns of Point Reyes, P.O. Box 145, Inverness, CA 94937; (415) 663-1420. Another referral service is Coastal Lodgings of West Marin, reached by dialing (415) 663-1351.

Mount Tamalpais State Park cabins • △ $

Off Highway 1 between Mill Valley and Stinson Beach; (415) 388-2070. Steep Ravine Cabins that sleep up to five, $30 per night. Reservations via Mistix, (800) 444-PARK. Cabins on a wooded bluff with awesome ocean vistas. Very rustic but in a great setting. Running water, no electricity, pit potties outside. Secluded beach reached by Steep Ravine trail.

Ocean Court • △△ $$$

18 Arenal (P.O. Box 94), Stinson Beach, CA 94970; (415) 868-0212. Kitchenettes $65 to $100, suites $85 to $110. MC/VISA. Attractive six-unit lodge with TV, full kitchens and patio or deck. Ocean or mountain views; a block from town.

Point Reyes Seashore Lodge • △△△ $$$$

10021 Highway 1 (P.O. Box 39), Olema, CA 94950; (415) 663-9000. Couples $85 to $130, suites $165 to $175. Major credit cards. Attractive lodge in wooded setting, with European dècor; 21 rooms with TV and phones; many with fireplaces and spa tubs.

Golden Hinde Inn • △△△ $$$ ∅

12938 Sir Francis Drake Blvd., Inverness, CA 94937; (800) 339-9398 in California only or (415) 669-1389. Couples and singles $69 to $95, kitchenettes $79 to $105, suites $125. MC/VISA. Well-maintained 35-room lodge a mile north of Inverness. TV, pool; continental breakfast; marina with launch ramp. **Barnaby's Restaurant** serves noon to 8 weekdays (to 9 Friday-Saturday) and 9 to 8 Sunday; dinners $6.50 to $15; wine and beer.

Motel Inverness ● ⌂⌂ $$$ Ø

12718 Sir Francis Drake Blvd. (P.O. Box 292), Inverness, CA 94937; (415) 669-1081. Couples $65, singles $60, kitchenettes $85; rates include continental breakfast. MC/VISA, AMEX. Well-kept eight-room motel with TV movies; large lodge with fireplace and big screen TV.

Valley Ford Hotel ● ⌂⌂ $$$ Ø

14415 Highway 1, Valley Ford, CA 94972; (800) 696-6679 or (707) 876-3600. Couples $63 to $80, singles $54 to $75, including continental breakfast. Major credit cards. Historic seven-room inn with comfortable, eclectic furnishings; sitting room with TV and VCR. **Duffy's** serves family style Basque fare 11 to 2 and 6 to 9; full bar service. Hotel and restaurant are smoke free.

Bed & breakfast inns

The Country House ● ⌂⌂⌂ $$$$ Ø

65 Manana Way (P.O. Box 98), Point Reyes Station, CA 94956; (415) 663-1627. Couples $85 to $125, singles $80 to $100. Three units with private baths; full breakfast. No credit cards. Ranch style home with California mission dècor and Victorian antiques; surrounded by English gardens and apple orchards. Large country kitchen-living room with fireplace and open beams.

Ferrando's Hideaway ● ⌂⌂⌂ $$$$ Ø

12010 Highway 1 (P.O. Box 688), Point Reyes Station, CA 94956; (415) 663-1966. Couples and singles $95 to $120. Three rooms with private baths and phones; full breakfast. No credit cards. Rustic-modern country home with contemporary furnishings; two rooms in main house plus a cottage. Hot tub, wood stove and attractive garden.

Holly Tree Inn ● ⌂⌂⌂ $$$$$ Ø

Three Silverhills Rd. (near Bear Valley Road), Point Reyes Station, CA 94956; (415) 663-1554. Couples $100 to $200, singles $80. Six rooms with private baths; full breakfast. MC/VISA. A touch of old Scandinavia in Marin, tucked into a grove of birches, laurels and buckeyes. Rooms furnished with antiques, designer linens and Laura Ashley prints; all with fireplaces or wood burning stoves. Spa; herb garden; creek nearby.

Olema Inn ● ⌂⌂ $$$$ Ø

10000 Sir Francis Drake Blvd. (at Highway 1), Olema, CA 94950; (415) 663-9559. Rooms $85 to $105. Six units with private baths; continental breakfast. MC/VISA. An 1876 inn converted into a comfortable B&B with antique furnishings, surrounded by attractive gardens. Non-smoking rooms; smoking permitted in parlor. **Restaurant** serves French-continental fare; lunch noon to 3, dinner 5 to 9; dinners $13 to $17; wine and beer.

Pelican Inn ● ⌂⌂⌂⌂ $$$$$

10 Pacific Way, Muir Beach, CA 94965-9729; (415) 383-6000. Couples and singles $140 to $150. Seven rooms with private baths; full English breakfast. MC/VISA. Luxurious English Tudor country inn with antique furnishings, half-canopy beds and Oriental rugs. Guest lounge with fireplace; fully stocked English pub with dart board.

Roundstone Farm ● ⌂⌂⌂ $$$$$ Ø

Sir Francis Drake near Highway 1 (P.O. Box 217), Olema, CA 94950; (415) 663-1020. Couples $115 to $125, singles $95 to $105. Five rooms with *private baths; full breakfast. MC/VISA, AMEX.* Modern ranch style inn on a large horse ranch, surrounded by gardens. Comfortable, attractive mix of antique and modern furnishings; fireplace in each room.

Ten Inverness Way • ⌂⌂⌂ $$$$ Ø
P.O. Box 63, Inverness, CA 94937; (415) 669-1648. Couples $110 to $140, singles $100 to $130. Five rooms with private baths; full breakfast. MC/VISA. Shingle-sided turn of the century home with plush country furnishings, surrounded by lush gardens. Comfortable living room with fireplace; decks; hot tub in back garden.

WHERE TO CAMP

State parks in the area accept reservations via Mistix; they can be made by phone with a major credit card: (800) 444-PARK.

Mount Tamalpais State Park • *Off Highway 1 between Mill Valley and Stinson Beach; (415) 388-2070.* Walk-in sites, tents only, $12. Hiker/biker sites $2.

Olema Ranch Campground • *Highway 1 (P.O. Box 175), Olema, CA 94950; (415) 663-8001. RV and tent sites, full hookups $23, water and electric $21, no hookups $16. Reservations accepted; MC/VISA, AMEX.* Showers, coin laundry, tables and barbecues, mini-mart, gasoline and rec hall. Near the national seashore.

Samuel P. Taylor State Park • *A few miles inland from Olema at Lagunitas, CA 94938; (415) 488-9897. RV and tent sites, $12 on weekdays, $14 on weekends, hiker/biker sites $3.* Barbecues and picnic tables, showers and flush potties. Hiking trails into nearby redwoods.

Lawson's Landing • *P.O. Box 97, Dillon Beach, CA 94929; (707) 878-2204. RV sites $10; MC/VISA.* Very rudimentary sites in a pasture near clamming area; pit toilets; no hookups.

Bodega & Bodega Bay

Population: approx. 500   **Elevation: 45 feet**
When Alfred Hitchcock came here in the early 1960s to film *The Birds,* he used clever camera angles and editing to lump the two towns together. Remember that scene where the kids ran in panic from the schoolhouse and fled to the shelter of the Tides Restaurant? Those attacking birds really had them moving, since they covered five miles in a couple of minutes.

Bodega is a small town a few miles in from the coast, and the famous schoolhouse is now a bed & breakfast inn (listed below). **Bodega Bay** sits on the shoreline of Bodega Harbor, offering a working waterfront and a few shops, motels and restaurants, including the Tides of movie fame. With a small craft harbor tucked behind the Tides, the place has an appealing Cape Cod look. At the **visitor's information center,** on the right as you enter town, you can discover what to do here.

Mostly, what to do is poke through the town's handful of curio shops and galleries, dine on fish with a harbor view and—if the tide's right—dig for clams on the mudflats. For that proper Cape Cod atmosphere, step out onto the salty old marina behind the Tides to watch fishermen fiddle with their nets. A drive out Westside Road will take you past some New England style rural homes and to a marine sanctuary at **Bodega Head.** For a quiet exploration of the bay, book a nature cruise on the **Electric Ferry,** operating out of Mason's Marina at 1820 Westshore Road; (707) 874-1000.

Beyond Bodega, Highway 1 presents views of the open sea for the first time since Stinson Beach, because the Pacific has been hidden by Point Reyes peninsula and assorted headlands. The vistas are impressive—a mix of steep seacliffs, seastacks and grassy or wooded hills. A string of public strands along here are wrapped into **Sonoma Coast State Beaches,** covering ten miles and 5,000 acres.

Shortly, you cross the mouth of the **Russian River** and enter the neat little community of **Jenner,** cantilevered into a steep, wooded headland. There's not much to see here, although you can go down to the mouth of the Russian for a visit with a harbor seal colony. Don't approach too closely, for they'll either panic or bite, ruining their day and yours.

A right turn onto State Route 116 takes you into the **Russian River resort area,** with an assortment of 1930s style streamside lodges—some scruffy, some refurbished. Swimming holes abound, including several nude beaches, and the slow moving Russian is pleasantly warm in summer. Canoeing is popular here, as well. If you continue inland past **Guerneville,** you'll enter the **Russian River wine country,** which we explored in Chapter three.

North of Jenner, Highway 1 elevates itself for particularly impressive views of this rocky coastline. Shortly, you encounter an 1812 Russian outpost that thrived during the sea otter slaughter:

☺ *Fort Ross State Historic Park* ● *Twelve miles north of Jenner; (707) 847-3286 or 865-2391. Daily 10 to 4:30; $5 per car, seniors $4. Living history demonstrations at noon and 3 p.m.* The Russians must have had an eye for beauty, for Fort Ross occupies a handsome redwood-shaded bluff above the rockbound coast. After they left, John Sutter bought the place and stripped it for his New Helvetia settlement at present day Sacramento, so only one original building survives. However, the stockade, Russian Orthodox church with its distinctive cylindrical wooden dome, blockhouses and other buildings have been restored with much attention to detail. A fine knotty pine visitor's center offers background on the Russians and the Máy-tee-nee Indians who preceded them.

North of Fort Ross, the Sonoma Coast offers an alternating mix of hideaway resorts and state or county parks. Lodgings range from simple sea view motels to the elaborate **Timber Cove** snugged into a coastal slope and the extensive **Sea Ranch** development. Its seacoast-modern homes are scattered over several thousand acres of moors. Sea Ranch Lodge (listed below) offers rooms and dining for passers-by.

☺ **Stillwater Cove Park,** between Timber Cove and Sea Ranch, is wedged into a dramatic, rocky enclave. A stairway leads down to a hideaway beach. This Sonoma County regional park is a fine spot for camping (listed below), picnicking and tidepool exploring.

☺ *Salt Point State Park* ● *(707) 847-3221 or 865-2391. Day use $5 per car; camping listed below. Picnic areas, hiking and riding trails, tidepools. Ranger activities in summer.* With 6,000 acres and six miles of beach, Salt Point is one of the coast's finest preserves. Attractions range from ecological stair steps rising from the beach to 1,000-foot highlands with a pygmy forest of redwoods, pines and cypress. Several sandy beaches are tucked into hidden coves and dozens of miles of hiking and horseback riding trails wind through grasslands and coastal thickets. Adjoining the park inland is **Kruse Rhododendron Preserve,** which bursts into brilliant bloom during April and May. Not commonly seen on this coast, hundreds of rhododendrons and azaleas took hold here several years ago, after a forest was destroyed by fire.

☺ Another Sonoma County Regional Park, **Gualala Point,** offers a particularly striking setting for its campsites (listed below) at the mouth of the Gualala River. Many are shaded by redwoods. The beach is across the highway ($2 day use), with tidepools, a bit of strand and a nice overlook above the river's mouth. Just beyond, you slip unnoticed into Mendocino County.

SONOMA COAST ANNUAL EVENTS

Fisherman's Festival, in Bodega Bay and Jenner, both in April; (707) 875-3422.

Festival of the Arts, Jenner in June; (800) 253-8000.

Living History Day, Fort Ross State Park in July; (707) 847-3286.

WHERE TO DINE ON THE SONOMA COAST
(In order of appearance)

Tides Wharf Restaurant ● ∆∆ $$$
800 Highway 1, Bodega Bay; (707) 875-2551. American, mostly seafood; full bar service. Breakfast, lunch and dinner daily; weekdays from 8 a.m. and weekends from 7. MC/VISA, AMEX. Dine where Tippi Hedren cowered from her fine feathered fiends. This simple family style place has nautical décor and a large seafood menu with a good shellfish selection, plus steaks, chickens and chops. Fish market is adjacent, so the fillets are frequently fresh.

Lucas Wharf Restaurant ● ∆∆∆ $$$
599 Highway 1, Bodega Bay; (707) 875-3522. American, mostly seafood; full bar service. Sunday-Thursday 11 to 9:30, Friday-Saturday 11 to 10. MC/VISA. Spacious, attractive San Francisco style restaurant built over the harbor, with redwood accents and a fireplace. Admire the fishing fleet at anchor while trying assorted seafood dishes, fresh oysters or chickens from over the hill in Petaluma. Inexpensive fare at an adjacent deli.

River's End Restaurant ● ∆∆ $$
Highway 1, Jenner; (707) 865-2484. International; full bar service. Daily 11 to 9:30. MC/VISA. Rustic haven perched over the mouth of the Russian River. The menu gallops the globe, from Indonesia's *bahmie goreng* (mixed grill with vegetable noodles and peach chutney) to medallions of venison and fresh fish.

Salt Point Bar & Grill ● ∆∆ $
23255 Highway 1 (near Salt Point State Park), Jenner; (707) 847-3234. American; full bar service. Daily from 8 a.m. MC/VISA. Rather inexpensive mesquite broiled specialties served in a spacious atmosphere, with picture windows onto an ocean cove. Dining moves to a sun deck when the weather's proper. Specialties include mesquite grilled fish, spiced shrimp and smoked ribs. Many dinners under $10.

Sea Ranch Restaurant ● ∆∆∆ $$$
60 Sea Walk Drive, Sea Ranch; (707) 785-2426. American-continental; full bar service. Breakfast daily from 8, lunch weekdays 11:30 to 2:30, dinner Sunday-Thursday 6 to 8:30, Friday-Saturday 6 to 9. Major credit cards. Elegantly rustic dining room with bentwood chairs, cathedral ceilings and rough wood walls; views of the moors and ocean beyond. The menu features seafood pasta, chicken cordon bleau, salmon and such.

Sizzling Tandoor Restaurant • △ $$

At Bridgehaven Campground, P.O. Box 59, Jenner, CA 95450; (707) 865-2473. Indian-American; wine and beer. Daily 11 to 10 New riverside restaurant featuring East Indian tandoori specials, plus American seafood, steaks and chops.

WHERE TO SLEEP

Bodega Bay Lodge • ⌒⌒⌒ $$$$$

103 Highway 1 (at Doran Beach Road), Bodega Bay, CA 94923; (800) 368-2468 or (707) 875-3525. Couples and singles $108 to $208, including continental breakfast. Major credit cards. Luxuriously appointed 78-room resort with TV movies, phones, pool; all rooms with glass-enclosed spa, fireplace and mini bars; ocean views. **Ocean Club Dining Room** offers an eclectic menu; 8 to 10 a.m. and 6 to 9 p.m.; dinners $25 to $49; ocean-view dining; wine and beer.

Inn at the Tides • ⌒⌒⌒ $$$$$

P.O. Box 640, Bodega Bay, CA 94923; (800) 541-7788 or (707) 875-2751. Couples and singles $105 to $210. MC/VISA, AMEX. Well-kept 86-room lodge near the boat basin; TV, room phones; pool. **Bay View Restaurant** serves continental fare Wednesday-Sunday 5 to 9; dinners $18 to $24; full bar service.

River's End Restaurant & Lodge • ⌒⌒⌒ $$$$$

P.O. Box 1800, Guerneville, CA 95446; (707) 865-2484. Couples $98 to $150; MC/VISA. Nine-unit lodge near mouth of the Russian River (close to Jenner despite the Guerneville address). Private beach on river; near ocean. **Restaurant** listed above.

Fort Ross Lodge • ⌒⌒⌒ $$$

20705 Coast Highway (at Timber Cove Road), Jenner, CA 95450; (707) 874-3333. Couples $60 to $175, suites $150 to $225. MC/VISA, AMEX. Nicely appointed 22-room lodge north of Jenner with TV, refrigerators, VCRs, patios with barbecues; some rooms with spas. Hot tub and sauna.

Bed & breakfast inns

Bay Hill Mansion • ⌒⌒⌒ $$$$$ Ø

3919 Bay Hill Rd. (P.O. Box 567), Bodega Bay, CA 94923; (707) 875-3577. Couples $95 to $150, singles $80 to $100. Five units; some private and some shared baths; full breakfast. MC/VISA. Newly built Victorian style inn at Bay Hill Road and Highway 1; furnished with Victorian and American antiques; complimentary wine and cheese.

☺ Murphy's Jenner Inn • ⌒⌒ $$$ Ø

P.O. Box 69 (Highways 1 and 116), Jenner, CA 95450; (800) 732-2377 or (707) 865-2377. Couples $60 to $150, singles $55 to $120. Eleven units with private baths; continental breakfast. MC/VISA, AMEX. Very charming hideaway with eclectically furnished rooms, suites and cottages; some units with fireplaces, kitchenettes or hot tubs; view decks. Activities include conducted walks and wine tasting tour. Home rentals also available.

School House Inn • ⌒⌒⌒ $$$$ Ø

17110 Bodega Lane (P.O. Box 136), Bodega, CA 94922; (707) 876-3257. Couples $75 to $90, singles $65. Four rooms with private baths; full breakfast. MC/VISA. Alfred Hitchcock's schoolhouse from *The Birds* reborn as a Victorian inn. Nicely furnished, with antiques and a few original artifacts from the 1873 school.

WHERE TO CAMP

Reservations for Sonoma Coast State Beach campsites can be made through Mistix by calling (800) 444-PARK.

Bridgehaven Campground • *On the Russian River at Highway 1 (P.O. Box 59), Jenner, CA 95450; (707) 865-2473. RV and tent sites $16.* Small, quiet campground on the banks of the river.

Porto Bodega RV Park and Marina • *Bay Flat Road (P.O. Box 456), Bodega Bay, CA 94923. RV sites only, full hookups from $12. Reservations accepted.* On Bodega Bay, with gravel sites, some pull-throughs. Showers, coin laundry, boat dock and ramp.

Doran County Park • *P.O. Box 372, Bodega Bay, CA 94923; (707) 875-3540. RV and tent sites, no hookups, $10.* Near the beach, a mile south of Bodega Bay; flush potties, boat ramp.

Sonoma Coast State Beach • *Two campgrounds between Bodega Bay and Jenner; (707) 875-3483. RV and tent sites, $12.* Bodega Dunes has showers, flush potties; no hookups. Wrights Beach has no showers or hookups. Both have beach access.

Salt Point State Park • *25050 Highway 1, Jenner, CA 95450; (707) 847-3221. RV and tent sites, $12; hiker/biker $6 to $7.* Flush potties; no hookups or showers. Hiking, riding trails, fishing.

Sonoma Coast Regional Parks • *Jenner, CA 95450; (707) 847-3245. RV and tent sites, no hookups, $13, hiker/biker $3.* Stillwater Cove just north of Fort Ross has flush potties and showers. Gualala Point, south of Gualala, has beautifully situated sites in a wooded enclave at the mouth of the Gualala River; flush potties.

Mendocino: a place and an attitude

Topographically, there's no difference between coastside Sonoma and Mendocino counties. The Gualala (pronounced *wah-LA-la*) River marks the boundary, but little else changes. However, Mendocino is a socio-ecological condition as well as a place. Flower children and seclusion-seeking artists began settling here in the 1960s to raise *cannabis* and paint seagulls and sunsets. Close on their liberal heels came environmentalists, fighting to save what was left of the redwoods, and now battling to stave off threatened off-shore oil drilling.

Bay Area schoolteacher and artist Bill Zaca arrived in 1959 and fell instantly in love with the area. He bought a Victorian house in the weathered old former lumber town of Mendocino, then established the Mendocino Art Center, which attracted other artistic types. Tourists followed, and soon charming Mendocino was being restored, renovated and loved to pieces. It became so popular and expensive that artists and other subsistence level liberals began migrating south to hamlets such as Gualala, Elk and Point Arena. Since most tourists approach Mendocino via Highway 128 which bypasses these places, folks there can paint and grow their pot in peace.

RV advisory: The highway from Gualala to Mendocino is particularly sinuous, with switchbacks and corkscrew dips through narrow creek valleys. Go slow, enjoy the spectacular scenery, and pull over for those in a hurry.

Your first Mendocino Coast encounter is Gualala, followed by Point

Arena, Manchester and Elk. Cut from the same weathered Cape Cod mold, they occupy a particularly scenic section of the coast, perched above rocky coves or atop grassy headlands.

Gualala sits in a wooded niche just above the beach and river. It features a few shops and little else. Most of what happens here occurs at the Gualala Hotel restaurant and bar (listed below). You might catch a glimpse of a harbor seal herd at **Del Mar Landing,** a rough-hewn piece of wilderness beach reached by a two-mile hike from **Gualala Point Regional Park,** on the south mouth of the river.

☺ Often bypassed by coastal travelers is rock-ribbed **Arena Cove,** a tiny harbor tucked into a ravine near **Point Arena.** It's particularly impressive on a stormy day when waves smash into the tilted strata of the cove. There's no marina here, only a weathered pier from which fishing boats are lowered by derrick. Galleria Restaurant (listed below) offers a view of all this. To reach the cove, turn left at a coastal access sign on the south edge of Point Arena and drive past the green slime ponds of a sewer plant. Point Arena itself offers an architectural mix of 19th century false front and 20th century Art Deco buildings. Most of them are unrestored.

Two miles beyond, follow signs seaward to **Point Arena Lighthouse Museum.** Built in 1870 and rebuilt after the 1906 shaker, the slender light occupies a precarious perch atop a rugged seacliff. The museum is open weekends 11 to 2:30; adults $2, kids 50 cents; (707) 882-2777. You can rent rudimentary lodging in some old Coast Guard billets here.

Manchester is one of the few uninteresting towns along this coastal stretch, occupying an open moor. **Manchester State Beach** just beyond offers camping at $7 per night and access to a sandy shore. Up the highway is **Irish Beach,** not a town but a gathering of upscale homes on a bluff above a rugged creek-fed cove. A bit farther along, note the strikingly beautiful estuary of **Elk Cove,** where waves burble and foam through sawtooth seastacks. Just beyond, you reach the juncture with Highway 128, with its attendant increase in traffic.

A right turn onto 128 will deliver you to **Anderson Valley,** a bucolic retreat lined with wineries and their tasting rooms. If you feel an urge to sip, this is one of the more appealing vineyard areas in the state, and wineries are rarely crowded. **Boonville** is an intriguing old town, with the popular old **Boonville Hotel** and very attractive **Buckhorn Saloon** brewpub with natural wood décor. Pressing north on Highway 1, you cross an imposing old wooden trestle to **Albion** and wind down through **Little River,** with its popular Victorian style Little River Inn.

☺ **Van Damme State Park** is one of our favorite coastal reserves, featuring a rocky, secluded beach popular with tidepoolers and divers, and a lush inland rain forest with campsites (listed below). Hiking trails lead up a fern-cloaked creek bed to a pygmy forest. As you drive north from the park, cross the highway (carefully) to a vista point. You'll enjoy your first view of the coast's penultimate art colony, standing on the headlands opposite.

Mendocino

Population: 1,000   **Elevation: 90 feet**

Mendocino's New England settlers brought their architectural heritage when they arrived in the 1850s. A thriving lumber boom brought prosperity and stylish homes. Then the mills died and the town went to sleep, to be awakened by artist Bill Zaca. Today's Mendocino is meticulously charming, and swarming with summer tourists. If you've followed our advice and come here in the fall or winter, you'll find the jewel-like town to be refreshingly uncrowded. You can browse its many shops, galleries, antique stores and boutiques without bumping elbows, and even find a place to park.

You might bump into a film crew as you browse, since Mendocino is the setting for Angela Landsbury's *Murder, She Wrote* TV series. Her house is a block north of the post office, at Little Lake and Ford streets.

Mendocino's 19th century business district poses handsomely atop an 80-foot headland. This offers a clear shot for photographers across the bay and for admiring strollers on the beaches of **Mendocino Headlands State Park,** which nearly circles the town. Among requisite stops are the exquisitely restored 1878 **Mendocino Hotel,** the landmark **Presbyterian Church** with its skinny steeple skewering skyward, the **Mendocino Art Center** with exhibits by local artists, the former **Mendocino Masonic Temple** (now a bank) with its unusual rooftop sculpture of father time and a maiden. It was carved more than a century ago from a single redwood log.

A pair of museums are worthy of pause:

☺ **Ford House** • *Main Street; (707) 937-5397. Daily 10 to 5; free.* Now headquarters for Mendocino Headlands State Park, this 1854 Victorian has exhibits on the area's Native Americans, lumbering and fishing. Particularly interesting is a three dimensional model of Mendocino in 1890.

Kelly House • *Main Street; (707) 937-5791. Weekdays 1 to 4; donations requested.* Fronted by elaborate gardens, this steep-roofed Victorian is head-quarters for Mendocino Historical Research, Inc. It exhibits the usual pioneer artifacts and photos. For $3, you can sign up for a walking tour past the town's historic sites.

☺ Immediately north of town, **Russian Gulch State Park** is something of an ecological twin to **Van Damme.** It also occupies a thickly wooded ravine that spills onto a rocky coastal cove. During incoming tides, waves surge into a collapsed sea cave, foaming into a wild witch's cauldron. Hiking trails lead several miles inland, through a redwood grove to a 36-foot waterfall. Thirty shaded campsites are available (listed below).

Jughandle State Reserve just north of **Caspar** is another fascinating state park in the Mendocino region. Its coastal terraces preserve half a million years of geological history, from a gravelly beach through thick stands of conifers to a pygmy forest. A bit farther along is **Mendocino Coast Botanical Gardens,** with several *thousand* plant varieties. Started by a retired nurseryman in 1961, this orderly jungle is now maintained by the Mendocino Coast Recreation and Parks District; (707) 964-4352

Fort Bragg

Population: 6,100   **Elevation: 80 feet**

While Mendocino basks in its busy glory, next door Fort Bragg shoulders the burden of providing basic services and housing. It is hardly a poor cousin, however. This sturdy, homely old town, founded in 1857, is the largest coastal community between San Francisco and Eureka. Georgia-Pacific's Union Lumber Company provides much of the economy, augmented by service people who work in Mendocino but can't afford to live there. For visitors who want to spend an extra day in Mendocino's upscale shops, Fort Bragg offers several affordable motels.

Before entering town, turn right just beyond Noyo River Bridge and wind down to **Noyo Harbor,** up the estuary from the Pacific. Not a cutesy tourist retreat, it's appealingly scruffy, with some honest seafood restaurants and a working marina. **Salmon Inn** sells smoked albacore, black cod and salmon, plus a very peppery salmon jerky.

Continuing into town, stop by the **Fort Bragg-Mendocino Chamber of Commerce** on Main Street to load up on local propaganda, including a walking tour map of the historic area. It's on your right; open 9 to 5 weekdays and 10 to 5 Saturday. During summers, check at the chamber for **lumber mill tours** at the Georgia-Pacific plant. Across the street from the chamber and up a bit is the **Guest House Museum** and behind that, Fort Bragg's major claim to tourist fame, the legendary **Skunk Train.**

Guest House Museum ● *Main and Laurel streets; (707) 961-2825. Open 10 to 4 Wednesday-Sunday, April to October, then Saturdays only the rest of the year. Free.* This city-run archive occupies a large multi-gabled house built by an early mill official. Exhibits focus on local logging and fishing.

☺ *California Western Railroad* ● *P.O. Box 907, Fort Bragg, CA 95437; (707) 964-6371. Round trip fare to Willits $23, kids $11; half way (to North Spur and back) or one way to Willits $18.50; kids $9. Full day departures 9:20 a.m., half day 9:30 in summer and 10 in the off-season; MC/VISA.*

Following the route of an old logging railroad, the Skunk Trains wind up steep ravines, across dizzying trestles and through hushed redwood groves on their daily 40-mile runs to Willits. Passengers catch either diesel or steam trains or small railway diesel cars, depending on the time of year. It was the bright yellow diesel-burners that inspired the "Skunk" name when they went into service on the line in 1925. In summer, you can make the round trip to Willits in a single day. With fewer trains running during the off-season, you must overnight in Willits. Any time of the year, you can catch a shorter round-trip to North Spur, a mid-point stop with a snack shop and beer garden among the redwoods.

MacKerricher Beach State Park just above Fort Bragg and still within its suburbs, offers a large campground (listed below) and beachside picnic area. You can stroll out to a viewpoint for glimpses of a harbor seal colony (and whales during migrating season), or walk as far as you want up an eight-mile beach. North of Fort Bragg, Highway 1 offers one final coastal town, **Westport.** It then swings eastward to merge with U.S. 101 for a trip through serious redwood country. There's not much reason to pause in tiny Westport, unless you need provisions from a community store. Slow down, however, to enjoy an impressive view of offshore seastacks.

A few miles beyond, the highway becomes a cliff-hanger notched into near vertical headlands. It swerves inland over Hardy Creek Bridge and suddenly the ocean disappears. You're climbing a serpentine canyon toward a crest in the Coast Range. Before you reach the summit, pause at the **Louisiana-Pacific Demonstration Forest,** for a walk beneath old growth and second-growth redwoods along a chortling creek. It's a pleasant preview of the mighty cinnamon-barked giants ahead.

MENDOCINO COAST ACTIVITIES

Bicycle and canoe rentals ● Mountain and road bikes, canoes, kayaks and sea cycles for rent from Catch a Canoe at Stanford Inn, Mendocino; (800) 439-5245 or (707) 937-0273.

Drama • Mendocino Theatre Company in Mendocino has a May-September season of classic and contemporary plays; (707) 937-4477. Gloriana Opera Company in Mendocino presents Broadway musicals; (707) 964-SHOW. Fort Bragg Footlighters present old-fashioned musicals May-September; (707) 964-3806.

Horse-drawn carriage tours • Mendocino Carriage Company, Mendocino, (800) 399-1454 or (707) 937-1640.

Horseback riding • Ricochet Ridge Ranch, Fort Bragg, (707) 964-7669.

Scuba rentals and classes • North Coast Scuba, Gualala, (707) 884-3534; Sub-surface Progression, Fort Bragg, (707) 964-3793.

Whale watching/deep sea fishing • Second Semester Charters, Point Arena, (707) 882-2440; Lady Irma II, Fort Bragg, (707) 964-3854; Cavalier Charter Fleet, Fort Bragg, (707) 964-4550; Misty II Charters, Fort Bragg, (707) 964-7161; Tally Ho II, Fort Bragg, (707) 964-2079.

ANNUAL EVENTS

Whale watch festivals—Mendocino, first weekend in March, (707) 961-6300; Gualala, second weekend, (707) 884-3377; Fort Bragg, third weekend, (707) 961-6300.

World's Largest Salmon Barbecue, Fourth of July at Noyo Harbor, Fort Bragg; (707) 964-6498.

Mendocino Music Festival, mid-July in Mendocino; (707) 937-2044.

Art in the Redwoods, mid-August at the Gualala Art Center; (707) 884-1138.

Paul Bunyan Days, Labor Day weekend, Fort Bragg; (707) 964-2477.

WHERE TO DINE ON THE MENDOCINO COAST

Gallery Restaurant • ∆∆ $$

Point Arena Cove, Point Arena; (707) 882-2189. American, mostly seafood; full bar service. Monday-Tuesday 11 to 9, Wednesday-Sunday 7 to 9. Major credit cards. The barn-like interior isn't much, but the views of narrow, rocky Point Arena Cove are nice. It features fresh local fish, plus specialties such as Cajun snapper and cioppino.

Giannini's Italian Restaurant • ∆∆ $$

174 Main St., Point Arena; (707) 882-2146. Italian-American; full bar service. Monday-Saturday 7:30 a.m. to 8 p.m., closed Sunday. MC/VISA. Pleasant oak-paneled dining room with full-course meals from $10 to mid-teens. Usual Italian fare plus steaks, chicken and chops.

Mendocino

Café Beaujolais • ∆∆∆∆ $$$$ Ø

961 Ukiah St.; (707) 937-5614. American nouveau; wine and beer. Monday-Thursday 8:30 to 2:30 and 6:15 to 9:30. MC/VISA. Luminaries such as Robert Redford and Julia Child have been lured to this outstanding cafè, occupying a 19th century house. *Prix fixe* dinner menu changes weekly, offering savories such as bistro Casoullete with duck, ham hocks, pork shoulder and pancetta. Breakfasts also are exceptional; try the buttermilk cornmeal waffles with maple syrup or apple-chicken sausages.

Mendocino Bakery • ∆ $

Lansing Street; (707) 937-0836. American. Daily 8 to 6. No credit cards. This survivor from the town's art colony days, complete with bulletin board announcing yoga lessons, is a good bet for quick, inexpensive fare. Try pizza by the slice, lasagna and a tasty Jewish dessert called *ruglach,* with sour cream, almond paste and fruit jam wrapped in *phyllo.*

Mendocino Café ● ∆∆ $$
Albion at Lansing streets; (707) 937-2422. Eclectic. Weekdays 11 to 4 and 5 to 8:30, weekends 9 to 4 and 5 to 10. MC/VISA. Recently renovated, this prim, bright little place in a clapboard house is all over the culinary map. Try spicy Bangkok chicken, Oriental stir fry, lentil pasta or hot shrimp pie. Breakfast burritos are a weekend feature.

Mendocino Hotel Dining Room ∆∆∆ $$$$ Ø
45080 Main Street; (707) 937-0511. American-continental; full bar service. Daily 8 a.m. to 9:30, to 10 Friday-Saturday. MC/VISA, AMEX. Choose between the utterly elegant Victorian dining parlor with polished woods, beveled glass and high-backed chairs or the less formal Garden Café and bar with its imposing leaded glass canopy. Eclectic menu ranges from Basque lamb chili to chicken Napoleon.

Fort Bragg

Egghead ● ∆∆ $ Ø
326 N. Main St.; (707) 964-5005. American; wine and beer. Daily 7 a.m. to 2 p.m. MC/VISA. A good breakfast spot, featuring 40 kinds of omelets, plus burgers, creative sandwiches, soup, salad and quiche for lunch. It's all made on the premises. Smoke-free.

Pasta House ● ∆∆ $
322 N. Main St.; (707) 964-8260. Italian; nonalcoholic wine and beer. Daily 11 to 7:30. No credit cards. Tiny, cheerful place with red checkered tablecloths, serving hearty Italian fare at bargain prices. Full dinners of pasta, lasagna, ravioli, Chicken Parmesan or scampi are under $10.

The Wharf ● ∆∆ $$
North Harbor Drive, at Noyo; (707) 964-4283. American, mostly seafood; full bar service. Daily 11 to 10. MC/VISA. Family style seafood parlor with views of Noyo Harbor. Ample dinners range from calamari steak and fresh-caught flippers to steaks and boneless chicken breast.

WHERE TO SLEEP

Bed & breakfast inns dominate the Mendocino sleeping scene, while Fort Bragg offers some inexpensive motels. Several resorts are tucked among the headlands and redwood groves along Mendocino coast. For hideaway homes, contact one of these agencies: **Coast Retreats**, P.O. Box 977, Mendocino, CA 95460, (707) 937-1121 or **Mendocino Coast Reservations,** P.O. Box 1143, Mendocino, CA 95460; (707) 937-5033.

Gualala

Seacliff ● ⌂⌂⌂ $$$$$
P.O. Box 697, Gualala, CA 95445; (707) 884 1213. Couples $155 to $180. MC/VISA. Opulent sea view lodging on a bluff overlooking the ocean and mouth of the Gualala River. Individually decorated rooms, each with a deck over the river or ocean. TV, refrigerators, fireplaces and spa tubs.

☺ Whale Watch Inn ● ⌂⌂⌂⌂ $$$$$ Ø
35100 Highway 1, Gualala, CA 95445; (800) WHALE-42 or (707) 884-3667. Units $160 to $250, includes full breakfast. MC/VISA, AMEX. Very luxu-

rious, modern 18-room coastal resort; individually furnished rooms with private decks, all with views of Anchor Bay. Some rooms with kitchenettes, spa tubs, saunas and fireplaces. Nearby beach access.

Mendocino/Little River

Agate Cove Inn • ⌂⌂⌂ $$$$ Ø
11201 N. Lansing St. (P.O. Box 1150), Mendocino, CA 95460; (707) 937-0551. Couples and singles $75 to $175. Nine cottages with private baths and TV; one room in house; full breakfast. Major credit cards. A renovated 1860s farmhouse with surrounding cottage units, perched on a bluff overlooking the sea. Country dècor with wallpaper, antique furnishings. Some rooms with fireplaces; ocean views.

The Headlands Inn • ⌂⌂⌂ $$$$$ Ø
Main Street (P.O. Box 132), Mendocino, CA 95460; (707) 937-4431. Couples and singles $98 to $164. Five rooms with private baths; full breakfast. No credit cards. Charming 1868 New England salt box Victorian furnished with American and European antiques. Located downtown, a short walk to shops and restaurants.

Joshua Grindle Inn • ⌂⌂⌂ $$$$ Ø
44800 Little Lake Rd. (P.O. Box 647), Mendocino, CA 95460; (707) 937-4143. Couples and singles $90 to $135. Ten rooms with private baths; full breakfast. MC/VISA, DISC. An 1879 New England style farmhouse surrounded by two acres of gardens. Light and airy early American furnishings; some rooms with ocean views, fireplaces. Short walk to downtown.

Little River Inn • ⌂⌂⌂ $$$$ Ø
Highway 1 (P.O. Drawer B), Little River, CA 95456; (707) 937-5942. Couples from $75, singles from $65, suites $155 to $255. No credit cards. Long-established 55-room coastal resort with TV, room phones; some fireplaces, refrigerators and spa tubs. Tennis courts, nine-hole golf course and pro shop. Garden view **Restaurant** serves "country cuisine"; breakfast and dinner daily; dinners $13 to $20; full bar service.

Mendocino Hotel • ⌂⌂⌂ $$$$ Ø
45080 Main St., Mendocino, CA 95460; (800) 548-0513 or (707) 937-0511. Rooms with private baths $65 to $180, without baths $50 to $80, suites $150 to $225. MC/VISA, AMEX. Meticulously restored hotel with Victorian and early American dècor; some rooms with fireplaces or wood stoves; modern amenities. Suites in adjacent cottages.

Mendocino Village Inn • ⌂⌂⌂ $$$ Ø
44860 Main St. (P.O. Box 626), Mendocino, CA 95460; (707) 937-0246. Couples and singles $65 to $185. Thirteen rooms, most with private baths; full breakfast. No credit cards. Charming bed & breakfast fashioned from an 1882 home, tucked behind lush gardens. Architectural mix of Queen Anne and Dutch colonial, with Victorian, early Californian and "coastal whimsy" furnishings. Opposite historic Presbyterian church.

Rachel's Inn • ⌂⌂⌂ $$$$ Ø
P.O. Box 134 (adjacent to Van Damme State Park), Mendocino, CA 95460; (707) 937-0088. Couples and singles $96 to $165. Nine rooms with private baths; full breakfast. No credit cards. Bed & breakfast fashioned from an 1860 Victorian, with a mix of antique and contemporary furnishings. Some rooms with fireplaces; some ocean views.

S.S. Seafoam Lodge • ⌂⌂⌂ $$$$ ∅
P.O. Box 68, Mendocino, CA 95460; (707) 937-1827. Couples and singles $85 to $150, kitchenettes $140 to $200; prices include continental breakfast. MC/VISA. A 24-room inn with TV, room phones and private decks. Ocean views from each room; beach access.

Sea Gull Inn • ⌂⌂⌂ $$$ ∅
44594 Albion St. (P.O. Box 317), Mendocino, CA 95460; (707) 937-5204. Couples $40 to $95; private baths; continental breakfast. No credit cards. A 19th century farmhouse near downtown Mendocino converted into a comfortable, nicely kept B&B. Rooms feature American antiques and works by local artists; some rooms with ocean views. Short walk to shops.

☺ Stanford Inn by the Sea • ⌂⌂⌂ $$$$$ ∅
Highway 1 at Comptche-Ukiah Road (P.O. Box 487), Mendocino, CA 95460; (800) 331-8884 or (707) 937-5615. Couples and singles $160 to $230, including continental breakfast. Major credit cards. A luxurious 23-room inn with TV movies and VCRs, room phones, fireplaces and refrigerators. Located on a wooded bluff with views of the ocean and Mendocino. Facilities include indoor pool, sauna and spa. Bike, canoe and kayak rentals.

Victorian Farmhouse Bed & Breakfast • ⌂⌂⌂ $$$$ ∅
7001 N. Highway 1 (P.O. Box 357), Little River, CA 95456; (707) 937-0697. Rooms $80 to $120. Ten rooms with private baths; full breakfast. MC/VISA. Sturdy 1877 farmhouse with antique furnishings; some rooms with fireplaces. Gardens, orchards and redwoods; short walk to the ocean.

Fort Bragg

Avalon House Bed & Breakfast • ⌂⌂⌂ $$$ ∅
561 Stewart St. (at Fir Street), Fort Bragg, CA 95437; (707) 964-5555. Couples and singles $70 to $135. Six rooms with private baths; full breakfast. Major credit cards. A 1905 Craftsman style home with a blend of antique and country willow furnishings. Some rooms with fireplaces and spas; private decks with ocean views; large garden.

Best Western Vista Manor Lodge • ⌂⌂ $$$ ∅
1100 N. Main St., Fort Bragg, CA 95437; (800) 821-9498 or (707) 964-4776. Couples $53 to $120, singles $46 to $85. Major credit cards. A 56-unit motel on six-acre grounds; TV, room phones; some rooms with ocean views.

Harbor Lite Lodge • ⌂⌂ $$$ ∅
120 N. Harbor Dr., Fort Bragg, CA 95437; (800) 643-2700 or (707) 964-0221. Couples $57 to $94, singles $53 to $94. Major credit cards. A 79-unit motel overlooking Noyo Harbor. Rooms with TV, phones, private decks; some with harbor views, refrigerators and spas.

Noyo River Lodge • ⌂⌂ $$$$ ∅
500 Casa del Noyo Dr., Fort Bragg, CA 95437; (800) 628-1126 or (707) 964-8045. Couples and singles $80 to $140, continental breakfast. MC/VISA, DISC. An 1868 lumber baron's home converted to a B&B; on a wooded slope with a view of Noyo Harbor. All private baths, some TVs and fireplaces. Furnished with American antiques; outdoor decks.

Old Coast Hotel • ⌂⌂ $$ ∅
101 N. Franklin St. (at Oak), Fort Bragg, CA 95437; (707) 964-6443. Couples $44 to $58, singles $38 to $46, kitchenettes $65 to $75. Major credit

cards. A 14-room 19th century hotel with simply furnished rooms; some with phones. Within walking distance of downtown Fort Bragg. Three small **cafès** serve American fare, espresso and Mexican fare; varied hours; dinners $3.50 to $21.50; wine and beer.

Old Stewart House Bed & Breakfast ● △△△ $$$
511 Stewart St., Fort Bragg, CA 95437; (707) 961-0775. Couples $65 to $95, singles $55 to $85. Six rooms with private baths; full breakfast. Major credit cards. Restored 1876 early American home across from Skunk Train depot. Rooms offer early American and Victorian furnishings; some refrigerators. Garden; spa.

Pudding Creek Inn Bed & Breakfast ● △△△ $$$
700 N. Main St (at Bush), For Bragg, CA 95437; (707) 964-9529. Couples $65 to $125, singles $50 to $115. Ten units with private baths; full breakfast. Major credit cards. Multi-gabled home built by a Russian count in 1844, now fashioned into an attractive inn. Victorian furnishings; some rooms with fireplaces. Garden, rec room, parlor with fireplace and TV.

Surrey Inn ● △△ $$$ Ø
888 S. Main St., Fort Bragg, CA 95437; (707) 964-4003. Couples $53 to $58, singles $46 to $51. MC/VISA, AMEX. A 53-unit motel just north of Noyo bridge; TV; room phones. **Perko's Coffee Shop** serves from 6 a.m. to 9 p.m.; wine and beer.

WHERE TO CAMP
State park reservations via Mistix: (800) 444-PARK.

Manchester State Beach ● *Manchester; (707) 937-5804. RV and tent sites, no hookups; $7 per night; hiker/biker $2.* Small camping area on an open moor above the ocean.

Albion River Campground ● *P.O. Box 217, Albion, CA 95410; (707) 937-0606. RV and tent sites, $8 to $10. Reservations accepted.* Simple, well-located private campground beside the Albion River near the beach; showers, boat launch, dock.

Van Damme State Park ● *Mendocino; (707) 937-5804. RV and tent sites, no hookups; $13.* Exceptionally attractive sites beside a thickly wooded creek. Flush potties, showers, barbecues and picnic tables; hiking trails.

Russian Gulch State Park ● *Mendocino; (707) 937-5804. RV and tent sites, no hookups; $13.* Sheltered campsites in a thickly wooded ravine. Flush potties, showers, barbecues and picnic tables; hiking trails.

Caspar Beach RV Park ● *14441 Point Cabrillo Rd., Mendocino, CA 95460; (707) 964-3306. RV sites, full hookups, $22. Reservations accepted; MC/VISA, AMEX.* Well-kept campground in a rock-walled cove just up from the beach, immediately north of Mendocino. Showers, mini-mart, playground, coin laundry.

REDWOOD COUNTRY
Botanists and park rangers call it *Sequoia sempervirens.* It was named in honor of Sequoyah, a Native American scholar who developed a syllabic alphabet for his Cherokee tribe in Tennessee. Sempervirens is Latin for evergreen. In 1769, Spanish Friar Juan Crespi gave it a simpler name—*palo colorado,* or red tree.

Redwoods are the tallest and among the oldest living things on earth.

They extend from southern Oregon through Monterey County, favoring moist, foggy basins of the Coast Range. Living links to the age of dinosaurs, they once ranged throughout the Northern Hemisphere. Fossil seeds and fronds from the Jurassic Period suggest that they have changed little in 160 million years. They're related to the bald cypress and they have a shorter, fatter and heavier cousin, *Sequoiadendron giganteum,* the big tree of the Sierra Nevada.

Although redwoods are huge, often topping 300 feet and weighing 5,000 tons, the seeds, cones and leaves are tiny. Needle-like fronds are usually less than an inch long, and the olive-sized cones contain seeds a bit larger than a pinhead. Tree ring counters have dated some redwoods back more than 2,000 years. The notion that the cinnamon barked tree standing in front of you was alive during the height of the Roman Empire is boggling. A thick, tannin-rich bark accounts for its longevity, making it resistant to insects and fire. The fine grained heartwood resists termites and other enemies.

This invulnerability to nature makes the noble tree vulnerable to man. Settlers began cutting the durable "redwood gold" for lumber in the 1850s. It was used in the construction of wine vats, boardwalks, balustrades, fencing and San Francisco's Victorian homes. Within a century, more than two million acres of virgin forest had been reduced to fewer than 300,000.

Fortunately, steps were begun early in this century to preserve the dwindling groves. A string of state redwood parks flank Highway 101 between Leggett and Crescent City. Additional groves were protected with the establishment of Redwood National Park north of Eureka in

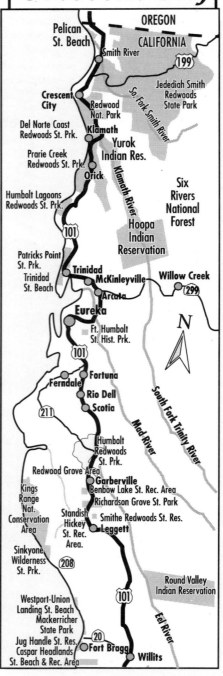

Fort Bragg to Crescent City

1968. Environmentalists issued new howls of protest several years ago when sections of Highway 101 between Leggett and Eureka were expanded to freeway status, wiping out more of the trees.

This destruction yielded a benefit, however. The Avenue of the Giants, following the original highway route between Phillipsville and Stafford, is free of through traffic. Liberated from snorting trucks and impatient motorists, this route through the hushed, eternal twilight of redwood groves provides one of America's most blissful driving experiences. It gets busy in summer, particularly on weekends. But at least the crowds are there to appreciate the redwoods, along with thee and me.

Incidentally, with preservation has come gimmickry—not by state and national parks, but by owners of private groves. Motoring through the redwoods, you'll pass a procession of drive-through trees, tree house trees, gift shop trees and grandfather trees. Most were created decades ago, when redwoods were regarded as curiosities instead of ecological entities. The beautifully grained redwood has been crafted into every imaginable souvenir, from earrings to toilet paper holders. Burls, irregular bumps that appear around a tree's base, are popular since they sprout when placed in water.

The redwood parade begins at **Leggett,** although the Avenue of the Giants is another 30 miles north, above Garberville. In Leggett, you'll encounter signs to **Drive Through Tree Park,** off Highway 1 before you reach U.S. 101. It'll cost you $3 to enter an attractive redwood park and pass through its Chandelier Tree, which is 315 feet high and 21 feet wide at its base. No surprise: beyond the drive-through is a gift shop.

RV advisory: Drive-through trees aren't high enough for most RVs and campers, so check before you lurch. Incidentally, several state park campgrounds are scattered through the redwoods, many with splendid sites right beneath the trees. Advance reservations are virtually mandatory during summer; use the Mistix number—(800) 444-PARK.

The drive north between Leggett and Garberville alternately travels through hushed groves of giants, then alongside the snaking Eel River. You'll pass an abundance of small motels, nondescript cafès and tourist gimmicks. You first encounter **Standish-Hickey State Recreation Area** (925-6482 or 946-2311), offering campsites for $12; day use is $3. Its redwoods are second-growth, although it's an attractive park, offering hiking trails and fishing and swimming in the Eel River.

Beyond the park is the **World Famous Tree House** (their name, not ours), once featured in Ripley's Believe It or Not. The "house" is a hollowed out trunk with windows. A gift shop is attached, of course. **Confusion Hill** at Piercy is your next tourist treat. It's one of those so-called gravitational force fields where people and things tilt at weird angles. It'll cost you $2.50 to lean funny and another $2.50 to ride the "Famous Mountain Train," a scale model choo-choo that chugs through a redwood grove. Next comes the **Grandfather Tree,** with a gift shop reached through an interesting colonnade of redwood carvings.

☺ Reality returns at **Richardson's Grove State Park,** where U.S. 101 loses its freeway status to pass beneath a magnificent stand of giants. The park has an extensive trail system, campsites and swimming beaches on the Eel River; (707) 247-3318. Richardson Grove Lodge offers books, maps, snacks and souvenirs in summer.

The freeway resumes and you can take the **Benbow** exit to reach **Ben-**

bow Lake State Recreation Area, with swimming, camping, non-power boating and ranger-led canoe hikes. The adjacent town is home to the historic Tudor style **Benbow Inn** (listed below). Just beyond is **Garberville,** with a couple of thousand people; it's the only town of substance along this redwood route.

At first impression, Garberville appears to consist mostly of motels and service stations. Closer inspection reveals a few gift, craft and curio shops, and a small community of tie-dyed dropouts from the 60s. A few galleries and natural food shops verify their presence. The **Garberville-Redway Chamber of Commerce** is on the main street (773 Redwood Drive) in the Jacob Garber Square building.

The Lost Coast

Garberville is gateway to the **King Range National Conservation Area** and **Sinkyone Wilderness State Park.** This is so-called Lost Coast—one of California's most remote regions. Isolated by the inland swing of Highway 101, this area contains more than 65,000 acres of rock-studded mountains, high grasslands, hidden redwood groves and 40 miles of wilderness beach.

King Range, administered by the Bureau of Land Management, spreads over 60,000 acres and the recently established Sinkyone Wilderness State Park to the south covers another 5,000. The only community of any size is **Shelter Cove,** a private enclave with basic essentials, lodging and RV park. Ordinary cars and carefully driven RVs can reach the coast at Shelter Cove, over a 24-mile paved and twisting road. Routes into King Range and Sinkyone are unpaved, often muddy and mostly suited to four-wheel drives. Rainfall in this region averages more than 100 inches a year, creating hazardous driving conditions even for the toughest four-wheeler.

The drive to Shelter Cove, through a mix of rocky grasslands and conifers, is pleasant if not awesome. Areas of the rockbound wilderness coast, harboring undisturbed seal and sea lion herds, tidepools and untrammeled beaches reached only by hiking trails, *are* awesome. For details on this area, contact the **Bureau of Land Management,** 555 Leslie St., Ukiah, CA 95482, (707) 462-3873; or **Sinkyone Wilderness,** P.O. Box 245, Whitethorn, CA 95989; (707) 986-7711.

Humboldt Redwoods\Avenue of the Giants

☺ California's biggest redwood preserve, 51,000-acre Humboldt Redwoods State Park, protects the world's largest surviving stands of virgin redwoods. More than 17,000 acres of old growth giants are within its boundaries. It also contains the mystical twilight zone of the **Avenue of the Giants.** An informational sign a few miles north of Garberville ushers you onto the 33-mile promenade. You can pick up a driving guide from a dispenser box near the sign. Park headquarters, with a visitors center and campsites among the redwoods, is at **Burlington,** about 14 miles north. For information contact: Humboldt Redwoods State Park, P.O. Box 100, Weott, CA 95571; (707) 946-2311.

Although you'll see fine stands of *Sequoia sempervirens* along this route, you can reach less crowded and more impressive groves by turning left under the freeway at **Dyerville** onto Mattole Road. You enter the magnificent 13,000-acre **Rockefeller Forest,** the largest surviving stand of old redwoods. Narrow but paved, Mattole Road takes you to trailheads, where you can get even further from the crowds. As you follow the Avenue of the Giants, frequent turnouts and occasional picnic areas invite you to pause and stroll beneath these eternal leviathans. Interspersed among the groves are a few motels, cafès and gimmicks such as the **Living Chimney Tree, One Log House** and the **Shrine Drive-Through Tree.**

Then suddenly, it's finished. North of Pepperwood, you merge onto the freeway and into the harsh light of day, like a kid emerging from a matinee, returning to the reality of life on the streets.

☺ Get off that freeway after two miles to explore the prim-as-a-pin Pacific Lumber community of **Scotia**, a classic example of a 1920s company town. Take the self guiding tour at the monster mill, check out the **Scotia Museum** with logging exhibits in the Greek style former bank building, and walk the imposing wood paneled hallways of the 1888 **Scotia Inn.** This baronial three-story structure, with wainscotting, high coffered ceilings and Victorian furnishings, is an outstanding example of a 19th century inn (lodging and dining listed below).

Pacific Lumber has been cutting—and even preserving—redwoods for generations, earning praise for its selective logging and care for its workers. In the past it has donated hundreds of acres of old growth trees for public parks. It's currently in the environmental hot seat, however, since officials of a hostile take-over have begun clearcutting company lands.

Beyond the reach of redwoods is a disarmingly charming Victorian town, reached by leaving the freeway at **Fernbridge** and driving southeast:

Ferndale

Population: 1,300   **Elevation: 30 feet**

Surrounded by pasturelands, Ferndale is a virtual living museum of 19th century architecture. Take a few hours to admire its elaborate brick and false front businesses along Main Street and its meticulously restored Victorian gingerbread gems in the neighborhoods. Discovered in recent years by guidebook writers and supported by shoppers from nearby Eureka, it offers many boutiques, galleries, antique shops and Victorian-trendy restaurants. The entire village has been designated as a state historic landmark. One of the North Coast's oldest communities, it was founded in 1852 as a farming and dairy center.

The prim little town made a different kind of news in 1992 when a powerful earthquake shook its historic foundations. A few buildings were destroyed or had to be dismantled, but today's visitor will find most of Ferndale intact.

Ferndale Museum ● *Shaw and Third Streets; (707) 786-4466. February through December Wednesday-Saturday 11 to 4 and Sundays 1 to 4 (open Tuesdays in summer); $1 donation.* This false front museum exhibits the usual pioneer relics, and displays on logging and a working seismograph. You can pick up a walking tour map here that will guide you past many of the town's historic buildings.

ANNUAL EVENTS IN REDWOOD COUNTRY

Scandinavian Festival in Ferndale, late June; (707) 486-4477.
Shakespeare Fest in Benbow, late July; (707) 923-2613.
Humboldt County Fair in Ferndale, early August; (707) 725-1306.

WHERE TO DINE IN REDWOOD COUNTRY
(In order of appearance)

Hartsook Inn • △△ **$$**
Piercy; (707) 247-3305. American; wine and beer. Daily 7:30 a.m. to 8:30 p.m. (Friday-Saturday to 9). MC/VISA. Comfortable, airy dining room in an old redwood inn. Although the setting is folksy, the menu is contemporary, with items such as honey lemon chicken and rock Cornish game hens.

Calico's Café • △△ **$**
808 Redwood Dr. (Highway 101), Garberville; (707) 923-2253. American; wine and beer. Monday-Saturday 7:30 a.m. to 3:30, Sunday 8:30 to 2:30. MC/VISA. Cute breakfast and lunch spot noted for creative omelettes. You can build your own at an assembly line; they're sticker priced at $4.59.

Trees Restaurant • △△△ **$$**
725 Redwood Drive, Garberville; (707) 923-3837. American-continental; wine and beer. Nightly from 5. MC/VISA. Cheerfully simple place with pink nappery, lattice screens and Bach in the background. The fare is creative for these parts, such as chicken Marsala and filet of sole *meuniere*.

☺ **Scotia Inn Dining Room** • △△△ **$$$**
Scotia; (707) 764-5683. American; full bar service. Dinner Wednesday-Saturday 5:30 to 9:30. MC/VISA. Dine like a lumber baron beneath high coffered ceilings in this Victorian inn. The menu features a few uncommon entrées such as roast pheasant and tenderloin of elk.

Bibo and Bear • △△△ **$$** Ø
460 Main St., Ferndale; (707) 786-9484. American; wine and beer. Monday-Thursday 5 to 8:30, Friday 11 to 3 and 5 to 8:30, Saturday 11:30 to 8:30, Sunday 4 to 8. MC/VISA. Stylish Victorian tearoom with print wallpaper, purple accents and café curtains. Catfish Louisiana, seafood sauté and chicken sauté emerge from the kitchen. Homemade desserts are a specialty.

Ivanhoe Roman's • △△ **$$** Ø
315 Main St., Ferndale; (707) 725-6358. Mexican-American; full bar service. Monday-Saturday 11 to 9, Sunday brunch 10 to 3 and buffet dinner 4 to 8. Inviting Latino place with leather-backed chairs and tile-topped tables in a 19th century storefront. The menu steps beyond tortilla-wrapped things to offer prawns in garlic and flautas, plus a few American dishes.

☺ **Victorian Village Inn** • △△△ **$$$** Ø
400 Ocean Ave., Ferndale; (707) 786-7400. American-continental; full bar service. Daily 11 to 9. MC/VISA. Very attractive Victorian dining room in a restored hotel (listed below) with elaborately carved chairs, print wallpaper and a crackling fireplace. Creative fare includes baked chicken breast stuffed with shrimp, plus a variety of steaks and chops.

WHERE TO SLEEP
(In order of appearance)

Hartsook Inn • ⌂ **$$$**
900 Highway 101, Piercy, CA 95587; (707) 247-3305. Couples $60 to $70, four people $90 to $100. MC/VISA. Oldstyle inn with rustic cottages tucked into a lush forest glen. Lounge with large fireplace; the **dining room** is listed above.

☺ Benbow Inn • ⌂⌂⌂ $$$$ Ø
445 Lake Benbow Dr., Garberville, CA 95542; (707) 923-2124. Couples $88 to $190, cottages $250 to $260. MC/VISA. Beautifully restored national historic landmark inn, built in 1926. Spacious rooms with country décor, TV and VCRs; some with fireplaces and spa tubs. **Dining room** serves breakfast, lunch and dinner; smoke free.

Ranch House Inn • ⌂⌂⌂ $$$$ Ø
2906 Alderpoint Rd., Garberville, CA 95542; (707) 923-3441. Couples $95 to $125, singles $75 to $85. Four rooms with private baths; full breakfast. MC/VISA, AMEX. Turn-of-the-century ranch house on 43 bucolic acres, with ponds, orchards and meadows. Large, comfortable guest rooms with country furnishings.

Miranda Gardens Resort • ⌂⌂ $$
6766 Avenue of the Giants (P.O. Box 186), Miranda, CA 95553; (707) 943-3011. Couples from $45, singles from $35, kitchenettes $70 to $155, suites $125 to $155. Major credit cards. Older resort with 16 rooms and four cottages; some with fireplaces and spa tubs.

☺ Scotia Inn ⌂⌂⌂ $$$
P.O. Box 248, Scotia, CA 95565; (707) 764-5683. Rooms $55 to $150. MC/VISA. Handsomely renovated redwood inn with early American and Victorian furnishings; two rooms with hot tub and spa. Large screen TV in lounge; comfortable cocktail lounge and **restaurant**, listed above.

Ferndale

Gingerbread Mansion Bed & Breakfast • ⌂⌂⌂ $$$$$ Ø
400 Berding St., Ferndale, CA 95536; (707) 786-4000. Couples $110 to $185, singles $95 to $170. Nine rooms with private baths; expanded continental breakfast. MC/VISA, AMEX. Beautifully restored 1899 Queen Anne Eastlake set amidst formal Gardens. Rooms with Victorian antiques; some with clawfoot tubs and fireplaces. Four guest parlors; guest bicycles.

Grandmother's House Bed & Breakfast • ⌂⌂ $$$ Ø
861 Howard St. (P.O. Box 1004), Ferndale, CA 95536; (707) 786-9704. Couples from $70, singles from $60. Three rooms with private baths; continental breakfast. MC/VISA. Turn-of-the-century Queen Anne home with American and Victorian antiques on the edge of Ferndale, with country views. Large yard; dining room with fireplace. Children welcomed.

The Shaw House Inn • ⌂⌂⌂ $$$$ Ø
703 Main St., Ferndale, CA 95536; (707) 786-9958. Couples $75 to $125, singles $70 to $120. Six rooms with private baths; continental breakfast. MC/VISA, AMEX. Attractive gabled carpenter Gothic house built in 1854 by town founder. Rooms decorated with a mix of Victorian, American and oriental furnishings and artworks. Fireplace in library and parlor; attractive garden; bikes available for guests.

WHERE TO CAMP

Redwood state parks • Camping is available in several state parks between Leggett and Pepperwood, with RV and tent sites for $12 and hiker/biker for $3. All have flush potties; some have showers. Reservations through Mistix, (800) 444-PARK. Campgrounds are at Standish-Hickey State park just north of Leggett, Richardson's Grove and Benbow Lake Recreation Area between

Leggett and Garberville and at Hidden Springs and Burlington Campground in Humboldt Redwoods State Park on the Avenue of the Giants.

Benbow Valley RV Resort ● *7000 Benbow Dr., Benbow, CA 95542; (707) 923-2777. RV sites only, full hookups $23. Reservations accepted; MC/VISA.* Very attractive full service resort with pull-throughs, showers, golf course, mini-mart, pool and spa and other rec facilities.

Richardson Grove KOA ● *750 Highway 101 (near Richardson Grove State Park), Garberville, CA 95440; (707) 247-3348. RV and tent sites, $11.50 to $17. Reservations accepted; MC/VISA.* Attractive spots beneath redwoods, some pull-throughs; showers, coin laundry, mini-mart, playground and rec room.

Eureka

Population: 27,000   **Population: 44 feet**

The largest coastal city between San Francisco and Portland, Eureka offers a good base for exploring the countryside. It's a sturdy, homely old town, rimmed by mudflats and perhaps suffering by comparison with redwood groves and scenic coastlines.

However, this tough old blue collar town is certainly worth a pause or two. It offers a goodly collection of Victorian homes, highlighted by the stunning Carson Mansion, and an interesting Old Town section. You can prowl the weathered waterfront, dig for shellfish in the mudflats of the huge bay and drive out to the Samoa Cookhouse for a lumberjack-sized meal that'll sink your boat (see box on page 136).

Approaching town from the south, take the **King Salmon Harbor** exit from the freeway if you'd like to explore an interesting bayfront marina. It has a couple of RV parks. Continuing toward town on 101, watch for signs to **Fort Humboldt State Historic Park,** on a bluff overlooking the broad bay. It's free, open 9 to 5 daily; (707) 443-7952. Little of the 1850s fort survives, although the complex has a rather well done museum of early day logging. Graphics will tell you that Ulysses S. Grant was stationed here as a young lieutenant. Probably depressed by the weather, he spent much of his time in local pubs.

About a mile beyond the fort, stop at the **Eureka Chamber of Commerce**. It's on the left at 2112 Broadway, opposite the Eureka Ranchotel; open daily 9 to 5. Fans of Victoriana will find plenty of material here, including a driving tour past some of the town's finer old homes. We'll give you an abbreviated version:

Continue past the chamber for several blocks and turn right onto one-way Seventh Street, just beyond the Safari Motel. Stop to stroll through the imposing Tudor style **Eureka Inn** at Seventh and F streets. To see a string of Victorian homes, turn right onto H street, follow it to Seventeenth, then loop back toward town on G Street.

☺ Follow G Street through the business district down to the waterfront and turn left on Second Street into **Old Town.** Locally called "Two Street," Second has been spruced up with brick crosswalks and old fashioned lamp posts. A few boutiques, galleries and restaurant occupy vintage brick buildings here, although several storefronts are still empty. **Clarke Memorial Museum** at Third and E streets has a nice display of antique weapons, Native American artifacts and stuff on local natural history. It's open Tuesday-Saturday noon to 4; donations appreciated; (707) 443-1947.

☺ The grand and green 1886 **Carson Mansion,** perhaps the most flamboyant Victorian in all of California, stands imperiously at the far end of Two Street. It's a private club, so you must admire it from the sidewalk.

After you've finished with Old Town's shops, drive up to Fifth Street (Highway 101 north), turn left and follow signs to Samoa/Highway 255. This takes you across viaducts over mudflat islands and peninsulas in Humboldt Bay. If you're a marina watcher, take the first exit to **Woodley Island Marina,** home to commercial and sportfishing boats. Then continue across another viaduct to the old mill complex of **Samoa,** turn left and follow signs to the **Samoa Cookhouse.** Even if you aren't hungry, check out vintage lumbering equipment and other museum artifacts in the far end of the barn-like dining room.

From Samoa, follow Highway 255 northeast across a mudflat sandspit to **Arcata,** Eureka's neighbor to the north. This smaller town is no poor sister, since it's home to Humboldt State University, with its attendant cultural offerings and scholastic leanings. Take a peek at Arcata's nicely maintained old business district by turning left onto G Street, just before you reach U.S. 101. Drive past the attractive town square to the **Natural History Museum** in an old Wells Fargo building at G and 13th. Operated by the university, it offers several interesting exhibits, mostly concerning prehistoric animals and plants. It's open Tuesday-Saturday 10 to 4; $1; (707) 826-4479.

Continue on G Street for a few more blocks, cross over the freeway, turn right onto a frontage road and you're beside the sloping hillside campus of **Humboldt State University.** If you'd like to prowl its attractive California mission style grounds, turn left onto Harpst Street and pick up a parking pass and campus map from a kiosk. From here, return to the nearby freeway interchange and continue your northward trek on Highway 101. After you pass the suburb of **McKinleyville,** the restless blue Pacific will reappear, holding promise of more windy moors, rocky headlands and beach parks.

ACTIVITIES

Carriage tours ● Old Town Carriage Company; Second and F streets; (707) 442-7264.

Charter boat fishing ● Contact the Chamber of Commerce for a list of operators; (800) 356-6381 or (707) 442-3738.

Harbor cruise ● Bay cruises aboard an old fashioned passenger ferry departs several times daily from the foot of C street. The Humboldt Bay Maritime Museum is adjacent; (707) 445-1910.

Historic home tours ● Eureka Chamber of Commerce, 2112 Broadway; five-hour bus tour, in summer only; (800) 356-6381 or (707) 442-3738.

Walking tour ● Old Town area; call (707) 445-2117.

ANNUAL EVENTS

Rhododendron Festival, first weekend in May; (707) 442-3738.
Redwood Acres Fair, June; (707) 445-3037.
Summer Arts Fest, all July; (707) 826-5401.
Christmas in Old Town with Victorian theme; (707) 442-9054.

WHERE TO DINE

☺ *Lazio's* ● ∆∆∆ **$$**
327 Second Street in Old Town; (707) 443-9717. American, mostly seafood; full bar service. Daily 11 to 9. MC/VISA. Established by an Italian fish-

HAVE SOME MORE AT THE SAMOA?

We were groaning with uncomfortable contentment, pushing our straight-backed chairs away from the table when the waitress returned: "Did you have enough of everything?"

Enough?

Half a dozen sausages, several eggs, a heavy wedge of hash browns, two slabs of buttered toast, biscuits and gravy, a pitcher of orange juice and a pot of tea.

We had just survived a monster breakfast at the legendary Samoa Cookhouse, on the Samoa Peninsula across from downtown Eureka. That pig-out breakfast cost an entire $5.85, for unlimited amounts of whatever you want. Lunch is $5.95 and dinner $10.65. Meals are served family style at long, oil-cloth-covered tables before an open kitchen. In front of you are pots of jam, jugs of juice and coffee or tea, assorted condiments, and napkins stuck in an old coffee can. To work off some of the calories, you can waddle over to a museum of old logging equipment, drag saws and lumber camp cooking utensils. It occupies one end of the barn-like dining hall.

The red and white-trimmed Samoa Cookhouse is open Monday-Saturday 6 to 3 and 5 to 9, and Sunday 6 to 9. Major credit cards are accepted; (707) 442-1659.

Claiming to be the last surviving cookhouse in the West, Samoa once served hungry lumberjacks. Now, it's the funky darling of the tourist set, challenging visitors with lumberjack-sized meals. Our favorite is breakfast, since we can throw culinary caution to the wind and pig out on all those cholesterol-rich calories.

Then, it's back on the road and back to Quaker oats and whole wheat toast, spread thinly with I Can't Believe It's Not Butter.

---

ing family in 1944, this venerable seafood café moved recently from its fish factory site into an attractive brick-walled facility in Old Town. Try the freshly caught local fish or specials such as *portacella* (shrimp in crepes and Newburg sauce). A few chicken and steak items also decorate the rather extensive menu.

Sea Grill ● △△△ $$

316 E Street in Old Town; (707) 443-7187. American, mostly seafood; wine and beer. Monday-Saturday from 11. MC/VISA. Extensive seafood menu features regional dishes such as cod Louisiana and Hawaiian mahi mahi, plus fresh filets, shellfish and Harris Ranch steak. The interior of this restaurant is cheerfully simple, done in beige and green.

Café Marina ● △△ $$

Woodley Island; (707) 443-2233. American; full bar service. Daily 7 a.m. to 9 p.m. Major credit cards. Nautically modern restaurant overlooking the marina opposite downtown, across the first Samoa bridge. Balanced menu ranges from bouillabaisse and Hangtown Fry (eggs and oyster omelette) to fresh seafood, steaks, chicken and chops.

WHERE TO SLEEP

Budget Host Town House ● ○ $$ Ø

933 Fourth St. (at K Street), Eureka, CA 95501; (800) 445-6888 or (707) 443-4536. Couples $38 to $55, singles $30 to $48, sites $55 to $85. Major *credit cards.* A 20-unit motel with TV movies; phones; some refrigerators and spa tubs. Near Old Town.

Carson House Inn • ⌂⌂ $$$$ Ø

1209 Fourth St. (between M and N), Eureka, CA 95501; (800) 772-1622 or (707) 443-1601. Couples $75 to $110, singles $60 to $85, suites $85 to $120. Major credit cards. A 60-unit motel with TV, room phones; some spa tubs. Pool, spa and sauna.

☺ Eureka Inn • ⌂⌂⌂ $$$$$ Ø

Seventh and F streets, Eureka, CA 95501; (800) 862-4906 or (707) 442-6441. Couples $110 to $135, singles $80 to $110, suites $150 to $250. Major credit cards. Grand old Tudor style inn, carefully restored to its 1922 opulence, with antique and modern furnishings. Three **restaurants** and lounges; polished-wood formal lobby.

Eureka Super 8 • ⌂⌂ $$$$$ Ø

1304 Fourth St., Eureka, CA 95501; (800) 235-3232 in California, or (707) 443-3193. Couples and singles $40 to $75. Major credit cards. Well appointed rooms with TV movies, room phones; spa, sauna, swimming pool and cocktail lounge.

Bed & breakfast inns

For reservations at any of nine area B&Bs, contact: Eureka B&B Reservation Service, P.O. Box 207, Eureka, CA 95502; (707) 441-1215.

A Weaver's Inn • ⌂⌂⌂ $$$$ Ø

1440 B St., Eureka, CA 95501; (707) 443-8119. Couples $65 to $85, singles $45. Four units, two private and two share baths. Major credit cards. Remodeled 1883 Queen Anne surrounded by elaborate gardens; furnished with Victorian and American antiques. Two rooms with fireplaces. Weavers' implements in owner-artist's studio such as a spinning wheel and loom.

Carter House • ⌂⌂⌂ $$$$ Ø

301 L St. (at Third), Eureka, CA 95501; (707) 444-8062. Couples $89 to $250, singles $79 to $240. Thirty rooms; most with private baths; full breakfast. Major credit cards. Reconstructed Victorian with bleached pine antiques in Old Town. Fireplace; some spa tubs and marina views; restaurant.

The Daly Inn • ⌂⌂⌂ $$$$ Ø

1125 H St., Eureka, CA 95501; (800) 321-9656 or (707) 445-3638. Couples $75 to $120, singles $65 to $110. Five rooms; four with private baths; full breakfast. MC/VISA, AMEX. Turn-of-the-century colonial revival home surrounded by gardens. Furnished American and European antiques; one room with fireplace. Comfortable parlor; patio and gift shop.

An Elegant Victorian Mansion • ⌂⌂⌂ $$$$ Ø

1406 C St. (at 14th Street), Eureka, CA 95501; (707) 444-3144. Couples $65 to $115, singles $55 to $105. Five rooms; some private and some share baths; full breakfast. MC/VISA. Nicely restored 1888 Queen Anne; former residence of Eureka mayor. Antique and turn-of-the-century furnishings. Victorian garden with croquet lawn; sauna; guest bicycles.

Old Town B&B Inn • ⌂⌂⌂ $$$$ Ø

1521 Third St., Eureka, CA 95501; (800) 331-5098 or (707) 445-3951. Couples $75 to $185, singles $55 to $95. Seven rooms; some with phones; private or shared baths; full breakfast. MC/VISA, DISC. Nicely restored 1871

Greek-Italianate home built for lumber baron William Carson. Rooms attractively furnished with antiques; some fireplaces; hot tub. Near Old Town.

WHERE TO CAMP

Ebb Tide RV Park ● *2600 Sixth St., Eureka, CA 95501; (707) 445-2273. RV sites only, $10 to $20. Reservations accepted.* Just south of the business district. Some pull-throughs, paved sites; coin laundry, showers; groceries adjacent.

Eureka KOA ● *4050 N. Highway 101, Eureka, CA 95501; (707) 822-4243. RV and tent sites, $18 to $23; Kamping Kabins $28. Reservations accepted; MC/VISA.* Just off freeway, a few miles north. Some shaded sites, pull-throughs; showers, barbecues, playground, rec room, mini-mart, coin laundry.

Johnny's RV Park and Marina ● *At King Salmon Harbor, 1821 Buhne Dr., Eureka, CA 95501; (707) 442-2284. RV sites only, $17. Reservations accepted.* Three miles south; take King Salmon exit from freeway. Some pull-throughs, showers, coin laundry, boat launch and slips; charter boat available.

EUREKA TO THE OREGON BORDER

A few miles north of McKinleyville, you top a rise and catch a magnificent view of the Pacific, with a scalloped surf rolling into a rocky bay. A freeway exit will take you to **Little River State Beach,** a dune-sheltered strand suitable for picnicking, strolling and clamming; (707) 677-3757. A few miles beyond is our favorite tiny town on the California coast.

Trinidad

Population: 432   **Elevation: 175 feet**

☺ Think of Trinidad as Mendocino in miniature, without the crowds and boutiques. This little New England style charmer perches atop Trinidad Head, 175 feet above a rockbound shore. It's the oldest incorporated town on the North Coast, founded in 1850, after an overland party discovered the narrow bay here the year before. The small fishhook cove became and important supply center and whaling port. Then business shifted south to larger Humboldt Bay and Trinidad was left to season in the sun and weather in the wind.

To fully appreciate the grandeur of Trinidad's setting, exit the freeway, then head south along a winding seacliff road. At **Luffenholtz Creek,** a trail leads out to a razor back ridge for awesome seastack vistas, and another leads down to the rocky shoreline and its hidden coves. Come during a storm and watch the waves slam into the rocks and catapult high into the air. Awesome! The skinny road, negotiable if carefully driven, rejoins the freeway a few miles south. You can then return and do the town itself.

Drive down to the harbor, noting the clapboard 1873 **Holy Trinity Church** and the now inactive **Trinidad Memorial Lighthouse** and a seafaring museum (open May through October Friday-Sunday 1 to 4). For a taste of spicy salmon jerky and other smoked fish, pause at **Katy's Smokehouse,** uphill on your right, before you drop down to the harbor. It's open daily 9 to 6; (707) 677-0151.

☺ The tiny nautically rustic harbor is tucked at the base of sheer Trinidad Head, offering as dramatic a setting as you'll find on the coast. There's no marina here; only a weathered pier with a boat hoist. Fishing boats bob at their moorings, adding color and motion to the setting. A system of trails crawls over the headland, offering predictably imposing views. If you'd like to linger over those vistas, how about lunch or dinner?

Trinidad Bay Seascape Restaurant ● △△ $$

At the harbor; (707) 677-3762. American, mostly seafood; full bar service. Daily 7 a.m. to 8:30 p.m. MC/VISA. The simple interior is vaguely nautical, although you'll probably be looking out the large windows to the harbor. Typical seaside menu lists fresh fish, herb chicken breast and teriyaki steak.

Three outfits at the harbor offer fishing trips: **Collins' Fishing Charters,** (707) 677-3625; **Shenandoah Salmon Charters,** (707) 677-3344 and **Trinidad Charters,** (707) 677-3874. **The Escape** conducts scuba trips; (707) 677-3625.

WHERE TO SLEEP

Bishop Pine Lodge ● △△ $$$

1481 Patrick's Point Dr., Trinidad, CA 95570; (707) 677-3314. Couples $70 to $90, singles $60 to $90, kitchenettes $5 extra, suites $80 to $100. Major credit cards. Rustic 1927 lodge; 13 cottage units with TV movies and phones; exercise room; close to parks and beaches.

Trinidad Bed & Breakfast ● △△△ $$$$$ ∅

P.O. Box 849, Trinidad, CA 95570; (707) 677-0840. Couples $105 to $145, singles $90 to $130. Four rooms with private baths; continental breakfast. MC/VISA, DISC. Very nice Cape Cod style home on a bluff overlooking Trinidad Bay. All rooms with ocean views; one with fireplace. Country and antique furnishings. Near beach, restaurants and shops.

Trinidad Inn ● △△ $$$ ∅

1170 Patrick's Point Dr., Trinidad, CA 95570; (707) 677-3349. Couples $45 to $60, singles $40 to $55. MC/VISA, AMEX. Rustic nine-room inn with TV; some kitchens. It sits among redwoods near beach and hiking trails.

North of town, follow signs to **Trinidad Beach State Park,** with a picnic area and beach access. Beyond that, Patrick's Point Road winds northward through an inland forest, passing tree-shaded homes and small resorts. After five miles, it ends at a freeway interchange, where you'll encounter a state park with some great Pacific vistas.

☺ **Patrick's Point State Park** (677-3570) covers several hundred acres of cedars, Sitka spruce and shore pines cloaking a bold headland. Drive out to "the point," where trails lead to viewpoints 200 feet above a broiling surf studded with seastacks. It's one of the finest whale watching areas on the coast. Day use here is $5 and three campgrounds have sites with showers for $12, hiker/biker $3. A few of the spots offer ocean views. Reserve through Mistix, (800) 444-PARK.

North of here is **Humboldt Lagoons State Park** (488-2171), where three saltwater basins offer calm water for wading and dipping and mud flats for clamming. Watch for herds of elk in the adjacent meadowland. Just beyond, you enter the North Coast's last major redwood enclave.

Redwood National Park ● *Mailing address: 1111 Second St., Crescent City, CA 95531; (707) 464-6101. Visitor centers located in Orick and Crescent City are open daily 9 to 5. Geology, flora and fauna exhibits and several videos on redwoods and other natural history subjects. Park admission is free. Camp-*

ing at three nearby state parks, **Prairie Creek Redwoods, Del Norte Coast Redwoods** and **Jedediah Smith Redwoods.** Most sites are $14, with showers and flush potties. Camping reservations through Mistix, (800) 444-PARK.

You'll see more beach than redwoods when you pause at the national park visitor center, on the left side of the highway just south of Orick. In fact, the federal reserve and its adjacent state parks enclose more than 30 miles of wilderness coastline. To find some redwoods, continue to a turnout above Orick and follow Bald Hills Road to **Lady Bird Johnson Grove.** Continue on the winding road to the impressive **Redwood Creek Overlook** and beyond for a pleasant drive, not thorough thick redwood forests, but over grassy, oak-studded hills.

RV advisory: Large RVs and trailers aren't recommended on the Bald Hills Road beyond Redwood Creek Picnic Area.

The long, skinny national park is strung out for 40 miles along the highway, wrapping around Prairie Creek and Del Norte Coast Redwood state parks. It also encircles the hamlets of **Orick** and **Klamath,** which offer small, often rather basic motels and cafés and a startling number of redwood burl and chain saw art places. Several hiking trails wind among the grand trees, and the Coastal Trail extends from Orick to Crescent City. Look for the trailhead at Skunk Cabbage Creek, off U.S. 101, about a mile beyond the Bald Hills Road turnoff. At the north end, the trail terminates at Crescent Beach overlook.

A new 12-mile section of freeway was opened above Orick in 1992, although we prefer the old route through the redwoods, now called **Elk Prairie Parkway.** Pick it up at the turnoff to Prairie Creek Redwoods State Park. Just above Requa is a nicely maintained tourist gimmick that's been around since Christ was a corporal:

Trees of Mystery ● *P.O. Box 96, Klamath, CA 95548; (707) 638-3389 or 482-2251. Daily 9 to dusk; adults $5.50, seniors $4.50 and kids $2. Lodging at adjacent Motel Trees; couples $44 to $48; MC/VISA.* I remember walking through this dark redwood grove as a kid to see the Candelabra Tree, Cathedral Tree and other living curiosities. Not much has changed, except the gift shop is larger now. Your kids will enjoy clambering about giant redwood statues of Paul Bunyan and Babe the Blue Ox, who've wandered a long way from their haunts in Minnesota's North Woods.

Crescent City

Population: 4,400   **Elevation: 44 feet**

Sitting just above Redwood National Park and uncomfortably close to the ocean, Crescent City is the seat of Del Norte (pronounced *Nort*) County. No tourist mecca, it does offer places to pause and refresh, and generally nicer motels than the simpler places you'll find in hamlets to the south.

We say it's uncomfortably close to the Pacific because its waterfront has been wiped out a time or two by tidal waves. Yielding to the demands of nature, citizens have now turned the seafront into a nicely landscaped park.

The present waterfront, **Citizens Dock,** is on your left, just off the highway as you approach town from the south. It offers the usual fishing fleet, nautical vibes and seafood restaurants. Just beyond is **Undersea World,** sort of a sunken aquarium with a gift shop atop, open daily from 9; adults $5.95, seniors and teens $4.95 and kids $2.95; (707) 464-3522.

As you approach the business district, turn left onto Front Street for a pause at the **Chamber of Commerce Visitor Center,** on the second floor of the Crescent City Cultural Center; open weekdays 9 to 5. For a quickie scenic drive through the area, stay on Front, which passes the new waterfront park. Just beyond is the **Battery Point Lighthouse Museum,** reached by a seawalk at the end of Battery Street. It's open Wednesday-Sunday 4 to 10; closed in winter; adults $2, kids 50 cents; (707) 464-3089. The oceanfront street then goes through various name changes as it zigs and wanders past sea bluffs and seafront homes.

A pair of other attractions aren't on our tour route, although this is a small town, so you can find them. **Del Norte County Historical Society Museum** is in the downtown grid at Sixth and H streets; open May through September, Monday-Friday 10 to 4; adults $1.50, kids fifty cents; (707) 464-3922. Stop at **Rumiano Cheese Company,** Ninth and E streets, to pick up some good Monterey style cheese (plain or peppery) and watch it being made through a viewing window. The Rumiano family has been making it since 1921, so the stuff's pretty good. It's open weekdays 8:30 to 5 and Saturday 8:30 to 4; (707) 465-1535.

ANNUAL EVENTS

World Championship Crab Races, late February; (707) 464-3174.
Del Norte County Fair, early August; (707) 464-3174.
Seafood Festival, Labor Day weekend; (707) 464-3174.

WHERE TO DINE

Captain's Table ● △△ $$
At Citizens Dock; (707) 464-9414. American; wine and beer. Daily 6 a.m. to 9 p.m. MC/VISA. Cute little place with cozy booths and drop lamps. The mostly seafood menu includes several Newburg dishes, and a fair sized chicken and chops selection. The moderately priced dinners include soup and salad.

Harbor View Grotto ● △ $$
At Citizens Dock; (707) 464-3185. American; full bar service. Daily from 11:30. Major credit cards. Basic Naugahyde place; not as attractive as the Captain's table, although you get a harbor view from this second-floor perch. It offers the usual seafood dishes, steaks, chicken and chops.

WHERE TO SLEEP

Bayview Inn ● △△△ $$$ Ø
301 S. Highway 101, Crescent City, CA 95531; (800) 446-0583 or (707) 465-2050. Couples $55 to $65, singles $45 to $55. Major credit cards. Very attractive 39-room inn with TV movies, phones; some in-room spas.

Best Western Northwoods Inn ● △△ $$$ Ø
655 S. Highway 101, Crescent City, CA 95531; (800) 528-1234 or (707) 464-9771. Couples $54 to $85, singles $45 to $69, suites $80 to $125. Major credit cards. An 89-room motel with TV movies, room phones; spa, picnic area. Near harbor and beach. **Northwoods Restaurant** serves from 7 a.m. to 9 p.m., dinners from $10; full bar service.

Royal Inn ● △ $$ Ø
102 L St., Crescent City, CA 95532; (800) 752-9610 or (707) 464-4113. Couples $42 to $58, singles $30 to $40, kitchenettes and suites $50 to $90.

MC/VISA. A 30-unit motel with TV and room phones; some small refrigerators and microwaves. Some rooms have ocean view. Adjacent **Hunan** Chinese restaurant serves from 10 to 9; wine and beer.

Valu Inn by Nendels ● ◠◠ $$ ∅
353 L St. (Highway 101), Crescent City, CA 95531; (707) 464-6124. Couples $35 to $75, singles $32 to $65. Comfortable, attractive rooms in 27-unit motel; TV movies, room phones; sauna.

WHERE TO CAMP
(See Redwood National Park for campgrounds in that area)

Crescent Redwoods KOA ● *4241 N. Highway 101, Crescent City, CA 95531; (707) 464-5744. RV and tent sites, $14 to $20; Kamping Kabins $29.50. Reservations accepted; MC/VISA.* Attractive sites under redwood trees; five miles north of town near U.S. 199 junction. Showers, rec room and playground, nature trails, mini-mart, coin laundry.

Shoreline Campground ● *900 Sunset Circle, Crescent City, CA 95531; (707) 464-2473. RV sites only, $13 to $15. Reservations accepted; MC/VISA.* Well located RV park just off the beach near Citizens Dock and shopping district. Showers, coin laundry, horseshoes and volleyball area.

Village Camper Inn ● *1543 Parkway Dr., Crescent City, CA 95531; (707) 464-3544. RV and tent sites, $12 to $15.50. Reservations accepted; MC/VISA.* Attractive park among redwoods just north of town. Full hookups, showers, coin laundry.

Highway 199 campgrounds

Hiouchi Hamlet RV Resort ● *2000 Highway 199, Crescent City, CA 95531; (800) 722-9468 or (707) 458-3321. RV and tent sites, $10 to $16.50. Reservations accepted.* Very attractive landscaped resort adjacent to Jedediah Smith Redwoods; pull-throughs, cable TV, rec room, mini- mart; restaurant and gas station adjacent.

Jedediah Smith Redwoods State Park ● *1440 Highway 199, Crescent City, CA 95531; (707) 464-9533. Reservations via Mistix, (800) 444-PARK. RV and tent sites, $12.* Tree shaded sites with barbecues and picnic tables. Showers, nature trails, fishing, swimming, boat ramp.

You have choices north of Crescent City. A right fork onto Highway 199 takes you through thickening forests to **Jedediah Smith Redwoods State Park** for a final walk among the noble giants (see camping above). Pressing north on U.S. 101, you swing inland, then touch the ocean at a coastal plateau famous for its Easter lily blooms in the spring.

Both routes take you into Oregon, and for that you should get our companion book, ***Oregon Discovery Guide.***

Chapter five
THE COAST SOUTH
Searching from San Mateo to Big Sur

HOLD A MIRROR to the coast north of San Francisco, and you see—to some degree—the coast south. They share many similarities. Their windy and often wooded headlands, seastacks and inland redwood forests are nearly interchangeable. Each offers a major peninsula with its own distinctive character—Point Reyes to the north and Monterey to the south. Both were first settled by expansionist foreign powers, Russia in the north and Spain in the south.

However, as you travel farther from the Bay Area, major differences become apparent. The more benign climate south of San Francisco encouraged earlier settlement. With the exception of the San Mateo coast and Big Sur, the shoreline south is more heavily populated. Indeed, Spanish California sunk its roots into the soil of the Monterey Peninsula, and the Latin character remains to this day.

Painted by summer sunshine, Monterey and Santa Cruz are among California's most popular beach resorts. The communities draw of thousands of visitors, and are particularly crowded on weekends. Fog is a frequent visitor, but the sun generally emerges shortly after lunch.

That sunny-foggy blend is ideal for a variety of row crops and several coastal communities between San Francisco and Monterey claim agricultural superlatives. Half Moon Bay in San Mateo County boasts of its great pumpkin patches. Farther south, Castroville calls itself the "Artichoke Capital of the World" and nearby Watsonville makes the same claim for strawberries. Inland Gilroy, full of Italians and good humor, is undisputed heir to the garlic crown. It's also one of the state's lesser known producers of premium wines, well worth the short diversion inland.

143

TRIP PLANNER

WHEN TO GO ● The coast south of San Francisco is an all-season area. There's nothing to keep you away except weekend summer crowds. It's prettiest in the spring when wildflowers bloom along the coast, and sunniest in the fall. Snowfall is as rare as a tax cut, so winter is great if you don't mind rain and you like to study a storm-tossed surf.

WHAT TO SEE ● Princeton and Pillar Point Harbor, Santa Cruz Beach Boardwalk and Municipal Pier, tidy little Capitola, Fisherman's Wharf and the Maritime Museum of Monterey, Monterey Bay Aquarium, Pacific Grove Natural History Museum, Pfeiffer Big Sur State Park, Hearst San Simeon State Historical Monument, Mission San Antonio at Fort Hunter Liggett, historic downtown San Juan Bautista, the wineries of Hecker Pass west of Gilroy.

WHAT TO DO ● Poke among tidepools of Fitzgerald Marine Reserve at Moss Beach, walk with the elephant seals at Ano Nuevo State Reserve, drive through the redwoods of inland Santa Cruz County and take a Roaring Camp train ride, walk the Path of History through Monterey State Historic Park, follow the Monterey Peninsula Recreation Trail to Cannery Row, have cocktails at Cannery Row's Outrigger restaurant, do the Pacific Grove beachfront drive and Seventeen Mile Drive, browse Carmel's boutiques, take a picture of Big Sur's Bixby Bridge (everyone else does), tour Point Sur Lighthouse, have a sunset glass of wine at Nepenthe, climb among the pinnacles of Pinnacles National Monument.

Useful contacts

Big Sur Chamber of Commerce, P.O. Box 87, Big Sur, CA 93920; (408) 667-2100.

Cannery Row Promotional District, P.O. Box 9214, Monterey, CA 93942; (408) 373-1902.

Carmel Business Association, P.O. Box 4444, Carmel, CA 93921; (408) 624-2522.

Gilroy Visitors Bureau, 7780 Monterey St., Gilroy, CA 95020; (408) 842-6436.

Monterey Peninsula Visitors & Convention Bureau, 380 Alvarado St., (P.O. Box 1770), Monterey, CA 93940; (408) 649-1770.

Monterey State Historic Park, 210 Olivier St., Monterey, CA 93940; (408) 649-7118 or 649-2836.

Pacific Grove Chamber of Commerce, P.O. Box 167, Pacific Grove, CA 93950; (408) 373-3304.

Salinas Area Chamber of Commerce, 119 E. Alisal St. (P.O. Box 1170), Salinas, CA 93902; (408) 424-7611.

San Juan Bautista Chamber of Commerce, 402-A Third St. (P.O. Box 1037), San Juan Bautista, CA 95045-1037; (408) 623-2454.

Santa Cruz-Monterey area radio stations

KDBQ-FM, 92.7—classic	KQKE-FM, 99.5/99.9—country
KMBY-FM, 107.1—rock	KBAY-FM, 100.3—easy listening
KOLN-FM, 105—rock	KTOM-AM, 1380—country
KTOM-FM, 100.7—country	KIDZ-AM, 540—easy listening
KWAB-FM, 96.9—adult contemporary	KLAU-AM, 1540—classic rock
KSUP-FM, 88.9—Nat'l Public Radio	KIDD-AM, 630—easy listening
KHKN-FM, 104.3—Christian	KSCO-AM, 1080—news & talk
KXTC-FM, 101.7—jazz, easy listening	KQKE-AM, 700—country

SAN FRANCISCO TO SANTA CRUZ

Highway 1, that grand asphalt carpet laid along much of California's coast, gets lost in the urban shuffle of San Francisco.

If you you're crossing the Golden Gate Bridge headed south, you can pick up Route 1 by taking the Park Presidio exit just south of the toll plaza. This landscaped boulevard skims through the **Presidio** and then twists through **Golden Gate Park.** After emerging from the park, the route loses its appeal. It becomes 19th avenue and trudges through a commercial and residential area. To escape a torment of stop lights, turn right onto Lincoln Boulevard just as you leave the park, follow it to the Great Highway at the oceanfront and head south. This blends onto Skyline Boulevard near **Daly City,** as you cross into San Mateo County. Signs will then direct you to Highway 1 and **Pacifica.**

If you're in downtown San Francisco, you can get to this area by heading south on the Bayshore (U.S. 101), and then switching to I-280. Head southwest to Daly City, and follow the Pacifica signs. Both towns are residential fringes of San Francisco, offering little visitor appeal.

Despite the lyrical name, Pacifica is a rather dreary place—a collective string of coastal communities known mostly for their fog. Seaward views can be impressive on sunny days, however. Residents prove their sunny dispositions by staging the annual Pacific Coast Fog Fest every September. If you'd like to enter a fog-calling contest or sip assorted versions of fog cutters, call (415) 346-4446.

The area also offers some attractive beach areas, wedged among coastal houses, service stations and fast food parlors. **Sharp Park State Beach,** where the Pacifica Pier stretches into the sea, is a good whale watching spot. To reach it, go seaward on Paloma Avenue. Just to the south, **Rockaway Beach** offers a rare black sand strand in a rocky cove. It's reached from the town of the same name—the southernmost of the Pacifica community complex.

Below Rockaway, civilization suddenly surrenders to a rocky, near-wilderness shoreline. The highway is chiseled out of steep headlands, offering dizzying views of seastacks and surf. Sections here are often blocked by slides and washouts, so avoid taking this route during a major storm. The name of a particularly notorious sections speaks for itself: **Devil's Slide.**

Nearly 20 miles of San Mateo County's 50-mile coastline is protected in **San Mateo Coast State Beach,** a string of strands offering picnicking, tidepooling, surf fishing and clamming (415-728-7177). Like those to the north, these are mostly bundling and strolling beaches. Chilly water, a hostile surf and nasty riptides discourage swimming. The area is popular with wet-suited surfers and windsurfers.

Pressing southward from Pacifica, you'll shortly encounter **Montara State Beach.** It's near the tiny town of that name, with family sunbathing at the south end and a total tanning beach at the north side. It's an attractive little beach, protected by rocky seacliffs. To reach it, take Second Street down from the town.

The **Point Montara Lighthouse** at 16th Street and Highway 1 has been restored and converted to a hostel, with overnight lodgings budget priced at $12, or $9 for American Youth Hostel members; family rooms are $5 extra. For details and reservations, essential on weekends, contact Point

Montara Lighthouse AYH-Hostel, 16th Street at Highway 1, Montara, CA 94037; (415) 728-7177.

☺ **Moss Beach,** the next town down the coast, is a little gem of a place. Its wind-graced homes are tucked beneath protective cypress and eucalyptus, perched atop 80-foot headlands. Much of its beachfront is within **Fitzgerald Marine Reserve,** one of the largest intertidal reefs in California. It extends along the base of the Moss Beach bluffs, stretching south to Pillar Point. To reach this beach, turn seaward onto California Avenue and follow it to a parking area. Operated by the San Mateo County Parks Department, the marine reserve's interpretive center has a couple of exhibits, with a picnic area nearby; (415) 728-3584. Trails lead down to the beach and up to a cypress grove on the bluffs.

Although Moss Beach is more of a residential cluster than a town, it does offer one restaurant worthy of pause. Nearby are paths leading to a section of the marine reserve. To reach the café, turn left from Highway 1 onto Cypress Avenue and follow the signs:

☺ **Moss Beach Distillery** • ΔΔΔ $$$

Marine Boulevard; (415) 728-5595. American-continental; full bar service. Monday-Friday from 5, Saturday from 2 and Sunday brunch from 11. Major credit cards. Handsome restaurant in an old Spanish colonial style Prohibition speakeasy, perched atop a seacliff. No longer a distillery, it serves a good assortment of seafood, Italian fare, chicken, steaks and lamb. The dining room, cocktail lounge and outdoor patio offer fine ocean views.

As you press southward, your eyes will be drawn to **Pillar Point,** a bold coastal promontory with a giant radar dish sitting atop. Part of a

San Mateo to Santa Cruz

Pacifica
Sharps Park Beach
101
San Bruno
380
S.F. Intl. Airport
Gray Whale Cove St. Beach
280
Montara
Moss Beach
San Mateo
Jms. V. Fitzgerald Marine Res.
1
92
101
Half Moon Bay St. Beach
Half Moon Bay
Menlo Park
84
San Gregorio Beach
Pomponio Beach
San Gregorio
Pescadero St. Beach
35
280
Pescadero
Skyline Co. Park
Pebble Beach
Pescadero Creek Co. Park
Stevens Creek Co. Park
Bean Hollow Beach
Saratoga
1
Butano St. Park
Sanborn Skyline Co. Park
Los Gatos
9
9
Big Basin St. Park
17
Ano Nuevo St. Res.
Boulder Creek
Ben Lomond
Davenport
Felton
Scotts Valley
Natural Bridges St. Beach
Santa Cruz
Forest of Nisene Marks St. Park
Twin Lakes St. Beach
Capitola St. Beach
Capitola
New Brighton St. Beach
Seacliff St. Beach
Aptos
Manresa St. Beach
1
Sunset St. Beach
Watsonville

U.S. Air Force tracking facility, it's closed to the public, but the hamlet at its feet is certainly worth a pause.

☺ **Princeton** is a Cape Cod copycat wrapped around nautically attractive Pillar Point Harbor, just south of the radar installation. A short, landscaped boulevard leads through the small community. However, Princeton's prim look is mostly a façade. Travel behind the landscaped harbor, shops and restaurants and you're in a scruffy clutter of boat yards and somewhat seedy homes. A fine tidepool beach is just beyond, noted for its mussel beds. The northern part of the beach beyond Pillar Point is part of the marine reserve, so mind the signs if you're going mussel collecting. To reach this beach, turn right onto Broadway, go immediately left onto Harbor, follow it until you bump into West Point and go around to your right. Stop just short of the radar facility, find a place to park and walk out to the tidepools.

Incidentally, this small town offers a pair of descent seafood restaurants:

Barbara's Fish Trap ● △ $$
Capistrano Road; (415) 728-7079. Seafood; wine and beer. Daily 11 to 9, until 9:30 Friday-Saturday. No credit cards. Charmingly funky cafè offering inexpensive seafood and nice harbor views. Outdoor dining on a deck over the water.

Shorebird Restaurant ● △△ $$$
Capistrano road; (415) 728-5541. Seafood; full bar service. Monday-Friday 11:30 to 3 and 5:30 to 9:30, Saturday 11 to 3 and 5 to 10, Sunday 10 to 2 and 5 to 9. MC/VISA. It's a classier place than the Fish Trap, although views are not as nice, since it's across the road from the harbor. The cafè has a stylish Cape Cod look and the menu features the usual fresh fish dishes, plus specialties such as salmon Princeton with tomatoes and basil, and prawns Dijon.

Below Princeton, the headlands surrender to a coastal plain that nurtures artichokes, Brussels sprouts and pumpkin patches. They surround a town that, despite its aquatic name, is mostly inland:

Half Moon Bay

Population: 8,900   **Elevation: 69 feet**
An old farming community originally called Spanishtown, Half Moon Bay is working to preserve its false front downtown area. To visit this agreeable collection of shops and antique stores, go east onto Highway 92 at the Highway 1 traffic signal, then turn right onto Main Street.

Cavanaugh Gallery at 415 Main is particularly appealing, offering a good selection of folk art. The town also has a fine place to dine and sleep:

☺ **San Benito House ● △△△ $$$ Ø**
356 Main St., Half Moon Bay, CA 94019; (415) 726-3425. American-continental; wine and beer. Dinner Thursday-Sunday 6 to 8:30, Sunday brunch 10:30 to 1:30. MC/VISA, AMEX. Very nice 19th century style restaurant and B&B in a white and gray Victorian with cheerful window boxes. Parlor dining room and garden patio. Menu offerings include filet of beef with wild mushroom sauce, and salmon with sweet red pepper and onion relish. Rooms, nicely done in European and American antiques, are $55 to $112 per couple with some private and some share baths; full breakfast included.

If you continue inland on Highway 92, you'll pass through an bucolic land of nurseries, Christmas tree farms and pumpkin patches. The annual

Half Moon Bay Art and Pumpkin Festival is held here every October. Visitors can sample every conceivable pumpkin-inspired delicacy and watch novice and advanced jack-o-lantern carvers at work. The **Chamber of Commerce** at 514 Main Street has the details; (415) 726-4841.

So much for bucolic Half Moon Bay. Where's the beach? From the highway, follow either Beach Avenue or Poplar Street about half a mile to **Half Moon Bay State Beach**. This level strand stretches for several miles along the concave shoreline that gave Half Moon Bay its name. Campsites with flush potties and showers are $12; they can be reserved through Mistix, (800) 444-PARK.

Half Moon Bay's suburbs and farmlands extend southward for several miles, then the headlands return to crowd Highway 1 tight against the ocean. **San Gregorio State Beach** occupies an attractive cove at the mouth of San Gregorio Creek. Turn inland and you'll shortly encounter the tiny town of the same name.

☺ The 1889 **San Gregorio General Store,** housed in an attractively scruffy Spanish colonial structure, has found its niche between the 19th and 20th centuries. Its floor-to-ceiling shelves are laden with tie-dyed T-shirts, whole earth breads, cast iron pots, coal oil lanterns, western wear and books on poetry, new age, natural sciences and "environmental politics." You can get international beers, home made sandwiches and pastries at the old fashioned bar, along with "advice, weather analysis and bull----."

A few miles south, also in from the highway, is **Pescadero.** Not much bigger than San Gregorio, it's worth a pause for the startling selection of fresh baked breads, from garlic-herb sourdough to Italian sesame wreath, at **Norm's Market**. This all-purpose grocery has been in the same family since 1929.

Eight miles south, you'll see **Pigeon Point Lighthouse,** offering economy accommodations at a hostel in former Coast Guard quarters. For information and reservations contact Pigeon Point Lighthouse AYH Hostel, Pigeon Point Road at Highway 1, Pescadero, CA 94060 (415) 879-0633. Lodgings are $12 per person and $9 for American Youth Hostel members; $5 extra for family units. The lighthouse has been automated, although it's still using its antique multi-faceted Fresnel lens. Tours are generally on Sundays at 10, 11:15, 12:30 and 3. Call the hostel for confirmation.

A few miles below is a place where nearly half a million people sign up each year to watch nature's ugliest sea mammals practice unsafe sex:

☺ ***Ano Nuevo State Reserve*** ● *C/o San Mateo Coast District, 95 Kelly Ave., Half Moon Bay, CA 94109; (415) 879-0595. Reserve open daily 8 to sunset, visitor center 8 to 5. Entrance fee $4. Elephant seal tours from December through March, $4 plus credit card surcharge. Tours should be reserved well in advance through Mistix, (800) 444-PARK. Weekend reservations are very difficult to obtain. However, you might be able to pick up a no-show ticket if you stop by the reserve.*

Ano Nuevo is an uptilted coastal shelf of mudstone formed of clay, silt and silica that extends into the Pacific just above the Santa Cruz County line. It was named for the day on which it was sighted by Spanish navigator Sebastian Viscaino—New Year's Day, 1603. A large herd of northern elephant seals has chosen this place to haul out and make whoopee during their December to March mating season. About 400,000 people a year come to watch the action.

Although they're graceful at sea and capable of diving 3,000 feet, they're among nature's most ungainly and comical creatures on land. The males, resembling giant slugs with long, floppy snouts, begin wriggling ashore in November. Emitting snorting bellows that sound like two cylinder tractors, these two-ton Tonys spend the winter fighting for the privilege of fornicating. The dominate alpha bulls, having intimidated less aggressive suitors, mate with a harem of females, who are one-third their size.

During the mating season, rookery tours are given by trained volunteers. They'll volunteer more information than you probably ever wanted to know about elephant seals. At other times, you can pick up a pass at the visitor center to visit the elephant seal area. There isn't much activity then, although some critters come ashore from late spring through summer to molt. Keep a safe distance between yourself and these funny looking creatures. There's nothing funny about two tons of snorting seal sitting on your chest.

The elephant seal show at Ano Nuevo is a relatively recent spectacle. Prized for their blubber, they were hunted to near extinction in the last century, and eliminated from the California coast. In 1922, the Mexican government gave protective status to the last surviving herd of fewer than 100 seals. The beasts slowly recovered from extinction's brink and some began moving north to settle on California beaches. The United States has joined Mexico in giving them protective status. A few arrived at Ano Nuevo Island offshore of the present sanctuary in 1955. The first pup wasn't born onshore until 1975. Now, as many as 2,000 sea slugs a year spend their winters here. Others haul ashore farther north, although Ano Nuevo is the only California sanctuary with visitor access.

South of Ano Nuevo, the headlands dissolve to make room for Santa Cruz County's thousands of acres of artichoke and Brussels sprout fields. Among them is an historic agricultural preserve:

Wilder Ranch State Park ● *Highway 101, Santa Cruz; (408) 688-3241. Park open daily 10 to 4; $6 per car.* Acquired in 1974 but not opened to the public until 1989, Wilder Ranch covers 2,800 acres of shoreline and inland forests. Focal point is Rancho del Matadero, a 22-acre cultural preserve containing 19th century farm houses, a Mexican adobe and some Native American shell mounds. Over time, this former dairy farm will be restored to reflect its original use, with live animals and functioning workshops. For the moment, you can stroll through some buildings and peek into others.

Santa Cruz

Population: 49,000   **Elevation: 20 feet**

Founded as a Spanish mission settlement in 1871, Santa Cruz is a tough little town that has learned hard lessons of survival. The name, incidentally, means "sainted cross." Despite this holy name, the mission collapsed in an 1857 earthquake and was abandoned. However, this south facing slice of Monterey Bay provided good ship shelter and a trading center developed.

By the turn of the century, Santa Cruz was Northern California's most popular beach resort, since its southern exposure offers the coast's best weather. Inland redwood logging provided more economic stimulus. Then most of the surviving redwood groves were placed in preserves—thankfully—and the economy nose dived. The town's Coney Island style boardwalk fell into shabby neglect. A few decades ago, Santa Cruz began to right itself again. Investors poured millions into a complete renovation the Boardwalk, creating the most appealing beachfront fun zone on the West Coast. Inland, urban renewalists fashioned a landscaped mall from the frayed downtown business district along Pacific Street. The selection of Santa Cruz for a new campus of the University of California in the 1960s provided added financial stimulus. (The experimentally liberal campus also radically changed the politics of this conservative blue collar town.)

A prosperous Santa Cruz was rolling along in fifth gear when the October, 1989, Loma Prieta earthquake struck. The showplace Pacific Garden Mall was nearly ruined. Tourists, seeing the drama of damage on TV, began staying away, although 97 percent of the town was still intact.

Gradually, perhaps even cautiously, prosperity is finding its way back to Santa Cruz. Business is booming at the Boardwalk and the Pacific Garden Mall is undergoing a multi-million-dollar restoration. Santa Cruz also is growing as a bedroom community for overgrown San Josè, just over the hill. In fact, it's the largest coastal town between San Francisco and Santa Barbara. Many visitors prefer its folksy appeal to the smaller, more stylish and more expensive Monterey on the opposite end of the bay.

Doing Santa Cruz

Most of the town's appeal lies in its old fashioned waterfront with its sandy beach, carefully maintained Santa Cruz Beach Boardwalk and adjacent Municipal Pier. Think of it as a safe, clean Coney Island without the oppressive crowds. Many small motels just up from the Boardwalk offer affordable lodgings. Some are a bit scruffy, although most are well maintained. Newer, more expensive tourist digs are inland, along Highway 1.

The highway turns into a freeway through Santa Cruz, which isn't very interesting, so we'll keep you close to the coast. Before it becomes a freeway, turn right onto Swift Street and follow sings to **Natural Bridges State Beach.** This rocky cove, where waves have battered holes through basaltic ridges, is open from 8 a.m. to sunset. Day use fee is $6 per car. If you just want a brief glimpse of these razorback ridges, you can avoid the entry fee by pausing at a short term parking lot just above the park entrance. Nearby, at the foot of Delaware Street, is the UCSC **Long Marine Laboratory,** with an aquarium and exhibits concerning marine research.

Pick up West Cliff Drive from here and follow it along the town's imposing 80-foot headlands. Stylish homes crowded together for the view are on the inland side of the street, so *your* view is unobstructed. At **Lighthouse Field State Beach,** pause for a visit to the **Santa Cruz Surfing Museum,** occupying an unusual square brick lighthouse. Just beyond is a surfer in bronze, heralding the fact that surfing came here from Hawaii way back in this century. Offshore, you'll likely see their descendants on surfboards and sailboards flirting with waves that crash into the headlands.

West Cliff Drive leads onto Beach Street and the venerable **Santa Cruz Municipal Wharf,** which dates from 1914. You can drive out to check on fish markets and seafood restaurants. The **Santa Cruz Beach Boardwalk** is just beyond, so this is a good time to park and start walking. Good luck on finding a parking place on summer weekends. Take plenty of quarters, since one buys you only 20 minutes.

RV advisory: All-day parking for RVs and trailers is available for $7 on a lot at the south end of Beach Street (at Third). Don't try to get onto the municipal wharf in with a large rig or a trailer.

If you need to get oriented, follow Front Street inland from the wharf and stop at the **Santa Cruz Conference & Visitors Council,** at 701 Front. It's open daily 9 to 5. Pick up, among other things, the "Historic Santa Cruz Walking Tours and Museum Guide" that will take you past some of the town's fine examples of Victorian architecture. A block to the left of the visitor center and parallel to it is the **Pacific Garden Mall.** Several gaping holes remain from earthquake damaged structures that had to be demolished, although much of the mall is intact. You'll find a good selection of restaurants and shops.

To continue your Santa Cruz tour, return to the waterfront, follow Beach Street until it bumps into Third Street and turn inland. To stay close to the beach, go right onto Riverside Avenue, cross the **San Lorenzo River** and swing left onto San Lorenzo Boulevard, which becomes East Cliff Drive. You'll shortly encounter the octagonal brick **Santa Cruz City Museum,** whose exhibits offer a blend of human and natural history.

Beyond the museum, the route is again pushed away from the beach to wrap around **Woods Lagoon,** an estuary containing attractive **Santa Cruz Yacht Harbor.** Turn right onto Lake Street to parallel the harbor, then left to pick up East Cliff Drive again. After a couple of miles, it becomes Opal Cliff Drive and leads you to one of the coast's more charming villages:

Capitola

Population: 10,200   **Elevation: 50 feet**

Dating back to the 1850s, tidy little Capitola was Northern California's first beach resort. During the state's formative years, folks pitched tents and built shanty resorts at "Camp Capitola" along Soquel Creek and on the ocean bluffs above. The name was inspired by wishful thinking: Promoters felt this would be a proper site for the new state capital.

Inland Capitola is growing rapidly; the county's largest shopping complex is within the city limits. With this economic strength, the town has impeccably maintained its prim 1930s style downtown. Think of it as an unpretentious Carmel, with smart shops, boutiques and galleries.

Beaches here are less crowded than those in Santa Cruz, but only slightly so on sunny summer weekends. A sand bar at the mouth of Soquel Creek gives sun seekers the option of fresh or saltwater swimming at **Capitola City Beach.** A pedestrian path up Soquel Creek provides a nice stroll through a narrow, tree-shaded ravine past creekside homes. If you like sea breezes with your walking, amble onto the 1857 **Capitola Wharf.** At its base, note the thick-troweled stucco cottages of the multi-colored **Capitola Venetian Hotel.** Started in 1923 as the Venetian Court, it's listed on the National Register of Historic Places as America's first beachside condo (see lodgings below). Just beyond Capitola are two state beaches, **New Brighton** and **Seacliff,** both offering camping, picnicking and beach play. New Brighton occupies wooded bluffs above the surf, while Seacliff sits at waters edge. Day use at each is $6; camping details are listed below.

Attractions
(In order of appearance)

Joseph M. Long Marine Laboratory ● *Foot of Delaware Avenue near Natural Bridges; (408) 459-2883. Tuesday-Sunday 1 to 4. Free; donations appreciated.* This UCSC research facility offers a small aquarium, hands-in tidepool, dolphin tanks and assorted marine life exhibits. The skeleton of an 85-foot blue whale is rather imposing.

Santa Cruz Surfing Museum ● *West Cliff Drive at Lighthouse Point; (408) 429-3429. Wednesday-Monday noon to 4; free.* Opened in 1986 as the word's first surfing museum, this archive traces the evolution of the surfboard, wetsuits and other water play gear. Check out the 15-foot 100-pound surfboard made of redwood. You can understand why those Hawaiian princes who developed the sport were so hefty.

Santa Cruz Municipal Wharf ● *Off Beach Street; (408) 429-3628. Daily 5 a.m. to 2 a.m.* Stroll out to the end of this fine old pier to commiserate with seagulls and perhaps drop a fishing line or crab net into the briny. Unfortunately, most of the old fish markets have been replaced by curio shops and seafood restaurants. A few commercial fishing boats still operate out of here. It's also the place to catch party boats and whale watching cruises.

☺ **Santa Cruz Beach Boardwalk** ● *400 Beach St.; (408) 423-5590. Coconut Grove events (408) 423-2053. Daily from 11 a.m. in summer, weekends only the rest of the year. Boardwalk admission free, unlimited ride tickets $16.95, individual rides $1.35 to $2.70.* Dating from 1907, it's California's only surviving beach fun zone, and probably the cleanest and best run beach amusement park in the country. Climb aboard the 1924 Giant Dipper roller coaster, rated among the nation's scariest, and the classic 1911 Charles Looff carousel. Both are national historic landmarks. The imposing **Coconut Grove** ballroom which once hosted Harry James, the Dorsey Brothers, Glenn Miller and other big band giants, has been faultlessly restored. You can dance again to those swingin' years sounds or enjoy a huge Sunday brunch under its massive greenhouse roof. Other Boardwalk attractions include a giant Ferris wheel that suspends you high above the beach, bumper cars, shooting galleries, a sky ride, large indoor miniature golf course, modern video games and an old fashioned penny arcade. You don't even have to spend a penny. Just stroll along this glittery, noisy fun zone and enjoy the good vibes of a more innocent era.

Santa Cruz City Museum ● *1305 East Cliff Dr.; (408) 429-3773. Tuesday-Saturday 10 to 5 and Sunday noon to 5. Donations appreciated.* It's old fashioned and maybe a tiny bit musty, but this is an interestingly varied museum. Exhibits range from area natural history and artifacts of the Ohlone Indians who were obliterated by the whites to the contemporary history of Santa Cruz, its beaches, Boardwalk, wharf and mission. The unusual brick octagon building itself is worth a look.

OTHER PLACES, OTHER ATTRACTIONS

Several other lures, although difficult to link together in a logical driving tour, are worth a stop. Start with the campus of the **University of California at Santa Cruz**, perched on a sloping moor with imposing ocean views. Its various colleges are scattered over this hillside, some on open headlands and others tucked into redwood groves. To reach it, follow Bay Street from downtown; it becomes Glen Coolidge Drive as it curves onto the campus.

If you loop the campus, you'll wind up on Empire Grade, which becomes High Street. Follow it back toward town, under the freeway to **Mission Santa Cruz** at High and Emmett streets. Unfortunately, little survives of the original mission, although you can step into a half scale model, now a chapel and gift shop. It's open daily 9 to 5; (408) 426-5686. The adjacent **Holy Cross Church** is an imposing structure, with vaulted arch ceilings and stained glass windows.

Antonelli's Begonia Garden is a perennial favorite for flower lovers, particularly in spring when it's bursting with begonia, rhododendron, azalea and other blooms. This huge nursery is a bit tatty, but you'll hardly notice during flowering season. It's at 2545 Capitola Road, open daily 9 to 5; (408) 475-5222.

Beaches are abundant in and about Santa Cruz. Expect cheek-to-cheek sunbathers on the popular strand adjacent to the Boardwalk. **Lighthouse Field State Beach** and **Cowell Beach** southwest of the pier are less crowded. At **Natural Bridges State Beach,** you can see trees laden with monarch butterflies from fall through spring. There's a heavy penalty for molesting them. Those inclined to skinny dip will not feel out of place at **Red, White and Blue Beach** south of **Davenport,** a small hamlet a bit north of Santa Cruz.

Most county residents live along a narrow coastal fringe. Much of the inland area is mountainous, with redwood groves and funky little towns such as **Felton, Ben Lomond, Boulder Creek** and **Bonny Doon.** They attract city weary refugees and back-to-nature dropouts. An inland tour will deliver you to other county lures, including lush redwood parks. For a scenic sampler, you can attempt to follow "Tree and Sea Tour" signs through the area. However, you have to stay alert, because the route involves some quick turns. Further, folks with a twisted sense of humor occasionally remove them. Highway 9 winds through the county's outback, offering quick relief from busy Santa Cruz. To reach it, head north on Front Street, which becomes River Street. You shortly shed the city and enter darkened redwood groves. A pair of redwood parks and an historic train ride await you:

Henry Cowell Redwoods State Park • *Felton; (408) 335-4598. Day use $5, camping listed below.* Sheltering some fine groves of big trees, it offers a nature center and gift shop, several miles of hiking trails, picnic areas and a large campground.

☺ *Big Basin Redwoods State Park* • *Northwest Santa Cruz County; (408) 338-6132. Day use $5, camping listed below.* Big Basin is the big daddy of area parks, in both size and age. Alarmed by rampant logging, several conservationists formed the Sempervirens Club and deeded 3,800 acres of redwoods to California in 1902. It was to become the first unit of the state park system. In the passing years, another 15,000 acres have been added. This richly endowed preserve features dozens of miles of hiking trails, darkened canyons of redwoods and Douglas fir, seasonal streams, waterfalls and breezy beaches. The park's developed end, skirted by State Highway 236, offers RV and tent sites, tent cabins, a store and gift shop. Folks averse to such conveniences can find six hike-in campgrounds away from the crowds.

☺ *Roaring Camp & Big Trees Railroad* • *Graham Hill Road, Felton; (408) 335-4400. Several departures daily in summer; less frequently in the off-season. Adults $11.15, kids $8.15. Major credit cards.* This narrow gauge railway takes visitors a-winding through the redwoods in open rail cars, departing from "Roaring Camp," which is a mockup of a frontier town. You can picnic on the grounds or dine at a barbecue to the tune of country and western music. Owners recently added a second excursion run, the **Santa Cruz Big Trees and Pacific Railway.** It follows the scenic Lorenzo

River Canyon from Roaring Camp through Henry Cowell Redwoods into Santa Cruz. Fare is $9 for adults and $3 for kids.

Both Henry Cowell and Big Basin are heavily used in summer, so expect crowds, and make campsite reservations as early as possible. Those seeking more solitude should seek out the **Forest of Nisene Marks State Park,** reached via Aptos Creek Road north of Aptos. It's a forest of second growth redwoods, offering a picnic area at road's end, and miles of hiking trails leading to remote pack-in campgrounds. The park also contains a new and rather disturbing marker: ground zero for the 1989 Loma Prieta earthquake that shook Northern California to its foundations. A two-mile trail leads to the spot, where fallen redwoods mark those few brief seconds of violence. For trail maps and hike-in campsite reservations, check with the regional state parks office at 7500 Soquel Dr., Aptos, CA 95003; (408) 688-2341.

Several **wineries** are tucked into the county's hilly uplands and the Santa Cruz Conference and Visitors Council can point you in their direction. Three wineries have tasting rooms in or about town. **Storrs Winery** is in the Old Sash Mill shopping center at 303 Potrero Street in Santa Cruz; (408) 458-5030. It's open from noon to 5, daily except Wednesday in summer and weekdays only the rest of the year. Long established **Bargetto Winery,** noted for both fruit wines and premium varietals, is perched above a wooded creek at 3535 Main Street in nearby Soquel; (408) 475-2258. Hours are Monday-Saturday 9:30 to 5 and Sunday noon to 5. Nearby, tucked into the hills at the end of Park Avenue in Soquel, is **Devlin Wine Cellars**; (408) 476-7288. It's open weekends noon to 5.

ACTIVITIES
(In Santa Cruz unless indicated otherwise)

Boat and yacht rentals ● Chardonnay Sailing Charters, 400 Beach St., (408) 423-1213; Pacific Yachting, 333 Lake Ave., (408) 476-2370; Santa Cruz Marine, 523 Seventh Ave., (408) 475-4600.

Bicycle rentals ● Dutchman Bicycles, 3961 Portola Dr., (408) 476-9555; Surf City Cycles, 1211 Mission St., (408) 426-7299; Surf City Rentals, 46 Front St., (408) 423-9050 or 426-7299.

Bicycle touring ● Santa Cruz County Cycling Club, 414 Soquel Ave.; (408) 423-0829.

Farmers' markets ● Downtown Farmers' Market held Wednesdays at the corner of Cathcart and Pacific in Santa Cruz; (408) 429-8433. Monterey Bay Area Farmers' Market happens on a Cabrillo College parking lot in Aptos Saturdays from 8 to noon; (408) 423-7308.

Fishing and whale watching charters ● Capitola Boat and Bait, 1400 Wharf Rd., Capitola, (408) 462-2208; Shamrock Charters, Municipal Wharf, 476-2648; Stagnaro's Fishing Trips, Municipal Wharf, 425-7003.

Roller skate rentals ● Go Skate Surf and Sport, 601 Beach St.; (408) 425-8578.

Kayak tours and lessons ● Kayak Connection, 413 Lake Ave., (408) 479-1121; Kayak Shack, Municipal Wharf, (408) 429-5066, Venture Quest, 931 Pacific Ave., (408) 427-2267.

Parasailing ● Pacific Parasail, Municipal Wharf; (408) 423-3545.

Scuba lessons and diving trips ● Adventure Sports Unlimited, 303 Potrero St., Suite 15, (408) 458-3648; Scubaventures, 2222 East Cliff Dr., (408) 476-5201.

ANNUAL EVENTS

(Call the Convention & Visitors Council at (800) 833-3494 or (408) 425-1234 for details.)

Vintners Passport, tour of county wineries in January.

Spring Wildflower Show, April in Santa Cruz.

Bluegrass Festival, May in Felton.

Shakespeare Santa Cruz, August theater festival.

1907 Week, August, celebrating old time days at the Santa Cruz Boardwalk.

National Begonia Festival, a major celebration with boat floats on Soquel Creek, September in Capitola.

Welcome Back Monarch Day marking the return of the butterflies to Santa Cruz in October.

Fungus Fair featuring growths from the wilds, December, Santa Cruz.

WHERE TO DINE
Santa Cruz

Anna Maria's Italian Restaurant ● ∆∆ $$

Municipal Wharf; (408) 458-9534. Italian and American; full bar service. Lunch and dinner daily from 11. Major credit cards. Occupying a prime spot at the end of the pier, this modern, attractive place offers the usual Italian fare plus a good seafood selection. To work up an appetite for chicken Milanese or fresh filet of sole, try Sex on the Beach. Put down the phone, lady; it's a drink with vodka, raspberry and melon liqueur and cranberry juice.

Benten ● ∆∆ $$

1541 Pacific Garden Mall; (408) 425-7079. Japanese; wine and beer. Lunch 11:30 to 2 weekdays, 12:30 to 4:30 weekends; dinner 5:30 to 8 weekdays, 4:30 to 9:30 weekends. MC/VISA. Bright, clean little place with blonde woods and a few Asian lanterns. In addition to the usual teriyaki and tempura things, it offers a complete sushi bar. It's relatively inexpensive for a Japanese place, with several dinners under $10.

Crow's Nest ● ∆∆ $$$

2218 East Cliff Drive (at Santa Cruz Yacht Harbor); (408) 476-4560. American; full bar service. Lunch and dinner daily from 11. Major credit cards. Large, nautically stylish place with views of the small craft harbor and ocean; outdoor dining. Offerings include fresh fish, several Mexican specials, the usual steaks, chickens and chops, plus an oyster bar and salad bar.

☺ Palomar Restaurant ● ∆∆∆ $$$

1344 Pacific Garden Mall; (408) 425-7575. Spanish-Mexican; full bar service. Lunch and dinner Monday-Saturday from 11, Sunday brunch from 10. MC/VISA. Exceptionally attractive Spanish colonial style restaurant with arched decorative ceiling, potted urns and plush booths. The menu rises above smashed beans and rice to offer sautéed prawns with red bell pepper and chili butter and red snapper topped with tomatillo sauce.

Georgiana's Café ● ∆ $

1522 Pacific Garden Mall; (408) 427-9900. Espresso bar; wine and beer. Daily 7:30 a.m. to 10 p.m. Nice place to start the day or grab a quick lunch. Snack indoors or outdoors on salads, sandwiches, soups, espresso bar or bakery goods, including great sticky buns. Bookshop Santa Cruz is adjacent.

Miramar Restaurant ● ∆∆∆ $$$ Ø
Municipal Wharf; (408) 423-4441. American, mostly seafood; full bar serv-ice. Monday 4:30 to 9:30, Tuesday-Thursday 11:30 to 9:30, Friday 11:30 to 10, Saturday 10:30 to 10:30, Sunday 11 to 9:30. MC/VISA. Longtime wharf fixture with simple, stylish dècor and fine nautical views through floor-to-ceiling glass walls. Creative offerings include prawns picata, snapper Dijon and oysters Lyonnaise (lightly breaded and pan fried with sautèed onions).

Riva Fish House ● ∆∆ $$
Municipal Wharf; (408) 429-1223. American, mostly seafood; wine and beer. Lunch and dinner daily from 11. No credit cards. There's nothing fancy about this simple cafè with folding chairs, but neither are the prices. Try the Portuguese shark or Creole linguine for around $10. Fish and chips or fried calamari provide a bargain fill-up for less than $6.

Santa Cruz Brewing Company ● ∆∆ $
516 Front St.; (408) 429-8838. Brewpub; beer and wine. Daily from 11:30. MC/VISA. Attractive microbrewery done with exposed beam ceilings and light oak trim. The fare is a mix of American brewpub and English pub—plowman's lunch, calamari, beer ribs and turkey *speidies* (charbroiled chunks marinated in herb garlic vinaigrette). You can watch the beer brew-ing kettles through a viewing window.

Sea Cloud ● ∆∆∆ $$$ Ø
Municipal Wharf; (408) 458-9393. American, mostly seafood; full bar serv-ice. Lunch 11:30 to 2:30, dinner nightly from 5. MC/VISA, AMEX. Nautical polished wood place with ocean views and California *nouveau* entrèes on the menu. Try warm salad of confit of duck, sautèed tiger shrimp or Mon-terey Bay red snapper with black beans and sautèed greens.

Capitola

☺ Coyote Café Taqueria ● ∆∆ $
201 Esplanade; (408) 479-4695. Mexican; wine and beer. Sunday-Thurs-day 11 to 9, Friday-Saturday 11 to 10. MC/VISA. One of our favorite places in this area. Mexican family owned and locally popular, it serves excellent fare at reasonable prices, including savories such as shrimp ceviche tostada and prawn tacos. The look is Mexican nautical rustic, with high arched win-dows for ocean views and an outdoor deck right over the beach.

Margaritaville ● ∆∆ $$
221 Esplanade; (408) 476-2263. Mexican; full bar service. Lunch and din-ner daily, weekend brunch. MC/VISA, AMEX. We usually ignore franchise places, but this one occupies a fine location, with beach views and indoor-outdoor dining. The look is canned-Margaritaville-Mexican, and the place does tasty *fajitas* in addition to the usual tortilla-wrapped things.

Sea Bonne ● ∆∆∆ $$$ Ø
231 Esplanade; (408) 462-1350. Continental-American; wine and beer. Dinner nightly. MC/VISA, AMEX. Very cozy dining room with an aquatic New England look, done in soft silver and blue. The creative kitchen issues mostly seafood, including steamed manila clams, seafood pasta, and shrimp stuffed with crab meat. Indoor and outdoor dining.

☺ Shadowbrook ● ∆∆∆∆ $$$$ Ø
1750 Wharf Rd., (408) 475-1511. American-continental; full bar service. Dinner week nights from 5:30, weekends from 4:30, Sunday brunch from 10.

Major credit cards. It may be a gimmick, but it's a delightful one. Catch a funicular down to this rustic, immaculately kept restaurant tucked into a lushly landscaped terrace over Soquel Creek. Pause on the terrace for cocktails, then adjourn to one of several small dining rooms. The fare is innovative and often excellent, from charbroiled swordfish with lime marinade and mango salsa to blackened tenderloin of lamb.

Wharf House ● ∆∆ $$
Capitola Wharf; (408) 476-3534. American, mostly seafood; full bar service. Breakfast and lunch 8 to 3, dinner nightly from 5. MC/VISA. Typical net and glass float décor with a menu to match. Try Cajun blackened snapper or calamari steak with Dijon sauce while enjoying the coastal view. A specialty is Caribbean jerk chicken, grilled and served with salsa and avocado.

WHERE TO SLEEP
Santa Cruz

Best Western Torch-Lite Inn ● ⌂⌂ $$$ Ø
500 Riverside Ave., Santa Cruz, CA 95060; (800) 528-1234 or (408) 426-7575. Couples $49 to $89, singles $49 to $74. Major credit cards. Well kept 38-room motel with TV, room phones, some kitchens; heated pool, putting green. Adjacent to tennis courts and playground; short walk to beach and Boardwalk.

Candlelight Inn ● ⌂⌂ $$$ Ø
1101 Ocean Ave. (Water Street), Santa Cruz, CA 95060; (408) 427-1616. Couples $48 to $110, singles $35 to $90. Major credit cards. A 42-unit motel with TV movies, phones and room refrigerators; pool. **Bakers Square Restaurant** serves 6 a.m. to midnight; dinners $10 to $15; wine and beer.

Carousel Motel ● ⌂⌂ $$$$ Ø
110 Riverside Ave., Santa Cruz, CA 95060; (408) 425-7090. Couples and singles $49 to $125; rates include continental breakfast. Major credit cards. Nicely maintained 34-unit motel across from the beach and Boardwalk with TV and room phones. All rooms have private balconies or patios.

Casa Blanca Motel ● ⌂⌂⌂ $$$$ Ø
101 Main St. (Beach Street), Santa Cruz, CA 95060; (408) 423-1570. Couples and singles $95 to $195, kitchenettes and suites $145 to $195. Major credit cards. Very nicely located inn with all ocean view rooms; TV, room phones, private balconies or terraces, refrigerators, microwaves and fireplaces. Half a block east of the wharf. **Casablanca Restaurant** serves California cuisine; nightly from 5 and Sunday brunch 9:30 to 2:30; dinners $16 to $26; award winning wine list; full bar service.

Dream Inn ● ⌂⌂⌂ $$$$$ Ø
175 W. Cliff Dr., Santa Cruz, CA 95060; (800) 421-6662 or (408) 426-4330. Couples $165 to $255, singles $159 to $255. Major credit cards. The town's only beachfront hotel, with 164 nicely appointed rooms, many with ocean views; balconies or patios. TV movies, room phones and refrigerators. Pool, sauna and spa. **Dining Room** and coffee shop serve 6:30 a.m. to 10 p.m.; dinner $13 to $24; full bar service.

The Inn at Pasatiempo ● ⌂⌂⌂ $$$$ Ø
555 Highway 17 (Pasatiempo Drive), Santa Cruz, CA 95060; (800) 834-2546 or (408) 423-5000. Couples $89 to $99, singles $84 to $94, suites $155 to $175. Major credit cards. Nicely landscaped 54-room with TV, room

phones and mini-bars; refrigerators and spa tubs in suites. Pool, attractive grounds with a gazebo; adjacent to Pasatiempo Golf Course. **Peachwood's Bar and Grill** serves lunch 11:30 to 2, dinner 5 to 10 and Sunday brunch 10 to 2:30; dinners $10 to $19; full bar service.

Harbor Inn ● △ $ Ø
645 Seventh Ave., Santa Cruz, CA 95062; (408) 479-9731. Couples $35 to $55, singles $25 to $45, kitchenettes $45 to $65, suites $65 to $75; rates include breakfast. Major credit cards. A 19-room inn with rustic antique furnishings, near beach. TV, room phones and refrigerators.

Magic Carpet Motel ● △ $$
130 West Cliff Dr., Santa Cruz, CA 95060; (408) 423-7737. Couples $35 to $125, singles $29 to $95, kitchenettes $45 to $160, suites $65 to $130. Major credit cards. A 30-unit motel adjacent to the municipal wharf; TV movies, room phones; some rooms with ocean views, waterbeds and spas.

Rio Sands Motel ● △△ $$$ Ø
116 Aptos Beach Dr., Aptos, CA 95003; (800) 826-2077 in California only or (408) 688-3207. Couples and singles $69.50 to $89.50, suites $89.50 to $99.50; rates include continental breakfast. MC/VISA, AMEX. Nicely maintained 50-unit motel with TV and room phones; pool. Short walk to the beach.

Riverside Garden Inn ● △△ $$$ Ø
600 Riverside Ave. (Barson Street), Santa Cruz, CA 95060; (800) 527-3833 or (408) 458-9660. Couples and singles $45 to $98, suites $125 to $300. Major credit cards. Well kept 79-unit motel four blocks from the Boardwalk; TV movies, room phones; pool, spas; tennis courts nearby.

St. Charles Court ● △△ $$ Ø
902 Third St., Santa Cruz, CA 95060; 423-2091. Couples $35 to $95, singles $30 to $55, kitchenettes $50 to $135, suites $110 to $145. MC/VISA. A 34-unit motel two blocks from the Boardwalk; TV, pool, some new units.

Bed & breakfast inns

Chateau Victorian ● △△△ $$$$$ Ø
118 First St. (near Cliff and Main), Santa Cruz, CA 95060; (408) 458-9458. From $105 to $135. Seven rooms with private baths; continental breakfast. MC/VISA, AMEX. Turn-of-the-century Victorian within a block of the beach. Handsomely restored with antique furnishings, plush carpeting and color coordinated rooms. Fireplaces in each room.

Cliff Crest Bed & Breakfast Inn ● △△△ $$$$ Ø
407 Cliff St., Santa Cruz, CA 95060; (408) 427-2609. Couples and singles $90 to $140. Five rooms with private baths; full breakfast. MC/VISA. An 1887 Queen Anne with light, air rooms furnished with antiques. Stained glass solarium; elaborate gardens. Short walk to beach; some ocean-view rooms.

Darling House ● △△△ $$$$ Ø
214 West Cliff Dr., Santa Cruz, CA 95060; (408) 458-1958. Couples $95 to $225, singles $60 to $220. Eight rooms; two with private baths; continental breakfast. Major credit cards. Handsome Spanish mission revival home overlooking Monterey Bay; views from the veranda and most rooms. Polished wood interior with open beam; furnished with American antiques. Extensive grounds with roses and citrus trees.

New Davenport Bed & Breakfast ● ⌂⌂ $$$ Ø
31 Davenport Ave. (north of Santa Cruz), Davenport, CA 95017; (408) 425-1818. Couples and singles $60 to $125. Twelve rooms with private baths; continental breakfast or breakfast discount at adjacent restaurant. MC/VISA, AMEX. Former bathhouse enlarged and converted to a comfortable inn; garden; ocean views; beach access across the street. Eclectically furnished with ethnic collectables, antiques and artworks.

Pleasure Point Bed & Breakfast ● ⌂⌂⌂ $$$$
2-3665 East Cliff Dr., Santa Cruz, CA 95062; (408) 475-4657. Couples and singles $95 to $125. Three rooms with private baths; continental breakfast. MC/VISA. A 1940s beachfront home converted to a nautically styled inn; just above the ocean. Some ocean views.

Capitola

Capitola Inn ● ⌂⌂⌂ $$$$ Ø
822 Bay Ave., (Soquel exit) Capitola, CA 95010; (408) 462-3004. Couples $85 to $105, singles $75 to $95, kitchenettes $15 extra, suites $125 to $175. Major credit cards. Very attractive new inn; large rooms with TV movies, room phones, some fireplaces and spa tubs. Swimming pool.

☺ Capitola Venetian Hotel ● ⌂⌂ $$$
1500 Wharf Rd., Capitola, CA 95010; (800) 332-2780 or (408) 476-6471. Kitchenette units from $50 for three to $200 for eight. MC/VISA. Intriguing multi-colored collection of cottages wedged between the beach and the wharf. All units have TV and kitchenettes (no cookware); some suites with fireplaces. Weekly rates from November through April.

Harbor Lights Motel ● ⌂⌂ $$$$
5000 Cliff Dr. (Wharf Road), Capitola, CA 95010; (408) 476-0505. Most units are kitchenettes; couples $70 to $95, suites $125 to $145. MC/VISA, AMEX. Ten-unit motel on the beach; TV, room phones; most rooms with ocean view balconies.

☺ Inn at Depot Hill ● ⌂⌂⌂⌂ $$$$$ Ø
250 Monterey Ave. (Park Avenue exit from Highway 1), Capitola, CA 95010; (408) 462-3376. Couples and singles $155 to $250. Eight rooms with private baths; full breakfast. MC/VISA, AMEX. A luxury resort fashioned from a 1901 railroad depot with each room styled after a country. "Train stops" include Paris, Stratford-on-Avon, Portofino and Cote d'Azur. Units have TV with VCR and stereo, phones and fireplaces; five have patios with hot tubs.

WHERE TO CAMP

Beach RV Park ● *2505 Portola Dr., Santa Cruz, CA 95062; (408) 462-2505. RV sites, full hookups $22. Reservations accepted; MC/VISA.* Small, rather basic park with showers, picnic area, cable TV.

Big Basin Redwoods State Park ● *21600 Big Basin Way, Boulder Creek; (408) 338-6132. RV and tent sites, $14 to $16. Reservations via Mistix, (800) 444-PARK.* Shaded campsites with picnic tables and barbecues; flush potties and showers. Also tent cabins, store and snack bar.

Henry Cowell Redwoods State Park ● *101 N. Big Trees State Park Rd., Felton; (408) 335-4598. RV and tent sites, $14 to $16. Reservations via Mistix, (800) 444-PARK.* Campsites under a mixed conifer and hardwood forest; barbecues and picnic tables. To reach the campground, drive through Felton and go right on Graham Hill Road, past Roaring Camp railroad.

New Brighton State Beach • *1500 Park Ave., Capitola; (408) 688-3241. RV and tent sites, $14 to $16. Reservations via Mistix, (800) 444-PARK.* Attractive tree-shaded sites on a bluff above the beach, some with ocean views. Picnic tables and barbecues. Hiking trails, beach access.

Santa Cruz KOA • *1186 San Andreas Rd., Watsonville, CA 95076. RV and tent sites, $25 to $31, "kamping kabins" $30. Reservations accepted. MC/VISA.* Full service RV resort with pool, spa, mini-mart, playground, coin laundry, rec room, tennis court and bike rentals.

Seacliff State Beach • *Seacliff exit from Highway 1, Aptos; (408) 688-3241. RV sites only, $23. Reservations via Mistix, (800) 444-PARK.* Close together sites right on the beach with full hookups, a rarity for state parks. Visitor center; picnic and swimming areas on adjacent strand.

CAPITOLA TO MONTEREY

Mostly lumpy Santa Cruz County flattens into a broad agricultural flood plain south of Capitola. If you'd like to shed the freeway temporarily, take Larkin Valley Road west and follow signs to **Manresa** and **Sunset** state beaches. This softly rolling terrain, mostly anchored down by agricultural fields, is known as Pajaro Dunes (*pa-JAR-oh*), built up centuries ago by sand from the **Pajaro River**. You may know that nearly all oceanfront sand dunes are formed of river silt, which is emptied into the sea and then swept inland by wind and tides.

Manresa State Beach, a day use area, is tucked between the surf and seaside homes. Head south on San Andreas Road, following signs to **Sunset Beach**. Artichoke, Brussels sprouts, broccoli and strawberry fields are your roadside companions until you reach this low-lying beach behind Pajaro Dunes; (408) 688-3421. Campsites, away from the beach and shaded by sea pines, are $14 to $16, with flush potties, picnic and barbecue tables. Do the Mistix thing for reservations: (800) 444-PARK.

Return to San Andreas Road, go south for two miles and swing east onto Beach Road. (If you miss your turn, you'll dead-end into a Pajaro Dunes housing development.) Beach road takes you back to Highway 1 and into the side door of **Watsonville.** It calls itself the strawberry capital, with the surrounding patches to prove it.

Continuing south on Highway 1, you cross the Pajaro River and slip unnoticed into **Monterey County**. If you'd like to check out **Zmudowski State Beach,** follow signs west, traveling through a tiring series of 90-degree turns that wrap around broccoli patches. There isn't much to the beach, just a bit of sand beyond the dunes, with pit potties, picnic tables and—for a change—no fee for parking.

Back on Highway 1, your next sandy encounter is **Moss Landing State Beach,** which allows overnight parking in self-contained campers and trailers for $7; day use is $2. You'll have to contend with pit potties. The Elkhorn Slough mudflats here are popular for clamming. That immense industrial presence across the slough is the Pacific Gas and Electric Company's Moss Landing generator station.

The town of **Moss Landing** consists mostly of a commercial fishing fleet and a few pleasure craft parked in an Elkhorn Slough marina. The hamlet's small, properly weathered turn-of-the-century business district is just west of the highway. Out toward the marina, **Phil's Fish Market** sells seafood cocktails and chowder to go, along with fresh fish. Just beyond is **April's Moss Landing Social Club,** a scruffily typical waterfront bar with an aquatic Salvation Army décor. You can get light snacks here. Don't trip over any motorcycles on the way out.

This rolling sand dune country continues as you press southward. Here, it's not agricultural fields but tract houses and a large military base that anchor down the silt. **Fort Ord** spreads its tank tracks over thousands of acres, flanked by nondescript towns of **Marina, Seaside** and **Sand City.** These are bedroom communities for the thousands who can't afford housing in next-door Monterey. Collectively, they out-populate their upscale neighbor to the south.

Monterey

Population: 29,410   **Elevation: 25 feet**

As we said before, the Gold Rush created the California which 30 million of us have grown to love, hate and grudgingly support through excess taxation. The state's deepest roots, however, reach back to a tiny mud mission on the shores of Monterey Bay.

Although California's first mission was founded at San Diego in 1769, that was intended merely as a stopover on the long journey north. After spending several months stabilizing this first outpost of Alta California, mission founder Junípero Serra boarded a ship and set sail northward. (See box.) He established his mission headquarters on a crescent bay, which had been praised more than a century earlier by Sebastian Viscaino. The Spanish navigator had spent a month exploring this area in 1602. He noted that a hilly promontory forming the bay was heavily wooded, providing ample game and building material, and that the climate was favorable for settlement.

That promontory, thrusting northwest into the Pacific, is the Monterey Peninsula. It provides an appealing setting for Monterey, Pacific Grove and Carmel, the three upscale communities tucked among its trees. Development was slow in coming, however. Bankrupt Spain couldn't afford to send settlers abroad and the peninsula lay untouched for 168 years after Viscaino's visit.

Father Serra arrived on June 3, 1770, and his Mission San Carlos Borromeo del Rio Carmelo took root. Monterey served as the capital of Spanish and Mexican California for 76 years. When Captain John Drake Sloat sailed into the bay in 1846 to snatch this land from Mexico, it was Alta California's only town of substance, other than Los Angeles. It was thus picked as the site for California's constitutional convention in 1849. However, gold fever was in the air. Shortly after their work was done, convention delegates and many others hurried away to blossoming San Francisco and the gold fields of the Sierra Nevada. San José, not Monterey, was picked as the state's first capital.

At the peak of its Spanish-Mexican period, Monterey never had more than a thousand residents. It had shriveled to a handful when a consumptive Scottish writer named Robert Louis Stevenson arrived in 1879. He wrote:

The town was a place of two or three streets economically paved with sea sand. The houses were, for the most part, built of unbaked adobe brick, many of them old for so new a country. It was a strange thing to lie awake in 19th century America and hear one of those old heart-breaking Spanish love songs, which strikes on the unaccustomed ear as altogether sad.

Another writer in another century, who grew up just over the hill in Salinas, wrote about the simple people of Monterey and its sardine canning industry. John Steinbeck's *Cannery Row, Sweet Thursday* and *Tortilla Flat* thrust Cannery Row into a fame from which it can never recover. Tons of sardines had been hauled from the bay until they were fished out in the middle of this century, sending the area into a serious decline. Today, tourism has replaced those "nets full of silver," yielding considerably more dollars.

Steinbeck reluctantly visited the gentrified waterfront after he had inadvertently made it famous. He commented:

The canneries which once put up a sickening stench are gone, their places filled with restaurants, antique shops and the like. They fish for tourists now, not pilchards, and that species they are not likely to wipe out.

Monterey to Carmel driving tour

Approaching Monterey from the north, pass through Sand City and exit onto Del Monte Avenue at the Pacific Grove sign. After about a mile, turn left onto Camino El Estero and drive a block to the **Visitor Information Center,** open Monday-Saturday 9 to 5 and Sunday 10 to 4. You can gear up for the intensive exploration ahead.

RV advisory: Parking is a tough ticket in Monterey in the summer, and you'll get one if you park illegally. Virtually every street within a reasonable walk of the city's attractions is metered, and spaces for large RVs are scarce. However, several public parking lots do provide RV parking. A brochure called *Smart Parking in Monterey* available at the visitor's center lists these lots. Also, RV parking is available on Cannery Row near Hoffman Street and RV camping is allowed in Veterans Memorial Park at the end of Jefferson Street (see "Where to camp" below).

Our suggested driving route is hardly original; millions have preceded you. However, it will take you past a varying panorama of vistas in Monterey, Pacific Grove and Carmel, including that famous Seventeen Mile Drive. If you're a AAA member, pick up a copy of the *Tour Map of Monterey Peninsula,* which details driving routes and lists dozens of attractions.

Continue along Del Monte Avenue and you'll shortly encounter **Fisherman's Wharf** on your right, in the heart of the downtown area. Much of California's history happened here. The **Presidio of Monterey,** where Father Serra's mission was first established, is just above. It now houses the Defense Language Institute and an interesting **Army Museum.** The mission later was moved to its present site in Carmel.

Commodore Thomas Ap Catsby Jones set foot on the old wharf in 1842 to seize Monterey from the *Californios*, mistakenly thinking that war with Mexico had started. (Communications were rather slow in those days.) He beat an embarrassed retreat. Four years later, after war *had* been declared, Commodore Sloat came ashore at this same spot.

Today, thousands of tourists set foot on the wharf to patronize curio shops, T-shirt parlors and chowder houses. While predictably tacky and groaning under its burden of touristic excess, it still maintains a level of rustic charm. Fortunately, it has been spared the invasion of wax museums and carny rides that have ruined San Francisco's Fisherman's Wharf.

JUNIPERO SERRA: CALIFORNIA SAINT?

He seemed an unlikely candidate for the formidable task before him. Barely five feet tall and asthmatic, Fray Junipero Serra was delegated to hike across the hostile Baja California desert to install a series of missions in the unknown land to the north.

Serra succeeded where sturdier men might have failed. Before his death in 1784 at the age of 71, the frail father established nine such outposts. Credited with planting Spain's imperial roots in Alta California and praised for bringing the Good Word to the heathen, he is now a candidate for sainthood.

If he is canonized, he would become California's first saint, and one of the few from the Western Hemisphere. It's a slow process that can take decades. Every aspect of his life must be checked to see if he is worthy. The ritual began in the 1940s with the examination of his remains at Carmel Mission. A church tribunal convened there again in 1950 to hear testimony from historians. He *is* making progress. In 1988, Pope John Paul II declared him to be blessed, a major step up the ladder to a saintly niche.

However, Candidate Serra is receiving some flak. Some historians point out that his "good works" among Native Americans destroyed their culture. It's well established that the arrival of the Spanish brought degradation and disease to the neophytes. Serra has been accused of being a cruel taskmaster who virtually enslaved the Indians and punished them for trying to flee. It was, in fact, the Indians and not the padres who built the missions.

The Church, not surprisingly, disagrees. "The Indians lent themselves willingly to the padres," says a Carmel Mission brochure. Some historians have suggested that it was the soldiers who abused the Indians; that the padres worked to protect them. It is true that some of the missions, including Carmel, were relocated to distance them from the military presidios.

A man of stature

Whether or not he gets the saintly nod, there's no question that this man of humble stature was a remarkable individual. Born on the island of Majorca in 1713, he entered the priesthood as a teenager and soon became a distinguished university professor. Eager to spread The Word to Spain's outposts, he was dispatched to Mexico in 1749 to work as a missionary among the Indians. Officials, impressed with his hard work and devotion, appointed him as president of the Baja California missions in 1768.

He held that post for less than a year. Concerned about Russian encroachment from the north, Spain decided to establish a chain of missions along Alta California's coast. Father Serra was picked for the job, to be accompanied by Baja governor Don Gaspàr de Portolà.

Bearing the cross and the sword, they set forth with only two reference points to guide them. More than 160 years before, peripatetic Sebastiàn Vizcalno had discovered, named and explored the bays of San Diego and Monterey. His papers, exhumed from musty files, described Monterey as "the best port that could be desired." This would become headquarters for Father Serra's mission chain, with San Diego as an intermediate stop.

Astride a mule, perhaps more resembling Don Quixote's Sancho than *grande presidente* of the Alta California missions, the diminutive friar rode into history. He was accompanied by several other priests, Portolà with a contingent of leather-vested soldiers and a few Indians. Although their party was decimated by disease and hunger and Serra was crippled after a fall from his mule, the group managed to establish a rude stockade on San Diego Bay. Several months later, they pressed on to Monterey and the colonization of California had begun.

The 1827 **Custom House,** oldest public building in California, stands opposite the pier. This and several other structures are part of **Monterey State Historic Park.** These history rich adobes are best explored on foot, since they're all within walking distance and parking is very difficult downtown. If you missed the visitor center off Del Monte Avenue, you can find another one downtown on Alvarado near Franklin, in the Rodrigues-Oslo Adobe; it's open weekdays 8:30 to 5.

Note: Several adobes within the historic park are open by guided tour only, so pick up a *Discover Monterey State Historic Park* brochure, which tells you what to visit when. You may find it difficult to schedule all of them in one day, but then, why rush away from such an interesting area?

The neighborhood's newest attraction is the outstanding **Maritime Museum of Monterey.** It was opened in late 1992 in Stanton Center, perched atop the Lighthouse Avenue tunnel adjacent to the wharf. It replaces the smaller Allen J. Knight Museum. The facility also houses the Monterey State Historic Park Visitor Center.

Once you've done the wharf and downtown area, head for the next bastion of tourist gluttony, **Cannery Row.** If you've found a place to park your rig near Fisherman's Wharf, leave it there. Parking is even more difficult on the "Row." Instead, enjoy a pleasant waterfront stroll along the **Monterey Peninsula Recreation Trail.** Following an old railbed that served the canneries, the walking-biking route runs for several miles along the Monterey-Pacific Grove waterfront. The walk from Fisherman's Wharf to Cannery Row is less than a mile, and the views of the bay are pleasant.

Cannery Row is looking remarkably clean these days. Those who remember the old corrugated cannery buildings may agree with Steinbeck: Gentrification may have eliminated the smell of rotting fish, but it has spoiled the Row's charm. Today's sanitized version with its hotels, boutiques and—good grief—a wax museum, offers little intrigue. However, it *does* offer the outstanding Monterey Bay Aquarium and some splendid views of the bay, along with a pair of good restaurants.

☺ First prize for sterling bay views goes to the **Outrigger Restaurant's** cocktail lounge in the Monterey Canning Company building. Sitting on a slender pier, the lounge offers vistas in both directions from. Go there on a stormy day, pull your chair up to the open fire pit and enjoy the spectacle outside.

This old cannery building also houses several boutiques and shops, tasting rooms of the **Paul Masson** and **Bargetto** wineries and that wax museum. You may choose to ignore Steinbeck's waxen image, although you might enjoy the winery historical exhibits at the Masson tasting room.

First prize for tourist excess goes to the **Edgewater Packing Company,** where plastic horses spin on a large indoor carousel. Within this carnival of chaos, you can have your face placed on a sexy body of your choosing at a computerized video photo gallery, or play tic-tac-toe with a caged chicken.

Cannery Row, now a street name as well as a place, ends at the **Monterey Bay Aquarium**. Swing left away from the waterfront, then go right onto Lighthouse Avenue. (We assume you've retrieved your vehicle. The upcoming Seventeen Mile Drive is a long walk.) After a few blocks, turn right toward the bay and follow Ocean View Boulevard along the beachfront through a the home of the monarch butterfly:

Pacific Grove

Population: 16,100   **Elevation: 55 feet**

Sandwiched between Monterey and Carmel, Pacific Grove is an often overlooked jewel, possessing some of the peninsula's finest beachfront. Considering the traffic jams that assault the other two communities, its residents probably don't mind being overlooked. The town's neighborhoods, predictably upscale, offer a mix of restored Victorians, ordinary but well maintained homes and an occasional beachfront mansion.

Historically, Pacific Grove was rather distant from sometimes unruly Monterey and bohemian Carmel. It was founded in 1875 as a Methodist retreat. It remained dry until 1969—the last California city shun demon rum. Steinbeck, hardly a teetotaler, lived here for a spell, commuting to the wicked back alleys of Cannery Row to carouse and gather material for his books. You can see his vine-entwined house at 147 Eleventh St. It's a private home, not open to the curious.

Pacific Grove's Ocean View Boulevard hugs the bayfront, skimming the edge of **Shoreline Park.** Many people prefer this to the Seventeen Mile Drive. The gently swerving boulevard unveils a panorama of rocky shoreline on one side and elegant homes on the other.

You'll be tempted to stop frequently and step down to the beach—all of it open to the public—to poke about tide pools or have a picnic. Or just sit on one of the many beaches and stare blissfully out to sea. The recreation trail continues along here, so you may want to park and stroll or sprint for a mile or so. Swing inland from the beachfront to visit the excellent **Pacific Grove Museum of Natural History** at Central and Forest Avenues. Then go up Asilomar Boulevard to **Point Pinos Lighthouse Museum.**

☺ Trees along here provide havens for the majestic orange and black **monarch butterflies.** They converge on Pacific Grove and other select spots by the hundreds of thousands each winter after arriving from Canada. It's one of the longest migrations of any bug. Clustering onto cypress, pine and eucalyptus trees, they sometimes completely coat the branches with their folded wings. They return to Canada in the spring to mate and their offspring mysteriously find there way here in the fall. Good places to see these winged wonders are on the **Asilomar Conference Grounds** at the end of Asilomar Avenue, at **Butterfly Grove Inn** at 1073 Lighthouse Avenue, on **Ridge Road** off Lighthouse Avenue and in **George Washington Park**. To reach the park, go east on Sinex Avenue from the conference grounds.

Admire these creatures, but don't touch. There's a thousand dollar fine for molesting a monarch.

Meanwhile, back on Ocean View Boulevard, the route curves around Lighthouse Point, becomes Sunset Drive and passes **Asilomar State Beach.** It swings inland and hits a stop sign at Seventeen Mile Drive. Turn right and head for the Pacific Grove gate of this famous loop.

Seventeen Mile Drive

On rare occasion, the hand of man can do beautiful things to the land—particularly when that hand is holding fistful of dollars. The wealthy have taken the tip of the Monterey Peninsula—already stunningly beautiful with rocky headlands, cypress forests and pristine meadows—and fashioned it into one of the globe's most striking communities. Technically, the town is Pebble Beach. It's rimmed by acclaimed golf courses and homes of the embarrassingly wealthy. The entire peninsula is privately owned. (An international furor ensued a few years ago when Japanese interests bought it, stirring unfounded fears that it would be closed to the public.)

The region's owners are so pleased with their peninsula that they charge $6 a carload just for the privilege of seeing it. (Bikes can enter free; motorcycles are not permitted.) Four gates protect Pebble Beach from those unwilling to pay. Those of us with six dollars in our jeans will be treated to a seventeen-mile saunter past awesome headlands, rocky coves, cypress and eucalyptus forests and exquisitely fashioned homes.

A brochure provided at the gate will tell you what you're seeing. You may want to get your money's worth and do the entire loop (which is precisely 17 miles by our odometer, plus a little extra for access roads). However, the beachside portion offers the finest views; the back nine wanders up through the Del Monte Forest.

Entering via the Pacific Grove gate, you'll pass the sumptuous beachside resort of the **Inn at Spanish Bay,** then begin skirting the shore front. The wealthy landlords have provided frequent turnouts for us envious visitors, and even picnic areas. Don't try pitching your pup tent, however.

Our favorite part of the drive is around Cypress Point, rimmed by a craggy coast and thatched by Crocker Grove, the largest Monterey cypress forest in existence. Just beyond the point stands one of the world's most photographed shrubs, the **lone cypress.** Growing weary with age and all that attention, it's cabled into place and must be fed and watered during the dry season. You can admire it from an elaborate view platform; the tiny peninsula from which it sprouts is off limits.

Beyond this singular cypress, you pass through the exquisite boutique-ridden town of **Pebble Beach,** with its ultra fashionable **Lodge at Pebble Beach** resort. After a two miles or so, you can depart the scenic drive through the Carmel gate or loop up into the highlands.

Carmel

Population: 4,200   **Elevation: 20 feet**

No town on the globe more typifies a love-hate tourist attitude than quaint Carmel-by-the-Sea. While presuming to scorn visitors, it embraces them with capitalistic zeal. Of course, despite what some travel writers infer, cities don't have emotions or personalities, only the people who live in them.

Thus, Carmel's "attitude" depends on whether you're a shopkeeper or a resident who just wants to be left alone.

This is an absolute charmer—a tree-canopied village that slopes gently down to a white sand beach, shaded by wind-bent cypress. This enclave first attracted an artistic-bohemian cult, then the wealthy and finally the tourists. The bohemians and reclusive millionaires succeeded in keeping it quaintly eccentric. The town has no street or house numbers since there's no mail delivery. Further, many residents don't care to advertise their whereabouts. Building codes insist that things be rustic and that signs be simple, with no neon.

This carefully controlled retreat has attracted the likes of Sinclair Lewis, Upton Sinclair and photographer Ansel Adams. It also attracted Clint Eastwood, who sent tremors through the town's artistic soul in the 1980s. He suggested that the place was too conservative, that shopkeepers should have the right to sell ice cream and T-shirts to tourists. Seeing the need for a little economic magnum force, he ran for mayor in 1986 and won easily.

Some have suggested that Clint's brief tenure "ruined" Carmel, giving it a fistful-of-dollars mentality. They say the place is now overrun with tourists and their rag-tag kids, clutching dripping cones of frozen yogurt. In reality, Carmel has been overrun with tourists for decades. When I first visited 30 years ago, downtown Ocean Avenue was lined with boutiques, galleries and restaurants designed to seduce visitors.

It's true that the town is more crowded than ever. What popular California tourist attraction isn't? However, it's still a charming and well-tended village, with no neon and no tacky souvenir shops. Dirty Harry's term of office didn't degrade it all that much. The Establishment's ruckus over his campaign probably attracted more visitors than the right to eat ice cream in public.

Incidentally, you won't have much luck finding a parking place on a summer weekend. To save the frustration, follow our driving route through town, park on the fringe and walk back. Don't tell anyone we suggested this, but shopping centers along Highway 1 have large parking lots, within a mile or so of downtown Carmel.

Enjoy a pleasant stroll through the wooded neighborhoods, or down along the beach. The doll-house sized residences and Hansel and Gretel cottages—many with cutesy names—are quite eye-catching. (Since residents don't have house numbers, they have a penchant for naming their hideaway abodes.)

A geographic note: There are several Carmels. The name was first given to the river running through the valley by Spanish explorer Sebastian Viscaino. Father Serra named the mission for St. Charles Borromeo of the Carmelite order. Today's incorporated Carmel covers less than a square mile, surrounded by a larger unincorporated area. (You can tell you've left the real Carmel when the house numbers begin.) South of town, off Highway 1 beyond Point Lobos, is the ultra-luxurious Carmel Highlands. Inland is the upscale Carmel Valley with its tennis resorts and posh ranch homes.

Doing Carmel

Leaving the Seventeen Mile Drive, you'll emerge onto San Antonio Road. Drive about three blocks to a stop sign and turn left up Ocean Avenue. Follow it through Carmel's quaint commercial district to Highway 1, then turn around and take Ocean down to the beach. Follow aptly named Scenic Road along the dazzling white sand of **Carmel Beach City Park**, with views filtered through bonsai shapes of cypress.

Near Scenic Road's juncture with Stewart Way, glance uphill to the bold stone **Tor House** and **Hawk's Tower** on Ocean View Avenue. They were built of beach stones in the 1920s by reclusive California poet Robinson Jeffers. Don't let your curiosity become too obtrusive, since his descendants still occupy the place. However, tours can be arranged with advanced notice. See "Attractions" below.

Just beyond the Tor House, you encounter **Carmel River State Beach,** where might find a parking place—if you get there early enough in the day. The road curves away from the beach here, becoming Carmelo Street. You'll encounter a stop sign at Santa Lucia. Turn right, hit a second stop at Rio Road and go right again to **Mission Carmel.** Graced with the weathered patina of time, marked by an unusual star window and rimmed by gardens, it's one of the most beautiful of California's adobe outposts.

Opposite the mission is the emerald swatch of **Mission Trails Park** (although no sign identifies it). Several miles of trails pass through redwoods and alongside seasonal creeks. This is a good starting point for your walk back downtown, since—with luck—you'll emerge from the park's north end near Crespi Avenue. Take it a block northwest to Mountain View and turn left; this street slants into Ocean Avenue.

From the mission, Rio Road intersects Highway 1. Across the way is **The Barnyard,** a lushly landscaped theme shopping center modeled after old California barns. Follow the Barnyard's windmill into a weathered-wood complex of boutiques, galleries and restaurants. Particularly noteworthy is the **Thunderbird,** a cultural blend of book shop and café, like a Greenwich Village retreat that happens to be housed in a barn.

The majestic sanctuary of **Point Lobos State Reserve** is immediately south, off Highway 1. Too close to Carmel for comfort, it's hopelessly crowded on weekends. Access is limited to fewer than 500 people at a time, so late arrivals will find themselves in long motorized queue outside. Pick an off-season weekday to enjoy the rocky headlands, hidden coves and lush forests of this "Point of the Sea Wolves." The name was inspired by barking sea lions lounging on offshore rocks.

To reach the "inland Carmel," follow Highway 1 north from Point Lobos and turn east onto Carmel Valley Road. It takes you through a bucolic playground for the rich, along the course of the Carmel River. About five miles from Carmel, pause at the imposing castle-like **Château Julien Winery** tasting room. A few miles beyond is the rhinestone cowboy town of **Carmel Valley Village,** rimmed by oak trees, finishing schools and riding schools.

If you continue beyond the village, you'll pass through *real* farming and ranching country for a few miles. Then the highway changes temperament quickly, from gentle curves to tight, uphill spirals. Like a stepped-on snake, it twists into the Santa Lucia Range. The transition here is dramatic, from the crowded Monterey Peninsula to a remote highland of grassy knolls and rocky creek canyons.

After crossing a saddle in the Santa Lucias, Carmel Valley Road tilts downward and merges with Arroyo Seco Road. If you head west on Arroyo Seco, you'll shortly encounter **Camp Arroyo Seco** and a picnic area. Beyond, the road becomes a rough, twisting dirt route leading into the **Ventana Wilderness.** This wild area of skinny canyons, serrated ridges, oak woodlands and high chaparral is a favored hikers' retreat. However, winter rains can erode roads and trails. Before entering, get a hiking permit from a **Los Padres National Forest** office. They're available at Arroyo Seco and Memorial trailheads in this area.

If you go east on Arroyo Seco Road, you'll enter an attractive farm valley tucked into the **Arroyo Seco Valley.** The winding road eventually delivers you to U.S. 101 at **Greenfield.**

RV advisory: Although inland Carmel Valley Road and eastbound Arroyo Seco Road can be negotiated by large RVs and trailers, they are busy with hairpin turns and steep grades. Eastbound Arroyo Seco Road into the Ventana Wilderness is *not* recommended for RVs. No vehicle should attempt it during a winter rainstorm.

ATTRACTIONS
(Monterey, In order of appearance)

Monterey State Historic Park • *20 Custom House Plaza., Monterey, CA 93940; (408) 649-7118 or 649-2836. Various open days and hours; generally 10 to 5 (until 4 in the off-season). Individual admission prices to historic buildings $2 and $5 for an all-building two-day ticket, or a combination ticket with Maritime Museum of Monterey, $10; kids less. Pacific House and Custom House on the plaza have no admission charge.*

The historic park is focused around several buildings adjacent to Fisherman's Wharf, and it includes other structures within a few blocks' walk. Casa Soberanes, Larkin House and Stevenson House may be visited by guided tour only, which are conducted several times daily. Check for specific days and hours. Walking tours of the park depart daily at 10:30, 12:30 and 2:30 from the state historic park visitor's center at Stanton Center.

A fine way to see the park's treasures and other historic sites is to follow a *Path of History* walking tour brochure, available from Stanton Center and other visitor centers. These are the main elements of the historic park:

☺ **Custom House** • *One Custom House Plaza, adjacent to Fisherman's Wharf. Daily 10 to 4.* The oldest public building in California, this 1820s structure was the commercial center of Mexican Monterey. At one time, all cargo from incoming ships was cleared through here. Smell the aromas of history as you examine bags of lentils, coffee and wheat, pots and pans, blacksmith tools and wagon wheels—everything needed for a comfortable mid-19th century lifestyle.

Pacific House • *Calle Principal and Scott Street, off Custom House Plaza. Daily 10 to 4.* Nearly lost to commercialism, this ancient structure housed legal offices, small shops and Monterey County's first courthouse before joining the historic park. It's now a fine museum of Monterey's Spanish era and Native American culture. Several exhibits recall the Ohlone people who greeted the Spanish and then were subjugated by them. The structure was built in 1847 as offices for the American military.

Boston Store • *Scott and Olivier streets. Wednesday-Saturday 10 to 5 and Sunday noon to 5. Free admission.* Now a gift shop of early American crafts, this small structure was built as a store during the early 1800s.

California's first theater • *Pacific and Scott streets. Live melodramas periodically by "Troupers of the Gold Coast"; call for schedule: (408) 375-4916. Open to visitors in summer Wednesday-Saturday from 1 until curtain time; the rest of the year Wednesday-Thursday 1 to 5 and Friday-Saturday from 1 until curtain.* This 1846 structure supposedly was California's first theater, although that's stretching a point. It was built as a saloon, residence and sailor's boarding house. Two years later, after it was commandeered by the Americans, it became one of the first facilities in California to charge for "entertainments." Restored as a brass rail bar, it contains pieces of sets, props, old booze bottles and other relics of that era.

Thomas Larkin House • *Calle Principal and Jefferson Street. Open only for tours, conducted three time daily, five days a week; call for schedule: (408) 649-7118 or check with the park visitor center.* A pivotal figure in the transfer of California to the United States, Thomas Oliver Larkin served as U.S. consul during the Mexican period. His wood frame and adobe home, a blend of Spanish colonial and New England architecture, is furnished with antiques from many countries, collected by his granddaughter, Alice Larkin Toulmin. She lived here from 1922 until 1957.

☺ **Cooper-Molera complex ●** *Polk and Munras. Daily 10 to 4. Tours of the Diaz and Cooper adobes given twice daily, five days a week; check with the Stanton Center visitor center for schedules or call (408) 649-7118.* Covering most of a city block, this facility in the middle of downtown houses the Cooper Store with a fine collection of folk craft and California history books, and the "Corner Store," now an historic park visitor center. A nicely done museum here focuses on Monterey under the flags of Mexico and the United States. An herb garden and farm buildings are adjacent. It was owned by Thomas Larkin's half-brother Juan Bautista Cooper, who married Encarnacion Vallejo, the sister of General Mariano Vallejo.

Casa Soberanes ● *336 Pacific Street at Del Monte Avenue. Tours twice daily, five days a week.* The 1842 adobe is a classic of Mexican colonial architecture, with thick adobe walls, cantilevered balcony, tile roof and surrounding gardens. Well preserved rooms contain fine antiques from several periods.

☺ **Stevenson House ●** *530 Houston Street, off Pearl Street. Tours three times daily, five days a week.* Although it was never the great author's "house," the former French Hotel is one of the park's more interesting buildings because of its treasure trove of Robert Louis Stevenson lore. Ailing, penniless Stevenson arrived in Monterey in 1879. He got a job with the local newspaper and took lodging in the hotel. The paper didn't really need another reporter, so a group of benefactors gave the editor $2 a week to pay Stevenson's salary—which all went for room and board. While gathering material for his future writings, he courted American Fanny Osbourne, who he had followed across the Atlantic. After a few months, he joined Fanny in the San Francisco Bay Area, where they were married. They honeymooned at an abandoned silver mine above the Napa Valley. Although his Monterey stay was brief, Fanny's descendants gave curators a wealth of Stevenson memorabilia. The rooming house thus has become one of the world's most complete Stevenson museums, with items such as his dining table, first editions and many of Robert and Fanny's personal belongings.

☺ **Maritime Museum of Monterey ●** *Five Custom House Plaza; (408) 373-2469. Tuesday-Sunday 10 to 5, closed Monday; longer hours in summer. Adults $5, students $3, kids 6 to 12, $2. A $10 combination ticket is good for the museum, a walking tour and four units of Monterey State Historic Park. The park's visitor center in Stanton Center is open daily.* From the arrival of Father Serra's supply ships to the bloodless conquest by Commodore Sloat to the sardine canneries, Monterey has been a city tied to the sea. This outstanding new museum, opened in late 1992, traces the maritime history of the Monterey Peninsula and the Pacific Coast. An obvious focal point is a 12-foot multi-faceted Fresnel lens brought here from Point Sur Lighthouse. A 40-watt bulb rotates inside, glittering brightly and giving hint to the lens' great power when a 1,000-watt bulb was used at the lighthouse. Artifacts and graphics take you step by step from the Ohlone Indians to Father Serra and Commodore Sloat's arrival to the "nets full of silver" of the sardine industry. Exhibits include a nasty looking harpoon from Monterey's offshore whaling days, ship models, scrimshaw and sailor's "fancy work" (knot-tying). In the History Theater, a film using costumed actors provides a 14-minute introduction to Monterey and the historic park.

Cannery Row has gone from sardines to tourists, who can taste wines and enjoy the view at the old Monterey Company Company building. — **Don W. Martin**

Presidio of Monterey ● *Enter via Artillery Street off Pacific Street.* Occupying a swatch of high ground above downtown Monterey, the Presidio offers sterling views of the town and the bay. Now open to the public, it's one of the oldest military installations on the West Coast, first used as a gun emplacement guarding the bay, and later as a military installation by the Americans. Wander its hilly streets, noting its many monuments to heroes past, and stop in at the small **U.S Army Museum** with military artifact from various wars. It was the U.S. military that named this the "Presidio," not to be confused with the original Spanish presidio and first mission site near Lake El Estero. There, the **Royal Presidio Chapel,** Monterey's oldest building still stands.

☺ **Monterey Bay Aquarium** ● *886 Cannery Row; (408) 375-3333. Daily 10 to 6. Adults $10.50; seniors, students and military $7.75; kids and handicapped $4.75. MC/VISA, AMEX.* When David Packard wrote a check for $40 million so his two daughters Nancy and Julie could create the Monterey Bay Aquarium, they proved a simple fact. With enough money, talent and dedication, one can build a science center so magnificent that it will be overwhelmed with visitors—even at amusement park prices. More than two million people swarmed here when the aquarium was opened in 1984, and the millions just keep coming, like sardines to the net.

When you step through the front door and stare upward at a giant kelp forest in a 30-foot-high Plexiglas tank, you know that you're in one of the world's great natural science centers. The Packards re-invented the aquarium, with realistic habitats, attention-grabbing videos, working tidepools and knowledgeable docents who can answer your every question. Pet a bat ray, study sea life through a microscope, go nose-to-glass with 6,500 kinds of sea creatures, then step onto the outside deck to see non-captive sea lions basking on the rocks of Monterey Bay. They probably wonder what all the excitement is about.

Plan most of a day here. There are films to view, tidal interactions to watch, sharks to follow along a 90-foot undersea tank, giant whale skeletons to study and—when you get hungry—an attractive café. If possible, visit on a weekday in the off-season, or you'll feel more hemmed in than those fish in the sardine tank.

☺ **Pacific Grove Museum of Natural History** • *Forest and Central avenues; (408) 372-4212. Tuesday-Sunday 10 to 5; free.* The Monterey Bay Aquarium is a tough act to trail, although this little natural science museum is surprisingly appealing. The focus here is Monterey Bay wildlife and botany. Say hello to a life-sized gray whale sculpture out front, then step inside to see a monarch butterfly film and exhibit, unusual dried seaweed display, large sea bird exhibit and endemic bugs. Exhibits change frequently, so don't let a previous visit keep you away. Incidentally, the Monterey Peninsula Recreation Trail ties the Monterey Bay Aquarium to the museum; it's about a 20-minute stroll.

Point Pinos Light Station • *Asilomar and Lighthouse avenues; (408) 372-4212. Open weekends only, 1 to 4; free.* Commissioned in 1856 when its light was powered by whale oil, this is the oldest still-operating lighthouse on the West Coast. The original Fresnel lens is still in place, sending its 1,000-watt bulb beam seaward. Within the granite structure, a museum traces the Coast Guard's history from the days when it was established as the U.S. Lifesaving Service.

Carmel

Tor House • *Ocean View Avenue (P.O. Box 1887), Carmel, CA 93921; (408) 624-1813. Tours on Friday and Saturday by advance reservation only; adults $5, teens $3.50; under 12 not admitted.* Although it's still occupied by members of the family, you can make arrangements to tour this personal fortress of poet Robinson Jeffers. A highlight is the author's collection of more than 100 unicorns.

☺ **Mission San Carlos Borromeo del Rio Carmelo** • *3080 Rio Rd.; (408) 624-3600. Sunday 10:30 to 4:30, Monday-Saturday 9:30 to 4:30. A dollar donation.* This noble mission is distinctive both for its architecture and historic role. Since it was founded as the mother mission for Alta California, it was built of sturdy stone—more substantial and imposing than the plebeian adobe of most other missions. The look is Romanesque, with a rounded Moorish dome. Visit the sanctuary, which has earned cathedral status because of its historic significance. Pause and reflect at the final resting place of Father Junípero Serra beneath the altar. Note the imposing sarcophagus of Serra in repose, with his lifelong friend Father Crespi at his head. Stroll through the elaborate gardens and the cemetery where more than 3,000 Ohlone converts hopefully met their Maker.

☺ **Point Lobos State Reserve** • *Route 1, Box 62, Carmel, CA 93923; (408) 624-4909. Day use only; $6 per vehicle. No large RVs or trailers because of winding roads.* If you drive into this preserve and merely follow the twisting roads to its various vista points and then drive out again, you will have missed the entire point. This 1,250-acre peninsula is perhaps the state's finest outdoor museum—an unblemished microcosm of plant, animal and sea life of the central California coast. Take time to watch sea otters at lunch, walk the tide pools among six miles of rock-studded coastline, scan the sea for migrating whales in winter, search hidden coves for bashful harbor seals and *los lobos marinos*—those gregarious sea lions. Follow trails down to secret coves and up the headlands to forests of Monterey pines and cypress. As you reluctantly depart, be glad you got here early—particularly if it's summer and you note that long line of people, just waiting to get in.

Château Julien • *8940 Carmel Valley Rd., Carmel Valley, CA 93923; (408) 624-2600. Tasting room open weekdays 8:30 to 5 and weekends 11 to 5; tours weekdays 10:30 and 2:30.* Sip a Chardonnay, Gewürztraminer or Cabernet Sauvignon in this elegant tasting room, and take a few bottles home (MC/VISA, AMEX accepted). Among California's more artistic wineries, it was designed in the grand style of a French manor house.

ACTIVITIES

Auto Racing • Laguna Seca Raceway at 1025 Salinas-Monterey Highway holds periodic racing events; (408) 422-6138.

Bicycle Rentals • Bay Bikes on Cannery Row at 640 Wave St. (646-9090) and Lincoln between Fifth and Sixth in Carmel (625-BIKE); Monterey Canning Company Bikes, 807 Cannery Row, (408) 373-6904.

Diving equipment rentals • Aquarius Dive Shop, 32 Cannery Row, (408) 375-1933.

Guided tours • A Seacoast Safari at (408) 372-1200 or Otter-Mobile at (408) 625-9782.

Hot air balloons • Balloons by-the-Sea, Salinas, (800) 464-6420 or (408) 424-0111

Kayak rentals and tours • Monterey Bay Kayaks, 693 Del Monte Ave., Monterey, (408) 373-KELP.

Sailing tours • Spellbinder Sailing tours, (408) 291-9568.

Sea otter tours • See "Whale watching" below.

Whale watching cruises and sportfishing • Monterey Sportfishing, Fisherman's Wharf, (408) 372-2203; Princess Monterey Cruises, Fisherman's Wharf, (408) 372-2628.

Wine tasting • (All but Château Julien are on Cannery Row): Bargetto tasting room, 700 Cannery Row, (408) 373-4053, open daily 10:30 to 6; Paul Masson Wine Tasting and Wine Museum, 700 Cannery Row, (408) 646-5446, daily 10 to 7 (shorter hours in the off-season); Roudon-Smith Tasting Room, 807 Cannery Row, (408) 375-8755, daily 11 to 6 (closed Tuesday in the off-season); Monterey Peninsula Winery tasting room, 786

Wave St., (408) 373-4053, Monday-Friday 10 to 5 and Sunday noon to 5; Château Julien, 8940 Carmel Valley Rd., Carmel Valley, (408) 624-2600, weekdays 8:30 to 5 and weekends 11 to 5.

ANNUAL EVENTS

AT&T Pebble Beach National Golf Tournament, early February; (800) 541-9091 or (408) 649-1533.

Hot Air Affair balloon races, Laguna Seca Raceway, late February; (408) 649-6544.

Monterey Wine Festival in Monterey, mid-March; (800) 525-3378.

Wildflower Show at Pacific Grove Museum of Natural History, mid-April; (408) 648-3116.

Annual Adobe Tour in Monterey, late April; (408) 372-2608.

Tor House Garden Party in Carmel, early May; (408) 624-1813.

Great Monterey Squid Festival at Monterey Fairgrounds and Exposition Park, late May; (408) 649-6544.

Old Monterey Birthday Celebration with crafts, food and music, Alvarado Street in Monterey, early June; (408) 373-3720.

Carmel Outdoor Summer Art Festival, mid-June at Sunset Center, Ninth and San Carlos in Carmel; (408) 659-5099.

Monterey Bay Blues Festival at Monterey Fairgrounds, late June; (408) 649-6544.

Sloat Landing Ceremony, re-enactment of American take-over of Monterey, at Custom House Plaza and the Presidio, mid-July; (408) 372-2608.

Carmel Bach Festival at Sunset Center Theater and Carmel Mission, mid-July through early August; (408) 624-1521.

Monterey County Fair at Fairgrounds, late August; (408) 372-1000.

Monterey Historic Auto Races at Laguna Seca Raceway, late August; (408) 648-5100 or 327-SECA.

Concourse d'Elegance at Pebble Beach Lodge, late August; (408) 372-8026.

Carmel Shakespeare Festival at the Outdoor Festival Theater, early September through early October; (408) 624-2522.

Monterey Jazz Festival, late September at Monterey Fairgrounds; mid-September; (408) 373-3366.

Sand Castle Contest, Carmel beach in October; (408) 624-2522.

Old Monterey Heritage Festival on Alvarado Street in Monterey, early to mid-October; (408) 373-3720.

Tor House Festival in Carmel, mid-October; (408) 624-1813.

Festival of the Trees, decorated Christmas trees at Monterey Fairgrounds; (408) 372-7591.

WHERE TO DINE
Monterey

Café Fina ● △△ $$ ∅
Fisherman's Wharf; (408) 372-5200. Italian and seafood; full bar service. Lunch weekdays 11 to 2 and weekends until 4:30, dinner nightly from 4:30. MC/VISA. Attractively simple little place with black lacquered chairs and white nappery. From the kitchen emerges homemade pastas, mesquite grilled fish, brick oven pizza and such. One dining room is smoke-free.

Casa Gutierrez • ΔΔ $$

590 Calle Principal in the historic district; (408) 375-0095. Mexican; wine and beer. Sunday-Thursday 11 to 9, Friday-Saturday 11 to 10. Major credit cards. Attractive oldstyle cantina housed in an ancient adobe. The menu features typical things wrapped in tortillas, plus some more interesting early California fare, including spicy seafood dishes.

Chef Lee's Mandarin House • ΔΔΔ $$

2031 Fremont St.; (408) 375-9551. Chinese; wine and beer. Lunch 11:30 to 2:30, dinner 4:30 to 9:30. MC/VISA. Delightfully gaudy Chinese palace done in red, white and gold lacquer, with upturned eves to divert evil dining spirits. It's like eating in a museum of Chinese architecture. The menu focuses on spicier Szechuan, Hunan and other Mandarin fare.

Domenico's on the Wharf • ΔΔ $$$

Fisherman's Wharf; (408) 372-3655. American, mostly seafood; full bar service. Daily from 11:30. Major credit cards. Modern, attractive bayview dining room with a good—if somewhat pricey—menu. Among its offerings are mesquite grilled prawns, marinated chicken, baked scallops and a good bouillabaisse. Extensive wine list.

Kiewels Café • ΔΔ $$

100 Heritage Harbor; (408) 372-6950. American; full bar service. Monday-Saturday 8 a.m. to 9 p.m., Sunday 9 to 9 (brunch 9 to 3). MC/VISA. Bright and airy café just above Fisherman's Wharf, with patio tables beside the walking/biking path to Cannery Row. Mixed menu ranges from curried chicken and roast pork loin to red snapper, pasta and sandwiches.

☺Old Fisherman's Grotto • ΔΔΔ $$

Fisherman's Wharf; (408) 375-4604. American, mostly seafood; full bar service. Daily from 11. Major credit cards. One of the wharf's better buys. This simple, unpretentious place offers a good selection of mesquite broiled fresh fish, flown-in live Maine lobsters and excellent thick clam chowder. The place has its own fishing boat, so ask what's just been caught. Many tables offer bay view dining.

The Outrigger • ΔΔ $$$

700 Cannery Row; (408) 372-8543. American, mostly seafood; full bar service. Monday-Friday noon to 10, Sunday from 11:30. MC/VISA. This tourist-oriented place with Polynesian dècor offers the best views at Cannery Row, with dining right over the water. The cocktail lounge is particularly well placed, on an enclosed pier extending into the bay. The menu offers the usual fisherman's platter, fresh local fish and a few steaks and chops.

Rapa's • ΔΔ $$

Fisherman's Wharf; (408) 372-7562. American-Italian; full bar service. Monday-Saturday 11 to 10, Sunday 4 to 6:30. MC/VISA. Italian sleek but not chic; green and russet tile and Naugahyde booths give it an upscale Denny's look. The menu features Italian pastas, bouillabaisse and cioppino, plus a good fresh seafood selection. End-of-pier location offers fine harbor views.

☺ The Sardine Factory • ΔΔΔΔ $$$$ Ø

701 Wave Street above Cannery Row; (408) 373-3775. Continental; full bar service. Lunch Monday-Saturday from 11, dinner Monday-Thursday 5 to 10:30 and Friday-Saturday 5 to 11, Sunday 2 to 10. Major credit cards. Very high class place aloof from its tacky Cannery Row neighbors; plush Victo-

176 — CHAPTER FIVE

rian interior with dark woods, crystal, crisp linens and tuxedo-clad waitstaff. Call well in advance and ask for seating in the striking glass domed Conservatory. The changing menu features European classics plus several fresh seafood dishes, lightly done and creatively spiced.

☺ Triples ● ∆∆∆ $$$
220 Olivier St.; (408) 372-4744. American-continental; wine and beer. Dinner Monday-Thursday 6 to 9:30, Friday-Saturday 6 to 10, Sunday 6 to 9. MC/VISA, AMEX. Very charming early American style dining room in one of Monterey's historic structures; pink nappery, bentwood chairs and wooden floors. Menu offerings include breast of Peking duck and rack of lamb with mustard and French herbs.

Warehouse Restaurant ● ∆∆ $$
Cannery Row at Prescott; (408) 375-1921. Italian-American; full bar service. Daily 11 to 10. Major credit cards. Victorian style dining room housed in one of Cannery Row's old brick buildings; lots of Tiffany style glass and brass. The mixed menu ventures from steaks to assorted Italian entrées to fresh seafood. Large soup and salad bar.

Whaling Station Inn ● ∆∆∆ $$$
763 Wave Street above Cannery Row; (408) 373-3778. American-continental; full bar service. Dinner nightly from 5. Major credit cards. Attractive restaurant done up in Tiffany glass and dark polished woods, with drop lamps over comfy booths. The versatile menu features *nouveau* touches in its charcoal broiled chicken breasts, mesquite grilled chops and seafood, plus fresh pastas.

Pacific Grove

The Old Bath House Restaurant ● ∆∆∆ $$$$
620 Ocean View Blvd.; (408) 375-5195. Continental; full bar service. Dinner Monday-Saturday 5 to 10:30, Sunday 3 to 10:30. Major credit cards. Handsome European style restaurant with dark woods and beveled glass. The dimly lit dining room offers excellent bay views from its perch on a low headland between Monterey and Pacific Grove. The menu focuses on French and Northern Italian; in-house desserts are exceptional.

Carmel

Caffée Napoli ● ∆∆ $$
Ocean Avenue near Lincoln; (408) 625-4033. Italian; wine and beer. Daily 11:30 to 10. MC/VISA. Very popular little bistro serving Italian fare at reasonable prices; the cannoli dessert is excellent. Snug seating in simple caneback chairs before blue-checkered oilcloth.

Diana at the Plaza ● ∆∆∆ $$$
Ocean Avenue at Junipero, in Carmel Plaza; (408) 626-0191. Greek-American; full bar service. Sunday-Thursday 11:30 to 10, Friday-Saturday 11:30 to 11. Major credit cards. A trim Grecian look with white wood booths and green drop lamps. The menu goes beyond Greece to offer several other Mediterranean dishes, in addition to nicely seasoned fresh fish. Outdoor dining patio around a fire pit is a nice warm-weather spot.

Hog's Breath Inn ● ∆∆∆ $$$
San Carlos Avenue near Fifth; (408) 625-1044. American; full bar service. Lunch 11:30 to 3, Sunday brunch 11 to 3, dinner 5 to 10 (Friday-Saturday

until 11). Major credit cards. Perhaps just to twist Carmel's conservative tail, Clint Eastwood picked an outrageous name for his macho, clubby restaurant, with wild boars' heads to enforce the theme. The place is nicely arranged around a quiet courtyard with indoor and patio dining. The menu is upscale meat and potatoes; try the chicken in whiskey.

Pine Inn ● ΔΔΔ $$$
Ocean and Monte Verde; (408) 624-3851. American-continental; full bar service. Breakfast and lunch Monday-Saturday 7 to 2:30, Sunday brunch from 10, dinner nightly. MC/VISA, AMEX. Extremely handsome dark-wood dining room with smoked glass windows, brick interior walls, lots of plants and a skylight. Offerings include veal piccata, pepper steak and stuffed chicken breast with herbs and jack cheese.

Plaza Café and Grill ● ΔΔ $
Ocean Avenue at Junipero, in Carmel Plaza; (408) 624-4433. American; wine and beer. Daily 8 to 9. Major credit cards. Cheery patio café that's handy for quick bites as you stroll among Carmel's boutiques. Heat lamps encourage outdoor dining. You'll find pastas, jambalaya, burgers and pizza on the light menu.

Scandia Restaurant ● ΔΔ $$
Ocean Avenue near Lincoln; (408) 624-5659. Continental; wine and beer. Daily 8 a.m. to 10 p.m. MC/VISA, AMEX. Primly white and bright café with quilted booths and lots of *ficus benjamima.* Menu hops from chicken *mutard* and bouillabaisse to salmon touched with basil.

Thunderbird Restaurant ● ΔΔ $
In the Thunderbird book store at the Barnyard Shopping Center, Rio Road and Highway 1; (408) 624-9414. American; wine and beer. Lunch daily 10 to 3:30, dinner Tuesday-Sunday 5 to 8:30. MC/VISA, AMEX. Dine among the bibliotheca or on a flower-rimmed patio in this bookstore café done up in rustic barnwood. The fare is light, ranging from pastas, vegetarian entrées and fresh seafood to salads and sandwiches.

The Tuck Box ● ΔΔ $
Dolores between Ocean and Seventh; (408) 624-6365. American-continental. Wednesday-Sunday 8 to 3:45. No credit cards. Impossibly cute doll house of an English tearoom; a favorite of locals and camera-clutchers for half a century. The featured fare is predictable: scones, Welsh rarebit and shepherd's pie, plus omelettes and light American meals.

WHERE TO SLEEP

Many of Monterey's motels are along Fremont Street, just north of town and Munras Avenue heading downtown. Pricier ones, of course, are near the waterfront. For aid in finding a room, dial **Resort to Me**, (408) 624-5070 or **Carmel Tourist Information Center**, (408) 624-1711.

Monterey

Bay Park Hotel ● ⌂⌂⌂ $$$ Ø
1425 Munras Ave., Monterey, CA 93940; (800) 338-3564 or (408) 373-4258. Couples and singles $69 to $129. Major credit cards. Attractively landscaped 80-unit inn with TV, room phones, refrigerators $10 extra. Bay views, pool and spa. **Crazy Horse Restaurant** serves from 7 a.m. to 9 p.m.; dinners $7 to $16 with salad buffet; full bar service.

Best Western Victorian Inn ● ⌂⌂⌂ $$$$$ Ø

487 Foam St., Monterey, CA 93940; (800) 232-4141 or (408) 373-8000. Rooms $99 to $209, including continental breakfast. Major credit cards. Victorian style 68-room inn three blocks from Cannery Row; TV, room phones, gas log fireplaces, honor bars. Patios or view balconies.

Casa Munras ● ⌂⌂⌂ $$$$

Fremont and Munras Avenue (P.O. Box 1351), Monterey, CA 93940; (800) 222-2446 in California, (800) 222-2558 elsewhere and (408) 375-2411. Couples $81 to $101, singles $71 to $125, kitchenettes and suites $140 to $350. Major credit cards. Older, very well maintained 151-room inn surrounded by landscaped gardens and trees. TV movies, phones; swimming pool.

Cypress Tree Inn ● ⌂⌂ $$$

2227 N. Fremont St., Monterey, CA 93940; (800) 446-8303 in California only, or (408) 372-7586. Couples $54 to $86, singles $52 to $82, kitchenettes $52 to $82, suites $95 to $195. MC/VISA. A 55-unit motel with TV, room phones and refrigerators. Hot tub, sauna, guest laundry, barbecue area; RV parking (see below under "Where to camp").

El Adobe Inn ● ⌂⌂ $$$$ Ø

936 Munras Ave. (near Eldorado), Monterey, CA 93940; (800) 433-4732 or (408) 372-5409. Couples and singles $79 to $89; rates include continental breakfast. Major credit cards. A 26-room inn with TV movies and room phones; spa. Near Fisherman's Wharf.

El Castell ● ⌂ $$ Ø

2102 N. Fremont St., Monterey, CA 93940; (800) 628-1094 or (408) 372-8176. Doubles from $30, singles from $28, suites $45 to $150. Major credit cards. A 51-room motel with TV movies, room phones; pool and sun deck.

Hotel Pacific ● ⌂⌂⌂ $$$$$

300 Pacific St., Monterey, CA 93940 (800) 554-5542 or (408) 647-9322. Suites $144 to $264; rates include continental breakfast. Major credit cards. Luxurious Spanish style 105-room hotel with TV movies, room phones, refrigerators and wet bars, fireplaces and private patios or balconies. Elaborate gardens with two spas. **Triples Restaurant** serves dinner 6 to 10; $15 to $23; full bar service.

Hyatt Regency ● ⌂⌂⌂⌂ $$$$$ Ø

One Old Golf Course Road, Monterey, CA 93940; (800) 824-2196 in California only, or (408) 372-1234. Couples $170 to $195, singles $135 to $150, suites $275 to $550. Major credit cards. Opulent 557-room full service resort with six tennis courts, two outdoor pools, health club with weight room and spa. Beautifully landscaped grounds. Stylishly furnished rooms have TV movies, phones; most with service bars. **Peninsula Restaurant** serves continental fare from 6:30 a.m. to 10 p.m.; dinners $15 to $32; full bar.

Monterey Bay Inn ● ⌂⌂⌂ $$$$$ Ø

242 Cannery Row, Monterey, CA 93940; (800) 424-6242 or (408) 373-6242. Rooms $119 to $299, including continental breakfast. Major credit cards. Nicely appointed rooms with TV movies, room phones, honor bars; all have balconies with harbor or bay views. Hot tubs, sauna, exercise room.

Monterey Marriott ● ⌂⌂⌂ $$$$$ Ø

350 Calle Principal, Monterey, CA 93940; (800) 228-9290 or (408) 647-4000. Rooms $149 to $179. Major credit cards. Very nicely appointed 341-

room resort with TV movies, room phones and refrigerators; some rooms with ocean view. Pool, spa and health club. **Dining Room** and **Characters Sports Bar & Grill** serve breakfast, lunch and dinner; $6 to $26; full bar service.

Monterey Plaza ● ⌂⌂⌂⌂ $$$$$ Ø
400 Cannery Row, Monterey, CA 93940; (800) 334-3999 in California, (800) 631-1339 elsewhere and (408) 676-1700. Couples and singles $150 to $300, suites $450 to $675. Major credit cards. Quite stylish 290-room resort on Cannery Row with ocean view rooms; TV movies, phones and honor bars; fitness room. **Delfino's** serves 6:30 a.m. to 10 p.m.; Northern Italian fare; dinners $30 to $50; full bar service.

Motel Six ● ⌂ $$ Ø
2124 N. Fremont St., Monterey, CA 93940; (408) 646-8585 or (505) 891-6161. Couples $46, singles $40. Major credit cards. A 51-unit motel with TV movies, phones and a swimming pool.

Scottish Fairway Motel ● ⌂ $$ Ø
2075 N. Fremont St., Monterey, CA 93940; (408) 373-5551. Couples $44 to $66, singles $40 to $60, kitchenettes $5 extra, suites $66 to $88. Major credit cards. A 42-room motel with TV, room phones; pool.

Spindrift Inn ● ⌂⌂⌂ $$$$$ Ø
652 Cannery Row, Monterey, CA 93940; (800) 841-1879 or (408) 646-8900. Rooms $149 to $389, including continental breakfast. Major credit cards. Very stylish rooms with TV, room phones, fireplaces, canopied beds. Views of bay or cannery row.

Monterey bed & breakfast inns

Del Monte Beach Inn ● ⌂⌂ $$ Ø
1110 Del Monte Ave., Monterey, CA 93940; (408) 649-4410. Couples $40 to $75. Eighteen rooms; some share and some private baths; continental breakfast. MC/VISA, DISC. Nice European style 18-room pension near El Estro Lake downtown. Comfortable rooms with early American furnishings.

☺ The Jabberwock ● ⌂⌂⌂ $$$$$ Ø
598 Laine St., Monterey, CA 93940; 372-4777. Couples $90 to $175, singles $90 to $165. Seven rooms; some private and some share baths; full breakfast. MC/VISA. Comfy, whimsically decorated inn tucked behind a large garden with bay views. Some rooms with fireplaces and bay views. Early American and Victorian furnishings, with touches of "Alice in Wonderland."

☺ Old Monterey Inn ● ⌂⌂⌂⌂ $$$$$ Ø
500 Martin St. (at Pacific Street), Monterey, CA 93940; (408) 375-8284. Couples and singles $160 to $220. Ten rooms with private baths; full breakfast. MC/VISA. English Tudor country house in a wooded setting; built as Monterey mayor's home in 1929. Beautifully furnished rooms with antiques and modern amenities; TV and room phones available; some fireplaces.

Pacific Grove

Asilomar Conference Center ● ⌂⌂ $$$$ Ø
800 Asilomar Blvd. (P.O. Box 537), Pacific Grove, CA 93950; (408) 372-8016. Doubles $52 to $59 per person, singles $63, suites $65 to $75 per person; rates include full breakfast. No credit cards. Historic conference center with 105 acres of forests and dunes, just off the beach. Swimming pool, gen-

eral store. **Crocker Dining Room** serves 7:30 to 9, noon to 1 and 6 to 7; dinners $11.24; no alcohol, although it may be brought in.

Gosby House Inn • △△△ $$$$ Ø

643 Lighthouse Ave., Pacific Grove, CA 93950; (408) 375-1287. Couples and singles $85 to $100, kitchenettes from $150. MC/VISA. Very attractive carriage house-style inn near beach; 22 rooms with two TVs, room phones; some with spa tubs and small kitchens. Near beach.

☺ Gatehouse Inn Bed & Breakfast • △△△ $$$$ Ø

225 Central Ave. (near Second), Pacific Grove, CA 93950; (800) 753-1881 or (408) 649-1881. Rooms $95 to $170. Eight units with phones and private baths; buffet breakfast. MC/VISA, AMEX. Beautifully restored 1884 Italianate Victorian, furnished with antiques and antique reproductions, plus Art Deco touches. Some rooms with wood stoves or fireplaces and private patios or decks. Located just off bay front with ocean views.

The Martine Inn Bed & Breakfast • △△△△ $$$$$ Ø

255 Ocean View Blvd., Pacific Grove, CA 93950; (408) 373-3388. Couples and singles $125 to $230. Nineteen units with private baths; full breakfast. MC/VISA, AMEX. Award-winning inn fashioned from an 1890s Mediterranean-Victorian mansion built by the Park-Davis Pharmaceutical family. Furnished with museum-quality American antiques. Woodburning fireplaces, library, billiards room, spa; early California landscape art collection and vintage auto display.

The Old St. Angela Inn Bed & Breakfast • △△△ $$$$ Ø

321 Central Ave., Pacific Grove, CA 93950; (408) 372-3246. Rooms $95 to $150. Eight units, six with private baths; full breakfast. MC/VISA, AMEX. Cape Cod style inn built in 1910 furnished with American antiques and folk craft. Just off the shoreline; some rooms with bay views. Garden patio, solarium and comfortable living room with fireplace.

Roserox Country Inn Bed & Breakfast • △△△ $$$$$ Ø

557 Ocean View Blvd., Pacific Grove, CA 93950; (408) 373-7673. Couples $125 to $205, singles $105. Eight units with private baths; full breakfast. No credit cards. Country Victorian fashioned into a stylish bed & breakfast; lofty redwood beam ceilings, patterned hardwood floors. On the edge of the shoreline; all guest rooms have water views

☺ Seven Gables Inn Bed & Breakfast • △△△△ $$$$$ Ø

555 Ocean View Blvd., Pacific Grove, CA 93950; (408) 372-4341. Couples and singles $105 to $205. Fourteen rooms with private baths; full breakfast. Elaborate, beautifully kept 1886 Victorian mansion across the boulevard from the beach. Formal 18th century furnishings, including stained glass windows, Oriental rugs, crystal chandeliers and carved armoires. Formal gardens; short stroll to the beach.

Carmel

Candle Light Inn • △△△ $$$$$ Ø

San Carlos between Fourth and Fifth (P.O. Box 1900), Carmel, CA 93921; (800) 433-4732. Couples and singles $119 to $139, kitchenettes $139; rates include continental breakfast. Major credit cards. Nice 20-room inn with TV, room phones, refrigerators, some fireplaces. Swimming pool; near downtown shops.

Carmel Normandy Inn ● ⌂ $$$$ ∅
Ocean Avenue at Monte Verde (P.O. Box 1706), Carmel, CA 93921; (800) 343-3825 in California only, or (408) 624-3825. Couples and singles $89 to $145, kitchen suites $165 to $185, three-bedroom cottages $250 to $300; rates include continental breakfast. MC/VISA, AMEX. Attractive cross timbered lodge near downtown Carmel with TV, room phones; pool.

Carmel Studio Lodge ● ⌂⌂ $$$$ ∅
Fifth and Junipero (P.O. Box 2388), Carmel, CA 93921; (408) 624-8515. Couples and singles $75 to $135, suites $115 to $135. Major credit cards. Inviting 19-room inn among the pines, near shops and the beach. TV movies, room phones; most rooms with refrigerators; swimming pool.

Carmel Village Inn ● ⌂⌂ $$$$ ∅
Junipero at Ocean Avenue (P.O. Box 5275), Carmel, CA 93921; (800) 346-3864 or (408) 624-3864. Couples $79 to $130, singles $69 to $125, kitchenettes $89 to $189. MC/VISA, AMEX. Nicely landscaped 32-unit studio apartment inn; TV, room phones and refrigerators.

Carriage House Inn ● ⌂⌂ $$$$$ ∅
Junipero between Seventh and Eighth (P.O. Box 1900), Carmel, CA 93921; (800) 433-4732 or (408) 625-2585. Couples and singles $169 to $185, suites $220 to $225. Major credit cards. Opulent 13-room inn with TV movies, room phones, fireplaces; open beam ceilings; some rooms with sunken tubs.

Hofsas House ● ⌂ $$$$ ∅
Fourth and San Carlos streets (P.O. Box 1195), Carmel, CA 93921; (800) 221-2548 or (408) 624-2745. Couples and singles $75 to $95, kitchenettes $110 to $120, suites $150 to $165; rates include continental breakfast. MC/VISA, AMEX. A 38-room inn with TV, room phones, some refrigerators; pool and sauna. Three blocks from downtown.

Sundial Lodge ● ⌂⌂ $$$$$
Monte Verde and Seventh (P.O. Box J), Carmel, CA 93921; (408) 624-8578. Couples and singles $105 to $170; rates include continental breakfast. MC/VISA, AMEX. Handsomely restored 1929 European style lodge built around a brick courtyard; near beach. Rooms furnished with antiques and Victorian wicker; TV, room phones; some kitchens; some ocean views.

Carmel bed & breakfast inns

Holiday House ● ⌂ $$$$ ∅
Camino Real at Seventh Avenue (P.O. Box 782), Carmel, CA 93921; (408) 624-6267. Couples $80 to $100, singles $80 to $95. Six rooms; some private and some share baths; full buffet breakfast. MC/VISA. California craftsman style home furnished with American antiques; some rooms with ocean view. Attractively landscaped grounds with flower garden and fish pond. Short walk to the beach.

Monte Verde Inn ● ⌂ $$$$ ∅
Monte Verde at Ocean Avenue (P.O. Box 394), Carmel, CA 93921; (408) 624-6046. Rooms $95 to $155. Ten rooms with TV, room phones and private baths. MC/VISA, AMEX. A nicely restored early 20th century inn. Comfortable with pine, wicker and an eclectic mix. Near Carmel's shops.

San Antonio House ● ⌂⌂ $$$$$ ∅
San Antonio between Ocean and Seventh (P.O. Box 3683), Carmel, CA 93921; (408) 624-4334. Rooms $110 to $155. Four units with TV, room

phones and private baths; continental breakfast; MC/VISA. An English style cottage fashioned into a cozy inn with country furnishings, near beach and downtown shops. All rooms have fireplaces, refrigerators, private entrances and patios.

Sandpiper B&B Inn at the Beach • △△△ $$$$$ Ø

2408 Bay View Ave. (at Martin Way), Carmel, CA 93923; (408) 624-6433. Couples $100 to $170, singles $100 to $160. Inn rooms and cottages with private baths; continental breakfast. MC/VISA, AMEX. Early California stucco home just up from the beach; cathedral beamed ceilings, stone fireplaces; English and French antiques. Rooms with views of the ocean or an attractive garden.

Sea View Inn • △△△ $$$$ Ø

Camino Real between 11th and 12th (P.O. Box 4138), Carmel, CA 93921; (408) 624-8778. Couples and singles $80 to $115. Eight rooms, six with private baths; continental breakfast. MC/VISA. Turn of the century country style Victorian with an eclectic mix of American and European antiques and local artworks. Secluded garden; living room with fireplace and small library.

Stonehouse Inn • △△ $$$$ Ø

Eighth Street near Monte Verde (P.O. Box 2517), Carmel, CA 93921; (408) 624-4569. Couples and singles $95 to $135. Six rooms with shared baths; continental breakfast. MC/VISA, AMEX. Interesting turn of the century stone house furnished with antiques. Casual atmosphere; garden and patio; massive stone fireplace in the living room.

WHERE TO CAMP

Camping is not plentiful on the Monterey Peninsula, although it's abundant as you head south into Big Sur. Within Monterey, we found two places:

Cypress Tree Inn • *2227 N. Fremont St., Monterey, CA 93940; (408) 372-7586. RV sites adjacent to a motel, water and electric $18. Reservations accepted; no credit cards.* This motel about a mile north of the downtown area offers a few RV slots. Guests have access to the motel's spa and sauna. The spaces go fast in summer and on most weekends.

Veterans Memorial Park • *End of Jefferson Street at Via del Rey; (408) 646-3865. RV and tent sites, $10. No reservations or credit cards.* Basic camping accommodations near the Presidio, with showers and flush potties. Get there early in the day to pick up a permit.

Outside Monterey

Lake Laguna Seca Recreation Area • *At Laguna Seca Raceway, 1025 Salinas-Monterey Highway, P.O. Box 367, Salinas, CA 93905; (408) 755-4899. RV and tent sites, $9.50 to $14. Reservations accepted; MC/VISA.* Hilltop sites above the raceway with barbecues and picnic tables, showers, rec hall and horseshoe pits. Some shaded sites and pull-throughs.

Marina Dunes RV Park • *3330 Dunes Dr. (Reservation Road exit from Highway 1), Marina, CA 93933; (408) 384-6914. RV and tent sites, $22 to $29. Reservations accepted; MC/VISA.* Well-kept park with full hookups; showers, cable TV, coin laundry, mini-mart, rec hall and game room.

Riverside RV Park • *Route 2, Box 827, Carmel Valley, CA 93923; (408) 624-9329. RV sites only, $28. Reservations accepted.* Small, attractive park with some sites on the Carmel River; showers. To reach it, go 4.5 miles east on Carmel Valley Road, then a mile southwest on Schulte Road.

Monterey to Big Sur

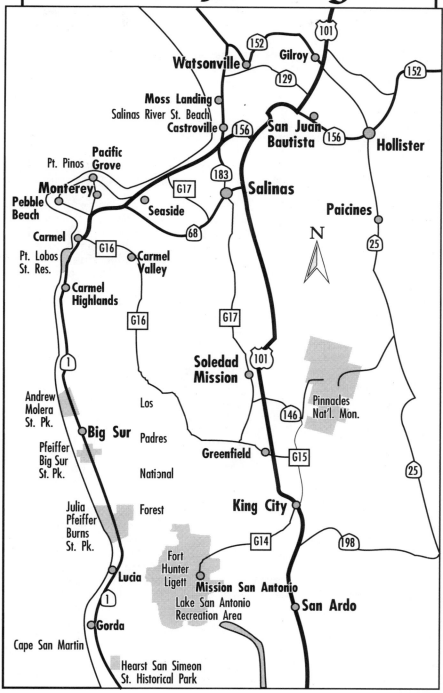

101

152 Gilroy

Watsonville

129

152

Moss Landing
Salinas River St. Beach
Castroville 156 San Juan Bautista 156 Hollister

Pacific Grove
Pt. Pinos
183

Monterey G17 Salinas

Pebble Beach
Seaside Paicines

Carmel 68 N 25

G16
Pt. Lobos St. Res.
Carmel Valley

Carmel Highlands

G16 G17

Soledad Mission
101

Andrew Molera St. Pk.
Los

Pinnacles Nat'l. Mon.
146

Big Sur Padres

Pfeiffer Big Sur St. Pk.
Greenfield G15 25

National

King City

Julia Pfeiffer Burns St. Pk.
Forest

G14 198

Fort Hunter Ligett
Lucia
Mission San Antonio

1
Lake San Antonio Recreation Area
San Ardo

Gorda
Cape San Martin

Hearst San Simeon St. Historical Park

"EL GRANDE SOUTH"

"There are mountains which seem to reach the heavens and the sea beats on them," wrote Portuguese navigator Juan Rodríguez Cabrillo when he passed this way in 1542.

Big Sur is a land tilted sideways, spilling downward as the steep face of the Santa Lucia Mountains, in collision with a wild sea. Nowhere else in America does *terra firma* incline so steeply and dramatically into the ocean. The Santa Lucias extend a hundred miles south of Carmel, often towering several thousand feet above the surf.

The vistas are stunning of course, and they must be earned, for this place of vertical beauty yields to roads only reluctantly. Indeed, chunks of Highway 1 periodically fall into the sea, as if the reclusive god of Big Sur is trying to throw pesky intruders from its back. A massive slide in 1983 closed the highway for a year and required the rearrangement of three million cubic yards of earth.

Big Sur is wilderness with a bohemian California attitude. It's a steep pathway to individualism where many may visit, but few find the means to stay. It may be America's last grand retreat—a judicious mix of reclusive artists, back-to-the-land dropouts and a few super rich determined to go beyond the reach of their cellular phones. Big Sur is road-hugging BMWs and rusty pickups and kids with backpacks. It's cliff-clinging mansions cloaked in trees, beachside crash pads fashioned from flotsam and weathered shacks draped around fieldstone fireplaces. And it was, until the arrival of satellite dishes, a land free of TV.

For decades, Big Sur successfully resisted intruders. The Spanish California government, busy with Monterey, claimed this land but did nothing with it, except to name it *El Pais Grande del Sur,* the big country to the south. In 1843, the Mexican government granted a large chunk to Juan Bautista Alvarado, who was to become governor of Alta California. He established El Rancho Sur along the banks of *Rio Grande del Sur.*

The area's current name is an odd English-Spanish mix. Following the same logic, would a Spaniard call it *El Grande South*?

As the 20th century approached, towns immediately north and south of Big Sur began to blossom. However, no through road punctured these vertical wilds. Highway 1 finally was completed in 1937, hacked out of coastal bluffs, mostly by convict labor from San Quentin. Thirty-two bridges had to be built to span many of the 50 creeks—mostly seasonal—that spill down from the heights. Bixby Creek Bridge, 260 feet above a steep coastal canyon, was the highest single-arch bridge in the world when it was finished in 1934. Initially called the Roosevelt Highway, it was changed to the Cabrillo Highway in the 1950s. Lady Bird Johnson and California Governor "Pat" Brown designated it as America's first scenic highway in 1966.

Writers and artists, who suffer no need to commute or to communicate directly with society, have been drawn to this area for decades. Poet Robinson Jeffers tramped these wilds from his lair in Carmel and author Henry Miller spent many of his creative years here. Others began braving the coiled highway to hike the heights of the Santa Lucias and seek out hidden beaches. Naturally, as each person arrives, he or she wants the door slammed behind. Big Sur residents resist development with a zeal bordering on fanaticism.

Business picked up when Hollywood brought Dick and Liz to film *The Sandpipers* a couple of decades ago. Nepenthe, a restaurant and art complex dating back to the 1950s, became a popular hangout for locals, drop-in film stars and star-gazing tourists. It survives today as an inviting lunch and dinner stop that's *de rigeuer* for the Big Sur visitor. There is no finer place on the coast to watch day's end than on Nepenthe's deck, with a glass of overpriced wine in hand.

Big Sur has no specific boundaries, since it is not a specific place. There *is* a community by that name. However, it's not really a town, but a thin scattering of settlements in search of their post office. Most folks have decided that El Grande South starts just below Carmel Highlands and ends somewhere around the Monterey-San Luis Obispo county border.

We'll go along with that reasoning, because that's where we've decided to end the southward thrust of this book. It's appropriate, since this central coastal region is a transition zone between northern and southern California. (Most residents of San Luis Obispo and Santa Barbara counties, however, scorn any ties with the Southland. They're part of *Central* California, thank you!)

The north-south coast takes an inside tuck below Point Sur and the climate becomes drier. Although upper Big Sur has some of the heaviest rainfall in California, the redwoods disappear and the mountains grow bald as you head southward. Approaching the San Luis Obispo County line, you note a distinct southern California look to the browning hills and roadside chaparral. The coast-hugging Santa Lucias persist for a few more miles. Then they begin drawing inland below San Simeon to leave a handy coastal shelf for the towns of Morro Bay and San Luis Obispo.

Although coastal vistas are awesome through much of Big Sur, the coast itself is difficult to reach. Much of the highway was cut into headlands a hundred feet or so above the sea. Travelers will find easier beach access as the highway approaches San Luis Obispo County.

Driving Big Sur

No place in California is so remote that a paved highway won't invite traffic jams. On summer weekends, Big Sur's asphalt artery can be a bumper-to-bumper nightmare. From fall through spring, it can be a scenic delight. If you must visit in summer, at least wait until Monday morning before sallying forth.

Advisory to RVers and others behind the wheel: Although the terrain is wildly pitched, Highway 1 is gently curved for the most part, since scores of bridges span the narrow coastal gorges. You'll likely encounter more twists and turns on northern Highway 1 above San Francisco, where the roadbed often winds down into canyons.

Heading south on Highway 1, you pass through **Carmel Highlands,** with elegant sea view homes graced by pines and formal gardens. To indulge in a brief fit of envy, take a short detour on Yankee Point Drive past some of this opulence. It loops back to the highway after less than a mile.

Below Carmel Highlands, the highway climbs into Santa Lucia's near vertical flanks, offering stunning vistas of seastacks with the surf frothing at their feet. The mountains, reaching thousands of feet above the sea, offer a mix of tilted forests and velvety pasturelands. Turnouts beg you to pause and reach for your camera, or at least for your adjectives.

Hikers can sample some of Big Sur's wilderness in the undeveloped 42,879-acre **Garrapata State Park,** about ten miles south of Carmel. You'll find no road entrance or developed parking areas. To explore the area, use turnouts near **Soberanes Point.** Trails lead through a varied terrain of moors, redwood groves and even cactus patches to the beach.

Two roads crawl up the Santa Lucia range from the Coast Highway to offer incredible aerial views and relief from summer traffic. Pick up paved but skinny **Palo Colorado Road** about four miles south of Soberanes Point for a dizzying climb into narrow **Palo Colorado Canyon**. The name means "tall red," certainly appropriate for the trees of the area. At road's end is **Bottchers Gap Campground** and picnic area, with primitive campsites and trailheads for the **Ventana Wilderness Area.**

About a mile and a half south, the **Coast Road** cuts upward and inland near picturesque concrete arch **Bixby Bridge.** (The bridge, incidentally, is perhaps the most photographed subject along the Big Sur Coast.) The only route south before the Cabrillo Highway was built, the Coast Road ascends the mountains' flanks and then tailspins back down to Route 1. It's unpaved, rutted and subject to washouts. Take great care as you follow its spiral roller coaster course through tree-canopied canyons to high points for incredible coastal views. Having survived, you will agree that it's one of California's grand side roads.

RV advisory: Both roads are narrow and winding, definitely not recommended for trailers, large RVs or the faint of heart.

About 15 miles south of Carmel, the Cabrillo Highway swings inland to avoid the imposing muffin-shaped promontory of **Moro Rock** at Point Sur. Perched on top is an historic lighthouse that now functions as a state park:

☺ *Point Sur State Historic Park* ● *C/o Pfeiffer Big Sur State Park, Big Sur, CA 93920-0001; (408) 625-4419. Accessible by guided tours only, conducted Saturdays at 9:30 and 1:30 and Sundays at 9:30. No reservations needed; be at the highway gate at the appropriate time. Adults $5, kids $2.* Tours take visitors up a spiral road to the top of Moro Rock, upon which is perched the finely crafted stone Point Sur Lighthouse and several outbuildings. You can follow your guide up a spiral stairway within the lighthouse and enjoy imposing views of the Big Sur Coast. The original Fresnel lens has been spirited away to the new Monterey Bay Maritime Museum, although most of the rest of the facility is intact. At the visitor center, you can watch a charming 1950s film about a day in the life of a Coast Guard lighthouse keeper and his family, and other videos on the history, flora and fauna of the area. Graphics advise you that you're standing atop a 300-foot basaltic mound known geologically as a *tombolo.*

Point Sur Light was completed in 1889 to join the network of light and fog signals that guided coastal shipping before the advent of north-south highways. Isolated in this wilderness, men of the U.S. Lighthouse Service tended the oil-burning lamp while their families tended gardens to keep food on the table. Supplies arrived only three times a year, hoisted by crane from a seagoing tender. Eventually, a rough wagon road was carved to Pfeiffer's resort, where families could pick up mail and essentials. The light was taken over by the Coast Guard in 1939, automated in 1974 and deeded to the state parks department in 1984.

Andrew Molera State Park, a few miles south of Point Sur, occupies a shallow inland valley on the Big Sur River. Several miles of hiking trails

Big Sur's Bixby Creek Bridge, 260 feet above a coastal canyon, was the world's highest single-arch span when it was completed in 1934. — **Betty Woo Martin**

wind through the park's undeveloped 4,800 acres. You can picnic near the parking area and hike or bike a short distance to a campground. A one-mile trail follows a riparian stream bed to an attractive wilderness coast. Day use fee is $6; hike-in/bike-in camping $3. The park, incidentally, occupies a portion of Juan Bautista Cooper's El Rancho del Sur.

South of the park, Highway 1 swerves away from the ocean to follow the lazy curves of the river and stitch together scattered pieces of the Big Sur community. Big Sur's **River Inn** here offers rustic lodging and casual dining. Its **Heartbeat Gift Shop** displays items typical of Big Sur's holistic-hedonistic boutiques, such as Kama Sutra oils, African drums and books on self realization and—uh—erection protection. Just beyond is an historic resort turned state park:

☺ ***Pfeiffer Big Sur State Park*** • *Big Sur, CA 93920; (408) 667-2315. Day use $6, camping $14 (details below). Lodge, restaurant, store, picnic areas and hiking trails.* California bought 680 acres of redwoods and creek valleys from the pioneer Pfeiffer family in 1933 as one of the early elements of its state park system. Included in the deal was Pfeiffer's Ranch Resort. Now Big Sur Lodge, it remains a focal point for this attractive park, along with several sturdy stone and log park buildings constructed during the Depression by the Civilian Conservation Corps. From the main visitor area, a short road and several hiking trails extend into a wooded haven of redwood groves, waterfalls and ferny canyons. An hour's hike will take you to Pfeiffer Falls. A two-hour grunt will get you to Buzzard's Roost atop Pfeiffer Ridge for splendid views of the ocean and Santa Lucia range. No wilderness experience, this. The park gets exceedingly busy with visitors in summer. Get your name in early for campsite or lodge reservations (listed below).

Just beyond the state park is **Big Sur Station,** an information center jointly operated by the state park and forest services. Open daily from 8 to 4:30, it offers lots of maps and books on the area. Helpful rangers can tell you where to hike and what to see. They'll also tell you how to reach one of the few beach accesses in the heart of this inland Big Sur area. Here's how:

☺ Half a mile from the station, watch on your right for a "narrow road" sign and follow it down through a ferny forest. It's called Sycamore Canyon Road, although no sign betrays this information. After 2.5 miles, you'll reach **Pfeiffer Beach,** a wonderful little bit of strand sheltered by a rocky cove. Note the offshore Arch Rock, with a square tunnel pounded through by the relentless surf.

RV advisory: The road to Pfeiffer Beach has its predictable twists, but carefully driven RVs—even large ones—can make it. If you're towing a trailer, you might want to leave it parked at the state park or in the Big Sur Station parking lot.

You'll find another fragment of "urban Big Sur" just below the Pfeiffer Beach turnoff. It has the post office to prove it, plus a deli café and general store. A short distance beyond is a left turn to **Ventana Inn** and beyond that, a right branch up to the legendary **Nepenthe.** Once you achieve Nepenthe's perch, you'll see that the Pacific—missing for the last several miles—is just down the hill, filtered through the trees.

☺ Pause for a drink on Nepenthe's deck or **Café Kevah** which sits atop the roof of the **Phoenix,** one of the more interesting gift shops you'll find anywhere. In addition to the usual sensual oils and regionally correct books, you'll encounter a fine selection of natural fiber clothing, both from area artists and from abroad, hand-knit woolens and earthy jewelry.

The **Henry Miller Library** just below Nepenthe houses a collection of the Big Sur author's writings and papers. It can be seen by appointment only; (408) 667-2574 or 667-2537. Next in line along Route 1 is **Deetjen's Big Sur Inn,** another early day hideaway. Beyond that, the highway again begins skittering dizzily above the Pacific.

☺ A short distance below Deetjen's, **Coast Gallery and Café** (408-667-2301) offers your last chance for a gallery browse. It features a fine selection of local artists' works, jewelry, crafts, books by Henry Miller and a small café. They're housed in three huge redwood water tanks once used by a naval hospital. The largest, 32 feet in diameter and 18 feet high, held 100,000 gallons. The café offers a scenic Pacific vista from its small patio.

Below here, the highway becomes a real cliff hanger. It's easy to see why pieces occasionally fall into the ocean. As you stare down from your asphalt perch, the term "edge of the continent" takes on real meaning. This is not a place for folks with vertigo or bad brakes.

Julia Pfeiffer Burns State Park is a day-use retreat ($6 per vehicle) with hiking trails leading into the Ventana Wilds. This spectacular 1,800-acre slice of Big Sur crawls high into the Santa Lucias and drops hundreds of feet from the roadway to the ocean. The short Waterfall Trail takes you to McWay Waterfall that plunges directly into the surf. A steep trail, 1.8 miles north of the park entrance, leads down to the beach at Partington Cove; use caution in getting there. (Get details on this park's trails and hike-in campsites at Big Sur Station.)

Pressing southward, you'll note that the landscape becomes drier and bushier; trees are confined to the higher crests. Clumps of pampas grass sprout from the roadside and you detect that subtle change to Southern Californiana. This is one of the least populated stretches along the entire coast of western America. You'll see little hint of humanity between the Coast Gallery and San Simeon. The map shows two communities along Big Sur's lower reaches—**Lucia** and **Gorda.** Each consists of a service station, cafè and mini-mart; Lucia has a few cabins. Gorda was conducting a going-out-of-business sale when we last passed.

Los Padres National Forest's **Kirk Creek campground,** between Lucia and Gorda, offers some great spots right over the ocean; $10 with flush potties. The balding Santa Lucia range retreats inland through this area, allowing the highway to drop down toward the water. Several national forest picnic areas offer beach access, particularly on a wide coastal shelf called **Pacific Valley** between Lucia and Gorda.

As you pass into **San Luis Obispo County** south of Gorda, you begin seeing vestiges of civilization. Particularly civilized is newspaper baron William Randolph Hearst's palatial hideaway, now a state park. Despite its remoteness, Hearst Castle is extremely popular, so make tour reservations *well in advance.* Like the highway that brought you here, the place should be avoided on summer weekends. During the slow season, you might catch a tour without a reservation, but don't bet on it.

Hearst San Simeon State Historic Monument • *P.O. Box 8, San Simeon, CA 93452; (805) 927-2020. Four 1.5-hour tours available; daily 8 to 5 in summer and 8:20 to 3:20 the rest of the year. Adults $14, kids $8; special evening tours $25. For tour reservations by phone contact Mistix at (800) 444-PARK, (800) 444-4445; or write Mistix, P.O. Box 85705, San Diego, CA 92186-5705. For wheelchair accessible tours, call the state park at (805) 927-2020. MC/VISA, AMEX, DISC accepted.*

Hearst's incredible Spanish renaissance *La Casa Grande* crowns a hill 1,600 feet above the ocean. It's surrounded by 127 acres of gardens and a private zoo. Convinced that "pleasure is worth what you can afford to pay," the newspaper baron filled his 165-room mansion with priceless European art and furnishings. His agents raided cathedrals, churches and monasteries for coffered ceilings, choir stalls and other relics to decorate his monument to excess. A museum in the visitor center at the base off the hill offers a retrospective of Hearst and Julia Morgan, the architect who designed the lavish complex. Plan an extra half hour or so to absorb its offerings.

Of the four available tours, the first is recommended for first-timers, taking them through the gardens, a guest house and ground floor of the main building. Tour Two goes to the upper floors of the mansion, housing Hearst's private quarters. Tour Three focuses on the lavish gardens, and includes the main building's guest wing, a guest house and a video about the castle's construction. Tour Four is a special behind-the-scenes look at the wine cellar, dressing rooms and guest house. Special evening tours cover highlights of the overall complex and feature a living history program.

WHERE TO DINE IN BIG SUR

Coast Cafè • △△ **$**

At the Coast Gallery; (408) 667-2301. American, wine and beer. Daily 9 to 4:30. MC/VISA. Pleasant place for a leisurely pastrami sandwich, salad or bowl of soup. It's housed in a giant former water tank, with sea views from a postage stamp of a patio.

Deetjen's Big Sur Inn ● ΔΔ $$$
South end of Big Sur; (408) 667-2377. Continental; wine and beer. Break-fast 8 to 11:30, dinner 6 to 8:30. No credit cards. Rustic old European red-wood dining room with antiques, open beams and crackling fireplace. The fare includes rock cornish game hen, vegetarian dishes, lamb and steaks with French accents in the seasoning.

Glen Oaks ● ΔΔΔ $$$ Ø
North of state park; (408) 667-2623. American regional; wine and beer. Dinner 6 to 10 p.m. MC/VISA. Elegant little candle-lit restaurant with Euro-pean touches in the décor and a California *nouveau* tilt to the menu. Settle into a bentwood chair, listen to soft music and dine on mesquite broiled fish, creative crepes and stir fried dishes touched with pineapple and ginger.

☺ Nepenthe ● ΔΔΔ $$$
South end of Big Sur; (408) 667-2345. American; full bar service. Lunch from 11:30 and dinner from 5. Reservations a must in summer. MC/VISA, AMEX. The word is Greek for "no sorrow," and you'll agree after enjoying the views. The menu features hearty, well seasoned American fare. Most dishes are well prepared, although we've had trouble with overdone and then un-derdone fish. We'll rate the food as average but the view and overall ambi-ance in this oak-shaded aerie as awesome. Prices are more digestible at adjacent **Café Kevah,** where an ambrosia burger with something to sip goes for under $10. The architecture fits the setting—an earthy Frank Lloyd Wright look with adobe brick, rough angular wood and lots of glass.

River Inn Restaurant ● ΔΔ $$$
North end of Big Sur; (408) 667-2700. American-continental; full bar serv-ice. Daily 8:30 to 10. MC/VISA, AMEX. This place fits the Big Sur mold with wood slab tables and walls and a fieldstone fireplace. Among the entrées are scallops Provençal, ravioli with crab meat sauce and linguine with mussels.

Rocky Point Restaurant ● ΔΔΔ $$$
Twelve miles south of Carmel (P.O. Box 223281, Carmel, CA 93922; (408) 624-2933. American-continental. Lunch 11:30 to 3, dinner nightly from 5:30; reservations essential. Full bar service. MC/VISA. More impressive than the menu, which offers a mix of American and European fare, is the stunning view from the restaurant's rocky perch above the Pacific. The maple dining room is simple, as if designed not to distract from the vista. Before or after dinner, have a drink on the patio for an even clearer vision. In fact, the parking lot here offers a better vista than most "view" restaurants.

Ventana Inn ● ΔΔΔ $$$$ Ø
South end of Big Sur; (408) 667-2331. American-California nouveau; full bar service. Lunch weekdays 11 to 3 and weekends noon to 3, dinner nightly 6 to 9:30. Major credit cards. This handsome, modern dining room with ex-posed beam ceilings is as elegantly woodsy as the posh hilltop resort sur-rounding it. The best views are from an outdoor deck. (They're better, however, from Nepenthe.) The pricey menu ranges from grilled fresh fish to rack of lamb and wild mushroom strudel with goat cheese.

WHERE TO SLEEP

Big Sur Campgrounds and Cabins ● ○ $$
Highway 1, Big Sur, CA 93920; (408) 667-2322. Cabins from $38, kitch-enettes $85 to $105, suites $72 to $105. MC/VISA. Rustic 13-room resort

with accommodations ranging from tent cabins to A-frames; many with fireplaces. Basketball and volleyball, fishing and swimming in nearby Big Sur River; campsites (listed below).

Big Sur Lodge ● ⌂⌂ $$$$$

Pfeiffer Big Sur State Park, P.O. Box 190, Big Sur, CA 93920; (408) 667-2171. Rooms $99 to $169, kitchenettes $20 extra, suites with kitchens and fireplaces $139 to $169. Rates include continental breakfast during the off-season. MC/VISA. Historic lodge within the state park, offering rustic, wood-paneled rooms and cottages. Gift shop and mini-mart; heated pool. **Trail Head Café** serves breakfast, lunch and dinner from 8 (no lunch in the off-season); dinners $8 to $20; wine and beer; outdoor deck.

Deetjen's Big Sur Inn ● ⌂⌂ $$$

Highway 1, Big Sur, CA 93920; (408) 667-2377. Units $66 to $136. No credit cards. Very rustic, comfortable accommodations in a 1930s redwood inn; old European atmosphere and attitude. Listed on the National Register of Historic Places, the inn was established in the 1930s by Norwegian immigrants. Wood-paneled rooms are simply furnished; some with share baths. **Restaurant** listed above.

Lucia Lodge ● ⌂⌂ $$$

Route 1 (Highway 1), Big Sur, CA 93920; (408) 667-2391. Couples and singles $66 to $121. No credit cards. Ten-room cliff-edge lodge with impressive ocean views. Restaurant serves 8 to 8 in summer and 8 to 6 in winter; dinners $13 to $23; full bar service.

Ripplewood Resort ● ⌂ $$$

Highway 1, Big Sur, CA 93920; (408) 667-2242. Couples and singles $45 to $80, kitchenettes $65 to $80. MC/VISA. Woodsy 16-unit resort a mile and a half south of Pfeiffer Big Sur State Park, with decks and fireplaces. A small **café** serves breakfast and lunch from 8 to 1; wine and beer.

River Inn ● ⌂⌂ $$$$

Pheneger Creek, Big Sur, CA 93920; (408) 625-5255. Couples $70 to $100, suites $125 to $145. MC/VISA, AMEX. Big Sur's oldest resort, dating from 1937 when it was operated as a roadhouse by the Pfeiffer family. Rustic motel style units; pool and lawns adjacent to Big Sur River. **Restaurant** listed above.

Ventana Inn ● ⌂⌂⌂ $$$$$ Ø

Ventana, Big Sur, CA 93920; (800) 628-6500 in California only; (408) 667-2331 or 624-4812. Couples and singles $165 to $785, suites $315 to $785, includes continental breakfast. Major credit cards. Opulent hideaway tucked into the woods; extensive grounds with hilltop views of the distant Pacific; two swimming pools, hot tubs, saunas and massage rooms. Elegantly rustic rooms with TV, VCRs and refrigerators; many rooms and suites with hot tubs and fireplaces. All public areas are non-smoking. **Restaurant** listed above.

WHERE TO CAMP

Big Sur Campground ● *Highway 1, Big Sur, CA 93920; (408) 667-2322. RV and tent sites, $20; Cabins listed above. Reservations accepted; MC/VISA.* Two miles north of Pfeiffer Big Sur State Park; shaded sites among redwoods by Big Sur River. Showers, coin laundry, playground, swimming and fishing in river.

Kirk Creek Campground • *Highway 1 near Gorda. RV and tent sites, $10. No reservations or credit cards.* Los Padres National forest campground; some sites with ocean views. Flush potties, barbecues and picnic tables.

Pfeiffer Big Sur State Park • *Big Sur, CA 93920; (408) 667-2315. RV and tent sites, $14. Reservations via Mistix, (800) 444-PARK.* Beautifully situated wooded sites beside the Big Sur River; flush potties and showers; picnic tables and barbecues. Hiking trails; restaurant and mini-mart nearby.

Riverside Campground • *Highway 1 (P.O. Box 3), Big Sur, CA 93920; (408) 667-2414. RV and tent sites, $19. Reservations accepted; MC/VISA.* Two miles north of Pfeiffer Big Sur State Park; shaded sites among redwoods by Big Sur River. Showers, coin laundry, playground, swimming and fishing in river.

SALINAS VALLEY LOOP

This one or two-day trip inland from Monterey Bay will touch three counties, two or three missions, a geological national monument and some fine wineries. And if that isn't enough variety, how about a huge reservoir and a place where you can get chocolate-covered prunes?

Incidentally, those three missions are a commentary on the ruggedness of Big Sur. Although most of the Spanish missions were located near the ocean, those impenetrable wilds pushed their connecting roadway, El Camino Real, inland through the present day Salinas Valley.

You'll be traveling for the most part through and around the Salinas Valley, a agriculturally rich basin cradled between the Santa Lucia Range and Gavilan section of the Diablo Range. To get there, we'll suggest two different exits from Monterey Bay. Your choice depends on how steady your hand is at the wheel.

The scenic but twisting route is out Carmel Valley Road, up through the mountains to Arroyo Seco Road, and on to Greenfield. We touched on this route during our Carmel Valley visit above. Nervous drivers and folks with trailers or large RVs may prefer to head out the Monterey-Salinas Highway (Route 68). Pick it up between Monterey and Seaside.

The first group will stay on Arroyo Seco until it becomes Fort Romney Road, and follow that north. The second will watch for a right turn from Route 68 onto River Road, just past Toro Regional Park, a mile or so short of Salinas. Southbound River Road eventually becomes Fort Romney Road, and both groups can meet in front of the loneliest of missions:

Mission Nuestra Senora de la Soledad • *36641 Fort Romney Rd., Soledad; (408) 678-2586. Chapel open daily except Tuesday, 10 to 4; free.* Perhaps it was that unlucky number 13. *Senora de la Soledad* translates as our lady of solitude and this was the sorriest of the missions. Established in 1791 as the 13th in California's 21-mission chain, it is one of the few that fell to total ruin. What you see today is a reconstruction of the original chapel, a pleasant garden and crumbling walls of the original mission. The walls have been capped with gunnite to prevent further deterioration.

If you don't mind driving about 40 miles out of your way, you can visit San Antonio de Padua, a mission that's rarely visited and very nicely preserved. To reach it, go briefly south on Fort Romney, turn east to get to Highway 101 and follow it to **King City.** Before continuing on to the mission, hop off at the first exit, turn left onto San Antonio Drive and follow it a few blocks to that town's fine little park and museum:

☺ **San Lorenzo Park** • *San Antonio Drive, King City; (408) 385-5964. Day use $4, camping $16 with water and electric and $12 with no hookups.* Missed by most travelers on U.S. 101, this park encloses the **Monterey County Agricultural Rural Life Museum.** Its centerpiece is a large unpainted barn housing farm implements, carriages, old cars, historic photos and pioneer relics. All are nicely arranged, with lots of room to move about. Surrounding the barn are several historic buildings moved here from elsewhere in the county. The park also has picnic tables, barbecue areas and RV camping. A **visitors information center** sits among the exhibits in the barn, offering maps and brochures concerning King City and Monterey county.

From King City, go briefly north over the Salinas River bridge and head south on Jolon Road toward **Fort Hunter Liggett.** It occupies a large swatch of dusty prairie and encircles this gem among the missions. There are no entry formalities for the army base.

☺ **Mission San Antonio de Padua** • *P.O. Box 803, Jolon, CA 93928; (408) 385-4478. Monday-Saturday 10 to 4:30, Sunday 11 to 4:30; $1 donation.* If you can ignore the tank tracks in the background, San Antonio enjoys the most authentic present-day setting of any mission in the chain. Surrounded by open fields, this handsomely restored brick and adobe complex reflects the spaciousness typical of these early California settlements. Note its burnt-brick bell tower, barrel-arched ceiling leading to the sanctuary with hand-painted illuminations, and classic arched colonnade. This was the third and one of the more prosperous of the missions, established in 1771 by Father Serra.

Return to King City and follow Broadway through town. Then pick up County Road G-13 (Bitterwater/King City Road) heading east. You'll climb gently through a low point in the **Gavilan Range** (some spell it Gabilan) and intersect State Highway 25. Drive about 14 miles north through the remote Paicines agricultural valley, and then turn west toward another divine temple. This one was shaped by erosion, not by Bible-toting padres.

☺ **Pinnacles National Monument** • *Paicines, CA 95043; (408) 389-4485. Entrance fee $4 per car. Commercial campground outside east entrance, $15 for water and electric, less for dry camping. Small campground on west side $8, no hookups.* The Pinnacles are fragments of a 23 million year old volcano, eroded into fantastic shapes by wind and rain. Like gnarled fingers, they reach skyward in stark contrast to the sensuously rounded contours of the rest of the Gavilans.

Too rugged to be crossed by road, Pinnacles has two approaches: from the east through Paicines Valley, and from the west off Highway 101 from Soledad. The eastern slope is the most interesting, containing the park's fieldstone visitor center with a small museum, built during Depression make-work days. The park can be crossed by a steep trail that winds up and among these tortured spires, ridges and peaks. From the top, which can be reached in an hour, the views of the Salinas Valley and its cradling mountains are awesome.

Pinnacles is a one-dimensional park, and that dimension is fascinating. Other than dusty oak-chaparral woodlands, it offers little to the car-bound visitor. If you hike, however, you'll travel among some of the most fascinating shapes in geology. Start with the so-called Bear Gulch Caves route, reached by a short hike from the visitor center. These "caves" were formed when giant boulders tumbled from above and wedged themselves into a narrow ravine. Watch your head in the low places and don't fret; these van-sized boulders haven't budged in centuries. Hike here in the spring, when a seasonal creek plunges and hisses through narrow cracks. You'll need a flashlight for some of the more enclosed areas.

Best time to visit the Pinnacles is during the March through May wild-flower season. (Avoid spring weekends, when herds rush in from surrounding areas. Because of crowds, camping isn't permitted on weekends on the west side.) With no sheltering trees among these barebones rocks, the park is sizzling hot in summer. If you must visit then, hit the trails at daybreak so the sun is warming your back, not frying your face. In any season, take lots of water and beware of rattlesnakes.

Incidentally, you're in the heart of earthquake country here. The notorious **San Andreas Fault** runs through the Paicines Valley on the eastern edge of the Pinnacles. Hollister to the north shakes so frequently that it's called California's earthquake city. Because of the torturous movement of the Pacific and North American plates at the fault line, the Pinnacles have shifted 195 miles north of their original location, northeast of Los Angeles!

RV advisory: The western access, Highway 146, is very steep and winding, not recommended for trailers or large RVs. The eastern approach is more gentle, easily handled by most larger rigs. The approach from King City or Hollister is all paved and relatively smooth.

From the Pinnacles, continue north on State Route 25 to **Hollister.** This small farming community looks reasonably intact despite frequent cases of the shakes. Our eventual destination is San Juan Bautista. However, we recommend that you first detour to a king sized specialty foods place that features chocolate covered dried fruits, which taste much better than they sound. Pick up State Highway 156 in Hollister and follow it five miles north to Route 152, then go northeast a mile to:

Casa De Fruta ● *6680 Pacheco Pass Highway, Hollister, CA 95023; (800) 548-3813 or (408) 842-9316.* A few decades ago, the farming Zanger brothers started a roadside fruit stand here. It has since ripened into the largest specialty foods operation in this part of the state. Chocolate-dipped dried fruits are only part of their huge line of specialty foods. The complex also has a wine tasting bar, small zoo, kiddie train and play area, large grocery and gift shop, service station, motel and RV park (see "Where to sleep" and "Where to camp" below).

Thirteen miles east of Casa de Fruta, over 1,368-foot **Pacheco Pass,** is **San Luis Reservoir State Recreation Area.** It doesn't dam a river, but provides storage for the huge California Water Project. The pond is of interest mostly to boaters (although it offers camping, picnicking and bird watching). We'll take a better look in Chapter 10. Retrace your route west on Highway 156, nip back through Hollister and head for a fine old Spanish town that's one of our favorite California retreats:

San Juan Bautista

Population: 1,600   **Elevation: 200 feet**

Sitting just off busy Highway 101 yet somehow undisturbed by it, San Juan Bautista dozes around an old Spanish plaza. It is little changed—in attitude, at least—from its mission days. Come on a weekday when the tourists have thinned out, and you can lose yourself in a kinder, gentler era.

Walk the cool stone colonnades of the handsome old mission and study the wagon tracks still evident in El Camino Real that passes nearby. Admire casually-kept gardens fronting weather-worn Victorian homes and white-washed adobes in the neighborhoods. Poke into the ancient structures of San Juan Bautista State Historic Park that rim the grassy plaza. End your visit with some spicy food appropriate to the setting. Second Street is lined with restaurants and they're nearly all Mexican. A few antique and gift shops are spaced among them.

Spanish padres arrived here in 1797 to establish their 15th Alta California mission. By 1814, a town had begun to develop around the plaza. San Juan Bautista is thus one of the state's older civil settlements. Many of its structures are preserved in the state historic park. The mission itself is not part of the park, but is an active parish church. Since it was never abandoned, it is one of the least modified of California's 21 missions. This is particularly remarkable since the venerable adobe structure sits beside the San Andreas Fault.

☺ **San Juan Bautista State Historic Park** • *P.O. Box 1110, San Juan Bautista, CA 95045; (408) 623-4881. Adult $2, kids $1. Most buildings open daily 10 to 4:30.* Start your visit with a 12-minute slide show on the town's history. It's shown on request at park headquarters in the **Plaza Hotel** at Second and Mariposa streets. Then poke about the hotel's rooms, downstairs and up, many with early 1800s furnishings. Note the nicely restored barroom, complete with green felt poker tables.

The next-door **Castro-Breen Adobe,** also with period furnishings, has ties to California's Mexican and Gringo history. Built by civil administrator Jose Tiburico Castro in 1840, the house was sold in 1848 to John Breen, whose family had survived the Donner tragedy two years earlier. Breen struck out for the Sierra Nevada gold fields, came home with $12,000 and bought the adobe along with 400 acres. Family members occupied it until 1933. Among other historic park structures is the **Zanette House,** built in 1815 as sleeping quarters for unmarried Indian women of the Mission. It's restored to a later period, when it served as a boarding house. Adjacent is the **Plaza Stable,** which offers a nice collection of old carriages. The town **blacksmith shop,** busy with tools and a forge, stands just behind.

☺ **Mission San Juan Bautista** • *Second Street at the Plaza; (408) 623-2127. Open March-October 9:30 to 5 and November-February 9:30 to 4:30. Admission by donation.* Little has changed in this white stucco, pink tiled mission named for St. John the Baptist. More restored than renovated, it still retains its heavy arched columns, tiles polished by nearly two centuries of footfalls and hand-painted trim in the sanctuary. The present church, built in 1812, is the largest of the mission chain and the only one with three aisles. Out back, you can walk through the casual, nicely kept garden where 4,000 Indians are buried. Out front is a commentary on the mission's amazing survival: A seismograph in an earthquake exhibit marks each moment this stubborn old town rocks and rolls.

South of San Juan Bautista, San Juan Canyon road hurries through farm fields and then crawls painfully to the top of Frèmont Peak in **Frèmont Peak State Park.** You'll find a primitive campground, picnic area and hiking trails that wind around the hot, dusty 3,169-foot mound. Originally called Gavilan Peak, it earned its new name after John C. Frèmont and Kit

Carson took the high ground here in 1846. They unfurled the American flag and dared the Mexicans to attack. Jose Castro demanded that they withdraw. After some touchy negotiations, they did so—"slowly and growlingly," according to Frèmont's journal.

WHERE TO DINE

Cademartori's ● ∆∆ $$
600 First St.; (408) 623-4511. Italian-American; full bar service. Tuesday-Saturday 11:30 to 2 and dinner from 5, Sunday 1 to 9. Major credit cards. Something of a local legend, this large barn-like place has been serving huge Italian meals since the 1950s. The exterior look is Spanish, but the accent inside is definitely *Al Italia.* Try hearty fare such as seasoned veal cutlet, chicken cacciatore and calamari steak Bordelaise.

Dona Ester Restaurant ● ∆ $
Third and Franklin; (408) 623-2518. Mexican; full bar service. Weekdays 11 to 10, Saturday 9 to 10, Sunday 9 to 9. Major credit cards. Brick walled place with oldstyle Mexican and early American dècor. The menu is mostly Mexican, with a Gringo touches like tiger prawn enchiladas. It's quite inexpensive, with several dinners under $10.

Jardine de San Juan ● ∆∆ $$
115 Third St.; (408) 623-4466. Mexican; full bar service. Daily 11:30 to 10. MC/VISA. San Juan's most attractive restaurant, built around a Spanish courtyard; indoor and outdoor dining. The interior is simply done, in salmon and turquoise with decorative Mexican mirrors. Try the *huachinango ala Alicia* (red snapper with sour cream on a bed of rice).

La Casa Rosa ● ∆ $
107 Third St.; (408) 623-4563. Mexican-American; wine and beer. Lunch Wednesday-Monday 11:30 to 3:30, dinner Friday-Saturday from 5:30, closed Tuesday. Early Mexican-American style cafè that serves three basic lunch offerings: two casseroles and a chicken souffle. Dinner menu is more versatile.

WHERE TO SLEEP

Best Western San Benito Inn ● ⌂⌂ $$$ Ø
660 San Felipe Rd. (Highway 156), Hollister, CA 95023; (408) 637-9248. Couples $50 to $55, singles $40 to $45. Major credit cards. Attractive 42-unit motel with TV movies, room phones and pool.

Casa de Fruta Motel ● ⌂ $$$
10031 Pacheco Pass Highway (Highway 152), Hollister, CA 95023; (800) 548-3813 or (408) 842-9316. Couples $55 to $59, singles $51 to $55; rates include continental breakfast. MC/VISA. A 14-unit motel with TV movies, phones and refrigerators; pool. Adjacent facilities include several dining areas, mini-mart, gift shop, service station, zoo, play area and RV park .

Hollister Inn ● ⌂ $$ Ø
153 San Felipe Rd. (Highway 156), Hollister, CA 95023; (800) 371-1641 or (408) 637-1641. Couples $38 to $64, singles $36 to $48. Major credit cards. A 31-unit motel with TV and room phones; some refrigerators and microwaves; spa.

Posada de San Juan Hotel ● ⌂⌂ $$$ Ø
310 Fourth St. (P.O. Box 2130), San Juan Bautista, CA 95045; (800) 742-3401 or (408) 623-4030. Couples and singles $58 to $98, suites $115 to

$130. *Major credit cards.* Spanish style inn with TV movies, room phones, gas fireplaces and spa tubs; some rooms with refrigerators and microwaves.

Ridgemark Guest Cottages ● ⌒⌒⌒ $$$
Ridgemark Golf & Country Club, 3800 Airline Highway, Hollister, CA 95023; (408) 637-8151. MC/VISA. Attractive 32-unit golf resort with TV movies, phones; some cottages with spa tubs. Tennis, 36-hole golf course. **Restaurant** serves 7 a.m. to 9 p.m.; dinners $11 to $20; full bar service.

WHERE TO CAMP

Betabel RV Resort ● *9664 Betabel Rd., San Juan Bautista, CA 95045; (408) 623-2202. RV and tent sites, $15 to $22. Reservations accepted; MC/VISA.* Well-maintained park with pull-throughs, showers, picnic tables and barbecues, TV cable, coin laundry, mini-mart, playground, lawn game area and swimming pool.

Casa de Fruta ● *10031 Pacheco Pass Highway (Highway 152), Hollister, CA 95023; (800) 548-3813 or (408) 842-9316. RV sites, $22. Reservations accepted; MC/VISA.* Tree-shaded sites, many pull-throughs; showers, cable TV; adjacent Casa de Fruta complex has a swimming pool, shops, mini-mart, zoo and various recreational facilities.

Frémont Peak State Park ● *San Juan Canyon Rd. (P.O. Box 1110), San Juan Bautista, CA 95045; (408) 623-4255. RV and tent sites, $8.* Primitive campsites with pit potties, barbecues and picnic tables; nature trails.

Mission Farm RV Park ● *400 San Juan-Hollister Rd., San Juan Bautista, CA 95045. RV and tent sites, full hookups $20. Reservations accepted; MC/VISA.* Attractive park set in an old farmyard. Shaded sites in a walnut grove; showers, coin laundry, mini-mart, rec hall and horseshoes.

Pinnacle Campground ● *Paicines, on State Route 146 outside east gate of Pinnacles National Monument; (408) 389-4485.* RV and tent sites, from $6 per person to $15 for water and electric. Reservations accepted. Some wooded sites; showers, mini-mart, pool.

Days of wine and stinking roses

From San Juan Bautista, westbound State Route 156 provides a quick run back to Highway 1 and Monterey Bay. But, what's your hurry? This is supposed to be a Discovery Guide. Instead, follow highway 101 about seven miles north to **Gilroy** in the southern Santa Clara Valley. It's the garlic capital of the world and home to a collection of small premium wineries.

More than 90 percent of America's garlic is produced hereabouts. As a visitor, you can immerse yourself in the essence and flavors of this "stinking rose" or "scented pearl," depending on your attitude toward garlic breath. Shops and some winery tasting rooms sell an alarming assortment of garlicky food items. Will Rogers once said that Gilroy was "the only town in America where you can marinate a steak by hanging it on a clothesline."

The Gilroy Garlic Festival, held the last full weekend of July, attracts more than 140,000 visitors each year. They gather for the *Tour de Garlique* bicycle run, Garlic Gallop, Garlic Squeeze Barn Dance and—hold your breath for the grand finale—the Great Garlic Cook off. The *Los Angeles Herald-Examiner* once called it the "ultimate summer food fair."

This garlic gathering gala isn't the only reason to visit the southern Santa Clara Valley. The area's small wineries, offering excellent premium wines, provide an even better excuse.

Gilroy

Population: 31,760   **Elevation: 194 feet**

Gilroy got its start in the mid-19th century when a dour Scotsman named John Cameron went AWOL from a British ship in Monterey Bay and scampered inland. Using his mother's maiden name of Gilroy—perhaps to avoid detection—he befriended the Ortega ranching family, married one of the daughters and settled down. The Ortega-Gilroys planted orchards and raised cattle, gradually forming the hub of a community. Several Italian families followed, guessed correctly that this was a good place to make wine and grow garlic for their pasta.

The wineries are small family affairs which never suffer the crowds of the more famous Napa-Sonoma operations. Further, the person who pours your wine might be the one who made it.

Before going wine tasting, pause to catch your garlic breath. In fact, you can do both simultaneously. At the point where the freeway portion of U.S. 101 ends just south of Gilroy, take a sniff-and-sip break:

☺ ***Rapazzini Winery & Garlic Shoppe*** • *Highway 101 at Hollister Avenue; (408) 842-5649. Daily 9 to 6 in summer, 9 to 5 the rest of the year. MC/VISA.* The Garlic Shoppe offers every conceivable application of the scented pearl. Try (hold your breath) garlic herb sauce, garlic mustard, garlic mayonnaise, garlic jelly, garlic barbecue and pasta sauce, garlic Bordelaise sauce and—good grief—even garlic ice cream. Many of these items can be sampled, including several non-garlic specialty foods. Garlic garlands are available, too, in case you want to start a new trend in costume jewelry. If the stinking rose starts getting to you, step up to the winetasting counter and sample Rapazzini's line of varietals. Don't forget to taste the *Chateau de Garlic.*

Another establishment, **Garlic World,** is just up the highway, offering more scented pearl fare.

Gilroy's wine country is focused along Route 152, the westbound Hecker Pass Highway. Several wineries stand alongside the highway, waiting for you to drop in. Here are some of our favorites, in order of their appearance:

A. Conrotto Winery • *1690 Hecker Pass Highway, Gilroy, CA 95020; (408) 842-3053. Weekends only 11 to 5 (11:30 to 5 in winter), MC/VISA, DISC.* Housed in a cute little red shed, Conrotto's rustic tasting room looks out over an orchard, not a vineyard. A deck invites visitors to linger. A small vineyard of Symphony grapes in the front reminds visitors that this is indeed a winery.

Live Oaks Winery • *3875 Hecker Pass Highway, Gilroy, CA 95020; (408) 842-2401. Daily 8 to 5, MC/VISA, AMEX.* Visitors wander through an old farmyard and follow a gravel road down into a hollow to find this rustic little place. Once there, you step into a long, rudimentary tasting room whose walls are lined—not with wine—but with glossies of TV and movie stars. Tasting room manager Al Whitaker collects celebrity photos, claiming an accumulation of about 20,000. He sells them, along with wines, in the tasting room.

Solis Winery • *3920 Hecker Pass Hwy., Gilroy, CA 95020; (408) 847-6306. Open 11 to 5, daily January through April and Wednesday-Sunday May through December; major credit cards.* Solis has one of the more appealing tasting rooms in the area. A curved tasting bar is matched by a curving bay window that offers a CinemaScopic view of vineyards and forested ridges.

Thomas Kruse Winery ● *4390 Hecker Pass Hwy., Gilroy, CA 95020; (408) 842-7016. Weekends 12 to 5; no credit cards. Most varieties tasted for $1 fee (refunded with purchase).* This laid-back winery sits among a casual scatter of rudimentary equipment—an old red tractor, plastic jugs and barrels for fermenting, a canoe paddle for stirring. Tasting occurs on a plank inside a battered building, or on a barrel head outside. "No loose pets, ill behaved children, bicyclists or large groups of Republicans," advises a sign.

☺ **Fortino Winery** ● *4525 Hecker Pass Hwy., Gilroy, CA 95020; (408) 842-3305. Daily 9 to 6; MC/VISA.* Fortino is the largest, busiest and most versatile of the Hecker Pass wineries. One can buy picnic fare from the Italian deli or have a hefty sandwich constructed, pick out a bottle of wine or a soft drink, and adjourn to a tree-shaded picnic area beside a vineyard. The Ernie Fortino family makes some of the valley's best wines and sells them at civilized prices. They're particularly noted for hearty reds.

Hecker Pass Winery ● *4605 Hecker Pass Hwy., Gilroy, CA 95020; (408) 842-8755. Daily 9 to 6; MC/VISA.* Pardon the pun, but the Fortinos seems to have bottled up this end of the Gilroy wine country. Ernie's brother Mario operates this next-door winery, engaging in friendly competition with his brother. The tasting room is a simple wood-paneled affair. A pleasant picnic area sits beside the vineyards, near the forested slopes of Mount Madonna.

Two other attractions also are up this way. **Goldsmith Seeds, Inc.,** presents a spectacular quilt of flowers in summer. Visitors are welcome to stroll among its brilliant fields to admire striking geometric floral patterns. Just beyond is **Hecker Pass Family Adventure,** a theme park owned by Nob Hill Foods. Presently accessible by group reservation, it's projected to open for the public in late 1994. Call (408) 842-6436 for an update.

From the Hecker Pass wine region, you can continue west through the Santa Cruz Mountains to Watsonville. Or, at the risk of going on a wild goose chase, return to Gilroy and drive a few miles up Highway 101 to **Morgan Hill.** The purpose? To see if an intriguing facility called Wagons to Wings and the adjacent Flying Lady are functioning. To get there, take the Tennant Avenue exit in Morgan Hill, go east for a mile, swerve around to the right onto Foothill, follow it for just under a mile, then go left into the complex. (The sign isn't large, so be alert.)

Wagons to Wings is a remarkable collection of old carriages and vintage airplanes, including one of the world's few functioning Ford Tri-Motors. Just beyond, above a golf course, is the large **Flying Lady Restaurant,** with a Victorian interior and a large collection of model airplanes dangling from the ceiling. When we last visited, the restaurant had cut back to weekends only (lunch and dinner), and Wagons to Wings was locked up. So call before you go: (408) 779-4136.

Chapter six

THE DELTA & SACRAMENTO
Cruising California's rivers of history

I AM NEVER ABLE to quite describe what it is that I love about the Delta. It does not have great beauty in the sense that mountainous places with forests of tall trees have. There are no surf and miles of sandy beaches. But to me it has a sense of honesty, a reason for being. And there is beauty in tule forests and the leaning trees and the blackberry thickets and the muddied sloughs. There is beauty in the easy bend of a river and in a crumbling old shack ready to fall into the water. There is beauty in the early morning light shining off a boat at tranquil anchorage. —**Dawdling on the Delta** © **Hal Schell**

A soggy patch of land between the San Francisco Bay Area and Sacramento seems somehow transported from Mississippi bayou country. Huck Finn would feel right at home here, adrift on a raft, netting for crawdads or idly dangling his bare feet in the water, seeking respite from a muggy September sun. (In fact, the area once was used as the setting for a Huckleberry Finn movie.)

The Sacramento-San Joaquin Delta is a tangled mass of waterways covering 600 square miles. It's formed by the convergence of five rivers—the Sacramento, San Joaquin, Mokelumne, Cosumnes and Calaveras. After creating a vast swampland—since reclaimed as farmland—the almagamated streams funnel through Carquinez Strait to become the great sprawling hand of San Francisco Bay. These inland waterways and their upriver cities of Sacramento and Stockton figured prominently in California's history. Before the invention of traffic jams, water offered the only practical means for moving quantities of people and cargo. Most of the world's cities are built alongside rivers or sheltered harbors.

TRIP PLANNER

WHEN TO GO ● Our favorite Delta time of the year is September through October, when days are warm, sunny and relatively wind-free. (This is important if you've rented a houseboat; they handle like barges in a wind.) Summer is fine, since it's rarely crowded, except at some recreation areas on weekends. The weather can get hot, but with all that water, there's no problem. Fog can be pesky in the winter, and possibly dangerous on winding levee roads. Sacramento is an all-season city; its attractions are open the year around.

WHAT TO SEE ● The Blackhawk museums, John Muir National Historic Site, Benicia Capitol State Historic Park; in Sacramento, the California Railroad Museum, Sacramento History Museum, Central Pacific Passenger Station, state capitol and grounds, Sutter's Fort and State Indian Museum.

WHAT TO DO ● Drive or hike the heights of Mount Diablo State Park, walk the weathered streets of Locke, rent a houseboat and dawdle on the Delta, ride a Delta ferry, prowl the shops and museums of Old Town Sacramento, then walk along Capitol Avenue Mall to the statehouse.

Useful contacts

Bethel Island Chamber of Commerce, P.O. Box 263, Bethel Island, CA 94511; (510) 684-3220.

Delta Chambers of Commerce, 49 Main St. (P.O. Box 177), Isleton, CA 95641; (916) 777-5007.

Delta Houseboat Rental Association, 6333 Pacific Ave., Suite 152, Stockton, CA 95207; (209) 477-1840.

Old Sacramento Citizens & Merchants Association, 917 Front St., Sacramento, CA 95814; (916) 443-7815 or 443-0677.

Rio Vista Chamber of Commerce, 60 Main St., Rio Vista, CA 94571; (707) 374-2700.

Sacramento Convention & Visitors Bureau, 1421 K St., Sacramento, CA 95814; (916) 264-7777.

Schell Books, (for guides about the Delta), P.O. Box 9140, Stockton, CA 95208; (209) 951-7821.

Stockton San Joaquin Convention & Visitors Bureau, 46 W. Fremont St., Stockton, CA 95202; (800) 888-8016 or (209) 943-1987.

Delta-Sacramento radio stations

Most Bay Area stations reach the Delta; Sacramento has these offerings:

KRAK-FM, 105—country
KXJZ-FM, 88.9—jazz & news
KXPR-FM, 90.9—NPR
KGBY-FM, 92.5—adult

KYMX-FM, 96.1—classic Top 40
KDRX-AM, 650—talk
KRAK-AM, 1140—country

— **Sketch courtesy of** *Spirit of Sacramento* **cruises**

Wily Swiss entrepreneur John Sutter saw the value of water transit when he conned Mexican officials out of 47,827 acres for his California empire. As the site for his New Helvetia, he chose the confluence of the Sacramento and American rivers. After his hired hand James Marshall discovered glitter while erecting a sawmill upstream, Delta waterways provided quick access to the new gold country.

San Francisco, Sacramento and Stockton were the state's three largest cities at the peak of the Gold Rush. Water traffic was heavy for the next several decades. As many as 200 paddlewheelers plied the Sacramento and San Joaquin rivers. Both the Pony Express and transcontinental railroad used the Sacramento as the final leg of their cross-country treks.

Before all of these intruders arrived, 30,000 Maidu Indians thrived on the Delta's plentiful game and wild fruits. However, when Spanish explorers Pedro Fages and Friar Juan Crespi saw this vast expanse from the slopes of Mount Diablo in 1772, they determined it to be a mosquito-ridden swamp best avoided. Tragically, the Maidus later were practically exterminated by a malaria epidemic, probably introduced by the Spanish.

Then in the 1850s, after the flush of gold fever cooled in the foothills, some argonauts returned to this wetland to try farming. The land, flooded each spring by fresh silt, was incredibly productive. In 1850, the new state of California passed the Swamp and Overflow Act and took control of the Delta. Later, it began selling potential farmland at a dollar an acre.

Unpredictable floods made farming difficult, so levees were built to keep the rivers out of the fields. The first ones were leaky affairs made of peat blocks. Later, thousands of Chinese—newly unemployed after completing the transcontinental railroad—were hired to build an extensive levee network. They were paid the princely sum of 12 cents for every cubic yard of dirt moved. Steam powered clamshell dredges then took up the task. By the time they were finished in the 1930s, more than a thousand miles of diked waterways had been shaped from this former soggy bottom.

Dredging produced a double bonus, since it also deepened and sometimes widened the channels for ship traffic. Both Sacramento and Stockton, 100 miles upstream from the Golden Gate, are deep water ports. Delta newcomers often do a double take when they see a freighter—its hull concealed by levees—apparently sailing through a cornfield.

A distinctive look

The levees give the Delta a unique topography. Instead of merely protecting against seasonal floods, the dikes were built high enough to drain thousands of acres that originally were below sea level. The result is 55 manmade islands, linked by 70 bridges and rimmed by retaining rings of mud. Most of the Delta's roads follow these crests, linked by an assortment of draw bridges and a few small ferries.

Although larger communities such as Antioch and Stockton border the Delta, the towns within this water maze are mostly tiny. They sit near or below sea level, perched on the dikes or tucked behind, relying on the levees to keep them dry. Many stores have their chins resting on a dike, with stilts holding up their back rooms. Occasionally, a levee will break or the rivers will rise suddenly, flooding a town or its surrounding fields. Rio Vista and Isleton have suffered serious floods in recent memory. One former farming island, Frank's Tract, is now an inland lake since levee breaks were too numerous to plug.

These Delta communities and farms are the focus of an ongoing controversy because of a phenomenon called saltwater intrusion. Continued upstream diversions for valley farms and California's cities has lowered the Delta's fresh water levels. Much of this water is sent all the way to Southern California. During high tides, salt water from San Francisco Bay intrudes, ruining crops, fouling wells and disrupting the ecological balance of wetland wildlife.

The recent seven-year drought forced federal water officials to make bitter choices between releasing fresh water to protect the Delta or sending it to farms in the arid Central Valley and the cities beyond. Salt water intrusion becomes a key issue each time another dam is proposed for one of the rivers flowing out of the Sierra Nevada.

DIABLO VALLEY AND CARQUINEZ STRAIT

Our approach to the Delta will be somewhat round-about, touching on some of the attractions of the Diablo Valley and Carquinez Strait. The valley borders the strait and the Delta's southwestern edge. Rising above it like an East Bay Kilimanjaro is **Mount Diablo,** one of the most isolated promontories in the United States. From its 3,849-foot summit, one can see on a rare clear day more than half the counties of California. As you travel through the Delta, its bold profile breaks the monotony of the flat countryside.

The Diablo Valley is actually more of a shelf, cradled between Mount Diablo, the Oakland-Berkeley hills, Carquinez Strait and the Delta. Reached via Highway 24 through the Caldecott Tunnel, it's home to a string of upscale bedroom communities. Orinda, Lafayette and Walnut Creek are attractive towns that offer little to attract to visitors. However, we will suggest a couple of interesting pauses.

After clearing the Caldecott Tunnel and passing **Orinda,** take the Acalanes/Mount Diablo Boulevard exit to the right and follow Mount Diablo east toward **Lafayette.** Before reaching the community, turn right and climb steeply up to **Lafayette Reservoir Recreation Area.** You can picnic or rent a boat for a float across this small lake cupped in wooded hills. Or, follow an attractive one-mile hiking-biking trail around its perimeter. The recreation area is open daily until 5:30. You can park all day for $4.50 or feed two-hour meters at the rate of 50 cents an hour.

Continue on Mount Diablo Boulevard, past the shops and occasional boutiques of downtown Lafayette. The road eventually merges back onto Highway 24. At the complicated Walnut Creek interchange, swing right onto Interstate 680 and head south about ten miles to Crow Canyon Road. Go left (east) over the freeway, following Crow Canyon about five miles toward the wealthy community of **Blackhawk.**

At a stoplight, turn right onto Camino Tassajara, go south for less than a mile and turn left into **Blackhawk Plaza.** It's an upscale Spanish style shopping center with a fountain-fed stream cascading pasts shops and boutiques. It features two remarkable museum discoveries:

☺ *UC Berkeley Museum and Behring Auto Museum* ● *3700 Blackhawk Plaza Circle, Danville, CA 94506; (510) 736-2277. Daily 10 to 5 (until 9 Wednesday and Friday), closed Monday in the off-season. Berkeley Museum $3 for adults and $2 for students and seniors; Behring Auto Museum $5 for adults and $3 for students and seniors; combination ticket $7 and $4. These new, beautifully designed archives offer attractions for many tastes. The Ber-*

keley Museum focuses on archaeology and anthropology, with exhibits ranging from life-sized carved Papua New Guinea male figures (very!) to saber
tooth cats, mastodons and other finds from the nearby Blackhawk Quarry.
Visitors can play pebble games from the Arctic or Nigeria and watch videos
tracing human ancestry.

The Behring Museum is a handsome study in marble, polished granite
and glass—every bit as elegant as the cars it displays. Stroll through this upscale automobile row and wish you were in the driver's seat of Ettore
Bugatti's personal black and yellow Royale, or assorted Delehayes, Rolls
Royces and Mercedes. Clark Gable's 1935 cream and red Duesenberg is
here, along with nostalgia cars such as early T-birds, Corvettes and fancy-
finned Caddy convertibles.

Return to Crow Canyon and turn right; the route now becomes Blackhawk Road. When F. Scott Fitzgerald said the rich really *are* different, he
could have had Blackhawk in mind. This community of 4,000, tucked into
wooded foothills, is comprised mostly of mansions of the super rich. Indus-
trialists and CEOs hang out in Blackhawk, and this is where John Madden

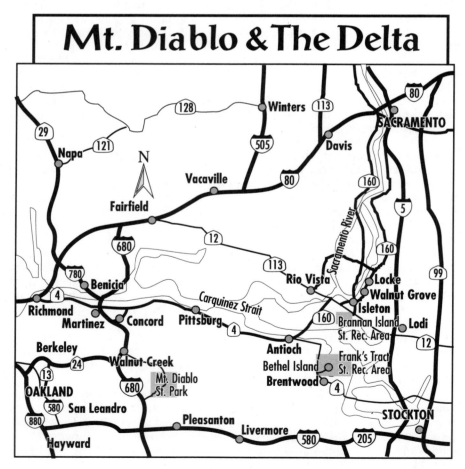

Mt. Diablo & The Delta

parks his Greyhound. Most of the homes are clustered behind gates, out of reach of the unwashed and envious. You can admire many of them as you drive past, brushing the edge of the golf course and country club. To see what the other half can afford, you can to inspect model homes and home-sites.

During this drive south from the Walnut Creek interchange, Mount Diablo has been a commanding presence. To reach its heights, follow Black-hawk Road north. The route becomes Diablo Road and within a mile, you're at the junction of Mount Diablo Scenic Boulevard, which leads you onto the mount itself.

☺ *Mount Diablo State Park* ● *P.O. Box 250, Diablo, CA 94528; (510) 837-2525. Day use $5, camping $12 with flush potties, barbecues and picnic tables; no hookups. Reservations via Mistix, (800) 444-PARK, or write: P.O. Box 85705, San Diego, CA 92138-5705.* The sign at the summit says you can see 40,000 square miles of California on a clear day. However, during 18 years' residence in the Diablo Valley, we never experienced a day that clear. Still, the views are awesome, and you can reach the summit in your vehi-cle—even a large RV, if it's driven with patience. These heights were critical reference points for the Spanish, guiding them to San Francisco Bay and other places. In 1851, Colonel Leander Ransome established the Mount Diablo meridian grid, surveying most of California and Nevada from here.

The peak was sacred to Miwok Indians. Its "Devil Mountain" name may have resulted from a Spanish corruption of their reference to "place of the spirits." Today's visitors can follow 50 miles of trails through oak-chaparral woodlands and an occasional conifer grove, while conferring with red fox squirrels, great horned owls and scrub jays. Even if you never leave your ve-hicle, you'll be treated to a constantly shifting panorama of Northern Cali-fornia as you wind toward the summit. A visitor center occupies an imposing Depression era stone octagon at the very top.

Although hardly remote—receiving half a million visitors annually—Mount Diablo is still a special kind of wilderness, aloof from the thick sub-urbs at its skirts. So high that it generates its own weather, it can be snowcapped in winter, cloud capped in summer when the foothills are sunny, or windy and cool when the valley is becalmed and hot.

Walnut Creek

Population: 60,600   **Elevation: 135 feet**

As you depart the park, head northeast on North Gate Road. Pick it up at a junction near a campground and park headquarters. North Gate will put you at the back door of Walnut Creek. It passes Northgate High School and a string of upscale homes before intersecting with Ygnacio Valley Road. Turn left and go about five miles downhill to the heart of town.

Once a rural enclave surrounded by walnut orchards, this suburban heartland of the Diablo Valley is now rimmed by bedrooms of the middle class and beyond. Developers have used its position on the Bay Area Rapid Transit line to turn it into an upscale office park. Thousands of Bay Areans commute here on BART to toil behind the smoked glass of architecturally pleasing buildings.

We've always liked downtown Walnut Creek, which offers some inviting cafès and shops. Extended sidewalks with landscaping, benches and foun-tains add to its appeal. To reach this area, turn left (south) from Ygnacio

Valley Road onto Main Street. Among the more interesting shops is **J.R. Muggs** at 1432 Main, peddling fresh roasted coffees and hundreds of styles of mugs. Nearby, at Main and Bonanza, is **Café Italiano,** an espresso place with soups, salads, sandwiches, Italian pastries and outdoor tables—a good lunch stop. It's open daily 6 a.m. to midnight. For something more extensive, try one of these:

Little Europe ● ΔΔ $$

1516 Main St.; (510) 945-1165. International; wine and beer. Monday-Saturday 11 to 9, Sunday noon to 9. MC/VISA. Rather cute European style place with arched windows, stucco interior walls and cozy seating. The menu is versatile, dancing from chicken curry to Hungarian goulash, shish kabab and assorted pastas.

Prima Walnut Creek ● ΔΔ $$

Main near Lincoln; (510) 935-7780. International; full bar service. Lunch Monday-Thursday 11:30 to 3 and Friday-Saturday 11:30 to 5, dinner Monday-Wednesday 5 to 9:30, Thursday-Saturday 5 to 10 and Sunday 5 to 9. MC/VISA. Sleek, intimate yet bright and airy café with wall murals, a fireplace and outdoor tables. From the kitchen emerges grilled scallops, eggplant with tomatoes and capers, feta pizza and other interesting dishes.

If you like animals (or have kids who do), you might want to visit the **Alexander Lindsay Junior Museum** at 1901 First Avenue; (510) 935-1978. It's open Wednesday-Sunday 1 to 5; free. This little museum offers nature exhibits and several live animals that like to interact with visitors. The Lindsay is where locals take injured wildlife for a little TLC. To reach it, head north on Main Street, cross under the freeway, turn left onto Second Avenue, right on Buena Vista and then left on First. It's in **Larkey Park**.

Continue north on Main Street (either from the museum or from downtown), and pick up Freeway 680/24. After a few miles, as you nip the edge of **Concord,** stay left to remain on I-680, then take the **Martinez** exit west onto Highway 4. After three miles, you'll reach the Alhambra Avenue interchange, adjacent to the former home of America's leading naturalist. Exit to the left and then immediately cross Alhambra avenue into the parking lot.

☺ *John Muir National Historic Site* ● *4202 Alhambra Ave., Martinez, CA 94553; (510) 228-8860. Wednesday-Sunday 10 to 4:30; admission $2. Self-guiding tours; one conducted tour at 2 p.m.* John Muir, who once said that "wilderness is a necessity," would be aghast to see that a freeway brushes past his two-story Victorian home and that his orchards are rimmed with fast food parlors. A small visitor's center offers a few exhibits regarding Muir and an extensive collection of Muir-related books. The nearby home is furnished appropriate to Muir's turn-of-the-century tenure. However, only the writing desk in his authentically cluttered study and a few other items belonged to the great naturalist.

Credited with sparking America's environmental awareness, Muir lived here until his death in 1914. Originally a 2,600-acre fruit ranch belonging to his wife's father, it provided his sustenance between tramps into the wilds. His success in operating the ranch and the sale of his books enabled him to become a man of means. He spent virtually all of it on "environmental awareness," writing, traveling and working to convince leaders of the need to protect the wilds. The Scottish-born naturalist persuaded President Theodore Roosevelt to set aside Yosemite as a national preserve, even as he chided the Rough Rider for his "childish" big game hunting. Muir founded the Sierra Club, but split with other environmentalists who saw conservation as a means to save resources for mankind's future use. Wilderness, Muir felt, was a resource unto itself, a place for human renewal.

Climb the mountains and get their good tidings. Nature's peace will flow into you as the sunshine flows into the trees. The winds will blow their own freshness into you...while cares drop off like autumn leaves.

Return to Highway 4 and continue east for 3.6 miles. Then, turn north onto McEwen Road and follow its twisting course down to **Port Costa.** There isn't much to this tiny town on the edge of the Carquinez Strait, although its scruffy charm is rather captivating. It has a few shabby Victorian homes, an antique shop or two and a weathered hotel and restaurant, all tucked beneath weeping eucalyptus trees.

Warehouse Café ● △ $$$
Canyon Lake Drive; (510) 786-1827. American; full bar service. Wednesday-Friday from 10 a.m. and weekends from noon. MC/VISA. This funky cafè in an 1886 concrete warehouse serves assorted lunch fare. At night you can order prix fixe dinners of lobster, steak, prime rib or scampi for $17.95, with an all-you-can-stuff salad bar.

Burlington Hotel ● △ $
Two Canyon Lake Dr., Port Costa, CA 94569; (510) 787-1827. Rooms $29 to $55. Private or share baths. Across from the cafè and matching its scruffiness, this old bay-windowed hotel offers very basic accommodations.

From Port Costa, pick up Carquinez Scenic Drive and head west toward Crockett. The route offers pleasing panoramas of the strait and its ship traffic. Earlier, one could follow this shoreline drive all the way from downtown Martinez. However, a piece fell into the channel a few years ago and has never been replaced. Sections of **Carquinez Strait Regional Shoreline** along this route offer a chance to hike among these grassy and occasionally wooded hills.

Crockett, larger than Port Costa and somewhat less scruffy, sits in the shadow of the twin **Carquinez bridges,** where I-80 spans the strait. It's basically an old company town gathered around the huge brick and corrugated metal **C&H Sugar Refinery.** There are no tours, although the sprawling complex is worth a look from the outside. Just down the street in a grizzled railroad depot is the **Crockett Historical Museum,** at Loring and Rolf avenues. Its undisciplined clutter of early day leftovers can be visited Wednesday-Saturday from 10 to 3. Donations are appreciated and obviously sorely needed. One of our favorite Bay Area escape restaurants resides in Crockett:

☺ Nantucket Fish Company ● △△ $$
Foot of Port St.; (510) 787-2233. American, mostly seafood; full bar service. Lunch Monday-Saturday 11 to 3:30, dinner Monday-Thursday 4 to 9, Friday-Saturday 4 to 10 and Sunday 11 to 10. MC/VISA. Wedged between the railroad tracks and the Crockett Marina, this long established place offers a New England style seafood menu, ranging from steamer clams to pan fried fillets and deep fried clams, scallops and oysters. The look is nautical funk with exposed beams, ceiling fans and feigned Tiffany lamps. From the shoreside deck, you can watch the river traffic pass and study the webwork of the Carquinez bridges above.

The Nantucket's a bit hard to find. From C&H and the museum, drive along the waterfront to the business district (Second Avenue), take a downhill right onto Wanda Street, then right onto Port Street and follow it past mud puddles to the marina. If that doesn't work, just ask someone.

Thither to Benicia

From downtown, climb onto I-80 freeway and cross the Carquinez Bridge toward **Vallejo.** If you'd like to talk to the animals at **Marine World Africa USA,** stay on I-80 for a few miles and take the Marine World Parkway exit. If not, swing left from I-80 onto I-780 and head for **Benicia,** which had its brief moment of glory as California's capital. Recently rediscovered, it's rapidly expanding as a bedroom community for Bay Area commuters.

Benicia was founded in 1847 and therein lies a bit of historic irony. Hulking Robert Semple (some said he was seven feet tall) was a principal in the 1846 Bear Flag Revolt in Sonora. During the ruckus, Semple and other Americans regional governor Mariano Guadalupe Vallejo and declared California to be a republic. Semple befriended his captive and learned that he held title to land along Carquinez Strait—a great site for a future town. He persuaded the deposed Mexican official to donate five square miles as a townsite. In exchange, Semple would name it for the general's wife, Dona Maria Francisco Benicia Carillo de Vallejo.

Later, as California officials cast about for a capital, Semple and others championed Benicia as the ideal site. They built a sturdy two-story brick building that presented "a most imposing appearance from the bays and Straits of Carquinez." However, the legislature moved in 1850 to San Josè, and then to Vallejo, and to Sacramento and back to Vallejo. The Semple crowd finally lured the legislature to their community in 1853. Said Monterey's *Alta California* newspaper:

Thither to Benicia that conveniently portable piece of public property, the State Archives, will next be trundled, and there the herd of politicians in the State be gathered together in the name of office. A pious conclave for which a better rodeo ground than Benicia could not have been selected.

Benicia lost its grasp on the capital just a year later. With appropriate fanfare, Governor John Bigler and assorted other politicians boarded a riverboat bound for Sacramento. That old red brick building still stands, now a state monument to California's peripatetic politicians. To find it, take the Second Street exit from I-780, head toward the bay, jog a block right on Military Road and then left onto First Street.

Benicia Capitol State Historic Park • *115 W. G St. (at First), Benicia, CA 94510; (707) 745-3385. Daily 10 to 5.* Fluted columns out front give the former capitol a proper touch of dignity. Inside, the senate and assembly chambers are faithfully reproduced, complete with quill pens, folded newspapers and legislators' hats sitting on their desks. Across an attractive garden is the **Fisher-Hanlon house,** a 14-room Victorian built in the 1850s. It's furnished to the period and can be toured on weekends, every half hour from noon to 3:30. Next door is a carriage house displaying assorted buggies and wagons.

After your visit with history, you might want to poke about downtown Benicia, which offers a few boutiques, gift shops and antique stores. Eastbound Military Road will take you to the old **Benicia Army Arsenal,** established in 1849. It's now the Port of Benicia's industrial park. There isn't much to see, other than a few old brick and concrete buildings and parking lots filled with Toyotas, inbound from Japan.

Return to I-780, then fork right onto I-680 to cross the **Benicia-Martinez bridge.** Note the **mothball fleet** of Navy ships parked upstream in the Carquinez roadstead. In the foreground is the **Glomar Explorer,** an expensive salvage vessel financed by Howard Hughes, intended for the Navy's use in rescuing crews of sunken submarines. Like Hughes' Spruce Goose, it never saw much service.

Across the strait, you're back in Contra Costa County and the Diablo Valley. Brush the edge of Martinez, then take eastbound Highway 4 toward Pittsburg, Antioch and the Delta. Yes, you did just go in a circle. We warned you that this was a Discovery Guide.

DOING THE DELTA

With a thousand miles of waterways, the Delta is California's grand aquatic playground. Obviously, it is best explored by boat. This certainly can be done by the visitor, since many marinas and waterside resorts rent assorted watercraft, from jet skis to ski boats to houseboats. Indeed, nothing could be finer than spending a few lazy days dawdling on the Delta aboard a houseboat. They come fully equipped, with everything from a barbecue and stereo to a refrigerator full of beer.

If you aren't aquatically inclined, you can still enjoy much of the Delta from your car or RV—particularly since most of the roads are elevated for views of all those sloughs. Our intent here is to steer you through some interesting areas of the Delta while transporting you to Sacramento.

To properly do the Delta, one should be as laid back as the people who inhabit the region. They like to call themselves river rats and many spend their spare moments in anything and everything that floats. The Delta is not a tourist trove of museums, fancy resorts and fine cuisine, but more of a place to lean back, relax and—well—dawdle. Some of the towns and resorts are a bit on the scruffy side. "Picturesque" would be a kinder description. Others, like downtown Rio Vista and the stylish Tower Park Marina Resort near Terminous, are as neat as a pin. Dining on the Delta fits the rest of the picture. Don't expect gourmet, but do expect good seafood, simply prepared and reasonably priced. Crawdads, abundant in these slow-water sloughs, are a specialty. Most cafès are linked to marinas, and we like to seek out those with channel views and outdoor decks. (Several are listed below, under "Where to dine.")

Don't hurry through the Delta. Pull over to a levee shoulder (when you can find one) and watch a cargo ship ply a deep water channel, steering a course between an asparagus patch and a cornfield. Drop a crawdad trap in the water, then ask the lady at the marina bait shop how to cook the squirming, nasty looking little things. Watch a sunset breeze fracture the perfect mirror of a sailboat's reflection. Count the kinds of drawbridges, from Bascule lift to vertical life to swing. Ride a ferry across a channel, even if you don't need to get to the other side. You can always ride it back because, like many of the Delta's lures, it's free.

Fisherfolk will find the Delta's quiet waters a haven for striped bass, catfish and the ubiquitous crawdad. Occasionally, an angler will land a salmon or sturgeon. Several years ago, a local fisherman hauled a 391-pound sturgeon from these waters. Fishing's best in the spring when the stripers are running. Visitors can angle from banks, boats or from public piers in Antioch and Rio Vista. Most marinas have bait shops offering appropriate lures and lots of free fishing advice.

The best visitors' guides to the area are written by Hal Schell, a writer who's regarded as the "voice of the Delta". His *Delta Map and Guide* is available at local shops and chambers of commerce. His illustrated hardcover guide, *Dawdling on the Delta* is on sale at area bookstores and other outlets. These and other items can be ordered by contacting: Schell Books, P.O. Box 9140, Stockton, CA 95208; (209) 951-7821.

RV advisory: The Delta is ideal country for RVers. Although the small towns offer few motels, the area has an abundance of RV parks. Many are at marinas and resorts, where you can rub elbows with a boater—or become one. In fact, you can rent a "Camp-a-float," a motor powered floating platform onto which you can install your RV.

Drive levee roads with caution, since many are quite crooked, offering the option of falling into an asparagus patch or into the channel. Use particular care when winds gust across the Delta, common in the springtime.

A river route to Sacramento

As you head east on State Highway 4, you nip the edge of the **Concord Naval Weapons Station,** often the scene of protests when the United States engages in unpopular wars. The highway parallels Carquinez Strait as it passes waterfront towns of Pittsburgh and Antioch, although it's too far inland for a view.

A brochure calls **Pittsburg** the Delta City, but it isn't quite, since it's still on the strait. However, it does have a modern new marina, part of an ambitious downtown restoration project. Here, you can rent a boat if you prefer to explore the Delta by water. Founded in 1849, it was the site of a large steel mill—thus the name—then it was home to a major commercial fishing fleet. The mill closed, the fleet sailed elsewhere and Pittsburg fell into decline. It's now resurrecting itself, with the downtown renovation project and new housing tracts in its sloping hills.

Antioch also claims to be a gateway to the Delta, and that *is* accurate, since it sits at the juncture of the San Joaquin and Sacramento rivers. Half a dozen marinas and small aquatic resorts line its busy waterfront. Much of its history parallels that of Pittsburg, since it also was established during that 1849 year of Gold Rush river traffic. It also slumped, and is being revitalized by a new waterfront. The downtown area, undergoing considerable restoration, is worth a brief diversion off Highway 4.

The freeway you've been following terminates at the base of the high, gracefully arched **Antioch Bridge** that crosses the San Joaquin River. You have a choice of two routes through the Delta from here. The bridge route becomes State Highway 160, an asphalt path into the upper delta. Highway 4 swings east to wander through the southern area, bound for Stockton.

If you want to hang out a few days on the Delta, a good base of operations is **Bethel Island,** off Highway 4 beyond **Oakley.** Bethel's waterfront and nearby **Dutch Slough** are lined with marinas. Many offer houseboat, ski boat and fishing boat rentals, along with several channel view restaurants. The area's aquatic front yard is **Frank's Tract,** the farm that became a lake when levees gave way in 1938. To reach Bethel Island, follow Cypress

Road east from Oakley, and then turn left onto Bethel Island Road.

However, our Delta route to Sacramento will go in the other direction, heading north across the Antioch Bridge. Highway 160 crosses the pancake flat agricultural fields of Sherman Island, then picks up the main channel of the Sacramento River. Here, you climb aboard a levee road and begin riding several feet above the channel and the sunken fields. On your right is **Brannan Island State Recreation Area,** wedged between the Sacramento River and Threemile Slough. It offers a boat launch, nice swimming beach and campground. Day use is $5, boat launch $10 and camping $12 (listed below).

If you'd like to explore a string of small marinas with their attendant channel-side restaurants, turn right onto Brannan Island Road just north of the recreation area. Follow its twisting course along Sevenmile Slough to the main channel of the San Joaquin River. You'll then pick up the Mokelumne River, where most of these marinas and a few Delta homes are nested. Note that some of the newer homes, sitting off the levee road below water level, are built on stilts for a channel view. Tucked behind the Delta Boatworks on the Mokelumne channel is **Moore's Riverboat,** a restaurant built into an old freighter. It's popular with area river rats. A few miles beyond, this squiggly levee road passes under Highway 12, and then wraps around to intersect with it. **B&W Resort Marina** here offers one of the few dry-land lodgings in the heart of the Delta.

Rio Vista

Looking like a topographer's mistake among these winding levee roads, Highway 12 cuts arrow straight across the fields. Follow it west about five miles to Rio Vista. It's a pleasant little town with a mix of false front stores and Victorian homes. If you haven't yet loaded up with visitor propaganda or purchased your Delta map, follow Front Street south from the bridge. Then turn left onto Main Street for a pause at the **Rio Vista Chamber of Commerce** at 60 Main. It's open weekdays 11 to 3.

Across the street is **Little Darling's Bakery,** a tiny place jampacked with goodies ranging from breakfast buns to whole wheat savories and tasty pastries. The assorted muffins are some of the best we've found anywhere. And we mean *anywhere.* (See listing below.)

Main Street bumps into the Sacramento River channel and a monument there marks the antics of **Humphrey.** He's the humpbacked whale who grabbed headlines in the fall of 1985 when he took a wrong turn through the Golden Gate. He spent nearly a month wandering Delta channels before he was successfully herded back to sea. The small **Rio Vista Museum,** capturing memories of early days on the Delta, occupies a storefront at 16 N. Front Street, just up from Main. It's open weekends 1:30 to 4:30.

Dozens of ferries once crossed the Delta's waterways, although most have been replaced by bridges. Five survive, and they're free. These are informal, one-man operations and they even break for meals, so you might have to wait a bit. If you'd like to ride a couple, head north out of Rio Vista on Front Street. Follow it 2.5 miles along the riverfront to the **Ryer Island Ferry.** After crossing to the island, follow Steamboat Slough briefly east and then north to the **Howard Landing Ferry.**

Make your crossing, go south briefly and then drive three miles east across Grand Island to **Ryde** on the Sacramento River. The only commercial

Assorted drawbridges, such as the Isleton bascule lift bridge over the Sacramento River channel are part of the charm of the Delta. — **Betty Woo Martin**

survivor of this tiny hamlet is the 18th century **Ryde Hotel**. It was an operating hotel and restaurant until recently; now, it houses an art gallery and the Ryde post office.

Head south along the Sacramento for five miles and cross a drawbridge to **Isleton.** With nearly a thousand residents, it's considered large by Delta standards. The weathered and pleasantly mismatched old business district provides basic essentials and a cafè or two. **Ernie's Restaurant and Saloon** (listed below) is popular with locals, featuring that ubiquitous Delta dish, crawdads. (Folks here never call them crayfish.) Isleton calls itself "Crawdad Town U.S.A." and stages an annual bash to salute the crustacean.

Retrace your route up the Sacramento River, this time staying on the east side of the channel until you encounter a pair of pieces of history. Walnut Grove was settled in 1851 by Caucasians and later by Chinese who had built the Delta's levees. Then in 1912, Tin Sin Chan moved a mile up the levee to start a new settlement. Asians weren't allowed to own land then, so Chan trusted a handshake by farmer George Locke, who leased him a few acres. When Walnut Grove's Chinatown was leveled by fire in 1915, most of its residents adjourned to Chan's new enclave, named for the farmer. It grew rapidly, becoming the only rural all-Chinese town in America.

Walnut Grove is scattered on both sides of the Sacramento River, although most of its battered old business district sits atop and below the levee on the eastern reach. Many of the buildings are boarded up, but a few shops function, including some Chinese establishments that didn't adjourn upstream.

Wonderfully ramshackle **Locke** dozes beside its sagging boardwalks down off the levee road. Since thrifty Chinese considered paint to be an extravagance, the weathered storefronts look considerably older than their 75-

plus years. No fancy turned-up eaves decorate this Chinatown. Visitors accept it for what it is, a tattered page out of the Delta's history. With its sagging balconies and unpainted wood, it looks more like a back alley in Singapore than a rural California town.

Most of the businesses are still Chinese, except for a some Caucasian-owned curio shops and the outrageously named **Al the Wop's** restaurant and saloon (listed below). Locke runs no great risk of becoming a tourist trap. Many storefronts are empty, with faded signs in Chinese characters or English giving clue to their former use. There has been talk of preserving it as a state historic park like Columbia in the Gold Country. Meanwhile, the town seems content to bask in its past, like the old men in quilted jackets, who sit in the sun reading Chinese language newspapers, and the ancient women who pass by silently, politely ignoring camera-clutching tourists.

☺ The **Dai Loy Museum**, operated by the Sacramento River Delta Historical Society, preserves Locke's memories. Exhibits recall wilder and raunchier days when gambling dens and prostitution rings thrived. Museum hours are 11 to 5 Thursday through Sunday. However, they're rather unpredictable during the off-season. Call (916) 776-1684 to see if anyone's home.

Continuing along the Sacramento River channel, you'll pass other hamlets—more modern but not much bigger than Locke. **Courtland** is the center of a pear-producing region and it stages a pear festival to prove it. **Hood** and **Freeport** are tiny rural trading centers that you'll miss if you blink. At this point, you've left the Delta and are nudging Sacramento's suburbs. Just beyond Freeport, your levee road touches I-80, providing a quick trip north to the California capital.

ACTIVITIES

About 40 marinas dot the Delta. Collectively they offer the full range of activities: boat launches, bait shops, all sorts of boat rentals, fishing, water-skiing and RV parks. For a complete list of marinas and their offerings, pick up a copy of Hal Schell's *Delta Map and Guide*. They're also listed in the free *California Delta* publication produced by **Delta Chambers of Commerce,** 49 Main St. (P.O. Box 177), Isleton, CA 95641; (916) 777-5007.

For houseboat rentals, contact: **Delta Houseboat Rental Association,** 6333 Pacific Ave., Suite 152, Stockton, CA 95207; (209) 477-1840.

WHERE TO DINE ON THE DELTA
Rio Vista

☺ Little Darling's Bakery ● Δ $
75 Main St.; (707) 374-6320. Light fare; no alcohol. Monday 7 a.m. to 1 p.m., Tuesday-Saturday 4:30 a.m. to 6 p.m., Sunday 7 to 3. Good breakfast or lunch stop, offering excellent pastries, assorted snacks and whole grain muffins to die for. The sausage, egg and cheese sandwich makes a good portable, cholesterol-rich breakfast.

The Point Restaurant ● ΔΔ $$
120 Marina Dr.; (707) 374-5400. American, mostly seafood; full bar service. Tuesday-Saturday 11 to 9, Sunday 1:30 to 9, closed Monday. MC/VISA, AMEX. Second-floor restaurant with nautical décor and views of the Sacramento River. Assorted fresh fish, plus steaks, chicken and chops populate the menu. (It may be changing ownership, so check before you go.)

Isleton

Several of these places are in marinas on the "Isleton loop" along Brannan Island Road, east of the community.

Croissanterie ● ∆∆ $$
Seven Main Street; (916) 777-6170. Continental; wine and beer. Daily 7 a.m. to 10 p.m. Major credit cards. Cheerfully simple new place in old town Isleton, with floral touches; outdoor dining patio. Continental menu offers chicken cacciatore, veal piccata and Creole baked catfish. The adjacent bakery issues fresh breads and pastries.

Ernie's Restaurant and Saloon ● ∆ $
Highway 160 downtown; (916) 777-6510. American; full bar service. Daily 7 a.m. to 2 p.m. MC/VISA. Oldstyle bar with a simple dining room, noted for its complete crawdad luncheons for $9.95. Other menu items include chicken dumplings, fried chicken and hamburgers.

Lighthouse Restaurant ● ∆ $
151 Brannan Island Road; (916) 777-5811. American; wine and beer. Daily 8 to 4. MC/VISA. Simple snack café that's appealing mostly for its outdoor deck over the Mokelumne River. Fare includes omelettes, sandwiches and baskets of fried fish or chicken.

Moore's Riverboat ● ∆∆ $$
Behind Delta Boatworks at 106 W. Brannan Island Rd.; (916) 777-6545. American; full bar service. Breakfast, lunch and dinner Tuesday-Sunday, closed Monday. MC/VISA. Nautically funky place built into an old freighter, with picture window views onto the Mokelumne channel. Crawfish is a specialty on the café's mostly seafood menu. Weekend dancing and entertainment.

Patty's Cookhouse ● ∆ $$
At Vieira's Resort, 15476 Highway 160; (916) 777-5857. American; full bar service. Daily from 8 a.m., dinner from 5. No credit cards. Basic Naugahyde café beside the Sacramento River channel, offering the usual local fish, chicken, steaks and chops.

Riverfront Pizza Café ● ∆ $
Near Spindrift Marina, Brannan Island Road; (916) 777-6409. Italian; wine and beer. Thursday-Friday 4 to midnight, Saturday 2 to 12, Sunday 10 to midnight, closed Monday-Tuesday. MC/VISA. Cute little knotty pine place with outdoor deck and river views. Pizza, pastas and assorted sandwiches.

Walnut Grove/Locke

☺ Al the Wop's ● ∆ $$
Main Street, Locke; (916) 776-1800. American; full bar service. Lunch Monday-Saturday 11:30 to 2, dinner Monday-Saturday 5 to 10 and Sunday 3 to 10. A favorite of locals and tourists since 1934, with a doodad-decorated bar up front and bare-bones dining room in back. Sit at wooden tables and tackle big steaks for $14.50, or chicken, hamburgers and such. The barroom ceiling is hung with dollar bills and it'll cost you one to learn how the barkeep gets them up there.

Locke Garden Restaurant ● ∆ $
13967 River Road, Locke; (916) 776-1405. Chinese; wine and beer. Tuesday-Thursday 11 to 8, Friday-Sunday 11 to 9, closed Monday. No credit cards. Appropriately shabby diner housed in an old shack that seems about to tip

backward off the levee. Prices are very reasonable for its long list of mild Cantonese and spicier Mandarin dishes; *mu shui* pork, beef, chicken or shrimp are specialties.

Whimpy's Restaurant • △△ $$

14001 W. Walnut Grove Rd.; (209) 794-2544. American; full bar service. Dinner Sunday-Thursday 5 to 9, Friday-Saturday 5 to 10, Sunday brunch 10 to 2. MC/VISA. Simple Delta cafè that's appealing for its levee perch with views of the Mokelumne River. Hearty menu offerings include pepper steaks, chicken livers, steaks and seafood. Sunday brunch is popular with local boaters.

WHERE TO SLEEP

Dry land lodgings are scarce in this water-oriented region, although they're plentiful in nearby Stockton and Sacramento. A few Delta marinas have cabins.

B&W Resort Marina • △ $$

964 Brannan Island Rd., Isleton, CA 95641; (916) 777-6161. Cabins $42 to $75. Simple resort near the Mokelumne River channel with housekeeping cabins that sleep two to six. Marina, mini-mart with snacks and boat launch.

Vieira's Resort • △ $$

15476 Highway 160, Isleton, CA 95641; (916) 777-6661. Cabins $40 to $65. No credit cards. Simple one-bedroom and two-bedroom housekeeping cabins sleep up to six; on the Sacramento River. Swimming beach, coin laundry, mini-mart, bait shop & marina. **Patty's Cookhouse** listed above.

WHERE TO CAMP

Brannan Island State Recreation Area • *17645 Highway 160, Rio Vista, CA 95471; (916) 777-6671. RV and tent sites, $12. Reservations via Mistix, (800) 444-PARK, or write: P.O. Box 85705, San Diego, CA 92138-5705.* Nicely-spaced sites with barbecues and picnic tables, some with views of the water. Flush potties and showers; no hookups. Picnic areas, boat launch and swimming beach.

Delta Marina • *100 Marina Dr., Rio Vista, CA 94571; (707) 374-2315. RV sites only, full hookups $14 to $22. Reservations accepted; MC/VISA.* RV park alongside the Sacramento River with some waterfront sites; showers, coin laundry, marina boat launch, boat shop, fishing pier; mini-mart. **Point Restaurant** listed above.

Duck Island RV Park • *16814 Highway 160, Rio Vista, CA 94571 (916) 777-6663. Adult park with RV sites only, full hookups $17. Reservations accepted; no credit cards.* Sites right on the water; no showers; self-contained RVs and trailers only. Rec room, boat launch and fishing access.

Island Park • *Gateway Road (P.O. Box 458), Bethel Island, CA 94511; (510) 684-2144. RV sites only, $17. Reservations accepted.* Full hookups, many shaded sites on lawns; showers, coin laundry, pool. Mini-mart, marina and golf course nearby.

Tower Park Marina & Resort • *14900 W. Highway 12, Lodi, CA 95242; (209) 369-1041. RV sites, full hookups $25, tent sites with no improvements $13. Reservations accepted; major credit cards.* Very well maintained full-service RV resort with barbecues and picnic tables, showers, coin laundry and play area. Adjacent marina, boat launch, **restaurant** and mini-mart. About 12 miles east of Rio Vista on Highway 12.

Sacramento

Population: 369,400   **Elevation: 30 feet**

Sometimes called River City, California's capital is an attractive grid, peppered with trees and spreading out from the banks of the Sacramento and American Rivers. Although not noted as a major tourist center, it offers a number of attractions worthy of a couple days' pause. Most are historic sites, since the city is woven intricately into the fabric of early California.

Sacramento is California's oldest non-Latin community, established by Sutter as New Helvetia in 1839. He built a civilian stockade and set about to carve an empire from the surrounding wilderness. In a sense, the Gold Rush started here, since it was from Sutter's Fort that Marshall ventured forth to build the mill that led to his discovery. It became an important staging area for gold-seekers hurrying up the Sacramento River from San Francisco.

When founders of the new state began casting about for a capitol site in 1850, Sacramento put in its bid. After false starts in San José, Vallejo and Benicia, it lured Governor Bigler and his troops here in 1854. Later, San José tried to get the capital back, along with Monterey and even Berkeley. However, Sacramento held on and its future as a pivotal California city was assured.

For decades, it reigned as the state's second largest city behind San Francisco. It was the western terminus of the Pony Express and transcontinental railroad. Rival San José has since surpassed it in size, along with Los Angeles and San Diego. However, it remains a key commercial center and the largest city in the agriculturally rich Central Valley. Obviously, it's the political nucleus of America's most populous state.

Sacramento is an easy city to navigate, particularly in the downtown area where north-south streets are numbered and east-west ones are lettered. It's boring, but efficient.

Since you left the Delta on I-5, stay aboard and pass through the heart of the city, watching for the exit to **Old Town Sacramento.** Signs guide you through several 90-degree turns to the place where the city began, alongside its namesake river. You could spend a day or two here, exploring the **California State Railroad Museum** and the **Sacramento History Museum,** plus several smaller museums and dozens of shops housed in old brickfront buildings.

From Old Sacramento, cross under the freeway, go south briefly on Third Street, turn left onto N Street and follow it a few blocks to the **State Capitol.** You can walk there by following the landscaped **Capitol Avenue Mall** from Old Town. It's less than a mile. After touring the impeccably restored statehouse, continue about 12 blocks up N Street, turn left onto 27th and you'll run into **Sutter's Fort** and the **State Indian Museum.**

ATTRACTIONS
(In order of appearance)

Old Sacramento ● *Between Second and Front streets, next to I-5. Two visitor centers offer information and guide maps: Sacramento Visitor Information Center near the* Delta King *at 1104 Front Street, (916) 442-7644. At the Sacramento History Museum, California State Railroad Museum or Central Pacific Passenger Station, you can purchase combination tickets good for admission to six historic sites in Sacramento. Walking tours of Old Sacramento are* *conducted between April and October, on a limited basis; call (916) 324-0040.*

Once a rundown waterfront area, Old Sacramento has experienced a remarkable transformation in recent decades. It's now a wonderful gathering of restored brick, stone and masonry buildings, cobbled streets and raised wooden sidewalks. It offers the city's largest collection of museums, boutiques, curio shops and restaurants. What the historic park lacks in authenticity (We've found no Gold Rush record of a Subway Restaurant) it makes up for with its many attractions.

☺ **California State Railroad Museum,** *Second and I streets; (916) 448-4466. Daily 10 to 5 (last entry at 4:30); adults $5, kids 6 to 17, $2.* We're tempted to call this the state's finest historical museum; it is certainly the best railroad museum anywhere. It features an imposing collection of full-sized trains in larger than life settings. You see the original Central Pacific Engine #1, poised to enter a Sierra Nevada tunnel hacked out by Chinese laborers. The gleaming red, black, brass and gold 1873 Empire locomotive is displayed in a hall of mirrors, creating a stunning kaleidoscopic effect. Admire Lucius Beebee's luxurious Gold Coast private railway car, and a full-scale Spanish Colonial California railway station straight out of the 1920s. Walk the narrow corridor of a Pullman coach as it hurries through the night; feel its gentle sway, listen to the rhythmic click of the rails and watch signals flash by at crossings.

☺ **Sacramento History Museum,** *Front and I streets; (916) 264-7057. Wednesday-Sunday 10 to 5, closed Monday-Tuesday. Adults $3, kids 6 to 17, $1.50.* Housed in a brick 1854 waterworks building, this large, nicely-done museum effectively captures Sacramento's yesterdays. Follow the city's development from John Sutter's arrival and the discovery of gold to the turn of the century and beyond. Featured exhibits include a mock-up of the 18th century *Sacramento Bee* newspaper, a gold miner's cabin and displays of Sacramento's various ethnic groups. Our favorite display concerns California agriculture, with old fruit box labels, farm equipment, an early kitchen set up for home canning and a conveyer belt that parades cans of Blue Diamond almonds throughout the exhibit.

☺ **Central Pacific Passenger Station** and **Freight Depot**, *Front Street between K and I streets. Daily 10 to 5; admission included with State Railroad Museum.* This is a reproduction of the terminal that served Sacramento during the 1870s. "Magic wand" audio tours take visitors through the ticket office, into a waiting room reserved for ladies, and to train-side where a steam locomotive chuffs quietly. The Silver Palace Refreshment Saloon is a replica of a depot diner, serving real food (listed below). A recent addition to the complex is the Central Pacific Freight Depot, with a collection of freight cars and stacks of cargo ready for shipping.

☺ ***Delta King*** *riverboat, at the foot of K Street; (916) 444-KING or (800) 825-KING.* Two grand paddlewheelers, the *Delta King* and *Delta Queen*, ran passengers between San Francisco and Sacramento from 1927 until 1940. The Queen eventually found a new life on the Mississippi but the King languished and crumbled at dockside for generations. It was rescued by a private firm in the late 1980s, returned to its original glossy elegance and berthed at Old Sacramento. The King offers staterooms done in the style of the Roaring Twenties (see "Where to sleep" below), the Pilot House restaurant, two cocktail lounges and a below-decks theater that hosts plays and musicales. Visitors may walk about the decks, peek into the theater and, of course, have dinner or drinks in the two lounges.

Citizen Soldier Museum, *1119 Second St.; (916) 442-2883. Tuesday-Sunday 10 to 5, closed Monday. Adults $2.25, seniors $1.50, kids 6 to 17, $1.* Sponsored by the California National Guard Historical Society, it traces the history of the state's part-time soldiers from the days of the Spanish to the present-day guardsmen. Its historic exhibits end in an Operation Desert Storm scene, with a guardsman sharing a tent with an Arab soldier; an Arabic-lettered can of Coke adds a nice touch.

Huntington and Hopkins Hardware, *Front and I streets. Daily 10 to 5.* This brickfront structure is part working hardware store and part exhibit center. Docents or park interpretive specialists will describe hardware stores of old or sell you a scythe, gold pan or oil lamp.

Wells Fargo Museum, *1000 Second St.; (916) 440-4263. Daily 10 to 5.* Wells Fargo's started as an express company during the Gold Rush and this museum traces its history. Exhibits include a strongbox, gold scales, bank drafts, a model stage coach and a display concerning Black Bart. There's also a cash machine, in case you spent too much at the shops.

Old Eagle Theatre, *925 Front St.; (916) 323-7234. Open weekends 10 to 4.* It's a reproduction of Sacramento's first theater, opened in 1849. A 14-minute slide show, given on the hour, focuses on Sacramento's history. A local theater group presents contemporary plays here on weekends.

☺ *California State Capitol* ● *Tenth Street at Capitol Mall; (916) 324-0333. Weekdays 7 to 6, weekends 10 to 5; docent tours on the hour, 9:30 to 4.* California's seat of government since 1869, the capitol still gleams from its six-year, $68 million restoration, completed in 1981. A study in turn-of-the century grandeur, it is even more elegant than the nation's capitol, of which it is a copy. Guided tours will take you down marbled corridors, beneath gleaming chandeliers, up grand stairways and past state offices with their tall wooden doors. Or, you can wander about on your own, rubbing shoulders with those who ponder various ways to spend our taxes. Everything you see here—except our legislators, of course—is a feast for the eyes. Admire the gold leaf, scrollwork, *fleur de lys* and filigree of the most meticulous restoration of a public building ever accomplished.

End your visit with the Capitol museum and book shop in the basement. You might want to schedule lunch down here. The inexpensive Capitol Restaurant cafeteria is a study in turn-of-the-century finery. After doing the capitol, explore the large surrounding park that covers ten city blocks. Then bid goodbye to the park squirrels who—like many capitol visitors—are seeking something for nothing.

☺ *Sutter's Fort State Historic Park* ● *2701 L St., Sacramento, CA 95814; (916) 445-4422. Daily 10 to 5. Adults $2, kids 6 to 17, $1.* This large quadrangle is a faithful reconstruction of the original. Although it's surrounded by homes and commercial districts, it's buffered by a large, shady park. Once inside the fort's protective walls, you can picture life as it was during Sutter's day. Peek into the tannery, blacksmith shop, cooperage, candelry and other shops. Docents and rangers recall the past with talks and demonstrations during "living history days" conducted several times a year. At other times, you can clap a "magic wand" to your ear, follow a numbered course and listen to the sounds of yesterday.

☺ **State Indian Museum** • *2618 K Street, Sacramento, CA 95814; (916) 324-0971. Daily 10 to 5. Adults $2, kids 6 to 17, $1.* This facility presents a realistic and sympathetic portrait of the peoples who were displaced, first by the Spanish and then by the Americans. Nicely done exhibits are thematic, with artifacts and graphics detailing the California natives' crafts, food preparation, weapons, social and spiritual lives. One leaves this place with a sobering statistic. Two centuries ago, 300,000 Indians lived in California. Within 50 years, at the peak of the Gold Rush, the population had been reduced to 30,000.

Other Sacramento attractions

These other lures in the capital city also are worth your consideration.

Crocker Art Museum • *Third and O streets; (916) 264-5423. Wednesday-Sunday 10 to 5 (until 9 Thursday), closed Monday-Tuesday. Adults $3, kids $1.50.* This is the oldest art museum in the West, started in 1873 and currently housed in a restored Victorian. Exhibits range from European masters and Asian art to works of California artists and photographers.

☺ **Governor's Mansion** • *Sixteenth and H streets; (916) 324-0539. Guided tours on the hour from 10 to 4; $2.* This beautifully restored Victorian was home to 13 California governors, from 1877 to 1967.

Leland Stanford Mansion • *802 N St.; (916) 324-0575. Tours generally on Tuesdays and Thursdays at 12:15 and Saturdays at 12:15 and 1:30; schedules vary so call first.* This brick Victorian, home to railroad baron and governor Leland Stanford, is still being restored. Tours focus both on its history and on the restoration work.

Spirit of Sacramento • *1207 Front St.; (800) 433-0263 or (916) 552-2933. One hour sightseeing cruises Wednesday-Sunday June through August and Friday-Sunday the rest of the year, 1:30 and 3 p.m. Adults $10, kids $5. "Happy Hour cruises" with music and hors d'oeuvres, Friday and Saturday April through October at 5 p.m., $10. MC/VISA.* This oldstyle paddlewheeler has been handsomely refurbished with teakwood, polished brass and beveled glass. In addition to sightseeing cruises, it offers meal trips (see "Where to dine").

☺ **Towe Ford Museum of California** • *2200 Front St.; (916) 442-6802. Daily 10 to 6. Adults $5; teens 14 to 18, $2.50; kids 5 to 13, $1.* Is there a Ford in your past? This museum houses the world's largest antique Ford collection, with 175 cars and trucks, starting with the earliest Tin Lizzies.

DELTA & SACRAMENTO ANNUAL EVENTS

Gold Discovery Days, late January in Sacramento; (916) 489-4918.

Opening Day Boat Parade on the Delta, Port of Stockton in April; (209) 943-1987.

Sacramento County Fair, early May in Sacramento.

Crawdad Festival, June in Isleton; (916) 777-5880.

Renaissance Fair, late June in Sacramento; (916) 966-1036.

Pear Fair, July in Courtland; (916) 777-5007.

Fifties Bash, nostalgia celebration on Bethel Island in August; (510) 684-3220.

Catfish Jubilee, August in Walnut Grove; (916) 777-2060.

California State Fair, late August through early September at Cal Expo, Sacramento; (916) 263-3000.

"A Taste of Sacramento" food fair, mid-September; (916) 442-8575.
Striped Bass Derby, mid-October in Rio Vista; (707) 374-2700.
RV, Sports & Boat Show in Stockton in October; (209) 943-1987.
Old Sacramento Holiday Festival, December; (916) 558-3912.

WHERE TO DINE

These are our favorites among Old Sacramento's restaurants:

California Fats Pacific Grill and Wok ● ∆∆∆ $$$

1015 Front St.; (916) 441-7966. California-Oriental; full bar service. Lunch Monday-Saturday 11:30 to 2, midday menu 2 to 5, Sunday brunch 10:30 to 2, dinner nightly 5:30 to 10. MC/VISA, AMEX. Intriguing *nouveau* machine shop décor with neon piping, open beams, assorted blue and red shapes and a 30-foot waterfall. The creative menu offers a mix of California and Pacific Rim fare.

Fanny Annie's ● ∆∆ $

1023 Second St.; (916) 441-0505. Light snacks; full bar service. Monday-Saturday 11:30 a.m. to 2 a.m., Sunday 11:30 to midnight. MC/VISA. Lively, cheerful old saloon decorated with an explosion of 19th century doo-dads. It's mostly a drinking establishment, with a limited menu featuring 'burgers, chicken fingers, buffalo wings and such.

Firehouse ● ∆∆∆ $$$$ ∅

1112 Second St.; (916) 442-4772. Continental; full bar service. Lunch weekdays 11:30 to 2:15, dinner Monday-Saturday 5:30 to 10:15. MC/VISA, AMEX. Old Sacramento's most elegant restaurant, with a posh New Orleans décor, inserted into an 1853 brick firehouse. It features an attractive court-yard for warm weather dining. Assorted European and a few American classics appear on the menu.

☺ Fat City Bar & Café ● ∆∆∆ $$$

1001 Front St.; (916) 446-6768. American-continental; full bar service. Lunch weekdays 11:30 to 2:30, brunch weekends 10:30 to 2:30, dinner Sunday-Thursday 5:30 to 10 and Friday-Saturday 5:30 to 11. MC/VISA, AMEX. Attractive 19th century restaurant and bar with polished woods, Tiffany style fixtures and leaded glass. The cocktail lounge is very alluring, with a mahogany, brass and glass backbar and Victorian couches.

Spirit of Sacramento ● ∆∆ $$$ ∅

On the waterfront at 1207 Front St.; (800) 433-0263 or (916) 552-2933. California nouveau; dinner, lunch and Sunday brunch cruises. Reservations essential; office hours 7:30 a.m. to 5 p.m. daily. MC/VISA. While the *Delta King* is anchored at dockside, the this venerable paddlewheeler chugs up and down the river with its dining guests.

WHERE TO SLEEP

We've focused most of our selected lodgings around Old Sacramento and the downtown area.

Clarion Hotel ● ⌂⌂⌂ $$$$ ∅

700 16th St. (H Street), Sacramento, CA 95814; (800) 443-0880 or (916) 444-8000. Couples $89 to $109, singles $79 to $99, suites $130 to $295. Major credit cards. Nicely furnished rooms in 239-unit inn; TV movies, room phones; pool. Free airport shuttle. **Mansion Court Restaurant** serves California cuisine 6:30 a.m. to 10 p.m., dinners $11 to $17; full bar service.

Crossroads Inn ● ⌂ $$ ∅
221 Jibboom St. (Richards Boulevard), Sacramento, CA 95814; (916) 442-7777. Couples $40 to $100, singles $38 to $100, suites $85 to $125; rates include continental breakfast. Major credit cards. A 28-room inn with TV, room phones and refrigerators; some rooms with microwaves.

☺ The Delta King ● ⌂⌂ $$$$$ ∅
1000 Front St., Old Sacramento, CA 95814; (800) 825-KING or (916) 444-KING. Couples $95 to $135, singles $84 to $125; rates include continental breakfast. Major credit cards. Restored riverboat staterooms with mahogany wainscoting, print wallpaper, oversized brass beds, TVs tucked into armoires and wicker furniture. **Pilot House Restaurant** serves continental cuisine; dinners $15 to $25; full bar service; lunch 11:30 to 2, Sunday brunch 10 to 2, dinner 5 to 10.

Holiday Inn Capitol Plaza ● ⌂⌂ $$$$ ∅
300 J St. (Third Street), Sacramento, CA 95814; (916) 446-0100. Couples $79 to $99, singles $69 to $99, suites $120 to $450. Major credit cards. A 368-room hotel with TV movies, room phones; some suites with wet bars. Pool, sauna. **John Q's** and **The Greenery** service breakfast, lunch and dinner; John Q's is a rooftop restaurant with city views; full bar service.

Hyatt Regency ● ⌂⌂⌂ $$$$$ ∅
1209 L St. (at 12th), Sacramento, CA 95814; (800) 233-1234 or (916) 443-1234. Couples $99 to $200, singles $89 to $175, suites $190 to $795. Major credit cards. Opulent full-scale resort hotel with TV movies, two phones per room and other amenities. Pool, workout room, spa. Adjacent to contention center and capitol. **Bugatti's** (Northern Italian) and **Dawson's** (American) serve from 6:30 a.m. to 10:30 p.m.; dinners $18 to $32; full bar service. Top floor lounge overlooks the city.

Mansion View Lodge ● ⌂ $$ ∅
711 16th St. (H Street), Sacramento, CA 95814; (800) 446-6465 or (916) 443-6631. Couples $34 to $48, singles $32 to $55, suites $48 to $70. Major credit cards. A 41-unit motel across from the historic governor's mansion; TV movies, room phones and refrigerators.

Ponderosa Inn ● ⌂⌂ $$$$
1100 H St., Sacramento, CA 95814; (800) 528-1234 or (916) 441-1314. Couples $75 to $100, singles $70 to $90, suites $150 to $200. Major credit cards. Attractive 98-unit inn; well-equipped rooms have TV movies, room phones; refrigerators on request; pool. **Bull Market** restaurant serves from 7 a.m. to 10 p.m.; dinners $10 to $20; full bar service.

Residence Inn by Marriott ● ⌂⌂ $$$$$ ∅
1530 Howe Ave. (near Cal Expo), Sacramento, CA 95825; (800) 331-3131 or (916) 920-9111. Studios $78 to $98, penthouse $98 to $118; rates include continental breakfast. Major credit cards. Attractive all-suite hotel with TV movies, phones, full kitchens and living rooms; most units with fireplaces.

Vagabond Inn ● ⌂ $$$ ∅
909 Third St. (near I Street), Sacramento, CA 95814; (800) 522-1555 or (916) 466-1481. Couples $65 to $70, singles $60, rates include continental buffet. Major credit cards. A 107-room motel with TV, room phones; microwaves and refrigerators for small extra fee. Across street from Old Sacramento. **Denny's** serves 24 hours; dinners $6.50 to $9.

Bed & breakfast inns

Amber House Bed & Breakfast ⌂⌂⌂ $$$$ Ø

1315 22nd St., Sacramento, CA 95816; (800) 755-6526 or (916) 444-8085. Couples $90 to $195, singles $85 to $135. Nine rooms with TV, room phones and private baths; full breakfast. Major credit cards. Two early 20th century homes fashioned into an elegant B&B, furnished with European antiques and reproductions. Some rooms with VCRs and oversized spa tubs. Eight blocks from the capitol and Sacramento Convention Center.

Aunt Abigail's Bed & Breakfast Inn ● ⌂⌂ $$$$ Ø

2120 G St. (near 22nd Street), Sacramento, CA 95816; (800) 858-1658 or (916) 441-5001. Couples $75 to $135, singles $70 to $95. Six units, some private and some share baths; full breakfast. Major credit cards. Cozy early American inn created from a 1912 colonial revival mansion. Victorian dècor with Edwardian antiques. Garden with spa.

Vizcaya ● ⌂⌂⌂ $$$$ Ø

2019 21st St., Sacramento, CA 95818; (916) 455-5243. Couples and singles $79 to $225. Nine units with TV, room phones and private baths; full breakfast. Major credit cards. An opulent turn-of-the-century colonial revival mansion furnished with American and European antiques and reproductions. Some suites with marble fireplaces and spas; landscaped gardens with a Victorian gazebo.

WHERE TO CAMP

Sacramento-Metro KOA ● *4851 Lake Rd., West Sacramento, CA 95691; (916) 371-6771. RV and tent sites, $25. Reservations accepted; MC/VISA.* Coin laundry, showers, mini-mart, pool, rec room and play area. Take West Capitol Avenue exit from I-80.

Stillman RV Park ● *3880 Stillman Circle, Sacramento, CA 95824; (916) 392-2820. RV sites only, full hookups $22. Reservations accepted; MC/VISA.* Mostly shaded sites, pull-throughs, showers, coin laundry, picnic area, rec hall and play area. In southwest Sacramento; take 47th Street exit from Freeway 99N, go one block west to a stop light and turn north.

Chapter seven
THE GOLD COUNTRY
Following an historic foothill highway

THERE ARE SEVERAL GOOD REASONS for calling California the Golden State. The golden poppy is the state flower, its foothill grasslands turn golden brown in the summer and—as the wealthiest state in the Union—it has provided golden opportunities for many.

However, it was real gold that inspired the state's nickname, and the lust for that gold which created today's California. The excitement began in January of 1848. Handyman James Marshall, building a water powered sawmill on the American River for entrepreneur John Sutter, discovered a bit of glitter in the mill's tailrace. The world's first gold rush began rather slowly after he found two tiny nuggets "about half the size and of the shape of a pea." It gained momentum in 1849 as each new strike drew more people in this "rush to riches." Within three years, prospectors were finding gold along a 300-mile stretch of the Sierra Nevada foothills, from a town called Coarsegold, northeast of Fresno, to Sierra City, northeast of Reno. This is the area we shall explore.

Geologists will tell you that the Sierra Nevada offered ideal conditions for gold deposits. The surface of east central California was uplifted and twisted by volcanic activity during the Jurrasic Period, about 160 million years ago. As it cooled, the igneous rock was shattered by cracks and fissures, where gold and other elements—in liquid form—gathered and congealed. Later erosion exposed these gold-bearing veins, or "lodes." Loose gold was washed downstream and deposited in gravel beds, where it awaited Marshall's dumb luck.

The Gold Rush inspired a kind of town that had never existed before. These were instant towns, hastily assembled from tents, replaced by shan-

TRIP PLANNER

WHEN TO GO ● Winters are mild in the Gold Country, so it's a year around vacation land. And of course, most of the state's ski resorts are in the Sierra Nevada just above. You'll find some nice fall color in autumn and summers are perfectly fine, since the area is rarely crowded.

WHAT TO SEE ● Marshall Gold Discovery State Historic Park, and handsome old Georgetown above Coloma; Empire Mine State Historic Park in Grass Valley; Malakoff Diggins State Historic Park above Nevada City; Sierra County Historical Park near Sierra City; Jackson Tailing Wheels and Amador County Museum in Jackson; Indian Grinding Rock State Historic Park and the town of Volcano; Columbia State Historic Park; Tuolumne County Museum in Sonora and the California Mining and Mineral Museum in Mariposa.

WHAT TO DO ● Pan for gold, run the rapids of the American River near Coloma or the Stanislaus in Tuolumne County, sip wine in the Shenandoah Valley east of Plymouth or in the tasting rooms around Murphys, hike to North Grove in Calaveras Big Trees State Park, ride a stagecoach at Columbia State Historic Park, ride a steam train in Jamestown's Railtown State Historic Park.

Useful contacts

Amador County Chamber of Commerce, 2048 Highway 88, Suite 3 (P.O. Box 596), Jackson, CA 95642; (800) 649-4988 or (209) 223-0350.

Calaveras County Visitor Center, Highway 49 at Highway 4 (P.O. Box 637), Angels Camp, CA 95222; (800) 695-3737 or (209) 736-0049.

Columbia State Historic Park, P.O. Box 151, Columbia, CA 95310; (209) 532-4301.

El Dorado County Chamber of Commerce, 542 Main St., Placerville, CA 95667; (916) 621-5885.

Marshall Gold Discovery State Historic Park, P.O. Box 265, Coloma, CA 95613; (916) 622-3470.

Mariposa County Chamber of Commerce, P.O. Box 425 (Ninth and Jones streets), Mariposa, CA 95338; (209) 966-2456.

Nevada City Chamber of Commerce, 132 Main St., Nevada City, CA 95959; (916) 265-2692.

Nevada County Chamber of Commerce, 248 Mill St., Grass Valley, CA 94945; (800) 655-4667 or (916) 273-4667.

North County Office, Mariposa County Chamber of Commerce, 5007 Main St. (P.O. Box 333), Coulterville, CA 95311; (209) 878-3002.

Placer County Visitor Information Center, 661 Newcastle Rd. (P.O. Box 746), Newcastle, CA 95658; (916) 663-2061.

Sierra County Chamber of Commerce, P.O. Box 222, Downieville, CA 95936; (916) 289-3560.

Tuolumne County Visitors Bureau, P.O. Box 4020 (55 W. Stockton Rd.), Sonora, CA 95370; (800) 446-1333 or (209) 533-4420.

Gold Country radio stations

KZSQ-FM, 92.7, Sonora—light rock, classic hits
KKBN-FM, 93.5, Twain Harte—adult contemporary
KNGT-FM, 94.3 or 103.1, Jackson—light rock, top 40
KVMR-FM. 89.5, Grass Valley—National Public Radio
KXSR-FM, 91.7, Groveland—National Public Radio
KNCO-FM, 94.3, Grass Valley—country
KVML-AM, 1450, Sonora—country
KAHI-AM, 950, Auburn—country, news & sports
KNCO-AM, 830, Grass Valley—news and talk

ties and log cabins and then by whipsaw board buildings. Inevitably, they burned down, supplanted by sturdy structures of brick, with steel doors and shutters to discourage further fires.

When the gold was exhausted, many of the towns were abandoned. Entire populations often shifted overnight, reacting to word of a new strike over the next hill. Gold production peaked within ten years, and then began a slow decline. Some communities survived for decades, others for only a few years. Many plodded into this century, as brick and stone shells of their former selves.

What remains is one of California's most inviting regions, rich in both historical and natural resources. Tourism has put the bloom back into many of the old towns. Gold Rush hotels are again hosting guests. Victorian homes are being renovated as bed & breakfast inns. Grizzled false front stores now contain boutiques and antique shops. Assay offices and stage stops have become museums. Several mining complexes are preserved as historic sites and communities proud of their rowdy past stage lively annual celebrations.

All of this happens in a handsome foothill area of oak groves and golden meadows, bullpine forests and narrow river canyons. The bold granite spires of the Sierra Nevada form an imposing backdrop. Their slopes embrace most of the state's winter sports areas. Most of the rivers that leached gold from the heights have been dammed to provide water and hydro power for much of Northern California, creating reservoirs for recreation (and consternation for environmentalists).

California's Gold Country towns are strung together by State Highway 49, which twists through the foothills like a stepped-on snake. The route climbs to high ridge lines for awesome views, then plunges dizzily down into river canyons. It dips into lowlands that sizzle like a miner's skillet in summer, and it traverses mountain passes dusted by winter snows.

RV advisory: National forest campgrounds and private RV parks are sprinkled liberally among the foothill trees. Several state parks offer camping as well. Also, most fairgrounds in the Gold Country's eleven counties have RV parks, often with hookups and showers.

Auto travelers have a good selection of pillow places, from renovated historic hotels and B&Bs to inexpensive motels and resorts.

This chapter can touch only the highlights of this rich trove of historic and recreational lures. For more thorough coverage, pick up a copy of our *Best of the Gold Country*. (Details in the back of this book.)

NORTHERN GOLD COUNTRY

Sacramento, which we explored in the previous chapter, is the gateway to the Gold Country, both historically and physically. As we noted earlier, it was here that Sutter established his fort, and it was from here that he dispatched Marshall to build his mill.

If you head east from here on U.S. 50, you'll hit the Gold Country roughly in the middle, so we'll explore it in two pieces. Beyond the capital city, you leave the broad, flat Sacramento Valley and begin climbing into the foothills that will be your companions for the rest of this chapter.

About the time the freeway starts to fizzle and become a surface highway, you'll hit one of the rowdier gold camps. In fact, things got so nasty there that it originally was called Hangtown.

Placerville

Population: 8,400   **Elevation: 1,860 feet**

Since James Marshall's gold discovery was just nine miles to the north in Coloma, it didn't take long for argonauts to find nuggets in areas nearby. Within two years, more than 30 mining camps had sprung up, including Placerville.

Today, its outer edges are strictly modern, since Highway 50 brings the world to and through town. However, several early day buildings survive along Main Street in the downtown area, which locals like to call "Old Hangtown." To reach it, take the downtown exit just before the freeway ends at a stoplight; Main Street parallels the freeway, one block to the south. Here, you'll pick up Highway 49, called the "Golden Chain" by tourism promoters. It coils through Placerville, skimming the edge of downtown and crossing Highway 50 at the first traffic light.

Among noteworthy buildings downtown are the brick Victorian **Cary House** hotel at 300 Main Street with an ornate 19th century lobby, **Placerville City Hall** in an old firehouse at Main and Bedford, and the **Placerville Soda Works building** at Main and Clay streets.

ATTRACTIONS

The town's three most interesting historic sites are randomly placed. You'll see the turnoff to the county fairgrounds and **El Dorado County Museum** on the freeway about a mile south of town. Once in the downtown area, watch on your right for the **El Dorado County Historical Society Museum** in the old Fountain-Tallman Soda Works building. Then turn left onto Bedford Avenue near the city hall and follow it out to **Gold Bug Park and Mine.**

☺ *El Dorado County Museum* ● *100 Placerville Dr. (county fairgrounds entrance west of town); (916) 621-5865. Wednesday-Saturday 10 to 4 and Sunday 1 to 4; free.* This large museum building with a rough-hewn "great hall" look is a treasure house of Gold Country yesterdays, including a finely appointed cream colored Concord stagecoach. The grounds contain all manner of equipment and vehicles used during the latter half of the 19th century.

El Dorado County Historical Society Museum ● *524 Main St.; (916) 626-0773. Friday-Sunday noon to 4; admission by donation.* This small, nicely maintained museum offers just what you'd expect—flatirons, high button shoes and other early day memorabilia. Perhaps the most interesting item is the building itself—a brick and fieldstone structure looking as rough and gnarled as a prospector's hands.

☺ *Gold Bug Park and Mine* ● *Bedford Avenue a mile north of downtown Placerville; (916) 642-5232.* The only city owned gold mine in the nation, the Gold Bug gives visitors a firsthand view of the excitement and drudgery of hardrock mining. The 61-acre park is in the midst of a major renovation and improvement project.

The **Pony Express** galloped through Placerville and you can trace its route by following Highway 50 farther east. Get off at **Pollock Pines** and visit **Sportsman Hall,** where you'll see a monument to those swift young mail carriers. An earlier version of the "hall" was a Pony Express stop.

If you continue west on Carson Road from Pollock Pines, you'll wind up

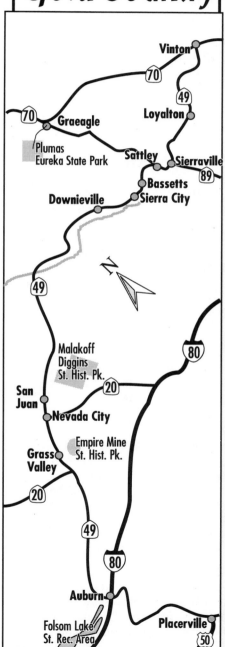

Northern Gold Country

in **Apple Hill,** an area thick with apple orchards and fruit stands. Get a map of these direct-to-consumer growers from the chamber of commerce back in Placerville (see "Trip planner" above) or from the Apple Hill visitor center at 4123 Carson Road. You'll also find some wineries in the area, listed on the Apple Hill map.

ANNUAL EVENTS

Pony Express re-ride, Fourth of July, Placerville, (916) 621- 5885.

El Dorado County Fair, August at fairgrounds in Placerville, (916) 621-5860.

Apple Hill Harvest, September-November, (916) 622-9595; apple specialty foods, apple bake-off, music, crafts and such.

WHERE TO DINE

Café Sarah's ● ΔΔ $ Ø

301 Main St., Placerville; (916) 621-4680. American; wine and beer. Daily 8 a.m. to 2 p.m. No credit cards. Comely early American style café in a 19th century building with a white embossed tin ceiling, maple chairs and modern art. Breakfasts and light lunches of burgers, sandwiches and elaborate salads.

Mama D Carlo's ● ΔΔΔ $$

482 Main St., Placerville; (916) 626-1612. Italian-American; wine and beer. Monday-Thursday 11:30 to 9, Friday 11:30 to 10, Saturday 3 to 10, closed Sunday. No credit cards. Locally popular spot; pleasant wood-paneled interior with an early American look. Menu ranges from scallop and scampi sauté through the usual cacciatores, Parmesans and pastas to American steaks.

☺ Sportsman Hall ● ΔΔ $$

5620 Pony Express Trail, Pollock Pines; (916) 644-2474. American; no alcohol but it can be brought in. Monday-Thursday 5:30 a.m. to 9 p.m., Friday-Saturday 5:30 to 10 and Sun-

day 6 to 9. MC/VISA, AMEX. Western style knotty-pine restaurant that's a virtual museum of early-day paraphernalia. Typical American fare in hearty portions—steaks, chicken and chops.

WHERE TO SLEEP

Best Western Placerville Inn ● △△△ $$$
6850 Greenleaf Dr. (Missouri Flat off ramp), Placerville, CA 95667; (800) 528-1234 or (916) 622-9100. Couples $64 to $75, singles $59 to $69, suites from $135. Major credit cards. A 105-unit motel with large, attractive rooms; TV movies, room phones. Pool and spa. **Brawley's Restaurant** serves from 5:30 a.m. to 11 p.m.; dinners $9 to $15; full bar service.

Mother Lode Motel ● △ $$ Ø
1940 Broadway, Placerville, CA 95667; (916) 622-0895. Couples $39 to $51, singles $39 to $43. MC/VISA, AMEX. A 21-unit motel with TV movies, some room refrigerators; pool.

Bed & breakfast inns and historic hotels

The Chichester House ● △△△ $$$$ Ø
800 Spring St., Placerville, CA 95667; (800) 831-4008 or (916) 626-1882. Couples from $60. Three units with half baths, tub and shower down the hall. MC/VISA, DISC. Beautifully ornate wood fretwork enhances this 1882 Victorian. Rooms are color coordinated and furnished with antiques.

☺ Combellack-Blair House ● △△△ $$$$ Ø
3059 Cedar Ravine, Placerville, CA 95667; (916) 622-3764. Couples $89 to $99. Two units with private baths; full breakfast. MC/VISA. This antique-rich Queen Anne classic is one of the most attractive of Placerville's many Victorians. Built in 1895, it perches on a hill like an elaborately coiffed Southern belle surveying her domain.

Cary House Hotel ● △△△ $$ Ø
300 Main St., Placerville, CA 95667; (916) 622-4271. Couples from $49.50 to $60.50. Twenty units, all with private baths. MC/VISA. Refurbished rooms are furnished with country oak, patchwork quilts and ruffled print curtains. The lobby is decorated in 19th century finery, with polished woods, beveled glass and chandeliers.

WHERE TO CAMP

Sly Park Campground and Recreation Area ● *c/o El Dorado Irrigation District, P.O. Box 577 (2890 Mosquito Rd.), Placerville, CA 95667; (916) 644-2545. RV and tent sites; no hookups; $9.* Wooded campground on Jenkinson Lake with pit potties, water but no showers. Fishing, swimming, boating, hiking. General store and gas station across the road.

El Dorado County Fairgrounds ● *100 Placerville Drive, Placerville; (916) 621-5860. RV sites only, $10 with hookups.* Clean, well-kept sites with water and electric hookups; flush potties and showers.

Coloma

Population: 1,100   **Elevation: 750 feet**

From downtown Placerville, a ten-mile drive along Highway 49 delivers you to **Coloma State Historic Park,** the site of Marshall's gold discovery. It's a twisting ten miles as the road coils over a couple of ridges and spirals down to the narrow American River valley.

THE GOLD RUSH: HOW IT BEGAN

A pair of improbable partners, interested only in land and lumber, were the instigators of the world's first gold rush.

Johann August Suter was a suave, free-wheeling entrepreneur from Switzerland. Fleeing debtors' prison and abandoning his family, he arrived in Monterey via Hawaii in 1839. There, he convinced Mexican officials to grant him a 76-square-mile tract of land to start a colony. Selecting a likely spot on the banks of the American river near present-day Sacramento, he began building his "New Helvetia." And he Americanized his name to John Sutter.

James Wilson Marshall was a wandering carpenter, probably more idealistic than clever. He contracted with Sutter to build a water-powered sawmill on the south fork of the American River, 30 miles east of Sutter's Fort. Sutter, who habitually operated on a shoestring and occasionally wrote rubber checks, provided Marshall with a crew but no funds. He agreed to give him 25 percent of the mill's output for supervising its construction and operating it.

The settlement around the mill was called Coloma, after the Cullooma Indians who inhabited this forested river valley.

The glint of history

On January 24, 1848, Marshall rose early to check the mill for damage after a heavy rainfall. Noting a glimmer in the millrace gravel, he bent down and picked up two tiny particles of gold, "about half the size and of the shape of a pea." It was worth maybe fifty cents at the going rate of $8 to $9 an ounce. He hammered the nuggets flat with a river rock to test their malleability, decided they were gold, and stuck them into his hat brim.

Four days later, after detecting more yellow flakes in the millrace, he rode through the rain to Sutter's Fort to share the discovery with his boss. The two agreed to keep it a secret until the mill was completed.

The secret soon leaked out, thanks mostly to another opportunist, capitalistic Mormon Sam Brannan, who was visiting the fort at the time. He hurried to Yerba Buena (San Francisco) and rode through the streets, waving a vial and shouting: "Gold! Gold from the American River!" However, he first bought up every pick and shovel he could find. Then he lit out for the discovery site and made a quick fortune selling them for $50 apiece.

Brannan thus set the pace for the rampaging inflation that marked the first years of the Gold Rush. During its peak, eggs brought a dollar apiece and rental for half of a leaky one-room cabin commanded $500 a month. More fortunes were made by speculators than by miners. This price-gouging was the origin of the present-day term "gold digger." Several other contemporary expressions emerged from the world's first gold rush, such as "panning out" (having your pan yield gold), "hitting paydirt" (finding gold-bearing gravel) and of course, "striking it rich"—which few did!

While Brannan thrived, neither Sutter nor Marshall fared well, and both died in poverty. Sutter lost his workers to the gold fields and his loosely assembled empire collapsed. His own efforts at prospecting were unsuccessful. He died in New York City in 1880. Marshall wound up a muttering, alcoholic eccentric, claiming mystical gold-finding powers. He ended his days puttering around his blacksmith shop in nearby Kelsey, and selling his autograph for pennies.

Sympathetic state legislators approved a small state pension for Marshal in 1872. But they declined to renew it after he appeared before that august body in 1878 to plead his case—and a brandy bottle dropped from his pocket. He died in Kelsey in 1885. Friends iced him down, returned him to Coloma and buried him beneath an oak tree overlooking his gold discovery site. He remains there today, beneath a bronze likeness erected in his honor in 1890.

Coloma was California's first golden boomtown, and the first to go bust. Nearly 10,000 miners were swarming about within a year of Marshall's discovery, but within two years the camp was practically abandoned.

It's a quiet little place today, more state park than town, with only a handful of homes scattered among the oaks and locust trees. Nearly everything worth seeing is visible from Highway 49, except for the **Marshall Monument.** It's reached by taking High Street to the left or following a tree-canopied hiking trail. A replica of **Sutter's Mill** stands just above the river, out of reach of the water needed to run it. Across the way is **park headquarters,** with a visitor center and fine museum. A few brick and cut stone buildings from yesterday survive, sharing the historic park's 275 acres with picnic areas and parking lots. Most offer historic exhibits; shopping is limited here.

☺ For a nice detour, follow Marshall Road northeast from Coloma to **Georgetown,** high in the Sierra Nevada foothills. It's a hidden delight, a well-preserved collection of wooden false front stores, Victorian homes and wide, tree-shaded streets. A few miles south on State Highway 193 is the shantytown of **Kelsey,** where gold-finder Marshall spent his final days as a reclusive blacksmith. A badly-done imitation of his blacksmith shop, built several decades ago as a tourist gimmick, stands abandoned on the southern edge of town.

ATTRACTIONS & ACTIVITIES

☺ **Sutter's Mill** ● *Just off Highway 49 in Coloma.* It's easy to believe that this simple structure, looking like an oversized shed without walls, was built nearly 150 years ago, with hand-hewn beams and simple mortise-and-tenon joints (basically, a square peg in a square hole). But it isn't that old, of course. It was reconstructed in the 1960s.

☺ **Marshall Gold Discovery Museum** ● *Across Highway 49 from the mill; (916) 622-3470. Open daily 10:30 to 4 except Thanksgiving, Christmas and New Year's Day. Day use fee $5 per carload (includes other park exhibits).* Graphics, artifacts, mini-dioramas and a scale model of the mill tell the oft-told story of The Discovery. Other exhibits concern the Cullooma Indians, the town that grew up around the discovery site then quickly shrank, and the Gold Rush in general.

American River Nature Center ● *8913 Highway 49; (916) 621-1224. Wednesday-Saturday 10 to 4, Sunday noon to 4.* While the state park interprets the area's human history, the non-profit American River Land Trust's Nature Center is concerned with the natural history of this river corridor. Dioramas and other exhibits focus on flora and fauna and a small gift shop sells things with wildlife themes.

Marshall Monument ● *On a hill overlooking the discovery site.* Four years after Marshall's death, state legislators appropriated $9,000 for this monument, which was cast in San Francisco and dedicated with much flourish in May, 1890. It stands over Marshall's grave, on a hill above a pretty thicket.

Hot air ballooning ● *c/o Coloma Country Inn, P.O. Box 502, Coloma, CA 95613; (916) 622-6919.* You can float blissfully above history on hot air balloon flights operating daily from Coloma, weather permitting.

River running ● The American River is just bouncy enough here to attract amateur rubber rafters and kayakers, and it's a launch point for more extensive voyages through the wilder American River Canyon beyond. These commercial operators can get you through the rapids wet but unscathed:

A Whitewater Connection, (916) 622-6446; Adventure Connection, (916) 626-7385; American River Recreation, (916) 622-6802; California River Trips, (916) 626-8006; Chili Bar Whitewater Tours, (916) 622-6632; Gold Country River Runners, (916) 626-7326; Mother Lode River Trips, (916) 626-4187; Outdoors Unlimited, (916) 626-7668; River Runners Inc., (916) 622-5110; Wilderness Adventures, (800) 323-7238.

WHERE TO DINE

Coloma Club Café ● △△ $$

Highway 49 at Marshall road, just east of Coloma; (916) 626-6390. American; full bar service. Daily 6:30 a.m. to 9 p.m. AMEX. Western style café, newly renovated with a pioneer town façade. Varied menu, ranging from Stroganoff to lasagna to steaks, chicken and chops.

The Vineyard House ● △△ $$

Cold Springs Road, Coloma; (916) 622-2217. American-continental; full bar service. Friday-Saturday 5 to 10, Sunday 3 to 8:30 (hours may be expanded later). MC/VISA, AMEX. An eye-appealing restaurant in an 1878 Victorian inn with plate rails, hurricane lamps and big oval rag rugs. Busy menu, ranging from papaya chicken and shrimp Dijon to beef stroganoff.

WHERE TO SLEEP

Coloma Country Inn ● △△△ $$$$ ∅

P.O. Box 502 (345 High St.), Coloma, CA 95613; (916) 622-6919. Doubles $89 with private bath, $79 with shared bath. Combination lodging-hot air balloon packages. Six units; full breakfast. Checks accepted, no credit cards. This 1856 yellow and white trimmed Victorian just above the historic park is nestled among green lawns and shady trees. The inn's interior décor is a mix of American country and Victorian furniture, accented by a large collection of antique quilts.

The Vineyard House ● △△ $$$ ∅

P.O. Box 176 (Cold Springs Road), Coloma, CA 95613; (916) 622-2217. Doubles from $70. Seven units with share bath. MC/VISA, AMEX. This 1878 country inn contains a restaurant (discussed above), a great bar and seven hotel rooms—but only one bath. Rooms are nicely appointed and color-coordinated with Victorian touches and antique furniture.

WHERE TO CAMP

Although there are no state park campsites at Coloma, several private campgrounds operate in the area. All are on the river, affording handy put-in and/or take-outs for rafters. Most are closed in winter.

American River Resort ● *P.O. Box 427 (Highway 49), Coloma, CA 95613; (916) 622-6700. RV and tent sites, from $12. Reservations accepted.* Water and electric hookups, flush potties, showers, picnic tables and barbecues. Swimming pool, kids' fish pond, water sports.

Camp Lotus ● *P.O. Box 578, Lotus, CA 95651; (916) 622-8672. RV and tent sites from $10. Reservations accepted.* Water and electric hookups; flush potties, showers, barbecues and picnic tables. Fishing, swimming, water sports, horse shoes, volleyball; small store.

Coloma Resort ● *6921 Mount Murphy Rd. (P.O. Box 516), Coloma, CA 95613; (916) 621-2267. RV and tent sites, $20 to $22.50. Reservations ac-*

cepted; MC/VISA, AMEX. Nicely landscaped campground across from the park, with water and electric hookups, flush potties, showers, picnic tables and barbecues. Shaded riverfront campsites; convenience store, fishing, swimming, water sports.

Auburn

Population: 10,600   **Elevation: 1,255 feet**

A dozen more miles of road—mostly winding—takes you to Auburn, founded by French immigrant Claude Chana. He was headed for the diggin's in Coloma when he stopped to do a bit of panning in a narrow ravine. He hit paydirt and went no further.

En route, you'll pass one of the more spectacular settings in the Gold Country—the twin canyons of the north and middle forks of the American River, which converge just outside of town. They've been the heart of a serious environmental dispute for decades, since a planned downstream dam would flood them. The project was on hold as of this writing, although a scaled-down version intended for flood control was in the works. **Auburn State Recreation Area** here offers hiking trails and river access, including swimmin' holes among the boulders, gold panning spots and put-ins for rafters.

Bisected by Interstate 80, Auburn is the largest town in the Gold Country. Although it suffers serious suburban sprawl, it has preserved its past in **Old Town**. Highway 49 twists up from the American River Canyon and enters Auburn's back door, becoming Lincoln Way. Instead of turning right at the Highway 49 north sign, continue on Lincoln, dropping downhill to the old town area. On the way, you'll pass the recently-restored yellow brick 1894 **Placer County Courthouse,** containing county offices and a new museum.

The town's other attractions are rather randomly placed, so pick up a direction map at the chamber (See "Trip planner"). Then cross the freeway and set your tires back on Highway 49, the Grass Valley Highway, for the Gold Country's most northern and most scenic reaches.

ATTRACTIONS

☺ *Gold Country Museum* • *1273 High St. (at the Gold Country Fairgrounds); (916) 889-4134. Tuesday-Sunday 10 to 4, closed Mondays and holidays; adults $1, kids 6 to 16 and adults 65 and over, 50 cents.* Built of rough stone and logs as a WPA project in the early 1940s, the museum offers a fairly complete study of gold mining in early Placer County. Exhibits include a walk-through model mine tunnel with displays of the various types of gold found in the area.

☺ *Placer County Courthouse and Museum* • *101 Maple St.; (916) 889-6500. Call for hours.* This imposing yellow brick structure was reopened in early 1991 after extensive remodeling. With its impressive capitol dome and four-sided matched entrances topped by Greek pediments, it's one of the Gold Country's most photographed structures. Courts occupy the upper floors and the Placer County Museum occupies several ground floor rooms.

Doctor Fox sculptures • *391 Auburn Ravine Rd.; (916) 885-2769.* Auburn dentist Kenneth H. Fox creates monumental concrete sculptures in his spare time. His main collection of statues, some as much as 40 feet high, occupy the grounds of his dental office and the public is free to browse.

They depict voluptuous Indian maidens and other figures done in a rough, textured finish with remarkably detailed features.

ANNUAL EVENTS

Wild West Stampede, April at the Gold Country Fairgrounds, Auburn, (916) 885-6281.

Firemen's Muster, late June at the Gold Country Fairgrounds, (916) 885-6281.

Gold Country Fair, early September at the Gold Country Fairgrounds, (916) 885-6281.

Auburn Air Fair, early October at Auburn Municipal Airport, (916) 885-5863.

Heritage Fair, mid-October in Old Town, (916) 885-5616.

WHERE TO DINE

All Auburn restaurants are smoke-free, by city ordinance.

☺ *Butterworth's* ● △△△△ *$$$* Ø

1522 Lincoln Way at Court Street (above old town), Auburn; (916) 885-0249. Continental; wine and beer. Lunch 11:30 to 2 and dinner 5 to 9 Monday-Saturday; Sunday brunch from 10 to 2 then dinner from 3 to 9. MC/VISA, AMEX. Auburn's most attractive restaurant, housed in an 1887 Victorian mansion. The fare, such as beef Wellington, tournedos Mecina, chicken with cider herbs and prawns with lime and cilantro, is as appealing as the décor.

Café Delicias ● △ *$* Ø

1591 Lincoln Way in Old Auburn; (916) 885-2050. Mexican; wine and beer. Daily 11 a.m. to 9 p.m. Major credit cards. Pleasantly funky Mexican café in the heart of Old Town with the usual smashed beans and rice dishes, plus specialties such as *carne asada, taquitos rancheros* and *flautas Juarez.* It's housed in an 1852 brick structure and decorated with brightly colored Latin posters and other South of the Border regalia.

Shanghai Restaurant ● △△△ *$$* Ø

289 Washington St., Old Town Auburn; (916) 823-2613. Cantonese; full bar service. Daily 11:30 to 9:30. Major credit cards. Local favorite that has been dishing up good Cantonese fare since 1906. Housed in the former American Hotel in Old Town, it has a mix of early American and Oriental décor, with cozy dining alcoves beneath 16-foot embossed metal ceilings.

WHERE TO SLEEP

Auburn Inn ● △△△ *$$$* Ø

1875 Auburn Ravine Rd. (Foresthill exit from I-80), Auburn, CA 95603; (800) 272-1444 (California only) or (916) 885-1800. Doubles $54 to $62, singles $48 to $56. Major credit cards. Attractive 85-unit motel with TV, room phones; some suites. Pool, spa, coin laundry; handicapped units.

Best Western Golden Key ● △△△ *$$* Ø

13450 Lincoln Way (Foresthill exit from I-80), Auburn, CA 95603; (800) 528-1234 or (916) 885-8611. Doubles $40 to $50, singles $38 to $44. Major credit cards. Nice 68-room motel with TV movies, room phones. Extensive landscaped grounds; indoor pool.

Elmwood Motel ● △△ *$$*

588 High St. (at Elm), Auburn, CA 95603; (916) 885-5186. Doubles $35 to $41; MC/VISA. Tidy little motel in downtown Auburn; cable TV, pool.

Bed & breakfast inns

☺ **Powers Mansion Inn** ● △△△ $$$$
164 Cleveland Ave., Auburn, CA 95603; (916) 885-1166. Doubles from $75. Fifteen units, all with private baths; full breakfast. Major credit cards. One of Auburn's most stylish inns. The rooms are color coordinated, with period furnishings and old fashion yet modern bathrooms.

The Victorian Hill House ● △△△ $$$ Ø
P.O. Box 9097 (195 Park St.), Auburn, CA 95604 (916) 885-5879. Doubles $65 to $85. Four rooms, three with shared baths and one with private bath; full breakfast. MC/VISA. One of Auburn's oldest Victorians, this white clapboard house with green trim sits on a landscaped slope above Old Town. Guest rooms furnished with antiques and assorted yesterday frills. Pool and gazebo with hot tub.

WHERE TO CAMP

Auburn KOA ● *3550 KOA Way (3.5 miles north, just off Highway 49), Auburn, CA 95603; (916) 885-0990. RV sites with full hookup $21, tent sites $15. Reservations accepted; MC/VISA.* Flush potties, showers, swimming pool and spa; store, playground, coin laundry, fish pond and rec room.

Bear River Park ● *Plum Tree Road, c/o Placer County Parks Division, 11476 C Ave., Auburn, CA 95603; (916) 889-7750. Thirty sites for tents or small self-contained RVs, $6. Pit potties, no hookups or showers.* Picnic tables and barbecues; fishing, hiking and swimming. Open all year, but no potable water available in winter.

Gold Country Fairgrounds ● *P.O. Box 5527 (1273 High St.), Auburn, CA 95604; (916) 885-6281. RVs and trailers only, $10.* Water and electric hookups, flush potties and showers, a few picnic tables.

Grass Valley

Population: 9,000   **Elevation: 2,420 feet**

The story goes that George McKnight tripped over a small quartz outcropping while chasing a cow in the moonlight. He noted a glint and, by George, it was gold!

No, this isn't how the term "moonlighting" originated.

This event, if it's true, heralded the beginning of the town of Grass Valley in 1850 and the beginning of serious hard-rock mining in the Gold Country. The techniques were developed here primarily by English copper and tin miners from Cornwall. Initially, gold-seekers had panned the streams, then rigged sluice boxes and other devices to sift gold-bearing gravel. However, the real treasure lay in veins beneath the ground. In fact, a single hardrock operation—Grass Valley's Empire Mine—yielded more ore than the entire Yukon Gold Rush!

The town's second claim to fame has nothing to do with gold. This briefly was the home of the notorious 18th century dancer-entertainer Lola Montez and her famous protegè, Lotta Crabtree.

Grass Valley today is a thriving bedroom community for the bustling Sacramento-Auburn suburbs. You noted, as you drove the 25 miles from Auburn, that much of the area suffers from strip commercialism. However, the town itself is rather attractive, set off by pine trees, since we're climbing higher into the Sierra Nevada.

Like Auburn, Grass Valley has an old town section, although many structures wear latter-day façades. Before you get there, take the Empire Street off ramp from Highway 49 south of town and follow signs to **Empire Mine State Historic Park.** Then cross back over the freeway, and—with some tricky turns—follow other signs to the **North Star Mining Museum.**

From the museum, head north into town on Mill Street. After a few blocks, you'll pass the shingled **Lola Montez house** which now contains the **Nevada County Chamber of Commerce.** Continue up Mill Street and you shortly reach the heart of the old district.

ATTRACTIONS

☺ **Empire Mine State Historic Park** ● *10791 E. Empire St.; (916) 273-8522. Daily 10 to 5 in summer; call for off-season hours. Adults $2, kids $1. Tours daily in the summer; weekends only in the off-season.* This was one of the oldest, richest and largest hardrock mines in America. More than 360 miles of underground passages were dug, fanning out from the main shaft. Its vertical drop was over 5,000 feet. A particularly striking feature of the complex is the boldly massive "cottage" of mine owner William Bourn, Jr., constructed of stone from mine tailings.

☺ **North Star Mining Museum** ● *Allison Ranch Road at Mill Street; (916) 273-4255. Daily except Monday 11 to 5 from late spring through early fall; closed the rest of the year. Admission by donation.* The powerhouse building of the defunct North Star Mine serves as an intriguing exhibit center for the county historical museum. Its excellent display of gold mining equipment includes a working Cornish pump developed by Cornwall miners to lift water, making deep pit mining possible.

Other attractions of interest in the Grass Valley area are **Mount St. Mary's Convent** at South Church and Chapel streets and the nicely restored 1862 **Holbrook Hotel** at 212 W. Main Street.

ANNUAL EVENTS

Living History Days, mid-April, mid-September and mid-October at Empire Mine State Historic Park, (916) 273-8522

Bluegrass Festival, June at Nevada County Fairgrounds, Grass Valley, (209) 464-5324.

Golden Empire Fly-in, early July, County Airpark, (916) 273-3046.

Nevada County Fair, August, County Fairgrounds, (916) 273-6217.

Cornish Christmas, early December in downtown Grass Valley, (916) 272-8315.

WHERE TO DINE

Arletta Douglas Room ● ∆∆∆ $$$ Ø

In the Holbrooke Hotel at 212 W. Main St., Grass Valley; (916) 272-1989. American regional-continental; full bar service. Lunch weekdays 11 to 2, dinner Monday-Thursday 5:30 to 9 and Friday-Saturday 5:30 to 9:30, Sunday brunch 10 to 1:30. MC/VISA, AMEX. Strikingly handsome Victorian dining room with print wallpaper, hunter green carpet and candle-lit tables. Grass Valley's most attractive dining parlor, with an innovative, versatile menu.

Tofanelli's ● ∆∆∆ $ Ø

302 W. Main St., Grass Valley; (916) 273-9927. American; wine and beer. Weekdays 7 a.m. to 8:30 p.m., Saturday 8 to 2 and Sunday 9 to 2 Sunday.

MC/VISA. Cute oldstyle cafè with remarkably inexpensive and tasty dinners, including soup or salad, potato or rice and veggie. Simple, attractive dècor: embossed tin ceilings, exposed brick walls, wainscoting and Boston ferns.

A distinctive feature of Grass Valley cuisine is the "pastie," a chubby turnover with spicy fillings of meat and other goodies. They were brought to the area by Cornish miners. Try the tasty specialty at these outlets:

Mrs. Dubblebee's ● *251-C South Auburn; (916) 272-7700. Weekdays 10 to 6 and weekends 10 to 5:30.* Housed in a cute cottage; dine in or take out.

King Richard's ● *217 Colfax Ave.; (916) 273-0286. Monday-Friday 9 to 6, Saturday 11 to 5, Sunday noon to 5.* Small cafè combined with **Antonio's Mexican Deli.**

Marshall's Pasties ● *203 Mill St.; (916) 272-2844. Daily 9:30 to 6.* Locateed in the historic district; dining room with balcony above.

Rachel's Pasties and Sweet Things ● *568 E. Main St.; (916) 273-2973. Weekdays 6:30 a.m. to 6 p.m., Saturday 10 to 6, closed Sunday.* Early American style cafè; eat there or take out.

WHERE TO SLEEP

Alta Sierra Resort Motel ● ⌂ $$$
135 Tammy Way (at the Alta Sierra Country Club), Grass Valley, CA 95949; (916) 273-9102. Doubles $64 to $85, singles $45 to $58; MC/VISA. Resort style motel with rustic dècor at Alta Sierra Country Club with a TV, pool, golf and tennis.

Best Western Gold Country Inn ● ⌂ $$ Ø
11972 Sutton Way (Brunswick exit from freeway), Grass Valley, CA 95945; (916) 273-1393. Doubles $46 to $54, singles $44 to $48, kitchen units $4 to $7 extra. Nicely-kept 84-unit motel between Grass Valley and Nevada City; TV, room phones, pool and spa.

Bed & breakfast inns and a historic hotel

Golden Ore House ● ⌂ $$$ Ø
448 S. Auburn St., Grass Valley, CA 95945; (916) 272-6872. Doubles $70 to $82. Six units, some private and some share baths; full breakfast. MC/VISA. Built in 1904, this Colonial style home has been nicely refurbished, accented with natural wood trim, lace curtains and antique furnishings.

The Holbrooke Hotel ● ⌂ $$$$
212 W. Main St., Grass Valley, CA 95945; (916) 272-1989. Doubles and singles $70 to $104, one suite $120 to $145. Seventeen units, plus 11 in the adjacent Purcell House, all with private baths; continental breakfast. MC/VISA, AMEX. Nicely restored hotel with gold rush-Victorian theme; rooms feature color coordinated print wallpaper, draperies and comforters on brass beds (some canopied). **Arletta Douglas dining room** listed above.

Murphy's Inn ● ⌂ $$$$ Ø
318 Neal St., Grass Valley, CA 95945; (916) 273-6873. Doubles $74 to $123. Eight rooms, all with private baths; full breakfast. MC/VISA, AMEX. Built in 1866 for North Star Mine owner Edward Coleman, this Early American style home with bold, squared lines and cheerful ivy-enlaced porch has been carefully restored and opulently furnished.

Annie Horan's Bed & Breakfast ● ⌂ $$$ Ø
415 W. Main St., Grass Valley, CA 95945; (916) 272-2418. Doubles $55 to $95. Four units, all with private baths; from $50 per couple; continental

breakfast. MC/VISA. This slender 1874 gingerbread-trimmed home is one of Grass Valley's more charming Victorians. The interior has been carefully restored and furnished in the typical Victorian manner, with lots of wood, brass and lace.

WHERE TO CAMP

Nevada County Fairgrounds • *Off McCourtney Road (P.O. Box 2687), Grass Valley, CA 95945; (916) 273-6217. RV and trailer sites, $12.* Flush potties, showers, some picnic tables. Open most of the year, except during major events at the fairgrounds.

Nevada City

Population: 2,900   **Elevation: 2,525 feet**

Perhaps the most attractive town in the Gold Country, Nevada City is an agreeable blend of Victoriana and the Old West, dropped among pine-clad hills. It shelters a sizable collection of artists, writers and musicians, along with folks who busy themselves renovating the town's many Victorian homes.

Tourism is taken seriously here. Glossy black surreys clip-clop along its streets, hauling camera-clutching visitors past old fashioned buildings containing boutiques and restaurants. With the Gold Country's largest collection of specialty shops, this stylish old town gets crowded on summer weekends. We prefer it on a quiet winter evening, when it becomes a Charles Dickens vision of flickering gaslights, frosty window panes and gentle voices of good cheer issuing from Friar Tuck's pub.

Nevada City was born of gold, of course. Glitter was found in Deer Creek shortly after the discovery in Coloma, and the town fanned out in all directions from the shallow ravine.

It has one significant archive, the **Nevada County Historical Society Museum** in an old firehouse on Main Street. You can sip the essence of the grape at the **Nevada City Winery** at 321 Spring Street, and admire the classic brick architecture of the **South Yuba Canal Building,** now housing the **Nevada City Chamber of Commerce** at 132 Main Street. Mostly, people come for the setting, the shops, the restaurants and the Victorian-yuppie ambiance.

The most extensive and interesting Gold Rush site in the region is **Malakoff Diggins State Historic Park.** It's reached by driving 11 miles north of Nevada City on Highway 49, then turning east onto Tyler Foote Crossing Road.

ATTRACTIONS

☺ **Nevada County Historical Society Museum** • *In Firehouse #1 at 214 Main St., Nevada City; (916) 265-5468. Daily 11 to 4 (closed Wednesdays from November 1 to April 1). Donations appreciated.* The slender old building is one of the Gold Country's more ornate wedding cake Victorians. Inside are displays of life in a 19th century gold camp, including antique guns, needlework, Maidu Indian artifacts and the usual pioneer relics.

☺ **Malakoff Diggins State Historic Park** • *23579 N. Bloomfield Rd., Nevada City, CA 95959; (916) 265-2740. Interpretive center open daily in the summer from 10 to 5; shorter hours in the off-season.* It looks like the surface of the moon after a flash flood, or perhaps the fantastically eroded cliffs of

The split-bucket Pelton wheel, invented by gold rusher Lester Pelton, used water to supply power to the mines. This one's in Nevada City. — **Don W. Martin**

Utah's canyonlands. This was the world's largest hydraulic mining operation until it was outlawed by America's first environmental legislation. The park also encompasses the old mining town of North Bloomfield.

More than a century ago, powerful blasts of water from "monitors" ripped apart the hillsides to reach gravel beds of a prehistoric river. One 10-inch nozzle could hurl water against the cliffs at the rate of 16,000 gallons per minute, nearly a million gallons an hour! The runoff silted up the Yuba River, ruined farmers' fields, caused a major flood in Marysville in 1875 and turned faraway San Francisco Bay to a murky brown. For years, lowlanders fought to have hydraulic mining stopped. Finally, in 1884, Judge Lorenzo Sawyer ruled that a mining company could not dump tailings into a stream. Malakoff Diggins went out of business and North Bloomfield went to sleep.

ACTIVITIES

Bicycle outings ● BikeSierra Adventure Company, Nevada City; (916) 265-9240. Bicycle rentals and conducted bike tours.

Carriage rides ● Nevada City Carriage Company, 17790 Cooper Rd., Nevada City, CA 95959; (916) 265-8778 or 265-5348.

Hiking, horseback riding and rock-hopping ● The South Yuba Recreation Area. For a map/guide, contact: Bureau of Land Management, Folsom District, 63 Natoma St., Folsom, CA 95630; (916) 985-4474. The South Yuba Trail extends for six miles through a rugged canyon of the South Yuba River. The area offers hiking, camping, picnicking, fishing and swimming.

ANNUAL EVENTS

Malakoff Homecoming, June at Malakoff Diggins State Historic Park, (916) 265-2740.

Victorian Christmas, early to mid-December, (916) 265-2692; decorated shops and carolers downtown, special events at Miners Foundry.

WHERE TO DINE

Cirino's Bar and Grill ● △△△ *$$$*

309 Broad St.; (916) 265-2246. Italian; full bar service. Lunch daily 11 to 4, dinner Sunday-Thursday 5 to 9 and Friday-Saturday 5 to 10. MC/VISA, AMEX. Upbeat, locally popular bistro with 19th century dècor. Menu runs the Italian gamut from veal parmagiana and scaloppini to picata and scampi, plus a goodly pasta assortment.

Country Rose ● △△△ *$$$* Ø

300 Commercial St.; (916) 265-6248. Continental; Wine and beer. Wednesday-Monday 5 to 9 p.m. (to 10 Friday and Saturday), closed Tuesday. MC/VISA. Stylish Country French cafè housed in one of Nevada City's old brick buildings, with high ceilings, lace curtains, candle-lit tables and early American dècor. Ivy-trimmed garden offers outdoor dining.

☺ *Friar Tuck's* ● △△△△ *$$*

111 N. Pine St.; (916) 265-9093. American-continental; wine and beer. Wednesday-Thursday 6 to 10, Friday 6 to 10:30, Saturday 5:30 to 10:30, Sunday 5 to 9:30; closed Monday and Tuesday. Major credit cards. One of the Gold Country's coziest and most cheerful restaurants, with brick walls, heavy ceiling beams, hanging plants and refectory booths. Diners have a choice of a dim, quiet back room or a more lively area adjacent to the wine bar, where they can dine to the rhythm of live music, usually guitarists or folk singers.

☺ *Peter Selaya's* ● △△△△ *$$* Ø

320 Broad St.; (916) 265-5697. California cuisine; wine and beer. Tuesday-Thursday 6 to 9 p.m., Friday-Saturday 6 to 9:30, Sunday 5 to 9, closed Monday. MC/VISA, AMEX. Both a culinary and visual treat; menu ranges from fresh salmon with mustard caper *aioli* to a gourmet vegetarian dish with vegetables and cashew-stuffed mushrooms in a baked pastry. The old fashioned dining room is cleverly styled to resemble a mine shaft.

WHERE TO SLEEP

National Hotel ● ⌂⌂ *$$*

211 Broad St., Nevada City, CA 95959; (916) 265-4551. Forty-three units, from $43 with share bath and $63 with private bath. MC/VISA, AMEX. Although not elegantly done, the National offers comfortable, clean rooms, many furnished with antiques. Some units are quite spàcious, with balconies overlooking the town.

Northern Queen Motel ● ⌂⌂ *$$$* Ø

400 Railroad Ave. (Sacramento Avenue exit from Highway 20), Nevada City, CA 95959; (916) 265-5824. Doubles and singles $43 to $51, cottages $75, chalets $85. Major credit cards. A 75-unit motel with TV, room phones, refrigerators; cottages with wood-burning stoves; chalets with full kitchens. Pool and spa. **Restaurant** serves 7 to 3 and 5:30 to 9; American fare; dinners $8 to $17; wine and beer.

Bed & breakfast inns

Flume's End Bed & Breakfast ● ⌂⌂⌂ $$$$ Ø
317 S. Pine St., Nevada City, CA 95959; (916) 265-9665. Doubles $75 to $125. Five rooms, plus a cottage with fireplace, all with private baths and decks; full breakfast. A mid-19th century Victorian tucked against a hillside with a creek splashing through the back yard. The landscaped grounds slope down to three wooded acres, where a flume once carried water to the mines. Tastefully furnished in country French.

Grandmere's Bed & Breakfast ● ⌂⌂⌂⌂ $$$$$ Ø
449 Broad St., Nevada City, CA 95959; (916) 265-4660. Rooms $95 to $145. Seven units, all with private baths; buffet breakfast. MC/VISA. An elegant example of Colonial Revival architecture with a marble entry, Corinthian columns and black wrought iron trim. Built in 1861, the house is listed on the National Register of Historic Places.

☺ **The Red Castle Inn** ● ⌂⌂⌂⌂ $$$$ Ø
109 Prospect St., Nevada City, CA 95959; (916) 265-5135. Doubles $70 to $110. Eight units; six private baths and two share; full buffet breakfast. MC/VISA, AMEX. Built by a wealthy mine owner in 1860, the four-story red brick mansion—rich with gingerbread trim—rises imperiously from a forested hillside. The home is opulently attired, with Victorian antiques and wicker baskets filled with silk flowers.

WHERE TO CAMP

Malakoff Diggins State Historic Park ● *23579 N. Bloomfield Rd., Nevada City, CA 94959; (916) 265-2740. Tent and RV sites, $14 in summer, lower in the off-season.* No hookups or showers; pit potties. Picnic tables and barbecues, swimming, fishing, small store. Located in a pine grove near the park interpretive center.

River Rest Campground ● *General Delivery, Washington, CA 95896; (916) 265-4306. RV and tent sites, water and electric hookups, from $12.50.* Flush potties, showers, picnic tables and barbecues. Swimming, fishing and tubing in nearby Yuba River; horse shoes, hiking, small store.

Sierra County

Downieville 400; Sierra City 100   **Elevation: 2,899 feet**

As you head north, you shed the upscale, upbeat tourist activity of Nevada City and enter the most remote and certainly the most scenic area of the Gold Country.

After passing through **North San Juan** and **Camptonville,** Highway 49 begins to twist and turn, although it's easily navigable. It passes a boulder-strewn crossing of the Yuba River, then begins wandering through the beautiful, narrow canyon of the South Yuba, flanked by forest-clad hills. Turnouts invite you to pause and dip a fishing line in the water or a gold pan into the gravel. Several forest service campgrounds and picnic areas line the river's edge.

About 40 miles along this idyllic drive from Nevada City, you encounter **Downieville**. It's an absolute jewel—a tiny tin-roofed hamlet tucked into a wooded canyon at the forks of the Yuba and Downie rivers. Its brick and stone buildings have survived the decades since William Downie found golden wealth in the two streams. (A legend claims that he caught a salmon, boiled it and found gold in the bottom of the pot.) Utility lines went underground a few years ago to give Downieville's tree-lined main street a clean, uncluttered look. A few boutiques and gold shops occupy the venerable buildings.

There are few specific attractions here; the town itself is charming enough. You might peek into the simple **Sierra County Museum** or catch a cup of coffee and sticky bun at **Downieville Bakery,** in the stone 1852 **Craycroft building.** Downieville is one of the smallest county seats in America and the **Sierra County Courthouse** is an interesting example of Art Deco—not early California—architecture. The gallows, still in working condition, stand outside, and exhibit of gold nugget replicas reside within.

A genteel version of the Gold Rush is still alive in Downieville. Sections of the Downie and Yuba rivers in this area are open to public panning and about 50 ounces of glitter are taken out by visitors each year.

Follow Highway 49 for another 15 miles along the rockbound river and you'll arrive in **Sierra City,** a smaller near twin to Downieville. You're now high among the pines, at 4,187 feet. Tiny Sierra City occupies a dramatic setting, sandwiched between the granite crags of the **Sierra Buttes** and the Yuba River. Like Downieville, it's a contented gathering of brick and cut stone buildings. The county's fine **Kentucky Mine Museum** is just north of town.

Pressing further north on Highway 49, you'll see the former road house of **Bassett's Station** on your left. A left turn here takes you to the **Gold Lakes,** a chain of alpine jewels behind the Sierra Buttes. They attract boaters, fly-casters and campers. Trails from here lead to the buttes' craggy heights. Beyond the lakes, this road reaches the woodsy resort town of **Graeagle** and **Plumas-Eureka State Park,** which preserves yet another 19th century mining operation.

Meanwhile, back at Bassett's, if you continue north on Highway 49, you top **Yuba Pass** at 6,701 feet. Pause at a turnout for a look down to the surprisingly flat **Sierra Valley.** Rimmed by mountains, this remote farming vale looks like a piece of Kansas dropped into the Sierra Nevada. Highway 49 winds down into the valley and hurries past its fields and pasturelands. After passing through the farm town of **Loyalton,** the historic Golden Chain finally comes to an end in the nondescript hamlet of **Vinton.**

ATTRACTIONS

Sierra County Museum ● *Main Street, Downieville, CA 95936. Open from Memorial Day to mid-October: 10 a.m. to 5 p.m. daily in summer; weekends only at the beginning and end of the season. Admission free, donations accepted.* The most interesting thing about this little museum is the building in which it resides—an 1852 mortarless schist structure with a brick front. Inside, you'll find the typical collection of pioneer artifacts, mining equipment and a stamp mill model. Exhibits are in a bit of a jumble.

☺ *Sierra County Historical Park and Museum* ● *A mile north of Sierra City, off Highway 49; (916) 862-1310. Wednesday-Sunday 10 to 5 from Memorial Day through September; weekends only in October, weather permitting; closed the rest of the year. Guided stamp mill tour $4, kids $2; museum admission $1; kids 12 and under, free with an adult.* Forty-five minute tours through this virtually intact stamp mill give visitors a quick and complete study of a typical hardrock mining operation. Elsewhere in this park, which occupies a pine-shaded slope, one can prowl through a scattering of mining equipment and visit a museum filled with Sierra County memorabilia.

☺ **Plumas-Eureka State Park** ● *310 Johnsville Rd., Blairsden; (916) 836-2380. Visitor center/museum open daily 8 to 4:30 in summer; shorter hours the rest of the year. Free admission.* Another fine example of hardrock mining has been preserved at Plumas-Eureka, within a beautiful 6,749-acre region of evergreen forests, glacier-shaped peaks and gemlike lakes. It offers an aging stamp mill, a display of mining equipment and a museum. The mill is undergoing restoration as funds become available.

Sierra Valley Museum ● *In Loyalton City Park, Loyalton; (916) 993-6750. Wednesday-Sunday 1 to 5. Free, donations accepted.* Although not professionally done, Loyalton's museum is a charming little exhibit center. Displays include pioneer artifacts, wooden skis and an exhibit of Depression glass—see-through dishes that were produced cheaply during the 1930s.

ANNUAL EVENTS

Kentucky Mine Concert Series, nine summer Friday evenings at Sierra County Historical Park; (916) 862-1310.

Miners Day Weekend and **Clampers Day Weekend,** on August weekends in Downieville; (916) 289-3560.

WHERE TO DINE

Cirino's at the Forks ● △△△ $$
Main Street, Downieville; (916) 289-3479. Italian; full bar service. Lunch daily 11:30 to 2, dinner 5 to 9. MC/VISA, AMEX. Italian fare served in a Western atmosphere: knotty pine, wagon wheel chandeliers and cowboy artifacts on the walls. Some tables overlooking the river; lunch served on a riverside patio during proper weather.

Downieville Diner ● △△ $
Main Street, Downieville; (916) 289-3616. American; wine and beer. Daily 7 to 7; closes at 4 in the off-season. MC/VISA. Typical rural American fare such as chicken fried steak, Southern fried chicken and roast beef. It's served in a simple American dining room in an 1860 building.

Sierra Buttes Inn ● △△ $$
Highway 49, Sierra City; (916) 862-1300. American; full bar. Friday-Monday 8 to 2, dinner nightly 5 to 9. MC/VISA. Pleasantly rustic family café with the usual steaks, chicken, chops, chicken fried steak and barbecued ribs. A salad bar is cleverly installed on a bed of ice in an old fashioned clawfoot bathtub. The restaurant is housed in a century-old wood frame hotel.

WHERE TO SLEEP

The Buttes Resort ● ◠◠ $$
P.O. Box 124, Sierra City, CA 96125; (916) 862-1170. Housekeeping units; $42 to $45, a two-room family unit $65. MC/VISA. Attractive little resort in a woodsy setting beside the Yuba River. Cable TV, pool, deck overlooking the river.

Coyoteville Cabins ● ◠◠ $$$
P.O. Box 553 (on Highway 49 south of town), Downieville, CA 95936; (916) 289-3624. Seven housekeeping cabins with kitchens, $40 per couple; MC/VISA. Rustic and appealing little units terraced into a steep ravine above the highway, alongside cascading Coyote Creek.

Herrington's Sierra Pines ● ⌂⌂ $$$
P.O. Box 235 (Highway 49 just south of town), Sierra City, CA 96125;
(916) 862-1151. Doubles and singles $49 to $65, cottage with kitchen and
fireplace, $75; MC/VISA. Nicely appointed 20-unit motel in wooded riverside
location with a trout pond. TV movies, balconies, many with view of Sierra
Buttes and river. **Restaurant** serves 8 to 11 a.m. and 5 to 9 p.m.; American; dinners $8 to $20; full bar service.

Sierra Buttes Inn ● ⌂ $$
P.O. Box 320, Sierra City, CA 96125; (916) 862-1300. Doubles from $39
with private baths, from $25 with share baths. MC/VISA. It ain't fancy, but
the rooms in this century old clapboard, tin roofed hotel in downtown Sierra
City are clean and neat. **Restaurant** listed above.

Bed & breakfast inns

Bush & Heringlake Country Inn ● ⌂⌂ $$$ Ø
P.O. Box 68 (Highway 49), Sierra City, CA 96125; (916) 862-1501. Doubles $75 to $110. Four rooms with private baths; continental breakfast. Sturdy
brick 1871 Wells Fargo Express and general store fashioned into an attractive inn. Wide plank floors and walls; rooms with oversized beds and early
American furniture. Its stylish **Carlo's Ristorante** serves Italian fare.

☺ Sierra Shangri-La ● ⌂⌂ $$$ Ø
P.O. Box 285 (Highway 49 three miles north of town), Downieville, CA
95936; (916) 289-3455. Doubles $49 to $88, four-person units $93 to $110.
Eight housekeeping cottages and three bed & breakfast units in the main building, all with private baths. MC/VISA. Cozy, rustic cottages and B&B units in
an impressive setting, perched on the brink of the cascading Yuba River.
Cottages have kitchenettes, decks and barbecue areas. Occupants of the
three B&B units in the main building are served a continental breakfast.

WHERE TO CAMP

Tahoe National Forest ● *Star Route, Box 1, Camptonville, CA 95922;*
(916) 288-3231. Several national forest campgrounds are alongside the
streams. A particularly appealing one, away from highway traffic, is Wild
Plum on Haypress Creek just above Sierra City. Other camp sites are in the
Gold Lakes area.

Sierra Skies RV Park ● *Sierra City, CA 96125; (916) 862-1166. RV sites,*
$15; reservations accepted. Full hookups, flush potties and showers. Lawn areas and horse shoe pits. On the north fork of the Yuba River, near Sierra
City. Open May through October.

Willow Creek Campground ● *17548 Highway 49, Camptonville, CA*
95922; (916) 288-3456. RV sites from $8 to $12. Reservations accepted.
Water, electrical hookups, flush potties and shower. Picnic areas, fishing;
river nearby.

SOUTHERN GOLD COUNTRY

If you drive south from Placerville on Highway 49, you'll see curiously
little hint of the Gold Rush for the first several miles. **Plymouth**, the first
town you encounter, is noted as the gateway to the **Shenandoah Valley
wine country.** Head east from here to taste some of the finest Zinfandels
in the state (see "Activities" below).

While exploring the Gold Country's wine country, pause in tiny **Fiddle-**

town east of Plymouth, one of the most unspoiled hamlets in the Sierra foothills. It has a fine collection of pleasantly seedy buildings.

Amador's hamlets

South of Plymouth, you encounter a string of towns noted for their boutiques, gift shops and cafés, housed in a grand collection of weathered wood, cut stone and brick storefronts. For you collectors of yesterday relics, this area offers the best selection of antique stores in the Gold Country.

The towns, in order of their appearance:

Drytown isn't much larger than the historical monument that tells of its past. Gold was discovered here in 1848, but it ran out after ten years. A few shops occupy its weather-weary buildings.

Amador City is a bit larger, with a few more shops, plus a fine restaurant and inn, the **Imperial Hotel.** It was renovated and reopened recently after a long sleep.

Sutter Creek is the only town of substance along here, with a population around 2,000. It offers one of the Gold Country's grandest façades, with a four-block business district rivaling Nevada City's architectural collection. Highway 49 traffic fails to detract from these false front stores, lining the high sidewalks, with thin wooden columns supporting upper balconies. They run the full architectural gamut from little yellow clapboards to bold brick and sturdy stone.

☺ Worthy of a visit is **Knight's Foundry,** the only one in America powered by water. It's a block east of the highway at 81 Eureka Street; (209) 267-5543. Although formal tours aren't given, you can stand just outside and watch the activity as workers prepare the castings. If you're there on a Friday afternoon,

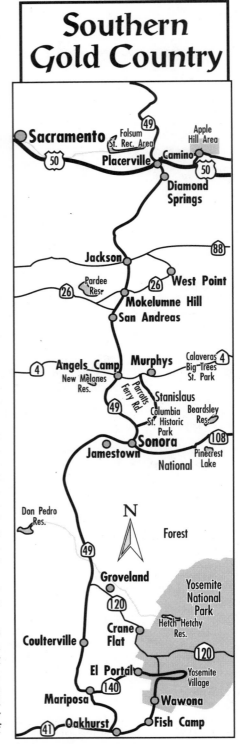

Southern Gold Country

you might see workers pouring molten metal into the molds.

Yes, the town was founded by John Sutter, whose sawmill project led to the discovery of gold. After all of his workers fled to the gold fields and his agricultural-business empire was ruined, he set out to find some gold for himself. But he was no mine boss. His men drank and gambled away what little gold they found, and Sutter soon gave up in disgust.

ACTIVITY

Wine tasting ● For a map and directory to the Shenandoah Valley wineries, contact the Amador County Vintners Association, P.O. Box 718, Plymouth, CA 95669.

ANNUAL EVENTS

Amador County Wine Festival, late June at the Amador County Fairgrounds, Plymouth; (209) 245-6921.

Amador County Fair, late July, county fairgrounds; (209) 245-6921.

Gold Country Jubilee, mid-September, fairgrounds; (209) 223-0350.

WHERE TO DINE

Bellotti Inn ● △△ $$$

53 Main St., Sutter Creek; (209) 267-5211. Italian-American; full bar service. Sunday-Monday and Wednesday-Thursday 11:30 to 9, Friday-Saturday 11:30 to 10, closed Tuesday. Oldstyle restaurant in an historic hotel with attractive although spartan 19th century décor. Usual pastas plus some American steak and prime rib dishes.

Imperial Hotel Restaurant ● △△△ $$$

Main Street, Amador City; (209) 267-9172. Continental; full bar service. Nightly 5 to 9, Sunday brunch 10 to 2. Major credit cards. Smart new restaurant in an 1879 brick Gold Country classic. High backed fabric chairs, ceiling fans and white nappery in the stylish little dining room. Attractive old fashioned saloon adjacent.

Pelargonium ● △△△ $$$ Ø

One Hanford St. (Highway 49 North), Sutter Creek; (209) 267-5008. Contemporary cuisine; wine and beer. Dinner Monday-Friday 5:30 to 9, closed Sunday. No credit cards. Comely restaurant in a Victorian house; all gussied up in geranium wallpaper and Americana frills. Daily-changing menu features entrées such as gallantine of chicken, pork loin, crepes Florentine and red snapper *amandine.*

Sutter Creek Palace ● △△△ $$$

76 Main St., Sutter Creek; (209) 267-9852. American; full bar service. Lunch Friday-Wednesday 11:30 to 3, dinner Friday-Tuesday 5 to 9, closed Wednesday night and all day Thursday. MC/VISA. A study in Victorian elegance, housed in an 1896 building that began life, appropriately, as a restaurant and saloon. Entrées include tournedos of beef, calamari *amandine,* wine country scallops and such.

WHERE TO SLEEP

Old Well Motel ● △ $$

Highway 49 (P.O. Box 187), Drytown, CA 95699; (209) 245-6467. Doubles from $32 to $40; MC/VISA. Rustic cabin type rooms with TV; swimming pool, picnic grounds, gold panning in nearby creek.

Shenandoah Inn ● ⌂⌂⌂ $$$

17674 Village Dr. (on Highway 49), Plymouth, CA 95669; (800) 542-4549 or (209) 245-3888. Doubles $55 to $65, singles $50 to $55. Major credit cards. Attractive new Spanish style 47-room inn on a knoll just outside of Plymouth. Large rooms with Southwestern dècor, TV movies and phones. On the edge of the Shenandoah Valley wine country.

Bed & breakfast inns and an historic hotel

☺ The Foxes ● ⌂⌂⌂⌂ $$$$ Ø

77 Main St. (P.O. Box 159), Sutter Creek, CA 95685; (209) 267-5882. Doubles from $95. Six rooms, all with private baths; full breakfast. MC/VISA, DISC. Occupying a beautiful 19th century home, sitting in a nicely landscaped garden off Sutter Creek's Main Street, it's the Gold Country's most impeccably appointed inn. Each room is color coordinated from wallpaper to drapes to chair coverings; half-canopied beds and massive armoires complete a vision of Victorian elegance.

Imperial Hotel ● ⌂⌂⌂ $$$ Ø

Main Street (P.O. Box 195), Amador City, CA 95601; (209) 267-9172. Doubles $75 to $90. Six rooms with private baths; expanded continental breakfast. Major credit cards. Individually decorated rooms are bright and sunny, with a mix of antique and modern furniture. **Restaurant** listed above.

Mine House Inn ● ⌂⌂⌂ $$$

14125 Highway 49 (P.O. Box 245), Amador City, CA 95601; (209) 267-5900. Doubles $55 to $65, singles $50 to $60. Eight rooms, all with private baths; continental breakfast. No credit cards. This 1880 office building for the Keystone Mine has been cleverly converted into a comfortable inn, nicely furnished with 19th century antiques. A swimming pool is open from May to October.

WHERE TO CAMP

49er Trailer Village ● *Highway 49 and Empire Street (P.O. Box 191), Plymouth, CA 95669; (209) 245-6981. Full hookups, $20 to $25. Reservations accepted; MC/VISA* RV resort with flush potties, showers, cable TV hookups, barbecue areas and general store. Other facilities include two pools, pool hall, rec hall, horse shoe pits, volleyball, fish pond and even a beauty parlor, deli and ice cream parlor.

Amador County Fairgrounds ● *Plymouth, CA 95669; (209) 245-6921. RV and tent sites, $10 with water and electrical hookups.* Well-kept fairgrounds with two camping areas. Flush potties and showers.

Jackson

Population: 3,600   **Elevation: 1,200 feet**

While Sutter Creek and neighbors are noted for their boutiques and antiques, the county seat of Jackson functions as the business end of Amador County. An attractive, prosperous town, it still preserves much of its yesterday look, with old storefronts downtown and a few Victorians tucked into the neighborhoods.

An important hardrock mining center, Jackson outlasted most of the other gold camps and its production continued well into this century. With this latter-day mining came the most unusual architectural objects in the Sierra foothills—the **Jackson tailing wheels.** These giant wooden and steel wheels, measuring 58 feet in diameter, were designed in 1912 to carry mine tailings away from streams, as per new environmental requirements.

To see these strange creatures, turn left from Highway 49 onto Jackson Gate Road in the community of Martell, and follow it to Jackson Tailing Wheels Park. The road then continues into town, taking you past the handsome, onion-domed **St. Sava Serbian Orthodox Church** on your left. You wind up on Main Street, lined with those now familiar wood front and brick front stores. Some have been modernized here, and they house conventional businesses as well as specialty shops. Note the old fashioned **National Hotel and saloon** at the end of the street, dating from 1863. A block above Main Street, reached by near vertical North Street, is the **Amador County Museum.**

A side trip into the hills from Jackson on Highway 88 is definitely worth the climb. After 17 miles, you reach **Pine Grove,** which offers little of interest. However, a left turn takes you another nine miles to **Volcano,** with an outstanding collection of early day buildings. It's just far enough off the beaten track to remain unspoiled. A short distance beyond is **Indian Grinding Rock State Park,** devoted not to the Gold Rush but to the Mi-Wuk Indian culture. If you're in the neighborhood in March or April, follow signs to **Daffodil Hill,** where a family has planted hundreds of thousands of daffodils that bloom in the spring.

ATTRACTIONS

☺ *Kennedy Mine Tailing Wheels* • *In Jackson Kennedy Wheels City Park, north of town on Jackson Gate Road.* Only two of the giant wheels remain standing, reached by short trails in either direction from the road. The others have crashed into ravines, scattered and broken in the underbrush, looking like crude space stations that fell from the sky.

☺ *Amador County Museum* • *225 Church St.; (209) 223-6386. Wednesday-Sunday 10 to 4; admission by donation. Kennedy model mine tour $1 for adults, kids under 8 free, conducted hourly on weekends from 11 to 3.* Located in a large 1859 brick home, the museum offers a quick study in the early day life of this small Gold Country county. Some rooms are furnished as they were during Jackson's heyday, with period cookware, an ancient piano and gramophone and other antiques.

☺ *Indian Grinding Rock State Historic Park* • *14881 Pine Grove-Volcano Rd., Pine Grove; (209) 296-7488. Museum open daily 10 to 5. Park fee $5 per vehicle.* This 135-acre state park in a pleasant pine grove protects the site of the largest grinding rock (chaw'se) in America. A typical Mi-Wuk village nearby features a ceremonial round house, tree bark dwellings and an Indian game field.

ACTIVITIES

Gold panning vacations • *Roaring Camp Mining Company P.O. Box 278, Pine Grove, CA 95665; (209) 296-4100.* Half-day to week-long gold prospecting vacations in the summer at an old mining camp on the Mokelumne River, far down a dusty road from civilization.

Water sports • Several fake lakes in the lower toes of Amador County's foothills lure the boating set: Camanche Reservoir North Shore, 2000 Jackson Valley-Camanche Rd., Ione, CA 95640, (209) 763-5121; Lake Pardee

Reservoir and Marina, 4900 Stony Creek Rd., Ione, CA 95640, (209) 772-1472; and Lake Amador, 7500 Lake Amador Rd., Ione, CA 95640, (209) 274-2625.

ANNUAL EVENTS

Daffodil Hill blooms, generally mid-March, above Volcano; (209) 223-0608 or 296-7048.

Chaw'se Native American Art Show, mid-August to late September at Indian Grinding Rock State Park; (209) 296-7488 or 267-0211.

Big Time Indian Days, late September at Indian Grinding Rock, (209) 296-7488.

WHERE TO DINE

Buscaglia's • ∆∆ $$
1218 Jackson Gate Rd., Jackson; (209) 223-9992. Italian-American; moderate; full bar service. Lunch Wednesday-Friday 11:30 to 2, dinner Wednesday-Saturday from 4:30 and Sunday from noon; closed Monday and Tuesday. MC/VISA. One of two longtime Jackson Gate restaurants, dating from 1916. Modern interior with candle-lit tables, offering little hint of its historic past as a miner's boarding house.

Teresa's • ∆∆ $$
1235 Jackson Gate Rd., Jackson; (209) 223-1786. Italian-American; full bar service. Lunch Monday-Tuesday and Friday-Saturday 11 to 2, dinner Monday-Tuesday 5 to 8:30, Friday-Saturday 5 to 9 and Sunday 2 to 8, closed Wednesday-Thursday. MC/VISA. The other venerable Jackson Gate restaurant, in business since 1921. A former miners' boarding house divided into several small Gold Rush era dining rooms.

WHERE TO SLEEP

Best Western Amador Inn • ⌂⌂ Ø
P.O. Box 758 (200 Highway 49 South), Jackson, CA 95642; (800) 528-1234 or (209) 223-0211. Doubles $60 to $66, kitchens $15 extra, singles $50. Major credit cards. Attractive brick-faced 119-room motel near downtown. TV, room phones; swimming pool. **Restaurant** serves 7 a.m. to 2:30 and 5 to 9:30; American fare; dinners $8 to $14; full bar service.

El Campo Casa Resort Motel • ⌂⌂ $$ Ø
12548 Kennedy Flat Rd., Jackson, CA 95642; (209) 223-0100. Doubles and singles $37 to $66. Major credit cards. An older, well maintained California Mission style resort hotel on landscaped grounds near highways 49 and 88. TV, pool, playground, barbecues.

Bed & breakfast inns and historic hotels

Gate House Inn • ⌂⌂⌂ $$$$ Ø
1330 Jackson Gate Rd., Jackson, CA 95642; (209) 223-3500. Doubles from $75. Four units in main house and a separate two-room summerhouse, all with private baths; full breakfast. MC/VISA, DISC. Ornate Queen Anne home in the Jackson Gate area with some original décor—even the wallpaper in some rooms. Spacious grounds, open porches and a swimming pool.

National Hotel • ⌂ $$
Two Water St. (at the foot of Main), Jackson, CA 95642; (209) 223-0500. Doubles from $42 with bath, $25 without. Thirty-five rooms, some private and

some share baths. MC/VISA. The rooms are minimally furnished but you can sleep with history for a modest price.

St. George Hotel ● △△ $$ Ø

P.O. Box 9 (16104 Volcano-Pine Grove Road), Volcano, CA 95689. Doubles from $39. Twenty rooms, 14 share baths, six private; full breakfast. MC/VISA. The 1862 St. George isn't completely refurbished, but it's clean and tidy, and it wears its age well. **Dining room** is locally famous for its hearty fare; single dinner sitting by advance reservation.

The Wedgewood Inn ● △△△ $$$$ Ø

11941 Narcissus Rd., Jackson, CA 95642; (800) 933-4393 or (209) 296-4300. Doubles $80 to $110, singles $70 to $100. Five rooms plus a carriage house, all with private baths; full breakfast. MC/VISA, DISC. Victorian replica offering a taste of yesterday with reliable plumbing. Rooms individually decorated, with special touches such as stained glass and Victorian lace.

Windrose Inn ● △△△ $$$$ Ø

1407 Jackson Gate Rd., Jackson, CA 95642; (209) 223-3650. Doubles $75 to $135. Four rooms, all with private baths; full breakfast. MC/VISA. Carefully restored century-old farmhouse sits in a pretty green vale in the Jackson Gate area. A glass solarium, grape arbor, fish pond and gazebo in the neat garden adds special charm to the place.

WHERE TO CAMP

Indian Grinding Rock State Historic Park ● On Pine Grove-Volcano Road (P.O. Box 177), Pine Grove, CA 95665. Phone reservations by Mistix, (800) 444-PARK. RV and tent sites, no hookups; $14 in summer and $12 the rest of the year. Attractive oak-shaded sites; flush potties; picnic tables and barbecues.

Camanche Reservoir North Shore ● 2000 Jackson Valley-Camanche Rd., Ione, CA 95640; (209) 763-5121. RV and tent sites in several campgrounds overlooking the lake; $11. Flush potties, showers, laundry, grocery store, service station, water sports.

Pardee Reservoir ● 4900 Stony Creek Rd., Ione, CA 95640; (209) 772-1472. RV sites with hookups $15, tent and RV sites with no hookups, $11. Flush potties, showers, marina, store, water sports. Open mid-February to mid-November.

Mokelumne Hill & San Andreas

Moke Hill 1,000; San Andreas 1,900   **Elevation: 1,008 feet**

Continuing south from Jackson, you enter an often-overlooked section of the Gold Country. With no main roads rising from the valley and no rows of boutiques or major historic parks, they attract few visitors. The small towns of **Mokelumne Hill** and **San Andreas** are set in oak and golden foothills, below the pine belt.

Since time and tide have passed it by, "Moke Hill" has changed little since gold was discovered here in the 1850s. It had gotten a bit seedy in decades past, but our recent visits revealed that several of its false front stores and Victorian homes are feeling the guiding hand of preservationists. Worthy of note is the 1851 **Hotel Leger** (pronounced *Leh-zhay*) and the modest little **Mokelumne Hill History Society Museum** housed in an old brick storefront.

You can drive right through **San Andreas** without realizing it was a

Gold Rush town unless you pause to peek down Main Street. A block-long stretch perpendicular to the highway contains a few olds buildings, mixed with more recent architecture. Note the the **Hall of Records,** housing the **Calaveras County Museum** and a jail cell where famous bandit Black Bart was held. Twelve miles east of San Andreas is **California Caverns,** the most elaborate of several limestone caves in the Sierra foothills.

ATTRACTIONS

☺ *Calaveras County Museum and Archives* ● *30 N. Main St., San Andreas; (209) 754-4023. Daily 10 to 4; donation 50 cents. Gift shop with extensive Gold Country book selection.* The museum covers a full spectrum of Calaveras County history, from the Mi-Wuk Indians to the Spanish, gold seekers and later settlers. Behind the structure is the cell where one Charles Bolton, alias Black Bart, was held to await trial after his capture nearby.

☺ *California Caverns* ● *Twelve miles east of San Andreas, off Mountain Ranch Road; (209) 736-2708. Tours hourly from 10 a.m. to 5 p.m. daily from June through October; weekends only in November; closed from about December through May due to winter rain seepage. Adults $5.75 for adults, kids 6 to 12, $2.75. Special four-hour spelunking tours $59, by reservation.* The regular "Trail of Lights" tour takes visitors past the cave's extensive formations. The Jungle Room, discovered only recently and therefore protected from vandalism, offers an excellent collection of limestone formations. Spelunking tours take adventurers into the caves' darkest recesses.

ANNUAL EVENT

Black Bart Days community celebration in Old Town San Andreas, early September; (800) 695-3737.

WHERE TO DINE

Nonno's Cucina Italiana ● △△ $$
In Hotel Leger, 8304 Main St., Mokelumne Hill; (209) 286-1401. Italian; dinners $9 to $15; full bar service. Thursday-Saturday 5 to 9; Sunday 3 to 8. MC/VISA. Nicely renovated oldstyle restaurant with print wallpaper, brass chandeliers and such. The usual fettuccini, tortellini, linguine and Parmigiana, plus specials such as rosemary garlic chicken.

Wendells Restaurant ● △△ $$
9036 W. Center St. (at Highway 49), Mokelumne Hill; (209) 286-1338. California cuisine; dinners $11 to $17; full bar service. Breakfast and lunch weekends 9 to 4, dinner Sunday, Wednesday and Thursday 5 to 9 and Friday-Saturday 5 to 10, closed Monday-Tuesday. MC/VISA. Attractive country style restaurant with lots of polished wood, wainscoting and ceiling fans.

WHERE TO SLEEP

Black Bart Inn ● ⌂⌂ $$
35 Main St., San Andreas, CA 95249; (209) 754-3808. Doubles from $40. Major credit cards. Modern rooms with TV; swimming pool. **Restaurant and coffee shop**, serving American fare from 6 a.m. to 10 p.m.; dinners $10 to $24; full bar service.

The Robin's Nest ● ⌂⌂⌂ $$$ ∅
P.O. Box 1408 (247 W. St. Charles St., downtown), San Andreas, CA 95249; (209) 754-1076. From $65 per couple. Three rooms, one private and

two share baths; full breakfast. Major credit cards. An 1895 blue-gray Queen Anne home on San Andreas' main street, enlarged and renovated into an attractive B&B. Each bedroom has a turn-of-the-century travel theme.

Hotel Leger ● ⌂⌂ $$$ Ø

P.O. Box 50, Mokelumne Hill, CA 95245; (209) 286-1401. Doubles $55 to $79. Some private, some shared baths; expanded continental breakfast. MC/VISA. Rustic rooms furnished with antiques. While not posh, they're neat, clean and comfortable. Some have fireplaces. Outdoor pool; massage therapy by appointment. **Nonno's Restaurant** listed above.

WHERE TO CAMP

Gold Strike Mobile Village ● 1925 Gold Strike Rd., San Andreas, CA 95249; (209) 754-3180. A mobile home park with 25 overnight spots for RVs. Full hookups $15, no hookups $10. Flush potties, showers, pool, laundromat.

Angels Camp/Murphys

Angels 2,400; Murphys 1,200   **Angels elevation: 1,379 feet**

Despite all that publicity generated by Mark Twain's *The Celebrated Jumping Frog of Calaveras County*, Angels Camp is a rather quiet little place. With a small old town section and a single museum, it does not draw large numbers of visitors. Coming from the north, you first encounter the **Altaville** section (literally, "Upper Town"). After passing through a mile of Altaville's too-modernized strip commercialism, you encounter Angel's small historic district.

Angels Hotel, where Twain first heard the yarn about the jumping frog filled with buckshot, still exists. However, it's been converted to a couple of small businesses. Naturally, there are frogs all over town, from a statue atop a monument across from the hotel to green silhouettes painted in the street. Several shops sell froggy curios.

Murphys, nine miles up State Highway 4 from Angels, is considerably more inviting, with an old fashioned downtown area canopied by giant locust and elm trees. With more than a dozen buildings in weathered brick and stone, it looks as though it never left the 19th century.

Both mining camps were established early in the rush to riches. Angels Camp was not heavenly; the name comes from Henry P. Angel, who set up a trading post there in 1848. "Murphys" is a plural without the apostrophe because it was established by the Murphy brothers in the same year.

Most of this area's attractions have little to do with the Gold Rush. Two limestone caverns are near Murphys—**Mercer Caverns,** just up from downtown and **Moaning Cavern,** to the south on Parrotts Ferry Road. This also is an important wine producing region. You'll find several tasting rooms in and about Murphys, and vineyards spreading over the hills. Two are downtown—**Millaire Vineyard Selections** at 276 Main Street and **Black Sheep Vintners** at Main and Murphys Grade Road. **Stevenot Winery**, a mile or so out of town at 2690 San Domingo Road, is the oldest and most interesting, set in a pretty valley with a tasting room in a sod roofed "Alaska House."

Continuing up Highway 4 from Murphys, you'll encounter **Calaveras Big Trees State Park,** offering hiking, camping and such among groves of sequoias. Beyond is the popular winter-summer mountain recreation resort of **Bear Valley**.

252 — CHAPTER SEVEN

ATTRACTIONS

Angels Camp Museum ● *753 S. Main St., Angels Camp; (209) 736-2963. Daily 10 to 3 from April until the day before Thanksgiving; Wednesday-Sunday the rest of the year. Adults $1, kids 25 cents.* Recently reorganized and expanded, this city-run museum offers the typical pioneer collection of old rifles, period china, cattle brands and probably even a butter churn if you look carefully enough.

Old Timers Museum ● *472 Main St. (Sheep Ranch Road), Murphys; (209) 728-2607. Thursday-Sunday 11 to 4 (weekends only in winter). Admission free; donations appreciated.* Built in 1856, this sturdy rough-cut stone structure is the oldest fully intact building in Murphys. The museum is a busy clutter of typical pioneer and Gold Rush regalia.

Mercer Caverns ● *One mile north of Murphys, off Sheep Ranch Road; (209) 728-2101. Daily 9 to 4:30 Memorial Day through September; weekends and school holidays 11 to 3:30 the rest of the year. Forty-five minute tour, $5 for adults and $2.50 for children.* Visitors descend the equivalent of a 16-story building through several chambers. One sees a goodly assortment of stalactites, stalagmites, helicites and flowstone, plus striking formations such as snow crystal-like Aragonite and delicate translucent "Angels Wings."

Moaning Cavern ● *Off Parrotts Ferry Road, Vallecito; (209) 736-2708. Daily 9 to 6 in summer and 10 to 5 in winter. Forty-five minute tour, $5.75 for adults; $2.75 for children. Special rappelling entry $24.50 by reservation; age 12 and over.* This is said to be the largest natural cavern in California, with a main room capable of holding the Statue of Liberty. Entry is gained through a series of wooden stairways, and an iron spiral staircase. For a more exciting entry, try rappelling down through a hole in the ceiling.

☺ **Calaveras Big Trees State Park** ● *Highway 4, above Arnold; (209) 795-2334.* This is a 6,000-acre preserve of beautiful foothills and mountain slopes, including two fine stands of sequoias. It's not uncrowded, since 250,000 people a year visit the popular North Grove, just inside the park entrance. Far fewer hike a mile along a brushy forest path to enjoy the imposing giants of the South Grove.

ACTIVITIES

Gold panning ● Jensen's Pick & Shovel Ranch, 4977 Parrotts Ferry Rd., Vallecito; mailing address: P.O. Box 1141, Angels Camp, CA 95222; (209) 736-0287. One hour to all day prospecting trips. Folks with campers can spend the night free at the ranch.

Whitewater rafting ● Oars, P.O. Box 67, Angels Camp, CA 95222; (800) 446-RAFT or (209) 736-4677. Whitewater trips on several rivers in the Gold Country and throughout the West.

Wine tasting ● For a locator map and list of wineries with tasting rooms, contact the Calaveras Wine Association, P.O. Box 1851, Murphys, CA 95247; (800) 999-9039.

ANNUAL EVENTS

Jumping Frog Jubilee, third weekend in May at the Calaveras County Fairgrounds, Angels Camp; (209) 736-2571.

Music from Bear Valley, in July; (209) 753-2574.

Murphys Gold Rush, community street fair the first weekend of October; (209) 728-3724.

WHERE TO DINE

Murphys Hotel Restaurant ● ∆∆∆ $$$
Main Street, Murphys; (209) 728-3444. American-continental; full bar service. Sunday-Thursday 7 a.m. to 8 p.m., Friday-Saturday 7 to 9. MC/VISA, AMEX. Victorian dining room in an historic hotel. American steaks and chops, plus continental fare such as lobster fettuccini, *coquilles St. Jacques*, veal Marsala and calamari. Slightly scruffy dining room but good food.

The Peppermint Stick ● ∆∆ $ Ø
454 Main St., Murphys; (209) 728-3570. Light lunches, desserts; no alcohol. Monday-Saturday 11 to 5, Sunday noon to 5. No credit cards. Cute ice cream parlor and lunch cafè. Oldstyle soda fountain chairs and tables, red and gold wallpaper and jars of candy along the walls complete the early American ice cream parlor look. The "miner's soup," served in a hollowed round loaf of sourdough bread, is intriguing and tasty.

☺ The Utica Mansion Restaurant ● ∆∆∆∆ $$$ Ø
1090 Utica Lane (opposite Utica Park), Angels Camp, CA 95222; (209) 736-4209. American-continental; wine and beer. Thursday-Monday 5:30 to 9:30, closed Tuesday-Wednesday. MC/VISA. Striking Victorian dining room in an immaculately restored 1882 mansion. Menu wanders from steaks, teriyaki chicken and stuffed Monterey chicken to calamari marinara, a couple of fettuccines and nightly specials.

WHERE TO SLEEP

Gold Country Inn Motel ● △ $$$ Ø
P.O. Box 188 (720 S. Main St.), Angels Camp, CA 95222; (209) 736-4611. Doubles from $39. MC/VISA, AMEX. A 41-unit motel in the Altaville end of Angels Camp. TV, room phones, some waterbeds, handicapped units.

Jumping Frog Motel ● △ $$
330 Murphys Grade Rd., Angels Camp, CA 95221; (209) 736-2191. Doubles from $39. MC/VISA. Small motel half a block off Highway 49 in the northern end of Angels Camp, with TV movies in rooms; barbecue area.

Bed & breakfast inns and an historic hotel

Dunbar House Bed & Breakfast Inn ● △△△ $$$$ Ø
271 Jones St. (P.O. Box 1375), Murphys, CA 95247; (209) 728-2897. Doubles $95 to $105. Four units with private baths; full breakfast. No credit cards. This grand 1880 Italianate home brims with European and early American antiques. Guests are served a buffet on arrival, and will find a free bottle of local wine in their room.

Murphys Hotel & Lodge ● △△ $$$ Ø
457 Main St. (P.O. Box 329), Murphys, CA 95247; (209) 728-3444. Nine historic rooms in hotel with share baths, $55 per couple including continental breakfast; 20 motel-type units with private baths and TV, $53 per couple. Major credit cards. Hotel rooms are nicely restored and furnished with antiques. Conventional motel units are next door.

Utica Mansion Inn ● △△△ $$$$ Ø
1090 Utica Lane (P.O. Box 1), Angels Camp, CA 95222; (209) 736-4209. Doubles $90. Three units with private baths; full breakfast. MC/VISA. This 5,000-square-foot mansion above Utica Park houses one of the Gold Coun-

try's most elaborately coiffed inns. Restored to exacting detail, it's a splendid study in print wallpaper, linquesta, polished woodwork, English-tile fireplaces and tulip chandeliers.

WHERE TO CAMP

Calaveras Big Trees State Park ● *P.O. Box 120 (four miles above Arnold on Highway 4), Arnold, CA 95223; (209) 795-2334. RV and tent sites in two campgrounds, $12 to $14 per night. Reservations via Mistix; (800) 444-PARK; MC/VISA.* Flush potties, showers, picnic tables and barbecues. Nice campsites under towering evergreens.

New Melones Reservoir ● *P.O. Box 1389, Angels Camp, CA 95222; (209) 984-5248. RV and tent sites, $10.* Camping at Glory Hole Recreation area just south of Angels Camp and at Tuttletown Recreation Area south of Highway 49 near Tuttletown. Flush potties and showers, no hookups. Picnic tables, barbecues, swimming, boating fishing.

Frogtown (Calaveras County Fairgrounds) ● *P.O. Box 96 (just south of town, half a mile off Highway 49), Angels Camp, CA 95222; (209) 736-2561. RV sites and separate tent area, $10. No credit cards.* Newly renovated campground with electric and water hookups, showers and potties.

Columbia

Population: 400   **Elevation: 2,143 feet**

If you have time to visit only one town in the Gold Country, it should be Columbia. Once one of the liveliest gold camps in California, it is now a state historic park. An eight block section of brick, steel-shuttered buildings has been preserved, offering visitors a goodly assortment of shops, restaurants and a pair of historic hotels.

During summers and most any weekend, one can board a stagecoach destined to be robbed by a lady Black Bart, listen to street musicians, pose for tintype photos in period costume, watch a working blacksmith, pan for gold and swagger into a saloon and order a mug of suds or sarsaparilla.

The most-visited attraction in the Gold Country, Columbia draws upwards of 400,000 a year. Millions of others have seen it on screen. Scenes from *High Noon* were filmed here, along with episodes of TV's *Paradise* and *the Young Riders* and many other horse operas.

With all this tourism, it's still a real town with its own Zip Code, a functioning bank and a corner grocery where we residents stop by for an occasional loaf of bread and quart of non-fat. And we grin when visitors think our century-old post office is a mock-up. ("Isn't that cute, Arnie. They've even put fake letters in those little post boxes!")

Gold was discovered here in March of 1850, and "Columbia, the gem of the southern mines" soon became the largest town in the entire Gold Country, with a population beyond 10,000. By the mid-1850s, it was the fourth largest city in California, behind San Francisco, Sacramento and Stockton.

ATTRACTIONS

☺ **The William Cavalier Museum** ● *Main and State streets; daily 10 to 4:30.* The museum, housed in a former general store, is a good starting point, providing a quick study of the Gold Rush and Columbia. Exhibits include curiosities such as a miner's washboard, just four by eight inches because only socks and neckerchiefs were washed regularly; and a "teamster's

Tens of millions of dollars in gold passed through this brick-front 1858 Wells Fargo office in Columbia State Historic Park.
— Arnie Martin

knife," a forerunner of the Swiss army knife with a cutting blade, saw, cork-screw, wood drill, leather punch and horse's hoof cleaner.

☺ **Columbia School** ● *School House Street, just above town.* The original wooden desks and other furnishings are still in place in this two-story brick schoolhouse. Built in 1860 for under $5,000, it was used until 1937.

Museum of the Gold Rush Press ● *In the Columbia Gazette book shop near the Fallon Hotel.* This basement museum features old printing presses and a "gallery of Gold Rush journalists," with brief biographies of folks like Mark Twain and the de Young brothers, who founded San Francisco's *Dramatic Chronicle* in 1865.

Nelson's Columbia Candy Kitchen ● *Main Street between Fulton and State.* This neat looking place with oiled floors brims with tasty diet break-ers. Third and fourth generations of the Nelson family operate it, using cen-tury-old recipes and equipment. Visitors can watch the candy makers at work through a window on Main Street.

St. Anne's Catholic Church ● *Crowning Kennebec Hill on Church Lane.* This sturdy brick structure with its impressive bell tower and flying but-tresses is thought to be the oldest brick church in California, dating from

1856. No longer active, it's open to visitors during summer weekends, generally from about 11 to 4.

Old time saloons ● Three Columbia saloons survive from the original 40. The **St. Charles** and **Jack Douglass** offer wine and beer for grown-ups and sarsaparilla for the kids. The **What Cheer** is a comely wood paneled establishment off the City Hotel Restaurant, offering full bar service.

ACTIVITIES

Gold mine tour ● Hidden Treasure Mine, P.O. Box 28, Columbia, CA 95310; (209) 532-9693. Tours daily in summer and weekends the rest of the year; adults $6, kids and seniors $5. Visitors are guided through a working mine in a nearby river canyon.

Live theater ● Columbia Actors Repertory, P.O. Box 1849, Columbia, CA 95310; (209) 532-4644. The group presents dramas, musicals and comedies the year around at the historic Fallon House Theater.

Stage coach rides ● (209) 785-2244. Adults $4, kids and seniors $3.50, "shotgun seat" beside the driver $1 extra. Daily in summer, weekends in the off-season. Also, horseback rides from a nearby stable.

Wine tasting ● Two tasting rooms just outside the park offer gratis sips and wine sales to visitors. **Yankee Hill Winery** is at 11755 Coarsegold Lane, about a mile up Yankee Hill Road (Jackson Street) from town, and **Gold Mine Winery** is at 22265 Parrotts Ferry Rd.

ANNUAL EVENTS

Firemans' Muster in early May; (209) 532-7423.

Columbia Diggins, late May to early June; reconstructed mining camp tent town with music, foods and customs of the period; (209) 532-3401.

Fathers Day Fly-in, Fathers Day weekend, air show at Columbia Airport; (209) 532-4616.

Old Fashioned Fourth of July Celebration; (209) 532-3401.

Christmas Lamplight Tour in early December; (209) 532-3401.

Miners Christmas and **Los Posadas** first and second weekends of December; (209) 532-3401; gold miners' rendition of the Nativity.

WHERE TO DINE

☺ City Hotel Restaurant ● △△△△ $$$ Ø
Main Street between Jackson and State, Columbia; (209) 532-1479. American regional; full bar service. Lunch Thursday-Saturday 11:30 to 2, dinner Tuesday-Sunday from 5, Sunday brunch 11 to 2. MC/VISA, AMEX. With attractive Victorian dècor, the restaurant recalls the opulence which prosperity brought to Columbia 135 years ago, yet the food is contemporary. It has earned plaudits from *Gourmet Magazine* and other restaurant-watchers.

Columbia House Restaurant ● △△ $$ Ø
Main and State streets, Columbia; (209) 532-5134. Western American; wine and beer. Breakfast and lunch daily 8 to 3, dinner Thursday-Sunday 5 to 9. MC/VISA. Old fashioned restaurant housed in a former saloon that started in a tent in 1850. Pleasant rural Americana look with wainscoting, print wallpaper and quilt panel wall hangings.

El Sombrero ● △△△ $ Ø
11256 State St. (between Main and Columbia), Columbia; (209) 533-9123. Mexican; wine and beer. Sunday-Thursday 11 to 9, Friday-Saturday 11

to 10. MC/VISA. One of the Gold Country's best inexpensive Mexican restaurants, housed in a turn-of-the-century cottage. Homey atmosphere and good food. Tacos, tamales, enchiladas and such, plus Mexican steak and remarkably tasty chili Colorado and chili verde.

WHERE TO SLEEP

Columbia Gem Motel ● △ $$
P.O. Box 874 (on Parrotts Ferry Road a mile from the historic park), Columbia, CA 95310; (209) 532-4508. Doubles $35 to $65. MC/VISA. Twelve-unit inn with small cottages and motel rooms tucked among the pines; TV, in-room coffee.

Columbia Inn Motel ● △ $$
22646 Broadway (P.O. Box 298) Columbia, CA 95310; (209) 533-0446. Doubles $46 to $56, singles $32 to $34. MC/VISA. A 24-room motel with TV, room phones; pool and hot tub. **Stagecoach Inn restaurant** adjacent.

Historic hotels, bed & breakfast inn

☺ City and Fallon Hotels ● △△△ $$$ Ø
P.O. Box 1870, Columbia, CA 95310; (209) 532-1479. Doubles $55 to $85, singles $5 less; rates include continental breakfast. Early California style rooms, all with half-baths; showers down the hall. Major credit cards. Columbia's two vintage hotels are jointly operated. The City Hotel has an 1860s look, while the Fallon is a bit more opulent, styled in the 1880s Victorian period. In both, fluffy robes and wicker baskets containing bath essentials are provided to simplify the short trip to the showers.

The Harlan House ● △△△ $$$ Ø
22890 School House St. (P.O. Box 686), Columbia, CA 95310; (209) 533-4862. Doubles $75 to $80. Three rooms with private baths; full breakfast. MC/VISA. This cheerful yellow Victorian, considered one of Columbia's finest homes in the last century, occupies a hillside niche three blocks above the historic district. Nicely appointed rooms feature a mix of Victorian and American antiques.

WHERE TO CAMP

49er Trailer Ranch ● *P.O. Box 569 (on Italian Bar Road, half a mile from the historic park), Columbia, CA 95310; (209) 532-9898. RV and tent sites, $17.50. Reservations accepted; no credit cards.* Well tended park in wooded setting with full hookups, flush potties, showers, cable TV, picnic tables and barbecues, games and square dance center in "Fun Barn"; laundromat.

Marble Quarry RV Park ● *P.O. Box 850, (a third of a mile east on Jackson Street/Yankee Hill Road) Columbia, CA 95310; (209) 532-9539. RV and tent sites, $17 to $22. Reservations accepted; MC/VISA.* In attractively wooded setting with full hookups, picnic tables and showers. Swimming pool, store, lawn play area, ping pong, volleyball, horse shoes, laundry.

SONORA/JAMESTOWN

Sonora 4,200; Jamestown 2,200   Sonora elevation: 1,796 feet
Sonora is the business end of Tuolumne County—the largest town, the only incorporated one and the county seat. A prosperous and growing community, it boasts one of the Gold Country's more inviting downtown sections. Several blocks of brick, cut stone and wooden buildings house a smart

mix of boutiques, specialty shops, galleries and restaurants.

Six miles down the road, venerable Jamestown exhibits an appealing selection of old buildings—mostly wooden false front—along its three-block Main Street. Not as upscale as downtown Sonora, it's scruffily charming, offering curio and antique shops, a gold prospecting operation, old hotels and several very good restaurants. **Railtown 1897 State Historic Park** is a few blocks up from Main Street.

To sample the historic charms of both places, follow Parrotts Ferry Road out of Columbia, turn south on Highway 49 and drive four miles into Sonora. As the highway swings to the left onto Washington Street, notice the handsome **St. James Episcopal Church** on your right. You'll see why locals simply call it the "Red Church." Explore the shops along Washington Street, then turn right onto Bradford Street in the middle of town and follow it to the fine **Tuolumne County Museum** at 158 West Bradford. Then continue downhill, blend back onto Highway 49 and follow it to "Jimtown."

Tuolumne County's roads invite exploration beyond Columbia, Sonora and Jamestown. If you drive north from Sonora on State Route 108, you'll encounter the attractive woodsy community of **Twain Harte.** Beyond are the lures of the Sierra Nevada and the handsome heights of **Sonora Pass.** If you follow Highway 120 southwest from Jamestown for about 20 miles, you'll hit the turnoff to **Knights Ferry,** a charming old riverside town that's often overlooked by travelers. Check out the **covered bridge** supposedly designed by Ulysses S. Grant. The **Stanislaus River Parks** here, operated by the Army Corps of Engineers, offer picnicking, fishing, swimming and stretches suitable for white-water rafting and gentle-water canoeing.

Pressing south from Jamestown on Highway 49/120, you'll hit the small Gold Rush hamlet of **Chinese Camp,** which is now little more than a ghost town. Just below, a swing inland on Route 120 takes you to the pleasantly rustic mountainside mining camp of **Groveland.** It's well worth a steep, spiraling climb up **Priest Grade.** Beyond is the jewel of the Sierra, **Yosemite National Park,** which we explore in the next chapter.

ATTRACTIONS

☺ *Tuolumne County Museum and History Center* ● *158 W. Bradford Ave., Sonora; (209) 532-1317. Monday, Wednesday and Friday 9 to 4:30, Tuesday, Thursday and Saturday 10 to 3:30 all year; plus Sundays 10 to 3:30 during the summer. Free admission, donations accepted.* The museum's main attraction is a glittering display of gold and quartz from the county's mining days. The structure itself once served as the county jail and several cells are used for exhibits. One houses a typical bunk house and another contains a gunsmith shop.

☺ *Railtown 1897 State Historic Park* ● *Fifth Avenue, Jamestown; (209) 984-3953. Grounds and gift shop open daily; various hours. One hour "Mother Lode Cannonball" stream train rides offered several times daily in summer and weekends only the rest of the year; adults $9, kids $4.50. Other more extended excursions, mostly in summer. Roundhouse tours daily May through September and weekends the rest of the year; adults $2.50, kids $1.50.* Railtown preserves memories and much of the equipment of the Sierra Railroad, established in 1897 to haul freight from the San Joaquin Valley into the Sierra foothills. It's also one of the county's best known film stars, having appeared in everything from *High Noon* to the recent HBO production of *Ishi.*

ACTIVITIES

Gold mine tour • Jamestown Mine, c/o Sonora Mining Corp., 17400 High School Rd., Jamestown, CA 95327; (209) 984-4641. One-hour tours of an open pit gold mine Wednesday at 1:30; free, reservations required.

Gold panning tour • Gold Prospecting Expeditions, P.O. Box 974 (18170 Main St.), Jamestown, CA 95327; (209) 984-GOLD. Programs range from half hour panning sessions to full day treks to nearby streams, gold dredging outings and five day helicopter trips into the wilds.

Live theater • Sierra Repertory Theatre, 2113 Mono Way (P.O. Box 3030), Sonora, CA 95370; (209) 532-3120; critically acclaimed professional troupe offering a year-around mix of dramas, comedies and musicals.

Whitewater rafting • The Tuolumne River is a popular rafting stream with stretches that pass through spectacular Sierra scenery. Commercial trips are offered by Ahwahnee Whitewater Expeditions, (800) 359-9790 or (209) 533-4101; American River Touring Assn., (209) 962-7873; OARS, (209) 736-4677; Sierra Mac River Trips, (209) 532-1327; and Zephyr River Expeditions, (209) 532-6249.

ANNUAL EVENTS

Mother Lode Roundup, second weekend of May at Mother Lode Fairgrounds in Sonora; (209) 532-8394.

High Sierra Music Festival over Fourth of July weekend at Leland Meadows, 39 miles east of Sonora on Highway 108; (800) 273-8813 or (209) 533-2851.

Gunfighters' Rendezvous, early July, Jamestown; (209) 984-3851.

Mother Lode Fair, in mid-July at the Mother Lode Fairgrounds; (209) 532-7428.

Wild West Days, last weekend of September in downtown Jamestown; (209) 984-3851.

Tuolumne County Wild West Filmfest and Rodeo, last weekend of September at Dreamwest and Memory Bank theaters downtown; (800) 446-1333 or (209) 533-4420

WHERE TO DINE

☺ **Hemingway's Café Restaurant** • ΔΔΔ **$$$** Ø
362 Stewart St., Sonora; (209) 532-4900. Contemporary cuisine; wine and beer. Open Tuesday-Saturday, lunch 11:30 to 2:30, dinner from 5. MC/VISA, AMEX. Eclectic menu wanders from Norwegian gravlox and "California stir fry" to fajitas and full-course dinners. The restaurant is housed in a charming ranch style structure, set in a garden-like atmosphere.

Jamestown Hotel Restaurant and Saloon • ΔΔΔ **$$**
Main Street, Jamestown; (209) 984-3902. American-continental; full bar service. Lunch 11:30 to 2:30, dinner 5 to 10, Sunday champagne brunch 11 to 3. MC/VISA, AMEX. Inviting yesterday atmosphere in a nicely appointed 19th century dining room with cozy booths, etched mirrors and glass flower-petal lamps; also patio dining. The menu offers a conventional selection of steak, London broil, barbecued spare ribs and country fried chicken.

National Hotel Restaurant • ΔΔΔ **$$** Ø
Main Street, Jamestown; (209) 984-3446. American-continental; full bar service. Lunch 11 to 4:30, dinner 5 to 10. MC/VISA. Excellent fare with a

small but versatile menu ranging from chicken Chelsea to lamb chops to New York steak. Served in a pleasant 19th century setting of polished woods, wainscoting, tulip glass and wafting ceiling fans.

☺ **Ristorante LaTorre** • △△△ $$$ Ø

39 N. Washington St., Sonora; (209) 533-9181. Italian-continental; full bar service. Lunch weekdays 11:30 to 3, dinner Monday-Saturday 4:30 to closing and Sunday 3 to 9. MC/VISA, AMEX. Striking second-floor restaurant in an 1889 brick and masonry building. Opulent Victorian décor with cozy high-back booths, lots of polished wood, brass and glass, old time photos and vertical striped wallpaper. Small, versatile menu.

The Smoke Café • △△△ $$ Ø

Main Street, Jamestown; (209) 984-3733. Mexican; full bar service. Tuesday-Saturday 5 to 10, Sunday 4 to 9; closed Monday. No credit cards, checks accepted. Stylish place in an old building with a Southwest look of beige, salmon and turquoise; dining rooms open to the street in summer. Some of the specials are excellent, such as carne asada—seared beef strips topped with fried onions and mild chilies.

WHERE TO SLEEP

The Gunn House • ⌂⌂ $$

286 S. Washington St., Sonora, CA 95370; (209) 532-3421. Doubles $40 to $70. MC/VISA, AMEX. Sonora's most historic lodging, occupying a picturesque two-story Spanish adobe dating from 1850. Comfortable rooms with rather eclectic furnishings.

Railtown Motel • ⌂ $$$

P.O. Box 1129 (Willow at Main Street), Jamestown, CA 95327; (209) 984-3332. Doubles $55 to $80, singles $50. Major credit cards. Small, nicely-maintained motel near historic area; TV, swimming pool and spa. Spa tubs in several rooms.

Sonora Country Inn • ⌂⌂⌂ $$$ Ø

18755 Charbroullian Lane, Jamestown, CA 95327; (209) 984-0315. Doubles $64, singles $54, suites $105. Major credit cards. TV, swimming pool, whirlpool. The motel sits a bit off Highway 49, in a quiet area.

Sonora Inn • ⌂⌂ $$ Ø

106 S. Washington St., Sonora, CA 95370; (800) 321-5261 or (209) 532-7468. Doubles $45 to $55, singles $32 to $50. Major credit cards. Refurbished rooms—not elegant but clean and comfortable—in a landmark Spanish style inn, dating back to 1896. TV, swimming pool, bar and **Restaurant**.

Sonora Towne House Motel • ⌂⌂⌂ $$$

350 S. Washington St., Sonora, CA 95370; (800) 251-1538 or (209) 532-3633. Doubles $50 to $65, singles $45 to $60; Major credit cards. A 112-unit motel in downtown Sonora. TV, room phones, wet bars; pool and spa.

Bed & breakfast inns and historic hotels

Barretta Gardens Inn • ⌂⌂⌂ $$$$ Ø

700 S. Barretta St., Sonora, CA 95370; (209) 532-6039. Doubles $80 to $95. Five units, all with private baths; full breakfast. MC/VISA, AMEX. This nicely appointed Victorian built in 1904 overlooks Sonora from its hilltop above terraced gardens. Rooms are furnished with antiques and those frilly extras that create an authentic Victorian atmosphere.

Jamestown Hotel ● △△ $$$
P.O. Box 539 (18153 Main St.), Jamestown, CA 95327; (209) 984-3902. Doubles $55 to $86. Eight rooms, all with private baths; continental breakfast. MC/VISA, AMEX. Handsomely furnished rooms in a sturdy brick, false front hotel building that stepped right out of the Gold Rush. **Restaurant** (listed above) and elegant old Western bar.

National Hotel ● △△ $$$
P.O. Box 502 (Main Street), Jamestown, CA 95327; (209) 984-3446. Doubles $65 to $75. Eleven units, five private baths, six share; continental breakfast. MC/VISA. One of the oldest continually functioning hotels in the Gold Country, dating from 1859. Authentically restored with some of the original furnishings. The small, neat rooms aren't opulent but they're clean and comfortable. **Dining room** listed above.

The Ryan House Bed & Breakfast △△△ $$$$ Ø
153 S. Shepherd St. (Theall), Sonora, CA 95370; (209) 533-3445. Doubles $75 to $80, singles $70. Three rooms, all with private baths; TV available on request; full breakfast. Major credit cards. An 1855 home in downtown Sonora with a nice mix of early American and Victorian furnishings. Surrounded by rose gardens, the home is within walking distance of Sonora's historic Washington Street shops and restaurants.

WHERE TO CAMP

Mother Lode Fairgrounds ● *220 Southgate Drive (off Highway 49 just south of town), Sonora, CA 95370; (209) 532-7428. RV sites only, $11. Reservations accepted; no credit cards.* Water and electrical hookups, flush potties, a few picnic tables.

COULTERVILLE/MARIPOSA

Coulterville 400; Mariposa 1,200   **Elevation: 1,200 feet**

Continuing south on Highway 49, you enter a precinct once called the "Mother of the Counties." When California became a state in 1850, a massive 30,000-square-mile chunk was designated as Mariposa County, with Mariposa as its seat. As other communities grew, pieces were carved off until only 1,500 square miles were left—rather medium sized as counties go.

Off the main stream of Gold Country and Sierra Nevada travel, this is one of the least visited and least populated areas in the Sierra foothills. The county's population is about 15,000.

Although it's bypassed by most Sierra foothills visitors, the county does have its appeal. Coulterville is a real charmer of a frontier town, and Mariposa—although it lost most of its yesterday charm to modernization—has a pair of excellent museums. Between them is one of the most dramatic highway passages in California, a wicked spiral down into **Merced River Canyon** aptly called **Hell's Hollow.**

RV Advisory: An RV or trailer can make it down and even back up Hell's Hollow, but take it slow on those many hairpin turns, and drop into a lower gear to keep your brakes from overheating.

ATTRACTIONS

☺ **Northern Mariposa County History Center** ● *Corner of highways 49 and 132, Coulterville; (209) 878-3015. Tuesday-Sunday 10 to 4 April through September 1; weekends and school holidays the rest of the year. Admission* *free; donations accepted.* This small, attractive museum occupies portions of two buildings that date back to the 1850s. Exhibits include a scale model stamp mill that clanks merrily at the push of a button, an 1890 Victorian living room and a model drug store where shelves brim with elixirs.

☺ *Mariposa County History Center* • *12th and Jessie streets, Mariposa; (209) 966-2924. Daily 10 to 4:30 April through October; weekends only 10 to 4:30 November, December, February and March; closed in January. Free admission, donations accepted.* The museum, which shares a low ranch style building with the town library, is another fine interpretive center. No disorganized collection of artifacts, this place offers a carefully assembled record of early Mariposa, from Native Americans to Spanish and Mexican explorers, through the Gold Rush to the turn of the century.

Mariposa County Courthouse • *Bullion Street between Ninth and Tenth, Mariposa; (209) 966-3222. Daily 8 to 5; free. Tours on weekends.* Built in 1854, this is the oldest continually used seat of government west of the Rockies. It's also one of the finest examples of Greek revival architecture in the Mother Lode. Visitors can stroll the hallways on weekdays and peek into the upstairs courtroom if it isn't in use.

☺ *California State Mining and Mineral Museum* • *At the Mariposa County Fairgrounds, a mile and a half south of Mariposa; (209) 742-7625. Daily except Tuesday 10 to 6 from May through September; Wednesday-Sunday 10 to 4 the rest of the year. Adults $3.50, seniors 60 and up and teens $2.50, kids free.* This nicely designed museum provides an excellent look at the state's mining history. Visitors receive a quick lesson in geology and mining as they view glittering exhibits of gold and other minerals, walk through a realistic mine tunnel mock-up, operate a mini-stamp mill and view scores of other displays.

ANNUAL EVENTS

Coulterville Coyote Howl in mid-May; (209) 878-3074.

Butterfly Days, June, County Fairgrounds, Mariposa; (209) 966-3686.

Mariposa County Fair, Labor Day, fairgrounds; (209) 966-3686.

Western Gunfighters Rendezvous in late September in Coulterville; (209) 878-3074.

WHERE TO DINE

The Banderita Restaurant ΔΔ **$$**

In the Jeffery Hotel; (209) 878-0228. American; full bar service. Monday-Thursday 7 a.m. to 9 p.m., Friday-Sunday 7 to 10. MC/VISA. Attractively refurbished restaurant off the hotel lobby done up in print wallpaper, historic photos and other early day lore. Basic American menu.

Charles Street Dinner House • ΔΔΔ **$$**

Charles Street (Highway 49) at Seventh, Mariposa; (209) 966-2366. American; wine and beer. Wednesday-Sunday 5 p.m. to 9 p.m. MC/VISA. An attractive Western theme restaurant serving creatively prepared and seasoned American fare. The interior is a pleasant clutter of old photos, Tiffany type lamps and wagon wheel décor. Waitresses in long gingham dresses scurry about, serving up good food and friendly smiles.

Yosemite Sam's • Δ **$**

5012 Main St., Coulterville; (209) 878-9911. Basic American; beer and wine. Daily 9 a.m. to 9 p.m. No credit cards. Funky old storefront saloon and restaurant that starts serving breakfast at 7, then turns into a pizza and burger parlor. Food service ends at 9; pool shooting and good ole boy drinkin' and hollerin' continue well beyond.

WHERE TO SLEEP

Best Western Yosemite Way Station ● ⌂⌂ $$$ Ø
P.O. Box 1989 (4999 Highway 140), Mariposa, CA 95338; (209) 966-7545. Doubles $66 to $76, singles $56 to $66. Major credit cards. Attractive, modern 78-room motel with TV, room phones; pool, spa. **Restaurant**.

Miners Inn ● ⌂⌂ $$$ Ø
P.O. Box 246 (Highways 49 and 140), Mariposa, CA 95338; (800) 237-7277 in California only or (209) 742-7777. Doubles $50 to $64, singles $40 to $44. Major credit cards. A 40-unit motel with TV, room phones, free coffee. **Restaurant** serves American fare; dinners $10 to $18; 6 a.m. to 10:30 p.m., full bar service.

Yosemite Americana Inn ● ⌂ $$
10407 Highway 49 (P.O. Box 265), Coulterville, CA 95311; (209) 878-3407. Doubles from $37. MC/VISA. Nine-room motel with TV, free in-room coffee and tea; just north of town.

Bed & breakfast inns and historic hotels

Jeffery Hotel ● ⌂⌂ $$$
One Main St. (P.O. Box 440-B), Coulterville, CA 95311; (800) 464-3471 or (209) 878-3471. Doubles $54 to $68 with private bath, $43 to $58 with shared bath; rates include continental breakfast. MC/VISA. While not luxurious, the newly restored Jeffery offers comfortable rooms with oldstyle brass beds and other yesterday furnishings.

Mariposa Hotel Inn ● ⌂⌂⌂ $$$ Ø
5029 Charles St. (P.O. Box 745), Mariposa, CA 95338; (209) 966-4676. Doubles $64 to $74. Six rooms, all with private baths. MC/VISA. Former stagecoach way station recently restored and opened as a cozy inn. The look is 19th century America with antique reproductions, oak wainscoting and trim, scalloped lace curtains and print wallpaper.

Meadow Creek Ranch Bed & Breakfast Inn ● ⌂⌂ $$$$ Ø
2669 Triangle Rd. at Highway 49 South, Mariposa, CA 95338; (209) 966-3843. Doubles $75 to $95. Three rooms with share bath and a cottage with private bath; full country breakfast. MC/VISA, AMEX may be used to secure reservations. Nicely refurbished 1857 ranch house that once served as a Wells Fargo stage stop. The rooms furnished with early American and European antiques; neatly groomed grounds and creek.

WHERE TO CAMP

Coulterville RV Park ● Highway 49, just north of Jeffery Hotel (P.O. Box 96), Coulterville, CA 95311; (209) 878-3988. RV sites $10 with full hook-ups, campsites $7. A new RV park with picnic tables, flush potties, showers, groceries and coin laundry.

Yosemite Americana Inn ● The inn (listed above) has several RV sites with full hookups, and tent sites; $10.

Bagby Recreation Area ● On Lake McClure, off Highway 49, 15 miles north of Mariposa; c/o Merced Irrigation District, 909 Lake McClure Rd., Snelling, CA 95369; (800) 468-8889. Camping $5.50, day use fee $3 per car and

$3 per boat. Tent and RV sites, no hookups or showers. Flush potties, picnic and barbecue areas, store, marina, water sports.

Mariposa County Fairgrounds ● *5007 Fairground Rd. (a mile and a half south of town on Highway 49), Mariposa, CA 95338; (209) 966-3686 or 966-2432. RV sites only, $12 per vehicle.* Hookups, flush potties, water, showers, picnic tables and barbecues, lawn area and playground. Closed Labor Day Weekend, when the county fair is in progress.

TO THE END OF THE GOLDEN CHAIN

Continuing south from Mariposa, you enter the northeastern tip of Madera County. Two towns, **Oakhurst** and **Coarsegold,** figure in the Gold Country's history, although both have been modernized beyond recognition. Oakhurst is little more than a string of service stations, shops and motels. They're patronized by San Joaquin Valley residents who come into the pines to escape the heat and monotony of the valley. Coarsegold is merely a wide spot in the road.

Highway 49 ends in Oakhurst, where it bumps into State Route 41. A **Gold Rush monument** at the entrance to the Golden Oak Village Shopping Center is set with chunks of native stone from each of the 11 Gold Country counties. You might ask directions to **Fresno Flats Historic Park** at 49777 Road 427 in Oakhurst. It's comprised of several early day buildings and a squared log jail, hauled here from other early communities.

From Oakhurst, Highway 41 provides a quick trip south through Coarsegold to Fresno and the San Joaquin Valley, or north to Yosemite National Park. If you go north, you might pause at **Yosemite Mountain Sugar Pine Railroad** (209-683-7273), which offers rides on an old log train into an attractive, thickly-wooded forest.

Chapter eight
THE HIGH SIERRA
Tahoe, the east side & Yosemite/Sequoia

IT WAS A CHINESE WALL to California's settlement in the last century. Historian Oscar Lewis called the Sierra Nevada a "bulky, awkward and inconveniently high barrier" that shut off the state from the rest of the nation. Now, it's a major drawing card—an alpine playpen of hiking trails, fishing lakes and streams, parklands and resorts.

The Sierra Nevada forms a great granite reef curving along the eastern edge of the state. The name, certainly appropriate, is Spanish for "snowy peaks." From 40 to 80 miles wide, the range stretches nearly 450 miles, from Mount Lassen to the Tehachapis east of Bakersfield. Although it achieves only moderate heights at the northern and southern ends, its mid-section crumples upward to form America's highest peaks south of Alaska. Mount Whitney, at 14,496 feet, is no alpine anomaly; ten other peaks in the neighborhood top 14,000. The terrain is so formidable that no road penetrates the Sierra from Yosemite's Tioga Pass to Sherman Pass, 155 miles south.

The range roughly separates California from Nevada, although the boundary itself was drawn with a straight-edge. A century and a half ago, the mountains tried to separate California-bound immigrants from their goal. This gigantic faulted block is tilted from west to east, like a monster chunk of broken sidewalk. The western side is marked by a wide band of foothills, while the eastern face is dramatically sheer, dropping nearly three vertical miles to the Owens Valley and Great Basin Desert. This steep escarpment presented the most difficult challenge for settlers and gold-seekers. Wagons had to be disassembled and carried in pieces up narrow river canyons and over high passes. After achieving the summit, weary travelers had to weave through miles of foothills before reaching the level Central Valley.

TRIP PLANNER

WHEN TO GO ● The Sierra Nevada is a four seasons playground, although one must compress summer and stretch winter in the high country. We like the fall, after crowds have thinned, the air is sapphire crisp and most high country trails are still open. Hardwoods add touches of autumn color, particularly in Sequoia National Park and along stream beds on the eastern slopes of the Sierra. All but a few of California's ski resorts are in the Sierra, mostly on the western slopes. Several highways cross the range, but only Interstate 80 and U.S. 50 are kept open after the first serious winter snow flies. They're frequently closed temporarily by storms.

WHAT TO SEE ● Historic downtown Folsom; Emerald Bay and Vikingshome at Lake Tahoe; Cal-Neva, Hyatt Lake Tahoe and Harrah's casinos; Bodie State Historic Park; Mono Lake; the wonders of Yosemite Valley and the high country of Tuolumne Meadows; Glacier Point Lookout in Yosemite; Grant Grove, Beetle Rock and Giant Forest in Sequoia/Kings Canyon National Parks.

WHAT TO DO ● Hike portions of the Tahoe Rim Trail; take an aerial tram ride at Heavenly Valley, Squaw Valley or Mammoth Mountain ski resorts; hike the Giant Stairway to Nevada Falls, the trail to Yosemite Falls and stroll down Four Mile Trail from Glacier Point in Yosemite; take the Congress Trail walk and climb to the top of Moro Rock in Sequoia; book an overnight trek to Bearpaw Meadow.

Useful contacts

Alpine County Chamber of Commerce, P.O. Box 265, Markleeville, CA 96120; (916) 694-2475.

Bishop Chamber of Commerce, 690 N. Main St., Bishop, CA 93514; (619) 873-8405.

Lake Tahoe lodgings and general information: (800) GO-TAHOE.

Lone Pine Chamber of Commerce, 126 S. Main St. (P.O. Box 749), Lone Pine, CA 93545; (619) 876-4444.

Mammoth Lakes Visitors Bureau, P.O. Box 48, Mammoth Lakes, CA 93546; (800) 367-6572 or (619) 934-2712.

Sequoia and Kings Canyon National Parks, Three Rivers, CA 93271; (209) 565-3311. **Lodging reservations:** Sequoia Guest Services, P.O. Box 789, Three Rivers, CA 93271; (209) 565-3381. **Camping reservations:** Mistix, (800) 365-CAMP, or write: P.O. Box 85705, San Diego, CA 92138-5705.

South Lake Tahoe Chamber of Commerce, 3066 Lake Tahoe Blvd., South Lake Tahoe, CA 95702; (209) 541-5355.

Tahoe North Visitors and Convention Bureau, P.O. Box 5578, Tahoe City, CA 96145; (800) 824-6348.

Yosemite National Park, P.O. Box 577, Yosemite National Park, CA 95389; (209) 372-0200. **Lodging reservations:** (209) 252-4848. This may change; see "Lodgings" under the Yosemite listing below. **Camping** reservations via Mistix, P.O. Box 85705, San Diego, CA 92138-5705; (800) 444-CAMP.

High Sierra radio stations

KRLT-FM, 93.9, Lake Tahoe area—light rock
KZFF-FM, 102.9, Lake Tahoe area—top 40
KIVS-FM, 97.7, Bishop—country
KIBS-FM, 100.5 and 100.7, Bishop—country
KMNT-FM, 102.3, Bishop—top 40, mostly rock
KOWL-AM, 1490, Lake Tahoe area—music & news
KTHO-AM, 590, Lake Tahoe area—music & news
KBOV-AM, 1230/1240, Bishop—easy listening

It was the steep eastern slope that trapped the Donner party in 1846. Three years later, argonaut Enos Christman wrote to his Philadelphia fiancè:

I now boldly turn my face toward the celebrated Sierra Nevada. What we may encounter I cannot anticipate; perhaps we shall have to engage with the native Indian in bloody conflict, or be hugged to death by the fierce and savage grizzly bear.

There is no record as to whether young Enos got rich, mugged by Indians or hugged by bears. John Muir, who began tramping the Sierra half a century later and brought the mountains to the world's attention, saw things differently:

Along the eastern margin rises the mighty Sierra, miles in height, reposing like a smooth cumulus cloud in the sunny sky, and so gloriously colored and so luminous, it seems not to be clothed with light, but composed of it, like the wall of some celestial city.

Even after rough trails where hacked over the Sierra, most California-bound traffic avoided it, preferring to travel either by sea or overland through the desert Southwest. It wasn't until a railroad was chopped and blasted through Donner Pass in late 1860s that Sierra transit became practical for the average commuter. In the 1920s, the first coast-to-coast highways were completed over the mountains. The Victory Highway was carved through Donner Pass beside the railway and the Lincoln Highway roughly followed the pony path. They are today Interstate 80 and U.S. Highway 50. Between them, they cradle Lake Tahoe, the Sierra's most popular and most commercialized playground. Each year, six million Tahoe visitors easily breach mountain passes that were titanic struggles for the pioneers. (During Sierra snowstorms, some travelers get a taste of their ancestors' ordeal.)

South of Tahoe are three of the nation's largest mountain national parks, Yosemite, Sequoia and Kings Canyon. Yosemite rivals Tahoe in its annual visitor count. The High Sierra is thus one of California's favorite tourist destinations, overdeveloped in many areas and often loved to pieces.

The birth of the Sierra

Foundations for this noble mountain range were laid down eons ago, although the present shape of the Sierra is relatively new by geological measure. Its footing was formed 500 million years ago as sedimentary accumulations on the bed of an ancient sea. The seabed wrinkled and began to rise as a "pre-Sierra Nevada" about 160 million years ago, during the Jurassic Period. Lava surged up from beneath and cooled as granite. Then, 65 million years ago, continental plates collided along California's shoreline, forming the Coast Range and tilting the Sierra back on its heels.

By this time, erosion had lowered the Jurassic peaks to around 3,000 feet, wearing away most of the sedimentary rock and exposing the granite beneath. Then, within the last two million years, today's peaks were buckled and thrust skyward in cataclysmic slow motion. Glaciers of the last Ice Age added a final sculptor's touch to this grand proscenium of broken granite. Yosemite Valley, the Sierra showpiece, was carved within the last few hundred thousand years. The Sierra Nevada is California's grandest biosphere, with the state's largest variety of landforms and climate zones. Within an hour, travelers can pass from the arid Central Valley through oak chaparral woodlands of the foothills, into a conifer belt and up to a sub-alpine tundra where naked granite juts skyward.

These peaks are the state's wellspring, leaching moisture from the east-bound jet stream and storing it as snowpack. Eleven river systems originate in the Sierra, and the region encompasses about 1,500 lakes. Most of Northern California's irrigation and drinking water issues from this watershed. When folks talk of drought—such as the record dry spell that ended in 1993—they refer not to wilting daisies in the valleys, but to reservoir water levels in the foothills.

The mountain range casts a rainshadow across Nevada, stealing most of the storm-driven moisture to leave the Great Basin high and relatively dry. Rivers flowing down the eastern slopes shrivel in summer, finally dying in alkaline lakes like Pyramid and Mono, or simply sinking into hot desert sands. Water diversion for Nevada's growing thirst is threatening these lakes with a premature death. On both sides of the Sierra, the demands of man versus the needs of nature have perpetrated an environmental and esthetic crisis. Lake Tahoe's once pristine shoreline is now an unplanned sprawl of strip commercialism. The lake itself was threatened with pollution until steps were taken to curb growth in recent decades. Yosemite Valley, overdeveloped by concessionaires, is jammed with summer visitors. A retrograde movement is underway to reduce facilities and restrict vehicle access.

The Sierra Nevada's resources are caught in an ongoing tug-of-war between developers and conservationists. The spotted owl issue has cost jobs in the lumber industry, and the threat of Delta saltwater intrusion has forced rationing of Sierra water to Central Valley farmers.

LAKE TAHOE

In taking you to the West's largest freshwater lake, we will not exclude lures on the Nevada side. The states' boundaries run right through it. The millions of annual visitors run all around it, indifferent to borders. It's a safe bet that more of them are drawn to Nevada's casinos than to the pines.

The irony here is that Nevada, noted for its garish flamboyance, appears to be kinder and gentler to its share of the lake than California. It is perhaps a pity that the Silver State controls only 29 miles of its 71-mile shoreline.

Much of the eastern shore is occupied by Lake Tahoe Nevada State Park, national forest lands and the planned community of Incline Village. This has deterred the unbridled development which has spoiled most of the California shoreline. "Cal-Tahoe" consists primarily of a disjoined string of motels, service stations and other small businesses, shimmering in their own sea of asphalt. As the beautiful Tahoe Basin gained popularity during the 1950s and 1960s, folks rushed in by the thousands to get their own piece of paradise while there was still some left.

In belated attempts at damage control, the two-state Tahoe Regional Planning Authority was formed in 1969 to control future growth and design. Fortunately, 85 percent of the greater Tahoe Basin is public land, so visitors can still retreat to their own personal patch of pristine—if second growth—ponderosas. However, 85 percent of the lakeshore is privately owned.

Nevada was not always so kind to its share of the lake. When silver was discovered in the 1860s, nearly all of the eastern side's timber was cut to shore up mine shafts and to build the towns of Virginia City, Carson City and Reno. Until that time, this amazingly clear mountain rimmed lake slept peacefully among the pines. Its few visitors came to admire, not to plunder. Wrote Mark Twain, who stopped by in 1861:

As it lay there with the shadows of the mountains brilliantly photographed upon its still surface, I thought it must surely be the fairest picture the whole earth affords.

John C. Frèmont apparently was the first outsider to see the lake, following the course of the Truckee in 1844. He gave it the unbecoming name of Lake Bonpland to salute a French explorer. It then became Lake Bigler in honor of California's third governor. But John Bigler turned out to be a rather unsavory character and a bit of a tippler. According to California historian Hubert Bancroft:

Nothing could have been in worse taste than in applying to a liquid so beautifully clear and cool the name of one who so detested water.

Finally, cartographers chose a Washo Indian term whose meaning is vague. Tahoe (from *Da-ow-a-ga*) may mean limpid water, big water, falling leaf or edge of the lake. Mark Twain insisted that Tahoe was Paiute for "grasshopper soup." The California legislature—presumably after consulting the Nevada legislature—made Lake Tahoe the official name in 1928. Northern Californians simply call it the Lake, as San Francisco is the City.

Nevada legalized gambling in 1931, but little of this activity found its way to the lake for several years. Then Sacramento meat wholesaler Harvey Gross opened a tiny bar with three slot machines in 1944. Others followed, setting the stage for the area's future as a major gaming destination.

Spectacular superlatives

The vision of Tahoe beguiles the eye and its statistics boggle the mind. Sitting at 6,229 feet and measuring 21.6 by 12 miles, it's the largest alpine lake in North America and the second largest in the world. It has 71 miles of shoreline—76 road miles. (Peru's Lake Titicaca is larger and higher, but murkier.) Further, it's the second deepest lake in the U.S., after Oregon's Crater Lake, averaging 1,000 feet. At its deepest point, 1,645 feet, the bottom is lower than the elevation of Carson City.

Tahoe's volume is so massive that it acts as its own insulator. Surface water temperature rarely rises above 60 degrees, even in August. Most attempts at swimming are rather brief, except in sun warmed bays. Six hundred feet below the surface, the water remains a constant 30 degrees. The lake's mass also prevents it from freezing in winter, except at sheltered inlets like Emerald Bay. Further, Tahoe is incredibly clear. Plants, which need sunlight to make fuel, have been found growing 400 feet below the surface. Unfortunately, runoff from the construction frenzy of the 1950s and 1960s introduced nutrients that encouraged algae growth. The water has lost an average 25 feet of its original clarity.

Getting there

Both I-80 and U.S. 50 offer relatively quick approaches to Lake Tahoe. Interstate 80 crests the dramatic Donner Summit and takes you to **Truckee,** from where you can drop down to the north shore on State Route 267. En route to Truckee, make it a point to stop the site where the Donner party spent its tragic winter:

Donner Memorial State Park ● *On Donner Lake, two miles west of Truckee; (916) 587-3841. Day use $5 per vehicle, museum open daily 10 to noon and 1 to 4; admission $2 per person. Camping available from May to October for $14; reservations via Mistix, (800) 444-PARK, or write: P.O. Box*

Lake Tahoe & Vicinity

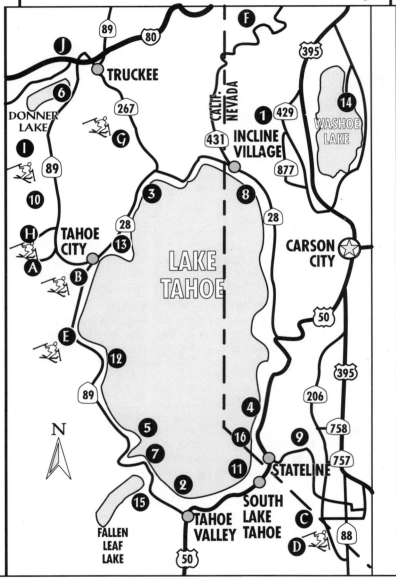

DIRECTORY (Recreation/Camping)

1. Bower's Mansion
2. Camp Richardson *(camping, boat launch)*
3. Carnelian Bay *(boat launch)*
4. Cave Rock *(boat launch)*
5. D.L.Bliss State Park *(camping)*
6. Donner Memorial State Park *(camping)*
7. Emerald Bay State Park *(camping)*
8. Lake Tahoe-Nevada State Park
9. Mormon Station State Historical Monument
10. Squaw Valley State Park *(camping)*
11. Nevada Beach *(camping)*
12. Sugar Pine Point State Park
13. Tahoe State Recreation Area *(camping)*
14. Washoe Lake Recreation Area *(camping)*
15. Visitor Center, U.S. Forest Service
16. Zephyr Cove *(boat launch)*

Ski Areas

A. Alpine Meadows
B. Granlibakkan
C. Heavenly Valley North
D. Heavenly Valley West
E. Homewood
F. Hunt Rose/Incline
G. Northstar
H. Squaw Valley
I. Sugar Bowl
J. Tahoe Donner

85705, San Diego, CA 92138-5705. Picnic areas, hiking and swimming in Donner Lake. The park's Emigrant Trail Museum recalls the harrowing winter of 1846-47 when the Donner-Reed emigrant party·was trapped by an early snowfall on the eastern side of the Sierra. Half of the party perished, and a few resorted to cannibalism to survive. Most of this occurred not at the encampment near Donner Lake, but within a group of men who had set out on foot over the pass to bring back help. They finally stumbled into the Sacramento Valley and were taken to Sutter's Fort. Sutter launched several rescue parties, who braved the Sierra winter to recover the others. The museum also covers construction of the transcontinental railroad.

☺ If you take the Highway 50 route from Sacramento, stop by **Folsom,** an 1860s gold rush town that has preserved much of its downtown area. Traffic-free Sutter Street is lined with false front and brick stores housing boutiques, antique shops and cafès. For a walking tour map, stop by the **Chamber of Commerce** in the Southern Pacific Depot at Sutter and Wool streets. Several pieces of old rolling stock are on display out front. The town's history is captured in a museum in the **Wells Fargo office,** dating from 1860. Nearby is the old **Folsom Dam Powerhouse,** displaying equipment and machinery used when it first sent juice to Sacramento in 1895. The large **Folsom State Recreation Area** is adjacent, with an information center at 7806 Auburn-Folsom Road; (916) 988-0205. It offers the usual fishing and water sports, swimming, picnic areas, miles of hiking trails and three campgrounds. Reservations are available through Mistix, (800) 444-PARK, or write: P.O. Box 85705, San Diego, CA 92138-5705.

RV and camping advisory: If you're driving a big rig or pulling a trailer, you may prefer the less winding I-80 approach, since you'll encounter some challenging twists and turns over Highway 50's Echo Summit. Campgrounds and RV parks are abundant in the Tahoe Basin. However, while casinos in most other Nevada gaming areas are quite generous about permitting overnight RV parking, you'll find the reverse at Tahoe. South shore casinos post nasty signs, threatening to have overnight RVs towed. (This conjures a vision of a couple sleeping in their Winnebago while it's being whisked away in the middle of the night.) On the north shore, the Tahoe Biltmore at Crystal Cover permits overnight RV parking.

From Folsom, route 50 takes you through **Placerville**, which we covered in detail in the previous chapter. You pass through **Pollock Pines, Kyburtz** and **Strawberry**, then spiral up to the crest of 7,382-foot **Echo Summit**. From this dizzying vantage point, you get your first dramatic view of the large blue pendant of Lake Tahoe, suspended in a green forest basin.

Highway 50 spins downhill quickly, joined at **Meyers** by State Route 89. The road then levels out a bit and skims through a ponderosa tableland. A few miles beyond **Tahoe Airport,** you enter the unsightly strip of businesses rimming the lake. Fork to the left at the Tahoe "Y" to stay with Highway 89. It travels up the western shore as Emerald Bay Road. Since this is a Northern California book, we'll do that side first.

South Lake Tahoe

Population: 21,650   **Elevation: 6,252 feet**

Several smaller south shore communities were incorporated a few years ago as South Lake Tahoe. Although the area from here west to Stateline is one long commercial sprawl, you'll see swatches of forest and scenic shoreline if you travel up the western shore. If you're here in winter, check to make sure the west side road is open, since it's sometimes closed by winter storms; call (916) 577-3550.

For heaps of outdoor information on the Tahoe Basin, stop at the **Forestry Supervisor's Office** and visitor center. It's about half a mile beyond the "Y" on the left at 870 Emerald Bay Road (in Plaza 89, opposite Emerald Palace Chinese restaurant). It's open weekdays from 8 to 4:30.

Just beyond the forest service office, you'll pass through **Camp Richardson,** one of the senior resorts on the lake. Built in 1923, this comfortably rustic facility still has rooms to let. A 230-unit campground is adjacent. (See "Where to camp" below.)

A bit farther along, the forest service is restoring several historic structures at the **Tallac Historic Site** in the **Pope-Baldwin Recreation Area.** Here, the super-rich came to play around the turn of the century. Tallac is a venerable shingle-sided retreat that hosts summer concerts (see "Annual events" below). The **Lucky Baldwin Mansion** and **Pope Mansion** are open to visitors in the summer. The **Tallac Museum** in the Baldwin mansion focuses on the natural and human history of the area. Hours are Monday-Friday 9 to 6 from Memorial Day through Labor Day Weekend.

The recreation area also offers picnic areas and hiking trails. Within this wooded and grassy complex is the Forest Service's octagonal **Lake Tahoe Visitors Center,** open Memorial Day through Labor Day weekend; (916) 544-5050. The Rainbow Trail leads from here to a stream profile chamber under Taylor Creek.

☺ After about ten miles, you'll climb a narrow ridge and witness Tahoe's most imposing vista—**Emerald Bay** on your right and **Fallen Leaf Lake** on your left. The slender bay, cradling wooded Fannette Island, is one America's most photographed spots. Now part of Emerald Bay State Park, it has been declared a National Natural Landmark. **Inspiration Point, Eagle Falls Trailhead** and **Vikingshome Vista Point** provide places to park and enjoy this imposing vista. The latter is the best, with a foreground of granite boulders to frame the bay and its island.

☺ From here, you can hike a steep trail down to **Vikingshome,** a lakeside mansion built in 1929. Now forest service property, this intriguing study in Scandinavian architecture is open for tours from mid-June through Labor Day, 10 to 4; adults $2, kids $1. Beyond Emerald Bay is the large **D.L. Bliss State Park** with a sandy beach, hiking trails and summer naturalist programs. Day use fee is $5. From here, you pass through the hamlet of **Meeks Bay** and hit **Sugar Pine Point State Park,** one of the few lakeside camping areas kept open in winter.

Civilization, such as it is, has claimed the shoreline from this point on. At **Tahoe City,** pause for a peek at **Gatekeeper's Museum State Park,** with a reconstruction of the dam attendant's log cottage. Exhibits concern flora and fauna, Native Americans and Tahoe's development. The park is open 11 to 5, daily in summer and Wednesday-Sunday from mid-May to mid-June and in September; it's closed in winter. Highway 89 peels off at Tahoe City, passing **Squaw Valley** and joining I-80. Your lakeside route becomes Highway 28, carrying you uneventfully through the wooded little communities of **Carnelian Bay** and **Tahoe Vista** to **King's Beach.** They offer lots of motels and small resorts, and not much else.

The shimmering sapphire of Lake Tahoe is particularly awesome in winter.
— **Photo courtesy Heavenly Ski Resort**

Taking a ride on the Nevada side

Nevada's gambling parlors are bunched near the California border on the north and south ends of the lake. The largest concentration is at Stateline on the southern tip. Between these casino clusters, much of the shoreline is protected by Lake Tahoe Nevada State Park and Toiyabe National Forest. You're first clue that you've entered the Silver State is a sign identifying **Cal-Neva Lodge and Casino.** You're in the town of **Crystal Bay,** consisting mostly of the Cal-Neva and a few smaller gaming parlors.

From here, the highway climbs a bit, affording views of the lake over condo rooftops. A mile or so beyond, fork to the right onto Lakeshore Drive and you'll be delivered to **Incline Village.** You immediately note the community planning here that is lacking on much of the California side. Although this is no pristine wilderness, homes and businesses are tucked carefully among the trees and lakeside condos march in an orderly fashion down to the shoreline. Most structures are dressed in properly muted browns and greens, going through the motions of forest camouflage.

The shoreline drive takes you through this appealing community to **Incline Beach,** offering a play area and picnic tables shaded by lakeside pines. A snack bar is open in summer. Just beyond, on your left, is **Hyatt Lake Tahoe,** the most elegant and pricey casino resort on this end of the lake. Opposite is **Country Club Mall,** with a few restaurants, assorted boutiques and real estate offices.

Incline is easily the most attractive and prosperous town on the lakeshore, now numbering about 6,500 presumably contented residents. Among its "residents" is a fictitious ranch inspired by history's most enduring TV western series. Since you followed Shoreline Drive, you missed the Ponderosa, which sits up on Highway 28. If you're a *Bonanza* fan or if you've got kids in tow, you may want to backtrack.

Ponderosa Ranch ● *State Highway 28 (P.O. Box AP), Incline Village, NV 89450; (702) 831-0691. May through October 9:30 to 5. Adults $9.50; kids 5 to 11, $7.50 and toddlers $2.* It's difficult to discern where one fable ends and the other begins at the legendary home of TV's Cartwright family. They galloped into 400 million living rooms, speaking 12 different languages during 239 episodes of *Bonanza* from 1959 until 1973. Sadly, only one member of this TV family of a father and three sons, Pernell Roberts (Adam), is still alive. However the legend of *Bonanza* seems destined to last forever. Nearly half a million people visit the so-called Ponderosa Ranch each year.

Wanna-be cowboys and *Bonanza* trekkies can explore a simulated Western town and the Cartwright ranch house; view a collection of antique cars, farm equipment and carriages; have an old timey photo taken; meet friendly critters at the Pettin' Farm and watch a shoot-out.

The unspoiled east shore

Beyond Incline, Lakeshore Drive rejoins Highway 28. You'll enter **Lake Tahoe Nevada State Park** in the basin's most pristine section. Let your eyes travel down through the pines to the boulder-strewn shoreline. Then peer across the great sapphire oval to the opposite shore, embraced by the snow-dusted granite peaks of the Sierra Nevada. You'll understand why Mark Twain called this "the fairest picture the whole earth affords."

The highway alternately hugs the shoreline, then climbs higher for an aerial view. Parking areas invite you to pull over for a more studied vista, allowing those less view-struck motorists to pass. At several points, you can follow trails down to the shore to peer into the clear ice blue depths.

Sand Harbor is an inviting public beach with picnic tables, potties, ranger station (open summers only) and a boat launch. Day use fee is $5 per vehicle and $1 for walkers and bikers. Just beyond, you enter "rural Carson City" (Carson is a combined city/county). And beyond that, a turnoff to the left leads a short distance to **Spooner Lake.** This little tree-rimmed pond has a picnic area and potties, plus 35 miles of groomed cross-country ski trails in winter. Entry is $5 per car and $1 for walkers and cyclists. Highway 50 joins the eastern shore just beyond Spooner Lake, bringing with it a quick increase in traffic. However, the area is still relatively free of development, except for the private community of **Glenbrook,** tucked down by Tahoe's edge. An historical marker at the Glenbrook turnoff discusses a lumbering operation based here in the 1860s.

☺ If you'd like to hike the **Tahoe Rim Trail,** follow Highway 50 east a short distance to **Spooner Summit,** where you can pick up the Nevada-side trailhead. Being built by volunteers, the path will circle the lake when it's completed in mid-decade. It will meander for 150, touching six counties, three national forests and—of course—two states. If you'd like to learn of its progress, or pitch in and help *make* it progress, contact: The Tahoe Rim Trail, P.O. Box 10156, South Lake Tahoe, CA 95731; (916) 577-0676.

☺ **Logan Shoals Vista Point** is a fine place to pause and admire the view. It offers your last chance to commune with the lake before you return to civilization. By scrambling carefully down through the trees, you can reach the water's edge. It's cobbled here by giant boulders that are favored retreats of summer sun lovers. In this undeveloped area, the water is amazingly clear, a soft turquoise at the edge, turning to a deep blue offshore. A trail leads in both directions from here along most of the length of the state park's three-mile lake front.

Beyond Logan Shoals, **Cave Rock** offers a boat launch and beach area, adjacent to the tiny community of the same name. **Zephyr Cove,** one of the area's oldest resorts and appropriately funky, is a good base of operations for lake play. Surrounded by national forest land, it was built in the early 1900s. The complex offers a restaurant, lodges and campgrounds (listed below), marina and boat landing, forested beach and picnic area. The **M.S. Dixie** is berthed here, offering excursions across the lake to Emerald Bay (see "Lake cruises" below).

The forest service's **Nevada Beach** is just beyond Zephyr Cove, down Elks Point Road, with lakeside picnic areas and campsites (closed in winter). Opposite the turnoff is **Round Hill Shopping Center,** a weathered mall with some shops and a restaurant or two. The **Tahoe-Douglas Chamber of Commerce** is here, open weekdays 9 to 5 and Saturdays 10 to 4.

Just beyond, you round a corner and there they are—four glass towers rising from what's left of the forest. Welcome to Glitter Gulch of the Pines!

Stateline

Population: about 3,000   **Elevation: 6,200 feet**

If you're a serious gambler, you'll probably like the setting, certainly prettier than downtown Reno or the Las Vegas strip. We'll add that the tower restaurants offer some of the finest dining views in the state. So do the rooms, which are rather opulent at the larger casino resorts. Of course, if you're a conservationist, you may be appalled at what's happened to the lake's south shore. Little survives of the natural terrain here. Stateline is a crowded collection of the Big Four highrise casinos—Caesars Tahoe, Harrah's, Harvey's and the Horizon—plus a few smaller ones. What space is left is taken up mostly by parking lots and parking structures.

Across the border, stretching into a cluttered California infinity, are the service stations, motels, cafés and other small businesses of **South Lake Tahoe**. You'll even see a few trees here and there—without which this business strip might as well be in Hayward or Hackensack. To load up on brochures, you can drive about a mile and a half beyond the casino center to the **South Lake Tahoe Chamber of Commerce** at 3066 Lake Tahoe Blvd., just beyond **El Dorado Beach**.

LAKE TAHOE ACTIVITIES AND ATTRACTIONS

Aerial trams ● These two ski resorts offer gondola rides (weather permitting) that provide imposing lake views: **Heavenly Valley Tram** at the end of Ski Run Boulevard in South Lake Tahoe (California side) operates daily between Memorial Day and Labor Day, and weekends the rest of the year; adults $10.50, seniors and kids $6.50; (916) 541-1330. **Squaw Valley Cable Car,** at Squaw Valley ski resort northwest of the lake, climbs up to the Pacific Crest Trail, daily throughout the year. Ice skating, swimming, hiking and horseback riding are available. Adults $10, kids $5; 583-6955.

Boating ● Lake Tahoe boat rentals are available from North Shore Sailing Inc., (916) 546-4333; North Tahoe Marina, (916) 546-8248; Sand Harbor, (702) 831-0494 and Zephyr Cove Marina, (702) 588-3833.

Hot air ballooning • Lake Tahoe Balloons, Inc., (916) 544-1221.

Fishing • Numerous outfits offer charter fishing on the lake. For a list, contact: Lake Tahoe Visitors Authority, (916) 544-5050.

Sightseeing • For tours between Tahoe and Reno, and around the lake, contact Reno Tahoe Company, (702) 348-7788; Showboat Lines, (702) 588-6633; Gray Line of Reno & Lake Tahoe, (800) 822-6009 or (702) 329-2877 and Travel Systems, (702) 588-4277.

Lake cruises

M.S. Dixie • *P.O. Box 1667, Zephyr Cove, NV 89448; (702) 588-3508. Emerald Bay cruise $12 for adults and $4 for kids, champagne brunch cruise $16 for adults and $7.50 for kids, sunset dinner dance cruise (kids not recommended), $31 with dinner. Mid-April through October. MC/VISA, AMEX.* Cruises are aboard a refurbished 1927 paddlewheeler that saw service on the Mississippi. It has a glass bottom for underwater viewing.

Tahoe Queen • *P.O. Box 14327, South Lake Tahoe, CA 95702; (800) 23-TAHOE or (916) 541-3364. Emerald Bay cruise $14 for adults and $5 for kids, dinner dance $18 for adults and $9.50 for kids (plus dinner from $14.95); all year. Also provides a winter ski shuttle to North Shore, adults $18, kids $9. MC/VISA, AMEX.* The "Queen" is a triple-deck oldstyle, newly constructed paddlewheeler, with glass bottom for viewing.

North Tahoe Cruises • *700 N. Lake Blvd. (P.O. Box 7913) Tahoe City, CA 96145; (916) 583-0141. Shoreline cruise, champagne continental breakfast cruise and Emerald Bay cruise, all $13 for adults and $5 for kids; also $12 adults-only "Casino Fun Package" cruise to Crystal Bay. Late April through November.* Sleek motor launches sail along the western shore.

Winter sports

The most complete information source for Tahoe Basin winter sports is the **Skier's Planning Guide**, P.O. Box 9137, Incline Village, NV 89450, with descriptions of major ski areas, casino resorts and ski packages. For a packet of travel and ski information, write: **Reno/Tahoe,** P.O. Box 9038, Incline Village, NV 89450. A newsprint guide, **Ski Tahoe** is available free at most casinos, ski shops and many other stores at the lake, with area maps, listings of ski resorts and discount coupons. Another good winter sports information source is the **Lake Tahoe Basin Management Unit,** P.O. Box 8465, South Lake Tahoe, CA 95731.

Most Tahoe Basin ski areas are in California; we list those in both states.

Downhill skiing • Alpine Meadows, (916) 583-4232, all day lift ticket $38; Granlibakken, (916) 583-4242, $12; Heavenly (sections on California and Nevada sides, above Stateline), (916) 541-1330, $38; Homewood, (916) 525-7256, $29; Mount Rose Resort (includes Incline), (702) 849-0706, $28; Northstar, (916) 562-1330, $38; Squaw Valley, (916) 583-6985, $38; Sugar Bowl, (916) 426-3651, $33 and Tahoe Donner, (916) 587-9400, $20.

Cross country • Squaw Creek, (916) 583-8951, trail pass $10; Diamond Peak, (702) 832-3249, $10; Eagle Mountain Nordic, (916) 389-2254, $11; Northstar, (916) 562-1330, $13; Royal Gorge, (916) 426-3871, $16; Tahoe Donner, (916) 587-9484, $13; Tahoe Nordic Ski Center, (916) 583-0484, $12; Hope Valley, (916) 694-2266, free; Lake Tahoe Winter Sports Center, (916) 577-2940, $5; and Spooner Lake, (702) 749-5349, $9.50.

Snowmobile rentals • The basin has more than 500 miles of groomed and ungroomed snowmobile trails. Call these outfits for rentals: Eagle Ridge

Outfitters, (916) 587-9322; Zephyr Cove Snowmobiles, (702) 588-3833; Mountain Lake Adventures, (702) 831-4202; Lake Tahoe Winter Sports Center, (916) 577-2940 and Snowmobiling Unlimited, (916) 583-5858.

Sledding and snow play • Hansen's Resort, 1360 Ski Run Blvd., South Lake Tahoe, (916) 544-3361, use fee, equipment rentals; Granlibakken, (916) 583-4242, free, equipment rentals; North Tahoe Regional Park end of National Avenue in Tahoe Vista, free; Incline Village, near the golf course driving range, free; Mount Rose Summit on Mount Rose Highway, free; Spooner Summit on Highway 50, free.

ANNUAL EVENTS

Snowfest, late February to early March at north shore, (800) 824-6348; Western America's largest winter carnival.

Valhalla Arts & Music Festival and **Starlight Jazz & Blues Festival,** June to early September at Lake of the Sky Amphitheater at the Tallac Historic Site above Camp Richardson; (916) 542-4166 or 541-4975.

Music at Sand Harbor, July at Sand Harbor State Park, Incline Village, (916) 583-9048; popular, rock, reggae and new wave jazz are performed at lakeside.

Shakespeare at Sand Harbor, August, (916) 583-9048; the Bard's works performed on an outdoor stage.

Cool September Days, early September at Stateline and South Lake Tahoe; (702) 588-8575; community celebration with car show, poker run and other activities.

Winter Festival of Lights, Thanksgiving through March at Stateline and South Lake Tahoe, with lights on homes and stores; (916) 541-5255.

WHERE TO DINE
California side

Cantina los Tres Hombres • ∆∆ $$
765 Emerald Bay Rd., South Lake Tahoe; (916) 544-1233; also at 8791 N. Lake Blvd., Kings Beach (north shore); (916) 546-4052. Mexican; full bar service. Daily 11:30 to 10:30. MC/VISA. Fun and funky place with a refreshing decorator twist for a Tahoe cantina—it's done in a bamboo Mexican tropical theme. Typical Cal-Mex dishes such as *fajitas* and mesquite-grilled meats, fowls and fishes, plus the usual tortilla-encased things.

Carlos Murphy's • ∆∆ $$
3678 Lake Tahoe Blvd., South Lake Tahoe; (916) 542-1741. Mexican-American; full bar service. Weekdays 11 to 10, Saturday 11 to 11, Sunday 10 to 10. Major credit cards. Bright and cheerful "Mexican-Irish pub" done up in sombreros and shamrocks. Fare includes contemporary Cal-Mex *fajitas, chimichangas* and other tortilla things, and American steaks and chops.

Old Post Office Coffee Shop • ∆∆ $
5245 N. Lake Blvd., Carnelian Bay; (916) 546-3205. American; no alcohol. Breakfast and lunch daily from 6 to 3. MC/VISA. Oldstyle cafè offering hearty flapjack, waffle and omelette breakfasts at modest prices. Lunch fare includes hefty 'burgers, salads and homemade soups.

Evans American Gourmet Café • ∆∆∆∆ $$$ ∅
536 Emerald Bay Rd., South Lake Tahoe; (916) 542-1990. American nouveau; wine and beer. Monday-Saturday 6 p.m. to 10 p.m. Major credit cards. Dressy, cozy cottage cafè done in soft blues and decorated with works of

area artists. Whatever's fresh goes into the tasty, innovatively seasoned entrées, ranging from American regional to Asian; smoke-free.

The Swiss Chalet ● ΔΔ $$
2540 Tahoe Blvd. (at Sierra Boulevard), South Lake Tahoe; (916) 544-3304. Continental; full bar service. Tuesday-Sunday 5 p.m. to 10 p.m. MC/VISA, AMEX. Snug Bavarian style restaurant that looks right at home among Tahoe's trees. European menu focuses on assorted schnitzels and other German and Swiss cuisine.

Tahoe House ● ΔΔ $$
Highway 89, half mile south of 89/28 junction, Tahoe City; (916) 583-1377. Continental; wine and beer. Dinner nightly from 5. MC/VISA. Cozy Swiss chalet style café on the west shore. Swiss-owned, it specializes in German-Swiss, French and Italian fare. Heartily-spiced entrées range from Swiss veal to fresh Italian pastas.

Zachary's ● ΔΔΔ $$$
In Embassy Suites (4130 Lake Tahoe Blvd.), South Lake Tahoe; (916) 544-5400. American; full bar service. Daily 11 to 2 and 5 to 11. Major credit cards. Stylishly modern place in the new Embassy Suites resort near the casinos. Assorted steaks, chicken and fish entrées are served with *nouveau* touches.

The Chart House ● ΔΔΔ $$$ Ø
392 Kingsbury Rd., Stateline; (702) 832-7223. American; full bar service. Sunday-Friday 5:30 p.m. to 10, Saturday 5 to 10:30. Major credit cards. Aquatic-woodsy dining room with a panoramic lake view. Versatile steak, seafood and prime rib menu, with a large all-you-can-eat salad bar.

Hacienda de la Sierra ● ΔΔ $ Ø
931 Tahoe Blvd., Incline Village; (702) 831-8300. Mexican; full bar service. Summer 11 to 10 daily, winter 4 to 10. MC/VISA, AMEX. Locally popular place with a woodsy-tropical look; outdoor deck and patio entertainment in summer. Wide range of Mexican dishes; specialties include *fajitas* and *carnitas de la Sierra* (mildly spiced chunks of pork or turkey with tortillas).

WHERE TO SLEEP
California side

Best Western Lake Tahoe Inn ● ⌂⌂ $$$ Ø
4110 Lake Tahoe Blvd., South Lake Tahoe, CA 96150; (800) 528-1234 or (916) 541-2010. Couples and singles $57 to $108. Major credit cards. A 400-unit lodge with TV movies, room phones. Two swimming pools, spa. **Angie's Cafe** serves 7 a.m. to 1:30 p.m.; $5 to $13; full bar service.

Best Western Timber Cove Lodge ● ⌂⌂⌂ $$$ Ø
3411 Lake Tahoe Blvd., South Lake Tahoe, CA 96150; (800) 528-1234 or (916) 541-6722. Couples and singles $57 to $98. Major credit cards. Lakeside lodge with TV movies, room phones. Attractively landscaped pool area, spa, beach with swimming area and marina. **Angie's Cafe** serves from 7 to 1:30 and 5 to 9; dinners $5 to $13; full bar service.

Franciscan Lakeside Lodge ● ⌂⌂ $$$
P.O. Box 280 (National Avenue), Tahoe Vista, CA 96148. Couples and singles from $50, suites $50 to $155. MC/VISA, AMEX. Rustic lakeside lodge with 57 units, some with lake views. TV movies, room phones; private beach, volleyball, lawn games, barbecues.

Inn by the Lake ● ⌂⌂⌂ $$$$$ Ø
3300 Lake Tahoe Blvd. (Fremont), South Lake Tahoe, CA 96150; (800) 877-1466 or (916) 542-0330. Couples and singles $98 to $175, kitchen units $250 to $330, suites $175 to $330; rates include continental breakfast. Major credit cards. Nicely appointed 99-room inn near the lake with TV movies, room phones, and view balconies. Hot tub, sauna, casino and ski shuttles.

Parkwood Lodge ● ⌂⌂ $$ Ø
954 Park Ave., South Lake Tahoe, CA 96150; (916) 544-4114. Couples and singles $38 to $58. MC/VISA, AMEX. A 20-unit motel with TV, room phones. Spa; continental breakfast on weekdays. Shuttle to casino and ski areas.

Tahoe Beach & Ski Club ● ⌂⌂⌂ $$$$
3601 Lake Tahoe Blvd. (Ski Run Boulevard), South Lake Tahoe, CA 96150; (800) 822-5962 or (916) 541-6220. Couples and singles from $75, kitchenettes and suites $75 to $290. Major credit cards. A 127-unit lakeside resort with a private beach, spa, sauna, ski shop, volleyball, badminton and croquet. Rooms with TV, phones; some with lake views and spa tubs.

Nevada side

Club Tahoe ● ⌂⌂⌂ $$$$$
914 Northwood Blvd. (P.O. Box 4650), Incline Village, NV 89450; (800) 527-5154 or (702) 831-5750. Two bedroom units with kitchens $110 to $155. MC/VISA. A 93-unit resort with TV movies and room phones. Attractive wooded grounds with pool, spas, sauna, racquetball, tennis, volleyball, exercise area, game room, cocktail lounge and deli.

The Inn at Incline ● ⌂⌂⌂ $$$$
Country Club Drive and Highway 28 (P.O. Box 4545), Incline Village, NV 89450; (800) 824-6391 or (702) 831-1052. Couples and singles $69 to $99, kitchenette condos $95 to $175; rates include continental breakfast. Major credit cards. A 50-unit resort with TV movies, room phones. Private beach privileges, sauna, spa and indoor pool.

Zephyr Cove Resort ● ⌂ $$
760 Highway 50 (P.O. Box 830), Zephyr Cove, NV 89448; (702) 588-6644. Rustic lodge rooms $45 to $50, mini-suites $75, cottages $39 to $85 for two, up to $185 for a two-story chalet that sleeps eight. MC/VISA, AMEX. Rustic resort with marina, beach, rental boats, parasails, jet skis, beachside bar and grill, stables. general store, video arcade, gift shop and winter snowmobile center with rentals. The **restaurant** serves American fare dinners $7 to $15; daily 7:30 a.m. to 9:30 p.m. (from 7:30 to 3 p.m. November-May).

Bed & breakfast inns

Chaney House ● ⌂⌂⌂ $$$$ Ø
West Lake Boulevard at Cherry (P.O. Box 7852). Tahoe City, CA 96145; (916) 525-7333. Couples and singles $95 to $110. Four units, two with private baths; full breakfast. No credit cards. European style 1928 stone house near the lakeshore with imposing stone fireplace and cathedral ceiling. Rooms furnished with European antiques; either lake or garden views.

Haus Bavaria ● ⌂⌂⌂ $$$$ Ø
593 N. Dyer Circle (P.O. Box 3308), Incline Village, NV 89450; (702) 831-6122. Doubles $72 to $90, singles $72 to $80. Five rooms, all with private

baths; full breakfast. MC/VISA, AMEX. Attractive European style guest house with rustic wood paneling, modern teak furnishings and German bric-a-brac. All rooms have balconies with mountain views.

NEVADA CASINOS
North shore

☺ *Cal Neva Lodge* ● △△△ $$$$$

Two Stateline Rd. (P.O. Box 368), Crystal Bay, NV 89402; (800) CAL NEVA or (702) 832-4000. Major credit cards. This handsome chalet style casino was renovated in the early 1990s. Frank Sinatra owned a piece of it in the 1960s but the Nevada Gaming Commission jerked his license for allowing Sam Giancana to hang out there. With an oldstyle bar offering a lake view, one may be more tempted to sit and sip than gamble. The Frank Sinatra Celebrity Showroom hosts live entertainment.

Dining: Cal Neva's early American style dining room, **Sir Charles,** serves continental fare, $10 to $15, nightly from 5 (weekends only in the off-season). The **Lakeview Restaurant** is certainly that, offering seating indoors and on a deck above the lake when weather permits; dinners $7 to $15; daily 7 a.m. to 11 p.m. (with seasonal variations).

Lodging: The rooms, all with lake views, are stylishly done in a blend of early American and modern. Doubles range from $99 to $149, suites (including cabins and chalets) are $199 to $259.

Tahoe Biltmore ● △△ $

Highway 28 (P.O. Box 115), Crystal Bay, NV 89402: (800) 245-8667 or (702) 831-0660. Major credit cards. Across the highway from the Cal Neva, this inviting mid-sized place has a sort of Mystic Seaport/Balboa Island look with a rounded glass front and blue-white color scheme. There's a kids' video parlor here and live entertainment in the Aspen Lounge. The Biltmore offers free overnight **RV parking** on a lot above. **Dining room** serves nightly dinners from $4 to $10, plus a 99-cent breakfast and cheap lunches.

Lodging: Room rates range from $27 to $33 in a motel unit and $33 to $44 in the casino hotel.

☺ *Hyatt Regency Lake Tahoe* ● $$$$$△△△ Ø

Lakeshore Boulevard at Country Club Drive (P.O. Box 3239), Incline Village, NV 89450-3239; (800) 233-1234 or (702) 832-1234. Major credit cards. With its sleek chalet style façade rising above the pines, the Hyatt looks right at home here. The casino is an interesting mix of woodsy class and flash—a kind of dark elegance with red and blue neon, accented by pine cones with twinkle-light needles. Singers, combos and the like perform in the Stage Bar, and Hugo's Rotisserie features live music.

Dining: Down by the lake with a view thereof, stylish **Hugo's** serves American-continental fare, $17 to $28; Sunday-Thursday 6 to 10 and Friday-Saturday 6 to 10:30. Back at the casino, **Ciao Mein** is Italian-Chinese, as dictated by that catchy name, with $14 to $26 dinners served Wednesday-Sunday 6 to 10. The 24-hour **Sierra Café** is a buffet.

Lodging: The Hyatt offers assorted handsomely-appointed accommodations, starting with tower room doubles from $152 to $239 and lakeside cottages and kitchenettes range from $237 to $564. Amenities at this full service resort include a pool, sauna and spa, tennis courts, golf at two nearby courses, and a private beach with boat rentals.

South shore

Harvey's Resort Hotel/Casino ● ⌂⌂⌂⌂ $$$$$ Ø

P.O. Box 128, Stateline, NV 89449; (800) 553-1022 or (702) 588-2411. Major credit cards. The oldest casino on the lake is now the largest, after a $100 million tower addition in 1986. Although the complex is handsome, it looks like an architectural mistake, since the blue tinted glass addition is fused to the original brown structure. The casino is roomy and glitzy, with red neon wagon wheels in alcove ceilings to mark the days when it was Harvey's Wagon Wheel. Scaled down versions of Broadway shows alternate with headliners in the Emerald Theater.

Dining: ☺ The headliner is the 19th floor **Llewellyn's,** an eye-catching space with chandeliers, marble, brocaded chairs and a striking lake view. The fare is international, $10 to $25, with lunch and dinner daily and a Sunday brunch. Others are the **Sage Room,** preserving a bit of the original Wagon Wheel, steaks and chops, $16.25 to $28.50, dinner nightly; **Seafood Grotto,** $7 to $26, lunch and dinner daily; **El Vaquero,** Mexican fare with fresh fish and a do-it-yourself taco cart, $3.25 to $14; lunch and dinner daily; **Pizzeria,** $4 to $7, lunch and dinner; **Classic Burgers** with a great 1950s look, from midday through late night; and the **Garden Buffet,** serving breakfast, lunch and dinner.

Lodging: Elegantly done rooms, many with lake views, range from $90 to $170 for doubles and $175 to $475 for suites. All include a free buffet breakfast. Non-smoking rooms available. Resort amenities include swimming pools, spa and health club, tennis courts, a lake view wedding chapel, video arcade for kids, specialty shops, barbershop and beauty salon.

Caesars Tahoe ● ⌂⌂⌂ $$$$$ Ø

P.O. Box 5800, Stateline, NV 89449; (800) 648-3353 or (702) 588-3515. Major credit cards. Although properly stylish and posh, this Caesars is modest when compared with the Las Vegas original. Caesar Augustus is out front to greet you, with a rolled up winning casino ticket in his hand, but that's about the extent of the marble statuary. Although it lacks the opulence of its Vegas cousin, it doesn't lack those sexy toga-clad drink girls. Circus Maximus features headliners, while lesser groups perform in the Emperor's Lounge, and magicians do their magic in Caesars Cabaret.

Dining: The clubby **Broiler Room** serves steak, seafood and Cajun, $14.50 to $30, dinner nightly; **Pisces** is the seafood place of course, $11 and up, Thursday-Monday 6 to 11; **Empress Court** features a mixed Asian menu, $12 and up, Friday-Tuesday 6 to 11; **Primavera** is a poolside Italian place, $11 to $18, Tuesday-Saturday 6 to 11 and **Café Roma** is the 24-hour space with an American-continental menu.

Lodging: The 440 rooms and suites are predictably opulent with the prices to prove it. They range from $115 to $175 for doubles and $300 to $650 for suites. All have refrigerators, and the hotel has several non-smoking floors. Resort amenities include a Romanesque indoor spa with a lagoon style swimming pool, weight and exercise room, racquetball and tennis courts, a large shopping arcade and a kids' video parlor.

☺ Harrah's Lake Tahoe ● ⌂⌂⌂ $$$$$ Ø

P.O. Box 8, Stateline, NV 89449; (800) 648-3773 or (702) 588-6611. Major credit cards. With a brown textured façade that tries to blend with the woodsy setting, Harrah's has the most attractive exterior of the resort towers here. This look of Sierran elegance carries into the large casino, with earth tones and natural textures. The South Shore Room alternates between Broadway shows and headliners, and the Summit Lounge features live music. The Stateline Cabaret offers adult revues.

Dining: ☺ The 18th floor **Summit** is a dressy American-continental place with awesome views, $15 to $30, nightly 6 to 10 (until 11 Friday-Saturday). Other gustatorial venues are the San Francisco style **North Beach Deli,** open daily with deli fare; **Andreotti,** regional Italian, $10 to $20, Wednesday-Sunday 5:30 to 10; **Asia,** serving Pacific Rim fare, $8 to $20, nightly 4 to 10; and **Sierra**, the 24-hour place with a basic American menu, $7.50 to $11.50. The clubby, lake-view **Friday's Station** serves steak and seafood, $19 to $37, nightly 5:30 to 10.

Lodging: These are the fanciest digs at the lake; each unit has twin bathrooms equipped with TV and phones. Prices for these and other amenities start at $139 for doubles and range up to $159; suites are $179 to $450. No-smoking rooms available. Resort amenities include a health club, shops, beauty salon and kids' video arcade.

Horizon Casino Resort ● ⌂⌂ $$$ ∅

P.O. Box C, Stateline, NV 89449; (800) 648-3322 or (702) 588-6211. Major credit cards. Originally Del Webb's Sahara, the Horizon has been renovated and stylishly dressed. Its casino is one of the prettiest around, with off-white coffered ceilings, fancy chandeliers and vivid red and white gaming tables and chairs. Two shows alternate at the Golden Cabaret. The "Bottoms Up" comedy revue is a good buy, $12 including buffet dinner. It cycles nightly with the *very* adult "Zoom!"

Dining: The dressy place is **Beaumont's,** serving steaks and seafood for $20 to $30, nightly 6 to 10:30. **Le Grande Buffet** comes in brunch and dinner versions, and **Four Seasons** is a 24-hour $7 to $13.50 coffee shop.

Lodging: Like the casino, the hotel lobby is striking, with marble floors and mirrored walls. Newly renovated rooms offer the usual amenities, from $65 to $139 for doubles; more for suites. No-smoking rooms are available. Resort goodies include a swimming pool, hot tubs and kiddies' wading pool.

Lakeside Inn and Casino ● ⌂⌂ $$$ ∅

Highway 50 at Kingsbury Grade (P.O. Box 5640), Stateline, NV 89449; (800) 624-7980 or (702) 588-7777. Major credit cards. This friendly little place east of Stateline offers a retreat from the overbuilt commotion of the casino center. It's a nice woodsy package with a small casino, 24-hour restaurant and 123 rooms. The 24-hour **Timber House Restaurant** serves a $5.99 prime rib dinner, Mexican and American fare from $6 to $16, plus $3 breakfast and $4 lunch specials.

Lodging: Nicely done rooms, some with stone wall accents, range from $59 to $89. A $99 package ($75 in winter) gets you week night accommodations, prime rib dinner, breakfast, champagne and a $10 gaming rebate.

WHERE TO CAMP

The Lake Tahoe basin has hundreds of national forest campsites, mostly away from the lake on the California side. That doesn't imply plentiful camping and RV parking, however. Spaces fill up quickly in summer and many campgrounds are closed in winter. For details on camping and other outdoor activities, contact: **Lake Tahoe Basin Management Unit,** P.O. Box 8465, South Lake Tahoe, CA 95731. To learn which units are on the forest service reservation system, call (800) 283-CAMP. The state park Mistix number is (800) 444-PARK.

Nevada Beach is the only lakeside national forest campground on the east shore. It's a *very* tough ticket in summer, since it doesn't accept reservations. Fees are $10 for camping and $2 per vehicle for day use. It's open Memorial Day through Labor Day.

Free RV parking is offered by the Tahoe Biltmore at Crystal Cove. However, signs at Stateline casinos forbid overnight RVing. Banned from resort parking, south shore RVers must resort to regular campgrounds. Most are on the California side, with the exception of Nevada's Zephyr cove.

Camp Richardson ● *P.O. Box 10648, South Lake Tahoe, CA 95731; (916) 541-1801. RV and tent sites, $20. Reservations accepted.* Shaded campsites in an historic resort, with showers, barbecue and picnic tables. Hiking trails, beach and marina adjacent.

KOA Kampground ● *P.O. Box 11552, South Lake Tahoe, CA 96155; (916) 577-3693. RV and tent sites, from $18. Reservations; MC/VISA.* Wooded pull-through sites on Highway 50, west of the "Y", eleven miles from Stateline. Showers, coin laundry, mini-mart, small pool, playground and rec room.

Sandy Beach Campground ● *6873 N. Lake Blvd. (P.O. Box 6868), Tahoe City, CA 95730; (916) 546-7682. RV and tent sites, $15 to $20. Reservations accepted; MC/VISA.* Tree-shaded sites across highway from the lakeshore. Showers, barbecues and picnic tables, beach.

Tahoe Pines ● *P.O. Box 11918, South Lake Tahoe, CA 96155; (916) 577-1653. RV and tent sites, from $16. Reservations accepted; MC/VISA.* On Highway 50, west of the "Y" with some sites on a stream. Showers, coin laundry, mini-mart and playground.

Tahoe Valley Campground ● *1175 Melba Dr. (P.O. Box 9026), South Lake Tahoe, CA 96155; (916) 541-2222. RV and tent sites, $16 to $23. Reservations accepted.* Near the "Y" at the end of C street off Highway 50. Some pull-throughs, showers, coin laundry, mini-mart, swimming pool, tennis court, rec room and playground; fishing in nearby stream.

Zephyr Cove Resort ● *P.O. Box 830, Zephyr Cove, NV 89448; (702) 588-6644. RV and tent sites; full hookups $22 a day or $140 a week, tent sites $15 a day or $95 a week. Reservations accepted; MC/VISA, AMEX.* It's a bit scruffy for the price, but it's in a woodsy setting. Facilities include showers, barbecues, pay phones, coin laundry, dump station, groceries, provisions and the many facilities of the adjacent resort (listed above).

THE EASTERN SIERRA

Highways heading south and east from the Lake Tahoe Basin take the traveler into a world of splendid isolation. The Sierra Nevada's eastern face, wrinkled brown and often snow-streaked, rises 10,000 feet from a broad valley floor, like a gigantic petrified wave. It is one of the most imposing escarpments in the world. A single north-south highway, U.S. 395, traverses this region. It undulates over the eastern Sierra's alluvial toes on its long trek from Canada to Mexico.

The rainshadow effect is dramatically evident here. From ponderosa forests, you drop quickly into an arid basin. With little to support the area except ranching and summer recreation, towns along here are small. The eastern Sierra counties—Alpine, Mono and Inyo—are among the most thinly settled in America. They are areas of deep topographical dimension, from the desert basins of the Carson and Owens valleys to the high Sierra ridgelines. Certainly the most impressive example is in Inyo County, where the Lower Forty-eight's highest and lowest elevations are 75 miles apart.

Despite this extremity, most of the "lowlands" along here are still rather elevated. In following U.S. 395 south, you'll stay well above 3,000 feet until you approach the Mojave Desert south of Lone Pine. Although this is foothill country, some of the highway's high points rival elevations of the trans-Sierra passes. This dictates a cool, dry and windy climate—perhaps another reason that the eastern Sierra does not encourage much settlement.

Summers are beautiful but brief, pleasantly warm under a canopy of crisp, blue sky. Temperatures can rise in this thin, dry air. It's a curious experience to be standing knee deep in summer heat shimmers while looking up at the snowy crests.

All of the trans-Sierra highways south of Lake Tahoe are closed in winter. East side residents thus relate more to Nevada and southern California than to the northern half of their state.

Three varieties of people are drawn to the eastern Sierra: seekers of solitude, seekers of splendid scenery and outdoor types tempted by the hiking, backpacking, camping and fishing lures in the mountains. If you're all of the above, this is your place.

Although snow keeps visitors from exploring the heights during winter, the drive along U.S. 395 can be stunningly beautiful then, as the snow-dusted Sierra becomes a giant confection. The highway itself is generally snow-free.

The High Sierra

TAHOE TO LEE VINING

You have choices in heading south from Lake Tahoe. If you seek a final gambling fling, you can follow U.S. 50 downhill to **Carson City.** Or, follow State Highway 207 (Kingsbury Grade) from Stateline to **Minden-Gardnerville,** and take Highway 395 south from there. The Kingsbury route is quite imposing. After a steep climb from Stateline up to **Daggett Summit**—thus proving that Tahoe is in a basin—you drop quickly toward the brown and green patchwork of tabletop-level **Carson Valley.**

If you choose an all-California route out, start climbing west toward Echo Summit from the South Lake Tahoe "Y" on U.S. 50, then head south on State Route 89. It takes you over 7,740-foot **Luther Pass** to the Pony Express stop at **Woodfords Station** and the mountain hamlet of **Markleeville.** You'll climb 8,314-foot **Monitor Pass** and pick up U.S. 395 south of Topaz Lake. This route offers exposure to the craggy granite beauty of the high Sierra. Aspens lining the banks of the Carson River and its tributaries dance with fall colors. You'll have to pick an alternate route in winter, however, since Monitor Pass is not kept open.

RV advisory: The southern descent from Monitor Pass, while certainly dramatic, is not recommended for large RVs and trailers. The tamest route out of Tahoe is U.S. 50. Kingsbury Grade is easily navigable after a few twists and turns in the climb toward Daggett Summit.

No matter which Tahoe escape route you choose, take time to pause at Markleeville. Even if Luther Pass is closed by winter snow (which it sometimes is), you can reach this little town from Highway 88 out of Minden-Gardnerville. On the way, pause at **Woodfords Station** at the junction of highways 88 and 89. Started as a Pony Express stop, it survives as a way station for traffic funneling through the Sierra. The first three stations burned down; the current version—a general store less than 15 years old—has a properly rustic look. Inside, you can get breakfast or a light snack, buy a few essentials and gossip with the proprietors.

If you press westward from Woodfords on Highway 88, you'll cross **Carson Pass,** a scenic spiral that delivers you to Jackson in the Gold Country. Below Markleeville, Highway 89 touches Highway 4, which takes you over our favorite Sierra passage, **Ebbetts Pass.** At 8,730 feet, you're elevated to an imposing alpine retreat of raw granite and ice blue lakes. **Hermit Valley,** cradled at 7,000 feet between Ebbetts Pass and Pacific Grade Summit (8,050) is a favorite playground of high country aficionados.

Markleeville

Population: 165   **Elevation: 5,501 feet**

This town tucked into a wooded stream valley is so darned cute, it's hard to believe that so few people live here. It's America's smallest county seat, sitting in the middle of California's least populated county. At last count, only 1,200 residents had chosen this idyllic county tilted against the eastern Sierra. The town got its start in the 1860s when prospectors began probing the hills for silver and gold. It got the county seat in 1875 when nearby Silver Mountain City's mines dried up and the town expired.

You can see all of Markleeville in a minute, although you could linger considerably longer. Among grizzled wooden structures is the **Alpine Inn,** built in 1862 in Silver Mountain City and moved here in 1886. Stop in at the good old boy **Cutthroat Saloon** for a round of beer and cheer. The inn also offers a family style restaurant (listed below). Appropriate to Markleeville's downsized environment, the **county courthouse** is little more than a stone cottage. Next door is the **Markleeville guard station** of Toiyabe National Forest. You can learn about the splendid wilds just above town, including the Mokelumne and Carson Iceberg wilderness areas. Two other structures worth a pause are the inviting **Coffee Bar Gallery** cafè and art shop (listed below) and the oldstyle **General Store.**

Just up Montgomery Street from the Alpine Inn, the **Alpine County Historical Society Museum** does a fine job of preserving the county's past. It's open daily except Tuesday, noon to 5; closed in winter. The collection includes the usual pioneer artifacts, plus an old school house, log jail and a stamp mill out front.

If you continue west past the museum, you'll happen upon **Grover Hot Springs State Park.** It's open daily in summer 9 to 9 and Friday-Monday 11 to 8:30 in the off-season. While a bit short on esthetics, the concrete-lined simmering basins are refreshing, particularly if you sink into the steaming water to drive away a winter chill. During summer, expect the place to be crowded. There's a campground adjacent with sites for $12 (see below). For specifics on the park, contact: Grover Hot Springs, P.O. Box 188, Markleeville, CA 96120; (916) 694-2248.

Moving south from here on Highway 395, you'll pass the drab hamlets of **Topaz, Coleville** and **Walker.** You're now in the gently rolling alluvial plain at the base of the Sierra Nevada. At **Sonora Junction,** Highway 108 takes you to the granite heights and down to Sonora and Columbia in the Gold Country. At 9,624 feet, **Sonora Pass** is second only to Tioga among the trans-Sierra highway routes. Back down on Highway 395, you climb briefly into steep foothills, top **Devil's Gate Summit** at 7,519 feet and drop down into an important mountain gateway.

Bridgeport

Population: 500   **Elevation: 6,465 feet**

Bridgeport's cultural message is telegraphed at the north end of town when you pass **Ziglar's Sporting Goods and Boutique.** That's about it, kids. Living mostly on tourism and outdoorsmen, the town is a modest mix of old false fronts and new motels. Take time to admire the architecture of the Italianate/federalist 1880 **Mono County Courthouse.** Also worth a look, and perhaps a meal, is the white, shingle-sided 1877 **Bridgeport Inn** (listed below). The small **Mono County Museum** occupies the town's 1880 elementary school, offering the usual pioneer relics and a few pieces of farm things out front. To find it, turn left onto School Street (beside the county courthouse), go a block and turn left again into **Bridgeport City Park,** beside and behind the Mono County Memorial Hall.

To pick up specifics on the area attractions—mostly focused on the Sierra looming overhead—stop at the **Bridgeport Chamber of Commerce** and the **Bridgeport District Ranger Station,** both on Highway 395. They're open weekdays, usually 9 to 5.

South of Bridgeport, the highway climbs again, carrying you 7,000 feet to a beautifully bleak world of sensuously rounded hills that are satiny with snow in winter. The Sierra peaks are strangely vivid now, poised before an empty sky as if marking the edge of the world. The stage is set for two of the eastern Sierra's most intriguing attractions. Seven miles below Bridgeport, follow signs east to a dusty slice of California history, preserved in a state of interrupted decline.

☺ **Bodie State Historic Park** • *P.O. Box 515, Bridgeport, CA 93517; (619) 647-6445. Daily 9 to 7 in summer, 9 to 4 the rest of the year; $5 per vehicle. Picnic areas, no camping. The park is open in winter although the road may be closed by snow.* Once the raunchiest, meanest mining town in California, Bodie now stands in perpetual freeze frame. After over 90 percent of this boomtown had burned or collapsed, the state park service stepped in to stop the clock. What survives is California's largest ghost town. More than 160 buildings are frozen in an historic bubble of careful maintenance. The state does not improve nor upgrade, but prevents more slippage into the dust. Walk with the tumbleweeds down the dusty streets of this forlorn town and peer through sagging windows at shabby relics of yesterday. There are no services or facilities here, only a ranger station, unshaded picnic area and pit potties. Bodie always *was* forlorn, located far afield from the other boomtowns, high up on a cold and windy desert slope at 8,369 feet. It was born in 1877 when gold was discovered in these ragged hills.

South of Bodie, U.S. 395 spirals up to **Conway Summit.** There, at 8,138 feet—the highest point on the highway—a haunting view is unveiled.

Mono Lake

☺ What is the world's fascination with **Mono Lake?** You may wonder this as you stare down upon a pallid blue surface, rimmed by bland gray desert, with dull gray volcanic cinder cones beyond. Fish can't survive in its water, 2.5 times as salty and 80 times as alkaline as the ocean. Along its shoreline are curious limestone tufa columns. They, too, are dull and bland, the color and shape of bleached dog dung, stood on end. This plain Jane of a pond, home to such unlovely creatures as brine shrimp and brine flies, is a *cause célèbre* for environmental groups Other travel writers seem moved to tears as they scatter their adjectives about this hallowed place.

All these people are worried about this stagnant pond because thirsty Los Angeles has been trying to drink it dry. Built upon a desert coastal plain, it must reach elsewhere for water. Its first reach (see box on page 295) was the Owens Valley, which we will enter later. After draining its once lush croplands, the powerful Los Angeles Department of Water and Power began drawing water from creeks that fed the Mono Lake Basin. Obviously, Mono Lake began shrinking. Alarmed local citizens, acting on the premise that it may be an ugly lake but it's *their* ugly lake, solicited the aid of environmental groups. Naturally, everybody went to court. The battle to save Mono Lake has been raging for several decades. As of this writing, compromises have been made to prevent further shrinkage.

There are good reasons for saving this unlovely puddle, other than the fact that those wormy looking brine shrimp need a home, just like everybody else. It's is a major stop for migrating waterfowl. We have seen most of the great wetlands of the West being sucked dry to divert water for farming. The notion that a surviving link in this critical flyway might be turned to dust to encourage growth for that awful sprawl of a city is unconscionable.

Before following the highway's steep descent into Mono Lake Basin, take time to enjoy the view from this lofty aerie. Although the lake has the vacant stare of a sightless blue eye, the surrounding terrain is imposing. You can see a grand proscenium of pinnacles from Conway Summit. Signs will direct your gaze to 13,143-foot **Boundary Peak,** the highest elevation in Nevada, and the **White Mountains** to the east, as lofty as the Sierra. They are home to the bristlecone pine, the world's oldest living thing.

From Conway Summit, the highway drops quickly, and you're soon skirting Mono's desert shoreline. If you'd like lunch or sunset dinner with your lake view, pause at **Mono Inn Restaurant** (listed below), occupying an upslope above the briny.

☺ A short distance beyond is the excellent **Mono Lake Scenic Area Visitor Center,** open 10 to 4, daily in summer and weekends only in winter; (619) 647-6572. Behind walls of glass offering imposing lake views, you can learn about the geology, flora and fauna of this intriguing basin. Nature trails take you toward the lakeshore and tell you what you're seeing along the way. Surrounding the pond is **Mono Lake Tufa State Reserve,** and a series of dirt roads can get you closer to the lakeshore. Take time for a dip to experience the mineral rich water's great buoyancy. If you're one of those people who swims like a rock, you'll be safe from sinking here. Don't let the water get into your eyes or a new cut, unless you want a harsh lesson in a body's physiological response to alkaline salt. The best tufa formations are on the south shore and we will direct you there later.

Meanwhile, Highway 395 takes you through **Lee Vining,** a town of 315 people and probably more motel rooms. It has a large number of "pillows" (the lodging trade's jargon for room capacity) because it sits at the junction of Highway 120, which climbs precipitous **Tioga Pass** into Yosemite National Park. If you have not yet visited Yosemite, this will provide a dramatic entry, taking you to the high country of Tuolumne Meadows.The town's odd name came from a literal source. Prospector Leroy Vining was poking around here in the 1860s. To learn more about Lee and the town named for him, stop at the **Old Schoolhouse Museum** in **Gus Hess Park.** It's open Thursday-Sunday noon to 4; (619) 647-6461 or 647-6530.

☺ Four miles south of Lee Vining, the **June Lake Loop** (State Route 158) takes you into the lower reaches of the Sierra and the **June Mountain Ski Area.** (For ski specifics: P.O. Box 146, June Lake, CA 93529, 619-648-7733.) Like Mammoth Mountain—owned by the same folks—June draws mostly from Southern California, although it's on the same latitude as San Francisco. It's usually less crowded than Mammoth, incidentally.

The 15-mile June Lake Loop offers splendid exposure to the high granite, with four alpine lakes chained along the highway. In the small village of **June Lake,** take a peek into the 1928 **June Lake Lodge** with its web-work of logs and large fieldstone fireplace. Once a temporary home for Bob, Bing and Dorothy during filming of *The Road to Utopia,* it now suffers the indignity of being a time share condo. The name has been changed to Heidelberg Inn. The loop drive is closed in winter, although the town and ski area can be reached via a lower turnoff from U.S. 395.

If you take the June Lake Loop, you'll miss the turnoff to Mono Lake's **South Tufa Area.** Go back to the State Route 120 junction, take it four miles east, then turn left at the South Tufa Area sign. A short drive delivers you to Mono Lake's shoreline, where you can walk among these curious pillars of limestone. They were formed underwater when calcium laden springs bubbled into the lake bed. Because of the lake level's drop—45 feet in recent decades—these pillars of calcium carbonate are now high and dry.

WHERE TO DINE
(in order of appearance)

Alpine Inn ● △ **$$**

14830 Highway 89, Markleeville; (916) 694-2591. American; full bar service. Breakfast, lunch and dinner from 7 a.m. MC/VISA. Basic wood-paneled cafe inside an historic hotel. The menu includes chicken fried steak, pork steak, scampi and *cordon bleu.*

Coffee Bar Gallery ● △△ **$**

14800 Highway 89, Markleeville. American; no alcohol. Thursday-Tuesday 8 to 3, closed Wednesday; shorter hours in winter. MC/VISA. This combined espresso bar and art and craft shop is styled as a comfortable living room. The simple menu offers various coffees and teas, plus breakfast croissants, muffins and pastries.

☺ **Bridgeport Inn** ● △△ **$$**

Main Street, Bridgeport; (619) 932-7380. American; full bar service. Lunch 11:30 to 3, dinner 5:30 to 8 (Friday-Saturday to 9). MC/VISA. Early American dining room in an 1877 hotel, with print wallpaper, wainscotting, folk artifacts and pink nappery. Menu items range from chicken, chops and steaks to pasta.

Mono Inn Restaurant ● △△ **$$**

Highway 395, Mono Lake; (619) 647-6581. American-continental; full bar service. Dinner Wednesday-Monday 5:30 to 10, closed Tuesday. MC/VISA. The most appealing thing about this simple dining room is its view of Mono Lake. It's perched right above the pond, with a deck. Versatile menu ranges from beef kababs and Cornish game hen to sirloin and shrimp.

WHERE TO SLEEP

In addition to the highway town motels, you'll find several rustic resorts tucked into the Sierra heights, often beside lakes and generally closed in winter. Local chambers can provide lists.

Alpine Inn ● △ **$**

14820 Highway 89 (P.O. Box 367), Markleeville, CA 96120; (916) 694-2591. Doubles $35, singles $32. MC/VISA. Basic accommodations in an historic hotel, built in 1862.

Bridgeport Inn ● △△ **$$**

Main Street, Bridgeport; (619) 932-7380. Couples and singles $48. MC/VISA. Simply furnished, comfortable rooms in a shingle-sided 1877 inn. Nicely restored and decorated with American folk crafts and antiques; Victorian parlor with wainscotting and an iron stove.

The Cain House ● △△△ **$$$$** Ø

Highway 395 (P.O. Box 454), Bridgeport, CA 93517; (619) 932-7040. Couples and singles $80 to $135; rates include full breakfast. Major credit cards. Attractively restored home belonging to prominent early family, converted to an attractive country inn. Six rooms with TV movies and phones. Sierra views; complimentary wine and cheese, social hour.

Silver Maple Inn ● △△ **$$$** Ø

Highway 395 at School Street (P.O. Box 327), Bridgeport, CA 93517; (619) 932-7383. Couples $55 to $85, singles $50 to $75. Major credit cards. A 20-room motel with TV movies.

Walker River Lodge ● ⌂⌂⌂ $$$$

Main at Hayes St. (P.O. Box 695), Bridgeport, CA 93517; (619) 932-7021. Couples $75 to $120, singles $65 to $95, kitchenettes $95 to $200, suites $115 to $160. Major credit cards. Attractive 36-unit riverside lodge with TV movies, room phones; some rooms with spa tubs, refrigerators and microwaves. Landscaped grounds with picnic and barbecue area beside the river; pool.

Best Western Lake View Lodge ● ⌂⌂ $$$ Ø

Highway 395 (P.O. Box 345), Lee Vining, CA 93541; (800) 528-1234 or (619) 647-6543. Couples and singles $48 to $78, kitchenettes $8 additional. Major credit cards. Well maintained 47-unit motel with TV movies, room phones; coin laundry, landscaped grounds.

Gateway Motel ● ⌂⌂ $$ Ø

Highway 395 (P.O. Box 250), Lee Vining, CA 93541; (619) 647-6467. Couples and singles $30 to $70. MC/VISA, AMEX. A 12-unit motel with TV, room phones; some refrigerators.

Murphey's Motel ● ⌂⌂ $$

Highway 395 (P.O. Box 57), Lee Vining, CA 93541; (800) 334-6316 or (619) 647-6316. Couples and singles $32 to $68. Major credit cards. A 43-unit motel with TV, room phones; sauna, spa and rec room.

WHERE TO CAMP

In addition to facilities listed below, there are dozens of campgrounds in adjacent national forests; check with area ranger stations.

Grover Hot Springs State Park ● *P.O. Box 188, Markleeville, CA 96120; (916) 694-2248. RV and tent sites, $12. Reservations through Mistix, (800) 444-PARK, or write: P.O. Box 85705, San Diego, CA 92138-5705.* Shaded sites; hot springs adjacent (adults $3, kids $2), fishing, swimming, trails.

Paradise Shores Trailer Park ● *P.O. Box 602, Bridgeport, CA 93517; (619) 932-7735. RV and tent sites, $9 to $12. Reservations accepted; no credit cards.* On Bridgeport Lake, about three miles from Highway 395 on State Route 182. Flush potties, cable TV, coin laundry; fishing on lake with cleaning and freezing facilities.

Willow Springs Trailer Park ● *Highway 395, Bridgeport, CA 93517; (619) 932-7725. RV sites only, $14. Reservations accepted; Major credit cards.* Adjacent to Willow Springs Motel, five miles south. Grassy sites, some shaded; showers, coin laundry, rec field, fishing pond with cleaning and freezing facilities.

Mono Vista Trailer Park ● *Highway 395, Lee Vining, CA 93541; (619) 647-6401. RV sites, $13 to $16. Reservations accepted.* Near Mono Lake, just north of town; some pull-throughs, shaded sites; showers, coin laundry.

MAMMOTH LAKES TO BISHOP

Below the turnoff to the South Tufa Area, Highway 395 brushes past the **Mono Craters,** arranged in a surprisingly orderly north-south rank. Dirt roads leading from highways 120 or 395 can get you to their base. South of the lower June lake turnoff, the highway tops 8,036-foot **Deadman Summit**. After less than five miles, a **Mammoth Lakes scenic loop** sign directs you to the right. You'll leave the dry high prairie and begin dancing among the ponderosas. After six miles, you hit a stop sign with choices. You can head uphill to the Mammoth Mountain Ski Area and Devil's Postpile National Monument, or go downhill to the town of Mammoth Lakes.

This area offers access to a fine collection of lakes and hot springs in Inyo National Forest, and it's a launching point for backpackers into Sierran heights. However, the region is noted mostly for skiing and earthquakes. One of the largest ski areas in the West, **Mammoth Mountain** offers two dozen lifts, a year around gondola ride and some glorious vistas of snow-dusted Sierra granite.

Cleverly disguised as an innocent basin, adjacent **Long Valley** is the remnant of a massive caldera that did a big bang number about 700,000 years ago. Scientists have determined that another magma mass is building far below, and it's blamed for triggering a series of recent earthquakes. Another major eruption is possible, they say. However, judging from the number of real estate offices in downtown Mammoth Lakes, most folks don't seem terribly worried.

☺ **Devil's Postpile National Monument,** with an intriguing collection of basaltic columns, is at the end of a steep and twisting road beyond the ski area. Not to worry if you're driving an RV or pulling a trailer. Rangers, concerned about traffic jams, offer a summer shuttle every few minutes from the Mammoth Ski Area parking lot to a trailhead. It operates between 7:30 a.m. and 5:30 p.m. From there, a half-mile trail takes you to the formations. It's worth the hike to bear witness to these octagons, hexagons and lesser-sided columns reaching hundreds of feet up a cliff face. Some have tumbled to its base, like a poorly constructed Greco-Roman temple. During late spring and fall, one can drive closer to the trailhead. In winter, the whole thing is closed. For information, call: (619) 934-2289.

The Postpile also provides gateway to the awesome reaches of the **Ansel Adams Wilderness,** dominated by the **Minarets,** a volcanic ridge fronting some of the Sierra's highest peaks. Backpackers find an inviting string of lakes, high meadows and tumbled granite hideouts.

Mammoth Lakes

Population: 4,800   **Elevation: 7,860 feet**

If you're a Southern Californian, you have reason to like this alpine-cum-jetset village. Unlike hamlets in mountains around the Los Angeles basin, Mammoth offers guaranteed relief from smog and crowds. With no historic nor cultural lures, it's not a place we'd drive a great distance to see.

Of course, it does occupy a nice wooded setting below a striking amphitheater of granite spires. And there's certainly nothing *wrong* with having veal *cordon bleau* and bottle of suitable Zinfandel after a day's hiking.

The largest community on the eastern slope, Mammoth Lakes is comprised mostly of condos, cafes and ski shops. During winter, it becomes Spandex City as skiers crowd the slopes above and the bars and restaurants below. For a quick pass through town, follow State Highway 203 (Minaret Road) downhill from Devil's Postpile and the ski slopes, then turn left onto Main Street at a traffic signal. The route passes through the strung out business district and shortly hits Highway 395.

Stop at the extremely well-stocked **Visitor Information Center,** open daily 8 to 6 (Fridays until 9). It's on Main Street, recessed into a shopping center on the right, and it may be a bit hard to spot. If you see the Polo-Ralph Lauren Factory Store, you've missed it. About half a mile beyond, also on the right, is the regional visitor center of **Inyo National Forest.**

ACTIVITIES

Skiing ● **Downhill:** Mammoth Mountain Ski Resort, P.O. Box 24, Mammoth Lakes, CA 93546; (619) 934-2571. **Cross-country:** Tamarack Ski Center, Tamarack Lodge, P.O. Box 69, Mammoth Lakes, CA 93546; (619) 934-2442 and Sierra Meadows Ski Touring Center, P.O. Box 2008; Mammoth Lakes, CA 93546; (619) 934-6161.

Bobsledding ● Sledz, (619) 934-7533.

Dog sledding ● Dog Sled Adventures, (619) 934-6270; Sierra Meadows, (619) 934-6161; Mammoth Adventure Connection, (619) 934-0606.

Gondola ride ● Daily in winter and summer 9 to 4; hours may be shorter in spring and fall; (619) 934-2571. Adults $8, kids $4; included in skiers' lift tickets. The enclosed sky bucket takes riders from the ski area to 11,053 feet for an imposing Sierra view.

Hot air ballooning ● Balloon Works, (619) 872-2610; High Sierra Balloon Co., (619) 934-7188.

Rock climbing and mountaineering ● Mammoth Adventure Connection, (619) 934-0606.

Sleigh rides ● Sierra Meadows Ski Touring Center, (619) 934-6161.

Snowmobile rentals ● Center Street Rentals, (619) 934-4020; DJ's Snowmobile Adventures, (619) 935-4480; Mammoth Snowmobile Rental, (619) 934-9645.

WHERE TO DINE

Golden Dragon ● △△ $$ Ø
3499 Main St.; (619) 934-2118. Chinese; full bar service. Lunch Wednesday-Friday 11:30 to 2, dinner nightly from 5. MC/VISA, AMEX. Smoke-free place that's a curious mix of Chinese art and woodsy Western décor. The menu is versatile, ranging from mild Cantonese to lively Szechuan. Try the Phoenix chicken with shrimp, walnuts, snow peas, bamboo shoots, water chestnuts and black bean sauce.

La Sierra's ● △△△ $$
Upper Main St.; (619) 934-8083. Eclectic cantina; full bar service. Lunch weekends from 11:30, dinner nightly from 4:30. MC/VISA. Trendy place with plush Naugahyde booths, thick beam ceilings and wrought iron accents. The jumping-bean menu hops from Mexican to Italian to American. Garlic chicken is good, along with designer pizzas and tortilla-wrapped things. It's a popular local hangout with live entertainment and a dance floor.

Matterhorn Restaurant ● △△ $$
In Alpenhof Lodge at 680 Minaret Rd.; (619) 934-3369. Continental; wine and beer. Daily from 7 a.m. MC/VISA, AMEX. Swiss style restaurant suited to its alpine surroundings, with a menu to match. Look for a lot of veal dishes, plus filet of pork with cranberry sauce and champagne poached salmon.

Mountainside Grill ● △△ $$
Opposite Mammoth Mountain Lodge; (619) 934-0601. American; full bar service. Daily 7 a.m. to 9:30 p.m. MC/VISA, AMEX. Very nice chalet style restaurant at the ski area with views of the surrounding peaks. California nouveau fare, plus fresh seafood and prime rib.

Whiskey Creek ● △△△ $$ Ø
Main and Minaret; (619) 934-2555. American-Latin; full bar service. Daily 5 to 10. Major credit cards. Attractive American country décor, with a lively

saloon adjacent, featuring entertainment and dancing. Menu ranges from California *nouveau* to Caribbean shrimp quesadillas.

WHERE TO SLEEP

Alpine Lodge ● △ $$$
6209 Minaret Rd. (P.O. Box 389), Mammoth Lakes, CA 93546; (800) 526-0007 or (619) 934-8526. Couples $66 to $89, singles $46 to $79, cabins with kitchens $140 to $155. MC/VISA. A 62-unit motel with TV, room phones; spa and sauna. Four housekeeping cabins.

Chalfant House Bed & Breakfast ● △△ $$$Ø
213 Academy St. (Warren Street), Bishop, CA 93514; (619) 872-1790. Couples $60 to $65, singles $50 to $55, kitchenettes $80 to $90, suites $65 to $75. Seven-unit inn decorated in antiques; antique store adjacent. All units with private baths; free breakfast and evening ice cream sundaes.

Econo Lodge Wildwood Inn ● △△ $$$ Ø
Main Street (P.O. Box 568) Mammoth Lakes, CA 93546; (800) 845-8764 or (619) 934-6855. Couples $49 to $99, singles $49 to $69, kitchenettes $84 to $99; rates include continental breakfast. Major credit cards. A 31-unit motel with TV movies and room phones; some microwaves and refrigerators. Pool, fish cleaning facility.

Kitzbuhel Lodge ● △ $
46 Berner Street at Minaret (P.O. Box 433), Mammoth Lakes, CA 93546; (619) 934-2352. Dorm facility from $15 to $20 per person. MC/VISA, AMEX. Chalet style dormitory catering to individuals and groups; community kitchens, spa; rec room with TV and fireplace.

Mammoth Mountain Inn ● △△△ $$$$
1 Minaret Road at the ski area (P.O. Box 353), Mammoth Lakes, CA 93546; (800) 228-4947 or (619) 934-2581. Couples from $80, singles from $75, condos $110 to $335. Major credit cards. Rustic-modern 214-room lodge at the ski slopes with TV, room phones; kitchens in condo units. Three spas, VCRs with video rentals. **Mountainside Grill** listed above; the **Yodeler** serves Bavarian style fare; 11 a.m. to 9 p.m.; dinners $9 to $21; full bar.

North Village Inn ● △△ $$$ Ø
103 Lake Mary Rd. (P.O. Box 1984), Mammoth Lakes, CA 93546; (800) 257-3781 or (619) 934-2525. Couples $49 to $69, singles $45 to $60, kitchenettes and suites $60 to $125; rates include continental breakfast. Major credit cards. A 20-unit motel near Minaret and Main; TV, room phones, refrigerators; pool and spa. Wooded setting with mountain views.

Ullr Lodge ● △ $
Highway 205 at Minaret (P.O. Box 53), Mammoth Lakes, CA 93546; (619) 934-2454. Couples $28 to $56, singles $15 to $56. MC/VISA. Basic budget accommodations ranging from dorms to individual rooms, some with TV; community kitchen, fireplace lounge and sauna.

WHERE TO CAMP

Scores of Forest Service campgrounds are in the mountains above and the Inyo ranger station visitor center can direct you to them.

Camp High Sierra ● *Lake Mary Road (a mile north of downtown), Mammoth Lakes, CA 93546; (619) 934-2368. RV and tent sites, $9 to $12.* Wooded sites, showers, rec hall and playground.

Mammoth Mountain RV Park ● *Highway 203 near town (P.O. Box 288), Mammoth Lakes, CA 93546; (619) 934-3822. RV and tent sites, $20 to $24. Reservations accepted; MC/VISA.* Wooded sites, showers, indoor pool and spa, coin laundry, mini-mart, cable TV. Near shops and restaurants.

As you continue southward, you might turn west opposite the **Mammoth-June Lakes Airport** and drive three miles up to **Convict Lake.** It sits behind a terminal moraine in a dramatic glacial-carved valley, rimmed by towering peaks. Below here, Highway 395 brushes the shoreline of **Lake Crowley,** a popular boating and fishing spot. And therein lies an irony. After Los Angeles drained Owens Lake, it created this blue pond—looking rather inviting in the brown desert—as a storage basin. Just beyond Crowley, swing westward briefly to check out a bit of history called **Tom's Place.** This roadhouse, trimmed with wood paneling and glassy-eyed game trophies, has been around since 1924. You can hang out with the good old boys at the bar or pig out on huge American style dinners for under $10.

South of here, the highway begins a steep, nine-mile tilt down Sherwin Grade into the **Owens Valley.** Before you pull out of your dive, you will have lost 2,860 feet. The flora changes from high desert chaparral to sage. The dusty pre-Mojave Desert look suggests that you've passed that invisible barrier from northern into southern California.

This narrow swatch of brown and gray desert is cradled rather dramatically between the walls of the Sierra Nevada and the White Mountains. Within this century, this was a green pastureland, until Bill Mulholland of the Los Angeles Department of Water and Power stole its water (see box).

Bishop

Population: 3,700   **Elevation: 4,147 feet**

If you measure a town by its setting, Bishop has no equal in California, and few in the rest of the country. The Sierra Nevada and the White Mountains, the state's two highest ranges, tower on either side. They look either threatening or protective, depending on your state of mind. If I lived here, I'd spend much of my time watching sunrises and sunsets. On sunny days—and most of them are—shadows, silhouettes and alpenglow take turns dancing on this mountain range and then that one.

The craggy face on the western side belongs to Kings Canyon National Park. Although no road crosses this wildest part of the Sierra Nevada, State Highway 168 leads high into the ramparts, providing fishing access and trailheads for hikers and packers. Several small resorts and pack outfits are tucked into these forest-clad ribs of granite.

Bishop looks surprisingly prosperous despite its loss of water to Los Angeles. It appears to have no visible means of support. The downtown area is so neatly tended that it's lost much of its old Western character. Ranching contributes to the local economy, focused higher up in the alluvial foothills, where there is still ample water. Also, the town thrives as a major provisioning point for backpackers and pack trips into the mountains. Further, it's midway between Los Angeles and the party centers of Reno/Tahoe. An large number of motels confirm its popularity as a place to pause. All those Western wear and sporting goods stores confirm that this is Marlboro country.

The **White Mountains Visitor Center** of Inyo National Forest is on your left at 798 North Main as you enter town. It's a good place to get infor-

THE WAR OVER WATER

It has been established by environmentalists and anyone else with a lick of sense that California's largest city was built in the wrong place. Who ever heard of six million people trying to survive on a coastal desert? The only way Los Angeles *can* survive is to buy, beg and borrow water from elsewhere. In the case of the Owens Valley Water Wars, it went a step beyond and stole it.

This saga, which sounds like the plot of a B-movie, began early in this century. The Los Angeles Department of Water and Power, headed by self-educated Irish immigrant William Mulholland, began secretly buying up the valley's water rights. The buyers concealed their L.A. connection and duped residents into thinking they were planning a local reclamation project. The people howled in protest when the scheme was revealed, but they had already signed away much of their precious resource.

President Theodore Roosevelt sealed the their fate in 1906 when he proclaimed: "This water is more valuable to the people as a whole if (it is) used by the city (of Los Angeles) than by the people of the Owens Valley." When speculators rushed in to buy land in the path of the new aqueduct, he declared the entire strip a national forest (Mojave Desert and all) and granted Los Angeles a right of way. The channel was completed in 1913 and the draining of the Owens Valley began.

The valley begins to die

Mulholland's henchmen continued buying land and water rights, manipulating high country ranchers against lowland farmers to divide the communities. As water tables fell, wells went dry and the valley's lush fruit orchards and farmlands withered and died. Owens Lake, no longer receiving runoff from the Owens River, became an alkaline dust bowl.

Locals fought back, first with words and then with dynamite. Night riders began blasting holes in the canal. Mulholland sent gun-toting sentries and threatened to call in the National Guard. An unexpected twist knocked the wind out of the resistance. Banking brothers Wilfred and Mark Watterson, leaders of the rebellion, were convicted of embezzling $2 million from their own bank to cover bad investments. They were packed off to San Quentin, and the resistance movement died a short time later.

Los Angeles still wasn't satisfied. In 1941, the aqueduct was extended northward to capture water from streams flowing into Mono Lake. That briny pond, a precious resource for migrating waterfowl, seemed doomed to join the fate of Owens Lake. The conflict over water diversion continues, and the locals have won a few rounds in court. Los Angeles has been ordered to cut back on its diversion. Hopefully, the level of Mono Lake has been stabilized.

Although Mulholland fulfilled his promise to "turn Inyo County dry," he met disaster on another front. His St. Francis Dam in Southern California, built to store Owens Valley water, burst in 1927, just two years after it was completed. A 125-foot wall of water rushed down the dry Santa Clara river bed, killing more than 400 people and destroying 600 homes. It was—and remains—the worst disaster in California's history.

The water chief had personally inspected the dam a few hours before and determined that a leak at one side posed no immediate threat. At a coroner's hearing, he was cleared of any wrongdoing, but the incident ruined his reputation and broke his health. "If there is any responsibility here, it is mine alone," he said at the inquest. "I envy the dead."

He resigned his office a few months later and died in 1935. Upon receiving word of his death, workers building the canal for L.A.'s next great water grab—the Colorado River—stopped to observe a moment of silence.

mation on the bristlecone pines; (619) 873-4207. A bit beyond, also on the left, is the **Bishop Chamber of Commerce** at 690 N. Main, in an A-frame in the city park

In a land hungry for good museums, Bishop has a couple of worthies. The first is reached by heading east out Highway 6 from the north edge of town. To find the second, continue into town, turn right onto Line Street (Highway 168) and follow it about two miles east.

☺ *Laws Railroad Museum* • *P.O. Box 363, Bishop; (619) 873-5050. Daily 10 to 4; donations accepted.* Five miles west of Bishop, Laws was a busy railroad center when the narrow gauge *Slim Princess* traveled between Nevada and California. It died during the 1930s water struggle, and is now preserved as a fine outdoor museum. Stroll through old railroad cars and poke into a general store, medical office and other weathered storefronts along a boardwalk.

☺ *Paiute-Shoshone Indian Cultural Center* • *2300 W. Line St., Bishop; (619) 873-4478. Weekdays 9 to 5, weekends 10 to 4; donations appreciated; gift shop accepts MC/VISA.* Bishop is surrounded by Native American lands and this fine cultural center portrays their past and present arts, crafts and lifestyles. A *toni* (tule shelter) out front speaks of their yesterdays and fine jewelry and other crafts in the gift shop talk of the present.

☺ A third Bishop attraction, certainly worthy of a grin, is the **Erik Schat's Bakkery** downtown. It's home of sheepherders' bread and uncountable other bakery goodies and specialty foods. Run by the third generation of Schats, it brims with Dutch, Scandinavian and American pastries and truffles. It also functions as a small cafe (see below) and gift shop selling Delft porcelains and other imported giftwares.

WHERE TO DINE

Amigo's • ΔΔ $
285 N. Main St.; (619) 872-2189. Mexican; wine and beer. Monday-Saturday 11 to 9, closed Sunday. MC/VISA. Simple, yet ingeniously decorated family cafe with *serape* table trim and *sombreros* on wood paneled walls. It serves typical Mexican fare, plus interesting entrées such as crab Vallarta, topped with white wine sauce and served in a tortilla. The *pico de gallo* (beak of the rooster) salsa is great.

Barbecue Bill's • ΔΔ $$
187 Main St.; (619) 872-5535. American; wine and beer. Daily 11 to 9. MC/VISA, AMEX. Nicely done country style barbecue cafe trimmed with farm implements and other rural artifacts. The barbecue sauce aroma will lure you to the walk-up counter, where you can pick up corned beef, ribs, chicken, prime ribs or a combination thereof, and assorted sandwiches.

Eric Schat's Bakery • ΔΔ $
Main Street; (619) 873-7156. Dutch-Swedish-American; no alcohol. Bakery open at 7, sandwich bar at 10. MC/VISA ($15 minimum). Local institution since 1907. The small cafe area serves breakfast pancakes and eggs, sandwiches and other light fare, plus assorted bakery goods.

Whiskey Creek • ΔΔΔ $$
524 North Main St.; (619) 873-7174. American, full bar service. Daily 7 to 9, Friday-Saturday to 10. MC/VISA. Very appealing early American style restaurant with maple furniture, folk artifacts and copper accents. The menu is

mostly American, with some spicy touches like Caribbean shrimp and chicken *caliente*. A saloon and folk craft gift shop are part of this complex.

WHERE TO SLEEP

Best Western Holiday Spa Lodge ● △△△ $$$ Ø
1025 N. Main St., Bishop, CA 93514; (800) 576-3543 or (619) 873-3543. Couples $60 to $75, singles $54 to $64, suites $82. Major credit cards. Attractive 89-room motel with TV movies, room phones and refrigerators; some microwaves. Pool, spa, coin laundry and fish cleaning area.

Bishop El Rancho Motel ● △△ $$
274 Lagoon St. (at Main Street), Bishop, CA 93514; (619) 872-9251. Couples $38 to $42, singles $36 to $38, kitchenettes $8 additional. MC/VISA. A 16-unit motel with TV; some refrigerators; fish cleaning area.

Bishop Days Inn ● △△ $$$ Ø
724 Westline St., Bishop, CA 93414; (800) 325-2525 or (619) 872-1095. Couples and singles $55 to $70. Major credit cards. New 34-unit motel with TV-VCRs, room phones and refrigerators; spa.

Bishop Elms Motel ● △ $$
233 E. Elm St. (half block off Main), Bishop, CA 93514; (800) 848-9226 or (619) 873-8118. Couples $37 to $49, singles $34 to $39. A 19-unit motel with TV; fish cleaning area; near park and tennis courts.

WHERE TO CAMP

Brown's Schober Lane Campground ● *Highway 395 at Schober Lane, Route 1, Bishop, CA 93514; (619) 873-8522. RV and tent sites, $10 to $13. Reservations accepted; MC/VISA.* Interesting frontier town façade with mini-mart, cafe, playground and showers. Shaded sites with views of the Sierra.

Habeggar's Resort & RV Park ● *South Lake Road (Route 1, Mountain View Estates), Bishop, CA 93514; (619) 873-4483. RV and tent sites, $15 to $21; rental trailers $40 to $52. Reservations accepted; MC/VISA.* Alpine setting on Bishop Creek; 15 miles west on Highway 168, then two miles south on South Lake Road. Showers, coin laundry, mini-mart, cafe and fishing.

Highlands RV Park ● *2275 N. Sierra Hwy., Bishop, CA 93514; (619) 873-7616. RV sites, $17. MC/VISA.* Some pull-throughs and shaded sites; showers, coin laundry and rec room. Two miles north on U.S. 395.

BIG PINE TO LONE PINE & BEYOND

The mountain patriarchs become increasingly craggy as you continue south from Bishop. Wrinkled and brown, they spill directly to the desert floor with nothing to break their fall but a gentle alluvial plain. You're staring up at the ramparts of Sequoia and Kings Canyon national parks.

Big Pine, with 1,500 folks sitting at 4,000 feet, comes and goes quickly. This small provisioning center offers no cause to pause unless you're hungry, sleepy or low on gas. You just might want to take a break here, for it's the gateway to the planet's oldest living forest.

Bristlecone country

☺ Those much-adored botanic dwarfs, the **bristlecone pines** of the White Mountains, can be reached via State Highway 168 northeast of here. Before heading out, top off your tank, check your radiator coolant and pack a lunch and water, for it's a long, steep drive. Follow Route 168 about 13 miles, then turn north on White Mountain Road, just below Westgard Pass. As you climb toward the 'cones, you pass **Grandview Campground** at 8,500 feet, and you might consider overnighting here. It's free, with pit toilets and no water.

At 10,100-foot **Schulman Grove** on the edge of the bristlecone preserve, you can pick up material on the pines at a seasonal ranger station, and perhaps join a ranger-led outing. The short Alpha Trail leads to the nearest grove and a 4.5 mile hike through this thin air delivers you to the **Methusaleh Grove,** home to the most ancient of these ancients. To protect it from vandals, no sign identifies the 4,700-year-old Methusaleh Tree, the world's oldest living thing.

A rough 11-mile road takes you to the **Patriarch Grove,** a strangely desolate lunarscape at 11,000 feet. Lichen, tiny flowers, scattered bristlecones and passing hawks are all that prevail at this altitude. You're on one of the highest roads in California and if you insist on going higher, a seven-mile hiking trail takes you to the top of **White Mountain** at 14,246 feet.

This strange "Paradise Lost" of the bristlecones is a chilly and harsh land of icy winds, bared rock, poor limestone soil and little water. This is either barren and bleak or hauntingly beautiful, depending on your poetic state.

Summers are brief in these arctic heights, with a four to six week growing season. These hostile climes are suitable only for the hardiest of creatures. And therein lies the success of this remarkable tree. Because the soil is poor and water is scarce, few other plants are able to compete with the hearty bristlecone. These gnarled bonsai crouch low to the ground, spaced far apart to share what little water is available and to avoid the spread of fire. Resin-rich wood discourages insects and the outer shell of these trees is dead wood, which resists rot and bug intrusion. Although bristlecones are common throughout the West, this specific genus, *Pinus longaeva*, is the only one to attain such an amazing age.

RV advisory: Although the White Mountain Road to Schulman Grove is paved, it's very steep and winding and not recommended for large RVs or trailer rigs. The unpaved road to Patriarch Grove is *definitely* not advised for large RV/trailer rigs. You may have second thoughts about taking the family sedan to Patriarch as well; inquire at Schulman about the road's condition.

Below Big Pine on U.S. 395, tumbled lava flows add to the drama of the setting. This may be the most imposing Sierra views yet. If you look carefully, you'll recognize some of the snow patches as the **Palisade Glaciers,** America's southernmost active ice floes.

☺ Watch on your right for a sign to **Mount Whitney Fish Hatchery,** just north of Independence. We normally don't go out of our way to visit a fingerling farm but this one's a classic. Constructed in 1916, the main structure is an ivy-entwined Normandy style building more resembling a monastery than a trout nursery. For a nickel, you can feed fish from a vending machine at a pond out front. A unmanned visitor center, open daily 8 to 5, has a few displays concerning fish hatching and the history of this facility.

Independence

Population 1,000   **Elevation: 3,925 feet**

Just beyond the hatchery, Independence is slightly smaller and a bit lower than Big Pine. Worth a peek is the 1927 California Mission style **Winnedumah Hotel** at 211 N. Edwards (Highway 395). It offers rooms and food (listed below) and a pleasing turn of the century interior with beam ceilings, polished woods and arched windows. Across the way, note the off-white federalist style **Inyo County Courthouse.**

Follow Center Street a block west for a gander at the 1871 white clapboard, steepled **Pioneer Methodist United Church.** Two more blocks will take you to the small **Eastern California Museum** in a cinder block building. It has a front yard full of farm equipment and some well-arranged historic exhibits inside. You'll also find a gift shop with a good selection of books on the area. Hours are Wednesday-Monday 10 to 4, closed Tuesday; donations appreciated.

The last cause for pause in Independence is the simple brown clapboard **Mary Austin home,** where the author of "Land of Little Rain" lived until her death in 1934. It's now privately occupied; a plaque marks its significance. To find the house, drive a block south from the Winnedumah Hotel on the highway, then turn west for a block on Market Street.

About four miles south of Independence, a pair of stone sentry stations mark one of the most disturbing episodes of American history. Two months after the Pearl Harbor attack, President Franklin D. Roosevelt signed Executive Order 9066, calling for the "relocation" of persons of Japanese ancestry to areas away from the war sensitive coastline. It amounted to arresting innocent people and placing them in remote concentration camps. Before this heartless, paranoid roundup was completed, more than 100,000 people had been pulled from their homes, farms and businesses.

Manzanar was the first of these relocation centers. Within a barbed wire enclosure, 10,000 people—most of them American citizens—lived in cold, leaky wood and tar paper shacks. Adding irony to insult, many of their sons and brothers were in the European theater, fighting the Axis powers.

Little is left to remind us of that unjust episode. The two sentry posts—whose pagoda roofs seem a cruel joke—stand just off the highway. A former auditorium, a large green structure, is off to the right in the distance. Designated a national historic site in 1992, Manzanar is not yet staffed and the sentry boxes are boarded up to curb vandalism. You can walk around this desolate patch of land—which the Japanese made briefly green with their small gardens—and look up at the contrasting beauty of the Sierra Nevada.

Lone Pine

Population: 2,060   **Elevation: 3,700 feet**

We're nearing the end of our journey south from Northern California. To the east is fascinating Death Valley and to the south is the vast expanse of the Mojave Desert, two major Southern California attractions.

Lone Pine is a busy provisioning center and jump-off point for treks into the Sierra Nevada and down to Death Valley National Monument. It's also the gateway for a popular act of masochism—climbing Mount Whitney. A highway reaches 13 miles up to **Whitney Portal**, trailhead for the hike. (See box on page 301.)

Even if you aren't planning this climb (which requires a permit), you'll enjoy the view and the nearness of the peaks from Whitney Portal. Trailheads will launch you on a variety of day hikes into the area, and you can angle for trout in a stocked pond. A small grocery peddles provisions and a campground provides a place to spend the night.

En route to Whitney Portal, follow signs along a dirt road to the **Ala-**

bama Hills. These tumbled granite columns, ledges and boulders have been the setting for more than 300 Western movies and TV shows. You can prowl where Roy Rogers, Ken Maynard, Tom Mix, Gene Autry, William "Hopalong Cassidy" Boyd and countless others shot it out with the guys in the black hats. Appropriately, the scenic drive through these hills is called Movie Road. In early October, Lone Pine stages a film festival, featuring movies shot here and inviting their stars to attend. When the fete was started in 1990, Roy Rogers showed up to dedicate a monument to the area's Hollywood role.

As you pass through Lone Pine, two information centers will steer you to the region's mountain and desert attractions. The **Whitney Ranger Station** is on the left at the southern edge of town, open weekdays 8 to 4:30. A couple of miles beyond, at the Highway 136 turnoff to Death Valley is the fine **Mount Whitney-Death Valley Interagency Visitor Center.** It's open Thursday-Monday 8 to 4:30; (619) 876-4252.

If you haven't yet spotted Mount Whitney among the jumbled peaks above, the interagency center guarantees you a sighting. Step into this well-stocked visitor's bureau and step on the red "X" on the floor. Arrows will point you to the noble crest. It appears lower than some of the other peaks because they're closer. If the visitor center is closed, an outside exhibit will help you find the famous mount.

As you head south from Lone Pine, look to your right for **Diaz Lake Recreation Area.** This Inyo County park offers a campground (see below), swimming area, boat launch, mini-golf and the **Tin Roof Restaurant.** It's rather scruffy, but it offers nice views of the small lake.

WHERE TO DINE
Lone Pine
Bonanza Family Restaurant ● Δ $

104 N. Main (at Mountain View); (619) 876-4768. American-Mexican, wine and beer. Daily 6 a.m. to 10 p.m. Major credit cards. Simple Western style cafe with a menu to match—broasted chicken, steaks, chops and a few Mexican entrées.

Mount Whitney Dining Room ● Δ $

227 S. Main St. (at Polk); (619) 876-5751. American; wine and beer. Daily 7 a.m. to 9 p.m. MC/VISA. Plain Jane restaurant with a vague cowboy look, noted for its hamburgers. Try the Alabama hills burger with mushrooms, Monterey jack and barbecue sauce. Other items include chicken fried steaks, steak fried steaks and chicken in a basket.

Sierra Cantina ● Δ $

123 N. Main St.; (619) 876-5740. Mexican; wine and beer. Daily 11:30 to 8. No credit cards. Go for the food, not the décor, 'cause there isn't any. The all-you-can eat buffet is a good buy at $10. Try the spicy chili Colorado or build your own taco. Or, rabbit-out at the salad bar.

WHERE TO SLEEP
Independence
Winnedumah Hotel ● △ $$

211 N. Edwards (P.O. Box 147), Independence, CA 93526; (619) 878-2040. Couples $42, including continental breakfast. MC/VISA. Refurbished 1927 roadhouse with a California-Spanish look to the parlor and dining

WHITNEY: THE MASOCHISM MARATHON

What's this fascination for climbing Mount Whitney? It's not a daring ascent up a granite spire, but a tough 10.7-mile trudge up a trail busy with fellow hikers. You aren't going where few have gone before, to plant a triumphant flag. You're getting in line, getting blisters and then wondering if it was worth all the pain and perspiration.

Certainly, the scenery is awesome, although this is hardly a wilderness escape. And hikers say the views are better from other peaks in the Sierra. It's even difficult to spot the darn thing, since Whitney is surrounded by other mountains of similar height.

Mount Whitney's lure lies in its statistic. At 14,496 feet, it's the highest American peak south of Alaska and therefore a prize. And that prize is attainable by thee and me. It doesn't necessarily take pitons and ice axes (except when snow is still on the route in early summer). It requires only an investment in backpacking, blisters and a lot of heavy breathing.

To keep the Mount Whitney trail from resembling the Venice Beach boardwalk, access is limited to 50 overnight hikers a day. Still, the route can be crowded, since many hikers come in from other trails. Also, many hearty souls attempt the round trip in a single day, which doesn't require an overnight permit. That, incidentally, is a tough workout, unless you've gotten in shape for a *Rambo* movie.

So many people want to make this climb that a lottery system is necessary. Obtain an application by contacting: Mount Whitney Ranger District, Inyo National Forest, P.O. Box 8, Lone Pine, CA 93545; (619) 876-6200. If you're in the neighborhood, you can pick up forms at the ranger station at the southern edge of town, or the Mount Whitney-Death Valley Interagency Visitor Center, south of town at the junction of State Highway 136. The form is good for other Whitney wilderness trails as well.

Applications must be postmarked between March 1 and May 22, and permits are drawn by lottery from same-day postmarks. Your odds are best if you have your request postmarked on March 1, *and* ask for midweek days, preferably after Labor Day Weekend. (The permit period is May 22 through October 15, but you generally have to deal with snow on the trail until mid-July.) If you try to fudge and send your request before March 1, it'll be returned unopened. Also, duplicate requests must not be sent.

If you do get a slot in the Whitney lottery, you'll find camping, water and a small grocery at Whitney Portal, 13 miles above Lone Pine, at 8,300 feet. Half the campsites are available for reservation through Mistix at (800) 283-CAMP. The remainder are first-come, first served. The hike is so popular that even parking is scarce at the trailhead. The Lone Pine Chamber of Commerce sometimes runs a shuttle from town; call (619) 876-4444.

It's possible—but not likely—that you can pick up a no-show permit at the ranger station on the day you want to hike. Folks who don't claim their passes by 8 a.m. lose them. However, according to Inyo National Forest's Wilderness Travel bulletin, "competition for those openings is intense."As a final resort, you can do your Rambo thing and try to make it up and back in a single day. But don't count on it. One steep section has 100 switchbacks.

room; simply furnished, comfortable rooms. Workout room, library and lobby TV. **Dining Room** serves lunch and dinner in summer; wine & beer.

Lone Pine

Best Western Frontier Motel ● ⌂ *$$$ Ø*

1008 S. Main St., Lone Pine, CA 93545; (800) 528-1234 or (619) 876-5571. Couples $46 to $75, singles $42 to $75. Major credit cards. Well-kept

73-unit motel with TV movies, room phones; some refrigerators. Pool, coin laundry, lawn picnic area.

Dow Villa Motel • ⌂⌂ **$$$** Ø
310 S. Main St. (P.O. Box 205), Lone Pine, CA 93545; (800) 824-9317 or (619) 876-5521. Couples and singles $54 to $60, suites from $60. Major credit cards. Attractrive motel with TV, refrigerators; pool, spa, tanning bed.

Lone Pine Budget Inn • ⌂ **$$**
138 Willow St. (P.O. Box 1013), Lone Pine, CA 93545; (619) 876-5655 or (619) 876-5738. Couples $42 to $48, singles $38. MC/VISA, AMEX. Small motel a block off the highway with TV movies, room phones; some spa tubs.

Mount Whitney Motel • ⌂ **$$$**
305 N. Main St. (P.O. Box 722), Lone Pine, CA 93545; (800) 845-2362 or (619) 876-5534. Couples $49 to $59, singles $39 to $59. MC/VISA. Simple units with TV movies and room phones; some kitchens; swimming pool.

The Portal Motel • ⌂ **$$$** Ø
Highway 395 (P.O. Box 97), Lone Pine, CA 93454; (619) 876-5930. Couples and singles $49 to $60. Major credit cards. A 17-unit motel with TV, room phones, refrigerators; some microwaves.

WHERE TO CAMP

Boulder Creek • 2550 S. Highway 395 (two miles south), Lone Pine, CA 93545; (619) 876-4243. RV sites, $20. Reservations accepted. New park with showers, pool, spa, coin laundry, rec room, clubhouse with kitchen and cable TV.

Diaz Lake • *Highway 395 (two miles south), Lone Pine, CA 93545; (619) 876-5656. RV and tent sites, $7, no hookups.* Inyo County park with some spots over the lake; cold showers, swimming, boating, fishing, mini-golf, restaurant (Tin Roof, listed above).

Whitney Portal • *C/o Mount Whitney Ranger District, Inyo National Forest, P.O. Box 8, Lone Pine, CA 93545; (619) 876-5542. RV and tent sites, $10; Reservations via Mistix, (800) 444-PARK.* Wooded sites near trailhead to Mount Whitney wilderness; picnic tables and barbecues; mini-mart, nature trails, fishing.

Below Lone Pine, you'll see the great white alkaline dust bowl that once was **Owens Lake,** drained dry so Los Angelenos could have ice cubes in their gin tonics. Farther along, a short and bumpy road leads you east to **Cottonwood Charcoal Kilns.** Looking like something out of a set for Yoda's scene in *Star Wars,* these conical adobe brick structures produced charcoal for smelters in nearby mining areas.

Pushing along, you begin to see Joshua trees and creosote bush, signaling the transition from Owens Valley to the Mojave Desert. You might glance to your right and stare in surprise. What happened to the mountains? The Sierra Nevada stages one last grand showing at Lone Pine and then diminishes rapidly. At some point south of here, known only to geographers and cartographers, your longtime pinnacle companions blend into the lower-elevation **Tehachapi Mountains.**

If you want to make a round trip out of this, take Highway 178 west over **Walker Pass** through the shrinking lower Sierra and drop down into **Kern River Valley.** It's a rather scenic route past rock-strewn hills and Joshua forests. On the other side, as you reach the **Lake Isabella** wetlands, follow

Mount Whitney is difficult to spot because of lower, closer foreground peaks. It's just under the flag in this view from Lone Pine's Interagency Visitor Center.

— Betty Woo Martin

signs north to **Kernville,** along the lake's upper shoreline.

Like Lone Pine's Alabama Hills, Kern Valley was popular with movie companies. At the **Kern Valley Museum and Gift Shop** (Big Blue and Whitney roads), exhibits focus on the films of Roy, Gene, Joel, Hoppy, Hoot, the Duke and others, along with stuff on local history. It's open Thursday-Sunday 10 to 4. Free; donations appreciated; (619) 379-5895. The town, obviously cherishing its cowboy movie heritage, is all done up in false front stores housing boutiques, antique shops and cafes.

From Kernville, Highway 178 takes you to Bakersfield and the San Joaquin Valley. Unless you like getting dizzy, don't be tempted to take Highway 155 from **Wofford Heights** into the valley. You'll be subjected to 30 miles of corkscrew turns as you crawl up to wooded **Greenhorn Summit** (6,102 feet) and down the other side.

To learn more about Kern Valley, call the Kernville chamber of commerce at (619) 376-2629 or the Lake Isabella chamber at (619) 379-5236.

EASTERN SIERRA BACKPACKING

For a list of horse packing outfits in Bridgeport, June Lake, Mammoth, Bishop, Big Pine and Independence, contact: **Eastern High Sierra Packers Association,** 690 Main St., Bishop, CA 93514, (619) 873-8405.

EASTERN SIERRA ANNUAL EVENTS

Snowmobile ride to Bodie from Mammoth Lakes, in February; (800) 367-6572 or (619) 934-2712.

Mule Days, Memorial Day weekend in Bishop; (619) 873-8405.

Old West Days, Fourth of July weekend at Sierra Meadows Ranch near Mammoth; (619) 934-6161.

Mammoth Lakes Arts & Crafts Show, Fourth of July weekend in Mammoth Lakes; (619) 872-1554.

Tri-County Fair, mid-July in Bishop; (619) 873-8405.

Sierra Summer Music Festival, July and August in Mammoth Lakes; (800) 367-6572 or (619) 934-2712.

Bishop Homecoming and Wild West Rodeo, Labor Day weekend; (619) 873-8405.

Labor Day Arts and Crafts Festival, Labor Day weekend in Mammoth Lakes; (619) 873-7242.

Lone Pine Film Festival, early October in Lone Pine, featuring films shot in the adjacent Alabama Hills; (619) 876-4314.

YOSEMITE NATIONAL PARK

No written word, no paintbrush, not even an Ansel Adams photograph can quite capture the drama. Only by standing at Glacier Point or Inspiration Point or perhaps the top of Yosemite Falls will you know that this is the grandest temple in California. Ralph Waldo Emerson may have expressed it best when he cast aside adjectives and said it was the "only spot that came up to the brag."

Embracing the best of the Sierra Nevada, Yosemite National Park is a wilderness trilogy: the Tuolumne high country, the vertical-walled Yosemite Valley and primeval stands of giant sequoias. It is a grand expanse that cannot be discovered in a day, a year or—as John Muir and Ansel Adams realized—in a lifetime.

Of course, you can't devote your life to this place as Muir and Adams did, and few of you share our privilege of having Yosemite in your back yard. We will thus suggest how to best invest what little time you spend there.

Our favorite part of the park is Tuolumne Meadows, crossed east to west by Highway 120. Since it is high above the busy Yosemite Valley floor, it's considerably less crowded. It offers striking scenery, tree-shrouded campgrounds accented by granite boulders, a lake or two and great hiking trails. We won't insist that the vistas here rival those of the Yosemite Valley. However, the bold and broken granite outcroppings and glacier-polished massifs up here are nothing short of spectacular.

No matter which way you approach, Yosemite is a grand granite cathedral. This is where John Muir fell in love with the wilderness, where he decided to get serious about conservation. It could be said that America's environmental movement started here—with Muir's ushering outdoor conscious Teddy Roosevelt into the Yosemite Valley, and his later creation of the Sierra Club, named for the peaks that rise above it. Yosemite Valley and portions of the Wawona area were set aside as a state park in 1864, then, at Muir's urging, Yosemite became one of the first national parks in 1890.

How ironic that this early wilderness sanctuary is now one of the most heavily impacted parks in America. During a recent summer, four-hour traffic jams were recorded on the valley floor. If you must come in summer, make reservations far in advance for lodgings or campsites.

The basics

When to come: Spring and fall are best, when all the park roads are still open and it's possible to get a campsite without advance reservations. Winter is beautiful in Yosemite, although trails and high country roads are closed. Highways into Yosemite Valley and up to Badger Pass are kept open all year, although they can be closed by storms, and they may be subject to chain controls.

Park entry is $5 per vehicle; free with a Golden Eagle, Golden Age or Golden Access pass. There are three westside entrances: through Groveland on Highway 120 (Big Oak Flat), from Mariposa through El Portal on Highway 140 (Arch Rock), and Highway 41 (Fish Camp) from the south. Eastern access, closed in winter, is through the Tioga Pass gate on Route 140.

Park information: Call (209) 372-0200 for specifics on roads, recreational activities, weather, and a campground update. Reservations can't be made through this number. The address for general information (not lodgings) is: Superintendent, P.O. Box 577, Yosemite National Park, CA 95389.

Road information: For approaches to Yosemite, call the CalTrans road information number, (800) 427-ROAD, and (209) 372-0200 for conditions within the park.

Campground reservations, may be made up to eight weeks in advance through Mistix, (800) 365-CAMP, or write: P.O. Box 85705, San Diego, CA 92138-5705. Without reservations, campsites in the valley are a *very* tough ticket in summer and most weekends in the spring and fall. Your best chances are weekdays or Sunday afternoons. Signs posted at the gates advise you of campsite openings.

Lodgings: As we went to press, the lodging number was (209) 252-4848, and reservations could be made up to a year in advance. However, that may be changed. On October 1, 1993, longtime concessionaire Yosemite Park and Curry Company was to turn the reins over to a new operator, owned by the Delaware North Company of Buffalo, New York. If the number changes, we assume that a recording will tell you so. If not, call (209) 555-1212 and ask for the Yosemite National Park lodging reservation number. Yosemite offers a wide range of facilities, from rudimentary tent cabins to the rustically refined Ahwahnee Hotel (see "Where to sleep" below).

Winter sports: Badger Pass Ski Area (209-372-1330) is a family winter sports area with beginners and intermediate runs set against striking scenery. It offers lessons and equipment rentals, plus Snow-Cat and snowshoe tours. Child care is available for toddlers. **Cross country skiing** is exceptional here, with 90 miles of trails beneath all that scenery. The Yosemite Cross-Country Ski School at Badger offers lessons, rentals and tours. Outdoor **ice skating** is available at Curry Village in the valley.

Backcountry activities: Wilderness permits are required for all overnight hiking and high country camping in the park. They must be obtained in person, although you can call (209) 372-0307 for information. There's a bit of potluck here, since access is restricted to avoid too much strain on the environment. Half of the allotted passes are reserved by mail from the first of March to the end of May, and the remainder are handed out on a first-come basis at the park, up to one day in advance of your trip.

RV advisory: The spiral up Tioga Pass is a difficult climb, but it can be managed by a large RV. The same is true of other park portals. Approaching Groveland on Highway 120, take the left side of Priest Grade; it's better engineered and lest twisting than Old Priest Grade. The two travel up opposite sides of a canyon. Within the park, most roads also are negotiable, although large RVs and trailers aren't allowed on the climb to Tuolumne Grove on Big Oak Flat Road.

Driving Yosemite

Roads cover only a tiny fraction of Yosemite's 1,189 square miles, yet they offer some of the park's most stunning vistas. An excellent milepost directory, the *Yosemite Road Guide,* is available at most park gift shops and visitor centers. Maps and descriptions in the guide are keyed to roadside markers.

Although we prefer the Tioga pass entrance, we'll guide you up Highway 120, since most travelers approach from the west. After surviving the wicked spiral up Priest Grade, take pause to explore the noble old brick and stone buildings of **Big Oak Flat** and **Groveland,** two early mining camps. Particularly appealing is the **Iron Door Saloon** in Groveland, one of the oldest drinking parlors in the West.

After entering the park through the **Big Oak Flat** gate, the highway passes the entrance to **Tuolumne Grove,** with an imposing stand of big trees. Just beyond, fork to the right onto Tioga Road, leading to Tuolumne Meadows. A long, winding climb carries you into a stunning high country of granite shaped into domes, tabular layers and concentric strata. Alpine meadows are alive with July flowers, and cobalt lakes shimmer in the crisp, thin air. Two campgrounds along Tioga Road, **White Wolf** and **Porcupine Flat** sometimes have mid-week vacancies in summer. Just beyond Porcupine, you can catch a view across precipitous **Tenaya Canyon** to far away **Half Dome,** that incredible monolith whose face was sheared away by glacial movement.

☺ After passing **Tenaya Lake,** you enter the lush green expanse of **Tuolumne Meadows,** one of the few relatively flat areas within the park. Cupped by granite domes and peaks, this 8,600-foot basin is one of the largest high meadows in America. At the Tuolumne Meadows Visitor Center, you can pick up hiking maps, the above mentioned road guide and assorted natural history publications. You'll find a campground, service station and cafè here as well. For a brief and particularly dramatic hike, follow a trail from the parking area up **Lembert Dome**. Your reward for a short, steep climb will be incredible views of this granite wilderness. For a longer and equally imposing hike, follow a trail eight miles down the Tuolumne River to **Waterwheel Falls.**

The **Tioga Pass** entrance station is a few miles beyond Tuolumne Meadows. At 9,941 feet, it's the highest road pass in the state. Several national forest campgrounds are along the highway just below the pass, possible alternatives if you fail to find space in the park.

Reverse your route, drop down from the high country and turn east onto Big Oak Flat Road, headed into Yosemite Valley. The road soon becomes a cliff hanger, notched from the lip of the **Merced River Canyon** and tunneled through a granite wall. Shortly after you merge with the road from Arch Rock, the curtain of granite parts:

The first view of this convulsion-rent valley, with its perpendicular mountain cliffs, deep gorges, and awful chasms, spread out before us like a mysterious scroll, took away the power of thinking...

Your initial impression of Yosemite Valley may not be as loquacious as that of James Hutchings. He was an early visitor who stayed to guide others. However, you certainly will be awe-struck by the perpendicular face of **El Capitan,** the misty shrouds of **Yosemite Falls** and **Bridalveil Fall,** and the signature profile of **Half Dome.** Incidentally, the two waterfalls often shrink to a trickle by midsummer.

From this vista point, simply called **Valley View,** the cliff-clinging highway coils down to the valley floor to join the Merced River. Here, wilderness surrenders suddenly to the loving chaos of nearly four million annual visitors. At some point, you should park your rig and explore the valley by foot or by free trams. They appear every few minutes to run endless loops past the valley's facilities.

Scattered across the valley floor are campgrounds, a riding stable, medical clinic and dental office, assorted lodgings, a nature center, supermarket, souvenir shops, pizza parlor, hamburger joints, post office, bank, beauty parlor, dog kennel, laundry, service station and repair garage, several saloons, a church and a brig. We have seen good sized towns not so well equipped.

Most of this commercial bounty is gathered in **Yosemite Village,** about mid-point in the valley. To help sort through all of the services, programs, activities, ranger talks and walks, stop at the **Visitor Center** and pick up a free copy of *Yosemite Guide,* the park's information-packed newspaper. The center, on the northern rim of the village, has a fine museum with graphics, videos and exhibits to help you understand the grandeur of the park. Out back is a simulate Miwok village, where Native Americans sometimes conduct living history programs. The **Backcountry office,** a required stop for overnighting in the wilderness, is nearby.

☺ You can escape some of the press of humanity with hikes out of the valley. The zig-zag climb to the top of **Yosemite Falls,** which starts north of Yosemite Lodge, is tough, but the straight-down valley view is rewarding. Our favorite is the six-mile round trip up the **Giant Stairway** to the glossy granite heights of **Vernal Fall** and **Nevada Fall.** The trailhead is at the **Happy Isles Nature Center** at the valley's east end.

Yosemite Valley is a wonderful place to go biking—peddling along while its grand dimensions swim past. Roads that are closed to vehicular traffic make fine bike routes, and there are several miles of biking/walking paths as well. Bicycle rentals are available through park concessionaires; check at Curry Village and Yosemite Lodge.

After you've done the valley, drive west along the meandering Merced River and branch to the left past Bridalveil Fall, following signs to Badger Pass and Glacier Point. This puts you on Wawona Road, headed toward the south entrance. Along the way, valley viewpoints will have you expending more film and adjectives. **Tunnel Viewpoint** is just east of the Wawona road tunnel, and the famous **Inspiration Point** is a mile or so beyond. At **Chinquapin,** take a hard left up Glacier Point Road. You'll pass **Badger Pass** ski area. (In winter, Badger is as far as you can get.)

☺ The road levels out a bit at **Mono Meadow** before its final descent to **Glacier Point.** This high, narrow peninsula offers Yosemite's most stunning vistas. Half Dome seems close enough to touch. Yosemite Valley is beneath your feet, 3,200 feet straight down. Yosemite Falls and the great wall of the Sierra are opposite. Off to the east, two miles away yet filling your right ear with its thunder, is Nevada Fall.

For a vista-rich return to the valley, hike down the **Four-Mile Trail,** which is much more dramatic than its name. It's a moderate stroll, if you don't mind what backpackers call "exposure." How do you get back up to Glacier Point? In summer, tour buses run to this lofty rampart.

To complete your driving tour of Yosemite, follow Wawona Road south to **Wawona,** which preserves much of the park's human history. Wawona, thought to be an Indian word for "big tree," was the site of a roadhouse built in 1857. The **Pioneer Yosemite History Center** exhibits wagons that made the hard pull up to the park in the early days, and several old structures that were brought here from other parts of Yosemite. Nearby is the nobly rustic **Wawona Hotel,** built in 1875 and still in use. **Mariposa Grove,** with the largest gathering of big trees in the park, can be reached by car or free bus from Wawona. During summer, tram tours make the run from the parking lot into the upper grove, or you can hike the trails.

Just below Wawona, Highway 41 drops southward toward **Fresno.** It becomes a freeway on the outer edge of this San Joaquin Valley metropolis. Thus, without becoming entangled in Fresno traffic, you can take the State Highway 180 exit and follow us to Sequoia-Kings Canyon National Parks.

WHERE TO DINE AND RECLINE
Within the park

As mentioned above, some of these details—and possibly phone numbers—may change because of the new management company's takeover. For the moment, the reservations number for lodgings is (209) 252-4848. In addition to restaurants in the hotels, you'll find assorted snack shops and cafeterias around Yosemite Village and—good grief!—even a pizza hut.

☺ *The Ahwahnee* ● △△△△ *$$$$$* Ø
Yosemite Valley. Couples from $208, singles from $201, suites $409 to $446. Major credit cards. This magnificent structure near Yosemite Falls is to be seen even if you can't afford the rates. The epitome of national park lodges, this 1927 castle is a regal study in stone and timber, with a rustic mix of Native American and Art Deco. Stroll the Great Lounge with its massive fieldstone fireplace and lofty log ceiling. Have a drink at one of the western style lounges and plan dinner in the baronial dining room, with its awesome valley views. The **Dining room** serves from 7 to 4 and 5:30 to 10; dinners $30 to $35; full bar service. Dinner reservations are essential (209-372-1000) and lodging reservations should be made far in advance—up to a year for summer weekends.

Curry Village ● △ *to* △△ *$ to $$$* Ø
Yosemite Valley. Couples and singles $33 to $75.75. Major credit cards. The village offers a wide range of pillow places, from basic tent cabins (which may be removed under the new management) to slightly less basic cottages. Because of fire hazards, cooking isn't allowed in the tent cabins. Cottages have full baths and a few have phones. Rental bikes are available. **Dining facilities** include a cafeteria, Fast Food Bar and Pizza Deck.

☺ *Wawona Hotel* ● △△ *$$$* Ø
Wawona area. Couples and singles $64 to $86. Major credit cards. This fine old complex includes a pool, tennis court, nine-hole golf course and riding stable. Rooms are properly rustic and neatly maintained. The **Wawona Dining Room** serves breakfast from 7:30, a buffet lunch and dinner from 6 to 8; dinners $12 to $25; full bar service.

Yosemite Lodge ● △ *to* △△ *$$$ to $$$$* Ø
Yosemite Valley. Couples and singles $47.25 to $89.25. Major credit cards. A cut above Curry Village, the lodge offers cabins without baths and newer

motel style rooms with; many have room phones. The lodge has a swimming pool and rental bikes. **Dining facilities** include an attractive woodsy restaurant, coffee shop and cafeteria; meals from 7 a.m. to 9 p.m.; dinners $15 to $25; full bar service.

Outside the park
Highway 120 approach (northwest)
Groveland Hotel ● ⌂⌂ $$$$ ∅
18767 Main St. (P.O. Box 289), Groveland, CA 95321; (800) 273-3314 or (209) 962-4000. Couples and singles $75 to $95, suites $155; rates include continental breakfast. Major credit cards. A restored 17-room hotel furnished with European and American antiques. This wood and adobe structure is one of California's oldest inns, dating from 1849. **Restaurant** serves lunch, brunch and dinner; $20 to $25; wine and beer. About 20 miles from the Big Oak Flat entrance.

The Hotel Charlotte ● ⌂⌂ $$$
Highway 120 (P.O. Box 787), Groveland, CA 95321; (209) 962-6455. Couples $49 with share bath, $60 with private bath, singles $40 and $49, suites $92 to $103; rates include continental breakfast. MC/VISA, AMEX. Neat, simply furnished oldstyle rooms in a refurbished 1921 inn, with iron beds, lace curtains and print wallpaper. **Dining room** serves dinner nightly except Tuesday 5 to 9 and Sunday brunch 9 to 2; dinners $9 to $15; wine and beer. About 20 miles from the Big Oak Flat entrance.

Highway 140 approach (southwest)
Cedar Lodge ● ⌂⌂ $$$$
9966 Highway 140 (P.O. Box C), El Portal, CA 95318; (800) 321-5261 or (209) 379-2612. Couples and singles $68 to $115, apartments with kitchens $275 to $375. MC/VISA, AMEX. A 206-unit lodge with TV, room phones; most units with refrigerators, some with spa tubs. Two swimming pools; in attractive wooded setting, five miles from park entrance.

Highway 41 approach (south)
Karen's Bed & Breakfast Yosemite Inn ● ⌂⌂⌂ $$$$ ∅
1144 Railroad Ave. (P.O. Box 8), Fish Camp, CA 93623; (800) 346-1443 or (209) 683-4550. Couples $85, singles $80. Three units with private baths; full breakfast. No credit cards. Country style home in a wooded setting, a mile from the park entrance. "Contemporary country" furnishings in guest rooms; living room and sitting room with wood stove, TV with VCR and small library; covered porch and deck.

☺ *Marriott's Tenaya Lodge* ● ⌂⌂⌂⌂ $$$$$ ∅
1122 Highway 41 (P.O. Box 159), Fish Camp, CA 93623; (800) 635-5807 or (209) 683-6555. Couples and singles $119 to $215, suites $179 to $350. Major credit cards. Stylish new 242-unit lodge with Native American and alpine dècor. Rooms with TV, pay movies, room phones and most resort amenities. Wooded grounds, indoor and outdoor pool, spa, sauna and steam rooms, exercise room; rental bicycles, coin laundry, gift shops. **Dining room** and coffee shop serve 7 a.m. to 10 p.m.; dinners $15 to $22; full bar service. Two miles from park entrance.

Narrow Gauge Inn ● ⌂⌂⌂ $$$$ ∅
48571 Highway 41, Fish Camp, CA 93623; (209) 683-7720. Couples and singles $80 to $120. Major credit cards. Very attractive old country inn with

room TV, view balconies; small swimming pool and spa. Smoke-free **Dining room** serves 7:30 a.m. to 10:30 and 5:30 p.m. to 9; Sunday brunch 10:30 to 1; dinners $15 to $25; full bar service. Four miles from park entrance; Yosemite tours arranged. Adjacent to historic Yosemite Mountain-Sugar Pine Railroad, offering excursion train rides.

The Redwoods Guest Cottages ● ⌂⌂⌂ $$$$
Highway 41 at Chilhualna Falls Rd. (P.O. Box 2085), Wawona Station, CA 95389; (209) 375-6666. Couples and singles from $68, suites $255 to $416. MC/VISA. Lodgings range from studio cabins to privately owned homes—two to five bedrooms with fully furnished kitchens; most in wooded settings. Seven miles south of park entrance.

WHERE TO CAMP

All campsites in **Yosemite Valley** are on the Mistix reservation system year around. All sites at **Hodgdon Meadows** near the Big Oak Flat entrance station and at **Crane Flat,** eight miles into the park, and half those at **Tuolumne Meadows** are on the system from spring through fall. The number is (800) 365-CAMP and reservations are accepted up to eight weeks in advance. Any sites not taken may be reserved in person at the Campground Reservation Office in Yosemite Valley. Other campgrounds in the park are on a first-come, first-served basis. RV and tent sites are available at all campgrounds; most have flush potties but no hookups or showers.

Valley camping is available the year around, although some of the sites are closed in winter. Spaces in the four campgrounds, **Lower** and **Upper River, North Pines** and **Upper Pines** are close-packed. Of these, Upper Pines is the farthest from congestion, and it's near the trailhead to Nevada and Vernal falls. **Tuolumne Meadows** campground is less congested, although it's a 50-mile drive back to Yosemite Valley. **Hodgdon** is 25 miles away. Sites at **Wawona,** about 30 miles from the valley near the south entrance station, also go fast.

Outside the park
Highway 120 approach (northwest)
Big Oak Flat area ● Several campgrounds are near Big Oak Flat and Groveland in Stanislaus National Forest, ranging from $8 to free. For information, contact the Groveland Ranger District, P.O. Box 709, Groveland, CA 95321; (209) 962-7825.

Highway 140 approach (southwest)
El Portal area ● Several Sierra National Forest campgrounds are near the El Portal entrance to Yosemite, ranging from $8 to free. Contact the Mariposa Ranger District, Highway 140 at Highway 49 (P.O. Box 747), Mariposa, CA 95338; (209) 966-3638.

Indian Flat RV Park ● *Highway 140 (P.O. Box 356), El Portal, CA 95318; (209) 379-2339. RV sites, $13 to $18. Reservations accepted; MC/VISA.* Wooded sites six miles from park entrance; some pull-throughs; water and electric, cable TV, showers. On the Merced river; fishing and swimming.

KOA Yosemite-Mariposa ● *6323 Highway 140, Midpines, CA 95345; (209) 966-2201. RV and tent sites, $18 to $25. Reservations accepted; MC/VISA.* Shaded sites, some pull-throughs; showers, coin laundry, mini-mart, swimming pool, pond with boat rentals and fishing, playground, rec room and horseshoes. About 23 miles from park entrance.

Highway 41 approach (south)

Big Sandy Campground ● *Five miles east of Highway 41; turnoff is just outside park entrance station; (209) 683-4665. RV and tent sites, free.* National forest campsites with picnic tables and barbecues, no hookups, drinking water or showers.

Summerdale Campground ● *Highway 41 near park entrance station; (209) 683-4665. RV and tent sites, $8.* National forest campground with picnic tables and barbecues, pit potties, no showers or hookups. Swimming, fishing; mini-mart nearby.

SEQUOIA/KINGS CANYON NATIONAL PARKS

In the rush to Yosemite, tourist crowds often overlook this double dish of Sierran beauty just to the south. Larger than Yosemite and rivaling its grandeur, Sequoia and Kings Canyon national parks receive only a third as many visitors. Both Sequoia and Yosemite became national parks in the same year, 1890. However, the magic of Yosemite Valley apparently captured folks attention more than the majesty of Sequoia's big trees. Yosemite got the baronial lodges, the good press notices from John Muir and stunning photos of Ansel Adams.

Thus, Sequoia and Kings Canyon have never suffered the impact of the Yosemite Valley's commercialism. They offer an alternative to the more popular park's summer crowds. Of course, they aren't exactly deserted at peak season. Although the parks are large, only a few areas are reached by roads, so visitors naturally congregate along them. Summer lodging and campground reservations should be made as early as possible.

Although Sequoia was among the first of the federal reserves, Kings Canyon wasn't added until 1940. This little-visited wilderness embraces the canyon of the Kings River and 717 square miles of high country. For some odd reason, it was designated as a separate entity. However, these Siamese twin parks are administered as one.

The nub of **Grant Grove Village** is technically a part of Kings Canyon, even though it's attached to Sequoia's northwestern shoulder. Originally, it had been General Grant National Park, established a few weeks after Sequoia. Within the main part of Kings Canyon, several miles east, facilities are limited. Its **Cedar Grove** area is open in summers only, offering a small lodge, mini-mart and ranger station.

The basics

When to come: As in Yosemite, spring and fall are best. Fall colors can be striking here, particularly when they're blended with the cinnamon colored bark of the big trees. The road through the park is kept open all year, although it can be closed by winter storms. Because of the relatively high elevation in the main visitor area—6,440 feet at Giant Forest—spring arrives around June. Wildflowers on the trails peak in June and July.

Park entry fee is $5 per vehicle; free with a Golden Eagle, Golden Age or Golden Access pass. Since the parks occupy the most rugged of the Sierra peaks, no road travels west to east. Approaches are from Fresno on State Highway 180 (Grant Grove Village) and from Visalia Highway 198 (Giant Forest). The two roads link to form a loop through the parks' western tip. An extension of Highway 180 curls into Kings Canyon to **Cedar Grove** and a high country trailhead beyond.

Park information: Call (209) 565-3134 for specifics on roads, recreational activities and weather conditions. Mailing address is: Sequoia and Kings Canyon National Parks, Three Rivers, CA 93271.

Road information: For approaches to Sequoia/Kings Canyon, call the CalTrans road information number, (800) 427-ROAD, and (209) 565-3134 for conditions within the parks.

Campground reservations, may be made up to eight weeks in advance for **Lodgepole,** the park's main campground, through Mistix, (800) 365-CAMP, or write: P.O. Box 85705, San Diego, CA 92138-5705. Other park campgrounds are on a first come, first served basis.

Lodgings: Accommodations are available at **Grant Grove Lodge** near the Highway 180 entrance, **Cedar Grove** in Kings Canyon, and **Giant Forest** above the Highway 198 entrance. Reservations may be made through Sequoia Guest Services, P.O. Box 789, Three Rivers, CA 93271; (209) 565-3381. A month's advance reservation is usually sufficient; two months for summer weekends.

Winter sports: Sequoia has some of California's most picturesque cross country skiing, beneath those giant trees. **Sequoia Ski Touring** at Wolverton near Giant Village offers Nordic ski sales, rentals and lessons; (209) 565-3435. More than 30 miles of ski trails are in the park, including some that traverse snowbound park roads. The road/ski trail up to **Moro Rock** is particularly appealing.

Backcountry activities: Wilderness permits are required for all overnight hiking and backcountry camping in the park. They're available at ranger stations in the park. If you like to hike light, get a reservation for **Bearpaw Meadow.** This hike-in camp perches on the crest of a Sierra canyon about 12 miles from Giant Forest. For a fee, you'll get a tent cabin, breakfast, dinner and a box lunch. From here, you can venture forth into the high country. You must get reservations *very* early. They go on sale the first working day of each year and are usually gone by the end of that day. Call (209) 565-3381.

RV advisory: If you're driving a large rig or pulling a hefty trailer, use the Highway 180 approach through Grant Grove. The climb from the Ash Mountain entrance station to Giant Forest is a veritable asphalt corkscrew. It's not recommended for rigs over 20 feet; towing combinations over 50 feet are prohibited.

Sequoia takes its name from its resident botanical star. *Sequoiadendron giganteum* is a shorter, fatter and heavier relative of the coast redwood. Like their coastal cousins, sequoias are among nature's oldest creatures, often surviving more than 4,000 years. The General Sherman Tree in Giant Forest is the largest thing alive. It's 275 feet high, 103 feet around at the base and weighs maybe 2.8 million pounds, with 52,000 board feet of lumber in its trunk.

These noble giants are variously called big trees and Sierra redwoods; the British call them *Wellingtonia.* The sequoia name comes from a curious source. Cherokee Indian scholar Sequoyah (1760-1843) created an 86-character written language so his tribe could read and write. He is the only man who ever created an alphabet single-handedly. An Austrian botanist, obviously a big Sequoyah fan, borrowed his name for the big red tree. The literal meaning of *sequoyah* is "neither this nor that," used by Cherokees to describe the opossum.

Fortunately, most of the big trees didn't suffer the lumber cutting fate of coastal redwoods, since the wood is too brittle for construction use. However, early "entrepreneurs" liked to strip the bark and reassemble it for exhibit back east. Some of the park's largest trees were thus felled before federal protection arrived. One massive stump was used as a dance pavilion during the park's earlier days.

Driving Sequoia/Kings Canyon

A drive through these parks is short and certainly sweet, passing through America's finest sequoian cathedrals. Mostly, these are hikers' havens, since trails reach into some of the highest and most spectacular of the Sierra Nevada's high country. Mount Whitney, the tallest American peak south of Alaska, sits on Sequoia's eastern border.

Approaching from Fresno on Highway 180, pause at the visitor center in **Grant Grove Village** to learn about these two parks, their wilderness and their big trees. It's open daily from 8 to 5. Exhibits focus on early logging efforts, Native Americans and the flora and fauna of the parks. Nearby Grant Grove contains the namesake General Grant Tree, 267 feet high and a chubby 107 feet at its waistline. You'll also see the stump of a fallen giant that was cut in 1875 for exhibit at the Philadelphia World's Fair.

☺ Start your visit by taking the serpentine 70-mile round-trip into Kings Canyon, along the frothy rapids of the Kings River. Continue past the visitor facilities at **Cedar Grove** to the end of the road. A grand proscenium of Sierra wilderness unwinds before you, served by more than 700 miles of trails. Reaching road's end is a tough challenge for large RVs and trailers, although the route is all paved.

Return to Grant Grove and head south into Sequoia. The aptly-named **Generals Highway** alternately winds through towering sequoias and climbs rocky ridges. It offers imposing views of peaks to the east and the San Joaquin Valley to the west. You'll be struck by the contrast between the cobalt blue sky above the high Sierra and the beige haze hovering over the "civilized" valley below. **Lodgepole** offers a visitor center and the park's largest campground, with attractive tree-shaded sites.

☺ Three miles beyond, pause to salute General Sherman. The **Congress Trail** here takes you two miles past several other sequoia titans. The park's main activity center at **Giant Forest** is a mile or so south of the Sherman tree, with lodging, dining, a mini-mart and service station.

☺ One of our favored haunts, often overlooked, is **Beetle Rock,** an enormous slab of exposed granite tilted high above the San Joaquin Valley. We like to spend lazy hours communing with chipmunks, ground squirrels, scrub jays and others whose antics inspired the Disney nature film, *One Day at Beetle Rock.*

☺ More popular and therefore more crowded is the granite dome of **Moro Rock,** reached by a short side road. From the top of the rock, the sawtooth crests of the Great Western Divide stand before you, in stark relief against the sky. Beyond Moro Rock, the road leads to **Crescent Meadow,** an emerald patch rimmed by quaking aspen. It offers one of the park's prettier settings in the fall. Trails lead into the high Sierra from this area, including the route to **Bearpaw Meadow.** Just beyond Bearpaw, hikers encounter the **John Muir Trail** that links Sequoia to Yosemite. It's a portion of the Canada-to-Mexico **Pacific Crest Trail.**

Continuing south on the park's main road, a branch to the right takes you 6.5 miles down to **Crystal Cave,** a pretty limestone cavern. Although not extensive, it offers an impressive variety of calcite formations. Hour-long tours are conducted from May through September. Take a wrap, since's it's below 50 degrees inside.

The **Ash Mountain** gate is 13 twisting miles below the Crystal Cave turnoff. Just outside the south portal, a tortuous route leads eastward to **Mineral King.** Once the center of a controversial plan for a Walt Disney resort, this wilderness enclave was added to the park in 1978. Trailheads lead from here into the heights and a ranger station is staffed in summer. There are no developed facilities, and the road—partly gravel—is not recommended for RVs or trailers.

WHERE TO DINE AND RECLINE

Cedar Grove Lodge ● △ $$$$ Ø
Kings Canyon Park, 30 miles from Grant Grove. Rooms $77.50. MC/VISA. Rustic lodge rooms on the banks of the Kings River. Open summers only. Coin laundry, fishing, hiking trails nearby. **Coffee shop** serves from 7 to 7; dinners $8 to $12; wine and beer.

Giant Forest Lodge ● △△ $$ to $$$$ Ø
Sequoia Park, in Giant Forest Village. Rooms $40 to $115. MC/VISA. Wide range of lodgings among the sequoias, from canvas-roofed cabins to knotty pine motel style rooms and two-bedroom cottages. Rooms and cottages have private baths; cabins use central restrooms and showers. **Lodge Dining Room** and lounge open in summer 7 to 7, dinners $10 to $30 with full bar service; **cafeteria** available the rest of the year.

Grant Grove Lodge ● △ $$$
Kings Canyon Park, in Grant Grove. Cabins $32 to $68.50. MC/VISA. Rustic cottages and tent cabins; some with and some without private baths. Adjacent **coffee shop** serves from 7 to 7; dinners $5 to $15; full bar service.

Stony Creek ● △ $$$$
Between Grant Grove and Lodgepole in Sequoia National Forest. Rooms $77.50. MC/VISA. Small lodge with **restaurant,** market and gift shop; all private baths. Open summers only.

WHERE TO CAMP

Lodgepole Campground ● *Near Giant Forest; (209) 565-3338. Reservations via Mistix, (800) 365-CAMP, or write: P.O. Box 85705, San Diego, CA 92138-5705. RV and tent sites, $8 to $10.* Flush potties, picnic tables and barbecues; no hookups. Attractive tree-shaded sites. Hiking trails nearby.

Other campgrounds are in **Grant Grove, Cedar Grove, Mineral King** and the foothills area. Sites are $4 to $8, with either flush or pit potties; no hookups. Primitive camping is available in **Mineral King** for $4. First come, first served; most are closed in winter.

Chapter nine
TOP OF THE STATE
Exploring lakes and lava lands

CALIFORNIA'S NORTHERN REACHES are among the least populated area of the state. Although the far north contains much of California's water resources and forests, most of the land is too rough and tumbled and the winters are too severe to lure many inhabitants.

Several mountain ranges run together at the top of the state to form this jumbled region. The Sierra Nevada range dissolves into the Cascades, and the Coast Range merges with the Siskiyous. Filling in the middle are the Salmon and Marble mountains and the rugged Trinity Alps. The Marble and Trinity wilderness areas are among the state's most remote alpine retreats, favored haunts of backpackers and horsepackers.

Standing tall above it all is **Mount Shasta,** one of the most isolated promontories in America. Five other California peaks are higher but none is more dramatic. She stands alone and aloof on the edge of the Shasta Valley just below the Oregon border. The peak will be your beacon as you explore this area, appearing unexpectedly as you round a bend or top a crest.

Isolated regions lend themselves to legend. For decades, northland residents have reported sightings of Big Foot or Sasquatch, their own personal abominable snowman. This hairy critter supposedly lopes through the forest with ten-foot strides, towering 14 feet high and weighing 600 pounds. Although there have been many sightings, "proven" by photographs and foot prints, Big Foot is a pussy cat who's never hurt anyone. He probably just wants to be left alone, like many others who choose this distant land.

Fifty years ago, folks in the area felt they were being ignored *too* much. Residents of Northern California and southern Oregon border counties, convinced that their respective states were neglecting road construction and

TRIP PLANNER

WHEN TO GO ● Even though the area is popular in summer, it's so remote and widespread that crowds are uncommon. Camping or lodging reservations are recommended but not critical in summer, except around the busy lakes. Spring and fall are nice if you like clear, chilly days. Winter comes early to much of California's far north and most high country hiking trails are open only from July through September or October. Snowstorms can inhibit travel, and at times even block I-5.

WHAT TO SEE ● Lassen Volcanic National Park, McArthur-Burney Falls, Weaverville and its Joss House, Shasta Dam and Lake Shasta Caverns, Castle Crags State Park, old town Yreka, Klamath National Wildlife Refuge and Lava Beds National Monument.

WHAT TO DO ● Hike to the summit of Mount Lassen and to the soggy base of Burney Falls, follow a trail to Lassen's Bumpass Hell, rent a houseboat on one of the Whiskeytown-Shasta-Trinity lakes, drive the Klamath River Highway and maybe run a rapid, scope out the birds at Klamath National Wildlife refuge, crawl through a few lava tubes at Lava Beds.

Useful contacts

Klamath National Wildlife Refuge, Route 1, Box 74, Tulelake, CA 96134; (916) 667-2231.

Lassen Volcanic National Park, P.O. Box 100, Mineral, CA 96063-0100; (916) 595-4444

Lava Beds National Monument, P.O. Box 867, Tulelake, CA 96134; (916) 667-2283.

Northern Klamath River Chamber of Commerce, P.O. Box 25, Klamath River, CA 96050.

Shasta-Cascade Wonderland, 1250 Parkview Ave., Redding, CA 96001; (800) 326-6944 or (916) 243-2643.

Trinity County Chamber of Commerce, P.O. Box 517, Weaverville, CA 96024; (800) 421-7259 or (916) 623-6101.

Weed Chamber of Commerce, P.O. Box 366, Weed, CA 96094; (916) 938-4624.

Yreka Chamber of Commerce, 1000 Main St., Yreka, CA 96097; (916) 842-1649.

Top of the state radio stations

KEKA-FM, 104.9, Shasta City—country
KPAY-FM, 97.1, Chico—rock
KWSD-FM, 95.3, Redding—rock
KARZ-FM, 106.1, Burney-Redding—classic top 40
KWHO-FM, 100.9, Mount Shasta—country
KKRV-FM, 106.9, Klamath Falls—rock
KCHQ-FM, 97.7 and 101.3, Klamath Falls—classic hits
KSHA-FM, 103.4, Susanville—easy listening
KYRE-FM, 98, Yreka—rock
KAGO-AM, 1150, Klamath Falls—music, news and talk
KCMO-AM, 570, Susanville—news and talk
KPAY-AM, 1060, Chico—talk radio
KSYC-AM, 1490, Yreka—country

other services, decided to secede and form the State of Jefferson. However, their half joking secession was ill-timed—November 27, 1941. Less than two weeks later, Japan's attack on Pearl Harbor turned peoples' attentions to more serious matters.

Eventually, the region did get its roads, including a major freeway, Interstate 5. The vast majority of folks living in the area are bunched along this corridor, particularly in Redding and Red Bluff.

Although this region is thinly settled, it does lure its share of visitors. Tourism is the area's economic mainstay, followed by lumbering and ranching. Most visitors are outdoor types, drawn to its lakes, rivers and wilderness areas. The Sacramento River, California's largest, drains this mountainous region. Dams on the Sacramento and its tributaries provide an abundance of flatwater fun, particularly in the Whiskeytown-Shasta-Trinity National Recreation Area. Farther north, the Klamath is a popular whitewater stream.

However, you don't need a tackle box, backpack or kayak to enjoy the region. Scenery is abundant from main highways and back roads. The area embraces two of America's more interesting yet often overlooked federal reserves—Lassen Volcanic National Park and Lava Beds National Monument. Old mining towns such as Yreka, Weaverville and Shasta have their special appeal. Bird lovers will see tens of thousands of winged critters at Klamath National Wildlife Refuge. We'll approach this land from the south on Interstate 5, a favored route from Sacramento—and from San Francisco, reached by cutting across on I-505 from eastbound I-80.

LASSEN LOOP

This discovery route can be accomplished in a day or two weeks, depending on your state of relaxation or sense of urgency. I-5 carries you quickly north past the rice paddies, pasturelands and orchards of the flat Sacramento Valley. As a diversion en route, head east from Colusa on State Route 20 and follow a series of rural roads around the **Sutter Buttes.** These strange, castle-like andecite crags were thrust through the earth's surface by a magma flow about two million years ago. From Route 20, turn north on Acacia avenue, follow it through tiny **Sutter**, then go east on Butte House Road. Left turns onto East Butte Road and then West Butte Road take you on a 40-mile loop around this curious mini-mountain range.

Bird lovers will want to investigate the wildlife refuges in this area, east of I-5. **Sacramento National Wildlife Refuge,** alongside the freeway between **Williams** and **Willows,** is the Pacific Flyway's most important stopover, attracting more than two million wintering birds. From I-5, Norman Road, about eight miles south of Willows, will take you into the refuge, where you can pick up a six-mile auto tour route. For specifics this and other area reserves, contact: Sacramento National Wildlife Refuges, Route 1, Box 311, Willows, CA 95988; (916) 934-2801.

Continuing north, you encounter **Red Bluff,** a town of 12,400 sitting in a transition zone between the valley and the northern mountains. Take time for a brief spin through its old red brick and false front downtown area. At the northern end, follow signs east to **William B. Ide Adobe State Park,** open daily 8 a.m. to sunset; (707) 527-5927. Ide was one of the leaders of the rag-tag band of Americans who seized Sonoma in 1846 and declared California to be a republic. His modest adobe home on the banks of the Sacramento River was built around 1850.

Top of the State

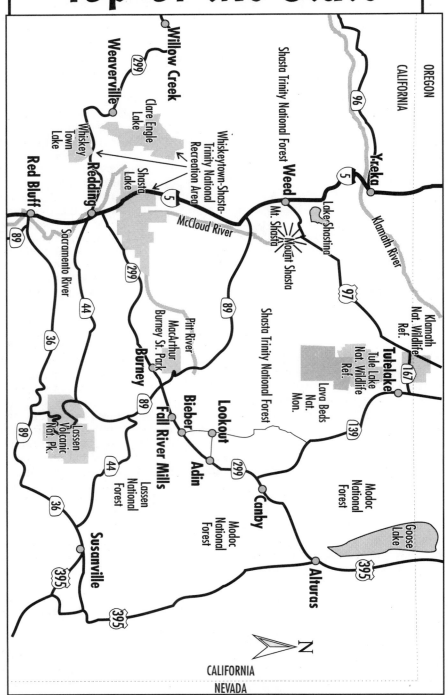

From the adobe, retreat south and pick up State Highway 36, heading east into the lower reaches of the **Cascade Range.** The gently winding route climbs easily from pasturelands and oak woodlands into conifer forests. Looking northward, you'll catch occasional glimpses of Mount Shasta. Just beyond the small mountain hamlet of **Mineral,** turn north onto Highway 89. You're headed for a national park that gets surprisingly little attention for such a grand place:

☺ *Lassen Volcanic National Park* • *P.O. Box 100, Mineral, CA 96063-0100; (916) 595-4444. Park headquarters at Mineral; other visitor centers near north and south entrances. Admission $5 per vehicle; free with Golden Eagle, Golden Age or Golden Access pass. Food and other services available at Lassen Chalet in the park's southwest area and at Manzanita in the northwest corner. Camping at Manzanita Lake, Summit Lake and Crags campgrounds, $5 to $7 a night. Other campsites in the surrounding Lassen National Forest. The only lodging within the park is at Drakesbaad in Warner Valley, which isn't directly accessible from the park's main visitor area. (Open in summers only; units book up very early.) Several resorts and motels are in nearby towns of Mineral and Lassen Lodge; see "Where to sleep" in the Lassen area below. Lassen Ski Area is near the south entrance. For ski information: 2150 Main St., Suite 7, Red Bluff, CA 96080; (916) 595-3376; snow phone 595-4464.*

Lassen Peak, a still active plug volcano, offers a rich trove of lures, from burbling thermal areas and jeweled lakes to high country hiking areas. Yet it's one of the least visited national parks in the country. It does draw summer weekend crowds from nearby Red Bluff and Redding, so plan your visit accordingly. Highway 89 snakes through the park, offering splendid vistas of these alpine heights. You'll pass broken lava flows, steaming fumaroles and the **Devastated Area**, still scoured clean of vegetation by Lassen's most recent eruption, in 1915. A driving guide available at visitor centers points out landmarks as you pass. The road is closed by snow in winter. Although the park is kept open the year around, only the southwest corner around Lassen Chalet and the ski area can be reached by car in winter.

For a good workout and an incredible view of the area, stop at the **Lassen Peak trailhead** for a steep but easily negotiable 2.5-mile hike to the top. An easier 1.5-mile trail leads from a turnout just beyond **Lake Helen** to **Bumpass Hell,** an area of sputtering mud pots, fumaroles and other intriguing thermal activity.

RV advisory: The 33-mile road through the park is very steep and winding in areas, although it can be negotiated by motorhomes and trailers. It's not recommended for motorhomes over 32 feet long.

Emerging from the park's northwest corner at Manzanita, stay with Highway 89 north, climbing over 5,920-foot **Eskimo Hill Summit.** The road begins unsnarling as it drops down into a pretty mountain meadow with a mix of ranch lands and forests. The near perfect volcanic peak of 7,247-foot **Logan Mountain** stands off to the left. Thirty-five miles from Lassen, you cross State Highway 299 and shortly encounter a handsome waterfall surrounded by a state park.

☺ *McArthur-Burney Falls Memorial State Park* • *Route 1, Box 1260, Burney, CA 96013; (916) 335-2777. Day use $5, camping $12 (see below).* President Theodore Roosevelt was so taken by the spectacle of this broad 129-foot waterfall that he called it the eighth wonder of the world. Spilling in dozens of rivulets over a lava face, the falls are within a short walk of the campground. You can follow a zig-zag (and eternally damp) trail down to a rainbow pool at its base. Several miles of other trails wind through the 875-acre park. Nearby **Lake Britton** reservoir offers assorted water sports.

If you like funky old forest towns, return to the junction of route 299 and follow it 12 miles east to **Fall River Mills.** There's a Lassen National Forest ranger station here, offering information on the abundant campgrounds in the area. Take a gander at the scruffy three-story cross-timbered Normandy-style **Fall River Hotel** in the middle of town.

From Fall River Mills, Highway 299 winds quickly down from the piney mountains into oak woodlands, heading for **Redding**, back on Interstate 5. With 66,500 residents, it is by far the largest community in the region. There's not much in town to entice the casual visitor, although Redding is the major gateway to California's far north. Tourist promoters call this region the Shasta-Cascade Wonderland. Redding is a good place to stock up on provisions and perhaps catch a motel room. More than a dozen line I-5.

Three different agencies can load you up with information: **Redding Chamber of Commerce,** 737 Auditorium Drive, open Monday-Thursday 8:30 to 5; **Redding Convention and Visitors Bureau,** 772 Auditorium Drive, Monday-Thursday 8 to 5:30, Friday 8:30 to 4:30 and weekends 9 to 5; and the **Shasta-Cascade Wonderland Association,** 1250 Parkview Avenue at Pine, weekdays 8 to 5.

Before leaving town, visit the **Carter House Natural Science Museum** at 1701 Rio Drive. It's a "living" museum with living creatures as well as natural history exhibits. It's free, open Wednesday-Sunday 10 to 4; (916) 225-4125. A short distance away, the **Redding Museum and Art Center**, at 1911 Rio Dr., has a fine Native American exhibit. It's also free, open Tuesday-Sunday 10 to 5; shorter hours in winter; (916) 225-4255.

WHERE TO SLEEP IN THE LASSEN AREA

Drakesbad Guest Ranch ● △ $$$$
In Warner Valley, Lassen Park; c/o 2150 Main St., No. 7, Red Bluff, CA 96080; (916) 529-1512. Couples $82 to $92, family units $110 to $125. Open from early June to early October. MC/VISA. Very rustic 110-year-old guest ranch with no electricity, phones or TV. Hiking, swimming, fishing, horseback riding; dining hall for guests. Units book up very early.

Fire Mountain Lodge ● △ $$
Route 5, Box 3500, Mill Creek, CA 96061; (916) 258-2938. Couples $40 to $50, singles $30 to $40, kitchenettes $40 to $60. No credit cards. Comfortably rustic 12-room lodge on a mountain stream, southeast of the national park. Game room with billiards, fireplace, country store and full hookup RV park. **Restaurant** open from 8 to 8; dinners $10 to $25; full bar service.

Hat Creek Resort ● △△ $$
P.O. Box 15 (Highway 44), Old Station, CA 96071; (916) 335-7121. Doubles and singles $37 to $52, housekeeping cabins $40 to $75. MC/VISA. Rustic resort with seven lodge rooms and ten cabins, near Highway 44/89 junction, 11 miles from Lassen park's northern entrance. RV hookups available.

Lassen Mineral Lodge ● △ $$
P.O. Box 160 (Highway 36), Mineral, CA 96063; (916) 595-4422. Couples $45 to $55, singles $40. MC/VISA. Comfortable 20-unit motel with pool, tennis courts. Some kitchenettes. **Restaurant** serves American fare; dinners $8 to $13; full bar service.

Mount Lassen becomes a Christmas card vision in winter. The view is from the national park's northern border.
—Betty Woo Martin

WHERE TO CAMP
(Also see Lassen Volcanic National Park)

Hat Creek Hereford Ranch RV Park ● *41397 Updyke Lane, Hat Creek, CA 96040; (916) 335-7171 or (916) 335-7519. RV and tent sites, $9.25 to $13.75. Reservations accepted; MC/VISA.* Wooded area between Lassen and McArthur Burney; some pull-throughs and shaded sites. Showers, coin laundry, mini-mart, playground, rec field; swimming and fishing.

Hat Creek Resort ● *P.O. Box 15 (Highway 44), Old Station, CA 96071; (916) 335-7121. RV sites, $15 for full hookups. Reservations accepted. MC/VISA.* Shaded sites 11 miles from Lassen's northern entrance; laundry.

McArthur-Burney Memorial State Park ● *Route 1, Box 1260, Burney, CA 96013; (916) 335-2777. RV and tent sites, $12. Reservations through Mistix, (800) 444-PARK.* Nicely located sites beneath trees near Burney Falls. Barbecues, picnic tables, flush potties; no hookups or showers.

Volcano Country Camping ● *Highway 36 (P.O. Box 55), Mineral, CA 96063. Full hookups $16.50, tent sites $14. Reservations accepted; MC/VISA.* Small campground in wooded setting with flush potties, showers, barbecues and coin laundry. Nine miles from Lassen's southwest entrance.

THE "GREAT LAKES" AREA

A glance at a Northern California map reveals three sprawling lakes north and east of Redding. These are key elements of the Central Valley Project, California's largest irrigation and hydroelectric venture, started in the late 1930s. Largest is **Shasta Lake,** a gnarled blue hand reaching into canyons formed by the Sacramento, Pitt and McCloud rivers and Squaw Creek. West of Redding along Highway 299 is smaller **Whiskeytown Lake** and northwest of that is long, skinny **Trinity Lake.** Each is rimmed by a segment of **Whiskeytown-Shasta-Trinity National Recreation Area.**

Fringed by trees and cupped by valleys, these could be pretty lakes except for the ugly bathtub ring of red dirt that rims their shorelines when the water is low. But never mind that. With plenty of room to run, they comprise California's most popular boating area. They're busy on summer weekends with speedboats, ski boats, house boats, jet skis and just about anything else that floats. Despite the area's popularity, the lakes are so extensive that boaters can find their own personal inlet for a bit of peace.

Redding to Weaverville

To begin your exploration of these lakes and beyond, head west from Redding on Highway 299. You'll shortly encounter a brickfront ghost town that looks like it belongs in California's Gold Country:

☺ *Shasta State Historic Park* ● *P.O. Box 2430, Shasta, CA 96087; (916) 243-8194. Visitor center/museum open 10 to 5, daily in summer and Thursday-Monday the rest of the year. Adults $2, kids $1.* At a glimpse, the gold rush ghost town of Shasta seems rather extensive. Closer inspection reveals that a sturdy row of brick-front, iron shuttered buildings is but a façade. They're only shells of their former selves, like a Western movie set. Some substantial buildings do remain. The former **Shasta County Courthouse** serves as the visitor center and a first rate museum of the area's yesterdays. An unexpected find here is an excellent collections of paintings by early California artists. Check out the grim jail cells downstairs and the grimmer gallows out back. Shasta thrived in the early 1850s as the center of the largest gold-producing region of California's far north. Once the largest town in the county, it served as the seat of government until Redding took it away in 1888 after the gold ran out.

Whiskeytown Lake ● *Whiskeytown National Recreation Area, P.O. Box 188, Whiskeytown, CA 96095-0188; (916) 241-6484. Visitor center open daily 9 to 4:30.* Three miles west of Shasta, you enter the Whiskeytown segment of the national recreation area. Its visitor center is up to the left, off Highway 299. Just beyond is **Brandy Creek** with a marina, boat launch and trailer camp. Several tent camp sites are south of here, along a twisting dirt road. Back on Highway 229, you'll encounter **Oak Bottom,** with another marina and a campground with RV and tent sites for $5, including cold showers (soap up quickly).

The smallest of the three major national recreation area lakes, Whiskeytown doesn't suffer from lack of popularity. To get away from summer crowds, drive to a trailhead beyond Brandy Creek at the end of the road. Trails lead from here into the far woods. With a permit, you can enjoy wilderness camping back there. West of Whiskeytown, you'll top **Buckhorn Summit** at 3,215 feet and follow Little Grassy Valley Creek toward the

Trinity River. Signs shortly will direct you six miles north to **Lewiston,** another old mining town, which still has a few inhabitants. Beyond is the third major NRA lake, whose name has been a poltical football for decades:

Trinity Lake • *Trinity Center, CA 96091; (916) 623-2121. Several campgrounds and marinas; small resorts with houseboat, fishing boat and speedboat rentals.* This fjord-like reservoir is officially called Clair Engle Lake, in honor of the California senator who campaigned for the damming of the Trinity River. Many locals didn't like that much and many still don't, so they insist on calling it Trinity Lake. It has the most impressive setting of the three ponds, stretching for miles into the flanks of the Trinity Alps. The least busy of the trio, it offers scores of hidden coves and creek inlets for solitude. The usual campgrounds, marinas with boat rentals and other water recreational facilities rim this slender pond. A smaller reservoir, **Lewiston Lake,** occupies a lower forebay between Trinity Dam and Lewiston Dam. Free of speedboats, it's a peaceful little strip of water noted for trout fishing.

Trinity County is one of the least populated in California, with nary a traffic light or elevator, and hardly a stop sign. A proposal to put a stop light in the county seat of Weaverville raised such a ruckus that it made national news. More than two-thirds of the county is national forest, so most of it is likely to remain uncrowded.

For a splendid drive through this little-visited land, follow Trinity Dam Boulevard along the Lewiston-Trinity lakeshore, then pick up State Highway 3 and head north. Trinity Alps Road leads to the foothills of those craggy, glaciated peaks adored by backpackers. Trails head into the heights from here. For information about travel into the 500,000-acre **Trinity Alps Wilderness,** contact the **Weaverville Ranger District,** Shasta-Trinity National Forest, P.O. Box 1190, Weaverville, CA 96093; (916) 623-2121. Wilderness permits and maps can be picked up from the office on Highway 299, open weekdays 8 to 5.

Continuing north on Highway 3, designated here as the Trinity Heritage National Scenic Byway, you'll hit the townlet of **Trinity Center.** It's a focal point for much of Trinity Lake's aquatic activities. Pause at the **Scott Museum,** offering the usual pioneer artifacts. Particularly noteworthy is a collection of hundreds of varieties of barbed wire. The museum is open mid-April to mid-October daily from 1 to 4. Beyond Trinity Center, the highway follows the Trinity River between the steep flanks of the Trinity Alps to the west and the Trinity Mountains to the east. The stream offers wonderful little places to pause for a picnic, pictures or a bit of fly fishing. After passing the hidden hamlets of **Etna** and **Fort Jones,** you hit I-5 at **Yreka,** which we will tend to later.

Meanwhile, back on Highway 299, continue west until you enter the metropolitan center of Trinity County:

Weaverville

Population: 2,800   **Elevation: 2,045 feet**

This charming old mining town is being discovered by tourists, although it's hardly crowded. Weathered yet prosperous looking, Weaverville boasts a few curio shops and crafts places. Don't call them boutiques; the friendly locals are touchy about things like that.

Park and walk about, perhaps following an historic guide available free at the **Chamber of Commerce.** It's in the middle of town on your left;

open daily 9 to 5. Notice the classic gold rush era balconies in the brick-front business area, some with distinctive spiral staircases to the sidewalk. Worth a peek is the **Weaverville Drug Store,** California's oldest. It has been in continuous operation for 140 years. While picking up your Advil, note the wonderful collection of old pharmaceuticals lining narrow floor-to-ceiling shelves. Nearby is the **Old Fashioned Ice Cream Parlor,** whose description fits its name. Close together on the east end of town are two interesting historic sites:

☺ **Joss House State Historic Park** ● *P.O. Drawer W, Weaverville, CA 96093; (916) 623-5284. Daily 10 to 5; adults $2, kids $1.* More preserved than restored, this is the oldest active Chinese worship temple in California, perhaps in the country. The Taoist joss house was built in 1853, rebuilt in 1874 after a fire and still in use. The Chinese comprised half of Weaverville's population during its heyday in the 1850s, and the visitor center offers fine exhibits concerning their daily lives. Ranger-led tours, given whenever enough people show up, take you to the red and gold lacquered temple, and the spartan attendant's quarters tacked onto one side.

J.J. Jackson Museum ● *C/o Weaverville Historical Society, P.O. Box 333, Weaverville, CA 96093; (916) 623-5211. Daily 10 to 5 in summer, Tuesdays only noon to 4 the rest of the year. Donations appreciated.* Housed in a brick building across the parking lot from the joss house, it offers a goodly record of Weaverville's past. Exhibits include mining gear, Chinese artifacts and the usual Native American baskets. Out back are a working stamp mill (ore crusher), a miner's cabin and blacksmith shop.

WHERE TO DINE

La Casita ● △ $ Ø
254 Main St.; (916) 625-5797. Mexican; wine and beer. Tuesday-Thursday 11 to 7:30, Friday-Saturday 11 to 8:30, closed Sunday-Monday. Housed in a white clapboard house with yellow trim, the "Little House" offers Latino fare at reasonable prices.

☺ **The Brewery Pub & Grill** ● △△△ $$ Ø
401 S. Main St.; (916) 623-3000. American; full bar. Daily 6 a.m. to 10 p.m. Major credit cards. This frontier style restaurant is housed in a brick 1855 former brewery. Check out the wagon hanging from the ceiling, then dine between knotty pine walls adorned with hurricane lamps. The menu is contemporary, with entrèes such as prawns stuffed with crab and cheese.

WHERE TO SLEEP

Forty Niner Motel ● ⌂ $ Ø
718 Main St. (P.O. Box 1608), Weaverville, CA 96093; (916) 623-4937. Couples $32 to $38, singles $30 to $34. Major credit cards. Simple 13-unit motel with TV movies, room phones and pool; in downtown Weaverville.

Granny's House Bed & Breakfast ● ⌂⌂⌂ $$$ Ø
313 Taylor St. (P.O. Box 31), Weaverville, CA 96093; (916) 623-2756. Couples and singles $65 to $75. Three units with private baths; full breakfast. Nicely restored 1897 Queen Anne near downtown. Attractively appointed rooms with Eastlake antiques. Parlor with fireplace; English country garden.

Lewiston Valley Motel ● ⌂⌂ $$
Trinity Dam Boulevard (P.O. Box 324), Lewiston, CA 96052; (916) 778-3942. Couples $40 to $45, singles $35 to $37.50. MC/VISA. Inviting little

knotty pine motel near Trinity Lake; TV movies, room phones; picnic tables and barbecue tables on wooded grounds. Near Lewiston Lake. **Mama's Restaurant** serves from 6 a.m. to 9 p.m. in summer, 7 to 7 in winter; dinners $6 to $11; no alcohol.

Red Hill Motel ● △ $$
P.O. Box 234 (Highway 244), Weaverville, CA 96093; (916) 623-4331. Couples $35 to $45, singles $30 to $35, kitchenettes $50 to $60. MC/VISA. Well kept, rustic motel tucked beneath pines off the highway.

Weaverville Victorian Inn ● △△△ $$$ Ø
1709 Main St. (P.O. Box 2400), Weaverville, CA 96093-2400; (916) 623-4432. Couples $53 to $59, singles $44 to $49, suites $105. Major credit cards. Appealing oldstyle inn; 60 rooms with TV movies and phones; some rooms with hot tubs; swimming pool.

TRINITY LAKE RESORTS & HOUSEBOAT RENTALS

Cedar Stock Resort ● Star Route 2, Box 510, Lewiston, CA 96052; (916) 286-2225. Lake-view restaurant and lounge, cabins and houseboat rentals; marina and store; rental canoes, jet skis, fishing and ski boats.

Trinity Alps Marina ● P.O. Box 670, Lewiston, CA 96052; (916) 286-2282. Marina, bar and restaurant, mini-mart; houseboat rentals; ski and fishing boats.

WHERE TO CAMP

Pinewood Cove RV Park ● HC Route 1, Box 500, Lewiston, CA 96052; (916) 286-2201. RV and tent sites, $13.50 to $18.50. Reservations accepted; MC/VISA. Tree-shaded sites with views of Trinity Lake; full hookups, showers, mini-mart, coin laundry. Dock with rental boats; water sports.

Trinity National Recreation Area ● Trinity Center, CA 96091; (916) 623-2121. RV and tent sites, from $8 to free. A variety of sites are available, many with lake views. Some flush potties; some pit.

Weaverville Ranger District ● Shasta-Trinity National Forest, Main Street (P.O. Box 1190), Weaverville, CA 96093; (916) 623-2121. Scores of campsites are available in the surrounding national forest.

Whiskeytown National Recreation Area ● P.O. Box 188, Whiskeytown, CA 96095-0188; (916) 241-6484. RV and tent sites, from $8 to free. A variety of sites are available, many with lake views. Some flush potties; some pit. Swimming, boating fishing.

From Weaverville, Highway 299 follows a fork of the Trinity River, winding past an abundance of campgrounds, picnic sites and fishing holes in **Six Rivers National Forest.** After topping a couple of modest passes—nothing higher than 3,000 feet—it spirals down to the coast, hitting U.S. 101 above Arcata.

Shasta Lake and north

Meanwhile, back on I-5, superlative-ridden Shasta Lake is the most imposing of the three oversized ponds. With a 370-mile shoreline (30 percent larger than San Francisco Bay), it's California's biggest reservoir. It's crossed by the world's highest double-deck bridge (measuring from the bottom of the pond), which carries I-5 and a railroad trestle.

Begin your Shasta exploration by driving north on I-5 from Redding, and then turning west at **Project City**. Ready for more superlatives?

☺ **Shasta Dam** • C/o Central Valley Project, Shasta Dam, Redding, CA 96001; (916) 275-4463. Visitor center open daily 7:30 to 4 in summer and weekdays 8:30 to 5 the rest of the year. Guided tours; 30-minute film on dam's construction, shown on request. The mighty plug that created Shasta Lake is America's second largest concrete dam and the second highest (602 feet), after Lake Mead's Hoover Dam. We don't know who figures these things out, but if the concrete used in the dam were fashioned into a sidewalk, it would reach around the world. This concrete colossus was born during America's Depression-inspired building era. Begun in 1938 as a federal reclamation project, it wasn't completed until 1945. From the walkway atop the dam, you can view the expansive mass of the lake and the distant snowy head of Mount Shasta, keeping watch over its domain.

Return to I-5 and head north, crossing that tall double-decker span over **Bridge Bay.** Just short of the bridge is the largest of several lakeside play areas, **Bridge Bay Resort,** offering lodging, a restaurant, houseboat and other watercraft rentals (see listing below). Above Bridge Bay, the freeway winds about the lake, offering occasional glimpses of tree-shrouded inlets, some with tucked away resorts. At **O'Brien,** catch a boat across one of the lake's many arms to a cavernous attraction:

☺ **Lake Shasta Caverns** • P.O. Box 801, O'Brien, CA 96070; (916) 238-2341. Guided tours hourly in summer from 9 to 4 and the rest of the year at 10, noon and 2. Adults $12, kids $6. Take the time to tour this fine brace of limestone formations; it's one of the West's best cave complexes. Lake Shasta Caverns is much more interesting than Oregon Caves to the north, which gets better press because of its national monument status. A trip to these caverns is, in a sense, three trips in one. You first cross an arm of the lake by boat and then climb a cliff-hanging road by bus before entering the cool depths of the caves. Within, you'll see a fine collection of stalactites, stalagmites, soda straws, drapes and other calcite creations.

North of O'Brien, I-5 crosses more arms of Shasta Lake, then it follows the Sacramento River appendage. It leaves the national recreation area north of a small commercial blob called **Lakehead,** staying with the Sacramento River, which is free flowing through here.

☺ About 30 miles past Lakehead, forsake the interstate for a visit to **Castle Crags State Park.** You'll see this craggy upthrust of a volcanic dike as you approach on the freeway. The park offers camping for $12 a night (flush potties, no hookups), picnicking and hiking trails. Climbing the crags should be attempted only be experienced rock scramblers. Several more negotiable trails wind around their base. For information: Castle Crags State Park, P.O. Box 80, Castella, CA 96017-0800; (916) 235-2684.

Pressing northward, you'll pass two mountain towns generally bypassed by the hurried interstate crowd. **Dunsmuir** and **Mount Shasta City** don't offer much for visitors, although curiosity might cause you to drive through their old fashioned business districts. The Dunsmuir look is turn-of-the-century front porch, while Mount Shasta City is somewhat less scruffy, with a larger and more modern business districts.

What these towns do offer is an impressive backdrop of **Mount Shasta,** becoming more dominant as you press northward. The great peak practically wears Mount Shasta City as a pendant. As you draw closer, you'll discover that the mountain has a little sister. **Shastina** grows from its western flank, topping out at 12,330 feet, compared with Shasta's 14,162.

From Shasta City, county road A-10 coils upward (not recommended for large RVs and trailers) into the mountain's rough-hewn flanks. Trails branch from **Panther Meadows** at the 6,800 foot level into the **Mount Shasta Wilderness.** The mountain itself is climbable, although only by folks with mountaineering skills, strong legs and a good set of lungs. Go aid your exploration of the Shasta area, pick up information at the **Mount Shasta Ranger District** at 204 W. Alma, Mount Shasta City, CA 96067; (916) 926-3781. You'll learn impressive stuff—that this is the largest volcano in the Lower Forty-Eight, that it has five glaciers on its flanks and that it isn't necessarily extinct. But don't hold your breath until it pulls a Mount St. Helens number. It last burped in 1786. A U.S. Geological Survey report guesstimates that it has a 250 to 300-year eruption cycle.

Also near the great peak is a community that's somewhat more inviting than its unfortunate name, **Weed.** It isn't the town's fault that a guy named Abner Weed came here in 1885 to establish a lumber mill. It's well preserved business district is worth a gander, so take the Weed/Klamath Falls Highway 97 exit. The **Weed Chamber of Commerce** visitor center occupies a little log cabin at the Highway 97 junction; it's open weekdays 10 to 2. To learn all about Abner Weed, ask directions to the new **Weed Historic Lumbertown Museum** at 303 Gilman. It's open May through October, Tuesday-Saturday 10 to 4 and Sunday 1 to 4; (916) 938-2352. You'll see some interesting exhibits on early day lumbering, several 18th century furnished rooms and the usual gathering of pioneer relics.

From Weed, head north on I-5 through bucolic ranch lands, across the surprisingly flat Shasta Valley. After 28 miles, you reach one of the senior cities of California's far north:

Yreka

Population: 7,000   **Elevation: 2,625 feet**

Yreka came to life in 1851 after gold was found at nearby Scott Bar. Many of its vintage downtown buildings have made the National Register of Historic Places. Start your prowl by picking up *A Door to the Past* brochure at the **Chamber of Commerce** at 1000 Main St.; open weekdays 9 to 5. It'll guide you past things historic, most of which are grouped around the juncture of Main and Miner streets. The **Siskiyou County Museum** at 910 S. Main offers some interesting pioneer relics. It's open Monday-Friday in summer from 9 to 5 and Sunday 1 to 5, and closed Sunday-Monday in the off-season; (916) 842-3836. **Siskiyou County Courthouse** at 311 Fourth Street exhibits an imposing gold nugget collection; open weekdays 8 to 5.

The friendly Klamath

☺ Overlooked by many but loved by whitewater enthusiasts is the **Klamath River** region northwest of Yreka. It's not a wilderness area, since the Klamath River Highway (Route 96) follows much of its course through a wooded canyon. It is, however, a user-friendly stream, with plenty of put-ins and take-outs for kayakers and baloney boaters and some deep holes for swimming. Since it originates at a low altitude, spilling out of 4,139-foot Klamath Lake in Oregon, the water is quite warm in summer.

A 16-mile stretch between I-5 and the town of **Klamath River** offers rapids sufficient to get you wet without any great risk. Camping is available for $5 a night at **Tree of Heaven,** a national forest site right on the river, between the freeway and Klamath River. Try to find a spot upwind of the pit potties. **Beaver Creek Lodge,** c/o Klamath River, CA 96050, has cabins at waterside and provides tubes for floaters, plus fishing guide service; (916) 465-2331. The Klamath is legendary for steelhead fishing.

To approach this region, follow Main Street north out of Yreka instead of returning to the freeway. It runs parallel to I-5, taking you through the stunning steep-walled canyon of Yreka Creek that flows into the Klamath. A hard left turn after crossing a high bridge puts you onto Route 96.

The highway follows the curving Klamath for nearly 150 miles before entering the **Hoopa Valley Indian Reservation** at Weitchpec. Winding Highway 169 then takes over, following the river 19 miles to a dead end. The stream, now designated wild and scenic, flows undisturbed from here to the sea. If you stay with Highway 96, you'll pick up the Trinity River and hit Highway 299 at **Willow Creek.**

RV advisory: The Klamath River Highway is navigable, but watch carefully for steep dropoffs. Keep an eye out for logging trucks, whose drivers seem unconcerned with their mortality.

YREKA/KLAMATH RIVER ACTIVITIES

Glider rides ● Montague Aviation; (916) 459-3456.

River running ● These outfits specialize in whitewater trips down the Klamath: Young's Ranch, Somes Bar, CA 95568, (800) KLAMATH or (916) 469-3322; Turtle River Rafting Company, P.O. Box 133, Mount Shasta, CA 96067, (916) 926-3223; Orange Torpedo Trips, P.O. Box 1111-D, Grants Pass, OR 97526; (800) 635-2925 or (503) 479-5061.

Scenic railroad ● Yreka Western Railroad runs its "Blue Goose" steam train through the Shasta Valley to Montague several times daily in summer. Three-hour excursions are $9 for adults and $4.50 for kids; (916) 842-4146.

WHERE TO DINE

Grandma's House ● ∆∆ $$ Ø

123 E. Center St.; (916) 842-7056. American homestyle cooking; wine and beer. Daily 6 a.m. to 9 p.m. MC/VISA, DISC. Cozy country restaurant featuring homemade soups and desserts. Seafood and steaks are specialties.

Old Boston Shaft Restaurant ● ∆∆ $$

1801 Fort Jones Rd.; (916) 842-5768. American and Swiss; full bar service. Lunch weekdays 11 to 2:30, dinner Monday-Saturday from 5, closed Sunday. MC/VISA. Stylish mining-theme restaurant with creatively prepared steaks, chicken, chops and prime rib, plus some continental fare; European accents to the desserts.

Yreka Bakery Café ● ∆ $ Ø

322 W. Miner St.; (916) 842-7440. American; beer and wine. Thursday-Sunday 7 to 2, Monday-Wednesday 7 to 5, open for dinner in summer 5 to 9. CB, DISC. Small café featuring hearty breakfasts and baked goods, plus basic American fare for lunch and dinner. Inexpensive place for a quick bite.

Wah Lee Restaurant ● ∆

520 S. Main St.; (916) 842-3444. Chinese-American; full bar service. Weekdays 11 to 10, weekends noon to 10. Major credit cards. Small family café specializing in Cantonese fare, plus some spicy Szechuan dishes. From the American side of the menu springs steak, prime rib and seafood. Cocktail lounge features tropical drinks.

WHERE TO SLEEP

Thunderbird Lodge ● △ $ Ø

526 S. Main St., Yreka, CA 96097; (800) 554-4339 in Western states only, or (916) 842-4404. Couples $32 to $40, singles $29 to $32. Major credit cards. A 44-room motel with TV movies, room phones and pool.

Wayside Inn ● △△ $$ Ø

1235 S. Main St., Yreka, CA 96097; (800) 795-7974 or (916) 842-4412. Couples $38 to $76, singles $30 to $60, kitchenettes $42 to $70. Major credit cards. A 44-unit motel with TV movies, room phones, some refrigerators. Pool, hot tub and RV parking. **El Rancho Café** serves 6 a.m. to 9 p.m.; dinners $5.50 to $10; wine and beer.

Lava Beds & Klamath Wildlife Refuge

We've never understood why so few people visit Lava Beds National Monument. We feel it's one of the most intriguing in the national park system, particularly when coupled with one of the state's premier birdwatching areas. This is the Modoc Plateau, a fascinating area with marshlands and farm fields a-swirl with birds, cindercones and broken lava flows touched by gray green junipers and sage, backdropped by the distant Cascades.

To reach this rough yet alluring land, backtrack to Weed and take U.S. 97 northeast. You'll enjoy splendid views of glistening, snow-streaked Mount Shasta along this remarkably straight route. You soon whisk through **Macdoel,** barely large enough to offer gasoline and a single store. Beyond, you drop down into **Butte Valley National Grassland,** a vast prairie rimmed by low hills. The highway takes several 90-degree turns through **Dorris,** a town with a few service stations and cafés, including one with a great name—Malfunction Junction. North of Dorris, turn left onto State Highway 161 and skim eastward just below the Oregon border.

☺ You soon enter the extensive grasslands and wetlands of **Klamath National Wildlife Refuge.** These vast marshes once covered 185,000 acres in California and Oregon. The turn-of-the-century Klamath Reclamation Project reduced them to a quarter that size to make room for potato patches and horseradish fields. Uncontrolled hunting and loss of habitat reduced the area's resident and transient bird population from six million to about one million.

Still, this is a *primo* place for bird watchers, one of the best sites in America. Clutch your binoculars and scan the wetlands for some of the 411 wildlife species that have been identified here. Peak viewing time is early November, when migrating and resident birds approach the million mark. For a brochure and self-guiding auto tour, watch for a sign that directs you four miles south to **refuge headquarters**. It's open weekdays 8 to 4:30 and weekends 8 to 4. A small, nicely done visitor center has stuffed versions of local critters, wildlife photos and exhibits on efforts to preserve them. For information: Klamath National Wildlife Refuge, Route 1, Box 74, Tulelake, CA 96134; (916) 667-2231.

From headquarters, you can continue southeast into Lava Beds National Monument or backtrack half a mile and follow East-West Road into **Tulelake.** It's an unlovely town, half boarded up, scattered over this flat basin. However, it offers a good place to eat and some basic places to sleep. It's evident that Tulelake is a bit off the major tourist routes. If you'd like to take home an authentic local souvenir, stop by **Mezzetta's Tulelake Horse-radish Company.** Our choice is the horseradish mustard. And yes, this is the horseradish capital of the world. I still have the T-shirt to prove it.

WHERE TO DINE & RECLINE

Mike and Wanda's Coffee Shop ● ▵▵ $
Modoc Street near Fourth; (916) 667-3226. American; full bar service. Daily 6 a.m. to 10 p.m. MC/VISA. It's a surprisingly attractive place in such a homely town, with barnboard walls etched with cattle brands. The entrée of choice is chicken fried steak, or go for the smoked ribs. Full dinners are under $10; there's a cocktail lounge in the adjoining Golden Hotel.

Park Motel ● ◠ $
Highway 139 (southeast of town), Tulelake, CA 96134; (916) 667-2913. Couples from $30, singles from $25. MC/VISA. Basic 12-room motel with TV in units.

Ellis Motel ● ◠ $
Highway 139 (a mile northwest), Tulelake, CA 96134; (916) 667-2913. Couples from $25, singles from $22. MC/VISA. Even more basic; spartan rooms with TV.

Although the land around Tulelake is as flat as a billiard table and not nearly as green, it's rimmed by nearby mountains. The Tulelake office of **Modoc National Forest** can provide useful information about camping, hiking and such. It's on Highway 139, just beyond the Park Motel, open weekdays 8 to 5; (916) 667-2246.

☺ *Lava Beds National Monument* ● *P.O. Box 867, Tulelake, CA 96134; (916) 667-2283. Visitor center open daily 9 to 6 in summer, 8 to 5 the rest of the year. Day use $4 per vehicle; campground with flush potties, water but no hookups, $6. (Campground water is turned off in winter, although it's available at the visitor center; no charge for winter camping.) No lodging, food services or gasoline in the park.*

When we last toured Lava Beds on a crisp November day, we were only the second callers to stop by in five days. Paper punch confetti still littered the visitor center counter where the ranger on duty had greeted the first group. Summer is busier, of course, and it's a good idea to get here early in the day to catch a spot at the campgrounds.

Lava Beds National Monument is three intriguing things: a dark and convoluted land of lava flows and lava tubes; a wildlife preserve busy with birds, jackrabbits and other critters; and the site of one of America's last Indian wars. Miles of hiking trails snake through the preserve, across lava fields and around cinder cones. During your visit, plan a night walk, when jack rabbits dance in your flashlight beam and kangaroo rats with silly-looking pom-pom tails perform erratic ballets.

As you approach the monument from Tulelake, across the squared shoreline of Tule Lake Sump, you'll encounter several sites of the Modoc War. Walk through the rough lava corridors of **Captain Jack's Stronghold,** where the Modocs held off an army force twenty times their strength for five months. Continuing on the black asphalt path that twists through blacker lava flows, you'll hit the visitor center. The campground is nearby. Although lava tubes are scattered throughout the monument, the greatest concentration is on Cave Loop Road, just up from the visitor center. Mushpot, adjacent to the center, is illuminated. For the others, you'll need your own light.

Chapter ten
THE BIG VALLEY
Shuttling through the San Joaquin

YOU'VE CERTAINLY HEARD that awful cliché that "it's a nice place to visit, but I wouldn't want to live there."

California's huge Central Valley gives that axiom a reverse spin. It's the state's fourth largest population center, after the Los Angeles Basin, the San Francisco Bay Area and San Diego, yet few people want to visit there. The valley's economic mainstay is agriculture. It's the largest farm belt in America, perhaps in the world. However, there's little in this flat landscape to tempt the tourist.

What hundreds of thousands of travelers do each year is go *through* the Central Valley, not *to* it. For those who choose not to fly, this great expanse offers the quickest land route between northern and southern California.

This chapter, then, provides a look at the valley for the incidental traveler, who might on occasion become an accidental tourist. If you've driven between the northern and southern ends of the state (and what Californian hasn't?), you may have wondered what lies on either side of the valley's two main arteries, I-5 and State Highway 99. This treatise intends to answer that question. Since few travelers stop, except for gas, we won't suffer you a lot of detail on lodging and restaurants.

We begin by discussing what the valley is and how it got that way. It's among the state's most distinctive topographical features, stretching more than 400 miles north to south, 50 miles sideways and covering 18,000 square miles. Looking more like Kansas than California, it's the largest piece of flatness west of the Rockies. The valley extends from the Siskiyou Mountains south to the Tehachapis just above Los Angeles. Although it's one contiguous piece of real estate, it carries two separate names, drawn from the

TRIP PLANNER

WHEN TO GO ● Some say that the Central Valley has two seasons—a hot and summer summer and a wet, foggy winter. That may be unkind, since spring and fall days can be quite nice. Given a choice, we'd go during the spring when orchard blossoms brighten the roadsides and scent the air, or in the fall and early winter when the hazy air isn't quite so. We'd certainly avoid the fog season, from mid-December to mid-February.

WHAT TO SEE ● Haggin Museum in Stockton, San Luis Reservoir near Los Banos, Kern County Museum and Pioneer Village near Bakersfield, Allensworth State Historical Park west of Earlimart, Metropolitan Museum and the zoo in Fresno, Castle Air Museum in Atwater, McHenry Museum in Modesto and the San Joaquin County Historical Museum near Lodi.

WHAT TO DO ● Drive or walk through Stockton's University of the Pacific campus, drag the main streets of Visalia and Merced, eat great steak at Harris Ranch restaurant near Coalinga, drive the foothills east of Visalia and the Fresno County blossom tour in spring, take the Hershey chocolate factory tour in Oakdale, get wet in summer at Manteca Waterslides, sip Zinfandel inside a giant wine barrel at Lodi's Oak Ridge Vineyard.

Useful contacts

Bakersfield Chamber of Commerce, P.O. Box 1947, Bakersfield, CA 93303; (805) 327-4421.

Fresno Convention & Visitors Bureau, 808 M St., Fresno, CA 93721; (800) 788-0836 or (209) 233-0836.

Lodi Chamber of Commerce, 1330 S. Ham Lane, Lodi, CA 95240; (209) 367-7840.

Modesto Chamber of Commerce, 1114 J St. (P.O. Box 844), Modesto, CA 95353; (209) 577-5757.

Stockton-San Joaquin Convention & Visitors Bureau, 46 W. Fremont St., Stockton, CA 95202; (800) 888-8016 or (209) 943-1987.

Visalia Convention & Visitors Bureau, 70 W. Mineral King Ave., Visalia, CA 93291; (209) 734-5876.

San Joaquin Valley radio stations

KATE-FM, 103.3, Stockton—country
KCJH-FM, 90, Stockton—Christian
KJOY-FM, 99, Stockton—business and news
KVFX-FM, 104.1, Stockton—rock and roll
KFMR-FM 100.1, Stockton—easy listening pops
KMIX-FM, 98.3, Turlock-Modesto—country
KTRV-AM, 860, Modesto-Stockton—top 40 and news
KFSO-FM, 92.9, Fresno—oldie pops
KEZL-FM, 96.7, Fresno—new wave and jazz
KSKS-FM, 93.7, Fresno—country
KBPR-FM, 89.3, Fresno—National Public Radio
KXSY-FM, 101.1, Fresno—easy listening
KFEQ-FM, 97-1, Lemoore-Hanford—rock
KBEE-AM, 790, Stockton—easy listening and news
KJAX-AM, 1280, Stockton—news and talk
KBLA-AM, 770, Stockton—talk radio
KRAK-AM, 1170, Stockton—country
KMJ-AM, 580, Fresno—talk
KFRE-AM, 940, Fresno—country
KRDU-AM, 1130, Dinuba—Christian

major rivers that run through it. The Sacramento Valley is the northern third, reaching from Red Bluff to some vague point below the capital city. From there south, it's called the San Joaquin Valley. Our chapter deals with the southern portion, since that's the main corridor for north-south traffic.

Every winter, millions of TV viewers see the valley—or at least its climatic effects—on satellite weather maps. It appears as a huge cigar-shaped pod of fog extending through California's heartland. The rest of Western America may be virtually clear, yet that off-white ellipse can persist for several days between rainstorms. After a rain, evaporating moisture is trapped between the Sierra Nevada and the Coast Range, creating this large pall of fog. National headlines are generated when the fog causes massive chain-reaction pile-ups. Some experts feel that the artificial greening of the valley through irrigation contributes to the haze.

There's no great geological mystery to the formation of this topographical anomaly. For eons, river runoff was trapped between the Sierra Nevada and the Coast range. This formed a giant inland sea that finally broke free at San Francisco's Golden Gate. What remains, only a hundred or so feet above sea level, is a giant settling basin of rich silt, sometimes reaching depths of over a thousand feet.

When early settlers came upon this valley, they saw—depending on the time of year—a vast grassland thatched with oak clusters and rich with spring wildflowers, or a tawny prairie. Today's travelers see wall-to-valley-wall vineyards, row crops, orchards and even fields of cotton. Agricultural superlatives flow here like irrigation water. The "Big Valley" is the nation's largest producer of vegetables, almonds, grapes, turkeys and rice (in flooded fields north of Sacramento); and it's a major cotton and citrus producer. It contains the world's second largest cattle feedlot and accounts for more than half of American's wine. Indeed, one-fourth of the nation's food supply comes from the valley; it's a $17 billion dollar a year industry.

Cities along the way offer several attractions for passing travelers, particularly along Highway 99. The newer route, I-5, planned during development of the 1960s California Water Project, travels through raw countryside on the valley's relatively undeveloped west side.

Longtime residents will recall that this project was a scheme to transport Northern California's water to the state's thirsty southern end. Several large corporate farms passionately pushed the plan, since it also brought irrigation water to tens of thousands of arid acres. Meanwhile, state planners sought a more direct north-south highway route to bring relief to the overcrowded Highway 99. A westside route was chosen, in some areas sharing topographic corridors with the aqueduct.

SOUTH ON I-5

The 235-mile stretch of I-5 between Manteca and Wheeler Ridge south of Bakersfield is the longest section of freeway ever completed as a single construction project. This thin ribbon of asphalt triggered special problems when it was opened in March of 1972. Since it passed through hot and dusty prairie wilderness for much of its route, few motorists' services existed. Hundreds of travelers eager to try this quick trip to L.A. found themselves stranded with empty gas tanks in the middle of nowhere. Auto clubs ran special rescue patrols and the news media carried advisories to top of your tank before starting out.

More than 20 years later, westside I-5 is still the loneliest busy highway in America, although clusters of service stations, motels and restaurants have sprouted at some interchanges.

Advisory for RVs and other motorists: Even with the growth of services at interchanges, you'll encounter stretches of 40 miles or more between fuel stops, so keep your vehicle tanked up. If possible, avoid driving either I-5 or Highway 99 during foggy periods. Motorhomes and trailers should be wary of high winds, common during the spring. In summer, the area is often baking hot; you might consider driving it at night. Although this asphalt ribbon seems endless and the scenery is something short of inspiring, quell that urge to press pedal to metal. The California Highway Patrol maintains a high profile along I-5, to ensure that bored drivers in a hurry don't get too lonely.

If you begin your run south from Sacramento, you'll pass farms and scattered homes instead of lonely prairie, since this end of the valley has been settled for decades. Still, you'll encounter no towns for the first 50 miles. The route brushes the edge of the California Delta, although its profile is too low to be evident from the freeway. Short drives westward will deliver you to the Sacramento River channel and its attendant Delta communities. We visited them in detail in Chapter 6. After an hours' worth of fields and farms, you'll encounter a town that figures prominently in California's history.

Stockton

Population: 215,058   **Elevation: 14 feet**

"Stockton is not just another Valley farm stop in the middle of nowhere," reads a visitors bureau brochure. Perhaps not, but it isn't a tourist mecca, either. Mostly, it's a thriving city galloping off in all directions, leaving its historic downtown area with an identity crisis. It wasn't always thus.

Pioneer Charles M. Weber had picked up a land grant from governor Manuel Micheltorena and began promoting settlement of the area in 1844. When gold was discovered in the nearby foothills, his hamlet of Tuleberg became a provisioning point on busy San Joaquin River route to the mines. In 1850, it was incorporated as Stockton; "Captain" Weber remained to shape and guide his city until his death in 1881. He created a planned community with wide streets, free public schools and a mixed economic base of business and agriculture. During California's formative years, Stockton was the state's first inland seaport, its second leading industrial center and third largest city, after San Francisco and Sacramento.

Stockton's University of the Pacific is California's oldest institute of higher learning, established in 1851. The town was one of the first in western America to build a streetcar system. It scored a different kind of history in 1904 when Benjamin Holt developed a tracked vehicle that wouldn't become mired in the boggey Delta farmlands. Onlookers said the contraption crawled along like a caterpillar, and a company was born. Military leaders came to study the device and they used Holt's design to develop the first successful tanks for World War I.

Today's Stockton is the third largest city in the Central Valley, after Sacramento and Fresno. It offers a couple of descent reasons to leave I-5. Approaching either from the north or south, take the downtown exit and follow El Dorado Street north a few blocks to Commerce. Go left one block through the civic center to the **Stockton-San Joaquin Convention and**

The Big Valley

Manteca
120
Oakdale
108
132
Modesto
5
99
N
Livingston
Henry W. Coe
State Park
Atwater
Castle
AFB
Gustine
140
Kesterson
Wildlife
Ref.
Merced
152
San Luis Res.
St. Rec. Area
33
Los Banos
152
Chowchilla
5
33
San Joaquin River
Firebaugh
99
Madera
Mendota
Mendota
Wildlife
Refuge
41
Fresno
198
Coalinga
41
Selma
198
Lemoore
Kingsburg
33
Hanford
J38
41
Visalia
Wood
Lake
198
Lemon
Cove
Delano
Wofford
Hgts.
Kernville
Isabelle
Lake
Bakersfield
178
58

Visitors Bureau; it's in a white masonry building at Commerce and Fremont. The bureau does a fine job of promoting Stockton and might even convince you to hang around for a bit. Driving brochures will take you through the downtown area, and into the nearby Delta and Gold Country.

Downtown Stockton is spacious in a disjointed sort of way, offering a mix of parklands, new buildings and empty lots. It's obviously in the midst of an ambitious renovation project, and all of this may make sense one day. A convention center, city hall and municipal auditorium are the area's focal points. A few old brick structures remain, many occupied by a Chinatown that has survived since the levee-building days of the adjacent Delta.

Return to El Dorado and continue north about 3.5 miles to Yokuts Avenue at the large **Sherwood Mall** shopping center. Turn left and follow Yokuts onto the campus of **San Joaquin Delta College**. It houses the **Earth Sciences Center,** open to the public on weekends, and the **Clever Planetarium**. Sky shows are presented Friday and Saturday at 7 and Sunday at 2; (209) 474-5110.

☺ The college borders on Pacific Avenue; just south is the **University of the Pacific.** With a wonderful Gothic-Ivy League look, this just may be the most attractive campus in western America. Particularly striking are the **Robert E. Burns Tower,** which hides a 150,000-gallon water tank, and the cathedral-like **Faye Stanos Concert Hall,** with a Gothic crown. Pick up a walking tour map in the lobby of Burns tower and follow it through this rich collection of fine old brick. Visitor parking is available in front of the concert hall.

Follow Stadium Way west through the campus, swing to the

left around **Tiger Stadium** onto Larry Heller Drive and you wind up on Pershing Way. Turn left and drive about a mile to Stockton's fine public museum, on the right, sitting in the middle of a park:

☺ **The Haggin Museum** ● *Pershing Avenue at Rose Street; (209) 462-4116. Tuesday-Sunday 1:30 to 5; $2 donation.* Occupying an imposing Greek style structure, the Haggin is at once an art gallery and Stockton's historical museum. The latter is the most interesting. Particularly noteworthy is the Benjamin Holt Hall, tracing the development of the tracked vehicle and the birth of the Caterpillar Tractor Company. A monster "Cat" and several other vintage pieces of farm equipment are displayed. Other exhibits include a Miwuk village with a bark shelter and stuff concerning the explorers, ranchers, trappers and gold- seekers who came this way.

From the museum, it's an easy hop back onto I-5. A couple of miles south on the freeway, you'll see a sign indicating **French Camp,** which is about a mile east. Stretching an historical point, it could be considered the oldest non-Spanish settlement in the state. It was established in 1828 as a rendezvous point for French-Canadian trappers. Charles Weber stopped by in 1844 to establish a farm colony. However, nothing survives of the original town. An historical landmark near the French Camp school will tell you all about.

South of here, I-5 continues its jaunt through the Central Valley, brushing and not quite touching the edges of **Manteca** and **Tracy.** Started as farm towns, they're now booming as bedroom communities to the San Francisco Bay Area, which hides just over Altamont Pass, west on I-205.

Then the final housing tract billboard—promising country living with modern amenities for under $100,000—flies past. You're in open farm country, and the highway begins playing tag with that large cement ditch. Originally called the California Aqueduct, it's now the **Edmund G. Brown Aqueduct,** in honor of the former governor who engineered the California Water Project. The foothills of the **Diablo Range** to the west add some contour to this land.

The monotony of I-5 begins. On your left, a mix of dusty prairie, croplands and orchards; on your right, the beige foothills of the Diablo Range. Ahead is the black asphalt strip, dancing in the heat like a pathway to eternity. Inviting lakes shimmer provocatively then vanish as mirages. Your companions are freight trucks droning monotonously at speeds well in excess of the limit, and lesser vehicles like yours—all in a hurry to get through this place. At roadside, you see an occasional fallen mechanical warrior with hood gaping open, a victim of too little fuel or too much speed on a hot day.

About the time you think this highway *does* lead to eternity, you see **Santa Nella,** a complex of service stations, motels and cafès. Like other I-5 interchange settlements, it isn't a town but a gathering of services supported almost entirely by passing traffic. The nearest town, **Los Banos,** is ten miles east on State Route 152. Several wildlife refuges—**Kesterson, Los Banos-San Luis, Volta** and **Merced**—are north of here, since the area lies in the path of the Pacific Flyway.

If you head west on Highway 152, you'll encounter the large **San Luis Reservoir State Recreation Area,** an inviting shimmer of blue that isn't a mirage. At the **Romero Visitor Center,** you'll learn that it's the largest reservoir in the San Joaquin Valley, with a capacity of more than two million acre feet. Further, San Luis Dam is the world's only major dam that isn't on a natural water source. It was completed in 1967 as a joint venture of the

Central Valley Project and California Water Project to create a storage basin for south-flowing aqueducts. The center is open daily 9 to 5; (209) 826-0718. recreation area rimming the lake's dry, grassy shoreline offers the usual water sports, swimming, hiking trails and picnicking. A tree-shaded campground off Highway 152 has showers, barbecues and picnic tables but no hookups; $12 per night. Call (209) 826-1196.

If you press west on Highway 152, you'll top 1,368-foot **Pacheco Pass** just above the lake. The highway then weaves through the Diablo Range and drop down into the Salinas Valley. Just east of the highway 152-156 junction, you might find **Casa de Fruta** worth a pause. It's a large specialty foods complex with an RV park, motel, service station, kiddie zoo, playland and gift shops. One of the specialties here, which sounds odd but tastes good, is chocolate covered dried fruit. For RV or motel reservations, contact: Casa De Fruta, 6680 Pacheco Pass Highway, Hollister, CA 95023; (800) 548-3813 or (408) 842-9316.

If you continue west beyond Casa de Fruta, you'll wind up in Chapter 5. Back on I-5, you're about to enter the loneliest stretch of this lonely highway. Between the Highway 152 interchange and the turnoff to Coalinga, you'll cover 65 miles of nothing but miles and miles.

After a weary hour, your first clue to civilization will be olfactory, not visual. The farther you drive, the stronger it becomes—the mother of all corral stinks. Top a low rise and you're greeted by a startling sight—about 100,000 beef cattle standing ankle-deep in their own doo-doo. It's the world's second largest feedlot (we'd hate to be downwind of the first), part of the extensive Harris Ranch operation.

Another three miles takes you to a considerably more attractive and aromatic phase of the ranch. In this remote land where one expects mirages, the vision of palm-shaded, Spanish colonial Harris Ranch Inn & Restaurant is real. It sits at the junction of I-5 and State Highway 198, safely upwind of the feedlot. The lavishly landscaped gathering of pink stucco looks more Palm Springs than westside San Joaquin Valley.

☺ *Harris Ranch Restaurant* ● △△△ $$
Route 1, Box 777, Coalinga; (209) 935-0717. American; full bar service. Daily 6 a.m. to 11 p.m. Major credit cards. Very stylish restaurant with beamed ceilings, high-backed chairs and tile accents. The adjacent coffee shop is equally appealing, done in a "California rural" mode with a packing crate label décor. The menu focuses strongly on beef and fresh produce from the extensive Harris Ranch operation. It also offers a good selection of chicken, seafood and other entrées. We've had several excellent meals here, and prices are reasonable.

☺ *The Inn at Harris Ranch* ● ⌂⌂⌂ $$$$ Ø
Route 1, Box 777, Coalinga, CA 93210; (800) 943-2333 or (209) 935-0717. Couples $80 to $85, singles $77 to $82, suites $86 to $215. Major credit cards. Like a proper oasis, this attractive complex has a swimming pool, spa and tennis courts surrounded by elaborate landscaping. Nicely done rooms have TV movies, phones and resort amenities. A private airstrip is nearby.

Fourteen miles west of here, reached either by Highway 33 from the feedlot or Route 198 from the inn, is the prim little town of **Coalinga.** It's prim primarily because the downtown area was flattened by an earthquake a few years ago and had to be rebuilt. The odd name comes from the town's roots as a coaling station for nearby mines in the 1890s. "Coaling Station A" was shortened to Coalinga as a settlement grew around the rail junction.

☺ Note the **oil pumping rigs** wearing whimsical animal faces, along the highway into town. Once in Coalinga, pause at the nicely done **R.C. Baker Memorial Museum** at 297 W. Elm Street (west side of town). It offers a extensive and orderly collection of pioneer artifacts, including oil-field rigging, stuff from local ranches, fossils and Native American exhibits. It's open weekdays 10 to noon and 1 to 5, Saturdays 11 to 5, and Sundays and holidays 1 to 5. Free; donations appreciated; (209) 935-1914.

The rolling landscape around Coalinga offers a nice break from the monotony of the San Joaquin Valley. Those attractively folded hills to the west are the **Gavilans,** part of the Diablo Range. A drive west on Highway 198 and then north on Route 25 will take you to **Pinnacles National Monument,** and other lures that we covered in Chapter 5. If you'd like to do a scenic if somewhat curving loop, continue north from the Pinnacles to **Hollister,** passing through the attractive agricultural valley of **Paicines.** Then go west to the charming old mission town of **San Juan Bautista,** and east on Highway 162 past **Casa de Fruta** and **San Luis Reservoir.**

South of Harris Ranch on I-5, settle in for 110 miles of serious monotony. No reservoir, ranch oasis or coaling station offers distraction along this barren stretch of highway. Dusty hills and angry summer heat tell you that you're approaching Southern California. This term of tedium finally is broken at **Wheeler Ridge,** where I-5 merges with Highway 99.

Ahead, appearing as formidable barriers, but pierced by the well-engineered I-5 freeway, are the **Tehachapi Mountains.** They mark an abrupt end to California's immense Central Valley, and the end of our journey south. If you're continuing over the hills and into the Los Angeles Basin, be advised that you have a long, tough climb ahead. On a hot summer day, try to avoid this grade around high noon so your vehicle won't overheat.

NORTH ON HIGHWAY 99

Peering north across the San Joaquin Valley from the foot of the Tehachapis, you'll note that I-5 veers off to the west and older Highway 99 fires straight ahead. It disappears into its own converging lines—and usually into a pall of haze or even light smog—on the far horizon.

If you're northbound on I-5 and have just completed that long spiral down the **Grapevine** from **Tejon Pass,** you'll be struck by the absolute flatness of the terrain ahead. ("Grapevine" was the name given to old highway 99 that twisted and writhed down the Tehachapi's steep north face.)

Unlike I-5, old 99 offers frequent encounters with civilization, since it dates back to 19th century wagon tracks. While the more glamorous El Camino Real to the west tied the coastal missions together, Highway 99 cut through the hot and dusty inland valley to serve early farm communities. Straighter than El Camino (which essentially became U.S. 101), it was the preferred route between Los Angeles and San Francisco.

Longtime Californians recall those days when two lanes of asphalt shouldered past auto courts, gas pumps and farm labor camps. Offering respite from miles of farmland were Bakersfield, Fresno and that string of "M-sisters"—Madera, Merced, Modesto and Manteca. Along the way, travelers stopped at Giant Orange stands—built in the shape of the citrus—to quench their thirst while letting their radiators cool.

Travelers in the San Joaquin Valley will encounter bits of whimsey such as this flowered teapot water tower in Swedish-style Kingsburg and the "iron zoo" of Coalinga's oil pumping rigs. — **Betty Woo Martin**

When Highway 99 became a freeway, it was hacked inelegantly through the middle of towns that were never elegant to begin with. We've always regarded it as a rather ugly freeway, lacking the scenery of Highway 101 and the engineering grace of I-5. The first town on northbound 99 relates more to Southern California. However, since you're in the neighborhood, we'll cover it briefly:

Bakersfield

Population: 174,000   **Elevation: 408 feet**

Bakersfield doesn't seem to belong in California. Surrounded by cotton fields and oil fields, it suggests a blue collar town of America's South. Its role as a major country music center further validates its apparent misplacement. However, thousands of acres of citrus in gently rolling terrain to the east confirm its geographic right to be in the Golden State.

Sitting in the bottled-up southern end of the San Joaquin, Bakersfield suffers both from summer smog and winter fog. However, lots of folks have found something to love, since the town has grown rapidly in recent decades. Agriculture and oil provide a solid economic base.

Residents seek refuge by heading for **Lake Isabella** and the **Kern River** to the northeast, where the Tehachapis collide with the Sierra Nevada. Although this southern extremity of the Sierra is rather barren in comparison with its higher reaches to the north, it does provide relief from summer heat. We touched on this area at the end of Chapter 8.

☺ Bakersfield offers at least one good reason to leave Highway 99. The **Kern County Museum** covers the oil and agricultural development of the area, as well as its natural history. Adjacent **Pioneer Village** is a collection of 56 old buildings moved here from elsewhere in the county. The 14-acre complex is east of town at 3801 Chester Avenue. To find it, take the Olive Avenue exit from Highway 99 near Oildale, drive about east two mile east to Chester and then head south for three miles. It's open weekdays 8 to 5 and weekends 10 to 5; last admission is two hours before closing. Adults $5, seniors $4 and kids $3; (805) 323-8368 or 861-2132.

Another outdoor facility, northeast off State Highway 178 (the Lake Isabella route) is the **California Living Museum** at 14000 Old Alfred Harrell Highway. It's a small environmental zoo, with species indigenous to the area. Hours are Tuesday-Sunday (plus Mondays on holiday weekends) 10 to dusk; adults $3.50, seniors $2.50 and kids $2; (805) 872-2256.

Heading north from Bakersfield on Highway 99, you pass the nondescript farm towns of **McFarland** and **Delano.** Just above **Earlimart,** head seven miles west on county road J-22 to visit town that began as a dream and ended in dust:

Colonel Allensworth State Historic Park ● *Star Route 1, Box 148, Earlimart, CA 93219; (805) 849-3433. Daily 10 to 4. Day use $3 per vehicle; camping $12.* California's only all-black community, Allensworth was established in 1908 as the utopian dream of a runaway slave. Allen Allensworth joined the Union army, served until retirement, became a minister and came west. In 1909, at the age of 66, he founded Allensworth, a town where Blacks could live, work and prosper, free of persecution and prejudice. He was killed five years later in an accident in Los Angeles, but his village continue to prosper. Then during the Dust Bowl era the water table dropped, and the local water company refused to service the town. Discrimination, which former slaves and their children had come here to escape, finally killed Allensworth. The last family moved away in 1959. At the urging of some ex-residents, it became a state historic park in 1976.

Budget constraints have limited restoration. A few buildings are being returned to their original condition, including Colonel Allensworth's home and the community school. They can be opened for viewing on request. In the small visitor center, exhibits and a 30-minute video trace the triumphs and tragedies of a peoples' pursuit of the American dream.

Continuing your trek north, breeze through **Pixley** and **Tipton,** then leave the freeway at **Tulare,** and head northeast on Highway 63. You might pause for a peek at the **Tulare Historical Museum** at 444 W. Tulare Avenue. It's open Thursday-Saturday 10 to 4 and Sunday 12:30 to 4; (209) 686-2074. In addition to the usual pioneer artifacts, it has some nicely done dioramas and furnished rooms from early homes and businesses. A six-mile drive northeast of Tulare takes you to a disarmingly charming town:

Visalia

Population: 81,685   **Elevation: 351 feet**

Visalia has an aura of comfortable prosperity. Handsome, well-tended old homes line streets shaded by mature trees. Its downtown area is an idealized California version of Main Street USA, with a mix of Spanish and middle America architecture. Sitting well off Highway 99, it doesn't have the unattractive commercial strip that's typical of many communities. Visalia fits comfortably into foothill contours, and the nearby Sierra Nevada provides a dramatic backdrop.

Dating from 1852, it's the second oldest city in the San Joaquin Valley, after Stockton. With its relatively mild foothill location, it thrived as a business center for surrounding ranches, farms and orchards.

Approaching from Tulare on Highway 63, you'll merge with State Route 198 (Mineral King Avenue) beside the **College of the Sequoias** campus. Several motels are clustered along Mineral King, since Visalia is a gateway to Sequoia National Park. Go east briefly on Mineral King, then turn left onto West Main and pass creekside **West Main Park,** shaded by giant oaks. Main curves around to the right to run parallel with Mineral King.

Visalia obviously has escaped suburban business flight, since the downtown commercial district is alive and thriving. Brick sidewalks and almond trees add visual enhancement. Note the wonderful old Spanish colonial **Fox Theater** at Main and Encina. If you'd like to prowl through Visalia's neighborhoods to see some elegant Victorian homes, stop by the **Convention and Visitors Bureau** at 720 W. Mineral King to pick up historical tour maps. Instead of returning to Highway 99, we're going to suggest an inland loop into pleasing foothill country. Continue through the downtown area on Main Street, go right onto Bridge Street and cross over Route 198, which has become a sunken freeway. Turn left onto a frontage road (Noble Street) and follow it several blocks; it merges with the highway in front of the Spanish style Mary's Vineyard Shopping Center.

Ahead is one of the California's more pleasing landscapes—gently rolling pasturelands, vineyards and orange groves, with the Sierran spires of Sequoia National Park rising behind. It's especially striking from December through March, when winter oranges are ripening on the trees and snow blankets the Sierra crests. Creamy white almond blossoms add further visual drama in late February. About ten miles from Visalia, you have choices. Continue on Route 198 to **Lake Kaweah Recreation Area** and Sequoia National Park, or turn north onto State Highway 245 toward **Woodlake.** (Sequoia was a High Sierra destination in Chapter 8.)

Along route 245, the lush orange groves crowd the roadway, tempting you to reach out and pluck some breakfast. (Resist the itch to snitch; there's a fine for stealing oranges.) Beyond Woodlake, rocky outcroppings and green foothills join this pleasing portrait of grove and mountain. Turn left onto State Route 201 at **Elderwood** and head back to the great flatness of the San Joaquin Valley. En route, you'll pass more exposed rock and a bucolic parade of almonds, fruit trees and vineyards.

Staying with Highway 201, you'll reach Freeway 99 at a town that's trying terribly hard to be Swedish.

Kingsburg

Population: 6,789   **Elevation: 297 feet**

"*Valkommen,*" says the sign. Visually, downtown Kingsburg almost works. Half-timbered buildings, scalloped shingles and dormer windows give the impression of a Swedish village. And the town's water tower fashioned into a flowered coffee pot is a delight.

However, the thing doesn't quite come together. We looked in vain for charming little Swedish cafès; we sniffed in vain for bakeries brimming with Scandinavian pastries. **Munson's Swedish Bakery** at 1508 Draper sells mostly American pastries, and **Ideal Home Bakery** at 1565 Draper is Mexican. **Draper Street Cafè** at 1332 Draper is cute, and it's inside an even cuter shopping mall, but the complex lacks Swedish ambiance.

The town does have a couple of gift shops with some Scandinavian stuff, and several antique stores. However, it's not a San Joaquin Valley version of southern California's famous Solvang. Curiously, the most Scandinavian building in Kingsburg is a Texaco service station, complete with windmill.

Certainly, Kingsburg's visual appeal is worth a pause, and you can get cardeman braided bread and ground beef and cabbage rolls at Munson's. Life becomes very Scandinavian during the annual Swedish Festival in late May, with ethnic music, costumes, dance and food. For specifics, call the Kingsburg Chamber of Commerce at (209) 897-2925.

Pick up the freeway at the base of Draper Street and continue north-ward. The Kamm/Bethel Avenue offramp takes you to the **Sun-Maid Raisin Store** at 13525 S. Bethel, open weekdays 9:30 to 4:30; (209) 896-8000. It offers raisins, of course, and a selection of other dried fruits, nuts and California specialty foods. **Selma,** a few miles north, claims with good reason to be the raisin capital of the world. More than 95 percent of America's shriveled grapes are produced within a 45-mile radius.

Ten miles north, take the Jensen Avenue offramp at **Calwa** and head east. After three miles, you'll encounter **Simonian Farms** at Jensen and Clovis avenues. The complex features a large farmers' market and specialty foods store, plus an extensive display of old farm equipment. It's open daily 8 to 6; (209) 237-2294. Back on Highway 99, the rural countryside takes on a distinctive urban sprawl. You're approaching the San Joaquin Valley's scattered population core.

Fresno

Population: 367,000   **Elevation: 294 feet**

Is poor Fresno really the Rodney Dangerfield of California cities? Did the *Fresno* TV mini-series that lampooned *Dynasty* and *Dallas* further corrode its tarnished image? Then why is it California's seventh large city, just behind Sacramento and Oakland?

According to Fresno's most famous son, the town really isn't all that bad. Mostly, it's just *there.* Wrote William Saroyan, after living in San Francisco, Hollywood, New York and Paris, and then returning home:

I don't think I know what it is precisely that Fresno has. Certainly, I don't know what it's got that some other town hasn't got. I do know that it's got me, because when I left Fresno in 1929, my idea was never to go back. That was a good idea until I discovered that New York was Fresno all over again.

The town began as a railway stop in 1885, taking its Spanish name from ash trees growing along banks of the nearby San Joaquin and Kings rivers. Irrigation ditches were extended from those streams, and Fresno just kept growing. It is today the center of the largest agricultural area in the United States, producing more than 200 varieties of crops. The county's $3 billion annual crop income is the highest in America.

What it makes up for in agricultural wealth, it lacks in charm. Mostly, it's a megasprawl of shopping centers and subdivisions, pushing agriculture beyond its ever-widening perimeter. For a quick peek at this giant king of cabbages and other things, take the Ventura Avenue exit into the downtown area. It's capped by a few modest highrises, with the old Spanish style Security Bank tower as a focal point.

After driving a few blocks northeast on Ventura, turn left onto Van Ness Avenue and pass between the **Civic Center** complex and **Fulton Mall**. Fulton is one of America's first downtown shopping malls, dating from the

1950s. Like much of the rest of downtown, however, it's looking a bit scruffy. Significantly, it's not listed among shopping areas in the convention bureau's visitor's guide.

If you want to pick up that visitor guide, stop at the **Fresno Convention and Visitors Bureau** at M and Inyo streets (open 8 to 5 weekdays). To reach it, turn right onto Inyo from Van Ness and drive two blocks to M. Back on Van Ness, continue a few blocks to Calaveras Street for Fresno's bastion of culture:

☺ ***Metropolitan Museum*** ● *1555 Van Ness Ave.; (209) 441- 1444. Wednesday 11 to 7, Thursday-Friday 11 to 5, weekends 10 to 5. Adults $4, seniors and kids $3.* Housed in the old square- shouldered *Fresno Bee* building, the "Met" covers a bit of everything, from American and European art to social science and nature. Kids will like the Playland Science Gallery, where they can fiddle with a plasma globe, chaotic pendulum and other scientific stuff. The museum's best exhibit is a fine retrospective on Fresno's Pulitzer Prize-winning author, William Saroyan. The son of Armenian immigrants, he was born here in 1908, went away to seek literary fame, ultimately returned to his hometown and died here in 1981. Graphics in the exhibit describe Fresno as a town he "loved, despised, tolerated and celebrated."

From the museum, go southwest on Calaveras for three blocks and turn right onto North H street. Follow it about a mile, then go left onto Belmont Avenue, ducking under a railway crossing. Loop through a traffic circle (following a "Highway 99" sign) and take Belmont to **Roeding Park** and the San Joaquin Valley's best zoo:

☺ ***Chaffe Zoological Gardens*** ● *Roeding Park; (209) 266-9543. Daily 10 to 6:30 in summer, 10 to 5 the rest of the year. Adults $4, seniors $2.50 and kids $1.50; plus $1 per car park admission.* This fine mid-sized zoo features a realistic rainforest exhibit (we went there to stare at a sloth after failing to spot one during an Amazon trip), the world's only computerized reptile house and a large Asian elephant compound. More than 600 species of mammals, birds and reptiles are counted among the zoo's critter collection. The surrounding Roeding Park has a kiddie playland with rides, historic fort reconstruction, picnic facilities an impressive batch of botanicals.

Fresno County in bloom

If you're planning a trip through the area in early spring, get the convention and visitors bureau's *Fresno Visitors Map,* which contains a blossom trail guide. A circuitous 67-mile route takes you past flowering almonds, plums, apples, citrus, apricots, peaches and nectarines. The map even tells you how to identify various blooms. Get a copy at the downtown office at M and Inyo streets (8 to 5 weekdays), or a satellite bureau at Simonian Farms (daily 8 to 6). Or contact: Fresno Convention & Visitors Bureau, 808 M St., Fresno, CA 93721; (800) 788-0836 or (209) 435-5545.

From Roeding Park, Belmont Avenue will return you to the freeway. You shortly cross into Madera County and pass its seat of **Madera,** another growing agricultural/commercial community. Twelve miles north, on your right near the Highway 99-152, you'll see a bit of history—one of the valley's few surviving **Giant Orange** refreshment stands. Just above, **Chowchilla** offers a large antique mall, for those interested in that sort of thing. The next town provides at least two excuses to leave the freeway, and maybe three if you're a gun nut:

Merced

Population: 53,550   **Elevation: 417 feet**

Like Visalia, Merced offers a nicely-kept middle America downtown, plus a couple of museums. It's a major gateway to Yosemite National Park and the Gold Country. Just beyond, between Merced and Atwater, is an excellent aviation museum.

Take the Highway 140 Mariposa/exit and follow it about a mile east to the **Yosemite Wildlife Museum.** The name may mislead you, however. The "museum" consists of stuffed critters in a display room beside a gun shop and shooting range. The message here is more NRA than environmental. Hours are Monday-Saturday 10 to 5; adults $2.50, seniors and kids $1.50; (209) 383-1052.

From the museum, reverse your route on Yosemite Parkway and take a quick half-right onto 21st Street. You'll pass through a well-tended neighborhood with some imposing Victorian and early American homes. You then encounter the **Merced County Courthouse Museum** at 21st and N streets. Built in 1875, this former courthouse is styled after California's capitol. Inside are the usual pioneer relics and exhibits tracing the area's agricultural history. It's open Wednesday-Sunday 1 to 3.

From the courthouse, follow N Street down to Main and turn right for a slice of Americana. Downtown Merced offers a pleasing mix of old brick and masonry buildings, most well-maintained, with extended and landscaped sidewalks. Drag Main until you've cleared the business district, then drop down a block to 16th street and continue northwest. You'll eventually blend onto Highway 99.

After four miles, take the Buhach Road exit and follow it north two miles to **Castle Air Force Base.** Just short of the gate, turn left onto Santa Fe Avenue. Within a few hundred feet is an archive to the wild blue yonder:

☺ *Castle Air Museum* ● *Santa Fe Drive (P.O. Box 488), Atwater, CA 95301; (209) 723-2178. Daily 10 to 4; free.* Anyone who loves combat aircraft—from the legendary Flying Fortress to the lethal-looking Blackbird—will love this place. Your eyes will first be drawn to the long, lean and black SR-17, parked beside Santa Fe Drive. Although retired, the Blackbird is still one of the fastest things a-wing, capable of Mach 3. Nearly 40 other aircraft are posted about this large outdoor compound, including a couple of contributions from Canada and Great Britain. The warplanes range from World War II bombers and cargo craft to a wide assortment of post-war jets. The collection includes a rare B-45, the world's oldest jet bomber, along with B-29 and B-50 superbombers. A small indoor museum displays armaments, insignia, combat photos and other military aviation memorabilia. A gift shop, snack bar, outdoor patio and a nearby picnic area complete the complex.

Incidentally, the museum will survive the planned 1995 closure of Castle Air Force Base. It will be turned over to a non-profit association.

Beyond Atwater is **Livingston,** who's claim to fame is that it has the only stoplight on Highway 99 between the Tehachapis and Sacramento. Since this breaks your flight pattern, you might consider a couple of nearby cafés for a lunch or dinner break.

Foster Farms Livingston Café ● Δ $

Highway 99, Livingston; (209) 394-7950. American; no alcohol. Sunday-Wednesday 6 a.m. to 3 p.m., Thursday-Saturday 6 to 10. Most Californians know that Foster Farms is a local chicken-plucking company that operates a few restaurants. Simple family-style places, they specialize in chicken dinners and they're generally excellent. You also can get steaks, chops and fish here, but go for the cluckers. Their chicken nuggets put the Colonel's to shame. The café is a block beyond the traffic light, on the east side.

Blueberry Hill Café ● △△ $

Highway 99, two miles north of Livingston; (209) 394-2733. American; wine and beer. Open 24 hours. MC/VISA. Various versions of this family restaurant have been around since 1959. The current rendition is fashioned of attractive stone and brick, with ceiling fans and open beams. The menu is exceedingly American, featuring breaded veal, fried chicken, and ham with sweet potatoes. The café's on the west side of the highway.

North of Livingston, **Turlock** has an old-fashioned tree-lined main street that is neither scruffy nor interesting. To the northeast is the new campus of **California State University, Stanislaus.** About 18 miles north of Turlock on Highway 99 is another "M" town which, believe it or not, was named after the Spanish word for modesty.

Modesto

Population: 172,000   **Elevation: 88 feet**

There's nothing modest about Modesto's reputation. Featured in native son George Lucas' hit film *American Graffiti*, it jealously guards this curious claim to fame. Each June, it stages the "Graffiti USA" cruising festival with cars, music and costumes of the 1950s. The grand cruise of vintage cars down McHenry Avenue is worth a special trip.

You can do your own cruise through Modesto by taking the 108/132 exit east, which puts you parallel to the freeway on Sixth Street. After a few blocks, turn right onto I street and pass under the old fashioned arch reading "Modesto: Water Wealth Contentment Health." Downtown has a sturdy, durable look, but without the charm of Merced or Visalia. A short distance beyond, at 14th and I, is a fine archive:

☺ *McHenry Museum* ● *1402 I St.; (209) 577-5366. Tuesday-Sunday noon to 4. Free; donations appreciated.* You won't find any chopped and channeled Chevys in here, but you will find a nicely restored 1881 stagecoach that ran between Sonora and Bodie. Other exhibits in this fine museum include a pioneer kitchen, children's room, McHenry Mercantile general store, dentist's office and a blacksmith shop. The federalist style building is a museum piece itself, built in 1912 as the town library. Note the wise old owls on the entrance rotunda. The building also houses the **Central California Art League Gallery,** open Monday-Saturday 10 to 4.

A block beyond the museum at 15th and I streets is the **McHenry Mansion,** an elaborate Victorian with 19th century furnishings. It's open to visitors Sunday and Tuesday-Thursday from 1 to 4; (209) 577-5344. As you've probably guessed, McHenry (Robert) was a leading Modesto citizen. He owned a ranch on the outskirts and the bank in town. The mansion was his town house.

Modesto's major employer is the world's largest vintner. **Gallo Winery,** established in the 1930s by Ernest and Julio, produces more than 100 million gallons of wine a year, nearly a fourth of America's total output. However, it doesn't offer tours and there's not even a sign out front to identify the complex. If you're curious to see the place, go south from the museum on 14th street, cross D street and blend onto Yosemite Boulevard, which swerves to the left. Cross a bridge by a small creekside park, turn right onto Santa Rosa Avenue and there it is!

There what is?

E&J Gallo Winery has all the glamor of a storage shed—actually, a lot of storage sheds. The sprawling complex, now surrounded by the town, consists of acres of windowless buildings and forests of fat storage tanks.

If you'd like to nibble some almonds and see how they're grown and harvested, return to the freeway, drive a bit over four miles north and get off at Kiernan Avenue (Highway 219). Take an immediate right onto Sisk Road and follow it south briefly to the **Blue Diamond Almond Growers Store.** It's open weekdays 10 to 5; (209) 545-3222.

Do you prefer your almonds in chocolate? Head inland to **Oakdale** for a visit to the large Hershey chocolate factory. It was established in this area because of easy access to almonds and dairies. To get there, take Kiernan east about five miles to its intersection with McHenry Avenue (Route 108). Turn north and follow 108 through Riverbank to Oakdale, where your route becomes F Street. At the stop light in downtown Oakdale, turn right onto Yosemite Avenue and then take a quick left into the parking lot of the Hershey Visitor's Center.

☺ *Hershey factory tour* ● *Yosemite and F streets, Oakdale; (209) 848-8126. Tours conducted weekdays 8:30 to 3; visitor center/gift shop hours weekdays 8:30 to 5 and Saturday 10 to 4:30.* A chocoholic's dream, the gift shop sells the full Hershey line, plus assorted chocolate curios and souvenirs. The plant is a couple of miles away, reached by tour buses that depart periodically. There, you'll see thousands of gallons of chocolate being stirred in huge vats, tens of thousands of Reese's peanut butter cups marching along conveyor belts and zillions Hershey's kisses tumbling into their foil wrapping machines. At the end of the tour, you'll be returned to the visitor center for a free Hershey bar.

Without almonds.

Incidentally, Oakdale is a great little wanna-be-cowboy town. If you need a new Stetson or Tony Lama boots, stop by **Oakdale Feed and Seed,** just down from the Hershey center on Yosemite. To find your way back to the freeway, head northwest on Yosemite Avenue (Route 120) through **Escalon** to **Manteca.** If it's a warm day and you have restless kids (or if you're restless), consider taking a break at Oakwood Lake Resort's water park. It also has a campground. To get there, stay with Route 120 as it zigs briefly south on Highway 99 and then swings west toward San Francisco. Take the Airport Way exit south and go right onto Woodward Avenue.

Manteca Waterslides ● *874 E. Woodward Ave., Manteca, CA 95336; (209) 239-2500. Open daily June through August, 10 to 7; weekends only in May and September, 10 to 6. Park admission $7.95; all day water slide pass $15.95. Campground open all year. Summer rates—water and electric $21 and full hookups $22 to $25; off-season rates—$16 and $17 to $20. MC/VISA, AMEX.* Get soggy on the Rapids Ride, Rampage or Turbo Tube, then adjourn for lunch at the snack bar or pizza shop. This large complex has 20 water slides, picnic areas and a 75-acre lake with swimming beaches, adjoining the San Joaquin River.

Continuing north from Manteca, Highway 99 brushes the eastern edge of

Stockton, which we discussed earlier in this chapter. At French Camp road just below Stockton, you might like to hop off for a visit to **Delicato Vineyards** tasting room and gift shop. It's open daily 9 to 5:30, winery tours Fridays only at 10, 2 and 4 or by appointment; (209) 825-6212.

A couple of miles above Stockton, the Eight Mile Road offramp will take you to **Pollardsville,** a dinner house and so-called ghost town on the east side of the freeway. For decades, the Pollard family dragged several old buildings to this spot and reconstructed them. We found the place to be rather scruffy and run-down, although it does contain some interesting old structures. The complex includes a run-aground riverboat used for dinner theater shows and the **Chicken Kitchen Restaurant.**

Before pressing northward, take time to visit an outstanding regional museum in **Micke Grove Park.** To get there, cross the freeway on Eight Mile Road, go west briefly, then north on Micke Grove Road.

☺ *San Joaquin County Historical Museum* ● *Micke Grove Park, (P.O. Box 21), Lodi, CA 95241; (209) 368-9154 or 463-4119. Wednesday-Sunday noon to 5. Adults $1, seniors and kids 50 cents; plus a modest per-car admission to the park.* The history of San Joaquin County is nicely presented in this large indoor-outdoor complex, which is a joint operation of the county and the local historical society. Check out the pioneer kitchen with its 1920s canning scene, the large farm tool collection, furnishings from Stockton's founding Weber family and Ben Holt's tractors. Then take a stroll along the "Sunshine Trail," a clever botanical trip across California, with streams, native stones and plants and a covered bridge. This regional park also includes a swimming pool, kiddie rides, picnic area and small zoo.

The **Lodi** wine producing area is just north of here. A few years ago, this was a popular winery touring area as well. However, all but one of its public tasting rooms is closed. The next-to-the-last one bit the dust in the spring of 1993. The lone survivor is certainly worth the brief detour from the freeway, since it claims to be the only tasting room housed in a wine barrel. To reach it, take the central Lodi/Highway 12 exit and go east toward San Andreas. The winery is about a mile in from the freeway, on your right.

☺ **Oak Ridge Vineyard** offers samples of its wines in a 49,429-gallon redwood tank, built originally for the old Roma winery across the street. Tasting hours are daily from 9 to 5; (209) 369-4758. The wines, incidentally, are quite good and very inexpensive.

Lodi hasn't lost its wineries, only its public tasting rooms. About eight of the area's vintners offer tasting and tours by appointment. For a map with addresses and phone numbers, contact the **Lodi Chamber of Commerce,** 1330 S. Ham Lane, Lodi, CA 95240; (209) 367-7840; or the **Stockton Convention & Visitors Bureau,** 46 W. Fremont St., Stockton, CA 95202, (800) 821-4441 or (209) 943-1987.

There's not much of interest on Highway 99 north of Lodi, with the obvious exception of Sacramento, which we gave a thorough going-over in Chapter 6. And so we end this book by approaching the capital city, where Gringo California began.

Chapter eleven
AFTERTHOUGHTS
The very best of Northern California

AFTER SPENDING the previous ten chapters exploring Northern California's diverse lures, let's have a bit of fun and select the very best that the region has to offer. We'll pick our favorite in each category, followed by the other nine in alphabetical order. Thus, we have no losers in the *Northern California Discovery Guide*, only winners and runners up.

THE TEN BEST ATTRACTIONS

1. Yosemite National Park, chapter 8, page 304.
2. Avenue of the Giants, chapter 4, page 130.
3. Columbia State Historic Park, chapter 7, page 254.
4. Golden Gate Bridge & Fort Point, chapter 2, page 38.
5. Lassen Volcanic National Park, chapter 9, page 319.
6. Lava Beds National Monument, chapter 9, page 330.
7. Monterey State Historic Park, chapter 5, page 169.
8. Northern Sonoma County wine country, chapter 3, page 76.
9. Point Reyes National Seashore, chapter 4, page 108.
10. Sequoia/Kings Canyon National Parks, chapter 8, page 311.

THE TEN BEST MUSEUMS

1. Monterey Bay Aquarium, Monterey, chapter 5, page 171.
2. California Academy of Sciences, San Francisco, chapter 2, page 46.
3. California State Mining and Mineral Museum, Mariposa, chapter 8, page 262.
4. California State Railroad Museum, Sacramento, chapter 2, page 217.
5. De Young and Asian Art Museum, San Francisco, chapter 2, page 46.

6. Maritime Museum of Monterey, chapter 5, page 170.
7. Metropolitan Museum, Fresno, chapter 10, page 342.
8. National Maritime Museum and Hyde Street Pier historic ships, San Francisco, chapter 2, page 47-48.
9. Oakland Museum, Oakland, chapter 2, page 63.
10. San Joaquin County Historical Museum, chapter 10, page 345.

THE TEN MOST INTERESTING TOWNS OR CITIES

1. Monterey, chapter 5, page 161.
2. Bishop, chapter 8, page 294.
3. Carmel, chapter 5, page 166.
4. Ferndale, chapter 4, page 131.
5. Mendocino, chapter 4, page 120.
6. Nevada City, chapter 7, page 237.
7. Sacramento, chapter 6, page 216.
8. San Francisco, chapter 2, page 35.
9. San Juan Bautista, chapter 5, page 194.
10. Trinidad, chapter 4, page 138.

THE TEN BEST RESTAURANTS

1. The Big Four, Huntington Hotel, San Francisco, chapter 2, page 52.
2. Butterworth's, Auburn, chapter 7, page 233.
3. Cafe Beaujolais, Mendocino, chapter 4, page 123.
4. City Hotel Restaurant, Columbia, chapter 7, page 256.
5. Donatello, San Francisco, chapter 2, page 53.
6. Evans American Gourmet Cafe, South Lake Tahoe, chapter 8, page 277.
7. The French Laundry, Yountville, chapter 3, page 98.
8. Manka's Inverness Restaurant, chapter 4, page 113.
9. The Sardine Factory, Monterey, chapter 5, page 175.
10. Silks, San Francisco, chapter 2, page 53.

THE TEN BEST HOTELS

1. Four Seasons Clift, San Francisco, chapter 2, page 58.
2. Eureka Inn, Eureka, chapter 4, page 137.
3. The Fairmont, San Francisco, chapter 2, page 57.
4. The Huntington, San Francisco, chapter 2, page 58.
5. Hyatt Regency, Monterey, chapter 5, page 178.
6. Hyatt Regency, Sacramento, chapter 6, page 221.
7. Mandarin Oriental, San Francisco, chapter 2, page 58.
8. Marriott's Tenaya Lodge, Fish Camp, chapter 8, page 309.
9. Monterey Plaza, Monterey, chapter 5, page 179.
10. Westin St. Francis, San Francisco, chapter 2, page 59.

THE TEN BEST RESORTS

1. The Ahwahnee, Yosemite National Park, chapter 8, page 308.
2. Auberge de Soleil, Rutherford, chapter 3, page 99.
3. Inn at Depot Hill, Capitola, chapter 5, page 159.
4. Madrona Manor, Healdsburg, chapter 3, page 83.
5. Meadowood Napa Valley, St. Helena, chapter 3, page 100.
6. Pelican Inn, Muir Beach, chapter 4, page 114.
7. Silverado Country Club, Napa, chapter 3, page 100.

8. Sonoma Mission Inn, Sonoma, chapter 3, page 90.
9. Ventana Inn, Big Sur, chapter 5, page 190.
10. Whale Watch Inn, Gualala, chapter 4, page 124.

THE TEN BEST BED & BREAKFAST INNS

1. Seven Gables Inn, Pacific Grove, chapter 5, page 180.
2. Amber House Bed & Breakfast, Sacramento, chapter 6, page 222.
3. Chateau Tivoli, San Francisco, chapter 2, page 61.
4. Forest Manor, Angwin, chapter 3, page 100.
5. The Foxes, Sutter Creek, chapter 7, page ??
6. Grandmere's Bed & Breakfast, chapter 7, page 240.
7. Old Monterey Inn, Monterey, chapter 5, page 179.
8. Red Castle Inn, Nevada City, chapter 7, page 240.
9. Utica Mansion Inn, Angels Camp, chapter 5, page 253.
10. White Swan Inn, San Francisco, chapter 2, page 61.

OTHER USEFUL BOOKS
Travel

The Best of the Sierra Nevada by Gerald W. Olmstead, © 1991; Crown Publishers Inc., New York.

The Best Places to Kiss in Northern California by Paula Begoun and Tomi Jo Taylor, © 1990, Beginning Press, Seattle, Wash.

California Escapes guide to state parks, available free from the Department of Parks and Recreation, P.O. Box 942896, Sacramento, CA 942896; (916) 653-4000.

California Handbook by Kim Weir and Elizabeth Sandbach, © 1990; Moon Publications, Chico, Calif.

California Whitewater: a guide to the Rivers by Jim Cassady and Fryar Calhoun, © 1989; Cassady and Calhoun, Berkeley, Calif.

Hidden Coast of California by Ray Reigert, © 1991; Ulysses Press, Berkeley, Calif.

Hidden San Francisco and Northern California by Ray Reigert, © 1990; Ulysses Press, Berkeley, Calif.

Places to go with Children in Northern California by Elizabeth Pomada, © 1989; Chronicle Books, San Francisco, Calif.

History and background

Anybody's Gold: The Story of California's Mining Towns by Joseph Henry Jackson, © 1970; Chronicle Books, San Francisco, Calif.

California Gold Camps by Erwin Gudde, © 1975; University of California Press, Berkeley, Calif.

Californians: Searching for the Golden State by James. D. Houston, © 1985; Creative Arts Book Company, Berkeley, Calif.

A Companion to California by James D. Hart, © 1987; University of California Press, Berkeley, Calif.

A History of California: the American Period by Robert Glass Cleland, © 1975; Greenwood Press, Westport, Conn.

The World Rushed In: An Eyewitness Account of a Nation Heading West by James Holiday; © 1981; Simon and Schuster, New York.

INDEX: Primary listings indicated by *bold face italics*